The Interpretation of
St. Paul's Epistles to the Colossians, to the Thessalonians, to Timothy, to Titus and to Philemon

By
R. C. H. LENSKI

AUGSBURG PUBLISHING HOUSE
Minneapolis, Minnesota

Printed 1964

Made in U.S.A.

ABBREVIATIONS

R. = A Grammar of the Greek New Testament in the Light of Historical Research, by A. T. Robertson, fourth edition.

B.-D. = Friedrich Blass' Grammatik des neutestamentlichen Griechisch, vierte, voellig neu-gearbeitete Auflage besorgt von Albert Debrunner.

C.-K. = Biblisch-theologisches Woerterbuch der Neutestamentlichen Graezitaet von D. Dr. Hermann Cremer, zehnte, etc., Auflage, herausgegeben von D. Dr. Julius Koegel.

B.-P. = Griechisch-Deutsches Woerterbuch zu den Schriften des Neuen Testaments, etc., von D. Walter Bauer, zweite, etc., Auflage zu Erwin Preuschens Vollstaendigem Griechisch-Deutschem Handwoerterbuch, etc.

M.-M. = The Vocabulary of the Greek Testament, Illustrated from the Papyri and other Non-Literary Sources, by James Hope Moulton and George Milligan.

R., *W. P.* = Word Pictures in the New Testament by Archibald Thomas Robertson.

St. Paul's Epistle
To the Colossians

INTRODUCTION

Lines drawn from Colosse to Laodicea, to Hieropolis, back to Colosse, outline a right-angled triangle. The little river Lycus flows west and empties into the Maeander. On its southern bank, on the road that leads west to Ephesus are situated Colosse and Laodicea, about eleven miles apart; while six miles north of Laodicea lies Hieropolis, about thirteen miles in an air line from Colosse. The great road from Attalia on the coast to the southeast crosses the road leading east and west at Laodicea, extends northward through Hieropolis, and then northwest through Philadelphia, Sardis, and Smyrna on to the coast. Laodicea thus occupied a most favored position. At the time our epistle was written Colosse had dwindled in importance and was outclassed by Laodicea.

These cities were located in Phrygia, which at this time was incorporated into the great Roman province Asia, with Ephesus as its capital. At Colosse the Lycus flows through a gorge having steep sides. Its waters, impregnated with carbonate of lime, form remarkable incrustations. From the glen occupied by the city rises Mt. Cadmus, reaching a height of 7,000 feet. This district is volcanic and subject to earthquakes; during the reign of Nero a disastrous tremor destroyed Laodicea and probably also Colosse. The soil is fertile; on its pastures grazed a noted breed of sheep. Both cities were famous for their manufacture of woolens, dyed a deep blue.

The bulk of the population was probably Phrygian with an admixture of Greeks. Laodicea and probably also Colosse had a number of Jewish inhabitants. These Jews seem to have compromised to a considerable extent with the Lyco-Phrygian paganism. The proportion of converted Jews in the Christian congregations of these cities is open to debate. Neither Epaphras nor Philemon were of Jewish extraction, yet the danger against which Paul's epistle warns came from a peculiar type of Judaizers who seem not to have emigrated to Colosse and Laodicea from elsewhere but to have been native to these cities themselves. Their fanciful doctrine and practice were intended to make a captivating impression on the Gentile membership of the church.

* * *

From the epistle we gather the impression that Christianity came to these cities through the work of Epaphras. Himself converted and grounded in the faith by Paul during the latter's long stay in Ephesus, Epaphras had established the faith in Colosse and probably also in Laodicea and in Hieropolis. Paul is not the founder of these congregations and had never paid them a visit. They probably came into existence toward the end of Paul's stay in Ephesus or shortly after his departure from that city. Epaphras had done most excellent work. The same compliment may be paid Philemon. After he and his wife had been converted by Paul in Ephesus they moved to Colosse and became prominent members of this congregation but cannot be designated joint founders with Epaphras.

A heretical movement had recently started in Colosse. Epaphras hastened to Paul in Rome, and our epistle is the result of his visit. The point that cannot be cleared up is that Tychicus, instead of Epaphras, is made the messenger to carry the epistle to Colosse. We know only that Paul sent Tychicus with the epistle to the Ephesians, the one to the Colossians, a third to Philemon personally in Colosse in regard to the slave Onesimus whom Paul sends back to his owner. The route followed by Tychicus was from Rome to Ephesus and then through Laodicea to Colosse. We know only what 4:16 states about Paul's epistle to the Laodiceans. The writer believes that this was a fourth letter entrusted to Tychicus, which he delivered to Laodicea while on his way to Colosse. Thus Paul orders the Colossians to exchange epistles with the Laodiceans. The epistle to the Laodiceans has been lost without further trace. See our comment on 4:16.

The purpose of the epistle to the Colossians is perfectly clear: Paul crushes the heretical teaching that had arisen in Colosse. As yet no actual inroads had been made into the congregation. The point that is unclear is whether the heretics, who were pretending Christians, were members of the congregation or not. It seems that they were not members — yet where and how had they learned about Christ? They were Judaizers, but of a type that was quite distinct from those who had come into the Galatian congregations from the outside (Palestine), and likewise distinct from those who had invaded Corinth in the same way. We may suppose that the Colossian heretics were native Jews, men who had adopted fanciful ideas that corrupted their Judaism and who, when Christianity entered the city through Epaphras, took up also with this and amalgamated it with all their other notions. Although they were not members of the congregation, they presently sought to win the members for their peculiar teaching. Then, before any real damage was done, Epaphras hurried to Paul, and this epistle followed which crushed the error completely. We take it that Paul sent a similar letter to Laodicea where this same heresy was seeking entrance, and that thus Paul wants each congregation to read and to study both letters.

* * *

The epistle itself is our only source of information regarding the Colossian heresy. It ought, then, to be an easy task to compile the data afforded by the epistle and to draw a fair picture of these errorists. Yet the investigators have gone beyond this safe procedure. They may be divided into two groups. The one thinks of Jewish, the other of Gentile errorists. The former group thinks of Pharisees, or of Alexandrine Jews, or of agents of the Jewish sect of the Essenes, or of Cabbalists. The latter group thinks of Epicurean Gentiles, Pythagoreans, Platonic Stoics, Gnostics, or incipient Gnostics, syncretistic universalists, syncretistic theosophists who combined nature mysticism with Christianity. Finally, some have thought of several of these classes whom Paul treated as one general class. Of late the debate has narrowed down to a choice between Essenes and Gnostics. Since Gnosticism takes us into the second century, this view asks us to give up the Pauline authorship of this epistle or to reduce the Gnosticism here combated to its very early beginnings.

The epistle itself shows us a peculiar type of Judaizers. They were certainly not Essenes, a small, inconspicuous sect located near the Dead Sea. Zahn, *Introduction* 1, 479, sums up the main data that oppose this view. These Judaizers did not demand circumcision, they only regarded it as being superior. They advocated some Jewish observances, but only those that were in line with their other ideas about earthly things which they deemed detrimental to the soul. They were not Gnostic, did not depreciate Christ, but did reduce Christ's work and its blessed effects for his followers— they regarded themselves to be his true followers.

The supposition that they advocated the worship of angels and thus in Gnostic fashion elevated angels rests on a strained interpretation of 2:18, to which later ideas are added. But no Jew would turn to the worship of angels. Paul presents the exalted deity of

Christ in this epistle, but not because these Judaizers denied it and elevated the angels to a position that was close to Christ, but in order to set forth Christ's work as destroying all the power of the evil angels for the true believers.

These Judaizers came with a show of wisdom and philosophy about earthly and material things. Evil angels worked through these things to man's hurt, hence their dictum (2:21): "Touch not; taste not; handle not!" Their idea was not that of acquiring merit by a kind of work-righteousness, which was the idea of the other Judaizers that we know; but they entertained the notion that by fasting and by refraining we are to supplement and to complete for ourselves the deliverance Christ wrought for us, without which supplementation we should after all be lost. The other Judaizers claimed to go back to the original, genuine Christianity, which, in their view, Paul had liberalized and emasculated in the interest of the Gentiles. These Colossian Judaizers claimed to have an advanced Christianity, Paul's being a back number, an inferior, imperfect article. Paul treats them with contempt, their supposedly superior ideas as puerile and foolish. He unfolds all the divine greatness of the person, the work, the position, and the power of Christ, all of them being infinitely beyond any other beings and powers. Connected with him as his own, we are lifted into a realm where no demon power, use what earthly elements it may, can ever harm us.

In this light we should read the hortatory section of the epistle (3:1-4:6) on the manner of the Christian life and conduct. Christ is the all, and is this in all ways, so that every difference between Greek and Jew, circumcision and uncircumcision, barbarian, Scythian, bond, free has disappeared, the new man being everything. When Paul describes the Christian life in all simplicity, he has not concluded his battle

against the Colossian Judaizers. He might so exhort
any congregation. The point of this Colossian epistle
is this very one that they need no new, advanced, philosophical ethics such as the commands given in 2:21;
the common Christian ethics constitute the height of all
advance, all pretended advance is utterly spurious.

* * *

Because they were written at the same time, possibly on the same day, Ephesians and Colossians present many parallels in thought as well as in wording.
Tables of these parallelisms have been constructed,
usually, however, in order to prove that one or the
other epistle is not written by Paul but by an imitator.
These similarities are most natural. Yet the differences are just as arresting. In Ephesians the subject
is the *Una Sancta;* in Colossians, Christ over all. In
the former there are no polemics, in the latter polemics
throughout. Each epistle has its own plan and its own
details.

The Christology of both is thought to be an advance
over the Christology of the other epistles of Paul. This
puts the matter in a wrong light. The advance is said
to consist in viewing Christ in relation to the whole
universe and no longer in his relation only to his followers or to men. This view, however, disregards the
respective readers. The Colossian errorists made it
necessary that, for their thorough refutation, Paul
present the Christological facts which he did set forth,
facts which it was not imperative to emphasize in
other epistles.

Paul's great arsenal held still other artillery. If
he had had still other opponents he would have drawn
on still other bolts and missiles to demolish their errors.
We do the same today. After using certain truths in
one battle we use still others in another somewhat dif-

ferent battle. Are our opponents free to use one and then another kind of attack while we are always and everywhere confined to only one kind of defense? Who will forbid the sword of Christology (or of any doctrine), after cutting down one error with a moderate blow, to cut down a greater enemy with a wider sweep and a longer reach?

*　　　*　　　*

It surely makes no difference which of the three simultaneously composed epistles was written first, which second, which last. Let the writer say for himself that, if he had written them, Philemon and Colossians would have been the first, Ephesians the last. Others may have other equally tenable views.

The fact that Paul wrote at Rome and not at Caesarea nor at Ephesus we have indicated in the introductory remarks to Ephesians. Philippians indicates its own date, namely, shortly before Paul was released from his imprisonment of two years in Rome. This trio of epistles was written weeks or months earlier. Haupt is a good illustration of the purely subjective feelings by which some men are swayed in matters of this sort. He says that unless we grant him Caesarea as the place of writing he will refuse to believe that Paul wrote these epistles at all! And why, pray, Caesarea at all costs? Because Haupt feels that he cannot imagine the right mental condition for Paul anywhere else! So the debate about the time and the place will probably go on.

The epistle has been dissected in the effort to arrive at the part that was composed by Paul and not by an imitator of Paul's. The case of Van Soden is an interesting one: after at first dissecting rather radically, in his later work he patches the letter together again and leaves out only 1:16b, 17. These operations will always be purely individualistic. So also will the effort to make the writer an imitator of Paul. Nobody names this forger or tells us how he passed off his forgery without detection. To claim a forgery is to reject all the solid tradition that runs through the ancient church, the data having been collected and presented often enough. If this epistle is forged, then its entire background is also forged. Why did the forger select Colosse and not Laodicea? Why did he stop after he had forged 4:16 and fail to forge also the epistle to the Laodiceans? These and other questions will always remain unanswered.

To go into the epistle itself, to rethink its inspired thought that is clothed in inspired language, to let the light and the power of this thought fill the soul and mold the life, this is enrichment for time and for eternity.

CHAPTER I

THE GREETING

1) Several things arrest our attention when we study this greeting although its form is stereotyped: Paul, etc. — to the saints, etc. — grace and peace! **Paul, apostle of Christ Jesus through God's will, and Timothy, the brother, to the saints and believers in Colosse as brethren in Christ: grace to you and peace from God, our Father!**

"Apostle of Christ Jesus" means that Paul is writing in his official capacity as the Lord's ambassador. The genitive is possessive. "Apostle" is to be understood in the narrow sense as also "through God's will" indicates. The possessive genitive, however, involves agency. As an apostle Paul belongs to Christ because Christ appointed and sent him. Paul did not receive his office by fortuitous circumstances, God willed his appointment (Gal. 1:15, 16). When he writes to the Colossians, Paul is discharging his apostolic obligation and a high responsibility. The genitive and the phrase indicate the dignity and the authority of Paul and thus the way in which this epistle should be received.

It is asked why Paul associates Timothy with himself as co-writer. The reason cannot be the same as that found in I Thess., II Thess., II Cor., and Phil., for in those letters Timothy is introduced as a person that is well known to the readers, which is not the case in this epistle. Neither Paul nor Timothy had been in Colosse. We find our answer in the apposition: Timothy, "the brother," combined with the predicative apposition: to the saints, etc., "as brethren." The

(15)

latter is distinctive in this greeting and thus makes Timothy's designation as "the brother" more distinctive than it is in II Cor. 1:1.

The authority of this letter is *apostolic* in the fullest *brotherly* sense. One of the writers is only "the brother" of the readers, and both writers address them as "brethren." As such "brethren" of Paul and Timothy, in a true fraternal spirit, the recipients are to read this letter which is both apostolic and brotherly in one. Paul could have written without a reference to Timothy and signed himself both "apostle" and "brother"; he does better than that, he lets this well-known assistant join him in sending this letter. Timothy is one who can claim as his highest position only that of a brother among brethren.

2) By taking this view we have already indicated that we regard τοῖς ἁγίοις καὶ πιστοῖς as nouns: "to the saints and believers," not as adjectives modifying ἀδελφοῖς: "to the holy and faithful believers." We do not regard the first expression as a noun and the other as an adjective: "to the saints (noun) and the faithful (adjective) brethren" (our versions). Eph. 1:1, which was written at the same time, treats the two words as nouns. If the one is a noun (and ἅγιοι is regularly so used), the other must be a noun also. We have indicated why the apposition: "brethren in Christ," is added. One article combines "the saints and believers." "In Colosse" is placed in the attributive position. In later times a variant form "Colasse" was used.

We need not repeat all that we have noted in regard to "saints," "believers," and the phrase "in Christ" in Eph. 1:1; see this passage. Here we may add that making "saints" objective and "believers" subjective is an inadequate way of defining the distinction. "Saints" is passive and wider, "believers" active and narrower. We are ἅγιοι or saints as ἡγιασμένοι, as having been sanctified and separated from the world unto

God and by God, the term referring to sanctification
in the wider sense. Our sins are forgiven. That act
took us out of the world; we are placed in a new life in
which we are daily made more and more holy, are more
and more drawn from the world to God. The essential
part of this separation is our faith. Brought to faith
by the gospel, by faith we ever hold fast to Christ, the
contents of our confidence and trust. The two words
thus form a unit designation for all Christians in their
relation to God and to Christ. "Brethren in Christ"
makes plain what we are to each other in this relation:
one family of brethren, all on an equality, but this
always and in every way "in union and communion
with (ἐν) Christ" alone. Paul, Timothy, the Colossians, all of them are "brethren in Christ."

The greeting itself: "grace to you and peace from
God, our Father," is explained in Rom. 1:7; I Cor. 1:3;
II Cor. 1:2, which see. The only question that arises
here is whether to add, as some texts do: "and the
Lord Jesus Christ." The question is one that concerns
merely the text. Paul may well have abbreviated; the
meaning of his greeting is quite the same as it is in the
other epistles.

I

The Preparatory Part of the Letter, 1:3-29

The structure of the letter is admirable in every
way and most effective. Its great purpose is to close
the door of the Colossian church against the peculiar
heretical teaching that had recently begun to knock
for entrance. No entrance had as yet been effected,
but there was danger that it might be gained. The
burden of the letter thus consists of warning. Paul
exposes the Judaizers and bids the Colossians "beware"
(2:1-23). This is only the half of his task. Paul completes it by showing in principle and in detail (3:1-4:6)

how the Colossians should meet this heretical teaching
by living the true Christian life they had learned to live
when they had been brought to Christ. Then comes
the conclusion (4:7-18).

The development and the elaboration are concise
and masterly. The situation is met in the most natural
and adequate way. In Galatians, Paul enters upon his
subject at once, for the churches he addresses were his
own churches, and he had only recently left them. This
case is different. Paul had never been with the Colossians. A preparatory section is needed in this letter,
and this section must truly prepare so that the warning
that follows will be fully effective, and so that the life
which is the best practical answer to the error the
Colossians are facing will be eagerly lived by them.

Paul's preparation for his exhortations could not
have been better. Examine it and see whether you can
suggest improvement. The same may be said with
regard to the other two main parts. Each paragraph
with its group of thoughts leads to the next in a way
that is so natural that one reads right on through the
body of the letter without halt or turn. It is like an
even, straight road from beginning to end. This church
that had never seen Paul or even Timothy, true brethren of theirs, could not but absorb this letter word for
word, and their faith and their life should rise to every
exhortation that is fraternally and convincingly offered
to them.

Paul and Timothy are Happy to Know the True Christian Character of the Colossian Brethren

3) It is on this basis that the letter is written.
There is no *captatio benevolentiae* that seeks to gain
good will by flattery. Here there is genuine, grateful,
sincere appreciation. "Brethren" in v. 2 is not a mere
formal term. This paragraph attests how fully the
Colossians deserve to be called brethren by Paul and

Timothy. Yet it faces forward. That is why it touches points that some have regarded as a mere jumbling together. If we keep in mind the purpose of the letter, every statement falls into proper focus, all are perfectly in line so that they prepare for what follows to the very end.

We are thanking God, Father of our Lord Jesus Christ, always concerning you when praying, having heard of your faith in Christ Jesus and of the love which you have toward all the saints because of the hope, the one laid away for you in the heavens, of which you heard in advance in the Word of the truth of the gospel present for you, even as also in all the world it is fruit-bearing and growing, even as also among you from what day on you got to hear it and to realize the grace of God in truth, even as you came to learn from Epaphras, our beloved fellow slave, who is a faithful minister of Christ on our behalf, the one also who informed us of your love in the spirit.

This is one sentence (see the two grand sentences in Eph. 1:3-23) which is formulated as one because it intends to convey one unified impression. The flexibility of the Greek makes this formulation possible; the Hebrew and the English would have to construct more than one sentence and employ other means to obtain such a unified impression. Some interpreters remind us of the fact that Paul likes to start a letter with thanksgiving. Of course he does, for his eyes are open to all the blessings he sees, nor does he write Eph. 5:20 only for others. But it is not enough to discover that Paul is ever a man who is most thankful to God; it is advisable in every instance to note *what* calls forth his gratitude. For he is not telling his readers what a grateful man he is but is drawing their attention to the great thankworthy things God has bestowed on them. Moreover, he does not enumerate a lot of

things in general for which his readers and he himself
may well thank God but names certain specific things,
with specific details, which bear upon the subject and
the purpose of his particular writing.

"We are thanking God" means: Timothy and I;
Paul is not writing a majestic or an editorial plural.
The texts vary; but just as we have Θεοῦ πατρός in v. 2,
so we now have Θεῷ πατρί *sine additum* (no καί, and no
second article) : "God, our Father," in v. 2; "God, our
Lord Jesus Christ's Father," in v. 3. The question
whether God is also "the God of our Lord Jesus Christ"
is answered in Eph. 1:17; it does not enter in here.
We do not agree that the adverb "always" is amphibolous (R., *W. P.*). As one reads the Greek he naturally attaches all three: adverb, phrase, and participle,
to the main verb: "We are thanking — always in regard to you when praying." Paul is not always *praying* for them (our versions) — he does a few things
besides; nor is he thanking God only when he prays for
them and not when he prays for others. What Paul
says is that, whenever he and' Timothy pray, they always include the Colossians in their thanksgiving to
God. The fact that they also petition God for the
Colossians is added in v. 9.

4) The participial clause is temporal: "having
heard of your faith," etc.; note the relative clause in
v. 9 : "since the day we heard" (it is like the ἀφ' ἧς clause
in v. 6). R. 860 is right: "antecedent action." Ever
since Paul and Timothy came to hear how Epaphras
planted the gospel in Colosse they thank God for what
was accomplished. As he did in Eph. 1:15, Paul mentions both the faith of the Colossians and their love to
all the saints. He acknowledges both as true. Love is
ever the fruit of faith, and both are here prominently
stamped as genuine because Paul intends to admonish
the Colossians that they permit no one to swerve them
from either. Faith connects them with Christ, love

marks them as thus being united with all the saints, but certainly not with the Judaizers who had a spurious faith and did not deserve the name "saints."

Paul and Timothy had heard about the Colossians from the beginning of the Christian work in their midst when Epaphras scored his first success, at least soon after that, and not merely since Epaphras had come to Rome. Paul thus refers to the faith and the love of the Colossians as both were first kindled and as both had continued to this time. The silent implication is that in the recent past their faith and their love were being threatened, and that if they should be destroyed, i. e., if under the influence of the Judaizers the Colossians should degenerate into a nominally Christian sect, neither Paul nor Timothy could any longer include them in their thanksgiving to God when they were praying.

When the Greek names the object of faith he uses the objective genitive: "faith *of* Christ." Here and in Eph. 1:15, "faith *in* Christ Jesus" does not name the object (contra R., *W. P.*). 'Eν denotes the sphere in which faith moves. But not as C.-K. 889 supposes: faith having its root in Christ. This is a form of Deissmann's idea (see Eph. 1:1), who states that "in" is local: "in Christ" like a bird in the air, a fish in the sea, etc. In all these phrases ἐν denotes the vital spiritual connection with Christ and not local inherence. The context indicates what this spiritual connection is; here "faith" indicates it: connecting with Christ by trustfully embracing him, confidently clinging to him. See Eph. 1:15.

Chrysostom calls faith and love "a wonderful pair of twins," yet they are never twins, they are mother and daughter, tree and fruit (Matt. 7:17), branches and grapes (John 15). Bengel has a better statement when he calls love the characteristic mark of Christianity, John 13:35; 15:12. The early pagans com-

mented on this Christian love: never having seen each
other, Christians treated each other as brothers. This
was astonishing to the pagan mind. In connection
with Eph. 1:15 we have pointed to the danger of laying
too much stress on love; see this passage. It is an old,
most dangerous error to neglect justification and faith
and to glorify love and works instead. This error generally also alters the Biblical conception of love and
makes it a love which disregards the essential matter
of doctrine. It was Pietism which produced Rationalism in Germany — a grave warning to us today.
Ἀγάπη is always the higher form of love, always based
on true intelligence and understanding, these always
coupled with corresponding purpose and action.

The reading τήν is textually inferior although it is
adopted in the A. V.; ἥν is the assured reading (R. V.).
Substantially there is no difference. "The love which
we have for all the saints" connects us with them as
"saints" but only because they and we have the identical faith in Christ Jesus. A love apart from this oneness of faith is a fictitious bond, however devoted and
fervent it may be. Nor is love ever stronger than the
faith from which it originates. All of its strength
comes from faith alone so that, in order to increase
our love, we must first nourish and strengthen our
faith. Paul places "all the saints" before the minds
and the hearts of the Colossians because he intends to
urge them as "saints and believers" and thus as "brethren in Christ" (v. 2) ever to remain in their blessed
connection with "all the saints"; note 3:14.

5) Paul and Timothy are thanking God concerning the Colossians because they heard of their faith
and of the love "which they have for all the saints
because of the hope laid away for you in the heavens,"
etc. Διά with the accusative states the reason or cause
of the love of the Colossians for all the other saints.
Why do we love all our fellow saints? Because for us

too, as for them, a great hope is laid away in the heavens. "Hope" is objective, for it is laid away in the heavens; it is the eternal "inheritance, incorruptible, and undefiled, that fadeth not away, reserved in heaven for us" (I Pet. 1:4). We love each other with intelligent and purposeful love that comes from faith because we are headed for the same great hope in heaven, for the same inheritance of glory, for the same blessed goal. That is why we cling together in love, support and help each other in love, so that none of us may fail of having that hope bestowed upon him at last.

Paul certainly has the trio: faith — love — hope. Yet it is not really the trio of I Cor. 13:13, for here "the hope laid away for you" is objective and not, like "faith and love," something subjective in our hearts, hope in the sense of our hoping. Paul does not merely say: we heard of your faith (believing), of your love (loving), and of your hope (hoping). He inserts the relative clause: "the love which you have for all the saints," so that he may add what is greater than the hope in our hearts, namely the heavenly treasure for which we hope, the mansions in our Father's house that are ready and waiting for our arrival (John 14:2).

Paul calls this hope the cause of our love to all the saints. Making it the cause of this love thus reaches back also to our faith in Christ, the source of love. Faith is the soil from which the fruit of love springs, and hope is the sunshine which ripens this fruit of love. By faith Christ unites all believers so that, joined thus, they love each other; Christ has laid away the treasure of hope in heaven for all believers so that, united by the hope of this expected treasure, we for this reason also love each other.

We should read together: because of the hope, "the one laid away for you in the heavens of which (one) you heard in advance in the Word of the truth of the gospel present for you," etc. The Colossians got to

hear about this hope πρό, "before or in advance" of the
coming bestowal of this treasure of hope, when the
gospel came to them through Epaphras, the gospel they
have had ever since, the gospel that is still present for
them. In both Ephesians and in Colossians Paul combines sonorous genitives like this, they make the main
concept weighty and rich. They are not different genitives; all three characterize. Λόγος = the Word which
is full of content; in this Word the Colossians heard in
advance about the hope laid away for them in the
heavens; the whole content of the Word centered in
this heavenly treasure. This Word is "of the truth,"
i. e., is marked by the divine verity. The genitive is
far stronger than the adjective "the true Word" would
be. This truth, moreover, is "of the gospel," it has the
quality of good news. Finally, this gospel has the
feature that it is still present for the Colossians.

Practically every word in v. 4, 5 is significant for
the purpose of this letter, which is to warn. We see
this also in the relative clause. Note how often the
verb "heard" occurs: v. 4, 5, 6, 9. Twice the Colossians "heard," twice Paul and Timothy "heard" that
the Colossians had "heard," and ever since Paul and
Timothy heard they are thanking God when they are
praying and are also asking God for the Colossians (v.
9). Faith and love came into their hearts because of
the great hope they had heard, heard from the start
(πρό) in the Word, the Word that was marked by the
divine truth, that truth having the character of the
gospel, that gospel being still present so that they ever
keep on hearing.

"For you" it is present, εἰς, which means more than
"among you," ἐν, "for you" still to hear. Another
"word" has recently come that is different from "the
truth" and not "the gospel" at all but false and dangerous. To hear and to accept this lying word is to
lose "the hope laid away for the Colossians," the love

this hope has caused and the faith from which this love has sprung. If Paul and Timothy ever get to hear that the Colossians no longer heard the Word, the truth, the gospel that is present for them, that they no longer let the great hope fill them with love and faith, this knowledge would turn their thanksgiving into lament.

This simple construction of Paul's clauses and phrases has been questioned. It is thought that Paul ought to say definitely for what he and Timothy are thanking God, and it is said that he does this in the διά phrase: "We are thanking God — because of the hope laid away for you," etc. The object, we are told, is placed so far away from the verb because there is no convenient place nearer to it. But Paul could have recast the sentence. But this construction yields a strange resultant thought, namely that after hearing of *the faith and love* of the Colossians Paul and Timothy are thanking God, *not* for this faith and love as we should expect but only for *the hope* laid away for the Colossians, this hope treasure of which they had heard in the gospel. No ordinary reader would refer the διά phrase back so far in order to get such a thought and then pass on. *What* Paul and Timothy are thanking God for appears in what they *heard* concerning the Colossians, and this is something that has come into the hearts of the Colossians and not something that is still far off in heaven. Besides, when we thank God in regard to certain people we may do so *because* God promised them or gave them something but not *because* of something about which there is still a doubt as to whether they will get it or not.

Nor should one say that it would be strange on Paul's part to make our objective hope the cause *only* of our love. This "only" is read into the words. Love is ever the product of faith, and all beloved saints are saints and brethren only because they are believers.

Does Paul not add that the Colossians heard the Word about this hope, meaning that they heard it with faith? And does he not say that this gospel about their hope is still present for them, meaning that they are ever to continue hearing it with faith? The very reason that Paul thus goes from *both* the faith and love of the Colossians (subjective) to this hope laid away in heaven (objective) is that they are in danger of not attaining this treasure. If they now start to believe and to love the Judaizers they will forfeit the great treasure in heaven. The point is the same as that made in Gal. 3:3: beginning in spirit, beginning with true faith and love, and then possibly ending with flesh, missing the inheritance of hope.

6) Paul says more about the Word of the truth of the gospel than that it is still present for the Colossians to hear as they had before heard about the heavenly hope; he adds: "even as also in all the world it is fruit-bearing and growing even as also among you from what day on you got to hear it," etc. Read all this together as one thought. The A. V. adopts the inferior text: καὶ ἔστι: "present for you even as in all the word, *and* it is fruit-bearing," etc., and then also lets the genitive participle mean: "which is come to you." Then εἰς ὑμᾶς and ἐν παντὶ τῷ κόσμῳ fail to harmonize as they should with καθὼς καί being between them.

The point of Paul's addition is the greatness of the gospel. The Colossians are to remember that its range is world-wide, the very opposite of the little Judaistic sectlet that has somehow appeared in their midst. The gospel is bearing its fruit and growing "in all the world" even as the Colossians themselves have witnessed this since the day on which they got to hear it (ingressive aorist, the day marking the start). What they witnessed in Colosse is happening "in all the world." The commentators call the phrase a popular hyperbole, but note the periphrastic present tenses, periphrastic in order to emphasize most strongly the fact that the fruit-bearing and the growing are in full force, ever progressing, never stopping with any nation or country. The whole world, nothing less, is the field for this activity of the gospel.

Καρποφορούμενον is the middle voice, yet not with intensive force compared with the active which has extensive force but to indicate that the gospel ever goes on bearing fruit spontaneously. Αὐξανόμενον is passive; the active = "to make grow" (although it, too, came to mean "to grow") ; the passive always = "to grow." Paul has just mentioned "all the saints" (v. 4) ; these were at this time widely scattered over the world and were ever entering into new territory. The fruit Paul refers to is the faith and the love mentioned in v. 4, and the growing is the further development of both, not, as some suppose, the increase in number of believers.

The ἐστί with its two participles forms a unit concept so that we should not think of the fruit-bearing as one thing and the growing as another. Paul never sought to make an impression with numbers and great crowds. That is a modern emphasis always to speak of *world* movements, *world* conventions, *world* this and that. When Paul speaks of "all the saints" and of "all the world" he has in mind the universality of the *Una Sancta* and of the gospel, which is different from boastfulness. The implication is that this universality of the gospel truth shall not be converted into a narrow sectarian heresy.

The two καθὼς καί are obviously to be paralleled: "even as also in all the world — even as also among you." What happened in Colosse the Colossians may take as an example of what is steadily happening far and wide in the whole world. In Colosse it dates "from what day on (antecedent drawn into the relative) you

got to hear and realize the grace of God in truth."
Then the great fruit-bearing and the growing of the
gospel began (ingressive aorists) in Colosse. The two
verbs aim to express the idea fully; they got to hear
effectively, i. e., got to realize.

We do not make "in truth" adverbial: "to hear and
realize truly," for the doubling of the verbs already
expresses this, as does also the strong verb ἐπέγνωτε,
which implies complete knowing and realization. "The
grace of God in truth" is one great concept. In v. 5 it
is "the hope laid away for you in the heavens," of
which the Colossians "heard in advance"; here it is
"God's grace in truth." The hope is the ultimate goal,
the grace is the present fountain and source. Both
come by hearing, are realized in the heart by this
means. The Colossians are ever to hear only these two,
are to keep their ears closed to every teaching that
would rob them of these two.

"Grace" has the same meaning as in v. 2: God's
undeserved, unmerited favor toward guilty sinners
which pardons and blesses them in Christ Jesus and
grants them, who, because of their guilt, have no hope,
the hope he has prepared for them in Christ. The
Colossians are to lose neither. Let them listen to nothing that is not pure grace, to nothing that offers only
an imaginary hope. We see why Paul does not say
merely "the grace of God" but adds "in truth." Although it is without the article, this is no other truth
than that mentioned in v. 5, the absence of the article
only stressing the more the quality just as it does in
Eph. 4:21 and 6:14. God's grace is ever connected
with (ἐν) what is truth and nothing but truth and
never is it connected with anything that is of a different
quality. Both "the truth" as contained in the gospel
(v. 5) and "truth" as connected with God's grace are
the opposites of all religious untruth, unreality. The
Colossians are to cling to the former and ever to keep

themselves separate from the latter. Let us keep the
purpose of Paul's letter in mind. His aim is to
warn, and this colors all that he says from the very
beginning.

7) The third καθώς amplifies the second and is thus
not followed by καί. It is epexegetical: "even as also
you got to hear and realize" = "even as you came to
learn (again ingressive) from Epaphras, our beloved
fellow slave who," etc. "You came to learn" repeats
by means of one verb what the two preceding verbs
contain. Yet it adds a new turn of thought: one
"learns" from a teacher, and Paul now wants to name
the teacher. One *"hears"* the gospel or the Word of
the truth of the gospel. When the Colossians got to
learn (ἐμάθετε) they became μαθηταί, "disciples." The
reason that Paul puts his stamp of fullest approval on
Epaphras is due to the fact that the Colossians are to
remain with this teacher and are not to turn from him
to the false Judaistic teachers who are trying to catch
their ears and to make them learn from them.

We are incidentally told how the gospel work
started in Colosse, namely through Epaphras. He
founded the congregation. It is difficult to say whether
it was he who did the same in Laodicea and in Hieropolis. It seems certain that Epaphras continued as
the head of the congregation at Colosse, that he was
now its head, and that he had come to Paul for help in
his fight against the Judaists.

Paul supports Epaphras in his entire teaching
when he calls him "our beloved fellow slave who is a
faithful minister of Christ on our behalf." Paul says
that Epaphras is a slave of Jesus Christ, just as Timothy and Paul are such slaves, and that they, too, love
him as such. These three are slaves, not merely in the
general sense as Christians who are attached to Christ
by faith and love, but in the sense in which Paul
denominates himself "a slave of Jesus Christ" (Rom.

1:1), as preachers and teachers of the gospel. As slaves they have no will of their own but in all their work are dominated only by the blessed will of their great Lord and Master, Christ. The point is again that the Judaizers are not slaves of Christ, do not bow their will to this Master's will and Word, do not teach what Christ bids his slaves teach. Let the Colossians heed Epaphras as they have done thus far, let them love him as Paul and Timothy love him. Also this thought lies in these words: that forsaking Epaphras means disowning also Paul and Timothy and their teaching. Yet Paul and Timothy were the persons who had spread the gospel in so many places which produced so many saints (v. 4) and in so many churches.

The relative clause says still more: Epaphras "is a faithful minister of Christ on our behalf," Greek: "a faithful on our behalf minister of Christ." The texts vary between "our" and "your" behalf. "Our" is, however, far more trenchant than "your." The fact that Epaphras ministered to the Colossians is declared in the statement that they came to learn from him, the verb even states how he ministered, namely by teaching them. Paul now aims to show why he and Timothy regard Epaphras as such a "beloved" fellow slave. Neither of them had been able to go to Colosse, there to slave for Christ; Epaphras had gone in their stead, Epaphras rendered Paul and Timothy this free service.

Διάκονος is the proper word to express this thought: one who renders voluntary service "in behalf of" other people so that they may have the benefit. Epaphras had so served to aid Paul and Timothy. They had every reason to love him, for he had proved himself a "faithful" *diakonos* on their behalf. The genitive "of Christ" is not objective as though Paul would say that the ministration served Christ. We ministers are Christ's ὑπηρέται, "underlings," his δοῦλοι, "slaves," and thus receive his commands; but as διάκονοι of his our service benefits the persons who need our service.

8) "The one also who informed us of your love in the spirit" adds this thought as an apposition to the relative "who." Epaphras had come to Rome, to Paul and to Timothy, and had told them all about the Colossians. But note how Paul writes about this. Not as though he personally has hierarchical jurisdiction over the Colossians, as though Epaphras had to report to him, the one who was in authority over him. This is a fraternal letter. It comes from two men and not from Paul alone. What Epaphras has achieved in Colosse is a free service that was rendered to Timothy as well as to Paul and thus to all others who preach the gospel and have been unable to go to other places such as Colosse.

In line with this conception is the fact that Paul does not say that Epaphras reported on his whole work, or on the state of the congregation, or on the danger that has recently arisen. There is not the faintest thought of lordship over the faith of the Colossians; Paul and Timothy are only joint helpers of their joy (II Cor. 1:24; I Pet. 3:5). So Paul says that Epaphras informed him "of their love in the spirit." With corresponding love this letter is sent by its two writers. It is love that unites writers and readers, the same love as that mentioned in v. 4; see the word in v. 4. This love Paul wants to preserve; let no Judaizers ever succeed in even lessening it.

All that this letter offers is intended for loving hearts, hearts that will read and respond in love. Although the readers and the writers had as yet not met, love unites them. The whole letter makes its appeal on this gospel basis. This is spiritual love. Some think that the last phrase means "in the Spirit" (our versions). But see the discussion on Gal. 5:16-6:8, where πνεῦμα occurs eight times and means "spirit" and not the Holy Spirit; this is also the case in numerous other passages. "Love in spirit" is love that is wholly spiritual. The fact that such love is due to the Holy Spirit goes without saying. "In spirit" the Colossians are joined by love to Paul and to Timothy and love them for their work's sake.

Paul and Timothy also Pray and Make due Petition for the Colossian Brethren

9) Paul proceeds with the preparatory section of this letter. Besides thanking God when they are praying in regard to the Colossians, Paul and Timothy ask God for what the Colossians need. Here, too, all that is thus asked has its direct bearing upon the special situation in Colosse, which had been made known by Epaphras; and it thus helps to prepare for the main purpose of the letter.

For this reason also we on our part from what day we came to hear do not cease praying in your behalf and duly asking that you may be filled with the knowledge of his will in all wisdom and spiritual understanding so as to walk worthily of the Lord, etc.

"For this reason also" does not refer to v. 8 alone, which is only appended as an apposition and a minor designation of Epaphras. Nor can the love of the Colossians be the reason that Paul and Timothy ask knowledge for them. Such connections in thought are linguistically and logically incongruous. "For this reason also" connects with the entire thought of the preceding paragraph. "We on our part" is scarcely in contrast with a "you" which is implied in the foregoing but is to be connected with the thought expressed in the temporal clause: "from what day we came to hear," i. e., *then,* from that day onward *we on our part* felt the obligation not only to thank God as has been stated but for this very reason also to ask certain things of God for you. "From what day we heard" refers to v. 4, "having heard," where what Paul and Timothy heard is stated. It is not the day when the Colossians got to hear the grace of God (v. 6); it was perhaps soon after this day. The formulation of the temporal clauses of v. 6 and v. 9 is alike, not, we think, accidentally but in order to parallel these hearings: the Colossians heard good things (v. 5, 6), and so Paul and Timothy got to hear good things about the Colossians (v. 4, 9). Shall this double blessed hearing not continue in the future?

In v. 3 Paul uses only the durative present: "we are (ever) thanking God"; now the duration of the activity is expressed by the verb itself: "we do not cease praying in your behalf and duly asking," etc. The second of the two complementary participles expresses the main thought, for the whole expression means: "we are always in our praying asking this for you that," etc. "Praying" is inserted as it was in v. 3: thanking and asking are naturally done by praying.

It is worth noting the middle voice of αἰτούμενοι. Blass says that this voice is used in business transactions when one asks and gives (B.-D. 316, 2); but the middle denotes an asking to which one is entitled. This may occur in a business deal, but it may also take place in far more refined relations when he of whom we ask in some way entitles us to do so. Note, for instance, that Herod had entitled Salome to ask for as much as the half of his kingdom. The reflexive idea "ask for oneself" is only the starting point of this use of the middle: ask as one who is entitled to ask. The entitling referred to here is the fact that God commands us to ask; the middle voice implies that only on this supposition do we ask.

Ἵνα is non-final and states what Paul and Timothy duly ask for: "that you may be filled with the knowledge (common accusative with passives) of his will in all spiritual wisdom and understanding." This is like the gift which Paul asks for the Ephesians (1:17, etc.). In both instances this gift is related to the body of the epistle and is not a general petition. To the Ephesians, Paul presents the vision of the great *Una Sancta;* to see it as they should the eyes of the Ephesians must be enlightened. The very formulation fits the object of the requested knowledge (Eph. 1:17, etc.). It is so here. For the Colossians, who are faced with errorists, Paul asks the knowledge they need in order to see through these errorists; and again the wording fits the special need: that you may be filled with full knowledge (ἐπίγνωσις), with no gaps in this knowledge that may lay you open to deception. They are to know fully "his (God's) will" so that no one may substitute something for what God has really willed. "His will" is a complete idea and = what God has willed for our salvation. "The knowledge of his will" is modified by the phrase "in connection with all spiritual wisdom and understanding," "all" and "spiritual" belong to both nouns.

We note the combination ἐπίγνωσις — σοφία — σύνεσις, the first dominating, the other two presenting its form. When it is connected with "wisdom" real knowledge of God's will knows how to use and to apply this knowledge in life's situations, for instance, when error confronts one. When it is connected with "understanding" (bringing this and that together) such knowledge will analyze and combine, will take one point after another of the error and will set against each point the part of truth regarding God's will which refutes and exposes that error. Both will, of course, have to be "spiritual" wisdom and understanding.

We do not view Paul's terms in an abstract light and say that his words would apply also to other congregations. They apply most exactly to the Colossian congregation; for that reason they may apply also to others, especially to such as are in similar situations, which enables us to apply the words to ourselves today. Paul is not writing appropriate things in general; he has a definite and specific purpose regarding definite people and is working in line with that purpose. He duly asks God to bestow the knowledge the Colossians need; God, however, uses his means when he answers such prayers, and one of his means is the apostle himself and this letter of the apostle. If you have bread, do not merely pray God to feed the hungry, pray and give them of your bread. So Paul, who has the real knowledge, prays for the Colossians, but prays and sends them the knowledge they need.

10) That you may be filled with the knowledge, etc., **so as to walk worthily of the Lord unto all pleasing, in every good work bearing fruit and growing by means of this knowledge of God; being made powerful in all power according to the might of his glory for all perseverance and longsuffering with joy; thanking the Father who made you fit for the** (your) **part of the lot of the saints in the light, etc.**

This infinitive is not appositional to the ἵνα clause but, as R., *W. P.* states it, consecutive and states the result of having been filled with true knowledge: "so as to walk worthily," etc. Right knowledge ever does bring forth the right result in conduct. *Right* conduct cannot be the product of *wrong* knowledge. But do many Christians not know better and yet do wrong? Is there no dead orthodoxy? On examination it will be found that such better knowledge and such orthodoxy are only superficial, not ἐπίγνωσις but lacking in vital parts. That is one point; the other is that in all of us the flesh prevents the perfect translation of knowledge into conduct.

Note that this is an aorist; hence it is not descriptive, "to be ever walking" but decisively final, "so as to walk" once for all and corresponds to the previous aorist, "to be filled" once for all. Paul regularly has a genitive with the adverb "worthily," nor is there any reason that he should not also here so construe this adverb: "worthily of the Lord." It is said that the genitive should be construed with the phrase: "unto all pleasing of the Lord" since he who is to be pleased ought to be named. But the expression is a unit: "worthily of the Lord unto all pleasing," i. e., so that he is pleased by our worthy walk. In ἀξίως there lies the idea of weight: the moral and spiritual weight of our conduct should balance the scales when it is laid in one pan and the Lord is laid in the other pan of the scales. "*All* pleasing" = not merely pleasing the Lord only in part.

It is grammatical quibbling when the nominative participles which follow are called irregular because the subject of the infinitive is an accusative. The infinitive itself depends on πληρωθῆτε, the subject of which is the nominative "you," and the nominative participles carry this subject forward in the most regular way: "*you* filled with the knowledge — *you* bearing fruit," etc. Paul repeats these two participles from v. 6: "bearing fruit and growing," save that the former is now active and not middle as it was in v. 6. The gospel bears fruit of itself, by its own inherent power (v. 6); not so we, for our fruit is borne in the power of this gospel. Just as in v. 9 both "all" and "spiritual" modify both nouns "wisdom and understanding," so now "in every good work" and "by means of the knowledge of God" are to be construed with both participles "bearing fruit and growing." Thus the whole expression is again a unit. We bear fruit and grow in every good work, and both bearing fruit and growing is accomplished by means of the knowledge of God. A fruit-bearing tree grows; one that does not grow ceases to bear and begins to die.

These participles expound what it means to walk worthily of the Lord unto all pleasing. What the aorist infinitive compresses into one these present participles unroll in its daily continuation. So they also expound what it means to be filled with the knowledge of God's will and now tell us that by means of this knowledge of God (the genitive "of God" = "of God's will") we bear fruit and grow. We regard the dative as a dative of means: "by means of the (this) knowledge of God." Ever and ever all our knowledge of God and of his will is not to be theoretical or abstract but fruitful, productive, molding conduct and life. That is why Paul uses ἐπίγνωσις which is not in the head alone but in the very heart. The dative of means seems better than the *dativus commodi*: "bearing fruit and growing *for* the knowledge of God."

11) The next participle shows *how* this knowledge is able to do *what* Paul has just said: "being made powerful in all power according to the might of his glory for all perseverance and longsuffering with joy." By means of this knowledge God ever keeps filling us with dynamic power. Gospel knowledge is power. Ἐν is not instrumental, "with." It does not state that God takes "all power," gives that to us, and therewith makes us powerful. We are not endowed with omnipotence. "Being ever made powerful *in* all (or every) power" is exactly like "bearing fruit and growing *in* all (or every) good work," in *no power* that we need for fruit-bearing and growing does God leave us deficient. If we ever prove deficient, it is never because he fails to supply us; it is always only because we do not let him "fill us with the knowledge of his will," with this knowledge that is so effective a means for making us bear fruit and grow.

Look well to the empty spaces in your knowledge. The fruit that is lacking in your life is due to the spaces that are still without full knowledge and thus

still without the power that should be in them. Here
we have an analysis that goes to the bottom. So many
think only of mere intellectual knowledge; even of that
they try to acquire only a little because they think it to
be enough. Think of this as heart knowledge, as spiritual power to do all things, yea, great things. Pray
as Paul and Timothy pray for the Colossians so that
you may not remain a sickly baby or child, a poor,
weak, helpless creature but a man in Christ Jesus full
of power.

God does not do this with half measures but "according to the might of his glory." Κράτος is might
that is put forth into action while ἰσχύς is strength
whether it is put into action or not. God's δόξα is the
shining forth of any or of all his attributes. Here the
context implies that we think of his love, grace, and
mercy as these shine forth in "the Word of the truth
of the gospel present with us" (v. 5). It is not his
omnipotence that fills us with power but his Word and
the knowledge of his blessed will in Christ Jesus. The
might of God's glory is as great as the glory of his
attributes, a might that is so great as ever ιο supply us
with spiritual power in every regard by means of the
gospel if only we draw on this might and use the
channel of the Word of the gospel (objective) and the
knowledge (subjective) of his will.

Paul does not revert to good works as requiring
this power from God (v. 10) but advances to the qualities in us from which such good works spring: God
empowers us "for all perseverance and longsuffering
with joy." By ὑπομονή, "remaining under," more than
"patience" (our versions) is meant: "It does not mark
merely the endurance, the *sustinentiam* (Vulgate), or
even the *patientiam* (Clarom), but the *perseverantiam*,
the *brave* patience with which the Christian contends
against the various hindrances, persecutions, and
temptations that befall him in his conflict with the

inward and outward world" (Trench). Thus it always applies to *things* and not to *persons;* thus it is also never ascribed to God but only to us.

Μακροθυμία = "longsuffering," holding out long against provocation to decisive action. It is used regarding both God and us and always refers to persons who provoke and should be dealt with. Chrysostom calls "perseverance" the queen of the virtues. "All" means every form of this perseverance and longsuffering as at any time or in any circumstance things or persons may distress us. Nor are we to make a long face about it, but all our perseverance and longsuffering are ever to be accompanied by (μετά) joy and not by a sickly smile behind which the weak heart longs only for relief, but by actual joy that reflects the power for which nothing is too hard, nothing is too long, this power that comes from the true knowledge of the gospel. All our good works are to be backed by these mighty virtues or qualities.

12) Thus Paul advances to the last step: "thanking the Father, him who made us fit for the part of the lot of the saints in the light." Because the participles occurring in v. 10, 11 are preceded by a modifier, some think that this is the case also here: "with joy giving thanks to the Father." The point is only rhetorical; in either case the sense is exceptional. Yet in v. 10, 11 the prefixed modifiers must be construed with the participles; here "with joy" is not necessary to complete the thought of the participle. As one reads he would not halt before "with joy" but after this phrase. The readings vary; "the Father" has the best authority, we drop the additions. The fatherhood here referred to ought not to be restricted to the relation to us; for in the next clause we have "the Son of his love."

"He who made us fit (sufficiented us) for the part (portion) of the lot of the saints in the light" is explained by what follows, which describes how the

Father did this, namely by a mighty act of rescue, a glorious act of transfer into saving possession. So we need not here expound "made us fit." "Us" is correct because the first person plural follows; "you" would be out of place at this point despite the texts that have it. Paul is including himself and Timothy with the Colossians.

We part company with those who refer the next phrase to heaven: made us fit "for the part of the lot of the saints in the light." Κλῆρος means "lot." When our versions and the dictionaries translate this Greek word "inheritance," and the Germans combine μέρος and κλῆρος into *Erbteil* as though two *articulated* Greek nouns could have the force of a compound, this is due to the conception that Paul is referring to our heavenly inheritance, and some refer to v. 5 as proof, "the hope laid away for us." Paul, however, speaks of "the lot of the saints" in this life. In this lot, Paul says, we have "the part (portion)" for which the Father has made us sufficient.

The debate about "in the light," as to whether it modifies the participle "made sufficient" or "the saints" (our versions ignore the article "*the* light"), is settled by the fact that the whole expression is a unit: "the part of the lot of the saints in the light," the part of the lot they have is entirely "in the light." This very definite light is "the Word of the truth of the gospel present for you" (v. 5); its rays are "the knowledge, wisdom, and understanding" in v. 9 ("knowledge" again in v. 10). The opposite of "the light" is "the darkness" mentioned in v. 13. Both "the light" and "the darkness" are viewed as powers, the former as the means for making us bear fruit and grow, the latter as "the authority or power" from which the Father has rescued us.

If anything more is needed to show that Paul is speaking of the part of the lot we have been fitted for

in this life, the series of participles used is sufficient:
the lot of the saints is to bear fruit and to grow in
every good work by means of the knowledge of God,
to do this as being empowered in all power for perseverance and longsuffering with joy, and while doing
this to thank the Father for this lot and for the part
of it for which he has fitted us. The three participial
statements with their modifiers are a whole, all take
place in this life; there is no sudden turn so that the
third which mentions thanksgiving looks up into
heaven and our coming lot in the inheritance that is
still awaiting the saints.

The saints here on earth have a blessed lot that is
lighted up by "the light" of the gospel, its knowledge
fills them with power to bear the fruit of good works.
Paul prays for ever more of this blessed knowledge
and this light for the Colossians (v. 9). These saints
have the blessed lot of bearing fruit of all kinds, being
empowered, as they are, for perseverance, etc. Among
all these saints Paul, Timothy, and the Colossians have
their place so that they, too, have been fitted for the
special part the Father wants them to occupy in the lot
of the great body of the saints. Paul has his portion
as an apostle, Timothy as Paul's assistant, Epaphras
as founder and leader of the Colossians, each of the
Colossians in his special place as one of the saints. The
whole great lot of them and the part of it that falls to
each person are "in the light," illumined by the gospel.

13) Here, as elsewhere, we see that ὅς is often
demonstrative (see v. 15) : **he, the One who rescued
us out of the authority of the darkness and transferred us into the kingdom of the Son of his love, in
connection with whom we have the ransoming, the
remission of the sins, etc.**

What a blessed lot is ours! Any person who has
part in this lot is blessed. But here we see how the
Father fitted us for our portion of the lot of his saints

in the light. *He* is the one, he who fitted us, "who rescued us," etc. All of these terms connote power. Ῥύομαι, "to rescue," requires a power that is greater than the power from which the rescue is effected. Already in connection with v. 11 we have said that this is the power of love, grace, and mercy. "Out of the authority" again involves power, ἐξουσία, the right and the power that goes with it; hence our versions translate: "out of the power," and others render: "out of the power domain."

"Of the darkness" plainly marks this darkness as a tyrant power. We need not say that "the darkness" is personified as we should scarcely say so much for "the light." But this we must say, especially when we follow the meaning of "the darkness" through the New Testament: it is conceived as a definite power that is horrible and monstrous. It holds all men in its authority, and all are powerless to escape. Only the Father, only he could effect our rescue, and the aorist says that he did so. In the verb "to rescue" redemption and justification are combined. To rescue anyone out of the authority of the damnable darkness is the negative for placing him "in the light," to have his lot there, the part of that lot for which God fits him.

This positive is, however, stated in a still grander and more blessed way: "and transferred us into the kingdom of the Son of his love." Matthew calls this "the kingdom of the heavens" and a few times uses the form that is found in the New Testament generally, "the kingdom of God." Nine times it is called the kingdom of Christ, beginning with Luke 23:42 and John 18:36 and ending with Rev. 1:9. On this kingdom see either Matt. 3:2, or Mark 1:15, or Luke 1:33, or John 3:3. It is present wherever God (or Christ) rules with love and grace. The very word denotes power as does also the verb "transfer." The idea that

Paul understands the kingdom in the eschatological sense, and that this aorist "transferred" is proleptic, is untenable. For this kingdom goes back to Adam and is now present wherever the gospel power rules.

Only here does Paul use the expression "the Son of his love," which the A. V. frankly regards as an attributive genitive, translates with a rather common adjective: "his dear Son," and thereby rather loses its force. It is attributive like "his beloved Son" and yet stronger than that. Augustine regarded it as a genitive of origin, and Lightfoot and others agree with him: the Son begotten in eternity of God who is love. The idea of deity lies in the word "the Son" and not in the term "his (the Father's) love." This genitive refers to the work for which the Father sent his Son, at the beginning of which the Father himself called him "my beloved Son" (Matt. 3:17) and did likewise when Christ was in the midst of it (Luke 9:35). Paul borrows his expressions from these utterances.

14) The thought is not yet complete; to the Father's making us fit, rescuing, and transferring us there is now added what has been bestowed upon us sinners to make us fit for the kingdom of the Son: "in connection with whom (faith making this connection) we have the ransoming, the forgiveness of the sins" which once held us bound under the authority of the darkness. In Eph. 1:7 this same statement about what we have in Christ follows his great name, "the Beloved One."

The word ἀπολύτρωσις denotes release by having a λύτρον, "ransom," paid for us. For a full discussion, including the synonymous terms as well as the pagan ransoming of slaves, see Rom. 3:24. In Eph. 1:7 the ransoming price, the sacrificial blood, is at once mentioned; here "the blood of his cross" is mentioned in v. 20. "The ransoming" is a better English term than "the redemption" because the latter has grown pale. We must ever resist the efforts to reduce the word to the meaning "deliverance" so that the idea of the ransom, the sacrifice, and the substitution is eliminated (λύτρον ἀντί, Matt. 20:28; Mark 10:45).

The ransoming is intended for all men, but only believers "have it" with all its blessed effects. It is theirs personally by faith alone. Hence the apposition "the remission of the sins," the essential effect of Christ's ransoming for all believers. The Scriptures never identify the ransoming with the remission. When this is asserted on the strength of II Cor. 5:19-21, this passage is misinterpreted; see the author on this passage. God remits the sins of those only who repent and believe, the sins of all others are "retained" (John 20:23), on them the wrath of God abides, they are already condemned (John 3:18, 36). Did Caiaphas, Annas, Pilate have the remission of their sins? Remission = justification by faith and is that act of God by which, the moment faith is kindled in a poor sinner's heart, God in heaven pronounces that sinner free from guilt and declares him righteous for the sake of Christ's merits.

Ἄφεσις = "remission," sending the sins away so far that they will never be found. How far that is Ps. 103:12; Micah 7:19; Isa. 43:25; 44:22 state. Our English "forgiveness" must always be understood in this sense. All the sweetness that lies in the word "grace" lies likewise in the word *aphesis*. "Sins" = "trespasses" in Eph. 1:7, everything wherein we have missed the mark set for us in the law by God. The sins cannot be separated from their guilt. The sending away of the sins sends away also all their guilt. In the final judgment (Matt. 25:34) not a single sin is mentioned in connection with a single believer; but look at those who did not believe — all their sins are there.

The ἵνα clause with its additions (v. 9-14) states the substance of Paul's prayer for the Colossians. He prayed thus since he first heard of their faith and he continues to pray thus even now when he has heard of their danger from Judaizers. It is perfectly true that Paul might pray in the same way for all his other congregations. This truth is often pointed to by those who wish to indicate that Paul's prayer is only of a general nature and without reference to the present dangerous situation in Colosse. What is true about this view is only the fact that the prayer contains no outspoken references to the dangers. What, however, is also true is the fact that the mention of this prayer is introductory to Paul's warning in this letter.

This prayer and similar ones for other congregations include times of peace as well as times of danger. It is one and the same "Word of the truth of the gospel present for us" (v. 5), one and the same knowledge, wisdom, and understanding, one and the same spiritual power thus conveyed to us that build us up in peace and give us the victory in war. The Ephesians were at peace. Note that after praying for knowledge for them Paul speaks of being built up (2:20), of continuous upbuilding (4:20), the whole organization of the *Una Sancta* being arranged accordingly (4:7-16). Yet even in this picture of unity, peace, family oneness in one body Paul touches also upon false doctrine and deception (4:14), against which the same knowledge is to protect us. So also in the case of the Colossians, who after a peaceful development are now at war, no new means are to constitute the defense but only the old means that built them up in peace. These must now be used for war. That is the connection underlying all that Paul writes in these preparatory paragraphs.

Read in this light, the things Paul touches on in his prayer were undoubtedly understood aright by the

Colossians as applying to their defense against the Judaizers. They must know fully the will of God in order to remain unshaken (v. 9), they must use this knowledge against their foes in all spiritual wisdom and understanding (v. 9). Their one aim must be to please the Lord in every way and not to be swerved aside to please the Judaizers (v. 10). They will please the Lord when they keep on bearing fruit and growing in every good work (avoiding every false work) in the true knowledge of God (v. 11) ; when they let God fill them with power to persevere in joy as they stand solidly in this power (v. 11) and ever thank him for their lot in the light of the gospel and never think of exchanging it for the darkness of the Judaistic error (v. 12). Did God not rescue them from the darkness and transfer them into his Son's kingdom (v. 12) where they have the ransoming and the remission (v. 13)? Shall these errorists ever induce them to turn from the Son and his kingdom, from all that they have in him? These are the implications of this prayer, which are all the stronger psychologically because they are only implications.

Paul and Timothy Recount for the Colossians the Glories of Christ and of His Position together with the Tremendous Effects of His Work

15) In the section v. 3-14 the "we" is prominent; v. 15-20 are entirely about Christ who has already been called "the Son of the Father's love," the King of the kingdom (v. 13). He and what we believers have in connection with him are thus introduced because of what is now to be said about his person, his position, and his work. These things are not new to the Colossians. In concise form they restate for the Colossians the mighty facts about the Son of the Father's love because these facts destroy root and branch the

error with which the Judaizers were operating in Colosse. We are glad to state that this is generally recognized. Here is the great ἐπίγνωσις (v. 9, 10) that is full of power when it is used in wisdom and understanding (v. 10, 11) and will overcome all this foolish error.

He who is the image of God, the invisible One, the first-born of all creation, because in connection with him were created all the things (that exist) **in the heavens and on the earth, the visible and the invisible, whether thrones or lordships or rulerships or authorities — all of them have been created through him and for him, and he is before all things** (whatsoever)**, and all the things** (that exist) **have their permanence in connection with him.**

This is the first unit of the great Christological section, the other is found in v. 18-20. The first deals with Christ's supreme position above the whole universe of creatures (Creator, Preserver); the second deals with him who is this in the universe as the head of the church. The parallel passages are Eph. 1:20-23 and Heb. 1:3, which should be compared.

Those who would begin a new sentence with v. 15 are undoubtedly correct: v. 15-20 form an objective unit about Christ and are thus distinct from the subjective "we" section that precedes and the subjective "you" section that follows. Those who differ and point to the relative ὅς are also right even as the subject of this section, the "who" of whom all this is said, is "the Son of the Father's love" of v. 13. We should combine both the independence and the dependence of these verses. The relative "who" is relative. Paul wants no complete break; at the same time the relative is of the greatest importance because of the mighty statements which it introduces. While it makes no break in the thought it has demonstrative force: *"He,*

HE who," etc. See similar demonstrative relative pronouns in Rom. 2:29; 3:8; 3:30; elsewhere.

The antecedent is "the Son of his love." We may as well right here answer the question that arises. Some of the things predicated of Christ reach back to a time before the incarnation, others follow the incarnation. The Scriptures freely name Christ according to his person, according to one or the other or both natures, and, no matter how he is named, predicate of him divine or human or both divine and human things. This is due to the personal union of the two natures, a union that involves the communication of the divine attributes to the human nature. The person is ever the eternal Son of God. Our poor intellect vainly seeks to conceive what the Scriptures state in this simple way. It will ever be beyond human conception even as in the whole universe no other being that has two such natures in one person exists.

The same is true with regard to time and dates in time regarding God and the God-man. The Creator of time is not bound by differences of time; our minds are chained to succession and limitation of time and cannot even conceive of the relation of the timeless God to events occurring in time. Before a thing occurs it is non-existent to us, then it occurs, and we date it and look back upon it as past. God and Christ are above anything like this. The Lamb was slain from the foundation of the world, Rev. 13:8, not ideally merely but in fact. It is useless for us to try to conceive this. All the saints stood before God ere the creation of the world as we shall see them after time shall be no more, not merely as a mental picture in God's mind but in a reality that was as factual as that of the last day. Second Peter 3:8 gives us a mere inkling. It is thus with regard to "the Son of his love." All the soteriology implied in the genitive existed in eternity as truly as when on a certain day God spoke Matt. 3:17 and on a later day Luke 9:35.

The same is true with regard to the acts of Christ. *We* cling to dates: the first six days of creation, the incarnation 4,000 years later, the resurrection and the enthronement thirty-three years after that. Accordingly our wisdom divides: these acts are placed *before* the incarnation, those *after;* these are ascribed to the Son ἄσαρκος, those to the Son ἔνσαρκος. Try as we will, our minds cannot rise above this divided conception. Even the miracle of the personal union of the natures with its communication of attributes is unable to lift cur minds high enough so that we can conceive how in actuality and not merely verbally or ideally the human nature of Christ took part in the creation of the world.

We stumble at the dates. Then we start to reason and rationalize; we are like a child that is flapping his arms and imagining that he is flying. We may land in the morass of denial and skepticism, at best in a learned, puerile theology. We need to read only a little philosophy to see how the greatest reasoners become confused when they try to conceive what time and space are. These are strong warnings for us lest we, too, go beyond our little shallow mental depth, not only in our natural thinking, but especially in our thinking regarding the God-man. The Scriptures present the facts, these are inconceivable but still eternal facts. Accept them, bow down and worship, leave a little to the light of glory, rejoice in Christ, God and man in one!

We translate: "*the* image of God, *the* first-born," although these nouns have no articles. It will not do to say with R., *W. P.* that these are predicates and for this reason lack the articles, for predicates have the article when, as here, they are identical and inter-changeable with the subjects (R. 767). The articles could, indeed, have been used. But they are often omitted when the noun names a person or an object, the duplicate of which does not exist (R. 794). This seems to apply here. "The image of God, the invisible One," expresses the relation to God, yet this relation as pertaining to men; the God-man is this image for our sakes. The second appellation is thus also appositional: "the first-born of all creation." The Son of his love is not two distinct and different things but, being the one, he is thereby also the other. As the first-born he is as such related to God and thus not only to men but stands in a certain supreme relation even to all creation.

Εἰκών, "image," is *Abbild*, which always implies a *Vorbild*, always implies derivation, hence is far more than ὁμοίωμα, "likeness," in which only resemblance and not derivation is implied (Trench, *Synonyms*). What derivation "image" implies is expressed already by the antecedent of ὅς, namely "the Son of his (the Father's) love." It is the derivation of eternal sonship in relation to the Father. The same thought lies in the synonym "the first-*born*." The eternal Son born of the Father is "the image" of the Father, "the effulgence of his glory and the impress of his substance (ὑπόστασις)," Heb. 1:3. Man was created (not born) in God's image. Man thus had the image, was in it, but was not the image. The difference is vast.

This, we think, answers the question as to whether the word "image" contains the idea of visibility, as some think it does. In man the image consisted in concreated holiness and righteousness which are not visible but are intended to appear in the character and the life of man. It would seem that a similar idea is expressed when the Son is described as "the image" of the Father. This visibility is here expressed by the genitive: "the image of God, the invisible One." It is not in accord with grammatical usage to say that the adjective that is added by a second article has no emphasis. It is used to add emphasis: the article makes an apposition and even a climax of the adjective (R. 776). The invisible God becomes visible to men in "the Son of his love" as "the image of the invisible God."

We have Christ's own word: "He that hath seen me hath seen the Father," John 14:9. Again John's testimony (1:14) : "We beheld his glory, glory as . . . of the Father" (see the author on this passage). Isaiah saw what John saw, what Philip saw (John 12:41) when he wrote Isaiah 53. This is not a visibility of the image that is comprehended by mere physical sight (John 12:40; II Cor. 4:4) but one for the eyes of faith (II Cor. 4:6).

The point of all this is the fact that these designations of Christ are soteriological and that, as such, they pertain to Christ's human nature and his saving work that was wrought by means of this nature. We have seen this in the designation "the Son of his love." We see it in the same way in "the image of God, the invisible One." This does not refer merely to the deity of the Son. The three persons are one in essence in their eternal existence. "Image" applies to none of them; in the oneness of their deity and their essence all are alike invisible. The Son "of his love" was such in his human nature by which he wrought out our salvation (Matt. 4:17; Luke 9:35; Eph. 1:6) ; this Son of his love as such was "the image of God, the invisible One," in his human nature. So Isaiah 53 saw him (John 12:41), Abraham likewise (John 8:56-58). But here again, as we have attempted to explain above, we must not tie our minds to time. The incarnation occurred on a certain date in time; but Rev. 13:8 lifts everything above time just as does every other passage which places the soteriology into eternity.

These terms should, then, not be dated from the *sessio* at God's right hand, nor ought one to say that

they do not apply to "the historic Christ," "historic"
being a modern term for what is more adequately
expressed by the state of humiliation. Christ is the
image of the invisible God not only during this state
but timelessly so that our powers of conception are
hopelessly left behind when we think of how this can
possibly pertain to his human nature. No human mind
can even conceive eternity (timelessness) ; our mind
ceases to function where infinity of any kind begins.
It is good to know this so that, when men confront us
with statements like this one about the historic Christ
and the glorified Christ, we may quietly lay them aside.
For John (1:14), for Isaiah, for Abraham, for Adam,
yea for the Father in all eternity the God-man was
"the Son of his love," "the image of God, the invisible
One," and thus also "the first-born of all creation."

There is no need to insist on the translation "every
creature" (A. V.) in preference to "all creation" (R.
V.) since in the case of abstract nouns the difference
between "all" and "every" (πᾶς and πᾶς ὁ) vanishes (R.
772). The ancient and the modern Arian contention
that Christ is here called a "creature" although the
chief one created by God is nullified by the very words
Paul uses. He does not write πρωτόκτιστος, "the first-
created," but πρωτότοκος, "the first-*born.*" Beside him
Paul places πᾶσα κτίσις, "all *creation.*" This is not a
comparison between creatures, the creature Christ and
all other creatures. Still less does "first" refer to time
and to a date. "First-born" denotes rank. Nor does
"all creation" = the new spiritual creation so that
Christ's pre-eminence over believers is expressed as
it is in Rom. 8:29.

Philo philosophizes about the Logos as a cosmic
principle, which was not even a person, to say nothing
of a person incarnate, see C.-K. 1076. "The first-born"
is used here as it is in Exod. 4:22: Ps. 89:27, late Jewish writers apply the word to even God himself

(Ewald). As the significance of the terms themselves shows, the genitive cannot be partitive; it is the genitive of comparison (here a superlative comparison, R., W. P.) : "the first-born as compared with all creation" (outranking all creatures) ; or, if one prefers, the genitive of relation, which expresses the same thought: "the first-born in relation to all creation," outranking all creatures in every relation. The God-man in both of his natures towers above the whole creature world.

We are to see him as "the image of God, the invisible One," for our salvation and thus "the first-born of all creation." As the one he is necessarily the other. His relation to God necessarily involves his relation to the creation. It is asked why Paul uses the term "first-born." The answer that the Colossian Judaizers used it and perhaps used also "the image," etc., is not satisfactory, whether it is supposed that they employed these terms in the later Gnostic sense which makes Christ an intermediate being, or indeed acknowledged his full deity and yet lowered his saving work.

We lack any indication that Paul is quoting either term from the lips of these Judaizers. We also do not know that these Judaizers had in any way become acquainted with Alexandrine speculation, which acquaintance would appear in these designations of Christ. No Alexandrine speculation dealt with Jesus Christ at this early date. It is doubtful whether Christianity had as yet been planted in Alexandria; it could at least not as yet have issued in such speculation and philosophical theory, to say nothing about such speculation having reached a distant little town like Colosse. These are Paul's own terms, both of them are pure and untainted by any speculation that had arisen anywhere.

Both get their light from "the Son of his love." This Son is the image of his Father, who possesses all his majesty, but in visibility. This Son is thus "the

first-born" who infinitely outranks all creation. "Born"
— not created. Paul's term "first-born" touches hands
with John's μονογενής, "the Only-begotten." Both of
these are as metaphysical as the term "the Son." Both
apply to the error of the Colossian Judaizers. This
error is not Gnostic as we shall see. Paul is not pitting
the true meaning of these terms against a false,
inferior meaning that was put into them by the
Judaizers.

These are also not strange, new terms which the
Colossians had as yet not heard. They are used as
though Paul's readers will at once assent to them as
stating exactly what the Son, the God-man, is. They
thus are the admitted major premise to which Paul
adds the minor and then draws his deduction, one that
destroys the entire inferior view the Judaizers had
of the extent and the power of Christ's work. So much
for the present. It is as though Paul says: "You and
we most certainly believe and confess that the God-
man Christ Jesus is the Son of the Father's love,
namely the image of the invisible God, the first-born
of all creation." The Colossians will answer, "Indeed,
we so believe and confess."

16) With ὅτι Paul adds the evidential reason for
these designations of Christ, the reason that was fully
known to his readers: "because in connection with him
all the things (that exist, τὰ πάντα) were created." Ἐν
is not instrumental: "by him were created" (A. V.).
It is an untenable idea to say that "in him" means that
Christ was the architype who in himself contained the
ectype, "all things," either in the sense that he furnished the pattern for them or that the eternal ideas
existed in him (Philo's Logos). Here and scores of
times ἐν means: "in connection with." What connection is referred to is left unsaid and is to be inferred
from the context. In v. 17 we have διά: "through
him all the things have been created." Add John 1:2,

"without him" nothing came into existence. The *opera ad extra sunt indivisa aut communa* and are thus ascribed to any one of the three persons although creation is ascribed to the first *per eminentiam*. Thus "in connection with him" does not exclude the Father or the Spirit. The aorist "were created" is historical and takes us back to Genesis 1.

The real problem for our mental powers is how this predication can possibly refer to the God-*man*. The usual assumptions are based on conceptions of time and operate with "ideal" pre-existence: all exists only in the mind of God. This is about the best one can do as long as one thinks that time binds God. If we drop this restriction and let the communication of the divine attributes bestow on the human nature also the acts of deity we may more nearly approach the facts regarding the God-man in his connection with the creation of all that exists although even then we shall never for a moment pretend to visualize or really to comprehend them. Apart from its connection with the God-*man* this creating, calling into existence from nothing, is so incomprehensible to our finite mentality that skeptics like Spencer make this incomprehensibility the ground for unqualified denial although they thereby gain nothing, for they run into the other incomprehensibility, a non-created world. Blind as we are to comprehend the first step, creation itself, we are not surprised at finding ourselves blind to comprehend the second, the connection of Christ's humanity with creation.

The emphasis is on the phrase "in connection with him." This does not, of course, suggest the contrast: "with him alone and not with another," but means that this astounding act is connected with him, this creation of all things. This would be a platitude if creation were predicated only of deity, only of the Son in his deity. Then, too, all these titles, "the Son of his

love, the image, etc., the first-born," etc., would end in
pointlessness.

This becomes even more obvious when we note the
specifications: "all the things in the heavens," etc.
That is the universe unlimited, but this universe with
its supermundane parts most impressively indicated.
To say that the act of their creation places the deity,
no matter which person is thought of, above them is
saying nothing valuable or pertinent; that this act
(rather *already* this act) establishes the supremacy of
the God-*man* also in his human nature above all that is
in the universe, in particular above all spirit beings, that
is the fact that is so pertinent for the Colossians. It is a
fact that was long known to them but is now one to be
used by them for ignoring all the Judaistic notions
which it helps to defeat. Paul draws on it for this
reason.

The listing of "all the things" as being those "in
the heavens and on the earth," etc., is very pointed.
First, it expresses absolute universality: "in the heavens and on the earth, the seen and the unseen." But
here there is already the second idea that those in the
heavens, or those unseen whether in the heavens or on
the earth, may control at least some of the things on
the earth, some of the seen things, so that the wise
Christians, as the Judaizers claim, need to employ
measures outside of the gospel to protect themselves.
This is folly when we look at "the Son of the Father's
love," etc., at the eminence of both of his natures, the
human being not less supreme over "all creation" as is
evidenced by the act of creation itself. The spirit
world is therefore mentioned in detail, in appositional
specifications of "the unseen things": "whether thrones
or lordships or rulerships or authorities." The Judaistic speculative philosophy had much to say about
these and showed how they operated with earthly ele-

ments, and how the gospel was not enough to keep Christians safe.

The four terms are arranged in neither a descending nor an ascending scale. The four terms do not designate four classes or ranks; neither do those listed in Eph. 1:21 and elsewhere. The idea that "thrones and lordships" = good angels, "rulerships and authorities" evil angels, is likewise untenable. The distinction between good and evil is not as yet made. The absoluteness of the God-man's supremacy is here expressed in all its absoluteness; what this involves follows presently. All these unseen beings have thrones, lordships, rulerships, authority, none are without the one or the other. Each has a higher or a lower throne and the corresponding lordship, rulership, and authority. Divide horizontally to obtain the ranks and not perpendicularly. Whether these spirits have been assigned their positions or have usurped them is still left unsaid, Paul has not as yet reached that point. We note only that the four terms are close synonyms (hence, perhaps, "powers" is not used here.)

Paul repeats and thus emphasizes, yet with additions: "all of the things (all of them) through him and for him have been created." There is no exception. They have their origin by creation, by nothing higher; they are to be classified with "all creation" (v. 15), are in the same class with the visible things such as stones and sticks. But now the perfect tense states that they remain as having been created, they never get beyond that state. Paul now also writes "through him" (the God-man), but R. 582, 820 should warn us not to put too little into διά which often names the agent with the passive. In Rom. 11:36 both διά and εἰς are used with reference to God as they are here used with reference to the God-man; only ἐκ is not used with reference to the latter.

This does not justify subordination, it ascribes the origin of all things to the first person only *per eminentiam* just as redemption is ascribed to the second and sanctification to the third. "For him" is to be construed with the perfect tense and = for him to control, for him to achieve his ends in them. As διά reaches back to the first origin, εἰς reaches forward to the ultimate goal. Both origin and goal and all that lies between as regards *all* created beings are connected with the God-man, with him as being infinitely supreme.

17) Two additional statements complete the immense thought so far expressed: "and he is before all things whatever (no article), and all the things that exist (once more the article) have their permanence in connection with him," in connection with whom they were created in the first place. Creation and preservation naturally go together. The latter is highly pertinent here. No created being in the universe is independent of Christ. All are "through him and for him" so that "he is before them," and all of them have their continuous existence only "in connection with him." Note the succession of the pronouns: δι᾽ αὐτοῦ — εἰς αὐτόν — αὐτός — ἐν αὐτῷ — all having equal emphasis and all of them carrying forward the emphatic ἐν αὐτῷ that occurs at the beginning of v. 16.

The interpretation that πρό is temporal but refers only to the deity of Christ is not correct. When I ask myself what point Paul makes in saying that the deity of Christ exists (some even accent ἔστι, "exists") prior to all created things I confess that I have no answer. This statement does not touch upon the Gnostic or even the Arian heresy, both of which are of a later date. The epistle nowhere indicates that in Colosse the Judaizers denied the eternal deity of Christ. If they had denied this they would not have been so dangerous to the Colossians; Paul would also have written otherwise in the body of his epistle.

Others let πρό denote rank: Christ is "ahead" of all things whatsoever. But the pre-eminence of Christ with regard to both of his natures has been most effectively stated in v. 15; this little πρό would be only a faint restatement of Christ's rank. Moreover, the use of πρό to indicate rank is doubtful. When one looks at the examples offered in the dictionaries and the commentators, all of them prove to be examples that refer only to time or to place: James 5:12 and I Pet. 4:8, "above all things" = first of all in time or in place.

The statement is a double one: *"he* is before all things in time, and in connection with *him* all of them have their permanent existence." He must most certainly be *before* them if their continuous existence is to depend on him. But this dependence is not divided so that up to the time of the incarnation (some say up to the glorification — Kenoticists) the deity of the Son ἄσαρκος preserved all things, and since that date both the deity and the humanity of the Son ἔνσαρκος do so. Paul cancels this division: "he is *before* all things" in both natures. Eternity is communicated to the human nature just as all the other divine attributes are. Inconceivable? Most assuredly! Even "eternity" itself, like every other essential divine attribute, is inconceivable. What lies in the statement: "in connection with him were created all the things that exist," namely that Christ in both of his natures is connected with the creation of all things, is now said outright when the preservation of all things is added: "he is before all things whatsoever," and so they all have permanence in connection with him. The perfect συνέστηκε is always used in the sense of the present.

18) We regard v. 15-17 as a unit: Christ in relation to all things, "all things" not only being repeated four times but even inventoried at length. So v. 18-20 are an additional unit: this Christ of v. 15-17 in his relation to the church. These same two units are com-

bined in Eph. 1:10, 11 and 21-23; but in Colossians both the creation and the preservation are mentioned and thus the eternity that was communicated to Christ's human nature.

The verbal formulation is another matter. By beginning v. 17 and 18 in the same way: καὶ αὐτός ἐστι, the end of the first unit of thought is amalgamated with the beginning of the second thought unit. Neither is complete without the other; together they are the full, complete unit. Creation and preservation are connected with the God-man, not for their own sake, but because of his relation to the church. The saving work of the God-man affects all creation. As its saving effects reached back timelessly to Adam, so its effects in the world extend to all things from their creation onward and throughout their preservation, timelessly, for creation and preservation are wholly ἐν αὐτῷ, "in connection with him." The full immensity of it all is here unfolded. Scores of other passages and also many statements of Jesus must be read in the light of this thought.

The immediate purpose Paul has in view in presenting this complex of facts is the annihilation of the Judaistic error in Colosse, which placed grave limitations on the saving work of Christ. No attack was made upon his person although, when it is carried to its logical extreme, the error would eventually extend that far; his work was reduced so as to leave unconquered or only partially conquered many earthly, material elements and the spirits that were supposed to control them, and the Judaizers offered means and methods by which Christians might make themselves safe against these still dangerous powers.

This Judaistic scheme of safety was really silly, and Paul treats it with a sort of lofty disdain. This whole Judaistic fiction collapses before the realities that the God-man, our Savior, as the Son of the Father's love

(v. 13), is his visible image, the first-born of all creation (v. 15), that in him and through him were created all things (see the list, v. 16) which are also
preserved in existence in him, that *he,* this great God-
man, is the head of the church, that his work extends
not to a few Christians alone in an incomplete way, but
to the whole universe in a complete way that exceeds
all comprehension. Seeing this, the Colossians, like
Paul, will disdain the puerile notions of the Judaizers.

**And he is the head of the body, the church, — he
who is the beginning, the first-born of the dead, so
that in all respects he got to be pre-eminent.**

"The head" is soteriological; the God-man is not
the head of all the things that exist. On this point see
Eph. 1:10 and the explanation of ἀνακεφαλαιώσασθαι, and
also v. 22. The God-man is in living, spiritual relation
only to the church, his body. Eph. 1:22, 23; 4:15, 16;
5:23 unfold this relation of headship. Rule and control are usually mentioned, but Eph. 4:15, 16 adds
more: all the spiritual life and the power of the church
are drawn from Christ, the head. But αὐτός includes
all that was said of the Son of the Father's love in v.
15-17 and even what is said of his kingdom in v. 14.
Here, as in Ephesians, "the church" = the entire *Una
Sancta* from Adam to the last believer at the Parousia.

Ὅς is parallel to the ὅς that occurs in v. 15 and just
as demonstrative: "*he,* he who is," etc. R., *W. P.,* calls
it causal: "because *he* is," which we may accept since
emphatic relatives often have causal force. The two
predicates lack the article for the same reason that the
two occurring in v. 15 are anarthrous and are appositional as were those used in v. 15. The God-man is
"the beginning"; this repeats the thought that he is
"before all things whatsoever," but does so in a more
impressive way. Compare Rev. 1:8: "I am Alpha and
Omega, the beginning and the ending," and v. 11, "the
first and the last." "The beginning" cannot be dated

at the resurrection of Christ but goes back to creation: "the beginning of the creation of God" (Rev. 3:14). This first predicate states that he who is the head of the church is the one who has been described in v. 15-17, all of which must be kept in mind when we consider what is now stated. Ἀρχή is, of course, not ἀπαρχή, "first fruits."

The appositional predicate "the first-born from the dead," repeats "the first-born" used in v. 15 and is used in the same sense of supreme rank, but now rank not in comparison with "all creation" but as regards the resurrection of the dead. Yet more is implied here than in Acts 26:23 where Christ is the first to arise, or in I Cor. 15:20, 23 that he is the first fruits. As "the first-born of the dead" he who is "the beginning" itself stands in absolute pre-eminence and supremacy over death and all the powers of death. In v. 15-17 he is presented as "the first-born" in his absolute supremacy as regards all creature *life and existence*, its very creation and its preservation; now he is presented as "the first-born" in the same supremacy as regards *death and its destructive powers*. The idea is not that suggested by "first fruits," that many shall follow in a blessed resurrection (these being the great harvest), that many shall be "later-born" by virtue of this "First-born one." No; as in v. 15, so here, "the first-born" is absolute for life and existence, created and preserved, irrespective of what or who the creature is and so for death and destruction, irrespective of who is involved.

We submit that the ἵνα clause is not final but consecutive. The debate about whether it states God's purpose or Christ's is beside the mark. Paul is stating result: "so that he got to be in all respects pre-eminent." The emphasis is on ἐν πᾶσιν αὐτός. The pre-eminence mentioned in v. 15, etc., is a pre-eminence in one respect or say in two (as far as creation and preservation are concerned), this added pre-eminence makes him pre-eminent *in all respects*, ἐν πᾶσιν, the phrase being just as adverbial (neuter) as it is in Eph. 1:23. If it is made masculine it would have to be: "among all the dead," which would be incongruous. He who is absolutely supreme *in all respects*, "he" (αὐτός) is the head of the church, is in this spiritual relation and connection with her. Note that the second αὐτός repeats the first.

The supposition that Christ's soul entered "the realm of the dead," *sheol*, hades, an intermediate place between heaven and hell, and remained there for three days is advocated in some books and deserves the condemnation which Paul here metes out to the Colossian Judaizers. The soul of Christ was in heaven in his Father's hands and returned to his dead body in the tomb, and thus Christ arose. Γένηται is the ingressive aorist "got to be," the present participle is its complementary predicate. The human nature is so plainly involved that no one even draws attention to it; yet "he" who is the subject in this passage is also the subject in v. 14-18, and we at least refuse to alter this subject — the God-*man*.

19) Ὅτι states the evidential reason by which we know that the God-man is what v. 18 states he is; it corresponds to ὅτι occurring in v. 16, which is to be understood in the same sense. **Because in him it well-pleased all the fulness to dwell** (permanently, aorist) **and through him to reconcile back all the things for him by** (once for all, again aorist) **making peace through the blood of his cross, through him, whether the things on the earth or the things in the heavens.**

The view that, because Christ is the subject in v. 18, he must be the subject also in this verse is negatived already by the emphatically placed phrase ἐν αὐτῷ (repeated from v. 16, 17), which shows that a different

subject follows. We need say no more. Our versions
assume that the unexpressed subject is the Father; a
number of commentators agree. We see no substantial
difference between this idea and regarding "all the
fulness" as the subject (R. V. margin) since the latter
means "all the fulness" of God. Compare 2:9. It is
not necessary that "all the fulness" have a specifying
genitive because this fulness itself is personified by what
is predicated of it in the verb plus its infinitives and
participle.

"All the fulness" pleased to dwell in Christ, not
only a part of it, not only most of it. No domain is
left in which the absolute supremacy of Christ and
of his work is not fully effective. The Judaizers
imagined such a domain into which Christ and his
work did not fully reach and had invented a system by
which Christians, as they claimed, could protect themselves from ill effects that came from this domain.

We need not specify what "all" this fulness includes, for it is equal to all that the absolute pre-eminence of "the first-born" in v. 15 and 18 embraces; it
is all that places the God-man in both natures above
the being and the life of the whole creation and above
every power of death and of destruction. Yet when
Paul writes "to dwell" in him, as he does in 2:9, this
indwelling refers especially to the human nature. This
indwelling is the preliminary part of the statement.

20) The main thought lies in the next infinitive:
by thus dwelling in the God-man it pleased this absolute fulness to show itself as such by completely and
fully reconciling all the things that exist (τὰ πάντα as
before) "through him — for him." Dwelling *"in* him,"
this fulness wrought "through him" and "for him"
just as it did in the act of creation (v. 16, 17), where
we have the same three phrases. The extent is also
the same, it includes "all the things" that exist and
makes the supremacy absolute. "Through him" is

repeated, and we once more have the all-comprehensive specifications: "whether the things on the earth or the things in the heavens," the terms being stated in the reverse order, cf. v. 16.

"To reconcile back all the things to him" is further explained by the participle of means: "by making peace through the blood of his cross." The infinitive and the participle are effective aorists and also historical: once for all, permanently. "The blood" = the sacrificial blood, it is more specific than "the death" and points more clearly to sacrifice. "Of his cross" notes the curse involved in the God-man's death (Gal. 3:13; Phil. 2:8).

All would be perfectly clear and simple if Paul had not written "all the things — whether those on the earth or those in the heavens," especially the latter. We have no difficulty in understanding the effect of Christ's redemption on the world in view of Rom. 8:19, etc., and Rev. 21:1, etc. The difficulty lies in a reference to the good angels in heaven and a statement such as that found in Heb. 2:16.

A great variety of interpretations is offered, among the most unlikely being an angelology which is built up on the basis of Jewish material and is then attributed to Paul, which claims that the good angels were faulty and thus themselves needed a reconciliation and the making of peace. As an exponent of this opinion see Peake (*Expositor's Greek New Testament*), especially his introduction. It is enough to say that the Scriptures know of no moral fault in the good angels. R., *W. P.*, follows Abbott and calls Paul's statement "hypothetical," "not categorical," which disregards the aorists and also leaves us in a haze.

The difficulty clears when we note that not all the objects of the God-man's reconciling act are affected alike by that act, but that each class is affected according to its nature, its condition, and its relation. We should also remember that "all creation" is a unit, is never viewed otherwise by the Scriptures, and always includes the whole angel world. "All creation" was disrupted: sin arose in heaven and entered men and the physical universe. The Son of God came to the rescue. But how? He became "the first-born of all creation" (v. 15, 16). But not by assuming the created nature of angels (Heb. 2:16). That means much for the angels with whom sin began. These evil angels are excluded from the rescue, are to be swept out of "the kingdom of the Son of God's love" (v. 13). The first-born of all creation became such by assuming our human nature. His work of rescue was accomplished "through the blood of his cross."

Now the effects. The evil angels were eliminated *eo ipso*. The blood of the cross has the same effect for all men who follow these angels and despise this blood; it rescues only the believers (v. 13). This rescue includes the physical creature world. How this is to be understood is shown in Rom. 8:19, etc. This creature world was "subject to vanity not willingly," it never willed sin. It shall be affected accordingly, i. e., according to its nature and its relation to us: a glorious liberation shall turn it into a new earth (Rom. 8:20), one that is joined to heaven (Rev. 21:1, etc.). Thus as "the blood of the cross" has its effects by *eo ipso* excluding the evil angels and then also all unbelieving men, as it establishes the eternal kingdom of the Son of God's love, it has its effects also on the good angels and on all "the things in the heaven," not, indeed, as though they needed a change in themselves (ἀποκαταλλάσσειν), a "being made other" (ἄλλος) in themselves, but as requiring a change and a new relation to the restored universe. Once there was war (note, for instance, Rev. 12:7) that involved all the good angels; by his cross "the first-born from the dead" has created peace, and this peace shall soon be absolute when the whole universe, heaven and earth united in one (Rev. 21:1, etc.), shall be one kingdom of eternal peace.

The cross affects "all creation." Each part of it is *not* affected in the identical way but according to the nature, the condition, and the relation of each part to the whole. We distinguish four grand parts. The cross affects each of them, but each of them differently: evil angels — good angels — man, believing or unbelieving — the physical universe. When we say "the blood of his cross," this means the act of reconciliation, the act of establishing peace. No less than "all creation" is involved in the act of "the first-born of all creation."

The double compound is stronger than καταλλάσσω. C.-K. 133 refers ἀπό to the situation to be left, and κατά to the new direction, "to reconcile back" to a former condition. It may also be possible that the single compound = to produce a condition that is *not* existing, the double to produce a condition that is *no longer* existing. C.-K. adds that it seems that Paul himself formed the double compound, which is found nowhere before his time, formed it in order to express most exactly the thought he had in mind.

The root idea lies in ἄλλος, "other," placing into a relation or a situation that is very much "other" than the existing one. The prepositions only add to this and intensify: completely other or: "away from" the old and "toward" the new. Thus the objects, "all the things that exist," may be diverse in themselves, the act changes their relation according to what their present relation in this πάντα may be. Moreover, εἰς αὐτόν is vital in its emphasis: "for him," for this great first-born of all creation, in whom all the fulness dwelt, effected the stupendous change of all that is on earth and in heaven. He is the King. The change was made by his establishing peace. We see the full, eternal results in his everlasting kingdom of peace.

*Paul and Timothy Remind the Colossians of What
Christ Has Done for Them through the Ministry
Committed to Paul*

21) No Judaistic error that would limit the work
of the God-man or its effect on the world of nature can
find lodgement where the God-man and the mighty
effects of his blood and his cross are known (v. 15-20).
From objective statement Paul turns to subjective experience, to the effects experienced by his readers.

**And you on your part, at one time being alienated
and enemies in your mind in your wicked works, yet
now he reconciled back in connection with the body
of his flesh through his death to present you holy
and blemishless and unreproved before himself —
if, indeed, you remain in the faith, grounded and
seated and not moved away from the hope of the gospel which you heard, that preached in all creation
under the heaven, of which I myself, Paul, got to be
a minister.**

The text that has the aorist active in v. 22 is so well
assured that the variants must be disregarded. West-
cott and Hort print their text with a parenthesis in
v. 22, which makes the construction of the verse very
difficult. They do this because of δέ, which, however, in
no way indicates a parenthesis. A new sentence (in
fact, a paragraph) begins with v. 21, καί connects the
reconciliation of the Colossians with that of all things.

The Colossians are to think of their terrible situation "at one time" so that they may fully realize the
vast extent and the power of the reconciliation which
reached to the eternal hope in heaven. Nothing is
left that might be added to the God-man's work. Robertson regards ὄντας ἀπηλλοτριωμένους as one of the two
periphrastic participles found in the New Testament,
but he does not state how he construes ἐχθρούς. Ὄντας
is the ordinary participle, and the perfect passive participle plus the noun "enemies" are its predicate. The

perfect participle describes the alienation that set in and then continued, and its passive voice implies that an evil power caused this alienation. From whom or from what the Colossians had been alienated need not be said; in Eph. 2:11 it is stated because of the different connection.

Thus turned away, they were "enemies" (the word is always to be understood in the active sense), and there is no need of stating whose enemies they became. The dative τῇ διανοίᾳ may be locative or indicate relation: "in" or "in regard to the mind," *Gesinnung*. They were at one time enemies with the whole moral bent of their mind and thus in connection with the deeds, and the second article emphasizes these deeds as being actively and viciously "wicked." Theirs was a desperate and an apparently hopeless case.

22) "Yet now" (see Eph. 2:13) you who were in this situation "he reconciled back," and this he did "in connection with the body of his flesh through the death" to which he submitted this body of his. Δέ is our ordinary "yet" and marks a contrast. The verb is the same as that used in v. 20, an effective aorist, and here indicates a making "other" so as to include the personal, inward otherness of contrition and of faith (II Cor. 5:20 has the ordinary compound). "The body of his flesh," like Heb. 5:7, "in the days of his flesh," has no relation with an incipient Docetic Gnosticism or with an inability of bodiless and fleshless angel beings; the added genitive helps to emphasize the physical nature of the body which suffered the (well-known) death; note "the blood of his cross" (v. 20). The great first-born of all creation (v. 15), the first-born from the dead (v. 18), is the God-*man* and accomplished the otherness in the Colossians by his bloody physical death. The all-sufficiency of his act is the point.

That is why the infinitive of purpose is added: "to present you holy and blemishless and unreproved be-

fore him" (compare Eph. 5:27), i. e., made thus by
the reconciling effect of his death. "Holy" = separate
unto God and Christ, the opposite of being in a state
of alienation; "blemishless" = without spot or wrinkle
in yourselves; "unreproved" ("unreprovable") = so
that no one can accuse you in any way. This is put in
so strong a way because the Judaizers claimed that
such a state could be attained only when their scheme
of purification and keeping pure is followed in addition
to faith in Christ. Errorists always like to add at
least something to faith in Christ's death, often even
the main saving thing. "Before him" is added emphatically at the end: he, he alone is the Judge on all three
points, let no one listen to any other judges.

We have no trouble as to the subject of the sentence and feel no jar in passing from v. 20 to the next
verses. He who has this body of flesh is so evidently
the subject that we scarcely need to say so. "All the
fulness" that pleased to dwell in him for his mighty
work (v. 20) is only what makes him what he is, and
so this fulness does what he does, and the change of
subject from v. 20 to v. 21, 22 is as natural as it can be.

23) Yet Paul does not fail to add the cautious condition: " — if, indeed (εἴγε)," etc. The Colossians were
troubled by errorists. Would they resist them? Would
they really? Would they abide by the great gospel
facts regarding the person, work, and extent of work
of the God-man? Paul voices no doubt regarding them.
This "if" contemplates reality, the reality that they
will remain what they have been made. Yet the "if"
bids them examine and watch themselves. We should
always have it in mind and especially when error is in
the air. We may here answer the question as to
whether the presentation which the God-man will make
is the one now before his judicial eye or the one at the
end of time. This "if" points to the latter just as does
"the hope of the gospel." Matt. 24:13; Rev. 2:10.

'Επιμένω is construed with the dative: "if you remain on the faith," with which also the three modifiers agree: "having been grounded and founded" on the faith — "seated" solidly on it — "not moved away," etc. But that makes "the faith" objective. We cannot accept the view that "faith" is always subjective (*fides qua creditur*); in many contexts it is *fides quae creditur*. Paul has here presented objectively this faith on which our subjective confidence rests (v. 15-20). On this the Colossians were founded as a foundation is laid on solid rock. They must remain so, solidly "seated" (this word is found in I Cor. 15:58) and "never moved." This last is a present participle to express a condition that continues from now on; the perfect participle is to express a condition that dates from the past and now continues. These two tenses finely match their meanings.

To be sure, "not moved away" implies not leaving the faith on which the Colossians rest. But this faith involves the great gospel hope, the goal of our lives. Hence Paul states it with this significant addition: "not moved away from the hope of the gospel which you heard." "The hope" is objective (see v. 5), "of the gospel" identifies it by means of a possessive genitive: belonging to the gospel, revealed by no other means. The gospel which the Colossians had heard Epaphras had taught them (v. 7, 8); "which you heard" once more approves his faithful work. What a loss: to have heard the true gospel, to have seen this great hope that the first-born will present us in glory as all-perfect before himself (v. 22) and then to let some errorists with foolish notions move us away from it all!

In the same pointed way as in v. 6 Paul adds the world-wide reach of the gospel. There he says that "in the whole world" it bears fruit and grows; here that it is "the one preached in all creation under the heaven." This is not hyperbole as some say; compare "all nations" (Matt. 28:19), "all the world, to every creature" (Mark 16:15), "unto the uttermost part of the earth" (Acts 1:8). It seems that Paul is using the language of Jesus. The point of his doing so is double. This Judaistic doctrine is an insignificant local heresy which Paul scorns as such, which the Colossians should scorn in the same way.

On the other hand, the world-wide gospel of the first-born of all creation — "all creation" is repeated from v. 15 — is not only already planted far and wide under heaven, this work has been especially assigned to Paul as the apostle of the Gentiles: "of which I myself (ἐγώ emphatic), Paul, got to be a minister," dispensing this gospel for the benefit of all men everywhere. This is the transition to what follows (v. 24 to 2:5). Will the Colossians let a few local errorists separate them from this immense gospel? Paul's object is to connect the Colossians with himself in this gospel. Epaphras was only the voice of Paul in Colosse, Paul's own agent in the gospel work entrusted to him by the first-born of all creation. When it is seen aright, all of this must hold the Colossians firmer than ever on their faith-foundation, looking up to their eternal hope.

24) One may make a separate paragraph of v. 24-29, for Paul now for the first time in this epistle begins to speak directly of himself: "I, Paul, became a minister of the gospel." **At present I am rejoicing in the sufferings for your benefit and am filling up in my turn what is lacking of the afflictions of Christ in my flesh for the benefit of his body which is the church, of which I got to be on my part a minister according to the administration of God, the one given to me for you, to fulfill the Word of God, etc.**

From what Paul got to be when he was made an apostle and "a minister" he turns to what he is "now" doing as a prisoner on behalf of the gospel and the church, especially of its Gentile portion. He is rejoicing "in the sufferings" which he is bearing "for your benefit," "on your behalf." A certain amount of suffering falls to the lot of the church because of its connection with Christ. A large part of it has to be borne by the leaders of the church, among whom God has placed Paul as the foremost. Thus he gets to bear the heaviest load of these sufferings. The Colossians are a part of the church; hence Paul says he is bearing these sufferings "for your benefit."

He rejoices to do so. It is a high privilege, a great honor, to have been placed in the position which brings these sufferings on his head instead of on the church generally. Grief and lament are far from Paul's heart; the more suffering comes to him because of his office, the more he rejoices. Is he not a διάκονος, all of whose work and suffering are intended for the benefit of others? The more suffering comes to him, the more is taken from others.

The second statement, which is ampler, elucidates. These sufferings are τὰ ὑστερήματα τῶν θλίψεων τοῦ Χριστοῦ, "the leftover parts of the afflictions of Christ." This does not mean that they are a part of the vicarious sufferings of Christ by which the world's sins are purged away, parts left over to be borne by the church. "It has been finished!" is true. Atonement and expiation are complete. That is why Paul calls what is yet left over literally "what comes behind," "the afflictions of Christ," and names them according to what they are for us, "afflictions."

All of these leftovers result from the hatred of the world toward the great substitute and expiator who died on the cross "for our advantage" and for all who cling to him by faith and follow him. On the road to

Damascus Jesus said to the persecuting Saul, "Why persecutest thou *me?*" As the good that we do the brethren is really done to him (Matt. 25:41), so all the evil that is done to us is really done also to *him.* There is no thought of further expiation in what we suffer for Christ's sake, but in a very real sense our sufferings are blows that are struck at Christ. Paul conceives these leftovers as bitter waters that are gradually being poured into a huge vessel until it is completely filled when at last the final day arrives. So he says: "I am filling up in my turn" my allotment of these leftover afflictions of Christ.

The verb Paul uses is rare. There is a question about the force of ἀντί in the compound. Is it only "in turn" (R. 574) or is it "in place of": *in Stellvertretung ausfuellen* (B.-P. 114)? The latter seems to say too much. In a way what Paul suffered ὑπέρ the church, for its benefit, might be considered as having been suffered also ἀντί, in its stead; for the lightning of persecution generally strikes the leaders of the church and thus spares the rank and file. Yet the verb can scarcely be stressed to mean that much. Paul is engaged in taking his turn in filling up the measure of the sufferings of Christ. Other *diakonoi* will have to have their turn; the great vessel will not be full until the last day arrives. Some interpretations convey a wrong meaning by regarding τὰ ὑστερήματα as "deficiencies," these tribulations of Christ have no "deficiency" of any kind.

Paul is not saying that something was lacking in what Christ had suffered, something that he could not suffer among the Jews, that only Paul in his position as apostle of the Gentiles could suffer. Christ suffered at the hands of both Jews and Gentiles, for Pilate had him scourged and mocked by his Gentile soldiers and then nailed him to the cross. Still less does Paul say that what he is now suffering is filling up what his own previous suffering still lacked. C.-K. 928.

25) All that any Christian suffers is in a way for the benefit of the church, especially for that part of it with which he is personally connected; Paul's office connected him with the entire Gentile church in the closest possible way. In v. 23, as already in v. 7, 8, we have noted his connection with the Colossians through Epaphras. He, therefore, repeats the statement made in v. 23 to the effect that he got to be a *diakonos* of the church. The great spiritual "body," which is the church, receives great benefit through the suffering endured in the physical "flesh" of this its *diakonos* who got to be this "according to the administration of God, the one (especially) given to me."

The measure or norm (κατά) to be applied to any διάκονος, to see what he is, is "the administration" committed to him by God. In v. 7 Epaphras is called a *diakonos*, but the administration committed to him was the leadership of only the one congregation at Colosse. Compare with that Paul's office, the tremendous "administration" entrusted to him. We at once see how the sufferings of this great apostolic *diakonos* were indeed "on behalf and for the great benefit of" the whole church, its vast Gentile section, and thus also of "you" (v. 24), the Colossians who had been converted through Paul's helper Epaphras.

Unfortunately, the R. V., here and in Eph. 1:10; 3:2, 9, translates this word "dispensation"; the A V. does likewise except in Eph. 3:9 where it follows a variant reading. All that we have said in connection with the passages in Ephesians belongs also here, note especially our discussion of Eph. 3:2. Οἰκονομία is not passive: "the dispensation" arranged by God, *Einrichtung* (C.-K. 785); it is active: "the administration," the divine apostolic office given to Paul, the office in its actual administration or operation in Paul's hands. The genitive is qualitative and not subjective. Paul always says that it was "given" to him and at times calls it "the grace" to mark it as an utterly undeserved gift to him who had at one time persecuted the church of God. Here he says "given to me for you" (Colossians) ; for they had been brought to Christ through Paul's apostolic office. In I Cor. 4:1 he calls himself and his assistants οἰκονόμοι of the mysteries of God; but here he refers to his superior office which had been given to him by the Lord in an immediate way (Acts 9:15), the apostleship in the narrow sense. To get the force of this word recall the fact that great lords appointed this and that slave as a steward (οἰκονόμος) over some great estate, gave them such an οἰκονομία. So Paul, the Lord's slave (Rom. 1:1), received his "stewardship" from his heavenly Master. Combine the two terms: Paul is a *diakonos* for the church and so serves men, and he does this because he is an *oikonomos* of God, appointed by him.

Both terms might refer to a minor position or to the highest position of all. Paul's is the latter. This he states in the infinitive clause which is in apposition with "the administration" given to him and which tells what Paul was to carry out by this administration: "to fulfill the Word of God." Some regard this as an infinitive of purpose: "given to me in order to fulfill" — which is less effective. In Rom. 15:19 we have the same expression: "I have fulfilled the gospel of Christ." The A. V. margin offers: "fully preach," which will do for conveying the general sense. "The Word of God" is something to be transmitted and thus to fulfill it is to give it what it wants, what it is for, namely to transmit it to those for whom it is intended. Note the aorist: effective, complete fulfillment. In Rom. 15:19 Paul states to what extent he had so fulfilled the gospel: in a vast circle he had carried it from Jerusalem to Illyricum.

26) We have already seen that his office is that of an apostle in the full sense of the word; but we

are to see that his was the greatest apostleship of all (I Cor. 15:10), the special one to the Gentiles: to fulfill the Word of God, **the mystery that has been hidden from the eons and from the generations, but now it was made public to his saints, to whom God willed to make known what** (is) **the riches of the glory of this mystery among the Gentiles, which is Christ in you, the hope of this glory; etc.**

The commentary is the parallel passage Eph. 3:9-11. "Mystery" = something that one cannot get to know of himself, something that is intended to be revealed. Here the mystery is "one that has remained hidden from the eons and the generations" until now. Paul is saying only how long this mystery has been kept hidden. The Greek counts from the far point forward, hence here has ἀπό, "from the eons on" "from the generations on," the count starting from the first one and moving forward. Eph. 3:10 shows that even the angels did not know this mystery. Here, however, "the eons" denote only the ages of time, and nothing is said about angels. The doubling: "and from the generations on" is done for the sake of impressiveness: so many generations of men during all these eons.

That is why Paul does not continue with another participle. The greatness of the thought is more adequately stated by a finite verb: "but now it was made public to his saints." This is neither irregular nor an anacoluthon but a simple, effective turn of phrase which is followed by the reader without the least effort. The Greek marks only the past fact (aorist); the English prefers the perfect to indicate a recent act: "has been made public," i. e., has been advertised far and wide "to his saints" (see 1:1), to all of them whether they are of Jewish or of Gentile origin.

27) Paul has thus far still left unsaid in what respect "the Word of God" remained a hidden mystery for so long a time and why it was only recently pub-

lished for the saints; this is finally stated: "to whom God willed to make known what is the riches of the glory of this mystery among the Gentiles, which is Christ in you, the hope of this glory." The fact that God had kept the mystery dark for so long a time is implied. It is he who finally willed its fullest publication to the saints, but his will was not that they were still to keep it only to themselves but, as the following shows, that they were to proclaim it so that men everywhere might share in its blessedness.

Read together: to make known (effective aorist) "the riches of the glory of this mystery among the Gentiles": this mystery contains all the riches of all the glory for all who really know it, they are to receive this richness and this glory. The main point lies in the phrase "among the Gentiles." All the riches of the glory contained in this mystery are not any longer to be confined to one nation but are so vast as to be told "among the Gentiles," even the pagan nations in all the world. "This mystery," the Word of God now fully uncovered by God, is full of glory, and this is vast in richness. The main concept is "glory": "what the riches of the glory." It is seen in all the saints; this glory is so rich because it appears "among the Gentiles," these, too — so many of them, in fact — were converted into saints.

There is no need to think of Messianic glory or of God's own glory. Paul himself defines: "which is Christ in you, the hope of this glory" (article of previous reference). The texts that have ὅς instead of ὅ only attract the relative to the gender of the predicate and thus do not change the relative in fact. This relative is naturally neuter, but not because it refers to only one neuter noun, its antecedent is the whole expression: "the riches of the glory of this mystery among the Gentiles," this is "Christ in you," and Christ in you is "the hope of this glory" (the main concept "glory" of the antecedent is repeated). This letter is intended for the Colossians who were former Gentiles. The whole blessed mystery is concreted in them.

Paul individualizes in the most telling way: "Christ *in you*," right in you Gentiles as in a large number of others. And what "Christ in you" means is no less than this in all its completeness: "the hope of this glory," the sure and certain hope that is backed by Christ that this glory of which the revealed mystery speaks will be yours in due time.

At one time Judaism was solid in the opinion that no Gentile could possibly be saved except by becoming a Jew. It was so inconceivable that Gentiles were to be saved without being incorporated into Judaism that it required a special revelation, almost a compulsion, to bring Peter to the level of the real truth (see Acts 10:1-11:18). It was not easy for the revelation of the mystery to penetrate, namely that "Christ in you," in any man's heart, meant "the hope of the (eternal) glory." At least this thought persisted, namely the Judaistic idea that something Jewish would have to be added, that it could not be otherwise. This precipitated the Jerusalem conference (Acts 15).

Even after that the notion persisted, and Judaizers appeared in Galatia who demanded the addition of circumcision, etc.; other Judaizers who made similar demands appeared in Corinth. Now, at this late date, the peculiar Judaizers appear in Colosse with the notion that their system for making earthly elements innocuous for Christians would have to be added to Christ. Against them all and especially against this new kind Paul sets the great first-born of all creation in the absolute completeness of his saving work (v. 15, etc.) and now the Word of God with its mystery that is entirely revealed: Christ in you, this is the hope of the glory, this alone.

The Old Testament Word revealed it all to the Jews; the prophets uttered it again and again. But the Jews refused to see it. The old covenant made them the chosen nation to prepare for Christ. They perverted God's plan so as to make it mean that they were the only nation, so that incorporation into their nation alone insured glory. They mocked Jesus when they said that he might go to the Gentiles (John 7:35). Jews were outraged everywhere when Gentiles were admitted into the kingdom by faith in Christ alone. This clash with the Judaizers in Colosse seems to have been the last that occurred during Paul's apostleship.

28) Paul returns to his office with the two closing relative clauses. "Christ in you," in whom God made known "what is the riches of the glory of this mystery among the Gentiles," of this Christ and "the hope of this glory" Paul says: **whom we on our part are proclaiming, exhorting every man and teaching every man in all wisdom in order that we may present every man complete in Christ, for which I even am toiling, straining according to the working of him which is working in me in power.**

"Christ in you" is the contents of this mystery, he is "the riches," etc., "the hope of the glory." The relative is thus emphatic and demonstrative: "*him* we on our part are proclaiming," *him* as here described. There is salvation and hope of glory in none other (Acts 4:12). Paul now rightly uses not the singular "I on my part" (ἐγώ) as he did in v. 23 ("I, Paul") and in v. 25 but ἡμεῖς, "we on our part." For Paul operates with a group of assistants. Timothy is joining him in this letter, and Epaphras was Paul's agent in establishing the Colossian congregation. With such assistants Paul operated "the administration," the work of the apostleship God had given him to fulfill the Word of God (v. 25). Paul multiplied himself through his assistants, multiplied the proclaiming and thus reached thousands whom he could not have reached single-handedly. This emphatic "we" endorses all Paul's assistants; at the same time this "we" places Paul and his assistant in opposition to any and to all Judaizers who do nothing but invade churches that are already established and spread their errors there.

"We are proclaiming, exhorting every man and teaching every man in all wisdom" describes the manner in which Paul carries out his office as a true apostle. Thus he fulfills the Word of God, the publication of the mystery, the substance of which is Christ.   Paul and his assistants do what God wants, go out in public, go out to "every man" to bring Christ, the hope of glory, to "every man," thus to fulfill the Word of God.   This is a picture that is quite different from that of the Judaizers who did not dream of going out with a public proclamation to "every man," whose work it was to bore into congregations and to undermine their faith in Christ, the hope of the glory.

Καταγγέλλειν is like κηρύσσειν and refers to a public proclamation.   The two participles are modal: "exhorting every man" = urging every person to forsake his idolatry and his wicked ways and to turn to Christ; "teaching every man" = informing and instructing every person in the saving truth about Christ.   "In all wisdom" is added (compare v. 9) because this work requires much wisdom in order to reach now this man, now that man with his wrong religious ideas and habits so as to win him for Christ, the one true hope of the glory.

The one purpose of this public work is "that we may present every man τέλειος in Christ," as having reached the τέλος or goal "in connection with Christ." In him alone it is reached.   The predicate adjective does not mean moral perfection, the "total sanctification" of perfectionists, but the completeness of faith, when a man fully reaches the goal in Christ.   To present every man as such does not here refer to the Parousia but to the present time: each and every believer is to stand forth so that all may see him as one who is spiritually complete and mature (Eph. 4:13, etc., no more babes swayed helplessly by every wind of doctrine, etc.). What a blessed work! How different from that of the Colossian Judaizers! This work had been wrought in the Colossians. Was it now to be ruined and nullified?

29) Reverting to himself as the apostolic leader in this work, Paul adds: "for which (the work just described, in which his assistants help him) I am even toiling, straining (like an athlete) according to the working of him which keeps working in me with power." Καί is the ascensive "even"; even with arduous toil, "agonizing" like an athletic contestant, Paul seeks to fulfill the Word of God (v. 25). God's working or energy is working and energizing in his person (ἐν ἐμοί, R. 587) in power. The accomplishment of this apostolic "administration" (v. 25) requires no less; he who gave Paul the task enables him to toil and strain for it in accord with (κατά) the energy which he himself (God) supplies, which ever energizes and works in Paul's person with power. Paul is only God's instrument; he toils and strains, but not with power of his own, the power comes from God. The results are great, but all are due to this communicated power (I Cor. 15:10). In every way this publication of the blessed mystery is God's work, the glory of it is his alone.

Let us say that this concludes the preparatory section of Paul's letter although we shall not quarrel with those who extend it to 2:5 or even to 2:7. We make the division at this place because 2:1, etc., turn to direct personal address and begin the warning (2:4).

CHAPTER II

II

The Burden of the Letter:
The Warning against the Judaizers, Chapter 2

Paul's Deep Concern Prompts His Warning

1) In 1:29 Paul makes the transition to what follows, and γάρ now completes the connection. Paul toils, "straining" (ἀγωνιζόμενος) with the energy God gives him in his office. **For I want you to know what great strain (ἀγών, matching the participle used in 1:29) I have for you and those in Laodicea and as many as have not seen my face in the flesh.**

In 1:28, 29 Paul speaks of what he and his assistants do for "every man," and thus in 1:29 his straining concerns his entire work. Now he specifies the strain for his readers in their present situation, who were being troubled by Judaizers. In "strain" the picture of a contestant seeking victory in an athletic contest is continued. We need not ask *how* Paul strains and strives; we have his own letter which speaks of his prayers and points to his discussions with Epaphras and with Timothy (1:1) regarding what to do for the Colossians. One preposition makes one group of those for whom Paul strains and not two or more groups: "for you" Colossians, "those of Laodicea," "as many as have not seen my face in the flesh."

Paul thus says that the Colossians and the Laodiceans had never seen him, he had never visited them.

(83)

He includes the Laodiceans because he asks that this letter be sent also to them (4:16). It is proper to conclude that they were facing the same danger as the Colossians. In fact, as we have already stated, we conclude that the letter to the Laodiceans, which Paul wants also the Colossians to read, was written and sent at this time through Tychicus and treated the same subject; hence the exchange of letters which Paul desires. "As many as," etc., certainly does not include *all* Christians who had never seen Paul's face but refers only to the general group here concerned, to which also the Christians in Hieropolis belonged. The reason that they are not named directly may lie in the fact that they were few in number and were not yet organized, perhaps, too, they were connected with Laodicea, see the introduction. Although Paul had not been in their midst, his concern for them is not less because of that fact.

2) We regard ἵνα as non-final, as a statement of what Paul strains and strives to attain: **that their hearts be encouraged — they having been knit together in love — even for all the riches of the full assurance of the understanding, for full knowledge of the mystery of God, (namely) Christ, in whom are all the treasures of the wisdom and the knowledge as hidden away.**

Παρακαλεῖν always gets its specific meaning from the context and here does not mean: "that their hearts be comforted" (our versions). In this trouble with errorists their need is not comfort. The verb is to be construed with the two εἰς phrases: "be encouraged for all the riches, etc., for the full knowledge," etc. The hearts of those here referred to are not to hesitate to draw on all the treasures of knowledge that are contained in the blessed mystery, the sum and substance of which is "Christ." There lies the danger as Paul sees it. These

Christians may be induced by the Judaizers to forget, to neglect, or to fear to use some of the knowledge and the wealth of assurance they have in Christ, they may then be deceived by the persuasive speech of the Judaizers. Paul's great object, therefore, is to encourage them to take and to use this full blessed knowledge, it will make them safe and immune against insidious error.

The aorist denotes actual, complete encouragement: "be fully, actually encouraged for" this riches. "Their hearts" = the mind and the will, yea, the very personality; in the Greek "heart" never refers only to the seat of the feelings as it so generally does in English. "Their" hearts = the hearts of those here mentioned: Colossians, Laodiceans, and the rest who are living in this Phrygian section that is now endangered. They are not to be intimidated by a "show of wisdom" (v. 23) on the part of the Judaizers; they are to place over against it the treasures of the real wisdom and knowledge in Christ (v. 3).

The aorist participle: "they having been knit together in love," is parenthetical, and since it is masculine does not modify "hearts" (feminine) but the subject of the subjunctive. Paul has mentioned all of them in v. 1. Why? Because they have long been knit together in love; the aorist indicates antecedent action. Love has made them one body, and a common danger now threatens them.

The Vulgate rendering "instructed" is inapplicable here and does not agree with "in love." It is love in which they have been knit together. It is impractical to try to connect: "in love and εἰς, unto all riches," etc. Καί does not here have the force of such a connecting "and." This εἰς phrase is to be construed with the main verb, and καί = "even": "that their hearts be encouraged . . . even for all the riches of the full assurance

of the understanding"; then follows another εἰς which
is appositional: "for the full knowledge of the mystery
of God." The idea to be conveyed is not encouragement for acquiring this wealth but for using it against
the Judaizers at this time in order to rout their philosophy (v. 8) and show of wisdom (v. 23). Some of this
wealth may yet need to be acquired by some, but that
is incidental as far as the double εἰς is concerned.

Paul uses many terms: full assurance — understanding — ἐπίγνωσις (twice in 1:9, 10) — wisdom (1:9)
γνῶσις. Then he attaches the first two to "all the riches"
and the last two to "all the treasures." All these terms
refer to "the mystery of God," which is expounded in
1:26, 27 and already there is said to = "Christ in you,
the hope of the glory," and which now are again briefly
summarized as: "Christ." What Paul prays for in v.
1:9, etc., all these Christians are told to use with full
assurance for routing the Judaizers.

Yes, this is "all the riches of the full assurance of
the understanding," i. e., "all the hidden treasures of
the wisdom and of the knowledge." The articles make
all of these terms definite, entities that are well known
to all the readers. They heap up the wealth and exhibit
it from all angles and also name its content: "the mystery — Christ." "The riches (wealth) of assurance"
is an incomplete concept, and "of understanding" completes it: "great wealth of personal full assurance connected with actual understanding and comprehension."

The Judaizers, like all errorists, also have a wealth
of personal assurance; but it is not connected with real
understanding. "Full assurance" (our versions) is
the correct rendering of πληροφορία; "fulness" (R. V.
margin) is a meaning that has been given to the word
because of the contention of some commentators that
the regular and established meaning cannot be applied
in this connection. They find the idea of quantity here
and support their argument by the claim that the

Judaizers charged the apostle with failure to supply his followers with the *full measure* of understanding while they, the Judaizers, promised to fill this lack. This was their charge and their claim, but it is taken care of by πᾶν πλοῦτος and by "all the treasures." The point contained in πληροφορία is far more vital than quantity of knowledge; it is *the personal full assurance or conviction* on the part of those who have knowledge, of which there is, indeed, much here. See C.-K. 931 which commends also Luther's adjectival rendering: "*aller Reichtum des gewissen Verstaendnisses.*"

Paul wants all of his readers actually encouraged "for all the wealth of the full assurance of real understanding" (the difference between πᾶς and πᾶς ὁ does not apply to abstract nouns). But what sort of "understanding" is this? The appositional phrase answers by substituting "full knowledge" for "understanding" and then adding the object of this understanding or knowledge; the encouragement is to be "for the knowledge of the mystery of God," i. e., this mystery is to be grasped by the understanding. We have been told all about it in 1:26-29. God published it, made it fully known to the saints. Its substance, named in 1:27, is now again named: "Christ." What this means has already been told at length in 1:15-22: Christ, the Son of the Father's love, the first-born of all creation, the first-born from the dead, the God-man, supreme in his deity, in his divine attributes communicated to his human nature, in his mighty work of reconciling back all that exists, reconciling also the Gentile believers, leaving nothing, nothing whatever to be added by any other power or means. Indeed, this understanding, this *epignosis* of the mystery of God, i. e., Christ, has all possible wealth of assurance for us so that we cannot be encouraged too much to use it. Χριστοῦ is the apposition to the genitive "of the mystery"; a look at 1:27 makes this certain. There has been much emending of the reading, see the critical notes in A. Souter's editions. All of the variants try to improve; some misunderstand the apposition.

3) No wonder the full knowledge (ἐπίγνωσις) of Christ has such a wealth of assurance of understanding, and thus no wonder that Paul strains to encourage his readers to use this wealth of assurance: "in him (Christ) are all the treasures of the wisdom and of the knowledge," they are all in him "as hidden away." This concluding relative clause has a causal effect. Where, save in Christ, are these treasures that we need? And *all* of them are in him, which is the point to be noted here since the Judaizers thought that they had a few extra ones which they had found elsewhere. But these extra ones were not wisdom but only "a show of wisdom" (v. 23). One naturally reads "in whom" as equal to "in Christ"; yet some interpreters prefer the rendering "in which," i. e., in which mystery of God. The sense of both renderings is the same.

There is also a grammatical debate about the last adjective, ἀπόκρυφοι. Few will agree that it is to be construed with the copula: "is hid" (A. V.) Some maintain that it is an ordinary attribute: "all the hidden treasures." So also making the adjective do adverbial duty is not good: "in whom are all the treasures in a hidden way." This adjective is added at the end for the sake of emphasis and is predicative: "as hidden away," not as lying open on the surface. For this reason an article would not be in place; such an article would alter the sense.

"Hidden away" matches "the mystery of God." While this mystery has been published so that all saints may know it (1:26, 27), the treasures are still in Christ "as hidden away." Not even the saints can find them unless they open this treasure chest, Christ. Judaizers open self-invented treasure vaults and find special kinds of wisdom. They find only tinsel, glass diamonds. "*All* the treasures," *all* of them are in Christ. It is already a wealth of wisdom to know this fact. In v. 1, "wisdom and understanding" are combined, here "wisdom and knowledge," wisdom as including the proper use of knowledge, and knowledge the apprehended and appreciated information as such.

The supposition that Paul's terms are, at least in part, quoted from the lips of the Judaizers is not maintainable. Nor is it correct to say that Paul "often took the very words of the Gnostic or Mithra cult and filled them with the riches of Christ." Paul's terminology is entirely original and is borrowed from no extraneous source or sources.

4) This is what I am saying, that no one is to engage in cheating you with persuasive argument. For though as to the flesh I am absent, nevertheless as to the spirit I am with you, rejoicing and seeing your good order and the firm condition of your faith in Christ.

"This is my meaning," Paul says, "no one is to try to cheat you," etc. Non-final ἵνα is in apposition with τοῦτο and thus states the point of what Paul is saying in v. 1-3. For this reason παραλογίζηται is the present tense, conative (R. 880): "no one is to try to cheat you," the verb meaning "to cheat by false argument or reasoning." The usual understanding of this expression is that "this I say" refers to v. 1-3, and that ἵνα states the purpose for which "this" is said. But purpose would require an aorist: "in order that no one may succeed in cheating you." Paul has more in mind than purpose; this ἵνα is just as appositional as the one used in v. 2. When Paul wants his readers to be decisively encouraged for all the riches, etc., this means, as far as the Judaizers are concerned, that none of them are to try their tricks on them. Πιθανολογία = persuasive argument (M.-M. 512 have one example from the papyri).

5) If Paul could visit Colosse he himself would soon rout all attempts of the Judaizers to carry into effect such cheating. But he has been a prisoner for over three years and is still without prospect of immediate release. This explains γάρ which puzzles some: "For though as to the flesh (dative of relation) I am absent (from you), nevertheless as to the spirit I am σὺν ὑμῖν," which does not mean that Paul is in thought and spirit present with the Colossians but that "as to his spirit," as to his real person, he is supporting them. As is the case so often, σύν has the connotation "with you" to support and to help you. Although he cannot be physically present in Colosse to rout these Judaizers and to prevent them from making even an attempt to cheat, the Colossians have all Paul's help right in this epistle, and with that help they can prevent any man from trying to cheat them. Εἰ καί = "if also," "though"; καί εἰ has a different force (R. 1026). The former belittles; the thing makes no difference.

We do not agree with those who think that the Judaizers faulted Paul for never having visited the Colossians. Such a charge would have been pointless, for Paul had been a prisoner for over three years, and, still more to the point, this Judaizing error had just recently begun in Colosse. How could Paul then in any way be blamed for not being present in Colosse? The words themselves also do not imply a Judaistic charge against Paul for his absence. The fact that Paul had *never* been in Colosse is not stated or implied in what he says here although his words are at times so understood. He speaks only of his present absence; the fact that he has never visited Colosse is shown elsewhere in this letter.

The two participles are appended and are placed in the proper order. So we do not combine: "rejoicing with you." This makes σύν merely associative: the

Colossians rejoice, and Paul rejoices with them. This
idea would erase the support and the help from this
preposition, which is the main thought. What Paul
says is that "as to the spirit he is with them," helping
them by means of this letter, and this he does "rejoicing." Why "rejoicing"? Explicative καί answers;
"and seeing your order and the firm stand of your faith
in Christ." The ranks of the Colossians have not been
broken; in his letter Paul is not hurrying to the rescue
of a congregation that has been thrown into disorder.
In Corinth the order had been broken; not so in
Colosse.

Στερέωμα is "what is made firm," stiff, hard; the
word is used with reference to the firmament. Paul
means "the firm condition" into which the faith of
his readers has been brought by the good work of
Epaphras. He is not hurrying to the rescue of a congregation whose faith has begun to lose its firm stand,
has begun to become unsteady. Εἰς = faith and trust
directed toward Christ.

No wonder Paul rejoices. Does he use the terms
in a military sense: "your battle line" — "the fortress
of your faith"? Scarcely. The context does not suggest a military setting; bulwark or fort would be expressed by a different term. It is enough to think of
the order and the firm stand of the Colossians. We
may note that the two ὑμῶν are placed chiastically, the
one before its noun, the other at the end of the sentence. Thus placed, they receive a degree of emphasis
although this is usually noted only with reference to
the first pronoun. The emphasis, however, is not that
of contrast: "your" good stand whereas other congregations are weaker; the thought is rather one of likeness: "yours" like that of others.

But if the Colossians stand so well, why does **Paul**
still come to their support, why does he still strain **to**

encourage them, meaning by this that no one is to try to cheat them? The answer is simple. We have already noted the force of the tense: "try to cheat you." Thus far the Colossians have stood in line with all firmness, but, like all errorists, the Judaizers are persistent, and this causes Paul's concern for the Colossians, he is thinking of the future days. He is not one who waits until the damage is done; he acts with promptness so that no damage shall ever be done, so that with his help the Colossians shall stand more firmly than ever. That is a far more joyful task than repairing damage after it has been done, especially when such damage might have been prevented by taking proper measures in time. Fortify in advance! is the proper procedure.

The Main Thing: To be Rooted and Built up in Christ

6) Verses 1-5 are the preamble to the warning which forms the body of the letter. Verses 6, 7 summarize its main contents in positive form. The R. V. does well by making these two verses a small paragraph. **Accordingly, as you actually received Christ Jesus, the Lord, in him continue to walk, continuing to be rooted and to be builded up in him and continuing to be confirmed regarding the faith even as you were taught, abounding in thanksgiving.**

The difficulty some interpreters have with the connective οὖν vanishes when the preceding verses are understood. There is no disharmony between the praise of v. 5 and the admonition of v. 6 as though such an admonition is not in harmony with such praise. Paul uses the full soteriological designation: "Christ Jesus, the Lord," he who is and has done all that 1:14-22 so effectively call to mind. This great Lord and Savior and the immensity and the completeness of his work the Colossians "did actually receive," the effective his-

torical aorist contrasts with the following durative
tenses. All that is needed is that the Colossians abide
by this reception of their divine Lord and thus go forward "in connection with him," ἐν αὐτῷ is placed emphatically forward. All the Judaistic vaporings that
the Colossians ought to add something are efforts to
cheat them with cunning, persuasive argument (v. 4).
They are like the sellers of fake stock, who try to persuade those who have made the most sound and perfect
investments to surrender these in exchange for their
worthless stock. These salesmen may *think* their stock
sound, but comparison with sound investments shows
that they themselves are deceived and cheated.

Περιπατεῖτε is strongly durative: "keep on, continue
walking." But the added participles show that this
imperative by no means refers only to Christian moral
conduct in distinction from faith. Here it means:
Keep on holding fast to Christ, keep on believing in
him, and then, of course, also keep on obeying him in
good works. "In him" = "in connection with him," in
the connection made when you truly and fully received
him by faith. Here, as well as in v. 7, Paul again most
thoroughly endorses the work Epaphras has done in
Colosse.

7) The four participles are not only a grammatical
addition to the imperative but also form one great
thought with the imperative, and each participle
stresses a part of what this continuous walking in
connection with the Lord implies. Thus also the four
participles are durative. The first is, however, properly a perfect passive, for the Colossians were rooted
in Christ the moment they received him. This participle reaches back to that moment, goes forward to
the present day, and continues on into the future. Yet
it is passive, for the Colossians did not root and do not
now root themselves in Christ. Another did and does
this: God or God's Spirit. As in Eph. 1:17 Paul com-

bines: "being rooted and having been founded," so he does also here. He, however, reverses the tenses and combines the closely allied figures: "having been (and thus continuing) rooted and continuing to be upbuilded in him." This second word is a present passive and marks only the continuance.

The progressive nature of all the participles suggests the idea of "more and more" just as a taproot goes down more and more, and as a building goes up more and more. These two participles and their respective ideas of down and up go together and are made a unit by Paul who gives them but one modifier. The two ἐν αὐτῷ are placed chiastically just as are the two ὑμῶν in v. 5, and this is done with even stronger effect since these are phrases.

The third participle is not number three in a series of three; it states the outcome and the result of walking as the first two participles describe. "And" is cumulative: "and continuing to be confirmed regarding the faith even as you were taught" (by Epaphras from the beginning, another endorsement of this missionary). We prefer the dative τῇ πίστει to the variant reading "in the faith, ἐν τῇ πίστει." But this is not a dative of means; it is a dative of respect. This view is confirmed by the meaning of the participle. Some interpreters regard it as a repetition of the idea of the two preceding participles and say that deeper rooting and fuller building establish (our versions) a person, which is an idea that is rather self-evident, which also the first two participles express more adequately than the third.

"Confirm" is here used in the technical sense: to confirm, guarantee, and make irrevocable legally. Hence "the faith" is objective. In scores of cases it is objective, and here we have one of them: "constantly receiving the divine confirmation in regard to the faith," i. e., in regard to the doctrine you hold, confirmation that it is lacking in no point, and that any claim which offers you additions and the like is spurious.

Moreover, read as a unit: "continuing to be confirmed regarding the faith (*what* you believe) even as you were taught (that faith, namely *what* you are to believe)." The faith Epaphras first taught the Colossians receives constant divine confirmation which shows that it is genuine, complete in every way. How does it receive this? "If any man will do his will, he shall know of the doctrine, whether it be of God" or not (John 7:17). Thus the confirmation comes continually, the durative tense of βεβαιούμενοι is in place and also the connection: "keep walking — constantly confirmed as to the faith" you embrace and have embraced since Epaphras taught you.

We thus see how finely the last participle is added: "abounding (overflowing) in thanksgiving." Who would not keep thanking God when he is living in the condition here described? No "and" connects this participle with the preceding, which means that, while it reaches back to the imperative, it is closely united with the confirmation that is constantly received. This completes the whole injunction. Yet the Colossians must understand it properly. People who received and were taught the correct faith by a true teacher from God, who were instructed in that great doctrine which was embodied in "Christ Jesus, the Lord," people who go on in it (walking), are constantly rooted more deeply and built up more fully in it, are thus constantly confirmed in regard to it by daily testing of it, are thankful for all of it, especially for the ever-renewed confirmation — what will they do? Why, laugh at all errorists who come along and try to alter any part of that faith and doctrine!

This is a most excellent summary, and it is placed exactly in the proper place. It surely helped the Colossians greatly (σύν to indicate help and support in v. 5).

*The Warning against all Philosophy which
Reduces what the God-man, who Is
Supreme over all Principalities
and Powers, has Done for
our Complete Salvation*

8) This is the first part of Paul's warning; hence we have no connective. **Beware lest there shall be anyone who makes booty of you by means of his philosophy and empty deceit in accord with the tradition of men, in accord with the elementary things of the world and in non-accord with Christ! Because in him there dwells all the fulness of the Deity in bodily manner, and in him have you been made full — he the One who is the head of all rule and authority!**

Βλέπετε μή is a plain warning, the only notable point being that μή is here followed by the future indicative, the only instance of such a construction in the New Testament (R. 995). Moulton, *Einleitung* 280, explains it as being *eindruecklicher* and translates: *vielleicht wird jemand kommen, welcher usw.* There are deceivers in Colosse at this writing, who are plying their nefarious work; that is why Paul is writing. The Colossians, however, are to see to it that there shall not be a single successful deceiver, no one who makes booty of *them* (ὑμᾶς is advanced before the participle), no one who leads them like so many captives taken in war. "Make spoil of" (R. V.) is correct. It is not "rob," for the idea is not taking something *from* you but taking *you yourselves* as booty. Paul's imagery is true to fact: error leads its victims away like booty. The thought that some single notable leader headed the Judaizing movement in Colosse has been found in Paul's use of the singular, especially in ὁ συλαγωγῶν ὑμᾶς. We have no objection to thinking that there was possibly a leader; but Paul says τὶς, "anyone," and thereby generalizes his whole statement so that it refers to no specific person such as the leader of a movement would be.

Paul names the means which the Judaizers employ: making booty of you "by means of his (the article with the force of the possessive) philosophy and empty deceit." But one article is used with the two nouns so that καί is explicative: this philosophy amounts to nothing but an empty show and deceit. It is speculation, devoid of facts, and thus deceives. "Philosophy" is here used in the general sense according to which we to this day call any speculative scheme a philosophy. Paul's use of the word does not justify the idea that the Colossian Judaizers had obtained their speculation from the universities of Alexandria or from some notable "philosopher" in the technical sense of the term. These Judaizers are not what we call men of learning, men of standing in the world because of their philosophical study. The whole epistle presents them as being ordinary men. They are like so many modern errorists who invent a specious scheme of reasoning and base their religious notions on it. See the details below where Paul deals with them.

He characterizes the philosophy and deceit by the three κατά phrases: "in accord with the traditions of men," etc. They are notions that men have invented and that these Judaizers have picked up and use for their purposes. This first phrase is general, hence Paul adds the second phrase which is in apposition: "in accord with the elementary things of the world" (see v. 20). Since στοιχεῖα has a wide range of meaning according to the use to which the word is put, commentators vary greatly in their conception of Paul's meaning in this passage, in v. 20, and in Gal. 4:3, 9; compare also II Pet. 3:10, 12; Heb. 5:12. Etymologically the plural means things placed in a row and thus the letters of the alphabet; since Plato's time it acquired the meaning the basic elements of which the world is composed, metaphorically, the elements or rudiments of knowledge. Of late the word has been defined: "The great angel powers which were said to preside over natural happenings and to rule over stars, wind, rain, hail, thunder and lightning," "the spirits of the elements," "astral spirits." These latter meanings are not connected with the word itself but are added speculatively from what Paul says in this epistle about angel powers.

The debate usually centers about the two meanings: elementary instruction and actual physical elements. Thus here: in accord with the A-B-C instruction of the primer departments; or in accord with physical, material elements of the world in which we live. The preference of meaning is not difficult to attain. "Of the cosmos" points to the physical. In Gal. 4:9, 10 these elements are called "weak and beggarly," observing days, months, times, and years. In v. 10 below Paul specifies the ordinances: "Handle not, nor taste, nor touch!" things which perish with the using, which are after the precepts and doctrines of men.

The idea that these *stoicheia* of the world designate personal beings is not in the context. The deceitful and empty philosophy of the Judaizers dealt with physical, material things, with humanly invented rules and regulations regarding these things. In Galatia the Judaizers were of the ordinary type and insisted on the Mosaic laws about using physical things and Paul refers also to the Gentile enslavement to such physical elements. In Galatians Paul preaches complete liberation from all such enslavement. In Colosse the Judaizers had their own empty, speculative system about the physical world and thus their own system of rules about physical things. Here Paul preaches the absolute completeness of Christ and of his work, the folly of regarding it as insufficient and as needing the addition of certain observances about physical things in order to assure our salvation.

Over against both positive phrases Paul sets the mighty negative: "and *not* in accord with Christ" or "in *non*-accord with Christ"; οὐ is used when a single concept is denied, οὐ is also used to express decisive denial. The Judaizers presented their philosophy as being in full accord with Christ, as completing the gospel and thus also the Christian faith and life. They were like some errorists of today. Unless you adopt their reasonings and their observances you are either no Christian or are a most inferior one. Rank inconsistencies in their doctrinal statements, flat contradictions are ignored. Enamored of their ideas, they seek to propagate them, generally with the pride of lofty superiority and fanatical zeal, and always only among Christians.

9) Why this judgment that these deceivers try to make booty of you, that they operate with empty, deceitful philosophy, that their doctrine is human invention in contradiction of Christ? "Because *in him* there dwells all the fulness of the Deity in bodily manner, and because *in him* (in connection with him) you have been made full — he the One who (demonstrative, emphatic relative as in 1:15, 18) is the head of all rule and authority." "Christ" — this is what he is, very God himself; and this is what he has done for the Colossians who are in connection with him — he, the head of all rule and authority in the whole universe! What a farce is a philosophy about physical substances that are ruled by an authority independent of this head, that necessitate that Christians use means other than Christ to escape the power of such rule and authority!

Θεότης = τὸ Θεὸν εἶναι, which is more than θειότης = τὸ θεῖον εἶναι. The former = *das Gottsein, das was Gott ist;* the latter *das was Gottes ist* (C.-K. 490). Thus

"Deity" — "divinity": the being of God, God himself
— divineness, divine quality (in Rom. 1:20 we have
combined: "his everlasting power and divinity," the
qualities of God that are visible in the things he has
made). "In him dwells all the fulness of the Deity" =
II Cor. 5:19: "God was in Christ" = I Tim. 3:16: "He
(God) was manifested in the flesh." "All the fulness
of the Deity" = the whole sum and substance of the
infinite attributes that belong to Deity and thus constitute Deity. This fulness "dwells in Christ." Some insert: since his exaltation. Paul does not say that.
Kenoticism is in error. So is all Socinianism and its
modernistic offspring. Christ is and ever was the God-
man.

The emphatic adverb σωματικῶς has caused much discussion, especially as to whether it refers to the body
of Christ or not. This word is rare, yet it is only the
adverb formed from the adjective, and both refer to
σῶμα, "body." See the adjective in the papyri (M.-M.
621). Luther has *leibhaftig,* our versions "bodily,"
"in bodily manner" or "corporeally" would be equally
correct. Some let the word mean "really," *so recht
eigentlich und im vollen Umfang;* but where is this
adverb used in such a sense?

The whole statement refers to "Christ." It cannot
even be said that "all the fulness of the Deity *dwells*
in God," for "Deity" is only the abstract term for God
himself. Deity *dwells* in Christ because of his human
nature, it could not "dwell," "reside" in him if he had
not become man. The adverb modifies the verb and
emphasizes the manner of the indwelling: this manner is "bodily," the idea to be expressed being that the
indwelling is not mystical, not spiritual, not in the
spirit of Christ alone, but in his whole human nature.

What Paul says here lies back of all statements
such as I Pet. 2:24: "bore our sins in his own body";
Col. 1:22: "reconciled in the body of his flesh through

death"; Heb. 10:5: "a body thou hast fitted for me,"
v. 10: "the offering of the body of Christ"; all those
passages that speak about the blood and the cross of
Christ. Note also Luke 3:22 regarding the Holy Spirit
in bodily form. The old Nestorian error which separated Christ's Deity from his human nature and body
is here excluded. The body and the blood that bought
our redemption did so and could do so because Deity
dwelt in them as in the whole human nature of Christ.

"The fulness of the Deity" can, of course, never be
divided. Wherever it dwells, "all" of it dwells. Division is unthinkable. Christ could not have omnipotence, for instance, without having "all the fulness of
the Deity." Yet we cannot agree to the view that the
Judaizers asserted a partial indwelling of deity in
Christ, and that Paul's thesis contradicts this idea.
Paul is not proving *that all* the fulness of the Deity
dwells in Christ bodily, by this fact he is proving that
the whole philosophy of these errorists is empty deception. Paul is bringing forward the immense fact that
is known to every believer because this fact destroys
the petty philosophy and the scheme the Judaizers had
devised for an all-around Christianity. The point of
Paul's statement lies, not in the fact as such, but in the
simple use here made of it.

10) It is, therefore, combined with the correlative
fact: "and *in him* (emphatic as in v. 9) you have been
made full," "in him" being made still stronger by the
pointed relative clause: "he the One who (strong ὅς)
is the head of all principality and authority." There
is no ὑμεῖς which might contrast the subject with somebody else. The periphrastic perfect has the strongest
present connotation: "you have been made full, are so
now, and continue so." The passive implies that God
made you full "in connection with Christ." The verb
and its phrase express a complete idea, so we need not
ask: "Made full of what?" One whom God "has filled

full in connection with Christ" has in this connection with Christ all that he needs spiritually for soul and for body, for time and for eternity.

"Have been made full" corresponds with what "all the fulness of the Deity" expresses. When we are connected with a Savior in whom all the fulness of the *Deity* dwells we are certainly made full to the limit, not a single need remains for *human* philosophy and human schemes that are built in accord with the tradition of *men*, according to *the elementary things of this world*, so that thereby we may be really and completely full. Christ as the *God*-man does not fill us merely in part and leave something to be added by means of philosophy so as to fill us to the brim.

We have seen that Christ is the image of the invisible God, the first-born of all creation, himself supreme because everything was created "in connection with him," the first-born from the dead, "through whom" all things were reconciled "for him." Also the Colossians were thus reconciled in order to be presented as holy, blemishless, unblamable (1:15-22). In this sense he, the One in whom all the fulness of the Deity dwells, is "the head of all rule and authority," 1:16 already having stated that beneath him are "all the things in the heavens and on the earth, the visible and the invisible, whether thrones or lordships or rulerships or authorities." "All rule and authority" summarizes all created powers, the two nouns express one concept: authoritative reign, reigning authority. As "head" the God-man is infinitely above them, all of them are in the hollow of his hand. What folly is the philosophy which pretends that such a rule and authority are able to interfere with Christ in giving us the fulness that we need! That was the figment of the Colossian Judaizers.

11) With καί Paul begins specification and starts with circumcision: **in connection with whom you also**

were circumcised with a circumcision non-hand-made, in the removal of the body of the flesh, in the circumcision of Christ, when you were jointly entombed with him in the baptism in which you also were jointly raised up by means of the faith in the working of God as the One who raised him up from the dead.

Note that in v. 9, 10 we have two ἐν αὐτῷ, and that καί does not add a third relative: "in connection with whom," which means that Paul now specifies what is included in our being made full, so entirely full that these Judaizers could not only not possibly point out some remaining emptiness or lack, but also that they are left far behind with all their schemes of adding to our alleged need; they are like beggars who with their philosophy about "weak and beggarly elementary things" (Gal. 4:9) would enrich those who are infinitely rich and are filled with what they have in the God-man himself.

Since Paul starts with circumcision, we conclude that the errorists in Colosse were Judaizers. Since, however, Paul's polemics deal with circumcision only here in this epistle and treat physical circumcision as being utterly inferior to what Christians have in baptism, we furthermore conclude that these Judaizers differed decidedly from those found in Galatia, that they did not make circumcision the *sine qua non*, did not demand it as an essential but only boasted of it: if circumcised men such as they were needed the asceticism and the careful observances they maintained, how much more did Gentile Christians need them, who were not even circumcised? This seems to be the argument regarding their circumcision. Paul points to the vastly superior circumcision which the Colossians have "in connection with Christ."

"You were circumcised with a circumcision non-handmade." That of the Judaizers was a poor "handmade" thing, "in flesh" only (Eph. 2:11), the cutting off of a little skin from the genital organ. That of the Colossians is one which consists "in the removal of the (whole) body of the flesh," of the entire old man. Physical removal of the bit of foreskin — what is that in comparison with the spiritual removal of the whole body of the sinful flesh? "The body of the flesh" is not the whole mass of sinful flesh, nor the whole physical body as composed of physical flesh, but the physical body as belonging to and dominated by sinful flesh. The Christian no longer has such a body.

"Of the body" is the objective; "of the flesh" is the possessive or the qualitative genitive (not the genitive of material). It is like the genitive found in Rom. 6:6: "the body of the sin." In 1:22, "in connection with the body of his flesh through the death," the genitive "of his flesh" (note "his") denotes the physical material of Christ's body, he died by means of his physical body which was composed of physical flesh.

The spiritual circumcision with which God circumcised us (he is the agent in the passive) occurred "in the removal of the body of the sin," in that act of God's by which he stripped off (ἐκ) and away (ἀπό) this body like an old, filthy garment that one throws aside to be rid of it for good and all. The Christian's physical body is thus a spiritually new one, not belonging to or marked by sinful flesh, but belonging to the spirit, marked and ruled by the spirit. His physical members are no longer instruments of the flesh but instruments of righteousness for God (Rom. 6:12, 13).

The dogmaticians make the distinction that this regeneration is perfect *a parte Dei*, imperfect *a parte hominum recipientium;* namely in this way: the flesh has been completely removed from its throne of ruling the body and its members, of making them serve the lusts of the flesh at the behest of the flesh; the spirit now occupies the throne, the body and its members obey the spirit, the flesh lurks about, seeks again to usurp the throne, invades our members, but succeeds only in making them sin here and there. Gal. 5:17.

The second ἐν phrase is appositional to the first. It thus elucidates: "in the removal," etc., means: "in the circumcision of Christ." This phrase tells us the kind of circumcision we received. This is, of course, not the objective genitive: "of Christ" when he was circumcised on the eighth day; it is subjective: the circumcision he inaugurated by baptism. There is a contrast between this and what the Judaizers had in the way of circumcision.

In this connection we should remember that the old covenant circumcision which was given to Abraham was a true sacramental seal of justification by faith (Rom. 4:11), the Old Testament anticipation of baptism; but the Jews had made it a mere legal rite that was disconnected from justification by faith, a piece of law and not a piece of pure gospel. These Judaizers in Colosse had made it even less than that: something on which they merely prided themselves. Moreover, Christ had brought in the new covenant which superseded the old and replaced the true circumcision given to Abraham by the baptism he (Christ) instituted. This circumcision which was instituted by Christ, Paul pits against the miserable, physical circumcision of which the Judaizers were proud.

12) The participle and the following verb state what was done by God (passives) when the Colossians were circumcised by God (passive) with the true spiritual circumcision: no less than this that "they were jointly entombed with Christ in the baptism" he instituted, and thus "also in connection with him they were jointly raised up by means of the faith" wrought by God. What a vast difference between this circumcision and that on which the Judaizers prided themselves! How ridiculous that they should boast of their

beggarly distinction which cannot even be remotely
compared with what *God* had bestowed on the Colossians in the mighty sacrament *Christ* had instituted!
The parallel passage is Rom. 6:3-5. Both deal with
baptism, both are couched in mystical language: "jointly entombed — jointly you were raised up." All three
occurred simultaneously: "you were circumcised," in
that instant entombed, in that instant raised up.
"Jointly entombed" is purposely a participle in order
to indicate a subsidiary act while "you were raised up"
is a finite verb in a relative clause, this being the main
act. The entombment is to be followed by the resurrection.

We should understand what mystical language is.
It is neither figurative (metaphorical) nor symbolical.
There is no thought of immersion, the plunge beneath
the water symbolizing burial in a tomb, the lifting out
of the water symbolizing resurrection out of the tomb.
What would be the symbolism in Gal. 2:20: "I have
been jointly crucified with Christ"? have been and so
remain? Moreover, a symbol does not consist in re-
enacting something; nor does a symbol picture something. A few drops of water may symbolize if a symbol is, indeed, desired. But we ought not attribute
such a thought to Paul. This is mystical language, a
concentrated statement of two immense realities by
means of one expression.

First, Christ was laid into his tomb; secondly, we
are laid into that very tomb jointly with him. Baptism joins us with Christ's entombment. The same is
true with regard to the raising up. Both joint acts
involve a joint death, i. e., a joint crucifixion (Gal.
2:20). The interval of time between what happened
to Christ and what happened to us is ignored. The
fact that Christ was actually buried and raised up is,
of course, beyond question. That implies that σύν in
the participles, *joint* entombment, *joint* being raised

up, cannot denote anything that is not equally actual, i.
e., cannot denote something that is only figurative or
symbolical, unreal, that may become real in some other
way, at some other time, by some other means. Christ's
entombment and his resurrection were actual and in
their actuality atoning, substitutionary, vicarious, full
of saving power. Duplication of this by having others
join him is impossible even as one world atonement is
sufficient, even as one God-man alone could and did
accomplish it.

But its very nature implies fullest impartation of
all that Christ achieved. Christ died, was entombed,
was raised up *for* us. The impartation *to* us of what is
for us is spiritual in its very nature. It demands a
spiritual joining to this Christ, to his crucifixion, etc.
This is the force of the σύν here and in Rom. 6 and in
Gal. 2. It leaves the saving power in these acts to
Christ and adds our being saved in these acts when we
are joined to them — both in fullest reality and actuality. This joining, so wonderful and blessed for us,
takes place "in the baptism," βάπτισμα, the suffix -μα
naming it as a result accomplished and wrought; in
Rom. 6:4 βαπτισμός = the act (R. 151; C.-K. 199).

Those who, like the Baptist R., *W. P.*, speak of "a
symbolic burial with Christ," "a picture of the change
already wrought," of Gnostics and of Judaizers as
beings "sacramentalists," of Paul as not being "a sac-
ramentalist," have a conception of baptism that is not
in accord with what Paul says of it here and elsewhere.
Our spiritual circumcision is real and not merely a
picture. These Judaizers, too, were not Gnostics. To
associate all those who adhere to the full spiritual efficacy of baptism as joining us spiritually to the entombment and the resurrection of Christ with Gnostics and
with Judaizers and labelling them "sacramentalists,"
does not separate us from Paul or from Jesus (John
3:3, 5), nor does this procedure make symbolists of

Paul and of Jesus. Although ἐν ᾧ is like the relative phrase at the beginning of v. 11, it is not a repetition of it: "in whom"; it resumes "the baptism": "jointly entombed with him in the baptism *in which* also you were jointly raised up" (with him), i. e., in that same baptism — no comma: "in the baptism in which," etc.

The idea that would make an *opus operatum* of baptism is excluded by Paul's phrase: "by means of the faith," etc. This was the false view of the Jews concerning their circumcision: the mere operation of cutting off the foreskin made them the chosen of God. Such a view of baptism is excluded by the very fact that it joins us to Christ's entombment, etc. Its efficacy is spiritual and not mechanical. Faith is ever the subjective means which is joined with baptism as the objective means in our joint resurrection with Christ. A man may be baptized a thousand times; but he is not jointly raised up with Christ unless he believes. Note that all the passives and baptism *bestow,* and that "through the faith" adds the thought that we *receive* what is thus bestowed.

That is why the phrase regarding faith, the ὄργανον ληπτικόν, is added to the positive statement: "you were jointly raised up by means of the faith," etc. But the idea that there are *two* blessings, one the entombment, the other the raising up, is untenable. We have *one* blessing, and that has a negative and a positive side. We are not entombed for a time and then after some time are raised to life. In the case of Christ three days intervened between these two events, in our case there is *no* interval of time. Yes, there is a removal for us, one that is vastly more than cutting off a bit of skin, the whole body of the flesh is removed by entombing us with Christ. This removal by entombment takes place "in that baptism in which" we are also raised up. The one objective means, baptism, accomplishes both. Not only is there a riddance of something bad which absolutely outclasses the riddance of a bit of foreskin, there is at the same time the production of a new life, something for which the Judaizers did not have even the least counterpart, for their removal of the foreskin was all they had, and even that amounts to nothing.

The reception of the new life in the resurrection of baptism involves faith. "In baptism you were jointly raised up (with Christ) διὰ τῆς πίστεως, through or by means of the faith," etc., the faith which receives all that God bestows in baptism. Luther: "Faith trusts such Word of God in the water." For baptism is not a mere symbol; it is "the washing of water in connection with a (divine) utterance" (Eph. 5:26), "the washing of regeneration" (Tit. 3:5).

The fact that in the case of adults faith precedes baptism causes no difficulty, for this faith promptly asks for baptism so that all the treasures of it may be possessed. He who scorns baptism has no faith to receive its resurrection power. "Raised you up through the faith" has been referred to our bodily resurrection which is said to occur "ideally" in baptism and is to be consummated at the last day. The baptismal resurrection is thought to be only "ethical," a start in good works. This baptismal resurrection is spiritual. A new spiritual life is produced. When this is present by faith, baptism seals, confirms, assures it. This faith is justifying faith. "Not the ethical life attitude but the religious treasures of justification and adoption constitute the contents of the συνεγερθῆναι." Haupt.

Luther heads the list of those who regard the genitive as a genitive of cause: "the faith which God works," etc., "of the operation of God" (A. V.), i. e., produced in us by his work. So this passage has come to be a *dictum probans* against synergism. The fact that faith is *in toto* of God's production is the teaching of all Scripture. Luther's causal genitive is made

doubtful by the fact that, when "faith" is followed by
a genitive, this genitive is either subjective, naming
the person who believes; or it is objective, naming the
person or the object which is believed.

The Greek fathers regarded this genitive as an objective genitive: "the faith *in* the working of God as
the One who raised him (Christ) up from the dead"
(R. V.). We see no escape from this construction. By
accepting this object, faith is, indeed, the subjective
means for our being raised up by God. The objection
does not hold that faith cannot be said to rely on only
one divine attribute. Why not? But this ἐνέργεια is the
energy or working of *all* God's saving attributes. All
of them are present in the raising up of Christ, and it
is jointly with him that we have been raised up in baptism. This is "the faith" (note the article), the one
holding to this object, which receives the resurrection
bestowed by God. This object of faith comes to us in
the objective means of baptism and is received as in
a cup by this faith as the subjective means of appropriation.

13)   We do not begin the new sentence with the
διά phrase: "By means of the faith . . . also you
. . . be quickened," etc. The ordinary reader begins the new sentence, as do our versions, with v. 13.
**And you, being dead due to the trespasses and the
foreskin of your flesh, he quickened you together
with him by forgiving us all the trespasses after
having blotted out the to us hostile handwriting in
decrees, which was opposed to us. And it he has
borne clear away by having nailed it to the cross.
Having stripped the rulerships and authorities, he
put them to shame publicly by causing a triumph
over them in connection with him.** Compare the
close parallel in Eph. 2:1, 5 where Paul writes about
the same deadness and the same quickening.

The entombment and the resurrection involve a
death and a quickening or making alive. The main
thought, however, lies in the two added participles
which show how this quickening was wrought. The
trespasses that rendered the Colossians spiritually
"dead," all of them God graciously forgave (χαρισάμενος)
and by this act quickened and made the Colossians
spiritually alive. This is justification by faith, "the
faith" whose object v. 12 describes.

Note the repetition of παραπτώματα and the "all" the
second time they are mentioned. No transgressions of
any kind are left in the spiritually quickened, which
they still need to trouble about and try to remove by
Judaistic regulations and observances. It is a farce
when the Judaizers claim to stand on a higher, cleaner
level than the Colossian Christians. These παραπτώματα
are not mere "lapses," the word does not have a mild
force; this word is never used in a mild sense in the
New Testament. These are "transgressions" that have
killed spiritually; no worse effect could be caused, and
in Eph. 2:1 Paul adds "sins." The dative is causal:
"dead due to the transgressions." God's forgiveness
destroys this cause and thus works spiritual life.

Because Paul has said in v. 11: "you were circumcised with a non-handmade circumcision," etc., he adds
as the cause of the spiritual deadness: "the foreskin of
your flesh." Καί is explicative; this foreskin is the
mass of the transgressions. The spiritual circumcision
which the Colossians had received took place "in the
removal of the body of the flesh" (v. 11). This body of
the flesh = the foreskin of your flesh. Cutting it away
in baptism removed the deadness and gave spiritual
life. In baptism the forgiveness took place, which removed the transgressions, i. e., this deadly foreskin,
this body of the flesh. There is no reference to the
physically uncircumcised condition of the Colossians.

Jews and Gentiles, physically circumcised and uncircumcised, are alike dead due to the transgressions and
the foreskin of their flesh or sinful nature. This spiritual foreskin that must be cut off if we are to be made
alive is a far different thing from the foreskin of the
penis, the removal of which the Judaizers made so
important.

We should not forget that we ordinarily entomb the
dead in order to be entirely rid of them. The entombment which the Colossians have undergone is totally
different. It joined them to Christ who was entombed,
not to decay in corruption, but to be raised up from
the dead. So the Colossians were entombed in order
to be raised jointly with Christ, to be "jointly quickened with him," the σύν of the verb is even repeated
with the pronoun, which is an exceptional usage with
this verb, and thus the union with Christ is strongly
emphasized. The expression is again mystical: what
occurred in Christ's physical quickening occurs spiritually in our quickening, his quickening effects and
produces ours. The expression, which has God as the
subject, is intended to make the facts stand out in their
absolute divine greatness and completeness so that the
ideas of the Judaizers may appear as utterly insane as
they really are.

"He quickened by forgiving," the participle is
modal, the action contemporaneous with that of the
verb. The preceding aorists also express activities
that are contemporaneous: "you were circumcised —
by being entombed — you were raised up." All of this
is one comprehensive act of God's in connection with
Christ Jesus and not a succession of acts that has intervals of time. As a diamond has many facets but
is only one diamond, so this one act has various aspects
and yet remains one. Facing the removal of the control exercised by our flesh, it is called circumcision, it
is also called an entombment; facing our deadness, it

is called an entombment, a resurrection, a quickening; facing our transgressions, it is called forgiveness. We cannot make the participle express antecedent action; the forgiveness does not precede the quickening in point of time. No spiritually dead first have forgiveness and then await the reception of life. This is the constant teaching of Scripture which no commentator is able to change by his conception of the grammatical relation of the participle to its main verb.

Von Hofmann, who is followed by Zahn (*Introduction* 1, 475), has ὑμᾶς = you Colossians who are Gentile Christians, and ἡμῖν = to us Jews, Paul and the Jewish Christians, and supports this view with an extended argument. We note the same type of exegesis in connection with Eph. 1:12, etc., where "we" and "you" are divided in the same way (see this passage). Why did Paul place this participial clause here if it means that God forgave *the Jews* their trespasses while he made alive the *Gentile* Colossians who had been dead in their trespasses? Separating the participle from its verb and letting it begin a new sentence does not yield the sense advocated by these expositors. The παραπτώματα which God forgave are the very ones which rendered all their owners dead. This word so unites verb and participle that they cannot well be separated. Paul's change from "you" Colossians to "we" combines him and Timothy (1:1) with the Colossians. The broadening into "we" indicates that others besides the Colossians have had God do for them what Paul says God has done for his readers in Colosse.

14) Not even this second participle begins a new sentence. Still less is this second participle modal to the first and thus simultaneous with it: "After God in grace forgave us (Jewish Christians) all our lapses by blotting out the bond," etc. (Zahn, *Introduction*). This blotting out occurred on Calvary long before Paul, Timothy, and the Colossians were raised to life, quick-

ened, and forgiven. This blotting out is the atonement made by God through Christ's death on the cross. It is applied to us in the forgiveness of our sins when we are brought to contrition and faith. This participle is antecedent: "after having blotted out the to us hostile handwriting in decrees," etc. On the strength of this act God forgives the penitent believer.

Καθ' ἡμῶν is used as an adjective and hence is placed between the article and the noun: this is "the down on us handwriting," the written law of God. Χειρόγραφον is "handwriting," a document in writing. The translation of the R. V. "bond" is not an improvement on that of the A. V. Misleading conceptions are introduced when the word is thought to mean *Schuldschein*, a "debtor's bond." It would then be the debtor who writes or at least signs the bond and states the amount owed as is done in a promissory note. Because they found this idea of a bond here some commentators searched the Old Testament for something that resembled a signature made by Israel, by which it obligated itself to keep the law; a few passages such as Exod. 24:3 were found. It is, however, too narrow a view to assume that "handwriting" always = "debtor's bond." Ewald finds that of thirteen such *cheirographa*, five were debtor's bonds, two concerned deposits made, two were labor contracts, one gave authority to act, three were business agreements. This diversity in meaning shows the range of the word.

The contents of this adversely written document are here indicated by the dative τοῖς δόγμασιν. The document contained the divine decrees (Eph. 2:15). No signature of ours is remotely thought of. *God* issued the decrees, he acted like the Roman emperor; he issued them in a written document with his signature and his seal affixed. This describes the divine law exactly: "written and engraven in stones" (II Cor. 3:7) and demanding, "Thou shalt! Thou shalt not!" It is

too narrow a view to say that this document of the law
was given only to the Jews. Rom. 3:9-20 (note v. 19)
shows that, by giving this law to the Jews, God shut
every mouth and made the whole world guilty before
him. By condemning the Jews this law condemned
every man on earth.

It was certainly "down on us," no man could meet
its demands. To speak of moral and ceremonial laws is
to limit this term unduly. Whether a man knew the
emperor's decrees or not, whether he knew some or
all of them, made no difference as far as the force of
the document was concerned. Luther's reference to
conscience is not in place when he regards it as *our*
signature, it is in place only when we regard it as
showing how absolutely the *divine* law and decrees
bind and convict us.

There is a diversity of opinion regarding the construction of the dative. The ancients construed: "having blotted out the to us hostile handwriting by the
decrees (of grace)," dative of means, but δόγματα never
means gospel "decrees." Today no one accepts this
view. A few draw the dative into the relative clause:
"which by the decrees (contained in the handwriting)
was opposed to us." But this gives an overemphasis
to the Greek dative which is placed before the relative
"which." Most of the grammars do not list this dative; Winer, 6th ed., § 31, 10, note 1, has: *den wider
uns (lautenden) Schuldbrief durch die Satzungen.* It is
certain that the dative, whatever one is pleased to call
it, is to be construed with the noun "handwriting" despite the fact that some call this construction "hard."
It will not do to construe it with καθ᾽ ἡμῶν: "against us
because of the decrees." If that were the sense, the
dative should be next to the phrase in its attributive
position between the article and the noun.

The relative clause: "which was contrary or opposed to us," seems redundant since the handwriting

has already been described as being "hostile to us."
But this is the very point that requires emphasis, one
form of such emphasis being repetition by means of
the same or by means of similar words. Completely,
utterly against us was this handwriting which no man
in the world could face and live. God blotted it out,
cancelled and annulled it completely! Remember that
this handwriting contained *all* the demands God made
upon us. The cancellation wiped out *all* of them. That
means that none are now left such as the Judaizers in
Colosse imagined, which required Christians to avoid
this and that (v. 20) and to observe this and that
(v. 16).

Paul might have continued with a participle: "by
having nailed it to the cross." But this act is too great
to be expressed only by participles which are so often
used to express minor actions. Paul repeats the
thought with a finite verb and by means of this tells us
what he means by the figurative blotting out: "And
it he has borne clear away by nailing it to the cross."
That was, indeed, blotting it out. The two αὐτό are emphatic: "it itself." Not only the writing was stricken
out, the very document itself perished on the cross.
This verb is used when Jesus is said to carry away the
sins of the world (John 1:29). Here the perfect tense
"has borne away" goes beyond the previous aorist "did
blot out" in that it adds the enduring condition to the
past fact: bore away so that it remains so borne away.
The phrase ἐκ τοῦ μέσου = "clear away." We need not
stress the idea that the document no longer stands "in
the midst" between God and us. Eph. 2:11, etc., speaks
of an entirely different subject, namely of the abolition
of the law which kept Jews and Gentiles apart, an idea
that is not touched upon here.

The climax lies in the arresting, concentrated statement: "nailing it (aorist, one act) to the cross." Christ
was so nailed to the cross, and in him the law was

nailed to it; Christ, when he was nailed up, died; so did the law. Christ rose again, but *not* the law; Christ rose because his death killed the law forever. If the law had not died in the blood of the cross, Christ could not have arisen. Since the law is dead and gone, spiritual quickening and resurrection are now ours.

As we read all this, passage after passage that Paul has written on the abolition of the law occurs to us. Here we have one of the strongest and the most expressive. Yet as we read we should not forget what precedes in 1:13-20 and in 2:9, 10 where Christ is called the God-man, supreme over all creation, very God himself. It is *his* cross that blotted out the law.

15) For us, in our ordinary situation, Paul might have stopped at this point: the whole handwriting and its decrees are nailed to the cross. But he cannot do so for the Colossians who have to face the miserable Judaizers. For them Paul must top the pyramid: "Having stripped the rulerships and authorities, he put them to shame publicly by causing a triumph over them in connection with him." The supposition that Paul changes the subject from God to Christ is answered by the closing phrase. The debate about the middle voice of ἀπεκδυσάμενος, as to whether it is reflexive or not, and if, to what extent and in what manner, need not delay us long. See Moulton, *Einleitung* 245-252, on the fluctuations between the active and the middle; B.-D. 316, the use of the middle for the active.

We regard Zahn's translation: "God put away from himself as a garment," as inaccurate, and R. 805 (not "undress" but "throw off from oneself") and the R. V. ("having put off from himself") are not improvements. The idea that *evil* spirits were in any way a *garment* of God, which he finally had to throw off, is untenable. Nor does Zahn improve this when he makes this garment a *mist* and tells us that this "mist" hid God from the Gentiles so that he finally put it away. But how could God take off this garment-mist and put it to shame publicly by having it carried in a grand triumphal procession!

This garment of mist is due to the distinction that is made between Jew and Gentile which some have found in the pronouns "we" and "you" in v. 13. Then the mist is advanced as an interpretation of the whole of v. 15, this mist is dissolved by the gospel preaching among the Gentiles who now see God, which is a great triumph for him.

The A. V. is correct: God "spoiled" or despoiled, he "stripped" the rulerships and authorities. In connection with Christ, "the Stronger One," he took away their armor wherein they trusted and divided the spoils (Luke 11:22; Matt. 12:29). Thus he exposed them to public shame, thus he caused them to be led in the triumphal procession which he granted to Christ. The Scripture substantiates this interpretation: Gen. 3:15; Ps. 68:18 (Eph. 4:8); Isa. 53:12; Matt. 12:29; Luke 11:22; John 12:31; 16:11; Heb. 2:14. Scripture is to be interpreted by Scripture. The difference between the noun ἀπέκδυσις used in v. 11 and the participle ἀπεκδυσάμενοι occurring in 3:9, on the one hand, and the participle ἀπεκδυσάμενος in our passage on the other hand, lies in the objects: in the former something that clings to us is stripped away, namely "the body of the flesh" (v. 11), "the old man with his practices" (3:9) ; in our passage persons or personal powers are stripped. The difference between the objects of the actions is so plain that the A. V. translates the former: "putting off" and "have put off," but the latter, "having despoiled."

Now we see why Paul in 1:16 writes about "thrones, lordships, rulerships, authorities" and again in 2:10, "all rulership and authority," and states that Christ, the God-man, is over them all also in his human nature. Paul had in mind the satanic powers, Satan and the evil angels. The good angels served (Luke 1:13, 26; Matt. 1:20; 2:13) and worshipped Christ (Luke 2:9-14) from the beginning; but the power of the evil angels he came to destroy (Heb. 2:14). The abstract terms "rulerships and authorities," of course, denote concrete beings who exercise rule and authority; but these abstract terms, each with its own article, imply that the beings referred to were stripped of all their ruling power, of all their authoritative power. They had usurped this because of hostility to God. God stripped them. For this reason Paul uses the middle voice in preference to the active. This usurpation of rulership and authority was a matter regarding *him* and not only regarding us. This rule and authority had set itself up in a war against *him*, we were only the victims that were struck down in the fight against *him*. On *his own behalf* God thus stripped them; the middle voice of the participle is correct, nor need the force of reflexive action be inserted.

Ἐν παρρησίᾳ is used exactly as it is in John 7:4, "in public," it is the opposite of ἐν κρυπτῷ, "in secret." "In public" is a better translation than the adverb "openly" (our versions). God "made a show of them in public," made a public example of them, i. e., "he put them to shame." The thought which is not yet quite complete is made so by another aorist participle that expresses simultaneous action: "by causing a triumph over them in connection with him" (i. e., Christ, the God-man). See this participle (present tense) in II Cor. 2:14: God "causing us a triumph in connection with Christ," i. e., making us (Paul and his assistants) march in a triumphal procession as *victors*. In our passage the *vanquished* are the direct object of the participle: "causing them (the stripped usurpers of rule and authority) to march in a triumphal procession." We find no difficulty between II Cor. 2:14 and our passage; the difference in the nature of "us" and of "them" makes everything plain just as does the difference between the objects of the first participle as used here and in 3:9 (the noun in 2:11) as explained above.

The Roman emperors or the senate granted a returning victorious general a grand triumph. This was a glorious procession through the streets of Rome: the general with his victorious legions, the captives bound with chains, all the spoils that had been taken displayed to the public (see further II Cor. 2:14). This is the imagery back of Paul's figurative participle. There is irony in his saying that God accorded *them,* these stripped captives in whom captivity itself was taken captive (Eph. 4:8), a public triumph. In such a triumph *they* marched as chained captives (Rev. 20:1, 2). The irony is deepened by the addition "in connection with him" (Christ); the very opposite of this phrase is found in II Cor. 2:14.

Yes, all the hellish spirits had a connection with Christ, so had Paul and his gospel assistants — need we state the difference? This irony manifests a keen contempt. The Judaizers in Colosse claimed that these spirits still exercised great power, and that all Christians must protect themselves against it by observing the rules and regulations which the Judaizers prescribed. Behold, Paul says, this is how God gave these spirits a Roman triumph "in connection with Christ" (just as he keeps giving us such triumphs in connection with him, II Cor. 2:14): they, stripped completely, march in shame as utterly crushed and vanquished, an example of all those who are in the same awful connection with Christ!

This is the climax of Paul's exposition. It harks back to v. 8: Watch out lest there come someone to make booty of you with his philosophy and empty deceit. Do you want to be the booty that is carried in such a triumph of the vanquished spirits of hell? The whole presentation is stunning because of its power of warning. The figures are powerful, every one of them is true to the reality it describes. The climax at the end is simply tremendous. Let nothing spoil it for you.

The aorists used in v. 15 are historical, they state facts that occurred. Zahn and others who follow him refer them to the progressive triumph of the gospel work among pagans. But these aorists designate acts that were completed a long time ago, they are history. When did they occur? When Christ descended to hell (I Pet. 3:18, 19). Then he took captivity itself captive (Ps. 68:18; Eph. 4:8), crushed the serpent's head (Gen. 3:15); follow out the other passages noted above. But literalize the figure from the facts. This means, do not lose the facts in the figures. There was no procession in hell, etc. The streets of hell were not lined with spectators to view the procession, etc. What does Paul then mean? What a Roman triumph meant to a conquered king and a vanquished army that is what God's destruction of the powers of Satan "in connection with Christ" means. It was victory, more than that, an absolute, final triumph.

It may be well to add a word. The old Judaistic notion seems to have perpetuated itself to the present day. Christians believe in signs, in charms. Read Wuttke, *Der Deutsche Volksaberglaube*, 2nd ed. All the German signs and charms he speaks of are also used here in America plus others that have other origins. Unseen powers, often conceived as spirits, are supposed to rule and govern the world of nature in thousands of ways, in thousands of things, in thousands of details. And these powers may either hurt or help us. Unless we do this, avoid that, use this and that we shall be harmed in this or in that manner. Here we have the medicine for all this witchcraft and its basis of superstition. When will Christians shake it off with finality? It has been kept alive to a large extent by the preachers themselves who, instead of rooting it out with Pauline con-

tempt and decisiveness, themselves still believe and
lead their own people to believe that, while 90 per cent
may be pure fake, a certain percent is genuine devil's
work.

The Warning against Grasping the Shadow and Losing the Body, yea, the Head, Christ

16) Both of the statements of warning are formulated in the third person singular imperative (v.
16 and 18). They continue the warning of v. 8:
"See to it lest there shall be," etc. Paul now specifies the Judaistic demands and claims. From what
is here said and implied the picture of these errorists
is largely drawn. **Accordingly, let nobody whatever
judge you in eating or in drinking or in the matter of festival or new moon or sabbath, which things
are a shadow of those coming, now the body is
Christ's.**

Οὖν makes this warning accord with the preceding
one (v. 8-15) which is general. Since no one is to
make booty of us with his philosophy and empty deceit
(v. 8) for the reason assigned (v. 9-15), we are to permit no person, no matter who he is (τὶς), to usurp judicial authority over us and dictate anything whatever
regarding the five points here specified. "Let nobody
whatever be judging you" means, whether he be one
of these Judaizers or somebody else.

The verb is neutral: "Judge with approval or with
disapproval"; to say that only condemning is intended
here is not tenable. The Colossians are not only to
avoid what such a judge forbids, they are also not to
do what such a judge approves. The latter would be
as serious a mistake as the former. The reasons for
which such a judge approves a thing are just as wrong
as the reasons for which he forbids it. For he is not
prompted by the gospel nor by Christ's words but by
his vapid philosophy and empty deceit (v. 8) and

would make booty of us either way. The main concern is always, not *what* we do or avoid, but *the inner reason* for our conduct.

Βρῶσις is "eating," not βρῶμα, "food"; πόσις is "drinking," not πόμα, "drink." Our versions: "meat or drink," are inexact. The distinction is material, for these Judaizers are not described as laying down rules about proper and improper food and drink, some being clean, others unclean, but rules about when to eat and to drink and to fast. They decree certain seasons of fasting as this is done to this day by certain church authorities. So also "in any festival matter," "new-moon matter," "sabbath matter"; ἐν μέρει is to be construed with all three genitives and means "any part or matter whatever" pertaining to festival, new moon, or sabbath, whether in the nature of approval or of disapproval, their "yea" as well as their "nay" would be the outcome of their false philosophy and deceit.

Five specifications, the broken ten, are not an accidental number but denote that these Judaizers have more judgments of this kind which the Colossians are to scorn and to reject altogether and never to act on. This verse shows that the errorists in Colosse were, indeed, Judaizers, for these specifications are plainly Jewish. Ἑορτή is not "holyday" (A. V.), nor "feast day" (R. V.), except in the sense of "festival." Since Paul tells the Colossians to scorn anything these errorists say about anything regarding these points, we are left to guess as to what they really did say, i. e., to what extent their philosophy incorporated Old Testament Jewish regulation or Pharisaic legal traditionalism. Only so much seems to be assured, that they insisted on the Jewish practice of fasting and on observing Jewish festivals, new moons, and the sabbath (the Greek plural is used also to designate a single sabbath).

The regular type of Judaizers demanded circumcision above everything else; the way in which Paul speaks of circumcision in v. 11 indicates that the Colossian Judaizers only boasted of their own circumcision and did not demand it as a *sine qua non* for all Christians. So also, as Paul's polemics show, fastings and festival days were not demanded legalistically as conditioning salvation but as great aids to the Christian life which freed the Christian from the dangerous influences of certain στοιχεῖα, earthly elementary things. The Galatian Judaizers were different. They demanded circumcision, the keeping of the law, all this as being essential to salvation; hence Paul writes as he does in Gal. 5:2, 3; 4:10, 11 and goes into the whole question of the law and of our liberty.

This point is most important for us. When law observance is demanded by present-day legalists, the gospel is upset and we must fight as Paul does in Galatians. But when certain observances, rules, and regulations are attached to the gospel, which are said to produce a much safer and superior Christianity, we must fight as Paul does in Colossians, scorn this fictitious safety and superiority with the absolute completeness and superiority of the gospel, with the infinite supremacy of the God-man, the utter fulness and completeness of his saving work, and the fulness (v. 10) which he has bestowed upon us. We must despise these rags of philosophy, traditions of men, elements of the world as not being in accord with Christ (v. 8) and not think for a moment of exchanging our perfect white silk robe for such rags or of sewing some of them onto this robe in order to make it really superior and beautiful. There is a queer and persistent tendency in the church to do this sort of thing, to pick up the fake excellencies of which errorists boast, to decorate ourselves with them when we ought to scorn the very idea.

17) The folly of the Colossian Judaizers calls for only a brief relative clause in order to expose it:

"which things are a shadow of those coming," and for the sake of clarity Paul adds: "now the body is Christ's." The relative "which things" refers to all of those mentioned in v. 16. We really have an understatement: these things are a shadow *at best,* especially when we consider how God used them in the old covenant. If one should consider how the Jews abused them by their Pharisaism, how they multiplied external, hypocritical traditions, far different language should be used.

Paul's understatement destroys the best that can be said for these regulations: they are at best out of date, long ago discarded by God himself, even when God was still using them in the old covenant he employed them only as "a shadow of the things about to come," to be superseded by these things when they arrived, i. e., by the great realities themselves, the actual substance or "body." What these substantial things are, and how all of them are "Christ's," i. e., belong to him, Paul has already set forth at length in 1:13-23 and 2:9-15. They are certainly tremendous. The old shadow has completely faded away before them.

This is not the adversative δέ, "but" (our versions). Δέ is explanatory, parenthetical, helping us to understand "shadow of the things coming." "Shadow" and "the body" are not in opposition or contrast but in conjunction even as we never have a shadow without the body by which it is cast. Both terms are figurative, the figure making clear the relation between God's Old Testament regulations and the New Testament realities: they are related as is "a shadow" to its "body."

Paul does not say that the body is "Christ." This would be out of the line of thought and thus not really correct. "The body," the coming realities, are "Christ's"; they belong to him, are his as shown in 1:13, etc.; 2:9, etc. We need scarcely say that the body does not here mean the church or anything else that is foreign to "shadow." Moreover, this whole statement is doctrinal; such statements use the present tense which simply notes the fact as a fact without regard to time. This disposes of the view that the "shadow" is all that we still have, that "the things about to come" are those that will arrive at the time of Christ's Parousia; that if the shadow refers to the old covenant which is now past and gone, and "the things about to come" refer to the new covenant that is now here, Paul should have written ἦν instead of ἐστί. If this contention were true, the shadow would now not be out of date, the Judaizers in Colosse would have been right in clinging to it, and Paul would be wrong in warning against them.

The picture is not that of a shadow cast by a body that is standing on the ground and thus waiting to step forward into full sight; this is the body of realities that are waiting to descend from heaven, its shadow is spreading beneath it, the body is already so near that its great shadow falls on those beneath who are standing in expectation. We should not think slightingly of the shadow. It was no less than the divine promise of all the heavenly realities about to arrive. The shadow proved the actuality and even the nearness of the realities, for only an actual body and one that is not far away casts a shadow. So the shadow called out all the faith and the hope of the Old Testament saints in the impending realities and guaranteed that faith and that hope in the strongest way. By faith Abraham saw Christ's day and was glad (John 8:56); Isaiah saw Christ's glory and spoke of it (John 12:41; Isa. 53).

Paul does not say that the regulations referred to in v. 16 formed "*the* shadow," they were only "*a* shadow." The whole of it was far greater, these few things were only a small part of this whole. If, however, one asks how these few things foreshadowed so much, the answer is that, if God had not intended to send the great body of coming things, all of which were Christ's very own, he would never have given Israel a single regulation, would have left it as he left the pagan nations. Jesus says: "Moses wrote of me" (John 5:46), which means that he did so, not in a few direct promises, but in *all* that he wrote, not a line of which would have been penned save for Christ and the things Christ would be and bring.

While the shadow and its every part dare not be discounted, once the body of the realities had descended, the whole shadow was superseded. To try to cling to the shadow or to any part of it now, could mean only one thing, namely that what the shadow had so long foreshadowed was not understood, was not appreciated and desired now that it had all come. To the extent to which the Judaizers clung to the past shadow as if it were still present, to that extent they abandoned the body which had filled the place of the former shadow. Instead of the gospel and its heavenly realities they had an empty, deceptive philosophy without the saving realities, traditions of men, poor earthly elements, not at all Christ (v. 8). The shadow is good for its time, by means of it faith and hope embrace the coming realities; but when men prefer the shadow instead of the realities they end with nothing, for even the shadow has disappeared when the shining, heavenly realities stand in its place. This is the point of Paul's warning.

Verses 16, 17 have been of the greatest value to the church. This passage appears in her Catechisms and in her confessions (*C. Tr.*) no less than seven times, it is repeatedly combined with v. 20, 21. Here all the conscience-binding power and the meritoriousness of church rites and observances are destroyed, in particular also all sabbatarianism, a substitution by divine right of the Christian Sunday for the abrogated Jewish

Sabbath (*C. Tr.* 91, § 57, etc.) You may also think
of the introduction of tithing with the attempts to
give it a Christian coloring. A study of the use which
the church has made of this passage is most illumi-
nating.

18) Now the second half of Paul's warning.
**Let no one deny you the prize by his mere will in
connection with (any) lowliness and worship
practiced by the angels, (such a person) going
in for (only) the things he has seen, vainly
puffed up by the mind of his flesh and not holding
fast the head, him from whom all the body, by
means of the joints and bands receiving supply
and being knit together, grows with the growth of
God.** Save for the clause about being puffed up, verse
18 is much debated. We consider it best to present
only our own views for the reader's consideration
without going into the many other views.

"Let nobody whatever" (v. 16) is not quite the
same as this downright: "Let no one." So also the
first imperative is general: "let nobody whatever judge
you," i. e., do you disregard anybody who arrogates to
himself the right in any way to dictate to you about
eating, etc. This second imperative is special: the self-
appointed judge may approve or condemn, the self-
appointed referee or judge in a contest is described
as doing only the latter to the Colossians: "let no one
deny you the prize" in such a way as is here stated by
the modifiers. This is more graphic. It pictures the
man who awards the prize in the athletic contests and
denies this prize to the true Christians in Colosse, and
does this mean thing in the way and on the grounds
now stated.

Paul says: "Let no one do this sort of thing to you,
i. e., disregard him who tries it, laugh at him; the
prize is yours whatever decision the fellow may hand
down. He acts as though he is the final arbiter, as

though he could award the prize to Judaizers at his pleasure, being one himself. Well, he is about the last man in the world who has such a right!" Some specify the prize to be the award that is accorded to the one who is considered the victor in a contest. Here we have the picture of the Colossians and the followers of the Judaizers being engaged in an athletic contest, and some leader of the Judaizers refusing the prize to the Colossians. Laugh at such an attempt of his! is Paul's meaning.

All the modifiers substantiate this imperative. First of all, the fellow does this θέλων, "of his own mere will." We regard the R. V. margin as correct on this point; the participle is adverbial (R. 551) and = "wilfully, arbitrarily" this man denies you the prize that in all fairness belongs to you as a reward for the true Christianity you have shown. We do not regard θέλων ἐν as a strong Hebraism: "delighting in" lowliness, etc. (Thayer and others). Paul does not use such bold Hebraisms (the New Testament has no duplicate), and it would here spoil what Paul is saying.

When an arbiter decides adversely in an arbitrary manner, he may have some odd reason that sways him. A Judaistic arbiter of the type found in Colosse would arbitrarily deny the prize to true Christians "in connection with (what he considers) lowliness and worship practiced by the angels." Note that the governing nouns are without articles and hence do not mean "*the* lowliness," etc., which the angels really have but "*some kind of* lowliness," etc., such as this arbiter imagines the angels to have. The fellow acts arbitrarily on a mere fiction and not with fairness in accordance with the rules of the game.

'Ἐν, "in connection with," is the proper preposition, the context indicates the connection: the Colossians are denied the prize of being honored and acclaimed genuine, superior, first-class Christians in comparison

with all others such as Judaizers and other errorists
because the denial as also the award are made by a
willful act (θέλων) which connects the decision of the
arbiter with a false criterion. Instead of using Christ,
"the head," and noting how closely the Colossians are
connected with him, from whom all life and all spiritual growth are derived, this arbiter in his arbitrari-
ness (θέλων) uses as the criterion "lowliness and worship as practiced by the angels" and so rejects the
Colossians as being far below par, as being far behind
in the race, and awards the prize to his fellow Judaizers as being up to par, as winning the race. Errorists,
especially rigorists, always set up false standards for
measuring people's Christianity. Unless you eat and
drink as they say, observe Sunday (they call it "Sabbath"!) as they prescribe, you are a most inferior
Christian; they generally say, no real Christian at all.
They by their will (θέλων) deny you the prize.

The two nouns are governed by one preposition:
ἐν ταπεινοφροσύνῃ καὶ θρησκείᾳ. We thus regard the genitive
τῶν ἀγγέλων as belonging to both. If it were read by
itself without the genitive, "in lowliness" would be an
incomplete concept. "Lowliness and worship" naturally go together, for θρησκεία, the worship in acts (*cul-
tus exterior*), is practiced in humility; the worshiper
approaches God in a humble, lowly attitude. We thus
regard the genitive as subjective: "the angels' lowliness with which they bring their worship to God."
The Judaistic arbiter sets up the angels as the standard and so denies the prize to the Colossians but accords it to Judaizers alone. "The angels" are, of
course, the good angels. C.-K. 499 translates: *Demut
in Betaetigung der Froemmigkeit, wie sie die Engel
ausueben.*

We have only the context to guide us in defining
this angelic standard and model of piety and worship.

Nothing is gained by going beyond this. The Judaizers taught that the evil angels had power to do great damage to Christians through the στοιχεῖα τοῦ κόσμου, the material, earthly elements of this world (see v. 8, 20). Hence there arose the Judaistic system for preventing this damage (v. 16, 20, 21). Hence the good angels are the perfect model. In their lowly worship these angels are superior to all earthly, material *stoicheia*, are wholly unaffected by them; no evil angel can in any way spoil their worship by detrimental contact with material things of the cosmos. Who, then, most nearly approaches this standard of the angels? Certainly not the Colossians who disregarded all of the Judaistic rules and regulations for keeping away from material elements; certainly only the Judaizers who observed these rules. They were accorded the prize; the Colossians were denied the prize. "Never let that bother you," Paul tells the Colossians.

He has already shown that Christ is infinitely superior to *all* angelic beings (1:16, 20), yea, that God has stripped the demons of their power and has let Christ celebrate a grand triumph over them (2:15). This takes the ground from under the feet of the whole Judaistic philosophy as far as the demonic damage done through earthly elements is concerned. The whole matter is "empty deceit" (v. 8), a bugaboo to frighten people, and nothing more. This causes the whole scheme of the Judaizers to collapse: their fastings, observance of Jewish festivals, new moons, sabbaths, their, "Touch not, taste not, handle not!" (v. 21) so as to escape diabolical danger. This wipes out their angelic model and their claim that we must be as free as the good angels from contact with the material things of the cosmos in which we live.

Luther has given the idea exactly in his masterly rendering: *in Demut und Geistlichkeit der Engel.* We

meet this ideal of angelic purity to this day and not
only in the false spirituality of monks and of nuns but
also in the sanctity that is supposed to develop from
a life that exalts itself above the common earthly contacts. This is that dangerous, morbid piety, which was
fought so strenuously by Luther, which despises the
robust Christian life of living the gospel in daily labor:
the workman in his trade, the housewife in tending her
home and her children (Luke 3:10-14). Note well that
Paul has used only a phrase to characterize this false
angelic, Judaistic ideal, which means that it was only
an incidental feature of the false philosophy of the
Judaizers. Paul may even be quoting the Judaistic
expression "lowliness and worship of the angels."

We cannot agree with the view of those who regard
the genitive as the objective genitive; this view attaches τῶν ἀγγέλων only to the second noun, θρησκείᾳ. The
Judaizers did not worship the good angels. This would
have been flagrant idolatry, and Paul would not have
dealt with it by a mere incidental phrase and in a connection that referred to denial of the prize. No worship of angels was known in Paul's day. To posit such
a worship on the strength of this genitive is asserting
too much as far as the genitive is concerned and as far
as Paul's whole statement is concerned.

In the Greek the four participles: θέλων — ἐμβατεύων
— φυσιούμενος — οὐ κρατῶν multiply the specifications by
which a Judaizer comes to deny the prize to the Colossian Christians: he does it 1) by acting arbitrarily in
setting up a false standard; 2) by thus going in for
only the things he has seen; 3) by being puffed up in
the mind of his flesh; 4) by letting go of the head,
Christ. Note the absence of connectives save with
the last participle. This means that by doing the one
thing he does also the next, and so on throughout. But
letting go of Christ is the effect of all three preceding
participles. By acting on his mere will in connection

with what he conceives the lowliness and worship of the good angels to be a Judaistic arbiter "goes in for (only) the things he has seen."

This is the most difficult of the four participial clauses. The reading itself is in doubt. Shall we retain μή: "going in for what he has *not* seen"? Yet why is μή and not οὐ used as it should be with a finite verb? The texts that have μή are not wrong linguistically; early copyists would have changed a *wrong* negative by replacing it with the linguistically correct one. Μή seems to have been considered correct because of the preceding μηδείς with the imperative.

At first glance the sense seems to require the negative: by setting up the angels as models of truly humble worship this arbiter goes in for things he has *not* seen, he has never seen the angels and the way in which they worship. True, indeed, but have we seen our model of worship? Do we, too, not walk by faith in things unseen? This "not" seems to have slipped into the text because the copyist thought that Paul was referring to the angels. If we omit the negative, "the things he has seen" (perfect tense: and still has before his eyes) would be the earthly, material elements, the things not to touch, taste, handle (v. 21) in eating or drinking, at festivals, sabbaths, etc. (v. 16), these being only samples of the Judaistic system of life. This seems correct. The Judaizer, who by his will sets up his angelic ideal, goes in for these visible, material things and demands avoidance in order to make us as angelic as possible.

C. K. 1164 translates ἐμβατεύω: *auf etwas ausgehen.* We do not accept the proposed textual alterations. The word is uncommon, and the task of the linguists is to find its meaning and not to substitute a word of their own choosing. "To go in for something" seems to approximate the true meaning. Of course, like any other word, this one, too, is used in various contexts;

the fact that it is used in the mystery cults does not make it technical, does not make Paul say that this Judaistic arbiter acts like an initiate of a secret cult.

The road is easier now: because of his notion about the earthly elements he has seen the Judaizer is described "as vainly puffed up by the mind of his flesh." That is why he acts as the arbiter, because he regards himself qualified to decree where the prize is to go. But he is puffed up "in vain." He has seen the *stoicheia,* the earthly elements, and that is all that he *has* seen; he has not seen the absolute supremacy of Christ over all things whether in heaven or in earth, the visible and invisible (1:15, etc.), the absolute victory and power of Christ over the whole hellish realm (2:15). This Judaizer's puffed up condition (durative participle) is caused (ὑπό to indicate the agent) "by the mind of his flesh" (qualitative genitive), by his blind, perverted "fleshly mind." When a man who has such a mind pretends to deny us the prize and calls us inferior Christians, we certainly will only smile at his silly dictum.

19) Καί can scarcely connect the last participle with only the third and ignore the other two; it implies that the three preceding participles involve the thought that the head is not held fast. When οὐ negates a participle, the negation is "clear-cut and decisive" (R. 1137-8): the thing is simply *not* so. In all that Paul has said of him this arbiter is simply "not holding fast the head," him who is over all things whatever (Eph. 2:22), the head of all rule and authority (v. 10); who as such is in a special sense the head of his body, the church (1:18; Eph. 2:22; 5:23), as its Savior (Eph. 5:23). How can a Judaist who does not see anything aright (the angels, the things on earth) be allowed in the puffed up condition of his fleshly mind to judge those who belong to the spiritual body of this head and

to decide that the prize is not theirs? The very idea of allowing him to do so is outrageous.

As is so often the case in Paul's writings, the relative is also here weighty and thus demonstrative: not holding fast the head, *"him* from whom all the body, by means of the joints and bands receiving supply and being knit together, grows with the growth of God." This great relative clause, which reminds of Eph. 4:16, does far more than to show *who* the head is (we have already been told that in 1:18, and in 2:10), or *how* he is the head; this clause shows that only he who holds fast the head is able to declare anything about the body of this head, and that, to be worth anything at all, every pronouncement of this kind must be based on the relation which the person or the persons pronounced upon sustain to this head.

"All the body" with all its members as a grand whole "grows with the growth of God" out of no one and out of nothing but this head. Who, then, deserves and must be accorded the prize? The pupils of the Judaizers who do not hold fast the head? Never! Only those whose spiritual growth is derived from this head, the God-man of 1:13, etc., and of 2:10, etc. For "out of *him* alone" (ἐκ) grows *"all* the body" with the growth of God.

In the entire universe there is no head like this head. All other heads grow, grow just as their bodies grow, head and body grow simultaneously. This head does not, could not grow, only its body grows. No ordinary body grows "out of" its head. But this body (the church) derives all of its growth "out of" its head, who is the sole source and fountain of its growth.

Is this a straining of the figure of head and body? It surely is: Paul intends that it shall be. He dominates figures, does not let them dominate him. These Judaizers go in for what they have seen and hand out their prizes accordingly. Fools! How can they pronounce any judgment at all on this body or on any member of it when the mind of their flesh has never had an inkling of a body growing out of its head, when they know nothing about this wonderful spiritual body of Christ and about its still more wonderful head, the fount of the whole body's growth?

The simple verb "grows" would not be strong enough; Paul adds the cognate object: "grows the growth (we say: with the growth) of God." This is, indeed, not the growing we see in nature. Plants grow out of their root; living creatures grow with head and body as one; nothing grows "out from" its head. Nothing makes "the growth of God" (characterizing genitive), this divine growth. This is not the genitive of author or source, for the author and source is the head.

Paul adds that the whole body does its divine growing "by (constantly) receiving supply (of vitality) and by (constantly) being knit together (as one developing unit) through its joints and bands." The participles denote means just as διά also denotes means. From the head the supply flows out through the joints and bands to every part of the body and at the same time knits it together into one spiritual, divine, living and growing organism. On "joints" compare Eph. 4:16; this plural cannot mean merely "contacts." As joints and ligaments connect the members in an ordinary human body, so the members of the church are joined and fastened together, their whole growth proceeds in this way.

Paul is not speaking of numerical growth. Every new convert, of course, belongs to the body, and this increases in great numbers, which is here taken for granted. Paul is speaking of inner, spiritual growth. He adds these participial amplifications, which his readers will know so well from their own spiritual experience in growth, in order to make plain to his readers that all that he says about the life of the real body is a closed book to the Judaizers. Not holding fast the head, they have never been a part of the body, jointed and ligated into it. What do they then know about it? How can they possibly judge the Colossians pro or con, either as to membership in the body or as to excellence in a membership which deserves recognition as a prize?

20) The two imperatives used in v. 16 and 18: "Let not somebody judge you — let nobody deny you the prize!" are now followed by a question of indignant feeling. It is as though Paul says: "These presumptuous fellows, why are we at all bothered with them?" With this rhetorical question Paul explodes the claim which the Judaizers laid to wisdom (see verse 8).

If you died with Christ away from the elementary things of the world, why, as living in the world, are you being pestered with decrees: Handle not! Neither taste!   Neither touch!   (which are all things for perishing by being used up) in accord with the prescriptions and teachings of men? things of a kind which have, indeed, a show of wisdom in connection with arbitrarily chosen worship and lowliness and not sparing the body, not in connection with a certain price toward satiation of the flesh.

The condition is one of reality; Paul takes it for granted that the Colossians have, indeed, died with Christ away from the elementary things of the world. "Died with Christ" continues the mystical language of v. 12: "entombed with him in the baptism in which you were also jointly raised up." This entombment and this resurrection with Christ include the death with Christ. Although it is implied in v. 12, this death is now mentioned and used and thus completes the circle of mystical thought. Baptism does not need to be mentioned again, for the fact that the death, like the entombment and the resurrection, occurred in baptism is understood. Christ died for our sins on the cross; we died in a spiritual way when baptism connected us with Christ spiritually, i. e., with all the power and the efficacy of his atoning death.

Here, however, Paul states to what we became dead. In Rom. 6:6, 7 he says it is the old man, the body of sin, the sin, thus to something that is *in our own selves*. Dead to this, we no longer respond to it as a dead slave no longer responds to his master's demands. Here, however, Paul says that we became dead to "the elementary things of the world," to something *outside of ourselves*. We are no longer concerned with these material elements as a dead man no longer pays attention to the earthly things around him. You died "away from" them repeats the preposition ἀπό which is a part of the verb, which is exact and fine in the Greek but cannot be reproduced in our idiom.

It is overdoing it when Christ's death is said to remove also him from "the elementary things of the world." We have already shown the difference between Christ's death, entombment, and resurrection (physical, vicarious, atoning, saving) and ours (by means of baptism, spiritual, receiving atonement and salvation). On this very difference rests the conjunction with Christ which is expressed by σύν. It never rests on mere likeness or similarity alone. Christ underwent no spiritual, inner change which placed his soul beyond effect from earthly things; he was sinless in his very nature.

We have defined "the elementary things of the world" in v. 8. The supposition that this expression refers to spirits of some kind, demons, astral spirits, and such like is refuted in the present connection. The prohibitions of v. 11 show exactly what is meant:

earthly, material substances, a whole row of them (στοιχεῖα = things in a row) which, according to the Judaizers, are not to be handled, tasted, or even touched.

Dead to these things, Paul asks, "why, as living in the world, are you being pestered with decrees: Handle not!" etc. The very idea of pestering people like you Colossians with such inapplicable decrees! Ὡς does not mean "as though" living in the world, for this would imply that the Colossians were not living in the world. "As living in the world" means that they *are* living in the world, and that the Judaizers think that for this very reason the Colossians need all the Judaistic decrees about the material elements of the world. These Judaizers have not the least conception that Christians, living in the world, are dead to these elements of the world, their death with Christ rendering them perfectly safe from anything belonging to the world. They come with their silly decrees and pester the Christians when 10,000 such decrees would produce not the least safety for themselves or for anybody else. These wise decrees are full of empty deceit (v. 8), the height of folly.

The verb δογματίζεσθε is passive: "why are you being decreed?" why are you being pestered with decrees by these Judaizers? The verb is *not* middle: "why do ye subject yourselves to ordinances?" (our versions). This would imply that the Colossians were already doing this whereas the entire epistle shows that they were not. They were being pestered by the Judaizers but had not as yet submitted to them. If they had "subjected themselves," Paul could not have expressed this with a mere verb form, and one that can be read as a middle and must not be read as a passive. The same may be said with regard to the permissive passive: "why are you letting yourselves be decreed?" The

Colossians were not telling themselves; like true errorists, the Judaizers were constantly trying to inflict their system of decrees upon the Colossians.

The verb is aptly chosen. It recalls the δόγματα of God's own divine law (v. 14), and δόγμα is the term for a "decree" issued by the Roman emperor (Luke 2:1) which tolerates no disobedience. Paul's verb implies that these Judaizers considered *their* rules and regulations as being no less binding than imperial, yea, divine decrees. So the Pharisees set aside God's laws in preference to the laws *they* made for men. Yet note that Paul's question: "why are you afflicted, pestered with decrees?" scoffs at these high and mighty decrees. They are like noxious insects that are to be brushed away and killed as being pestiferous.

21) Paul quotes tersely three samples of these Judaistic decrees without further introductory particle or phrase: "Handle not! Nor taste! Nor touch!" The objects are omitted, and thus the emphasis is placed on the decreeing verbs. The next clause takes care of the objects. Negative aorist commands are expressed by the subjunctive and not the imperative, and aorist commands are peremptory and therefore exactly suited to express decrees that brook no violation. Some find a gradation in the three decrees, but since "taste not" stands between the handling and the touching, gradation is not apparent. The main point is the fact that all three prohibitions deal with physical, earthly, material elements. "Taste not!" reverts to the eating and the drinking mentioned in v. 16; the other two are broader but refer equally to material *stoicheia*.

The prohibitions imply that, if certain things were handled, etc., the Christians would thereby be hurt in some way. Why and how can be inferred only from the rest of the epistle, from what it intimates about the evil spirits and the powers that the God-man has crushed in every way. The Judaizers seem to have

limited or minimized Christ's work as though it still
left us subject to harm from these spirits so that only
by observing the Judaistic decrees regarding material
things could we escape the harm. Pagan superstition
may have been the soil for these ideas. We say pagan,
not because only pagans had such superstition, but
because to this day such really pagan superstition lurks
in Jews, in Christians, in skeptics, in all kinds of
people. Only the fulness of Christ (v. 10) completely
expels it and all its outgrowths.

22) The relative clause is parenthetical and is
inserted in order to show the folly of such decrees from
already this minor angle: "which are all things (destined) for perishing by being used up." Ἀπόχρησις is
not *Gebrauch*, the using of a thing (our versions), but
Verbrauch, using the thing up. We see this most readily in the case of food and drink: we use these up. This
explains the phrase of purpose εἰς φθοράν, which recalls
John 6:27: "Work not for the eating which perishes."
These earthly, material things with which the decrees
of the Judaizers deal are by their very nature intended
"for perishing by being used up." Since that is what
they are for (εἰς), it is ridiculous to treat them in any
other way, to build around them a philosophy of superstition and demonic powers, and then to set up a system
of decrees in order to shield Christians.

Paul uses only negative samples of these decrees
but does not thereby imply that all the Judaistic decrees were negative. Negatives are the basis of the
positive: Do not do this in order that you may do that!
Paul destroys the very foundation; after that is shattered, the whole superstructure crashes in ruins. The
ἅ, "which are all," does not refer to the decrees: "Handle not!" etc., as if these decrees are intended "for
perishing by being used up." This relative is construed *ad sensum;* it takes up the objects that are left
unnamed in the three decrees so as to tell us their

nature and their purpose, and already this takes away the ground on which such decrees try to stand.

The κατά phrase is not to be construed with the parenthetical relative clause but with the three decrees; these decrees are "in accord with the prescriptions and teachings of men." Men everlastingly set up rules and regulations and combined these with their teachings; and all of these Judaistic decrees are of this type. Paul properly uses two nouns, for every human rule and regulation is connected with some sort of teaching: the teaching justifies the rule, the rule is the practical application of the teaching. So the Judaistic philosophy (v. 8) produces the Judaistic decrees. The trouble is not in the fact that teachings produce ἐντάλματα, "precepts." Christ's teachings do the same (John 14:15, 21, 23, 24; 15:10: ἐντολαί). Paul properly does not use δόγματα, "decrees," but the milder word "precepts"; for only the extremists, such as the Judaizers, make ironclad "decrees" of their teachings. Saner men are satisfied with precepts.

The point of Paul's phrase is the fact that all these precepts, in which class also the Judaistic decrees belong, are only "of men" (the Greek article is generic); together with their supporting teachings they are man-made (Isa. 29:13; Matt. 15:9). Some think that Paul had this passage from Isaiah in mind. Why not? But he surely also thought of Christ's word which reflects Isaiah's. "Of men" is ample, the Colossians have something to teach and to direct them that is *of God*.

23) All that Paul appends from v. 22 onward is construed *ad sensum* in order to show his readers how preposterous it is for these Judaizers to pester them with their decrees which deal with things to be used up, which decrees with their support are entirely man-made. And now he adds the last and worst indictment: these decrees are of a kind that make a show in a certain connection but in a connection where making

a show would be a rather damning revelation. The ἅ occurring in v. 22 is definite: "which things"; ἅτινα now = "things of a kind which," i. e., having a certain characteristic or quality. The qualitative neuter relative has its *ad sensum* antecedent: all such Judaistic decrees and all with which they deal. They are of a kind that, "indeed, have a show of wisdom" in a certain connection, λόγον is used in the sense of "show." These things appear mighty wise, Paul says, yes, wise "in connection with arbitrarily chosen worship and lowliness and not sparing the body."

We differ with R. 1152 regarding the present μέν *solitarium*. Some think that it calls for a contrasting δέ, and B.-D. 447 even calls μέν anacoluthic without its δέ. This claim is serious because it is thought that the contrast is indicated in οὐκ ἐν τιμῇ τινί, a construction that has made the interpretation of this passage extremely difficult. The interpretation is so difficult that B.-P. 1307 writes: *hat noch keine annehmbare Deutung gefunden*; and that Peake, after passing in review the interpretations of the commentators, joins Hort in supposing that the text has been corrupted. It thus seems well-nigh hopeless to find a satisfactory interpretation for this passage. It might be helpful if μέν is not regarded as calling for a δέ and thus a contrast. Μέν is truly solitary, its sole function is to lay a slight stress on λόγον ἔχοντα between which it is placed: which "have, indeed, a show," etc. This should, in fact, be plain, for μέν is *not* placed after ἐν and hence in no way indicates a contrast between the positive and the negative ἐν phrases.

These are the kind of things, Paul says, that have a show of wisdom — mark it, only a show! — "in connection with self-willed worship and lowliness and not sparing the body." These three terms describe the piety of the Judaizers. In the compound ἐθελοθρησκεία we have the same meaning as that of θέλων in v. 18

where both θρησκεία (the other half of the compound) and ταπεινοφροσύνη occur. The term means just what Luther says: *selbsterwaehlte Geistlichkeit,* a self-chosen worship that is willed by the will of those who want it and *not* a type of worship that is willed by God. These Judaizers invent their own worship. In connection with that kind of worship their decrees and their philosophy "have, indeed, a show of wisdom" although, of course, only a show (μέν after λόγον).

To be sure, "lowliness," which is now added gets the same color. It is not, indeed, a hypocritical or merely pretended lowliness but one that in its way is sincere enough and matches the self-chosen worship of these Judaizers. This is also true with regard to their "not sparing the body," their laws about eating and drinking (fasting, v. 16; "taste not," v. 21) and about treating the body severely in other ways. Grant them their philosophy with its superstitious fears regarding material elements, then all their decrees look wise although they only *look* so.

It is the negative phrase οὐκ ἐν τιμῇ τινὶ πρὸς πλησμονὴν τῆς σαρκός that causes difficulty for the translators (Luther, our versions, and others) and for some commentators. It would take considerable space to make an inventory of their efforts. The first point to be noted is that τιμή does not mean "honor" (A. V.) nor "value" (R. V.) but "price," and πρός is construed with it in a natural way: we pay a price *toward* a thing, meaning that more will still have to be paid. Hence also Paul writes ἐν τιμῇ τινί, "a certain price," not the entire price; the remainder, the bulk of the price will fall due presently and will then be paid.

Paul tells the Colossians toward what the Judaizers are really paying this advance price: "toward satiation of the flesh," i. e., to satiate and satisfy the cravings of the flesh. But let us keep to the context. Paul is not speaking in general of the common bodily vices of the flesh, of carousings, sexual excesses, etc. The Judaizers seek satiety for their pride in their peculiar philosophy, in judging others as to whether they are up to par in their Christianity (v. 16), in assuming the position of a referee who has the power to award or to deny the prize (v. 18), in inflicting their peculiar decrees upon the Colossians (v. 21), in posing as men of the greatest wisdom. Like a flash this final phrase: "toward satiation of the flesh," floods the whole Judaistic system with a light that horrifies all true Christians. It is this final phrase that exposes the whole inwardness of the Judaistic position to the Colossians so as to make them recoil.

Now let us note the connection. Yes, these are things of a type (ἅτινα) that have a show of wisdom, namely these decrees, regulations, and Judaistic teaching and philosophy; they have such a show "in connection with arbitrarily chosen worship and lowliness and not sparing the body" as these are exhibited and advocated by the Judaizers. That is, however, the limit of even this show of wisdom. These things have a show of wisdom that is *"not at all* in connection with a certain price," οὐκ ἐν τιμῇ τινί, which all these Judaizers are paying for what they really desire, a price "toward the satiation of the flesh." This satiation is what they are really buying and making payments on.

Paul does not say what the final payment will be, he leaves that to his readers; it will be eternal perdition. *"Not* in connection with a certain price" is a powerful litotes: in connection with this price there is not even a show of wisdom but the absolute opposite, there is sheer folly. It is frightful folly even to want satiety of the flesh, to say nothing of paying a price toward (πρός) securing such satiety.

In his interpretation Meyer notes the fine points in this masterly clause. Πρός implies that, in spite of the price that is being paid, the Judaizers and any who would follow their show of wisdom do not get even full satisfaction for the flesh. The devil always cheats even in this respect. See the fine balance: "not sparing the body — satiation of the flesh." Twice an objective genitive; all four nouns are exact even also "of the *body* — of the *flesh*." Ἐν and οὐκ ἐν are equally balanced. Masterly is the manner in which Paul reserves the crushing phrase "for satiation of the flesh" until the very end.

M.-M. 520 state that πλησμονή is used only *in malam partem* for repletion or satiety; Luther missed the meaning. "Will-worship" in our versions is meaningless. The question that Paul answers is simply how far the show of wisdom reaches. Whatever show of wisdom may be put forth, in all errors there is always a point at which even the show ceases, at which the deadly, terrible folly stands out fully.

Severe, unsparing were these Judaizers toward their *body* like the Romish monks and nuns. And yet all of them are after satiation of the *flesh*. Luther scourged the monks for this much as Paul scourged the Colossian Judaizers. Rules — rules — rules, severe as possible for the body but all to buy food for their pride of monkery. They are the paragons in all Christendom, they alone! Read Luther. Protestantism has allied types.

CHAPTER III

The Complementary Part of the Letter:

Sketch of the True Christian Life without Judaistic Taint, 3:1-4:6

Paul has concluded his warnings: "See to it lest," etc. (2:8); "Do not let anyone judge you" (2:16); "Let no one deny you the prize" (2:18). These warnings are concluded with the rhetorical question asked in 2:20-23. These are followed by exhortations throughout this third part of the letter, and all of them deal with the life the Colossians must lead as true Christians. The life sketched for the Colossians differs in no way from the life which Christians in any congregation should lead. This is exactly the point the Colossians should note, who are being pestered by the decrees of the Judaizers (2:20-23). The Colossians should ignore all these pestiferous Judaistic rules and regulations and simply live the plain, true, joyful, prayerful Christian life. That is to be their answer to the Judaizers.

The Life that ever Looks upward to Christ

1) Accordingly, if you were jointly raised up with Christ, keep seeking the things above, where Christ is, sitting at God's right hand!

Paul has an "if" of reality just as in 2:20; "if you were jointly raised up with Christ" is the counterpart of "if you died together with Christ." This links the new part of the letter to the part preceding; yet a new part begins at this point, it is not a continuation of 2:20-23. The new part is evident from the series of exhortations that now begins, all of which deal with the true Christian life.

(147)

These exhortations, i. e., this part of the letter, are not intended to meet a second and different need of the Colossians, not one that is apart from their need of warning against the Judaizers. The very way in which Paul links this new part to the preceding excludes this idea. Moreover, the answer which the Colossians give to the Judaizers must not consist only in doctrine but must also include the practice and the life based on the doctrine. Thus Paul recalls for the Colossians all the doctrinal facts about the absolute supremacy of the God-man, which he has pointed out in the second part of his letter, together with all the absolute completeness of his work; this shall utterly destroy the fictional Judaistic doctrine.

Now he proceeds to delineate the true Christian life which results from the true doctrine; and he shows that this is the opposite of the life the Judaizers try to live in accord with their doctrine. Through Paul's entire outline of the Christian life runs this deep and vital opposition. The Colossians are not to adopt some peculiar type of Christian life in order to meet the kind of life the Judaizers advocate, there is only one type of Christian life. It is this genuine Christian life that ever stands like a rock against all errorists, hence also against the type of life these Judaizers would foist upon the Colossians. Paul's task is to sketch this true Christian life in such a way that its opposition to all Judaistic life appears. This he does in this part of his letter. It would be a misunderstanding of Paul's purpose to regard this part as a general sketch of Christian ethics.

"If, then, you were jointly raised up with Christ," is a condition of reality (like the one in 2:20) and implies that the Colossians have, indeed, been so raised up. All of the following admonitions are based on this fact, which Paul assumes to be a fact. To be sure, "were raised up" is the positive counterpart of the

negative "died" in 2:20, but the connection does not
stop there. "You were raised up" reaches back much
farther, for it repeats the "you were raised up" used in
2:12. Οὖν thus refers back to the whole of the previous
part, in particular to what the Colossians have themselves experienced in their vital connection with the
supreme God-man and his work which is so complete
and mighty in every respect.

We need not again explain the mystical expression
"jointly raised up with Christ"; see the exposition of
"entombed with him," "raised up" and "died with
him" in 2:11, 12, 20. "Jointly raised up with Christ."
By this resurrection a new, spiritual life is created in
us. Paul now describes its vital activities. The Judaizers had not experienced such a spiritual resurrection. No wonder their religious life consisted of decrees about material earthly things (2:16, 20, 21), the
peculiar worship, humility, and severity to the body
backed by an empty philosophy (2:8) and show of wisdom (2:23)! The spiritual life of those who have been
raised up with Christ is the opposite of the Judaistic
religious life. Paul might merely have stated the objective fact that it is the opposite; he does better, he
admonishes his readers to live the new life and to exhibit it as such an opposite. They must ever manifest
the power of Christ's resurrection as it is comprehended in their own spiritual resurrection and thus
shows itself in their spiritual vitality.

"The things above keep seeking." By transposing
the verb and the object Paul emphasizes both. "Above"
means "where Christ is," our risen Lord, whose resurrection gave us our spiritual resurrection. He is in
the glory of heaven, "sitting at God's right" (with the
feminine δεξιᾷ we supply χειρί, dative of place). The
mystical language of this epistle does not go beyond the
death, the entombment, and the resurrection; in Eph.
2:6 it touches also the enthronement of Christ. The

right hand of God (Ps. 110:1) "is no fixed place in heaven, as the Sacramentarians assert, without any ground in the Holy Scriptures, but nothing else than the almighty power of God, in possession of which Christ is installed according to his humanity, *realiter*, that is, in deed and truth, *sine confusione et exaequatione naturarum*, that is, without confusion and equalizing of the two natures in their essence and essential properties," *C. Tr.* 1025, 28.

One should study as a unit all the passages that speak of God's right hand and of Christ's sitting there. Then the view will disappear that Christ is in heaven as Enoch and Elijah are, of neither of whom it is said that they are at God's right hand. Christ's sitting at God's right hand is the exercise of all the majesty and the power of deity according to his human nature. One cannot exalt only Christ's divine nature, for this is incapable of exaltation since from eternity it is in the same infinite glory as the Father and the Spirit, yes, one in essence with them.

If this is understood (see also Eph. 1:20), two things will be noted: 1) death, entombment, resurrection, sitting at God's right, all of which are possible only to the human nature and equally soteriological, all of which once more state what 1:13-23 and 2:9-15 say about the absolute supremacy of the person, power, work, and results. All of this the Judaizers did not perceive, as we have shown. 2) The absolute extent of Christ's saving power above everything in nature and above all spirit beings (1:16; 2:10; and especially 2:15, on which see the exposition). This the Judaizers did not perceive; they imagined that demons still controlled material elements, and that, therefore, in order to shield ourselves we have to guard ourselves according to their Judaistic rules and regulations (2:16, 20, 21) and adopt their type of worship (2:18, 23). For that reason the exaltation of the human nature of the

God-man is introduced at this point: he is sitting at God's right hand.

2) **The things above keep minding, not the things on the earth!**

We have the same reversal of the verb and the object. "Keep seeking" and "keep minding" have practically the same force. Lightfoot's note: "You must not only *seek* heaven, you must *think* heaven," puts too little into φρονεῖν which means not merely "to think" but "to mind," to attend to, to devote ourselves to. And "the things above" are not heaven. These two admonitions do not say that we must ever strive to attain heaven and let earth go. "The things on the earth" are the στοιχεῖα τοῦ κόσμου (2:8, 20), the material, elementary things of the world. The religion of the Judaizers minded these things; hence their decrees about not handling, tasting, touching certain things, about eating and drinking, festivals and sabbaths. All these religious rules pertained to "the things on the earth" and feared that they were dangerous, that spirit powers were behind them, etc. Such minding of such things is not for the Colossians, but the very opposite, ever minding the things above.

We note that Paul repeats, again in the emphatic position, "the things above." Of these he can say that we are both to seek and to mind them; "the things of earth" (when rightly understood) one minds only as the Judaizers do. Seek would not be fitting because 2:21 shows that they are to be avoided as being dangerous. If by their decrees the Judaizers not only forbade some things but also demanded certain others, Paul mentions these others nowhere, hence we do the same. "The things above" are defined as to their high nature by the clause "where Christ is" in his supreme exaltation, and thus they are the very opposite of the things on the earth of which the Judaizers were afraid. Note that they shunned these earthly things because they imagined them to be dangerous. The Colossians are to scorn this whole show of wisdom and the superstition which prompted the Judaizers. They were perfectly free to use all earthly things; no devils control any of them, Christ has utterly stripped all devils of power (2:15).

The things above are all the great and blessed, truly spiritual things that are where Christ is, that come from him to us who are joined spiritually to his death, entombment, and resurrection, things that we must ever seek and mind. We need not guess what these things are, Paul has told us: "the ransoming, the remission of our sins" (1:14), "all the treasures of the wisdom and the knowledge hid away" (2:3), all that he as the head supplies to all the body to make it grow with the growth of God (2:19). These things we must want and occupy ourselves with and not fill our religion with rules about material things and with superstitious philosophy regarding them. "Set your mind" (our versions) would be ingressive, but the two present imperatives occurring in v. 1, 2 are alike, are durative and not ingressive. Regarding φρονεῖν as meaning more than to think see its use in Phil. 2:2 (twice) and especially in 2:5.

3) "For" substantiates the admonition about seeking and minding "the things above." Unlike "the things on earth," the *stoicheia* (2:8, 20) of which the Judaizers made so much in their religious philosophy (2:8) and manner of worship (θρησκεία, 2:18, 23) and their decreeing (2:20, 21), "the things above" are truly spiritual and hence invisible while "the things on earth," which must not be handled, are plain and visible. It is then no wonder that when a Judaizer judges anyone's religion he does so "in connection with eating and drinking or in the festival matter," etc. (2:16), on the basis of tangible, visible things; he refuses the prize to anyone who does not worship

according to his style with "the things he has seen" (2:18). Paul has told the Colossians to scorn all such judging and withholding of the prize and has added the reasons for such scorn (2:18-23). They are to keep on seeking and minding "the things above" which are truly spiritual and invisible. **For you died, and your life has been hidden together with Christ in God; when Christ, your** (some texts read "our") **life, shall be made visible, then also you together with him shall be made visible in glory.** For this reason you are now to go on seeking and minding the invisible things above.

"You died" = 2:20: "died with Christ away from the elementary things of the world." By means of that death which connected you with the saving death of Christ you became like a dead man as far as religious response to human tradition and decrees about earthly, material things is concerned. All paganism, all Judaism, and all Judaistic perversions of Christianity operated with scores of material things, "the things of the earth"; see the discussions of στοιχεῖα in Gal. 4:3, 9; Col. 2:8, 20.

"You died" = you got away from every bit of religion that operated with material things and with doing this or that with them. What does it matter to a dead man what anybody does with material, earthly things whether these are a part of his religion or otherwise? Paul might also have said, "you were entombed" (2:12), for a man who is entombed is dead and cares nothing for earthly things. Paul does touch upon this after a fashion when he writes: your life "has been hidden" just as he touches upon our spiritual resurrection with Christ when he speaks of our ζωή, our new, spiritual life. But "you died," which repeats in brief the fuller statement of 2:20, expresses his thought in the clearest way.

This very death, however, gave us a "life" through
our resurrection with Christ (2:12; 3:1), a life such
as Judaizers know nothing about, one that from the
beginning and even now "has been hidden together
with Christ in God." It is spiritual and thus invisible
and hidden; full of vitality, indeed, so vital that it will
pass through temporal, physical death unharmed, but
operating with the intangible things it has in Christ
(1:14; 2:3; we having been, filled in him, 2:10). It is
hidden "with Christ in God," with the Christ sitting at
God's right hand (v. 1), he, in fact, being "our life"
(v. 4) as he himself is "the Life" (John 14:6). To all
who in their religion deal only with "what things they
have seen" (2:18) Christ is hidden (II Cor. 4:4) and
is revealed only to those who are risen with him (II
Cor. 4:6).

Hidden with Christ "in God" is our life — a tremendous thought. Yet God is the only fount of life;
God raised up Christ to the life of infinite glory, and
God raised us up to spiritual life with Christ. First
John 3:2 also speaks of the hidden nature and the
invisibility of this life: "Beloved, now are we the children of God, and it is not yet made manifest what we
shall be," and then adds, as does Paul: "that when he
(Christ) shall appear, we shall be like him." A death
of this kind and a life of this exalted nature concern
themselves with "the things above where Christ is at
God's right hand" and never with "the things on the
earth" with which the Judaizers — and we may add
pagans and Jews — are occupied religiously.

4) Our life shall not remain thus hidden forever.
It shall remain thus only until the time "when Christ
shall be made visible" (note that Paul uses the same
verb that is found in I John 3:2: be made manifest,
public, visible) at his Parousia. This date is mentioned because then our bodies, too, shall be glorified.
Paul significantly adds the apposition: Christ, "your

(our) life"; Phil. 2:21: "for me to be living (is) Christ." This is not substantial identification, nor is it only rhetorical. Joined spiritually to Christ, he is in us, and we in him, i. e., in a living connection by which he, the Life, fills us with spiritual, eternal life.

When that great day comes, Paul says, "then you, too, together with him (all the σύν are associative) shall be made visible in glory," "we shall be like him" (I John 3:2). Rom. 8:17. What shall then happen to the judgment of the haughty Judaizers who refused us the prize because we discarded all their decrees about earthly elements (2:16, etc.; 2:20, etc.)? What shall become of all their philosophy (2:8) and show of wisdom (2:23)? Well, here we have the reason that throughout our Christian life our one concern shall be with the things above and not with those on earth that fill our religion with the observance of things that perish by being used up (2:22).

In this first paragraph Paul sums up the whole Christian life in a comprehensive and a fundamental admonition which also carries us to the last day and to our final glorification. He often does this and lets the specifications follow as an elaboration.

The Life that Breaks with all the Old Vices since the New Man Has Been Put on

5) **Accordingly, render dead the members that are on the earth — as to fornication, uncleanness, passion, base desire, and the covetousness, which is of the nature of idolatry, because of which things there comes the wrath of God upon the sons of the disobedience, among whom you also walked at one time when you were living in these things.**

In v. 3 (2:20) we have the fact: "you died." When Paul now demands: "Accordingly deaden your members," this does not mean that this dying was only ideal and is now to become real when we deaden our members. This view confuses regeneration and sanctification. Nor is our having died partial and is made complete by now striking dead our members. "You died" is an aorist, the act is complete; so also is its positive side, "you were raised up" (v. 1; 2:12). In accord with this very completeness of our death and our resurrection with Christ we are to render dead our members.

In Rom. 8:13 we have θανατοῦτε: "keep bringing death" upon the deeds of the body; in Gal. 5:24 we have ἐσταύρωσαν, "nail on the cross" the flesh. Both are conceptions that are somewhat different from the thought of our passage: "strike dead the members that are on the earth," especially as to the object involved.

Romans 8:13 pictures the negative *process* of sanctification, bringing θάνατος or *death* upon the *deeds* of the body, which process continues as long as we have the body and its deeds. In Gal. 5:24 the aorist refers to *the decisive act* which nails the flesh to the cross in order cruelly, painfully to murder it there so that its career of crime shall cease once for all. In our passage, which also has the aorist, *the decisive act* is to strike dead the bodily members so that, being νεκρά or dead, they shall become incapable of being used for any of the vices here listed and indicated. Yet our passage, like Rom. 8:13, is written to Christians. Galatians 5:24 states that the thing has already been done, the other two passages that we are now to do it. All of these passages express a truth: we constantly kill off the deeds of the body just as we crucified the flesh in the first place. We strike our members dead summarily and leave them useless for all vices. The flesh is dethroned in us, its attempted usurpations for deeds of the body are constantly put to death as rebellious citizens are suppressed (Rom. 8:13), even the bodily members, which the flesh must have for its deeds, are

struck dead so that, like dead things, they become quite
useless instruments for the flesh.

The attributive phrase "upon the earth" gets its
point from v. 2 where "the things on the earth" (the
elementary, physical στοιχεῖα of the world with which
the Judaizers busy themselves in their religion, (2:20;
2:8) are contrasted with "the things above" (1:14;
2:3, 10, "having been filled"). Our bodily members
certainly do have to be used for the things on earth;
but the way in which the Judaizers propose to use them
in their decrees (2:16; 2:20, 21) ends only in satiating
their flesh (2:23). A religion that operates with decrees about earthly things and bodily members on
earth ("Handle not, nor taste, nor touch," 2:21; do
not eat or drink but fast as prescribed by the Judaizers; and do not do this or that on the festival and on
the Sabbath, etc., 2:16), such a religion remains on the
low level of the flesh which also has to have the bodily
members for its deeds.

The attributive phrase "those on the earth" is thus
decidedly pertinent. If regeneration has not taken
place, whatever the members that are on earth do in
the things that are on earth, whether they commit
vices or do things that are decreed by Judaizers, is
quite the same, for they achieve nothing but satiation
of the flesh, now in one way, now in another. As we
must ever turn to the things above and away from the
things on earth, so once for all we must strike dead
even our members on the earth so that they may be
useless for the things on the earth.

We do not regard the accusatives that follow as
appositions but as adverbial accusatives of reference
or specification: "as to fornication," etc. Compare
this passage with Eph. 5:3-6. All of Paul's lists are
carefully arranged. Both here in v. 5 and again in v. 8
Paul has five, the half of the completeness expressed

by ten. Let the reader himself complete these fives.
Five is also secular, these are vices. "Fornication" and
"uncleanness" go together as forming a most nasty
pair, the one being specific, the other broad. "Passion"
and "base desire" likewise form a pair, both are inward. Πάθος is not used by Paul in the sense of the
Greek schools of ethical philosophy (C.-K. 842; Trench,
Synonyms). Bengel defines it as the *morbus libidinis*.
It is like an inward fire that is kindled in the heart.
Ἐπιθυμία is a *vox media* although it is usually used in
an evil sense, which is placed beyond question by the
adjective: "base desire," reaching out for an object in
order to satisfy itself.

These four are sexual and are thus joined to "covetousness" as is so often done in Scripture apparently
because greed of money is also filthy. The idea that
we have this grouping because it takes money to in-
dulge in sexual vices is unsubstantiated. In most cases
of sexual vice money is not even involved, and thousands of covetous men and women cling to their money
and never use it for sexual vices. Here, as in Eph. 5:6,
the damnableness of covetousness lies in the fact that
its quality or nature (ἥτις, qualitative, also causal) is
"idolatry," worshipping gold instead of God. The
clause is needed in order to show the enormity of the
sin which even Christians often fail to recognize. A
Catholic priest states that during his long years of
service all kinds of sins and crimes were confessed to
him in the confessional but never the sin of covetousness.
Why is the article used with this fifth noun? Not, as
has been supposed, because it is the last of the group
but because it alone has an attached relative clause
(R. 758).

6) "Because of which things there comes the
wrath of God upon the sons of the disobedience." This
wrath is the reaction of God's holiness and righteousness against sin. See Rom. 1:18. It comes not merely

on the day of final judgment but whenever this wrath
blazes forth in judgments on individuals and even on
rotten nations. "Comes" is an iterative present tense.
Considerations of grace and mercy hold back the coming; this is God's long-suffering. But when the evil
cup is full, the wrath descends.

Critics of the text debate as to whether the phrases
"upon the sons of the disobedience" is genuine or is introduced from Eph. 5:6. The writer's opinion is that
the words are genuine; his reason for this opinion is
the fact that both epistles were written at the same
time, that in both epistles many expressions thus correspond in the most natural way; in fact, here not
merely this phrase but the entire clause is found in
both. The question as to how the phrase came to be
omitted in some texts is like that asked regarding
thousands of variants, for none of which the critics
have a satisfactory explanation. We also note that the
omission of this phrase leaves the clause just as incomplete as would its omission in Eph. 5:6.

On "the sons of the disobedience" see Eph. 2:2.
This is the old, original disobedience, hence the article
is used. "The sons" of it are brought forth by it and
as "sons" continue it as their disobedient fathers did
before them. Unbelief is also called disobedience, but
why introduce such a restriction here? The Gentiles
stifled even the voice of conscience and of the *lex nat-
uralis* (Rom. 1:32). To make these sons of the disobedience Gnostic heretics is venturing upon the un-
provable.

7) Those who cancel the phrase from v. 6 naturally translate: "in which things" also you walked.
This, however, produces an awkward repetition when
Paul now adds: "when you were living in these things."
We retain the phrase in v. 6 and thus translate: "among
whom also you walked at one time when you were living in these things." As former Gentiles the Colos-

sians, too, had walked among their pagan neighbors and were altogether like them. The constative historical aorist is in place, as is also the descriptive imperfect in the temporal clause: "when you were living in these things." This imperfect, however, leads us to expect the next statement which by means of an aorist tells us how this former living in such vices is to cease.

8) **But now do you also put away from yourselves** (middle; aorist; definitely, once for all) **all of them — wrath, exasperation, meanness, blasphemy, shameful language out of your mouth! Never lie to each other — you having put off once for all the old man together with his practices and having put on the new man, the one made over new for real knowledge according to the image of him who created him, etc.**

"Now" = since that fearful former time is past, thank God. "You also" = like other Christians. The aorist = "put away from yourselves for good and all"; yet this verb is not figurative for taking off clothing, as R., *W. P.*, states, it is literal: rid yourselves completely of all these things. Paul cannot list them all; he has mentioned one sample group and now adds another, but the complete list would be much longer, and in other connections Paul lists also other items.

Here we again have five. Those listed in v. 5 harm the sinner himself; these harm other people. "Anger" and "wrath" are quite the same in English. It is true that the corresponding Greek terms are also often used in the same sense (Trench), the one only to strengthen the other (C.-K. 805). But in lists such as this and in Eph. 4:31 ὀργή and θυμός preserve their difference; θυμός = boiling agitation of the feelings, i. e., "exasperation." See also Eph. 4:31 where the two are reversed. In both passages we have a climax. The exasperation (θυμός) may rise to wrath (ὀργή) (Eph. 4:31), or the wrath, getting beyond control, may rise to exasperation (our passage). We may have the words in either order because either word may be conceived as being the stronger.

The next step is κακία, "baseness" or "meanness" toward the person or the thing because of which a person is exasperated, *Schlechtigkeit*. This is not "malice" (our versions), for κακία = moral inferiority, "good-for-nothingness." The next step is to curse or damn by "blasphemy." The fifth, to hurl "out of his mouth" αἰσχρολογία, "vile or shameful language, dirty epithets." A true progression indeed! Like the five items listed in v. 5 the five items of this verse stop short at the half and let the readers add the other five: to strike, to wound, etc.

9) Lying is a different sort of harmful sin and is therefore listed separately with its own imperative: μὴ ψεύδεσθε. In the New Testament it is always used in the middle voice. As a translation for the negative present imperative R., *W. P.*, offers us the choice between, "Stop lying," and, "Do not have the habit of lying." Still other turns are offered in R. 854. "Stop lying!" would, however, imply that the Colossians have hitherto been given to lying, which Paul certainly does not want to intimate. This present imperative wants to exclude all lying; we should translate: "Never lie to one another!" The reciprocal pronoun does not restrict the injunction to Christians as though we may lie to non-Christians, for the sense is: "to one another" no matter who the other person may be. The ethical question as to whether a lie is ever justified under any circumstance of life has been answered in connection with Eph. 4:25.

The two aorist participles — remember that in the Greek they have number, gender, and case — apply to the subject of the imperative which is also the subject of the previous imperative (v. 8) and also of the one preceding that (v. 5). So these aorist participles and their antecedent actions extend back through the entire exhortation: "you who have put off — and who have put on," i. e., because you have done these two fundamental things. The figure is that of drawing off and drawing on a garment; we get away from the one (ἀπό), we get to be in (ἐν) the other. The idea of the garment is, however, not strong in the Greek (see the participle in 2:15): slip out of and *away from* — slip into and get to be *in*. But these are not two separate acts, the two are one; for never for an instant are we, as it were, naked; nor is there an interval between the getting rid of the old man and the acquisition of the new. *We* put off and put on just as *we* repent and believe, etc.; but in the very nature of the case, *we* do these things when grace with its divine power works this putting off and putting on.

"The old man" is old because he is derived from Adam by way of our natural birth. It is the inborn sinful nature plus its *habitus* with all the sinful thoughts, motives, emotions, volitions. Not merely this or that was wrong with us and had to be put off and removed; but our whole old nature must be removed. The figure of a garment should not mislead us; we should read it in the light of the death and the resurrection mentioned in 2:20; 3:3; 2:12; 3:1. The operation is by no means painless; it is violent, it is called a crucifixion (Rom. 6:6). The old man is not converted, he cannot be; he is not renewed, he cannot be. He can only be replaced by the new man, by a creative act of God and by no less.

10) The Greek has two words for "new," νέος and καινός, both of which are opposites of παλαιός or "old." We get the sense of "old" from Eph. 4:23; it means old as being full of the destructive corruption of lust and deceit — rottenly old. The new man is "new" (νέος) in the sense that he did not exist before, that God created him, that his being then began in us. Yet this

newly created man is one who is being constantly renewed by God (καινός in the participle), he undergoes
the newness of being continuously renovated, of having
every stain cleaned off, of having the original newness
restored. In v. 9 the two aorist participles ἀπεκδυσάμενοι
and ἐνδυσάμενοι denote a decisive momentary act while
the present participle in v. 10, ἀνακαινούμενον, denotes
continuousness and iteration.

Paul writes, "the old man together with his πράξεις,"
"practices," which word is at times used in the evil
sense of what is perpetrated. The old man and all his
products are abolished. Paul has just named some of
them. The new man who is newly created takes his
place, and this man is constantly restored to his original newness "for ἐπίγνωσις, genuine spiritual knowledge, according to the image of him who created him."
Yes, God created him, not by the use of omnipotence,
but by the creative power of grace and the gospel. Nor
is this man who is thus created left to shift for himself,
he is constantly renewed by God.

But now, instead of saying renewed for good works
(as in Eph. 2:10) and thus stating a direct opposite
of the evil "practices" of the old man, Paul goes deeper
and says: "constantly renewed for *epignosis* in accord
with his Creator." For out of this true, spiritual
knowledge arise all true spiritual good works. It accords with the image of God (on εἰκών see 1:15). Ephesians 4:24 informs us that the image consists in
righteousness and holiness which belong to truth. With
it goes this knowledge as being in accord with the
image of God. Adam was created in God's image. In
Adam this image existed in its pristine newness and
made him like God in righteousness and holiness. And
it was combined with true knowledge and thus with
truth as held by this knowledge. In these respects
Adam was a miniature copy of God. This image which
was lost in consequence of the fall God re-creates by

grace and constantly renews unto the spiritual knowledge which keeps the image clean and unspoiled in us.

How, then, can we Christians go back to the filth of the old man (v. 5), to all his old viciousness (v. 8)? These have been swept out of us by God's creative grace, and our new man who is ever renewed in true knowledge will certainly deaden our bodily members to sin and will make them instruments of righteousness (Rom. 6:13). Paul reserves the presentation of this activity of the new man for his next paragraph and thus in this verse does not go beyond true knowledge.

11) Paul concludes: **Where there is not Greek and Jew, circumcision and foreskin, barbarian, Scythian, slave, free, but everything and in every way Christ,** and his "where" refers to the condition just described: where the old man is abolished and the new has been created, anywhere where this is the case "there is not" Greek and Jew, etc. Ἔνι is the strong form of ἐν; ἐστί is always understood, and this word is always used with a negative, οὐκ ἔνι. Wherever what Paul says exists there is (not: "cannot be," R. V.) no human prerogative or human deficiency in religious standing, let the Judaizers judge and refuse or accord their prize as they will (2:16, 18).

Paul runs through a list of the most vital differences found in his day. "Greek and Jew" were opposed to each other, the Greek emphasizing his Greek culture and high social standing, the Jew boasting of his divine religion. Both prerogatives disappear before the spiritual glory of the new man. "Greek" does not mean "Gentile" nor "pagan" nor a native of Greece but any man who was educated in Greek culture. "Circumcision and foreskin" were also opposed to each other, the Jews and the Judaizers regarding the former a high prerogative and the latter either a fatal or a serious deficiency. In Colosse the Judaizers, as we have seen,

at least boasted of their circumcision. Where the new
man is, this boast evaporates.

The next four terms are independent, hence there
are no "ands." "Barbarian" (Rom. 1:14) is one who
cannot speak the Greek language (not just a savage);
a "Scythian" is not simply a native of Scythia but the
climax of barbarism, a savage. The Greek despised
the Jew; circumcision despised foreskin; even a barbarian scorned a Scythian.

In the last of the four pairs the words occur in
reverse order: "slave — free," a difference that ran
through the whole world at that time when millions
were slaves. The poor slave was looked down upon by
the free man. By reversing the last pair Paul closes
the list rhetorically in a skilful way. The view that
Paul could have continued with rich and poor, old and
young does not take into account Paul's rhetoric.

Were all of these types members of the church in
Colosse? This list does not prove that fact as some
think. The point of this list is not by means of examples to be found in Colosse to show the highest human
prerogatives and the lowest human deficiences but to
show that both were found in the world of that day,
that men in general made these distinctions.

There is one prerogative in Colosse and everywhere
else in the church that erases all differences between
high and low. This is the new man. Paul phrases this
thought in a striking way: "but everything and in
every way — Christ." Note that "Christ" is most emphatically placed last. He is indeed absolutely "everything" in the new man, and all that men may name
beside him in a religious way is — nil.

Some overlook what the emphatic "Christ" means,
namely *all* that Paul has said of him in this epistle,
notably in 1:13-23, and in 2:9-15, but also all else. This
God-man is the Christ who is everything in every way.
He is τὰ πάντα (definite): "all things" that are; outside

of him none exist. Neither here nor in Eph. 1:23 nor elsewhere is ἐν πᾶσι masculine as the preceding τὰ πάντα indicates. Read the whole together: Christ is "the all in all ways." On the phrase "in all ways" (adverbial) see the examples given in B.-P. 1012.

Some misunderstand Paul's thought and quote various passages to show that we are all one in Christ Jesus, that all national, social, and other differences are wiped out, that "brother" should be substituted for all of them. But that is *not* what Paul says here although he says it elsewhere. Here he says that *the new man* alone counts, that *Christ* is everything in all and every way, that all else is nothing in religion. The whole epistle is based on this thought because this meets the Judaizers who claimed that Christians needed also a few other things to make their religion what it ought to be (2:16, etc.; 2:20, etc.). Only by observing their decrees will Christians be safe from what devils can do to them through the material, earthly *stoicheia* or elements. This perverted notion Paul explodes. The things that are dangerous are the old vices — these avoid! These hurt the new man, these militate against Christ. Away with the superstition about earthly elements! For all of us Christ is the all in all ways!

The Life Full of Christian Virtues, Rich in the Word

12) Here is the positive side of the Christian life, here are the virtues. This paragraph is the complement to the preceding, the two together are the elaboration of the summary paragraph (v. 1-4). **Accordingly put on, as elect of God, saints and beloved ones, tender feeling of compassion, kindness, lowliness, meekness, longsuffering; enduring one another and forgiving each other if anyone against anyone may have complaint, as also the Lord forgave you, thus you, too.**

Like the οὖν occurring in 2:16; 3:1, 5, this connective "accordingly" also here does not connect one sentence with the preceding sentence but one paragraph with the preceding paragraph. Risen with Christ (v. 1-3), we get rid of the old vices (v. 5-11) and thus put on the real Christian virtues. Paul continues the idea of putting on which he mentioned in v. 10, for the new man there spoken of is the possessor of all the virtues now listed. In regeneration we put on the new man, we receive the new, spiritual life. Verse 10 adds the thought that its Creator constantly renews this new man unto true knowledge. It is this renewal of which Paul now speaks.

"Accordingly put on" these Christian virtues. We have already noted that the figure of a garment should not be stressed. These virtues, like "the new man," are not a mere garment that one puts on outwardly and then also takes off again and that in time wears out and must be thrown away. The aorist indicates the permanent acquisition of these virtues.

We should note that this is the only place in the entire letter where Paul inserts something that resembles an address to his readers, and that this form of address is not "brethren" or "my beloved," which would express their relation to him, but a triple designation that indicates their relation to God: "as elect of God, saints, and beloved ones." All Christians, of course, deserve these titles. "As" does not mean "in so far as" but "as in fact you are" what these titles convey. Yet Paul is not using them because they are merely beautiful and expressive terms in general; they are the proper and the most pertinent terms for this epistle.

The Judaizers did not judge the Colossian Christians to be "elect of God"; the Judaizers did not accord them the prize "as God's elect," etc. (see 2:16, 18).

According to the Judaizers the Colossian Christians had no such standing because they did not observe the Judaistic decrees (2:20), did not observe what the Judaizers regarded as essential in warding off spiritual harm that might come to them from earthly, material elements (*stoicheia,* 2:8, 20) which demon spirits used to damage men's souls. Over against this judgment of the Judaizers Paul does not, indeed, set *his* judgment but *God's;* "as" implies that the Colossians, like Paul himself, are accepting *God's* judgment about themselves and not that of the Judaizers.

The absence of articles means that there are many others, all of whom are Christians like the Colossians, who are also "elect of God" and must be considered "as" such by all. *God* accords them the prize, *he* is the arbiter and not the self-appointed Judaizers. God regards the Colossian Christians as his elect, as his saints, as those who have been beloved by him (perfect tense: continuing to be so beloved now and ever). We regard all three as coordinate nouns and do not regard the last two as adjective modifiers of the first: "holy and beloved elect ones." Ἅγιοι has the same force it had in 1:2: "saints," people separated unto God by justification and regeneration, by the death, entombment, and resurrection of which Paul speaks in 2:12, 20; 3:1, 3, by the reconciliation of which he speaks in 1:21, etc. At that time they entered into possession of God's love in Christ Jesus ever after to receive this love and its blessings. The three terms are synonymous, each casts light upon the other.

The verbal noun ἐκλεκτοί is like a passive past participle, "of God" is the genitive of the agent. Some are inclined to date the election at the time the Colossians were efficaciously called (v. 15). If Paul had intended to say this he would have used κλητοί (Rom. 1:6). These two verbals are not identical. "Elect of God" must be dated in eternity (Eph. 1:4). Like the ἐκλεκτοί occurring in Matt. 22:14, the verbal contains the entire elective act of God who, with the whole *massa perdita* of the whole of mankind before his omniscient eyes, chose as his own all those whom his grace in Christ Jesus would succeed in saving and bringing to glory. These are God's saints, his beloved, his elect. Because they are such and because they are of this number Paul calls upon the Colossians to put on all that ought to grace them in their lives. The three titles are positive designations, hence Paul does not use them in the negative paragraph (v. 5-11) which points out the things Christians must put away but does use them here in the positive paragraph which indicates all that Christians ought to put on.

Instead of being influenced by superstition regarding earthly elements and observing silly human decrees (2:20, etc.) Christians put off all the vices of the old man and put on all the virtues of the new, spiritual life. Note that, like the vices, the virtues here listed by Paul pertain to the second table of the law. Our relation and our devotion to God ever show themselves in our attitude and our conduct toward our brethren and our fellow men. I John 4:20, 21. Our love to God is attested by our love to men in Christ Jesus. Away with the philosophy, tradition of men, decrees about material elements (2:8), all of which are an empty show of wisdom (2:23) !

In Phil. 2:1, σπλάγχνα and οἰκτιρμοί are two virtues; these terms are there used as a synonymous pair. The former really means "viscera" and not "bowels" (A. V.), which latter makes us think of the intestines. The Greek connects the tender emotions with a stirring of the inner physical organs. Thus to the Greek "viscera" means "tender feeling" (as in Phil. 2:1) ; yet a genitive may be added, which specifies the kind of tenderness. This is the case in our passage: "tender feeling of compassion," "compassionate feeling." "Kindness," χρηστότης (Rom. 2:4), is broader. Compassion goes out to the distressed and the suffering, goodness or kindness to all whom we can benefit. These two are a pair. They both prompt us to bestow something and thus in a way place us *above* those upon whom we make the bestowal.

The next two may be paired with the first two, but they place us *below* others: "lowly-mindedness, meekness," etc. On the former consult Phil. 2:3 and the great example of Jesus (Phil. 2:5, etc.). The virtue admired by pagans was domination, powerful self-assertion, assuming a position above other men; hence ταπεινοφροσύνη was despicable to the pagan mind, a poor, low mind that could not assert itself and lord it over anybody. The Christian idea of humility lay beyond pagan ethics. A noble sense was put into the word by the spirit of Christ. Pride has vanished. Others are not beneath our feet. We ourselves are poor sinners. We do not lower ourselves while we are great as Chrysostom thought; we know that we are *not* great, hence we never even pretend that we are great. So we move among men.

Allied with humility is "meekness," here meekness toward men. Read Trench regarding the two terms. Of the latter he says: "He that is meek indeed will know himself a sinner among sinners; or, if in one case (meaning Christ's case, Matt. 11:29) he could not know himself such, yet bearing the sinner's doom. And this will teach him (the meek Christian) to endure meekly the provocation with which they may provoke him, not to withdraw himself from the burdens which their sin may impose upon him, Gal. 6:1; II Tim. 2:25; Tit. 3:2" — three excellent examples in these three passages. Meekness was elevated to this height by Christianity.

Comporting with these two is "longsuffering," the mind holding out long under provocations, injustice, inflictions, not giving way to resentment and retaliation.

We thus have five virtues like the two fives found in v. 5 and in v. 8 and yet not like them after all, for Paul adds two more that are expressed by two participles that denote actions. In this way he gets the sacred seven. For the five are Christian virtues and deserve to be completed so as to obtain seven. Otherwise five is the number of rhetorical incompleteness and ten the number of the greatest completeness. Thus when the writer stops with five items, the reader is asked to add the other five so as to have ten.

13) "Enduring one another" means holding out when burdens are heaped up. These need not be insults and injuries, they may be labors for us; they may be faults, thoughtlessness on the part of others. Finally, "forgiving each other if anyone against anyone (note the juxtaposition) may have complaint," ἐάν implying that such instances may be expected to occur. Μομφή is *Beschwerde, Vorwurf*. The point to be noted is that this word includes both justified complaint and complaint about fancied wrong. Paul says: "Suppose anyone of you has such a complaint against someone else, no matter who it may be, then graciously forgive."

This does not mean: Complain a while until pardon is asked and amends are made to satisfy you and then at last condescend to forgive. That is what too many think. Hence we have so many complaints and complainers. Then the pastors, too, think that they must step in and decide the merits of the case, with the result that both parties often complain against the pastor and his unfairness in judging. That is the wrong way to settle quarrels and complaints. Paul says: "The moment you have a complaint against anyone, graciously forgive. Bury it at once in genuine forgiveness." This is what pastors must insist on when complaints are brought to them. When this is properly done, no quarrel will arise; it will be extinguished at the very source. See the fuller elaboration in Eph. 4:32.

Do this, Paul says, "as also the Lord forgave you, thus you, too." The latter expression needs no verb. This is the model for us because it is at the same time the most impelling motive. Matt. 18:21-35. Since everything has been forgiven us, how can we hold a little complaint against anyone? The reading that has "Lord" seems correct; "God" is used in Eph. 4:32, forgiveness being attributed equally to both.

14) Paul has a cluster of seven in v. 12, 13; he crowns it with love. **Above all these things, moreover, the love! which means bond of the completeness. And the peace of Christ, let it be arbiter in your hearts! for which you were also called in one body. And (ever) be thankful!**

Some interpreters think that "put on" is to be supplied and then make love the grand outer robe to be put on over the seven virtues and call this the bond that holds them together. Paul begins a new sentence; he omits the verb and thus has an exclamation with its own imperative force. "Above all these things" = as being of even greater importance. "The love" with the article as well as "the completeness" speak of these as definite ideas. The German understands at once, for he, too, says: *die Liebe, die Vollstaendigkeit*. We are not to think of love as a general quality nor of completeness as a general condition but of the specific love and the specific completeness known to Paul and to all his Christian readers. If someone's English-thinking mind feels it necessary to supply a verb, let it reconstruct the thought in this way: "Above all these things *have* the love," the article to indicate what we Christians call genuine love.

Ἀγάπη = the love of intelligent comprehension and of corresponding purpose (see John 3:16; 21:15; Matt.

5:44) ; it is distinct from φιλία. Our love is always the
product of faith, for Paul is here addressing believers.
Warfield's idea that love sees value in its object is incorrect. When God loved the world which was full of
sin he saw that all value had departed from the world,
yet his love resolved with corresponding purpose to
restore and even to increase the value that had been
lost.

The relative ὅ, neuter, agrees in gender with
neither "love" (feminine) nor with "bond" (masculine) ; when B.-D. 132 changes the gender, he does so
without a warrant. The antecedent is "love," but love
as to what it *means* in this connection and not as to
what it *is* in itself. Ὅ ἐστι = "which means." Here
love means: "bond of the completeness," of the τελειότης
or condition that has reached the τέλος or goal, call it
"perfectness" as do our versions as long as perfectionism is not thereby understood. Paul might have said
simply that the real "love" means the real "completeness" (attainment of the goal). He says just a little
more when he adds "bond" of this completeness: love
is the completeness as to its binding power. State it in
this way: the (real) love of which we Christians speak
means for us a cementing bond that belongs to the completeness which we Christians know as our goal.

The genitive is possessive. It is not objective, for
this completeness needs no bond to hold it together. It
might be a subjective genitive: this completeness uses
a bond, one that binds us Christians together whenever
and wherever this completeness or goal attainment is
reached in any measure. The context does not suggest
that the bond is a girdle, that love holds all the gar-
ments, the seven virtues, together (R., *W. P.*). The
appositional as well as the adjectival genitive are excluded by the article with the genitive. Love is "a
perfect bond" (adjectival genitive) seems to be an at-

tractive thought but overlooks both the relative ὅ and the article with the genitive.

The seven virtues which Paul lists in v. 12, 13 help to bind together and thus are already bonds. Paul says: "Do not fail to add love, namely as the true perfection's own most essential bond." The thought is not that love binds the seven virtues together; they need no tie to bind them together, for they of their own accord unite in drawing and in keeping Christians together. Love, however, stands above them, for it is true perfection's own most wonderful bond.

But why should Paul speak about completeness and about a bond and about virtues that unite Christian hearts? The answer is that the Judaizers denied the Colossians the prize (2:16-19), denied that they had reached the true mark and goal with their type of Christianity, denied it because the Colossians did not observe the Judaistic decrees about eating, drinking, festivals, superstitious avoidance of many physical things. The Judaizers gave the prize to those who zealously observed their decrees as the bond of completeness. Over against all such Judaistic decrees about material things Paul sets the seven distinctive Christian virtues that hold our hearts together, and true Christian love crowns them, the genuine perfection's bond. The Lord awards the prize to those who have this τελειότης, this completeness. Human decrees are nothing in his sight. Dealing, as they do, with στοιχεῖα or material things, such decrees of men never unite hearts spiritually. The seven Christian virtues do, and love crowns them as perfection's own best spiritual bond.

15) Therefore Paul adds: "And the peace of Christ," the peace he bestows, "let it be arbiter in your hearts, for which (peace) you also were called in one body, and (ever) be thankful" for that. This is the

peace of Paul's greeting (1:2); it refers to a state when God is our friend and all is well with us, it is the objective condition that comes from God as our Father (1:2) through Christ as the giver who has made this peace for us. It is ever to be the arbiter in our hearts, the judge and referee who decides to whom the prize must be accorded. This is the verb that was used in 2:18. The Judaizers wanted to set themselves up as arbiters by awarding the crown and prize according to obedience to their decrees and denying it to true Christians like the Colossians. Paul says the true arbiter is right in your own hearts; it is Christ's own peace and no outside, self-appointed Judaizer.

Paul might have said that Christ is the arbiter; but the Judaizers claimed that their decrees accorded with Christ who observed the ceremonial Jewish laws. The peace of Christ does not come through regulations about material things but through Christ's ransoming and remission of sins (1:14), through his reconciliation which was effected in the body of his flesh by means of his death (1:22). This peace is the true arbiter when we are presented as holy, blemishless, and blameless before Christ (1:22). Ever do what accords with this peace of Christ, and this peace will crown you with the prize, let Judaizers say what they will.

"Rule" in our versions misses the point of $\beta\rho\alpha\beta\epsilon\acute{v}\omega$ which means "to act as an umpire," as an arbiter to decide with finality to whom the prize is to go. Nor is "arbitrate" (R. V. margin) correct, for this means to compose differences in a dispute. When a race is run, there is nothing to arbitrate, someone comes out ahead, the umpire gives him the prize. Let the Judaizers shout that the Colossians lack Christian completeness and dare not be accorded the prize. The Colossians are to listen to Christ's own peace speaking in their own hearts. Paul, as it were, personifies peace, for that peace speaks with Christ's voice. It accords the prize to those who have this peace in their hearts, who live and act accordingly. We may translate: "Let the peace of Christ accord the prize in your hearts." Indeed, there is where it is accorded and not before the reviewing stand of the self-appointed Judaistic umpires.

For this peace, Paul says, you were also called in one body, i. e., to have this peace, thus to have it award the prize to you for being complete, "in one body," that is not tied together, like the Judaizers, by their man-made decrees but by genuine Christian virtues (v. 12) and true Christian love (completion's highest tie or bond). "You were called" means effectively called by the gospel, by grace. That call, which made you one body of true Christians, gave you the peace of Christ, which is ever to assure you in your own hearts that yours is the prize, and let no voice of a Judaizer cry down the voice of this peace in your hearts. "In one body," not merely as separate individuals, were the Colossians called for the peace of Christ. The Judaizers vilified them as a body and tried to destroy the bond that kept them one body that had the assuring voice of Christ's peace in their hearts.

Let that peace accord the prize, Paul says, "and be thankful" (present imperative: ever thankful). Indeed, who would not be ever and ever thankful to have Christ's peace acting the umpire in his heart, assuring him and the whole body of Christians of the prize of being true Christians, elect of God, saints, and beloved ones (v. 12)? The translation, "Keep on becoming thankful," overlooks the fact that γίνεσθαι is extensively used in place of εἶναι; "ever be thankful" is entirely correct.

16) Instead of paying attention to the Judaizers or to any others who may try to disturb them with their notions, the Colossians are advised to abide by

the Word. **The Word of Christ, let it dwell in you richly in all wisdom, you teaching and admonishing yourselves with psalms, hymns, spiritual odes** (see Eph. 5:19 on these three terms), **with grace singing in your hearts unto God! And everything whatever you may be doing in word or in work,** (do) **all in the name of the Lord Jesus, thanking God the Father through him!**

"The Word of Christ" matches "the peace of Christ" used in v. 15. This is the Word of that Christ whom Paul has described at length in the infinite supremacy of his nature, his power, and his saving work. *His* peace, *his* Word are, indeed, the supreme gifts for Christians.

"The Word of Christ" does not exclude the Old Testament but includes the additional Word that Christ gave to his apostles who were to transmit it to the church. Although it was as yet only partly written, the New Testament was abundantly transmitted orally. "Let it dwell in you richly in all wisdom" = let it inhabit you as if you were the house and home of this Word, let it do this in a rich way by filling every nook and corner of your being with its blessed, spiritual wisdom. Wisdom is the ability to use knowledge in the right and the wise way. This Word of Christ is supreme and not the philosophy of empty deceit, the tradition of men (2:8), the decrees of Judaizers with their show of wisdom (2:20-23).

The Greek participles have number, gender, and case and are thus used with more precision than English participles. That is the case here: "you teaching and admonishing yourselves with psalms," etc. Our versions make ἑαυτούς reciprocal: "one another"; it is reflexive: "yourselves." When we sing our psalms and our hymns in our Christian worship, all of us sing together, and we by no means chant the instructive and the admonitory words only to our fellow singers, nor do they chant them to us, we all say them first and foremost to our own selves. We speak as one body with this body present. The reflexive pronoun is correct. Think how rich our hymns are in doctrine. Thus they teach and instruct in a most beautiful form, in a form that is readily memorized and thus easily retained. Psalms and hymns are full of imperatives such as: "O bless the Lord, my soul!" This is self-admonition.

The texts vary between "in grace" and "in the grace," but there is no appreciable difference between these two readings. The commentators, however, offer various interpretations such as: singing "about" grace, singing in a lovely, gracious way, singing in thankfulness (χαρίς being taken in the sense of "thanks"). "In your hearts to God' is by some referred to silent singing that is heard by God alone. But this can scarcely be the meaning of Paul. Psalms, hymns, spiritual odes are to be sung aloud. Paul is thinking especially of congregational singing, "in one body" (v. 15). This singing is ἐν χάριτι, "in connection with" God's grace, the grace that has made us what we are, the grace in which we live spiritually. It is this connection (ἐν) that makes us sing.

So also this singing is in our hearts and not only on our lips and in our mouths. All of this music with all its instructive and admonitory words resounds in our inmost hearts when our lips sound it forth in the congregation. Many church choirs and many other singers in the church might note this phrase. All this singing is to be "to God," to his praise and his glory. The more its instruction and admonition fill us with wisdom, the more God's grace overflows in our hearts, the more will it be "to God," acceptable to him. This is the θρησκεία or worship that is acceptable to God, the very opposite of the self-chosen worship of the Judaizers

(2:22, 23) which is in accord with the precepts and teachings of men and has only a show of wisdom.

17) Paul has just spoken about public worship; but the spirit of it and the riches of the wisdom of the Word of Christ permeate the entire life, everything we may do "in word or in work." Πᾶν views a matter as a whole (singular), πάντα as a multiplicity (plural). It is typical of Paul to combine the two numbers. To do "all things in the name of the Lord Jesus" means "in connection with the revelation of the Lord Jesus." Ὄνομα is frequently used in the New Testament and always means "name" in the sense of revelation by which the Lord makes himself known to us, by which we know and apprehend him. All that reveals him is his ᾽ONOMA, his NAME. Note that "the Name of the Lord Jesus" (articles are not needed in the Greek) follows and matches "the Word of Christ."

"In" is not mystical; the phrase does not mean merely "in the spirit of the Lord Jesus" or "with his authority." It means that absolutely everything (even our eating and drinking, I Cor. 10:31) is to be done in the light of the revelation of our Lord and harmonize with that revelation. It ever reveals Jesus as our Savior-Lord to whom we belong absolutely and altogether. The omission of the imperative makes the injunction stronger.

"And be thankful" (v. 15) is repeated with a participle which is enriched by the dative and by the phrase: "thanking God the Father through him" (compare Eph. 5:20). Indeed, when we do everything in our Lord's name we shall constantly be reveling in the sunshine of gratitude to our heavenly Father, all this gratitude being mediated by our Lord Jesus (διά) in whose name and revelation we live our lives with all that we speak and do. Ὁ Θεὸς πατήρ is really one term although the second noun is an apposition; that is why the second noun needs no article. The English rendering "to God the Father," with its article before the second noun, is only our idiom for the First Person of the Trinity.

Paul pictures the true Christian life in contrast with the life of the Judaizers and with the way in which these Judaizers wanted the Colossians to shape their lives: full of superstitious fears about earthly material things, carefully observing their rules and regulations (verses 16, 20, 21) lest demon powers damage them through earthly elements. The whole worship of true Christians is filled with the Word of Christ, its teaching and its admonition in psalms and hymns, all pure grace makes their hearts happy and joyful; the whole activity of this Christian life moves in the sphere of the name and revelation of the Lord Jesus, and they are filled with thanksgiving to God through him. All superstition has disappeared. What can harm them when they are with this Lord? Only thanksgiving overflows from their happy hearts and lips, thanksgiving to God the Father.

Apply all this to ourselves today over against all errorists who in new ways want to foist upon us their human decrees and regulations for producing the complete Christian life. Away with fears about this and that. Christ's Word and his Name are our delightful guide.

The Christian Life for the Various Groups in the Congregation

18) Compare Eph. 5:22-6:9. Yet in Ephesians the whole section is dominated by the great conception of the *Una Sancta* in which the family relation is placed. In Colossians the true Christian family life is placed in opposition to the Judaistic misconceptions which do not find the Christian τελειότης or completeness in obedience to the Word of Christ (v. 16), not in doing all things in the name of the Lord Jesus (v. 17) but

in obedience to the philosophy (2:8)and show of wisdom (2:23) embodied in Judaistic decrees (2:20). Over against such silly notions Paul here places what the Lord in his wisdom and his grace bids wives, husbands, etc., do in their connection with him. These directions are not novelties but the simple, fundamental obligations of the Word. As is done in Ephesians, so here wives, children, and slaves are placed first.

You wives, submit yourselves to your husbands as was (ever) **fitting in the Lord.** The articles "the wives" "to the husbands" are intended to distinguish classes and thus make the terms objective although we translate "you wives," "to your hubands." Christian subjection to the husband is the obligation of the wife. The very brevity of the statement shows that we should not read an ulterior application into Paul's word as though in Colosse the wives were emancipating themselves from proper submission. We cannot say that the Judaizers were trying to alter the status of wives. All that we are able to gather from what Paul says about the Judaistic decrees is that they were imposed as being vital for the true Christian life and were thus superior to the simple obligations which the Lord imposes, as upon wives, so upon husbands, children, etc. Keep to these obligations, Paul says. The wives measure up fully and completely to their obligation as wives when they submit themselves (probably a direct middle, R. 807) to their husbands "as it was (ever) fitting in the Lord."

B.-D. 352, 2 and R. 887 and 919, etc., do not explain this imperfect tense. It is idiomatic and conceives the fittingness as continuing in the past. Thus this tense was used when the present showed a violation of this past condition; but also, as here, when no such violation is occurring in the present. The idea is that it was ever fitting, is so now, and that it is recognized by Paul's readers who thus also will keep on doing what was ever fitting "in connection with the Lord." However, all that Paul has said about "the Lord" and our connection with him should be borne in mind when we now read the phrase, especially 1:13, etc.; 2:9, etc. The Lord directs. What is fitting in our connection with him is the one thing we do "in his name" (v. 17).

19) **You husbands, love your wives and do not be bitter toward them.** These articles have the same force. The verb means intelligent and purposeful love which goes beyond mere affection (φιλεῖν). If it be asked why in the case of wives and of children Paul introduces a reference to the Lord and does not do so in the case of the husbands, the answer is that in v. 18 "in the Lord" is by no means applicable only to the wives (Eph. 5:25, etc.) ; we may also add that husband and wife are one to Paul (Eph. 5:28-33). The whole Christian marital relation is "in the Lord."

"Be not bitter toward them" is added because the wives are to be subject to their husbands. One easily becomes bitter toward an inferior. A husband is not to treat his wife as a subject, as an inferior person in the home. This negative is on the order of a litotes: ever be considerate toward them in the way described in Eph. 5:28, etc.

20) **You children, be obedient to your parents in all things, for this is well-pleasing in the Lord.** Here father and mother are placed on the same level as far as the child is concerned, and the child's obedience is his one obligation, all is to be done "in connection with the Lord," which this epistle applies to the parents as well as to the children. We thus raise no question about the phrase κατὰ πάντα, "in all things" or "in all respects."

21) In order that no improper commands be given to children Paul now writes: **You fathers, provoke not your children lest they be disheartened.** Although this is addressed to the fathers, the mothers

are not to be excluded. Yet the father is the head of
the house. The verb forbids every action of this kind.
Although the verb is a *vox media* (it is used in the
good sense in II Cor. 9:2), it is here to be understood
in the evil sense of stirring up improperly by incon-
siderate or even unjust or wrong treatment. No par-
ent who wants his child to obey him "in the Lord" will
treat his child so that it becomes downhearted, gives
up, loses its cheerful willingness. Paul uses but a few
words, yet volumes might be written on the sorrows
and even the tragedies of children as R., *W. P.*, points
out. Paul demands Christian parental consideration
for children.

22) **You slaves, obey in all things your masters
according to the flesh, not in eyeservices as men-
pleasers but in simpleness of heart, fearing the Lord.
Whatever you may be doing, work from the soul
as for the Lord and not for men, having come to
know that from the Lord you will duly receive the
due return gift of the inheritance. For the Lord
Christ keep slaving! For he who does wrong will
carry away what he did wrong, and there is no
respect of persons.**

The brevity of what Paul says to all the other
groups makes the expanded form of what he says to
slaves stand out the more. The reason is obvious: Paul
is returning the slave Onesimus to his master Philemon to be received by him as a Christian brother. None
of the Christian slaves in Colosse are to get wrong
ideas about their relation to their earthly masters,
about the kind of service they owe their masters as
slaves, or about the gravity of any wrong they may do
their masters. Onesimus had gravely wronged Philemon by running away. Paul condones no wrong of any
kind on the part of any slave. On the question of
slaves and also their number in the empire see
Eph. 6:5.

The Christian slave's great obligation is obedience "in all things (the same phrase that was used with reference to children) to his master according to the flesh," meaning the body. We may translate: "their bodily masters." The whole relation is one only of this transient, earthly type and not a matter of the spirit. This obedience is not to manifest itself "in eyeservices as men-pleasers (so many workers who are not slaves render only that kind of service) but in singleness or simplicity of heart (without a fold in the heart, under which to hide a false motive, without duplicity or ulterior motive), fearing the Lord" whose eyes see through and through us. This is the proper fear and not that caused by the lash which the human master may apply or have applied. Paul's language is exceedingly plain.

23) He expands: "Whatever you may be doing, ever be working from the soul (see this phrase in Eph. 6:6) as for the Lord and not for men." Here is the secret for all who work for other men, whether they are slaves or free employees: "Throw your soul into the work as if your one employer were the Lord!"

24) The aorist participle is causal: "because you have come to know," aorist: have reached that point of knowledge. Earthly masters may reward a good slave; again they may not. A good Christian employee must never get the thought that his employer will give him no more for throwing his soul into the work than for just working along like other employees do. He has come to know that he is working for the Lord, no matter what his lowly job may be, and "that from the Lord (emphatic) he will duly receive the due return gift" of what is more than wages or pay in money, of what is far beyond all earning, namely "the (heavenly) inheritance" (appositional genitive, R. 498). 'Aπό in both the verb and the noun = duly, measured, however, not by human desert or claim but by the gen-

erosity and magnanimity of the Lord's grace. 'Aντί in the noun = return, δόσις = gift: the Lord will give in due return what in infinite grace he desires to give.

No wonder Paul exclaims: "For the Lord Christ keep slaving!" The imperative is so much more force-ful than the indicative would be, so we prefer to call this the imperative. The R. V. has the latter; the A. V. even adds "for" on most slender authority.

25) "For" belongs in this verse. The δέ is a mis-taken reading, "but" in the A. V. This δέ rests on the assumption that Paul is comforting the slaves who are mistreated by their masters by telling such slaves that their bad masters will carry away the wrong they are doing, and that God will not respect their persons. That idea is unchristian. No injured Christian is to harbor the secret thought: "He who wrongs me will get paid by God!" Lightfoot applies this verse to both slave and master: if either does wrong to the other, God will pay the guilty one without partiality. But masters are not mentioned until later.

Paul tells the slave that, if he wrongs his master, the very wrong he has committed he, the slave, will carry away, κομιεῖται, the future tense of κομίζω, "to carry off," not "receive again" (our versions). The wrong done remains on the slave's back, and he will carry it to judgment. In that judgment "there is no respect of persons," no looking at a man's face, letting him off because it is he. The view that this statement can refer only to a mighty person of high standing who, because of his standing, expects to be let off, is untenable, that just because a slave is only a lowly slave he may expect God to excuse him for shabby serv-ice to his earthly master. He is very much mistaken: just as a high standing counts for nothing in the judg-ment, so also a low standing. The latter is the point for the slave. If Paul had meant: "the one who wrongs you slaves" he would have had to add ὑμᾶς, the pronoun "you."

Here is Christian completeness (τελειότης, v. 14) for the Christian slave. It, too, has nothing to do with Judaistic decrees and observations.

4:1) **You masters, render what is right and equal to your slaves as having come to know that you, too, have a master in heaven.** Τὸ δίκαιον offers no difficulty, the neuter adjective has taken the place of an abstract noun; the sense is: "Do the right thing by your slaves!" the thing that God will approve when as your master he looks into your conduct.

There is also no difficulty in regard to Paul's adding a regular abstract noun: "the equality." The commentators waver in regard to the meaning of this noun. Most of them understand ἰσότης in a modified sense, not as meaning "equality," but "equity, what is fair and equitable." They then give the words the general sense: "Treat them decently!" They endeavor to make the two abstract terms match and seek for this modified meaning in secular writers. Meyer is an exception, for he rejects these efforts and prefers "equality," not the equality of social standing, but that of Christian brotherhood and appeals to Philemon 16 to support this idea; he restricts Paul's admonition, as to *Christian* masters, so the *Christian* slaves, brethren in the congregation: "Treat them like Christian brethren!"

Paul, however, here defines what he means in Eph. 6:9: "Keep doing *the same things* to them," i. e., the same things that correspond to the difference in position. "Equality" thus = "the same things": as you masters want the slaves as slaves to do the right thing by you, do you as their masters do the equal thing by them. Meyer goes too far in one direction, the rest go too far in the other. We shoud not restrict this injunction to the treatment of *Christian* slaves, it applies to *any and all slaves* of Christian masters.

The causal participle is the same as that used in
3:24: "because you have come to know that you, too,
have a master in heaven." As you serve this master
and want him to treat you, so as masters treat the
slaves of whom you ask that they serve you as you
serve your master. The whole admonition is an application of the Golden Rule. In Colossians Paul tells the
slaves that God does not respect person; in Ephesians
he tells this to the masters. It is typical of Paul to
vary in just this way. Once more we note that Paul
points to what constitutes Christian completeness for
Christian owners of slaves, something that is far different from the empty rules of the Judaizers.

CHAPTER IV

Additional Features of the Christian Life

2) In Ephesians there follows the famous section on the Christian hoplite, his unseen enemies and his armor, to which Paul adds prayer. In Colossians Paul at once proceeds to prayer. Yet in Colosse but not in Ephesus Judaizers were advocating their peculiar philosophy that demon powers could work harm to Christians through the στοιχεῖα of the world, through physical, earthly elements, and were offering their system of regulations for protection against such harm. Should not Eph. 6:10-17 or a paragraph similar to it appear in Colossians instead of in Ephesians? Certainly not.

In Ephesians, which presents a view of the great *Una Sancta*, we must have mention made of the great enemies of the Holy Christian Church and the armor which vanquishes them. These enemies are powers that do not operate by means of physical substances but by means of deception; the armor that vanquishes them is according. The fiction promulgated in Colosse was nothing but fiction. Paul has revealed it as such by calling it a mere show of wisdom (2:23). It is brushed aside as being silly; there is no need of hoplite armor. The God-man is absolutely supreme (1:13, etc.; 2:9, etc.). Through him God has stripped the demon powers of their armor and has given Christ a glorious triumph over them (2:15). That is the answer to the Colossian Judaizers.

Our Christian life proceeds on its simple course, undisturbed by any Judaistic superstitions. This is the burden of Colossians. In Ephesians Paul looks farther and therefore introduces our battle and our firm stand against the temptations and the deceptions of the hellish spirits. The two letters are companion pieces, yet each keeps to its proper subject. Colossians refutes the Judaistic fiction, one that is so empty and silly; Ephesians presents the *Una Sancta,* its enemies being unable to harm it, clad, as it is, in the panoply of God.

In the Christian life that Paul has portrayed in 3:1-4:1 prayer occupies a most important place. Remember, Paul's account shows in what Christian τελειότης or completeness consists. The Judaizers denied it the prize because it lacked observance of their decrees (2:18, 20, 21). God accords the prize to this life which, in addition to its other features, is filled with prayer.

Hold fast steadfastly to prayer, watching therein in thanksgiving! The verb means holding to something with strength and hence not neglecting or letting it drop. So the first Christians held fast to the doctrine of the apostles and to the fellowship, to the breaking of bread and to the prayers (Acts 2:42). Προσευχή is the sacred word, prayer to God, and is here and in a number of other places used in the wide sense as including all forms of prayer and devotion to God. Hence the Greek article "the prayer" which includes more than prayer in general, which also points definitely to the whole Christian prayer worship, public and private, for which the Colossians had been trained. In that, Paul says, go on with full strength of mind and heart.

In Eph. 6:18, "watching *unto it* in all steadfastness," etc., means never neglecting it or growing careless; hence εἰς αὐτό is placed forward. Here Paul writes: "watching *in it,*" and the phrase is added without emphasis. This means that watching is to be added to prayer as an adjunct: ever praying and at the same time watching. The two are combined: Watch and pray (Matt. 26:41) ; to watch is an independent act. Here it is subjoined to prayer. Hence, not: "Watch so

as not to neglect prayer!'" nor: "Watch and be atten-
tive during prayer!" but: "Pray, and at the same time
be watchful!"

A third point is added in briefest form by means of
a phrase: "in connection with thanksgiving." Let us
leave the phrase where Paul places it. Ἐν αὐτῇ = "in
prayer" so that "in thanksgiving" forms the sphere for
all our praying and our watching. This indicates
Paul's meaning: our great thankfulness for all that
Christ has done for us and all with which he has filled
us (2:9); see also 3:15, 17. He has freed us from all
superstitious fears; he has placed us into the pure and
happy Christian life. Cling to him in prayer and
watch that nothing removes us from him and constantly thank him for all that we have in him.

3) Paul continues by mentioning a special
phase of this activity of prayer: **praying withal also
concerning us that God open for us a door for the
Word, to utter the mystery of Christ because of
which I am also in bonds, that I may make it public
as I ought to utter it.**

The thought is the same as that found in Eph.
6:18, 19. Paul solicits the prayer of the Colossians
for himself especially and also for his assistants. Ἅμα
= at the same time: when you pray do so also "concerning us" (R. 1140). "Us" means Paul and Timothy
(1:1) and thus naturally includes other assistants of
Paul's. This "us" is not a majestic or an editorial
plural that designates Paul himself; no writer uses
such a plural and the singular in the same sentence.

Ἵνα is non-final and states what the Colossians are
to pray for: "that God may open for us a door for the
Word" (objective genitive). The infinitive is scarcely
epexegetical (R. 1086) but rather indicates result: "so
that we may utter the mystery of Christ." God's opening the door (aorist, one act) is to have this result:
effective utterance (aorist) of the mystery of Christ.

To utter a mystery is to make it known (Eph. 6:19), to reveal it. What Paul means by this "mystery" he has stated in 1:26, 27 and 2:2, namely the whole blessed gospel mystery of Christ's universal redemption which opened salvation for all men equally on the one basis of his blood through faith alone without any human requirement whatever. To open a door for the Word is to provide a free opportunity for the proclamation of the Word of the gospel so that its contents, the mystery of Christ (one may regard this genitive as objective), may be freely uttered.

God opens the door by his providence. Many fail to note this and try to open doors for themselves. When we are spreading the gospel we must follow God's providential indications as to where we ought to work. Louis Harms tried to send his missionaries to the Gallas, but the door was shut, God had another place open. Paul could not enter Bithynia (Acts 16:7) ; God opened the door into Europe, into Macedonia. Again, not until after Paul had preached in Europe did God open the door in Ephesus and in the Roman province of Asia. The Word and the work are his. Paul is not asking that a certain door be opened but for the opening of "a door" wherever God may have one. We need not puzzle about Paul's meaning. He is thinking of the time when in all probability he will be released (Philemon 22). Then, he hopes, God will have a door open for him and for his assistants that will lead them into new, fruitful mission work.

4) Now he uses the singular because he is speaking for himself alone: "because of which (mystery) I have been placed in bonds (and am still in this condition, perfect tense)." Paul had planned to go to Spain (Rom. 15:23, 24), but God had kept that door closed. It was God's plan to have Paul first testify in Rome (Acts 23:17), especially to the many Jews in Rome (Acts 28:17, etc., see the author's exposition of Paul's

great success among the Jews in Rome, which began
so promptly after his arrival in that city). The reason
for Paul's captivity was, indeed, the mystery of Christ.
The Jews would not believe that Gentiles could be saved
without first becoming Jews. Their rage against Paul
for preaching such a doctrine had brought about his
long imprisonment.

The relative clause regarding Paul's imprisonment
enables him to add a second non-final ἵνα which states
what he wants the Colossians to pray for for him personally regarding his imprisonment. Before God opens
a door into some new territory for him and for his assistants (Paul hoped that this might be Spain), he has yet
to face the imperial court when his case is brought to
trial. Then he wants to make public the mystery of
Christ (φανερώσω) in the court of the whole empire,
wants to do this "as he ought to utter" the mystery at
that critical time, literally: "as it is necessary that
I make utterance" (aorist infinitive, effective utterance
on that occasion). We are not left to surmise Paul's
meaning. Not long after this time he wrote Philippians and in that epistle reports that at his trial the
great fact that his bonds were connected with Christ
was published in the whole Prætorium (the imperial
Roman guard of 9,000 soldiers) and in all the rest of
Rome (see the exposition of Phil. 1:13, etc.). God had
granted the prayer which Paul here asks the Colossians
to make.

Paul's missionary plans for the future were of interest to the Colossians as they were to all the churches
which Paul had founded. They would surely pray that
another great door might be opened for him. Note
that in II Cor. 2:12 he states that such a door was
opened to him in Troas. But before those plans regarding the future could be realized, Paul had to face
the imperial court where he was obliged to show that
his imprisonment was due to the Jews, to their hate

against the gospel of Christ preached by Paul. All
Paul's work in the future depended on the manner in
which the court would regard this gospel. In fact, all
the congregations founded by Paul, including Colosse
which was founded by Paul's pupil Epaphras (1:7),
would be involved in the favorable or the unfavorable
outcome of Paul's trial. So much depended on how
Paul would speak when his case regarding the gospel
came up before the imperial supreme court.

5) The Colossian congregation is to pray for
the progress of the Word in the world as a unit.
Then the Colossians will, indeed, not hinder the gospel by their conduct in their own city. **In wisdom**
(ever) **walk toward those without, buying up the
opportunity.** See Eph. 5:16: "Those outside" are
all the non-Christians. Christian wisdom in our daily
contact with them will avoid everything that may prej-
udice them against the gospel and will do everything
that may win them for the gospel. It will make the
most of every opportunity that offers itself as one does
when he gets a good chance to buy up something and
then buys to the limit. In Eph. 5:16 the context is
somewhat different. Some endeavor to erase this difference by identifying Eph. 5:16 with Col. 4:5. Here,
as elsewhere in the two epistles where the wording is
similar, we should leave each modification of thought
as Paul has it.

6) **Your discourse** (ὁ λόγος = *what* you say)
**ever with grace, seasoned with salt, so that you
know how you ought to make answer to every single
one.**

To say that Paul writes carelessly in this last admonition is to fail to note the incisiveness of Paul's
brevity. Moulton, *Einleitung* 289, calls Paul's word
interjectional. Hence the imperative ἔστω or some
other verb form is not found. "Ever with grace"
means with graciousness, in a kindly spirit. The addi-

tion "seasoned with salt" (perfect passive participle: "having been seasoned") conceives the discourse as food that is duly seasoned before it is served and is thus palatable when it is served. "Have salt in yourselves!" Mark 9:50. "Salt is good," Luke 14:34. Salt is neither the wisdom nor the graciousness we are to use; it is the wholesomeness of what we say. Salt is not used in the sense of wit like the spice of Attic salt (wit). We need not introduce the power of salt to prevent decay; only its commonest use for making food palatable lies in the context.

Some have regarded the infinitive as a substitute for an imperative, but an infinitive of result (R. 1090) completes Paul's thought: "so that you get to know (aorist) how you ought to make answer to every single one." By using wisdom and clothing this in graciousness and giving it a wholesome taste we shall soon get to know just how to answer every person with whom we get into a discussion so that we may make the most of all such opportunities. Paul wants to say just the right thing at the critical time of his trial so as not to damage the cause of the gospel in any way. But this is what we should always strive to do in all our contacts with those outside. Foolish remarks, ungracious, surly, or cutting retorts, finally saltless talk that is vapid and from which the hearer's mind turns away because it is not worth considering, never do the Christian cause any good. These three qualities here touched upon briefly by Paul are only too often missing from what Christians say especially also to outsiders.

This concludes the description of the Christian life which is deserving of the Lord's prize and commendation. Let the Judaizers talk their show of wisdom (2:23), it is even tasteless, to say nothing about being foolish. It has neither the sound content of wisdom nor the attraction of grace and seasoning; men set such a dish aside. Our *logos* is to be such as will make men seek it more and more until they become Christians. Paul's words apply to much of the sermonizing of our day. The pulpit needs wisdom, the grace and the salt of the gospel. The food it offers is often too cheap in both content and seasoning.

The Conclusion

*Tychicus is to inform the Colossians about
Paul's affairs*

7) **All the things concerning me shall Tychicus make known to you, the beloved brother and faithful minister and fellow slave in the Lord, whom I have sent to you for this very thing in order that you may get to know the things about us and that he may comfort your hearts, together with Onesimus, the faithful and beloved brother, who is from you. They shall make known to you everything here.**

Therefore Paul sends no information about his present situation. The Colossians will want to know everything; Tychicus will give them all the information they desire. See the close parallel in Eph. 6:21, etc. See this passage regarding Tychicus. He was to take the three letters (Ephesians, Colossians, Philemon) to their respective destinations; we think he was also to deliver the letter to the Laodiceans.

In Eph. 6:21 Paul calls Tychicus "the beloved brother and faithful minister in the Lord"; here Paul adds a third term, "fellow slave." All three terms are objective, and hence no possessive pronoun such as "my," "our," "your" is added. "Beloved brother" places Tychicus among all the Christian brethren as being one of them, who has become beloved by those who know him. At the same time he is a "faithful minister" who as such has rendered true service to the church, which all should appreciate. With this second designation goes "fellow slave," a fellow slave of Paul and of Timothy (1:1) who submitted his will completely to the Lord. The last two terms refer to work done and being done and are thus modified by "in the Lord," "beloved brother" is quite complete in itself.

8) Ἔπεμψα is an epistolary aorist; we should say, "I am sending." The Greek thinks of the arrival of the letter and its reading in Colosse; the English of the time of its writing. Paul is sending his letter by a man such as Tychicus "for this very thing that you may get to know (ingressive aorist) the things concerning us (Paul and Timothy, etc., 1:1), and that he may comfort your hearts" (non-final ἵνα). Some other messenger might not have been able to supplement Paul's letter in this way. So the Colossians may ask Tychicus everything; that is why he is being sent. "The things concerning us" has the same plural that is used in Ephesians (which see). Although the Colossians had never had Paul in their midst they are deeply concerned about him and would like to know how he is faring in Rome. Tychicus will comfort their hearts by relieving all anxiety they may have. Things are going well enough for Paul and for the friends about him.

9) Associative σύν adds the thought that Paul is sending Onesimus along with Tychicus. All that Paul says is that he is "from you." Read Philemon. This slave ran away from his master in Colosse, came into contact with Paul in Rome, and was converted and completely changed. Paul is now sending him back to his master. Tychicus is serving as his protector, for a runaway slave was liable to arrest anywhere by the *fugitivarii* or slave catchers who were everywhere on the lookout for such slaves. Paul does not say what the congregation is to do with this slave; he says only that he is sending him back as "a faithful and beloved brother" who is from their city (ἐξ ὑμῶν). The rest is to be found in Paul's letter to Philemon. This desig-

nation is quite sufficient. The Colossians will receive Onesimus as "a faithful and beloved brother" (these same three words are also used to characterize Tychicus).

The implication that the Colossians will receive Onesimus as a brother lies in the last brief addition: "They shall make known to you everything here," a quiet but significant plural. Onesimus is to help Tychicus tell what the congregation will want to know. They will receive him in the congregation, will accept him as a brother, one of Paul's own converts who was brought to Christ in such a strange way. Paul dictates and commands nothing; he has the fullest confidence in the Colossians. Their hearts will tell them what to do. Let your imagination picture the scene when Tychicus brought Onesimus back to Colosse, when the remarkable news spread, when Philemon had his slave back with a special letter from Paul, when the congregation met, heard Paul's letter to them, etc. Wonderful, indeed! the whole of it exceedingly fine.

Salutations from Paul's friends

10) Paul sends salutations from six men; so together with Timothy (1:1) there were seven with him at this time, Epaphras having recently come from Colosse and belonging there. We have discussed the question of the salutations at the end of Ephesians and need not repeat, as to why there are none in Ephesians, why there are some in Colossians. Aside from Epaphras none of these men had had personal contact with the Colossians. Their salutation thus means that all these assistants of Paul's as well as Paul and Timothy are solicitous about the Colossians, concerned in their spiritual welfare. By sending their salutation they concur in all that Paul has said in this letter about the Judaizers. These salutations are far more than a mere courteous gesture.

There salutes you Aristarchus, my fellow war captive, and Mark, the cousin of Barnabas, concerning whom you received directions. If he comes to you, receive him.

It is customary in such salutations to place the verb first and thus to emphasize both the verb and the subject (see Rom. 16:21-23). The verb really means to draw one to oneself, to embrace, and is used to designate a salutation on arrival and on departing and then in letters to indicate the sending of the salutation from a person and having certain persons saluted. Aristarchus came from Thessalonica; he was a member of the delegation that took the great collection to Jerusalem (Acts 19:24; 20:4). He accompanied Paul when the latter was sent from Caesarea to Rome as a prisoner. Whether he had remained with Paul during his imprisonment at Rome we are unable to say, we know only that he was now in Paul's company.

Paul calls Aristarchus "my fellow war captive"; in Philemon 23 Epaphras receives this title, Aristarchus that of fellow worker. In Rom. 16:7 Andronicus and Junias are termed fellow war captives. The word does not mean fellow prisoner (our versions), one who was arrested and jailed with Paul as Silas was in Philippi. Paul does not have in mind spiritual war captives who are held as such by Christ's grace. This would be a strange figure and would apply to all Christians. Some have thought that the friends of Paul were allowed to share Paul's confinement under certain regulations, turn and turn about; that Aristarchus was now having his turn, Epaphras when Philemon was written. But both letters were written at the same time and most likely on the very same day. "Fellow war captive" means that Aristarchus shared the special hardship that was incident to Paul's gospel warfare.

"Fellow worker" means that one shares in Paul's labors. Either term can, therefore, be applied to Aristarchus. The one is not more distinguished than the other. The only difference is this, that the fellow captive is fellow to Paul while Paul is in confinement while a fellow worker may be fellow to Paul whether Paul is confined or not.

The second person is John Mark, the writer of the second Gospel, who is named also in Philemon 24 as being among Paul's fellow workers. Paul and Barnabas took him along on their first missionary journey, but Mark left them and went home; therefore Paul refused to take him on his second missionary journey (Acts 12:25; 13:5; 13:13; 15:36-40). We hear no more about Mark until this time. Now he is again with Paul in Rome. We should certainly like to know how he came to be here, how he had regained Paul's full confidence and was now one of Paul's assistants. It is worth noting that both Mark and Luke are now with Paul. It is, however, taking too much for granted when R., *W. P.*, supposes that both of them possibly had their Gospels with them. As far as Luke is concerned, he had for a long time been gathering material and may have had this material with him; but both Gospels were written a little later.

'Ανεψιός means "cousin" and not "nephew" as some suppose (see the evidence from the papyri). Mark is introduced to the Colossians as "the cousin of Barnabas" (Doric genitive), not in order to distinguish him from some other Mark, but in order that the Colossians may associate him with Barnabas, the latter being well known to them through the early work of Paul and Barnabas in Galatia which was not far from Colosse.

Mark is serving Paul: "concerning whom you received directions," then the addition: "If he comes to you, receive him." Mark is now with Paul and sends his salutation. The "directions" (ἐντολάι, plural) cannot be the statement to receive him when he comes. All our information is to the effect that Paul's first communication to the Colossians is found in this epistle. We thus dismiss the idea that either by letter or by a verbal message Paul had sent directions to Colosse regarding Mark although some think that the aorist ἐλάβετε indicates this. This is another epistolary aorist like the one used in v. 8. Paul is now sending directions regarding Mark through Tychicus; an English writer would say, "concerning whom you are receiving directions."

Paul is evidently sending Mark on some commission, in the course of which Paul expects him to arrive also at Colosse some weeks after the arrival of Tychicus. We, of course, do not know where Mark was to go on his route, what he was to do, and what directions Tychicus conveyed to the Colossians regarding Mark. "Receive him" means no more than to lodge and to entertain Mark; yet, since Paul asks this, Mark is to be received as Paul's friend and assistant. Although he is confined in Rome, we see that by means of his faithful assistants Paul is able to reach out into all his congregations far and near.

11) **And Jesus, the one called Justus, they being of the circumcision, these alone, fellow workers for the kingdom of God of a kind that have come to be a consolation for me.**

"Jesus" was a name that was frequently found among Jews, "Justus" a surname which was also common among Jews (Acts 1:23; 18:7, the Latin for the Hebrew *Zadok*). We know nothing further about this man. He is not mentioned in Philemon among those who are sending greetings, a fact which weighs against those critics who deny the authenticity of Colossians. A forger would not have inserted the name of this Jesus in Colossians alone.

It is well to note that Aristarchus has the apposition: "my fellow war captive," which completes the mention of him. Mark and Jesus have the minor appositions, which state only who they are, Mark being the cousin of Barnabas, Jesus the man called Justus, neither designation indicating their relation to Paul as "my fellow war captive" states the relation of Aristarchus to Paul. Hence Paul adds to Mark and to Jesus an apposition of this kind as he does to Aristarchus: οἱ κτλ. We thus see that this plural applies only to Mark and to Jesus and not to Aristarchus also, which agrees with the fact that Aristarchus was not a Jew. He was a Thessalonian and thus not a Jew; he was one of the delegation which took the collection that had been raised by the Gentile converts to Jerusalem (Acts 20:4); none of this delegation were born Jews, nor was it proper that this delegation should have born Jews. We thus cannot translate as our versions do; we refer the whole apposition only to Mark and to Jesus: "they being of the circumcision the only ones, fellow workers for the kingdom of God (see 1:13 on the kingdom), such as have come to be (ingressive aorist) a consolation for me." This is their relation to Paul as the relation of Aristarchus is the fact that he is Paul's fellow war captive.

"Of the circumcision" is a partitive genitive; it is not the predicate of ὄντες but modifies οὗτοι μόνοι: "these only of the circumcision." The predicate is συνεργοί . . . οἵτινες: "they being . . . fellow workers . . . such as have proved a consolation for me," the only Jewish Christian fellow workers who proved to be such a consolation for Paul. There were other fellow workers, both Gentile and Jewish, in Rome (Philemon 24). All of these Jewish fellow workers with the exception of Mark and Jesus worked for the kingdom as Phil. 1:15, etc., states: they preached Christ, indeed, but from envy of Paul by trying to put Paul into the shade (see this passage). They were no consolation for Paul in his confinement. Mark and Jesus were the exception in this respect. This was their distinction. With οὗτοι μόνοι Paul makes this fact emphatic. The Greek is without the slightest irregularity, is neat and most precise.

12) There salutes you Epaphras, one from you, a slave of Christ Jesus, ever striving in your behalf in his prayers that you may stand as complete and as fully assured in all the will of God. Indeed, I testify for him that he has much concern about you and those in Laodicea and those in Hieropolis.

Epaphras is the founder of the Colossian congregation and perhaps also of the other two (Laodicea and Hieropolis). See the introduction. Paul has characterized Epaphras in 1:7, 8; what is here said of him is additional. He had told Paul about the situation in Colosse, Paul's letter being the result. Epaphras is apparently not yet hastening back to Colosse; what is detaining him in Rome we are unable to say. The best surmise is that he expected to return in a short time. Having come such a distance, he would want to spend some days with Paul to learn more and more from him in order the better to serve his congregation and its two neighbors.

Ἐξ ὑμῶν is to be understood as it was in v. 9; both Onesimus and Epaphras are thus marked as coming from Colosse. "A slave of Christ Jesus" = one whose will is wholly governed by Christ, his Master. Paul applies this epithet to himself in Rom. 1:1. Thus, not with himself but with Christ Jesus does Paul connect this spiritual leader of the Colossians. They are to esteem Epaphras as one who obeys Christ alone in all things; Paul so esteems him.

As such Epaphras ever "agonizes" for the Colossians with strong pleading in his prayers, and his

prayer for them is that they may "stand" firm and
solid, "as complete," as having reached the goal and
lacking nothing to make them true Christians in every
way. Note this adjective in 1:28: "every man complete in Christ." Note Paul's "agonizing" for this
same thing in his work (1:29). See how the noun
"completeness" is used in 3:14. Τέλειοι is significant
here, for the Judaizers advocated a far different kind
of completeness, one that was attained by observing
their foolish decrees about material things.

In order to bring out the full difference Paul adds
with epexegetical καί: "and having been fully assured
(perfect participle: continuing now and ever in this
assurance) in all the will of God," i. e., God having
fully assured them in regard to all that he wills regarding them. The Judaizers follow their own will (θέλων
in 2:18; ἐθελοθρησκεία in 2:23) by setting up their own
philosophy and human tradition about material things
(2:8) in a false humility and show of wisdom (2:23).
We should read this whole clause in the light of all that
precedes. This true slave of Christ had no will of his
own as the Judaizers did, no false completeness and
fake assurance for the Colossians, but brought them
God's will according to which they should shape their
faith and their life. Paul puts this stamp upon Epaphras. Would that every minister of Christ deserved
this stamp!

13) We regard γάρ as confirmatory: "Indeed, I
testify," or: "Yea." Πόνος is broader than agonizing in
prayers, it means *viel Muehsal*, "much concern" ("zeal"
in the A. V. follows an inferior variant); "labor" is
not exact enough. When Paul says, "I testify" he
refers to what he has seen, that Epaphras talked and
talked with him and was full of deepest concern to
bring these churches through the Judaistic attacks so
as to lose no members. Here Paul mentions also the
people of Laodicea and those of Hieropolis. Epaphras

had all of them on his heart. See the introduction
regarding the close proximity of the three towns. Epaphras felt responsible for all three. He may have
founded the church in all three places; that he was the
spiritual leader of all three seems certain; compare
v. 16 and note also 2:1 regarding Paul's concern.

14) **There salutes you Luke, the physician, the
beloved, and Demas,** both of whom are in Philemon 24
listed among Paul's fellow workers. The apposition
that states that Luke is a physician is like the one that
calls Mark "the cousin of Barnabas" and the one that
is added to Jesus "called Justus." But Paul adds the
verbal with a second article, which makes it a further
apposition and thus a climax (R. 776). The fact that
Luke looked after Paul's health goes without saying
although Paul does not say "*my* physician." The service rendered Paul was wholly incidental and is not
stressed by Paul's apposition. The fact that Luke was
a medical doctor only differentiates him just as Mark
and Jesus have their differentiation. Paul's attachment to Luke lies in the word "the beloved."

To Demas, Paul adds nothing. This does not mean
that he is not beloved; it rather suggests the opposite
since his name is combined with one who is beloved.
The idea that already at this time Paul felt that Demas
might become unfaithful as he indeed did (I Tim.
4:10) is decisively excluded by Philemon 24 because
there his name appears between Aristarchus and Luke.
Bengel thinks that Demas was Paul's scribe; Ewald
adds that he also asked to send a salutation, that Paul
assented, and that Demas thus simply put down his
name and nothing more. Ingenious and yet not sub-
stantiated.

Why does Paul say so much more about Aristarchus, Mark, and Jesus than about Luke? Why is Jesus
omitted in Philemon? Why are the four men mentioned in Philemon 24 alike called "my fellow work-

ers"? All these questions center in the same thing, call it the personal equation. Paul reaches the end of the group that sends salutations so he becomes rather brief with regard to Luke and briefest with regard to Demas.

Salutations from Paul plus Two Directions

15) Do you salute the brethren in Laodicea and Nymphas and the church in his house. And when this epistle has been read among you, cause that it be read also in the church of the Laodiceans, and the one from Laodicea that also you may read it.

When Paul bids the Colossians do the saluting of others for him he unites them with himself as his agents to express his love for the persons he names; see Rom. 16:3, etc., where the Roman congregation is to salute person after person in its membership. Here the Colossians are to salute all the brethren in Laodicea.

There is much dispute about the additions. Is the name Νυμφᾶν, a masculine, or Νύμφαν, a feminine? Is this a person residing in Laodicea or in Hieropolis? Is the reading: "his" — "her" — or "their house"? We need not decide the question as to whether this is a man Nymphas or a woman Nympha although the writer inclines toward the former view. But we do place this person in Hieropolis for the reason that Paul would not leave the Christians in Hieropolis without a salutation, it would be too unlike Paul. So we reject the plural "their" house. We may well take it that the group in Hieropolis was small and met in the house of Nymphas but that it was affiliated with the church in Laodicea, i. e., was really a part of this church.

16) This explains the exchange of the two letters. When Epaphras had explained the situation to Paul, the apostle wrote two letters, one to the Laodiceans, the other to the Colossians, both on the same subject:

the Judaistic error. Tychicus had to pass through Laodicea in order to reach Colosse. He did so and left the one letter there and then went on with the second. These two letters were to be exchanged as Paul here directs. A special letter to the small group in Hieropolis was not necessary, for Paul included this group with "the church in Laodicea" (now he writes "the church"). Yet Paul does not fail to send a salutation to this little group (v. 15). Since Epaphras was so deeply concerned about all three places (v. 13), Paul would include all three as indicated.

The idea that the letter to Laodicea was one that had been written by Paul at some earlier date has little in its favor. So also the view that this was the letter to the Ephesians on the hypothesis of a circular letter (see the introduction to Ephesians). Both ἵνα introduce object clauses after ποιήσατε. We take it that the letter to Laodicea contained corresponding directions about the exchange. This letter has not come down to us.

17) And tell Archippus: Take heed to the ministry which thou didst receive in the Lord in order to fulfill it.
We think that Archippus was a member of the family of Philemon (Philemon 2), perhaps his son. We think that the ministry he had received was the service committed to him when Epaphras left for Rome. We see no reason for thinking of general evangelistic service. Why should Paul feel it necessary to refer to diligent execution of such service? With this injunction we should combine the honorable epithet found in Philemon 2 where Paul calls Archippus his fellow soldier. Epaphras had left Archippus in charge of the three places. Paul seconds the appointment, but not by way of his apostolic authority, but only by way of the Colossian congregation which is to tell Archippus to carry out his ministry as this had been re-

ceived. The appointment was made with the consent
of the congregations before Epaphras left for Rome.
The injunction which Paul wants delivered to Archippus resembles the one given to Timothy (I Tim. 4:16),
neither of which implies that the persons concerned
had been dilatory and needed prodding. The point
has been noted that a congregation is asked to tell a
minister to take heed to his work. The congregation
is as much concerned as the minister. But here Paul
speaks to the congregation and thus indirectly to the
minister.

18) **The salutation with my own hand,** (that)
of Paul! Remember my bonds! Grace (be) **with
you!**
The first statement is the duplicate of I Cor. 16:21
and II Thess. 3:17. The letter was dictated. Paul, as
it were, now signs his name to it, "with my own hand,
Paul's," the genitive being in apposition to the possessive pronoun (R. 685). By signing thus Paul sends
his own salutation to all his readers.

The plural "my bonds" does not refer to chains.
Whether it is regarded as masculine or as neuter it
always refers only to imprisonment. When Paul refers
to a chain or to chains he says so with the proper word.
"Remember my imprisonment!" is, of course, not a
plea for sympathy but recalls v. 3, Paul's being imprisoned for the sake of the great gospel mystery he
preached. Remembering Paul's bonds should stimulate
the readers to stand firm as Epaphras also ever prays
in their behalf (v. 12).

The last word is a benediction (see 1:2), "the
grace." This is definite in the Greek, the infinite *favor
Dei*, this be with you in Christ.

Soli Deo Gloria

St. Paul's First Epistle
to the Thessalonians

INTRODUCTION

Paul founded his second church in Europe in Thessalonica. Acts 16:38-40 informs us that he and Silas left Philippi after severe mistreatment, to which experience I Thess. 2:2 refers. Luke and Timothy were left in Philippi. No stopover for work was made in Amphipolis or Apollonia, apparently because neither place had a synagogue in which work could be begun. Following the great Egnatian Way, a distance of 100 miles, the two came to the great seaport Thessalonica, the capital of the second of the four great divisions of Macedonia, which finally became the capital of the entire province. When Cassander rebuilt it he changed its original name Therma to Thessalonica in honor of his wife, the sister of Alexander the Great. It shared the commerce of the Aegean Sea with Corinth and Ephesus. Politically it ranked with Antioch in Syria and with Caesarea in Palestine. It is now called Saloniki and played a part in World War I.

First Thessalonians 1:8 shows the wisdom of Paul's choice of Thessalonica. It was to serve as a strategic center from which the gospel should be spread in all directions as it actually was. When Paul passed by other cities such as the two named above, this only meant that they, too, would soon be reached.

All that we know about the founding of the church in Thessalonica is recorded in Acts 17:1-10. Luke does not say precisely when the uproar occurred that caused the brethren in Thessalonica to send Paul and Silas to Berea, 50 miles away. He merely mentions three Sabbaths in connection with Paul's success. Paul and Silas expected to stay for a longer period of time; we gather from I Thess. 2:9, and II Thess. 3:8, 9 that they were earning their own living in Thessalonica, which indicated that they were preparing for continued work. Their whole stay extended over little more, we judge, than four weeks. Yet in so brief a time they founded a permanent congregation in this great city, one that stood firm amid the persecutions that followed. The Lord was moving Paul about rapidly, but the work did not suffer.

The stay at Berea was again brief. Acts 17:14 reports that Paul left Silas and Timothy in Berea. Timothy must have come on from Philippi to Berea when he no longer found Paul in Thessalonica. See Acts 17:14. A party of Bereans accompanied Paul to Athens. Throughout Paul's travels friends accompany him a part of the way, at times as here, the entire way. When these Bereans left Paul at Athens, Paul ordered them to send Silas and Timothy on to him as speedily as possible. The two duly arrived. Yet because of his anxiety about Thessalonica Paul sent Timothy back to this city (I Thess. 3:2). Likewise, as we conclude from v. 1 where Paul is left "alone in Athens," he must also have sent Silas back, perhaps to Philippi. While these men were absent, Paul journeyed on to Corinth. Here Silas and Timothy return to him from Macedonia (Acts 18:5), the latter with a most encouraging report from Thessalonica. This report induced Paul to write his first epistle to the Thessalonians.

We can designate the exact year. In 1909 a whitish grey limestone inscription from the Hagias Elias quarries near Delphi was discovered which immortalized a letter from the Emperor Claudius to the citizens of Delphi, which contains not only the name of Gallio (Acts 18:12): "Lucius Junius Gallio, my friend and proconsul of Achaia," but also a most valuable date: the twelfth tribunian year of Claudius, for the twenty-sixth time acclaimed Imperator. This statement places these events between January 25 and August 1 of the year 52. The proconsuls were appointed for a year only, seldom for two. Imperial orders designated the time when the appointed proconsul was to leave Rome for his province as April 1 and later as April 15.

Thus Gallio came to Corinth before May 1 of the year 52. Deissmann's date, about July of the year 51, is incorrect. See Zahn's *Apostelgeschichte*. Zahn desires that all of the dates given in his *Introduction to the New Testament*, chronological table, III, 482, be likewise corrected in accord with this find.

Since Gallio came to Corinth about May 1, 52, Paul, who arrived six months earlier, came in the fall of 51. How soon did Silas and Timothy join him in Corinth (Acts 18:5)? On this point opinions may vary in view of I Thess. 1:7, 8 where Paul writes that the good example of the Thessalonians had become known to believers in Macedonia and Achaia because the Word of the Lord sounded forth from them in both provinces and news of their faith had spread abroad generally. Our estimate is that an interval of about two months is sufficient. Our epistle was then written in the late fall of 51. The content of the second epistle is such that the interval between the two letters cannot have been greater than two or three months. Thus they were written either quite late in 51 or during the first month of 52.

The sequence of events plus the exact date for Gallio's proconsulship rest on Luke's record in Acts and on I Thess. 3:1, etc. They are solidly assured and thus obviate all supposition as to place and date of composition. In our introduction to Galatians we have presented the evidence for the time and the place of its composition. Galatians was written *before* Silas and Timothy joined Paul in Corinth; First Thessalonians *after* they joined him. We thus regard Galatians as the first extant epistle of Paul, the two to the Thessalonians as the next in order.

We see at once why in both of our epistles Silas and Timotheus are made co-writers with Paul. Silas helped to found this congregation. When Paul sent him back to Macedonia from Athens, Silas must have made a brief stop at Thessalonica. He also touched this city when he returned to Paul at Corinth. Timothy had been sent to Thessalonica from Athens and together with Silas came to Paul in Corinth. The news that Timothy brought from Thessalonica prompted the writing of this letter.

What the character of this news was the letter itself shows. Although Paul and Silas had been able to work in Thessalonica only a few weeks, the congregation thus founded stood firm. For this fact the writers thank God and encourage the young church. Persecution and attacks upon its faith continue. The worst feature of this attack was the vilification that the missionaries were like the many drifting charlatans who were infesting the Roman world at this time and seeking glory and money for themselves. Chapters two and three answer these slanders most thoroughly. The doctrine Paul and Silas preached was the gospel. They took not one penny from the Thessalonians but labored as no charlatans would think of doing. The Thessalonians were one with all the Judean churches of Christ (2:14), one with all the churches in the Gentile world, against which the Jews raged from the start, even having killed the Lord Jesus himself (2:15). Paul was far from simply moving on when this Jewish opposition flared up in Thessalonica and seeking new pastures; he had twice endeavored to return, and when Satan hindered this (2:18), he sent Timothy in his stead (3:1, etc.). And now Paul, Silas, and Timothy are writing. They are doing their utmost for the Thessalonians. This is the main burden of the letter.

To this are added the admonitions given in the last two chapters on points of importance for the youthful congregation. Outstanding is the section 4:13-5:11. The death of believers before Christ's Parousia must not trouble the Thessalonians. Christ will raise them up to glory. Those living at the end will be caught up into the same glory. No man knows when the end will come; the thing to be done is ever to live as children of light. Embedded amid other pertinent injunctions, this is the second burden of the letter. This whole letter rests on the information brought by Timothy (3:6).

The second letter advances all that the first contains. We have no details as to what intervened between the writing of the two epistles. All that we can say is that further information reached Paul, Silas, and Timothy who were now working with all ardor in Corinth and its environs. The Thessalonians are holding out manfully. The question of Christ's Parousia, however, is still very much alive among them. Faked communications as coming from Paul were used to disturb the Thessalonians. Paul touches on them in 2:2, 3; 3:17. The main burden of this letter is found in 2:3-12: Paul repeats what he originally taught the Thessalonians about the Antichrist and his manifestations before the Lord will destroy him. This amplifies I Thess. 4:13, etc. God will take vengeance in due time (II Thess. 1:5-10); the Thessalonians are to stand firm in what Paul has taught and written them (2:15). Those who refuse to do this and act disorderly are to be disowned (3:6-12, 14, 15). The conduct of Paul and Silas in Thessalonica may serve as an example for all who are faithful (3:7-10). This second letter is altogether plain as to its connection with the first. The interval between the two cannot have been very extensive.

Radical criticism of the two epistles offers so little as to be almost negligible for those who deal with their interpretation. The second letter has been subjected to the severest attacks: it is either a complete forgery or is so in greater part. These critical assaults have succeeded only in their negative way in more firmly establishing the genuineness of these two epistles.

CHAPTER I

The Greeting

1) In both epistles the greeting is succinct; in the second it is amplified by only a phrase. **Paul and Silvanus and Timothy to the church of Thessalonians in connection with God the Father and the Lord Jesus Christ: grace to you and peace!**

We read the latter as an exclamation and supply neither ἐστί, ἔστω, or εἴη. In ancient times letters always had these three parts in the opening address or greeting: 1) a nominative to indicate the writer; 2) a dative to indicate the person addressed; 3) a word of greeting. In secular letters the latter was the infinitive χαίρειν (which is used in Acts 15:23; James 1:1); Paul substitutes two nominative nouns in his letters: "grace and peace." All three or any one of the three items may be amplified to accord with the nature of the letter. Here only the second has an amplifying phrase.

Comparison with other letters is instructive, most highly so a comparison with the greeting found in Gal. 1:1-5, Paul's very first letter which was written, let us say, four to six weeks before First Thessalonians. See how he amplifies item one, leaves totally unmodified item two, again most strikingly amplifies item three and even adds a doxology. The greeting found in Galatians reflects its militant contents and the intense feeling of Paul. The greetings used in the two letters to the Thessalonians are in strong contrast to the one found in Galatians and reflect the most normal relation between writers and readers; they are introductory to simple instruction and admonition.

After having separated at Athens (see the introduction) the three workers are again together: "Paul

and Silvanus and Timothy." The first two had founded
the congregation during their short stay of about four
weeks. Paul is the leader and is thus mentioned first;
Silvanus, his companion, is naturally mentioned next.
Luke calls him Silas (Acts 15:22) which was his Hebrew name, Silvanus being his Roman name. He was
a Roman citizen and thus had this second name just as
Saul had the added Roman name Paul, both names having been given to him by his father at the time of his
circumcision.

From Acts 16:37 we know that Silas was a Roman.
The added Roman name of a native Jew was often
chosen because of a similarity in sound. Silas was
prominent in Jerusalem; he was chosen to help to
convey the resolution of the Jerusalem conference to
the church at Antioch and to other churches. Acts
15:36-41 reports that Paul chose him as his companion
for his second great missionary journey. His name is
properly second in this greeting. Timothy was the
younger man; he had been with Paul since the events
recorded in Acts 16:1, etc., and was as yet but little
known to the Thessalonians.

The Thessalonians had come into personal contact
with these three men. This letter is the voice of these
three although Paul will at times speak alone and will
also refer to Silvanus and to himself apart from Timothy. There is no indication as to who took the dictation of the letter, some think Timothy did so. It is well
to note that no distinction between these three is made.
Elsewhere Timothy is called "the brother," Paul, "an
apostle" or "a slave of Jesus Christ." Paul wants no
distinction made because the contents of this letter call
for none. These three writers are men whom the Thessalonians know; that suffices.

The second member of the greeting is equally appropriate: "to the church of Thessalonians in God the
Father and the Lord Jesus Christ." Recently con-

verted, these Thessalonians were a "church," an assembly "in connection with" God and the Lord Jesus Christ. Ἐκκλησία always suggests to the Greek ear the idea of καλεῖν and ἐκ; yet to Christians, not the secular notion of calling out citizens for an assembly to transact the business of the commonwealth is prominent, but the spiritual implication that as believers Christians have received and accepted the κλῆσις or "call" of God and Christ unto life eternal, and that they thus form a spiritual body, an *ecclesia* under this permanent call. Hence we so often have the addition of a modifier to emphasize this spiritual nature of their *ecclesia*.

Here it is the ἐν phrase. We need not puzzle about the meaning of the preposition. It is neither mystical nor mysterious, nor profound. Ἐν is to be understood in its original sense: "in connection with," and the evident connection is that involved in *ecclesia*, namely faith. The fact that this *ecclesia* is an organized body is not the thought but that it is a distinct spiritual body which is made thus by the fact that its members are in the connection indicated. R. 780 does not solve the question of the absence of the article with "of Thessalonians." The article would be out of place, for not "*the* Thessalonians" but only *a few* "Thessalonians" formed the *ecclesia;* for this reason the Greek article is not used. Paul might have said: "to the church *in* Thessalonica," but this would add another "in," which the genitive avoids. Since these Thessalonians form the church, the ἐν may be construed with either noun, preferably with both as a unit: "the church of Thessalonians in," etc.

Proper names need no article; hence we have none with "God Father" or "Lord Jesus Christ." Both are soteriological, the first person of the Godhead and the second, incarnate in Jesus. Paul at times writes "our Father" and "our Lord Jesus Christ"; the pronoun emphasizes the relation to us and is thus confessional.

Yet this relation lies already in the preposition ἐν. "Father" names the first person as such. But every one of the persons is named only in order that we may know how each together with the other two works out our salvation. This is the Father of the Son and through him our Father.

"Lord" is to be taken in the same soteriological sense: he who bought us, to whom we belong with body and with soul in blessedness forever. His significant personal name as man, "Jesus," is joined with the name taken from his office, "Christ," God's Anointed. "Lord Jesus Christ" is the full designation and is always highly confessional, reverent, and worshipful. In II Thess. 1:2 both divine names are solemnly repeated. These two names occur so regularly in Paul's epistolary greetings that we cannot accept the opinion: "God Father" is used in opposition to the pagan gods, and "Lord Jesus Christ" in opposition to the Jewish rejection of Jesus; or that "Lord" is a pointed reference in opposition to the pagan deification of the Roman emperor as "Lord" or against the pagan gods and their "Lord" titles.

Regarding "grace to you and peace" see the other epistles: all the grace of God with the bestowal of its unmerited favors upon which we constantly depend (John 1:16), together with the objective peace of God, the blessed condition when God is our friend and all is well with us in time and eternity, and both are mediated by Christ.

The Defensive Section of the Epistle

The Thanksgiving

2) **We thank God always concerning all of you when making mention (of you) in our prayers, unceasingly remembering your work of faith, and toil of love, and perseverance of hope in our Lord**

Jesus Christ before our God and Father; having come to know, brethren beloved by God, your election, seeing that our gospel got to be for you not in connection with word only but also in connection with power and in connection with the Holy Spirit and much assurance, even as you know what kind (of men) we were among you for your sakes; and you, etc.

Also in other letters Paul begins with thanks to God. His first consideration is ever to fill the mind with all that God has so wonderfully bestowed and to let the heart overflow with gratitude. This letter is written in such a spirit. All that God has done for the Thessalonians the three writers regard as having been done for themselves. This is the purest, most unselfish gratitude toward God.

Construe together: "we thank God when making mention of you in our prayers" (ἐπί, "on the occasion"), i. e., whenever we pray we include you in our thanksgiving to God. There may be faults to be mended and further gifts to be asked of God, yet Paul and his helpers always keep in mind what God has already bestowed. To say that "distance lends enchantment to the memory of slight drawbacks" is to spoil the purity of Paul's thanksgiving. To ask: "Did Paul have a prayer list of the Thessalonian disciples which he read over with Silvanus and Timothy?" is to attribute to Paul a mechanical system for intercessory prayer.

3) Adverbs are generally placed next to the verb form they modify. Thus "unceasingly remembering" goes together; the adverb is not amphibolous, leaving us in doubt as to which participle it modifies. Paul, etc., give thanks whenever they pray; this they do because they ever remember what God has accomplished in the Thessalonians. The whole statement is strictly true and without the slightest hyperbole.

The arrangement of the objects has been made plain to the eye by the following diagram:

The participle has three genitive objects: "your work — toil — perseverance." Each of these has a subjective genitive attached: the work done by the faith — the toil endured by the love — the perseverance shown by the hope. "Your" (ὑμῶν) belongs to all three. The objective genitive: "of our Lord Jesus Christ" belongs to all three subjective genitives: the faith — the love — the hope that embrace "our Lord Jesus Christ" and do this "in the presence of our God and Father." The striking feature is this series of ten genitives with not a single other word breaking the line. Even the last phrase adds more genitives.

Here we have a summary of what fills the memory of Paul and of his companions. We note the trio: faith — love — hope. All of these are attached to "our Lord Jesus Christ." We note how "work — toil — perseverance" rise to a climax. Finally, we see that all is placed "in the presence of our God and Father," who as our Father will accept it all.

The attempt to restrict "your work of faith in our Lord Jesus Christ" so that it shall be distinct from "your toil of love for the Lord Jesus Christ," is misdirected. This love is itself the product of faith; this work is accomplished by the toil (κόπος) that fatigues. Plurals would not be in place, namely "works" and "toilings," for the writers think of all the work and the toil as a unit and not as a multiplicity. The faith is manifested in work: in confessing its trust in the Lord in a thousand ways. As one looks at all this work, the faith that is back of it is seen. This is not self-chosen work but the work that the Lord wants and that the Father approves. It is work full of toil, and this toil reveals the love that prompts it, love for the Lord, love and toil that he inspires and that please the Father. Hope looks forward to the last great day and to eternity. It is full of perseverance, ὑπομονή, remaining under any load the Lord imposes, ever looking with brave endurance to the day of fulfillment promised by the Lord, always holding out as in the Father's presence.

The articles are in place with the nouns because ὑμῶν makes all the nouns definite as applying to the Thessalonians. Faith — hope — love are subjective: the Thessalonians believe with true confidence and trust in the Lord; they love the Lord with the love of intelligence and corresponding purpose (ἀγάπη, which is more than φιλία, see John 21:15-17); they hope in him with the sure hope that is based on who he is, what he has done and promised to do, a hope that will be more than fulfilled. The work, the toil, the perseverance are all centered on Christ and the Father. That means that all we do for others is done for Christ (Matt. 25:40). Faith, love, and hope are wrought in the Thessalonians by the Lord and the Father. The very thought that the Thessalonians produced them of themselves is impossible. Even false faith, love, and hope are never self-wrought; they are the product of the deception that men offer to poor souls. By praising the Thessalonians, Paul does not fear that he will make them vain. Honest, sincere acknowledgment encourages and stimulates; censoriousness discourages.

4) Construe: "unceasingly remembering — having come to know your election"; the latter is an in-

gressive aorist. This natural construction is better than to leap over the remembering and to connect with "we thank God." In all that the writers remember about the Thessalonians the conviction is involved that the Thessalonians belong to God's elect. Εἰδότες is the proper word (the relation of the object to the subject, C.-K. 388); the knowledge and the conviction came into the mind of the writers. How this came about is recorded in the following, namely through what they saw: that the power of the gospel was so effective in the Thessalonians.

These writers have no access to the throne room of God nor a special revelation about certain persons which shows them that these are God's elect. The writers have what we all have, the plain evidence of faith, love, and hope (v. 3); where this is found, we know that we see God's elect. So we judge also concerning ourselves (*C. Tr.* 1071, 28, etc.; 1083, 65). The fact that some after all fall away is evidence to us that they are not the elect. Our knowledge is thus not absolute but rests on such evidence as we have. It is like our knowledge of a person's faith. We cannot look into his soul to see his faith, we are able to recognize it only by means of the evidence his faith furnishes.

Some take ἐκλογή in a double sense: at times it is dated in eternity (Eph. 1:4), but here it is dated in time and refers to the time when the Thessalonians were converted. Paul, however, knows of no twofold act of election. If he had referred to an act in time he would have written κλῆσις, "the effective and successful call."

When they make this statement about the election of the Thessalonians the writers address them as "brethren having been beloved by God," true, spiritual brethren of Paul, Silvanus, and Timothy, and, like all such, loved by God and continuing in this love (the extensive perfect participle). We take this to be the

love that embraced the Thessalonians when they came
to faith and continued to embrace them ever after that
even as they then came to be "brethren." God's love
to believers is able to shower gifts upon them which he
cannot bestow on others because they would not receive
them. The fact that the election of all the elect is due
wholly to God's love that reaches out to them from
eternity goes without saying; yet the perfect participle
does not refer to *this* act of love, nor to the universal
love of God for the whole world (John 3:16), but to
the love of God for his elect children from the moment
they are made his children.

5) The alternatives usually discussed are causal
ὅτι (A. V., "for"; R. V. margin, "because") or declarative, "having come to know . . . that" (R. V., "how
that"). We submit that we here have the ὅτι *consecutivum* (R. 1001) which is best rendered, "seeing that."
In consequence of the fact now stated the writers have
come to know of the election of the Thessalonians. This
evidential fact is that "our gospel got to be for (regarding) you not in connection with word only but also in
connection with power and in connection with the Holy
Spirit and much assurance." Both verbs are historical
aorists that report facts; the first may also be considered ingressive: "our gospel got to be regarding you,"
etc. "Came to you" (our versions) is not the thought
to be expressed; ἐγενήθη is not = ἦλθεν. The gospel always comes with power, for it is power (Rom. 1:16).
This statement deals with the effect which the gospel
produced when it came to the Thessalonians. They
were converted, and thus this gospel "got to be regarding (εἰς) them not in connection with (ἐν as in v. 1)
word only but also," etc. One could see this on the
basis of what the gospel wrought in the Thessalonians.

"Our gospel" — Paul says also "my gospel" — is
not a peculiar form of the gospel as though what Paul
preached differed from what the other apostles

preached; the pronoun merely indicates who the preachers were in this case. The noun simply means the gospel as to its contents and not the activity of εὐαγγελίζεσθαι as some suppose. The very nature of the εὐαγγέλιον is such that it must be told; good news is not news unless it is told. But when this gospel is rejected it gets to be in regard to those who reject it "word only." They hear it as mere "word," as something told, and stop with that and ignore what is told.

Not so the Thessalonians. When they got into connection with its "word" part through their ears and their minds, the gospel achieved a still greater connection; it got to be in their case "in connection with power," etc., i. e., the power of the gospel got through to their hearts and converted them. To be sure, the gospel is itself power, and every time it is preached this power goes out to the hearer. Yet this power uses the ear by means of λόγος or "word"; hence a hearer may treat it as only "word," may deny what the gospel says, argue against what it says, refuse to believe what it says, and may thus bar out of his heart the gospel's "power."

Not so the Thessalonians; all the saving power reached their hearts. This still leaves the thought incomplete; hence the epexegetical καί: "and in connection with the Holy Spirit (proper name, no article) and much assurance." But one preposition is used with the two terms. The Holy Spirit explains "power," he is its agent, the one who exerts the power. That makes plain the objective side of the reality of the gospel power. Coupled with this is the subjective effect in the Thessalonians themselves when this power and the Spirit reached their hearts: "much assurance," much full conviction (C.-K. 931). This explains the power as a spiritual power, its effect regarding the Thessalonians being the mighty assurance of faith which is wrought in them.

"Power" has no connection with the miracles wrought in Thessalonica; nor does it refer to the powerful way in which Paul preached. It is the power mentioned in Rom. 1:16, the power of grace unto salvation. Πληροφορία is not the fulness of spiritual gifts bestowed on the Thessalonians; not the fulness and the completeness of Paul's instruction; in fact, not "fulness" of any kind. It is the "assurance" or "confidence" produced by the Spirit's power of grace in the hearts of the Thessalonians through the gospel word. Seeing all this, Paul and his companions knew that these Thessalonians were the elect of God.

The καθώς clause rounds out the thought: "even as you know what kind (of men) we were among you for your sakes." "We got to know," the writers say, "regarding you," and you, they say, now know in regard to us "the kind of men we were among you (we read ἐν ὑμῖν in preference to plain ὑμῖν) for your sakes." The kind of men who preach the gospel means a good deal regarding the effect their preaching produces. This does not imply that they add to the power of the gospel, they may, however, decrease its all-sufficient native power. They may be a clogged channel through which only a little power can flow. The Thessalonians know the writers to be men who are wholly devoted to the gospel, totally unselfish, doing their work entirely for the sake of their hearers (δι᾿ ὑμᾶς). The Thessalonians had had them "in their midst" and thus know the kind of men they were. The more readily was "much assurance" regarding the gospel wrought in their hearts.

Some commentators connect this clause with v. 6 as though οὕτως followed. The terms εἰδότες and οἴδατε match: we have come to know, etc., even as you know, and what we got to know about you corresponds with what you continue to know about us since you had us in your midst. This last clause is not the main thought; it merely rounds out what precedes.

All that Paul says about the gospel's power as this
is evidenced in the Thessalonians, and about the kind
of men the Thessalonians know him, Silvanus, and
Timothy to be, carries an implication. The opposition
in Thessalonica identified Paul and his companions with
the roving charlatans of that day. Some of these practiced sorcery and claimed to possess occult powers, and
all of them had their peculiar systems of doctrine which
were composed of ideas that had been borrowed from
the east and been dressed up to impress such people as
they found susceptible. These quacks remained in a
place as long as something was to be gained and then
moved on to another place. They were of the type of
Simon Magus (Acts 8:9, etc.) and of Elymas (Acts
13:8, etc.). Their quackery was "word only" over
against which Paul places the gospel with power, the
Holy Spirit, the great assurance, and thus the faith,
love, and hope wrought in the Thessalonians. Paul
likewise points to the kind of men the Thessalonians
know him and his companions to be, men whose whole
work was δι᾽ ὑμᾶς, "for your sakes" alone without a
trace of self-interest. More to this effect follows. Paul
dwells on it in order to fortify the Thessalonians
against the slanders of the opponents of the gospel in
Thessalonica. He had been driven out of Thessalonica
after a few weeks of work, but the gospel and its divine
effects remained. This gospel and the kind of men who
were spreading it attested themselves in a way that left
no doubt for those who had received this gospel and
had had these men in their midst. This is the point of
all that Paul writes.

6) So he continues: **And you on your part became imitators of us and of the Lord by having received the Word in much affliction together with joy
of the Holy Spirit so that you became an example
to all those believing in Macedonia and in Achaia,
for from you there has sounded forth the Word**

of the Lord not only in Macedonia and Achaia,
but in every place your faith (directed) toward
God has gone forth so that we do not need to
say a thing, for they themselves are reporting concerning us what kind of entering in we had unto you,
and how you turned toward God, away from the
idols, to be slaves to a God living and genuine and
to await his Son out of the heavens, whom he raised
from the dead, Jesus, the one rescuing us from the
wrath to come.

The aorist states the fact that the Thessalonians
"became imitators of us and of the Lord" (objective
genitives.) Because the verb is placed between the two
genitives, the second genitive is the more emphatic of
the two.   Paul and his helpers were themselves imitators of the Lord; hence those who imitate them imitate the Lord. Why, then, is the first genitive used,
and why is it placed first? Because the Thessalonians
came into contact with the model, Christ, through the
model copies of Christ, Paul and his companions. If
they had not been attracted by the latter they could not
have known the former, the chief attraction. So it is
the reflection of Christ in us that today induces others
to become Christlike. The order and the position of
Paul's two genitives are most instructive.

"By receiving the Word in much affliction together
with joy of the Holy Spirit" (genitive of source) indicates what likeness is referred to. The action of the
participle is simultaneous with that of the main verb:
when the Thessalonians received the Word, then began
their great θλῖψις, *Bedraengnis*, the pressure of hostile
opposition and persecution; yet this was accompanied
by joy wrought in their hearts by the Holy Spirit.
These two, affliction and joy, go together (μετά), for
they rejoiced to be like the Lord in affliction. Note that
the Holy Spirit (again no article) again mentions this
person who was mentioned in v. 5 and thus continues

the thought of experiencing his power and the resulting great assurance. The important matter that Paul says about the Thessalonians is the fact that from the very start, when they first came to faith in the Word, they were beset with "much affliction" and that they endured it with divinely wrought joy. Although they were so young and untried in the faith, they bore persecution with joy.

This is generally true in the case of converts from heathenism and from Judaism. The example of such converts shames many of us who, when we are finally called upon to bear a little persecution, take it with anything but joy. Paul refers to what John 15:19-21 states regarding the treatment the Lord received, which also his followers are bound to receive. "You became imitators" = you did this of your own will and under no compulsion.

7) The result was that because of this joyful acceptance of affliction the Thessalonians became an example to all the believers in Macedonia and in Achaia, an inspiring example, indeed. Τύπος is the blow struck so as to leave a mark as when a die strikes the image and the inscription on a coin and in this sense means a sample or an example to others. The present tense, "those believing," is descriptive of continuing faith. Paul names only the provinces of Macedonia and Achaia because in this territory the story of the Thessalonians became known quite rapidly. We know about the planting of the gospel only in Philippi, Berea, Athens, and the start Paul was making in Corinth, where Paul is writing and had only recently begun work. As yet the believers in the two provinces mentioned were few; but the example of the Thessalonians was intended also for all who would yet come to faith as it stood for those already won.

Thessalonica was a great center for all of southern Europe. News from this great seaport spread rapidly.

A joyfully suffering church in Thessalonica meant exceedingly much for believers elsewhere, who in most cases also had to face vicious opposition. We see the broadness of Paul's view. The steadfast joy of one church means so much for others. When we suffer, let us think not only of ourselves but also of all the others whom our joy in endurance may aid.

When he says this to the Thessalonians, Paul is not only encouraging them to continue as they began, he is at the same time connecting them with all other believers and thus fortifies them against the slanders that Paul and his assistants are only roving religious quacks whom everybody ought to despise. The great gospel and the power of the Holy Spirit are building up the Church of God in many lands. The work has only begun in Macedonia and Achaia, but it is God's work and will go on to divine success. The Thessalonians stand in the forefront and thus bear the brunt of opposition, their position is the more glorious for that very reason. The A. V. follows the variant reading τύπους, "ensamples"; this plural speaks of the individuals, the singular of the congregation as a unit.

8) "For" elucidates what Paul means. "From you (Thessalonians) there has sounded forth the Word of the Lord (his gospel) not only in Macedonia and Achaia (in general)" so that near and far men are getting to hear about the Word and what it contains, which arouses their interest as being something entirely new. This is the first thought Paul intends to express by v. 6, 7. The position of the Thessalonians is strategic for the gospel. Word of the gospel planted in Thessalonica has run rapidly through both provinces; the perfect passive means that it is still doing this. "There has sounded forth" (and is still sounding forth) does not mean that the Thessalonians are evangelizing Macedonia and Achaia (let us not strain the meaning of the verb); it means that reports are

spreading. Some of the Thessalonian Christians had to travel and thus spread reports; other Thessalonians who knew what the Thessalonian Christians believed, including also such as opposed this faith, likewise spread their reports. Thessalonica was like a great sounding board (R., *W. P.*) ; reverberations promptly reached in all directions. Smaller places that were differently located could not produce such an effect.

We may compare this city with Ephesus; news of what occurred there was rapidly carried throughout the great province of Asia and adjacent southern Galatia. The greatest sounding board of all was Rome, the capital of the empire. It is not correct to call Paul's statement hyperbolical; the perfect tense reports the literal fact: the sounding forth has begun and still continues wave upon wave.

Note that "but *also*" follows "not only." This means that "but" (we might translate "yea") adds another notable fact: "yea, in every place (in Macedonia and Achaia where the reports from Thessalonica spread) your faith toward God has gone forth," i. e., all the reports about the Word of the Lord, this new religious gospel doctrine, include the report of your faith in the the God of this Word. The men who travel from Thessalonica, and the hundreds who also come there on business from the far parts of the provinces, carry away reports about this Christian church in the great city of Thessalonica.

Paul states it beautifully: "your faith has gone forth" like a traveler to all manner of places. Paul properly writes: this faith of yours πρὸς τὸν Θεόν, and not "in the Lord," "in Christ," or an objective genitive τοῦ Θεοῦ. He is practically quoting the actual words of all these news carriers. Note the same phrase in v. 9; there it is used in contrast: "toward the (living and genuine) God, away from the idols." Pagan news carriers would word it this way: "your faith toward the

God," the article to designate the God your faith embraces. In only a few instances is πρός construed with πίστις; R. calls it "the face-to-face preposition," which brings out the idea; your faith and trust faces this God as he faces your faith. The tense is again perfect: has gone and still goes forth.

The result is that Paul and his helpers need to say nothing, λαλεῖν, to open their mouths. When people already have the news, it is not news to tell them again. Paul is not referring to his preaching but to the Thessalonians. He and his helpers did not need to say anything in Corinth, where this letter is being written, or in other places about the faith of the Thessalonians who give up idols for the true God, people had already heard the story. Paul means that the way is in no small degree already everywhere prepared for him to preach the gospel.

9) Γάρ elucidates the extent of the information thus spread throughout the provinces: "for they themselves (αὐτοί *ad sensum,* the people in all these places) are reporting concerning us (what they have heard, namely) what kind of entering in we had (aorist to indicate the historical fact) unto you, and how you turned (the same aorist) toward God, away from the idols, to be slaves to a God living and genuine," etc. This is what the people themselves "keep duly (ἀπό in the verb) reporting concerning us," and they state it correctly. Paul does not say: "are reporting *to us*" so that *we* are surprised to hear what these people say about us. These people spread this report generally, and that "duly" as they have themselves heard it.

They tell "what kind of entering in we had to you," one that was so different from that of the charlatans and religious quacks who try to steal people's confidence to their own advantage. By εἴσοδος Paul refers to the whole approach to and dealing with the Thessalonians, which has already been touched upon in v. 5:

"what kind of men we were among you for your sake."
In v. 5 he refers to character and motive; here he refers
to the way of dealing, to which he adds the result. Πρός
has the same face-to-face idea.

Yes, religious teachers who acted like these were a
novelty, they became current news. Paul touches this
point again for the same reason: the Thessalonians
will not listen to any vilification, the purpose of which
is to turn them against the gospel by discrediting its
missionaries. At the same time the Thessalonians are
to know how helpful to Paul's work these reports are,
coming, as they do, from the Thessalonians themselves
and reaching so far. Yet this is only the preliminary
and subordinate part of what people report.

The main part is the result of this *eisodos*, "how
you turned," etc., which elaborates what Paul has just
said about the going forth of the faith of the Thessalonians. People speak of the radical turn the Thessalonians have made to the one great God, away from the
many idols. The very fact that there is such a God is
news to these people. This is not another god in addition to their host of gods but "the God" before whom
all other gods are nothing. These "idols" are both the
images and the beings they represent. This, however,
is Paul's own term which was not used by the people in
their reports. The verb ἐπιστρέφω is used to designate
conversion, and this is its meaning also here, save that
here conversion from pagan idolatry is referred to.
Acts 14:15.

The two infinitives are epexegetical: this turning
means: "to be slaves to a God, etc., and to be awaiting
his Son," etc. The idea of "to be slaves" is not that
of working for God ("to serve," our versions). The
fact that slaves work is self-evident although everybody ought to work (II Thess. 3:10); the point is that
slaves yield their will completely to that of their master. What people report is that the Thessalonians have

cast off all subjection to idol gods and are now subject solely to "a God living and genuine." This is the very reason for the turn they have made. It is silly to be subject to idols who are not living but imaginary beings and hence not ἀληθινός, real, genuine, but unreal, mere fiction. Perhaps for the first time the people who report this about the Thessalonians heard about this Christian God who lives and is really what the name "God" implies.

R., *W. P.,* thinks the absence of the article makes no difference here, and that we should translate "the God living," etc. But the absence of the article makes the noun qualitative, the two modifiers state the qualities, the whole expression thus justifies the action of the Thessalonians. Moreover, people are telling what the Thessalonians have done and the reason that the Thessalonians say they have done what they did. The good feature is the fact that the report thus spread has the facts quite correctly. These people thus will be interested to know more about this great God. Should they not also turn to him and give up their idols? Also, when the Thessalonians read what Paul says about these reports throughout the whole country they will stand the more solidly against opposition, never shall the report go out that they after all turned back to the idols.

10)   But this report contains still more. The first great requirement made of pagans is that they give up idols and bow only to the one living and real God. With this goes the hope of eternal blessedness through God's Son (see "the hope in the Lord Jesus Christ" in v. 3). So Paul adds by extending the epexegesis: "and to await his Son out of the heavens, whom he raised from the dead, Jesus, the one rescuing us from the wrath to come." This report states the main gospel facts correctly. This is, indeed, the Christian hope and its basis. The Thessalonians are, indeed, "awaiting his

Son out of the heavens" (Acts 1:11). This is a report
that was spread by pagans, yet they state it correctly:
"his Son," the Son of the God who lives and is real.
They also state correctly that his Parousia is connected
with his resurrection. This Son became man, died on
the cross, "whom he, the God living and real, raised
from the dead." They know his name: "Jesus," which
he bore on earth and still bears, to which is added the
great apposition: "the one rescuing us (you Thessalonians and Paul and his helpers) from the wrath, the one
coming" at the final judgment.

What a blessed report to come from the Thessalonians and to penetrate so far! What a help to Paul
and to his assistants! It breaks the ground for their
work among pagans. These will be eager to hear from
Paul and from his assistants themselves all about this
living God and his Son Jesus, all about his resurrection,
his coming out of the heavens, his rescuing men from
the final wrath. The Thessalonians will ever want to
substantiate the report that they forsook the idols and
put their trust in this God and his Son.

Paul might have worded the report differently,
without placing such an emphasis on the Parousia and
the deliverance from the wrath to come. For he is only
summarizing, touching only a few items. This summary is not made with reference to the people who
spread this report about the Thessalonians in the two
provinces but with reference to the Thessalonians
themselves. The two epistles show that the Thessalonians were especially concerned about the Parousia. Paul
answers the questions they have regarding this subject, the one regarding those who die before the Son's
return and about those who are then still living (4:13,
etc.) and the one about the time (5:1, etc.; II Thess.
2:3 etc.); he corrects also the mistake some are making by the way in which they live by expecting the
Parousia so soon that they give up their daily work.

True, we must ever be awaiting the Son from heaven; in this the Thessalonians were right, Paul does the same. But this means constant readiness and not foolish conclusions and conduct which the Son cannot approve. We thus see the trend of this epistle. Paul will presently add his instruction; he has not reached that point as yet.

When we say that Paul's summation is not made with reference to the people spreading the report we mean that it is not made in their interest. Paul does take the items from their actual report, but the Thessalonians are his interest. Some of the words here employed by Paul seem to be taken verbatim from the report as it was circulated, thus ἐπιστρέφειν, "a God living and real," ἀναμένειν τὸν υἱὸν αὐτοῦ ἐκ τῶν οὐρανῶν, "Jesus," perhaps all the rest also.

Some, following the historical method, attempt to draw a summary of Paul's missionary preaching from this chapter. In the writer's judgment such procedure abandons the historical method. This epistle is written for a specific purpose, and the historical method ought to read the epistle in the light of that purpose. To seek for more than this is not warranted. We may get a few incidental hints on this or that but very little more. So the way in which Paul speaks of "your election" shows that during the few weeks he spent in Thessalonica he expounded this act of God's most adequately. Let us say that during those few weeks his teaching had very few gaps. Both of these epistles contain only a part of his teaching. The more important feature is the fact that in so few days he built up a congregation that was so firm, in a large city, amid strong opposition, that needed only two brief letters from Paul to keep it firm. Have other men duplicated this? The secret of it is revealed in these very letters. The man who handles the Word and men as this man did will show equal results.

CHAPTER II

The Spirit in which Paul and Silvanus Worked in Thessalonica

1) "For" continues the elucidation; we note that γάρ continues on through v. 1, 3, 5, 9. Αὐτοὶ γάρ matches the αὐτοὶ γάρ occurring in 1:9: the people *themselves* report what Paul states — the Thessalonians *themselves* know what the facts are. This paragraph, then, presents what the Thessalonians themselves well know about the spirit in which Paul and Silvanus worked in their midst when they were founding the congregation.

We have already stated why Paul finds it necessary to remind the Thessalonians of all this. The news which Timothy brought from Thessalonica evidently reported the slanders that the opponents were resorting to in order to damage the faith of the congregation by depicting Paul and Silvanus as religious mountebanks who had come into the city and had gone out again, who were neither pagan nor Jewish, who had a quack doctrine of their own, who deserved to be driven out because they only upset people (Acts 17:6). So Paul follows the method he uses so effectively against the Judaizers in Galatians 1 and 2: he lets the facts speak by showing first that people in the entire two provinces of Macedonia and Achaia talk about the entering in of these missionaries in Thessalonica, and that the Thessalonians left their idols and turned to God and his Son Jesus (1:8-10), next, that the Thessalonians themselves know how Paul and Silvanus entered in, how despite all persecution they preached the gospel with a spirit that was faithful to God, with motives that were pure, unselfish, full of tender love. Religious quacks do not operate in this way. The Thes-

salonians know the facts in the case better than anybody else, they know that what disinterested people in
the entire provinces report is true indeed; they know
even more than all these people relate. The opponents
in Thessalonica may continue to rave, the church will
laugh at them.

**For you yourselves, brethren, know our entering
in unto you** (the entering in to you already mentioned in 1:9), **that it has not been an empty one.
On the contrary, although having suffered before
and having been outraged as you know in Philippi, we were free and open in our God to speak to
you the gospel of God with much agonizing.**

Yes, this was the one side of "our entering in unto
you"; εἴσοδος refers not to the first arrival in Thessalonica but to the whole work of Paul and Silvanus by
which they won the hearts of the Thessalonians. The
emphasis is on "you yourselves know, brethren," you
are the ones who experienced it. The people in the
provinces talk about it far and wide, they have only
heard the story, *you* are the ones who *know*.

What you know is that this our entrance unto you
"has not been an empty one," κενή, hollow, like a vessel
that has nothing in it. This is a litotes which states
the matter negatively but intends it positively: "not an
empty one" = one filled to the brim with most blessed
effects. The perfect "has been" = and still remains
so to this day. We place a period here, for not only
v. 2 shows how full and rich the entering in was for
the Thessalonians. Verse 2 shows only the preliminary part of it so that all that follows sets forth what
"not empty" means.

2) Ἀλλά, "on the contrary," our entering in to
you has been the absolute opposite of empty. You
Thessalonians know how we came to Thessalonica.
"You know" continues the appeal to the facts. We
came to you Thessalonians from Philippi where we

had suffered severely (explicative καί) by having been outraged in the most shameful way. Paul refers to Acts 16:19-40: he and Silvanus, Roman citizens, had been dragged before the authorities who had allowed them to be beaten by their lictors and had thrown them into the deepest dungeon as though they were the worst criminals. Instead of bringing these authorities to account for their criminal violation of the rights of Roman citizenship Paul and Silvanus had suffered the outrage. This showed their spiritual character, their motives, and their purposes. Men of this kind (1:5, 9, οἷος and ὁποῖος) were not engaged in empty work.

We regard the participles as concessive as does the A. V.: "although having suffered before, etc., in Philippi." In spite of this, when Paul and Silvanus came to Thessalonica, "we were free and open in our God to speak the gospel of God to you," etc. As "our entering in" covers the whole work in Thessalonica, so this aorist ἐπαρρησιασάμεθα is constative and, therefore, covers the whole free and open procedure in Thessalonica; hence also λαλῆσαι is an aorist, again constative to indicate all the speaking done in Thessalonica.

The R. V. and R., *W. P.* makes the aorist ingressive: "waxed bold." Uncowed by the fearful experience in Philippi, Paul and Silvanus freely and openly did their work in Thessalonica. They hid nothing of what they had suffered in Philippi, only the Philippian authorities had reasons for hiding the matter. This does not imply that the fearless courage of Paul and Silvanus was due to themselves as being men who were naturally strong and brave. That would really have been an emptiness in their spirit; Paul writes: "we were free and open in our God," in our blessed connection with him. They were preaching God's gospel as men sent by God, under God's protection; whatever they might suffer happened under God's direction. This is the connection indicated by ἐν. There is certainly no emptiness to be found here. Religious quacks, as the Roman world of that day knew them in plenty, would have operated very carefully after an experience such as that of Paul and Silvanus, would have kept it secret, and, when it was brought to light, would have lied about it.

"The gospel of God" = the one emanating from God, ordered to be proclaimed by God. Twice Paul writes the word "God," and it refers to the "God living and real" of 1:9, the absolute opposite of empty idols. Twice also Paul writes πρὸς ὑμᾶς, the same "face-to-face preposition" which he twice used in 1:9. It is well not to overlook these little details. The final phrase ἐν πολλῷ ἀγῶνι is certainly emphatic. It excludes the idea that, when Paul and Silvanus came to Thessalonica, they merely put on a bold front as charlatans who had been defeated elsewhere would try to do — an empty pretense. Paul and Silvanus spoke the gospel of God "in much agonizing," straining like athletes who try to run so as to gain the coveted prize. This agonizing was undergone in order to obtain the prize of success for the gospel in Thessalonica. Paul and Silvanus strained in their heart and their soul with fervent prayer and with utmost devotion, ever thinking only of this one thing.

The phrase is not incidental. Some would regard it as expressing a fear of a repetition of the experience met in Philippi, of a battle against opposition in Thessalonica, or in general of difficult and trying circumstances. Likewise, the phrase is thought to express more fully the "joyfulness" of the preachers although free and open speaking is not the same as joy. These ideas disregard the figure back of the phrase. The ardor, the strenuous effort of Paul and Silvanus was not in the least relaxed in Thessalonica after the reward it had met in Philippi. The Thessalonians saw this beyond question, they still know it. This is the same

spirit as that shown in Acts 5:40-42, the absolute opposite of emptiness.

3) "For" adds further significant elucidation
as to how Paul and Silvanus preach the gospel of
God. **For our urging (is) not (does not flow) out
of error, nor out of uncleanness, nor (is it) in connection with cunning. On the contrary, just as we
have been tested by God so as to be entrusted with
the gospel, just so we speak, not as pleasing men,
but (as pleasing) God, the One (ever) testing our
hearts.**

Paul is describing how he and his assistants ever do
their gospel work, which includes how they did it in
Thessalonica. The context always indicates what παράκλησις means; here it is the "urging" with which the
gospel of God (v. 2) is pressed upon people; "our
exhortation" (our versions) seems less proper.

Paul denies three things regarding his urging:
1) it is not due to error, 2) not due to uncleanness,
3) not connected with cunning. The objective source
is not error; the subjective source is not uncleanness;
the means employed is not cunning. The R. V., which
translates πλάνη "error," is correct; the A. V., which
translates it "deceit" (M.-M. 516), is incorrect. Paul
says that our zeal in urging the gospel does not spring
from error. So many of the greatest religious lies are
propagated with fanatical urging. The fanatics themselves believe the error; but the way in which this word
is used in the New Testament shows that it implies
the gravest guilt for those who hold to error. If Paul
and his helpers were enamored of error and thus propagated it they would *eo ipso* stand condemned. This is
where the opponents in Thessalonica classed him. Self-
deceived, he deceived all who followed him.

"Nor out of uncleanness" denies impure motives.
The word is broad; it covers covetousness (v. 5) but
also seeking glory from men (v. 6). Sexual unclean-

ness does not lie in the present connection. The opponents in Thessalonica classed Paul and his helpers with the selfish deceivers who were so numerous in the empire, whose secret motives were anything but clean. This mode of attack is especially difficult to meet, but Paul could and did meet it in the most crushing way, not by swearing that his motives were clean, but by letting incontrovertible facts speak. The unclean motives were those of his opponents and their efforts to support the vain errors they held.

The two ἐκ (source) are followed by ἐν (mode or method) : "nor in connection with cunning," the German *List,* which is attributed to Elymas in Acts 13:10 and denied with regard to Christ in I Pet. 2:22. Luther says of the devil: *Gross' Macht und viel' List sein' grausam' Ruestung ist.* The effort to discredit Paul as being one who used cunning tricks to lead people by the nose was easily met.

4) Over against all three slanders Paul sets another strong ἀλλά which he then expands by a further array of facts. "On the contrary," the fact is that "just as we have been tested by God so as to be entrusted with the gospel, just so we (ever) continue to speak," namely "not as pleasing (perhaps conative: trying to please) men, but (as pleasing) God, the One (ever) testing our hearts." "We have been approved" (R. V.) is inexact and necessitates "proveth" as a translation of the same word in the participial form. Δοκιμάζω and its derivatives are favorites with Paul. Here he twice uses the simplex, a perfect passive and an active participle: to test as metals and coins are tested for genuineness and for weight.

It is impossible to believe that the God who is living and real (1:9) would entrust his precious gospel to men whom he had not himself tested. This testing by God, Paul claims for himself and his assistants: "just as we have been tested by God" and now stand as thus tested (perfect tense). There is no need to insert more into the verb, for the context implies that God's testing did not find Paul, etc., unfit. The infinitive denotes result: "so as to be entrusted with the gospel," the usual accusative with the passive.

But how can the Thessalonians know that Paul and his helpers have been tested by God and were thus entrusted with the gospel by God? May not any errorist or fake religionist set up the same claim? He may, but he will be exposed at once. If he does not bring the gospel, and that the pure gospel, that already exposes him as *not* being attested by God, as *not* being entrusted with the gospel by God. With this goes the fact that he must ever speak exactly as he is tested and entrusted, not as trying to please men, but as pleasing God alone irrespective of men, the God who ever continues to test our hearts, yes, our very hearts. This will always show whether the claim is true or fictitious.

Of course, pagan and Jewish opponents of the gospel, who know neither the true God and his Son (1:9, 10) nor his gospel, cannot judge God's tested and entrusted preachers. They are the very ones who want preachers to please *them* and not the true God. But true Christians are always able to judge the claims of preachers. All they need to do is to listen how the preachers speak, to note whether they seek to please men with their religious notions, and especially also to please themselves and their unclean hunger for gain and glory, or whether they aim to please God alone and have the constant consciousness that God ever tests them to the very bottom of their hearts. It will never take long until true Christians can be quite sure. Paul is writing to the Thessalonians as being such Christians, people who have had the fullest opportunity to hear just how Paul and his helpers speak, not to please men, but ever only to please God.

5)   Another γάρ specifies and makes the matter clearer than ever. This connective often introduces elucidative specification. **For we were not at any time in connection with speech of flattery as you know, nor in connection with pretext for covetousness — God a witness! — nor seeking glory of men, neither from you nor from others, as being able to appear with weight as Christ's apostles. On the contrary, we were gentle in your midst as when a nurse warms her own children; thus, as being affectionately anxious about you, we were pleased to impart to you not only the gospel of God but also our own souls because you were beloved to us.** So far, says Paul, were we from even a trace of selfishness. The passive form ἐγενήθημεν (also found in v. 8) does not have a passive meaning; in the Koine this form is often preferred to the aorist middle. The aorist states the simple historical fact.

At no time, as the Thessalonians know, did Paul and Silvanus descend to a word of flattery (qualitative genitive) in order to ingratiate themselves. They were above that. They likewise never used a pretext for covetousness (either objective genitive: to cover up secret covetousness; or subjective: covetousness using a pretext). "Cloak of covetousness" in our versions is a good translation although "cloak" is figurative while πρόφασις, "pretext," is literal. They never put on a fair front to hide their covetousness while they sought to satisfy it by mulcting the Thessalonians. Paul cannot here say, "as you know," for covetousness is hidden in the heart of the greedy man, and it might be there even when we are unable to see any evidence of it. So Paul adds the nominative absolute: "God a witness!" Paul repeatedly appeals to God when he makes statements about things hidden in the heart. It is extravagant to call this an oath; it is the natural assurance of a Christian who constantly lives under God's eye.

6) The trio of expressions is completed by a participle: "nor seeking out of men glory," honor, acclaim, reverence, "neither from you" Thessalonians when you came to faith, "nor from others," no matter who they may be. The participial addition indicates in what manner Paul and Silvanus might have sought glory, literally, "as being able to be in weight as Christ's apostles" = as able to impress people with the dignity of being Christ's apostles. Paul and Silvanus put on no grand apostolic airs in order thereby to obtain glory from men (ἐκ and ἀπό are used with little distinction). They were not after such glory. As far as they were concerned, they were, indeed, "Christ's apostles" and not a whit less; but that very fact implied making no show of it, in no way capitalizing their office for the least personal end. Accountable to Christ as his commissioned representatives (ἀπόστολοι), their one aim was to carry out what Christ, through their commission, intended to bestow on men.

Paul puts himself, Silvanus, and Timothy on the same level. The view that this plural refers to himself alone is not tenable. The very heading of this epistle (1:1) makes no distinction between these three men. The fact that Paul alone was called immediately while the other two were called mediately is immaterial for the purpose of this epistle. "Apostles" is here used in a broader sense as it is in Acts 14:14 where also Barnabas bears this title. The very fact that Paul here classes Silvanus and Timothy as "apostles" together with himself shows the unselfish spirit which animated him.

Βάρος = *gravitas* and thus *auctoritas*. Some think that Paul is speaking of the financial support that he might have demanded as an apostle. Our versions seem to have this idea in mind. Their translation: "when we might have been burdensome," is inexact, for the participle is not potential. As regards money and support, ἐν βάρει εἶναι, without a pronoun referring to the Thessalonians, is far too broad to express something so narrow especially in a connection that speaks of seeking glory.

7) We decline to construe the clause beginning with δυνάμενοι with v. 7. This ἀλλά is like the two that precede, and it is best to regard it as introducing a new sentence. "On the contrary," etc. The question is asked whether this contrary conduct is the opposite of all three preceding items (flattery, covetousness, seeking glory) or of only the last of these, or the opposite of the desire to be honored as apostles. The question really answers itself. It would be strange, indeed, if Paul linked three negatives together as he does and then offered a contrary positive to only one of them; still stranger if he offered no contrasting opposite to the three negatives but one only to the subordinate participial modifier. Is not flattery used for selfish ends? Does not covetousness use its cloak for selfish ends? Is not all seeking of glory selfish throughout? Over against all three Paul places the pure unselfishness with which he and his assistants worked as apostles.

We consider the reading νήπιοι incongruous although Origen, Augustine, and a few others seek to justify it. The reading ἤπιοι is much rarer, hence it was easy to repeat the ν of the preceding word and change ἤπιοι into νήπιοι. R., *W. P.*, is uncertain. Wohlenberg thinks that Paul used the progression: Paul and his helpers were "infants" among the Thessalonians — infants that acted as "a nurse" (this is changed into "a mother") — next, infants who acted as "a father" (v. 11). Now, little ones may *play* mama and papa; but it cannot be imagined that the apostles ever used such a figure.

A few commentators call this mixing of figures: *"infants* in your midst as *a nurse* warms her own children,"* typically Pauline, but such a statement is not just to the apostle; it is typical of him to avoid all incongruities especially also in the use of figures. He may use closely allied figures, but babies who *need* care and a nurse who *bestows* care are opposites.

Moreover, here the ὡς clause completes the sense of the main clause. Does a *nurse* warming her own children complete the idea that some persons were *infants?* Can we think of accepting such an idea in place of the beautiful thought Paul expresses: "We were *gentle* in your midst as when a *nurse* warms her own children"? To say that a nurse would not treat children placed in her care so tenderly, that only a mother would do so, and that, therefore, Paul has a mother in mind, is a slander on all faithful nurses. A nurse even feeds, guards, and otherwise tends her own children, she dearly loves them as "her own." Committed to her care, they are in a very real sense "her own."

Ἐγενήθημεν = "we were" (as in 1:5; 2:5) ; in 2:9; 1:6, "you were," not "became"; and ὡς ἄν = "as when." Θάλπειν is used in Eph. 5:29; "to warm" is more definite than "to cherish" (our versions). When the Thessalonians came to faith they were like τέκνα, "dear children" who needed unselfish gentleness. Paul says we treated you thus, we did not exploit you by means of flattering talk, with cloaked covetousness, seeking glory from you as men who were able to put on the high dignity of Christ's ambassadors.

8) "Thus, as being affectionately anxious about you (ὁμειρόμενοι, the etymology is still in dispute, see R. 198, 206, 225, *W. P.,* also *M.-M.*), we continued to take pleasure (εὐδοκοῦμεν, present) in imparting to you not only the gospel of God but also our own souls because you were (historical fact, aorist) beloved to us." Οὕτως resumes v. 7 and emphasizes it. The figure

is dropped and the reality substituted. Instead of any selfish motive that might have been lurking in the hearts of Paul and his companions there was the very opposite, namely tender solicitude for you (ὑμῶν, genitive after a verb of emotion, R. 508). In εὐδοκοῦμεν there lies the thought of freely willing to do something good, the tense is descriptive: "we continued to take pleasure" in imparting to you. The infinitive is an aorist: actually and completely to impart. Instead of wanting to get something the apostles wanted to share something; and since they were true apostles they shared the greatest thing they had, "the gospel of God," in order to enrich the Thessalonians for time and for eternity.

This alone would have been sufficient. Paul, however, says: "not only the gospel of God," which we had from him, "but also our own souls." Lightfoot translates "lives," which does not fit the next clause: "because (διότι for the reason that) you were beloved to us," i. e., because we loved you so dearly. This explains what sharing our own souls with you means, namely becoming one heart and soul with the Thessalonians (Acts 4:32). The aorist "you were" beloved to us again states the fact. Here we have the true missionary, pastoral, and Christian spirit: voluntary and happy desire to bestow the divine gospel and all the love in our souls upon others. When soul goes out to soul, the gospel so offered will be the more readily accepted. Then soul will also be bound together with soul by the bond of love that reaches out to embrace the other's soul. Here there is a part of the secret of Paul's great missionary success. He offered the gospel and his own soul in love.

9) Γάρ again (as in v. 5) specifies but now adds a positive feature. **For you remember, brethren, our toil and hardship: working by night and by day so as not to be a burden upon anyone of you, we**

preached for you the gospel of God. You yourselves (are) witnesses, also God, how holily and righteously and blamelessly we showed ourselves in the judgment of you, the believers, just as you know how each one of you, as a father his own children, (we were) admonishing you and encouraging and testifying for you to walk worthily of God, the One calling you into his own kingdom and glory.

The specification carries forward the idea of a nurse doing everything for her children and thus shows the apostles imparting everything. Neither a nurse nor the apostles expect anything from their charges. So Paul says: "You remember that we earned our own living while preaching the gospel for you; we did not make ourselves a burden to anyone of you." "You remember" is only a variation for "you know" (used in 1:5; 2:1, 11).

Κόπος and μόχθος are close synonyms, "toil" that induces fatigue, the second term, toil as a hardship. The genitives νυκτὸς καὶ ἡμέρας denote time within which, thus a part of the night, a part of the day, and not all night and all day long (accusatives of extent). Πρὸς τό with the aorist infinitive denotes either purpose or result: "working in order not to be burdensome," or, "working so that we were not burdensome." The aorist infinitive (historical) leads us to prefer the latter.

Paul here says what some would insert into ἐν βάρει in v. 6. The infinitive ἐπιβαρῆσαι is derived from the same root as the noun but is a compound and is used in a totally different context and in no way affects the sense of the phrase used in v. 6. Paul and Silvanus had a rather hard time of it in Thessalonica. We see what moved the Philippians to send two gifts to Paul at this time (Phil. 4:16). These were gifts of love, which for that reason Paul could not refuse; they were not pay, wages, support, not a violation of Paul's principle ever to preach the gospel gratis. Paul says:

working thus for our own support and burdening not
one of you, "we preached for you the gospel of God"
(the same expression that was used in v. 8).

Κηρύσσειν = to act as a herald, to herald something,
to proclaim it aloud and publicly as having been commissioned to do so by authority (king, government,
general of an army, etc.).   When we translate "to
preach," the latter thought should not be forgotten, for
a herald dare announce only what he is ordered to announce, no more and no less; he must also word it just
so and not otherwise.   The herald is only the loud-
speaker of the radio.   Many preachers want to be
more.   But they always become less.   Whoever does
not sound forth "the gospel of God," this whole gospel
and nothing but this gospel, is no true herald.   God
wants heralds, *he* supplies the grand announcement to
be made, and no herald can improve upon it.

Εἰς ὑμᾶς does not mean: we heralded *"into you"* as
has been thought; "unto or for you" is correct.   The
whole expression harmonizes.   This God who sends *his*
heralds with *his* announcement and the people to whom
he sends *his* heralds are not expected to pay those heralds.   When *we* today send missionary heralds we do
not expect the people to whom we send them to pay
them.   When we as congregations appoint heralds for
ourselves, we, who appoint them, pay them.

The great wisdom of Paul in preaching the gospel
gratis appears very clearly here in Thessalonica just
as it does in Corinth.   The opponents tried to class
Paul and his assistants with the roving charlatans of
that time, who were out for what they could get from
the people.   Every Christian saw at once that the
apostles were the very opposite: wholly unselfish, asking and desiring nothing, heart and soul being bent
only on bestowing upon others.   Slander to the contrary fell flat.   Paul had a still higher reason for

preaching the gospel gratis (see the exposition of II
Cor. 9:15-18).

10) "You yourselves (are) witnesses, also God,"
is stronger than "you remember" occurring in v. 9;
for what is now added is much more important than
preaching the gospel without pay, asking nothing for
self, only enriching others. Acceptance of the gospel
means henceforth to walk "in a way worthy of God"
(v. 12). Preaching the gospel means to induce people
to live an entirely new life. The preachers of this gospel must thus themselves exhibit this new life. How
can they ask others to be sanctified when they themselves lack this sanctification? The preacher's life
shouts louder than his words. A preacher was once
told that his unsanctified life "hollered so that no one
could hear what he was saying in the pulpit."

The Thessalonians themselves are witnesses, as also
is God, in what a holy, righteous, blameless way the
apostles conducted themselves just as the Thessalonians know how the apostles admonished them to walk
in the same way. This is the simple meaning of v.
10-12. The wording ἐγενήθημεν (the same verb that was
used in 1:6; 2:5, 7; the second person in 1:6) with a
dative of persons and with adverbs (in v. 7 with an
adjective) is highly idiomatic and cannot be adequately
reproduced in English. The passive form is *not* passive in meaning; nor is the meaning, "we *became*." R.
545 is probably right when he states that this verb is
here not a mere copula; this is due to the adverbs and
the dative.

The aorist is plainly historical: the Thessalonians
are witnesses of a past fact. The adverbs are not equal
to adjectives; ὡς speaks of a degree of manner: "in
what a holy and righteous and blameless *way*" we were.
Grammars and dictionaries are unsatisfactory with
regard to the adverbs and with regard to the dative.

The latter is not "among you," which = εἰς ὑμᾶς (R. V.). The idea of the *dativus commodi* has the first adverb against it: "how holily — for your benefit." The thought that the apostles acted in the way in which they did only as regards "the believers" and *not* as regards others is manifestly not Paul's meaning. Yet, why does he add this apposition?

Some of the ancient commentators who are followed by Alford and Meyer solve the dative; it is "the dative of opinion or judgment" (Meyer), we prefer to say the dative to indicate the persons whose judgment as witnesses is of value in regard to how holily, etc., they saw the apostles conducting themselves. "You yourselves *witnesses*" explains "you, the believers." The judgment of nonbelievers is valueless; men who do not know what true holiness, etc., are, cannot testify regarding the presence of these qualities in other men; only believers can do this, only they can testify "how holily, etc.," a man lives and acts. One can have "a good report from those without" (I Tim. 3:7), but this is not a testimony in regard to one's holiness, etc. Only "those within," i. e., "the believers," are able to offer competent witness regarding this.

Since Paul's meaning is clear, we translate the idiomatic Greek as best we can. The verb does not mean, "we showed ourselves," "we behaved ourselves" (R. and A. V.); the German *wir traten auf* is the best (in John 1:6 ἐγένετο is thus used regarding the Baptist). "Holy and righteous" are often combined; here they are amplified by "blameless" (all three are adverbs). The view that "holy" refers to God and "righteous" to men cannot be maintained. All three terms refer to God's judgment even as God is here made one of the witnesses.

"How holily" = how we shunned sin, how we kept ourselves separate unto God. "How righteously" = how we obeyed God's norm of right, his judgment approving and vindicating us. The former is not to indicate what is in the heart in contrast to the latter which indicates what lies in the outward acts; both apply to heart and to conduct. "How blamelessly" rounds out and = in consequence no one could justly cast blame or reproach upon us. Paul says ὡς, "how," and thus does not claim for himself and for Silvanus perfect holiness, complete moral perfection (in the sense of perfectionism); he does claim a high degree of holiness, etc.

This makes plain why he here again makes God a witness; see the explanation of v. 5. The Thessalonians are able to bear witness to a degree; they judge what is *in* a man by what they see *of* a man just as we do. Their witness is competent to that degree. God sees the whole heart directly; his witness is still more competent and valuable. We should not object that God's witness cannot be obtained in this life; we have his witness in his Word, for there we hear whom he judges to be holy, righteous, and blameless. That is why Jesus spoke John 12:48b. We thus see how the two witnesses agree, you Thessalonians and God. All true believers are guided by God's Word in their judgment and testimony and have the fullest intent to judge only as God himself does and as he already judges and testifies in his Word.

11) Καθάπερ = "according to the very things which," i. e., "just as" you know, how, etc. This ὡς does not repeat the substance of the preceding ὡς but advances to what the apostles as men who lived in a holy, righteous, and blameless way did to make the Thessalonian believers live in the same way. Καθάπερ expresses this correspondence between the two ὡς. "You know" (see 1:5; 2:1) continues the appeal to what the Thessalonians know about this corresponding fact: "how each single one of you, as a father his own children, (we were)admonishing you and encouraging

and testifying for you to walk in a way worthy of God," etc. The participles are not equal to finite verbs as some assume; nor are they anacoluthic. The verb ἐγενήθημεν, used in the preceding ὡς clause, is also to be construed with this second ὡς clause. The present participles unfold descriptively what the aorist verb simply states as the succinct historical fact.

The personal object is placed forward for the sake of emphasis, which makes also the participles emphatic, the more so since they are again a trio. To add another "you" after saying "each single one of you," seems pleonastic, but it seems far less so in the Greek than in the English. Paul purposely stresses "each single one of you" and then combines all of them in ὑμᾶς, "you." He does this regularly with the singular and the plural, with individuals and with the whole group. He always has a view which takes in all sides. He dealt with every single person, he dealt with all of them as a body. Individual pastoral work, public admonitory preaching. Especially the former was "as a father his own children." The Thessalonians were, indeed, the spiritual children of Paul and Silvanus, and τέκνα connotes dearness as well as immaturity. They needed a nurse (v. 7) for one purpose; they needed a father for another. "Father" is the proper word to be used with these participles, "mother" would not be. In Gal. 4:19 the figure of the mother is highly effective. This fatherly action is a part of v. 10, "how holily," etc.

"Admonishing you," as Bengel states it = moving you to do freely; παραμυθούμενοι, to do with pleasure (*ut cum gaudio*) ; μαρτυρόμενοι, to do with fear (*ut cum timore*). The second is best taken in the sense of "encouraging"; some, like the A. V., prefer comforting since affliction seems to be involved. But one is comforted *after* affliction: to *face* it he needs to be strongly encouraged. Some think the third participle means "adjuring you," which, indeed, makes it the climax. Neither C.-K. nor B.-P. list this meaning. The word is not used in this sense in Eph. 4:17 where the context is the same. We retain the meaning "testifying," which affords even a better climax, for to the two subjective participles it adds a third that points to something objective. Paul and Silvanus testified to God's will and Word in order thereby to move the Thessalonians. As Bengel states it: "as with fear"; the Thessalonians would not want to go against God's will and Word. So these participles also reflect v. 10.

12) We do not think that εἰς τό expresses purpose because it plainly states the contents of the admonition, encouragement, and testimony: "for you to walk in a way worthy of God, the One calling you into his own kingdom and glory." We might have had ἵνα. The sense would be the same, it would be an object clause. R., *W. P.*, regards the expression as being one of purpose, some find in it an expression of result; only a few regard it as introducing an object clause although ἵνα as the equivalent of εἰς τό introduces many object clauses. Moulton, *Einleitung*, 347, is correct: "contents of a command or request," "purpose is so far away that it is practically disappearing."

We should read the whole of v. 12 as a unit. But τοῦ καλοῦντος is timeless: God is "the Caller" into his own kingdom irrespective of when and where and whom he calls. The present tense should thus not be translated: "who ever keeps calling you." The participle is really an apposition: "the God, the One calling you." Some texts have the aorist: "the One who did call you," but the present tense seems textually assured.

"His own kingdom and (his own) glory" are not hendiadys; καί is epexegetical, for "his own kingdom" would mean the kingdom in general, "and glory" narrows down to the consummation of the kingdom when all the heavenly glory shall be ours. We should not conceive the kingdom in the common, earthly manner of kingdoms. This King makes his kingdom, it is not the kingdom which makes him. Where he is and rules, there *eo ipso* is his kingdom. In the kingdom to come, the kingdom of glory, he rules with all his glory, the radiant effulgence of all his attributes. Those called into his kingdom and his glory are not made subjects under this King. The very word καλεῖν excludes this idea which is drawn from poor, earthly kingdoms; nobody is ever called into an earthly kingdom. We are called to be partakers of God's kingdom and glory, to inherit both, to share in the rule of God's glory, to be kings in this subjectless kingdom. See the author's volume *Kings and Priests*.

To walk ἀξίως, "worthily," is a common expression in Paul's writings and is also found elsewhere. Paul writes "worthily of the Lord" (Col. 1:10), "of the calling with which you were called" (Eph. 4:1), "of the gospel" (Phil. 1:27). The force of the adverb is that of weight: our whole walk from day to day is to be of equal weight with God as the One who calls us, etc. Place the way in which we live into one pan of the scales and God with his call into the other pan, then the two ought to balance, the one that has our conduct in it ought not to scale upward because of the heavy weight in the other. For the Thessalonians this ἀξίως = v. 10.

"Worthily" has nothing to do with work-righteousness. Our call makes us princes and kings; we should act as such. Where shall we get this weight? From him who calls us. What if we still sin? His grace removes our sin, gives us Christ's righteousness, and ever renews our life. If we are day by day replenished with newness (Rom. 6:4), the weight will be there. We must never take this matter lightly and become indifferent; the three participles take care of that.

The Spirit in which the Thessalonians Responded to the Work of Paul and Silvanus

13)   After describing the spirit in which Paul and Silvanus brought the gospel to the Thessalonians and worked among them so as to excite them to walk worthily Paul speaks of the way in which the Thessalonians responded to the gospel. **And for this we, too, on our part are thankful to God without ceasing that, on getting to receive God's Word by a hearing (of it) from us, you obtained, not man's word, but, as it truly is, God's Word, which also is effective in you, the believers.**

This still describes the spirit in which Paul and Silvanus labored among the Thessalonians. But the thought now progresses. In the first place, "we are thankful to God unceasingly" reaches to the present moment, to the constant thankfulness of Paul and his assistants. To what the Thessalonians know (v. 1), remember (v. 9), and testify (v. 10) about them when they were in Thessalonica is added what Paul and his assistants feel to this day, namely unceasing gratitude to God. This advance is joined with another: from the way in which Paul and his assistants *acted* in Thessalonica the thought advances to what they *brought* to the Thessalonians, to what the Thessalonians thus *received*, and thus to what they *were* (v. 14). It is essential to note this advance, otherwise we shall not keep step with Paul's thought.

Some commentators think that διὰ τοῦτο refers to what precedes, either to the last verse or two, or to the whole of v. 1-12. They translate accordingly: "for this reason . . . because," etc. Τοῦτο, however = ὅτι (explicative). To be sure, this is the same thankfulness of which Paul speaks in 1:2, yet the object of the gratitude is not the same. Compare the object as stated in 1:3 and the object here stated by the ὅτι clause. Here it is the Word of God which was obtained from the apostles by the Thessalonians and not, as in 1:3, what had appeared in the Thessalonians in the way of faith, love, and hope. Paul now goes back to the ultimate basis of faith, love, and hope, namely to the Word of God imparted to the Thessalonians.

The observation is correct that in the preceding Paul speaks of the gospel in various ways (1:6, "the Word"; 1:7, "the Word of the Lord"; 2:2, "the gospel of God"; 2:4, "the gospel"; 2:8, 9, "the gospel of God"); Paul has also touched on bringing this gospel to the Thessalonians and on their receiving it: we spoke it, imparted it, preached it to you (2:2, 8, 9), it came to you (1:5), you received it (1:6). While this observation is correct as regards the connection with what precedes, we should note that all this is now brought to its great focus: λόγον ἀκοῆς παρ' ἡμῶν τοῦ Θεοῦ, οὐ λόγον ἀνθρώπων, ἀλλὰ, καθώς ἐστιν ἀληθῶς λόγον Θεοῦ, ὅς κτλ. The preceding terms: "Word *of God, of the Lord,*" are now made to stand out in all their greatness and power: Word of God, *not* word of men, *but, as it truly is,* Word of GOD, *effective* in you believers as such. This, this is what all the preceding references mean!

The Thessalonians have full assurance about *the kind of men* who brought this Word to them (this is the burden of 1:5-2:12), and they are still the same men (in their thankfulness to God); the Thessalonians have the still greater assurance about *the Word itself* which these men brought to them. Let the Thessalonians look at *this Word itself,* at what it truly is! The two, of course, go together: *this* Word would be brought by *such* men; *such* men would bring a Word like *this.* But now the entire stress is on this Word and on its Author.

The opponents in Thessalonica would turn the Thessalonians from the Word of God by attacking the character of the men who brought that Word. The Thessalonians have the double answer: they *know* the

true character of these men, know it from their most
intimate contact with them, from their inside view of
the absolute unselfishness and devotion of these men;
they *know* the nature of the Word these men have
brought them, what this Word is in truth and thus
has effectively wrought in them. This double assurance fortifies the Thessalonians against all attacks
from no matter what opponents.

So much, we see, depends on the kind of men who
preach the gospel. Let all preachers keep this in mind!
In the last analysis, however, the decisive assurance
for all believers is the Word itself with its divine effects. See Gal. 1:8. In Thessalonians, too, the ultimate ground of assurance is the Word.

The idea that both καί belong to διὰ τοῦτο is not tenable; the second καί is to be construed with ἡμεῖς. And
this pronoun is emphatic; if it were not, the "we" in
the verb suffix would suffice. Paul says and means:
"we, too, on our part are thankful to God without
ceasing" just as you Thessalonians are on your part.
Who should be more constantly thankful to God than
the Thessalonians themselves, for what they received
was God's own Word? Those who brought that Word to
them are "also" thankful. With a verb such as this διὰ
τοῦτο and its explicative ὅτι might be conceived as cause
or reason: "for this cause" (our versions), "that" (R.
V.), "because" (A. V.). Yet it seems better to let the
phrase and its ὅτι express only the object of the thankfulness: "for this we thank God that," etc. Here the
verb is general: "ceaselessly we are thankful"; in 1:2
prayers are mentioned in which the thankfulness becomes thanksgiving uttered in words. Here no prayers are mentioned, and the verb thus denotes the constant feeling of gratitude to God.

The aorists παραλαβόντες and ἐδέξασθε (the participle
in 1:6) express simultaneous action, both are ingressive and closely synonymous. The synergistic ideas of

some commentators become evident when they distinguish between the two verbs and stress the human willingness and activity found in the second verb. But C.-K. 279 defines the verb in the present connection: *Anerkennung der evangelischen Verkuendigung und das Sichbestimmenlassen durch dieselbe,* acknowledging the evangelical proclamation and being determined thereby. Neither verb contains even a trace of synergism as little as does the verb πιστεύειν, "to believe or trust." We see this when we consider the object. Nothing in the word of mere men deserves reception, acceptance, or even consideration for our soul's salvation even as this word is totally ineffective in those who do receive it. But the Word of God, so blessed and mighty to produce saving effects, deserves the promptest and the completest acceptance and ever and ever by its own nature and its own power *produces* this acceptance just as *truth* produces *conviction* despite the fact that many men love lies more than truth (John 8:45; 3:19), just as *blessings* produce joyful *acceptance* despite the fact that many men want what they know will be a curse to them.

"On getting to receive . . . you obtained" = by taking the Word of God you accepted and got what is, indeed, the Word of God; we, too, we apostles, are thankful to God for this. Regard as one concept: λόγον ἀκοῆς παρ᾽ ἡμῶν τοῦ Θεοῦ, which the flexibility of the Greek is able to express as a unit object while the English finds it difficult to do this. The two anarthrous nouns are qualitative and yet are made definite by the phrase and by the genitive: "God's Word of hearing from us," the genitive is placed last in the Greek and is thus emphatic: a Word that you heard from us apostles (2:6), whose author is God himself.

᾽Ακοή is much like a technical term which is used, not to indicate the *actus audiendi,* but to designate the κήρυγμα, the proclamation as it is actually heard. The

R. V. tries to retain the qualifying genitive: "word of message" (although "message" is not exact) while the A. V. frankly paraphrases: "word which ye heard." Instead of using another genitive, ἡμῶν, to indicate the source of the Word heard and thus to bring together three genitives Paul uses the phrase "from us"; yet this is to be construed with the noun and not the participle. The ultimate source or author is expressed by τοῦ Θεοῦ, which genitive modifies the whole expression: "Word of hearing from us." Since it is "God's" Word, its nature, power, and effect are thereby also indicated.

When the Thessalonians got to receive this they got to obtain (two ingressive aorists) "not man's Word." Not "word of men" like the teaching of the religious quacks and charlatans that appeared in the entire empire to exploit people for their own selfish ends (v. 5, 6) but the very opposite, "Word of God" with all that this source implies. It is the assurance of the writers (1:1) that this is truly "God's Word," but the relative clause: "which is also effective in you, the believers," adds the evidence in support of the fact that this is truly God's Word, namely its divine effectiveness in the Thessalonian believers.

This Word works in the Thessalonians what Paul states in 1:3; it came to them with the power of the Holy Spirit and much assurance (1:5); it turned them from the idols to the living God, to him who raised up Jesus from the dead, the Savior from the wrath to come (1:9, 10). This effect, wrought by the Word, convinces all believers, all who experience this blessed effect, that this is, indeed, *God's* Word.

Ὅς does not refer to "God"; it refers to "Word" because the middle voice ἐνεργεῖται is never used with reference to God, only the active is so used. The apposition τοῖς πιστεύουσιν is the same as that found in v. 10: only "those believing" experience the effects of the Word and are thus able to know of a certainty that it

is "*God's* Word" and not the word of men although
God uses men to bring it as an ἀκοή, something heard.

Our versions regard οὐ λόγον, ἀλλὰ λόγον as predicative accusatives: "not *as* men's word but *as* God's
Word." But if this were Paul's meaning, he would
have written, οὐ ὡς λόγον ἀνθρώπων, ἀλλὰ ὡς λόγον Θεοῦ. To
regard these as being only predicative accusatives is
to reduce Paul's meaning. He tells the Thessalonians
that they did not receive men's word but did receive
God's Word; he does not tell them merely that they
regarded it *as* God's and not *as* men's. What Paul
states is objective; he is not referring to what the
Thessalonians subjectively thought about the Word
they heard.

14) "For" points to some of the plain evidence,
not merely in support of the fact that this divine
Word works in the Thessalonian believers (relative
clause, v. 13), but that this Word is, indeed, not man's
but God's own. **For you on your part were imitators,
brethren, of the churches of God that are in Judea
in Christ Jesus because you yourselves also suffered the same things at the hands of (ὑπό) your
own countrymen as also they at the hands of (ὑπό)
the Jews, they who both killed off the Lord Jesus
and the prophets and drove out us, both not pleasing God and contrary to all men by trying to prevent us from speaking to the Gentiles in order that
they be saved; so that they fill up their sins alway;
moreover, there did come upon them the wrath to
the uttermost.**

Ὑμεῖς is emphatic because it resumes the subject
of the object clause used in v. 13: *you,* the ones who
received not man's but God's Word, the Word that
works in you, the believers, *you* have this plain evidence that what you received is no less than God's own
most effective Word, *you* were imitators of the churches
of God in Judea. On ἐγενήθητε, "you were," see 1:5, 6;

2:5, 7, 8, 9, the aorist states the past fact. In 1:6 Paul has already said that the Thessalonians were "imitators of us and of the Lord" when they received the Word "in much affliction." This is now amplified. For not only we, the Lord's apostles (2:6), are like the Lord who sent them to suffer affliction because of the Word; all of the churches of God are alike in this respect. The very first ones, those that were organized in Judea, had to suffer because of the Word. They received the Word *of God* and thus are churches *of God,* and thus *men* hate and persecute them, namely men who want only the word *of men* and refuse to believe the Word *of God.*

Some think that it would be enough to say "the churches of God that are in Judea," that the addition "in Christ Jesus" is really not needed. Paul does not think so, for Judea is the Jewish land which always had the Word of God and professed to believe that Word, yet when Christ Jesus, the very embodiment of that Word came, the nation of the Jews rejected him and showed that they did not in reality believe God's own Word. These churches in Judea, however, of which Paul speaks are true churches of God because of their connection with (ἐν) Christ Jesus (office and person). The ἐν phrase is by no means unnecessary especially when there is a reference to Jews and to God. It differentiates the Jewish believers from all other Jews. Paul inserts the address, "brethren," in order to express the *Herzlichkeit* with which he writes and to voice the spiritual connection between himself and the Thessalonians in all that he writes.

῞Οτι states the evidential reason for the fact that the Thessalonians were imitators of the Judean churches. This ground of likeness is striking. The Thessalonians suffered the very same thing from their own countrymen which the Judean believers suffered from theirs, namely the Jews: "also you — as also they."

The question is asked as to why Paul makes the comparison with the Judean churches, and the answers offered are often strange: Paul wanted to vent his wrath upon the wicked Jews, the Jews in Corinth where he is writing had roused his ire, the opponents in Thessalonica had pointed out that the Thessalonian believers were becoming embroiled in Jewish controversies, and other ideas of this kind. Paul's idea is plain and to the point. He does not say, "You Thessalonians are like other *Gentile* churches who had to suffer persecution for the Word of God." Persecution is not a special mark of Gentile churches. Hostility against God's Word and Christ Jesus is not a special mark of Gentile unbelievers.

This hostility goes back to the unbelieving Jews, not only to those in Thessalonica and in the Diaspora, but to those in Judea itself, and not to those who are now living in Judea, but to those who lived in the days of the Lord Jesus himself (1:6). The Jews themselves started the fires of persecution, started them against their own believing countrymen; these fires have burned ever since. These unbelieving Jews keep them burning in the Diaspora; Thessalonica has also seen the fire (Acts 17:5, etc.), the Jews in Thessalonica raged just as they originally did in Judea against the Lord Jesus and against the churches of God in Christ Jesus.

"The same things" always happen: you at the hands of your own countrymen, your Gentile fellow citizens; the Judean believers at the hands of their countrymen, the Jews, the latter being the very first ones in this hostility, yea, the ones who fire others in this opposition. Paul states it in a striking way when he says that the Thessalonians were "imitators," as if *they* copied the Judean Jewish believers in the mat-

ter of getting themselves persecuted. One might expect Paul to state it in the opposite way, namely that
the Gentile *persecutors* copied the Judean Jewish persecutors. Yet the main point is that the Thessalonian
believers accepted the Word of God (v. 13), that *they*
thus entered the fellowship of the Judean churches,
and thus "suffered the same things," suffered them
also "at the hands of their own countrymen." Paul
sees all of it in its true inner relation and not in a
superficial light only.

15) That is why the whole guilt of the Jews is
unrolled. We translate καί — καί "both — and": "both
killed off — and drove out." The one act was not
enough, they must needs add the other in order to make
the measure overflow. Paul combines "the Lord Jesus
and the prophets" and yet names Jesus first because
killing him off is the greatest of the Jewish crimes.
The Greek can separate τὸν Κύριον from Ἰησοῦν and place
a strong emphasis on the former: "the Lord they killed,
Jesus," him who is the divine Lord himself. The Jews
did that; so the Scriptures constantly testify. All
modern Jewish efforts to cast the chief blame upon the
Gentile Pilate are futile. As the Jews forced the Gentile Pilate to act as their tool, so the Jews in Thessalonica made the Gentile rabble of Thessalonica their
tools and stirred up the Thessalonian Gentile authorities (Acts 17:5-9).

From Jesus, Paul reaches back to the prophets;
Stephen states these two in reverse order (Acts 7:52)
although he also combines Jesus and the prophets. The
Jewish persecution extends far beyond the time of
Jesus. Jesus himself mentions the killing of the prophets (Matt. 23:37), the Jewish prelude to the killing
off of Jesus himself (Matt. 21:34-39). The fact that
some of the prophets of old were not literally killed off
was not due to the love of the Jews for them. "And us
they drove out," this verb with ἐκ is used to designate

the exiling of fugitives. With "prophets" Paul reaches backward, with "us" forward. As far as Paul is concerned, Acts 9:29, 30 is sufficient.

Some think that "us" refers also to the other apostles (Peter in Acts 12:17). This is a direct reference to Paul and Silas (not to Timothy), but this "us" names Paul and Silas as representatives of a class so that those who know the whole story naturally think also of the other apostles. Yet Paul does not write the word "apostles" (see v. 6); the Thessalonians will think also of other preachers in Judea, who were persecuted and even driven out. When Paul comes to "us" he does not mention Stephen and the Apostle James who were actually killed in Jerusalem as the prophets and Jesus had been (Matt. 23:34, 35), "drove out" is enough; those who know will think of the rest which this participle and the pronoun "us" merely touch. With "us" Paul reverts to this same pronoun which he employed in 1:6.

Again we translate καί — καί "both — and": "both to God not pleasing and to all men contrary by trying to prevent," etc. "Not to be pleasing to God" is a strong case of litotes and meiosis. The matter is stated negatively whereas the thought is decidedly positive; the matter is purposely understated, and yet the effect is the stronger for that very reason. To call this hyperbole (overstatement) confuses matters. In both clauses the datives are placed emphatically forward.

16) "To all men contrary" has no relation to the charge which Tacitus (*Hist.* V, 5) makes against the Jews, of whom he says that they were filled with *adversus omnes alios hostile odium,* hostile hatred against all other people, despising all non-Jews as dogs. Paul himself explains in what way the Jews were ἐναντίων to all men: "by trying to prevent us from speaking to the Gentiles in order that they be saved." Jesus

makes a similar statement in Matt. 23:13. This is the same "us" that was used in v. 15.

The present participle κωλυόντων is conative: the Jews were trying to prevent, they did not succeed. Paul states it briefly: "to speak (aorist, effective) to the Gentiles in order that they be saved." The Jews wanted to silence him and all others. See the first unsuccessful effort of this kind in Acts 4:17, 18 and the next in Acts 5:40. The enormity of this crime against all men is touched upon in the purpose clause "in order that they be saved," this is, of course, the purpose of the speakers, "us." By preventing the speaking these Jews were set on frustrating the purpose of the speaker, were determined to rob the whole Gentile world of the heavenly salvation which they, the Jews themselves, scorned. The worst feature of unbelief is not its own damnation but its effort to frustrate the salvation of others.

Unbelief in salvation through Christ is the height of unreason for the unbeliever himself; for when a man who is lost and doomed in sin and guilt spurns divine salvation, this is the opposite of intelligence and saneness (II Cor. 4:3, 4). This unreason is multiplied when it demands that all other men should also be prevented from obtaining divine salvation. Why can unbelievers not let other men alone? The devil rides them. They must doubly damn themselves. They must come with the blood of other men upon their hands. Note the passive; the Savior implied is God. To this day the delight of some Jewish professors in our great universities is to poison the minds of their students, to prevent their being saved; many Gentile teachers ape their destructive work.

Eἰς τό with the infinitive denotes result. Those who regard it as expressing purpose find God's purpose in it: God wants the Jews to fill up their sins. This is true as John 2:19 and other passages show. When the sinner casts off all restraint, God lets him fill up the measure of his sins until his doom sweeps him to destruction. Is this what Paul wants to express? Paul generally uses εἰς τό to indicate a result. The next clause about the wrath surely states result. The result which the Jews always attained most exactly fits all that Paul says about the damnable crimes of the Jews against God; this would not be true of a statement that God wanted them to fill up their sins alway.

"To fill up their sins" is a concentrated expression for filling up a measure with their sins; the sins themselves are said to be made full. Πάντοτε means "alway" and not "in every way," πάντως or παντελής. This adverb is more than a lax addition which denotes only "completely fill up," it has the emphasis: always, always the result is that these Jews fill up their sins. That does not mean that they are ever engaged in this filling up and will finally fill them up and then receive the wrath. Every time they persecuted and killed a prophet the measure was full. It was so when they killed off Christ, when they drove out the apostles. To this day the Jews keep their sins full. "As your fathers, so you," Acts 7:52.

Hence also the statement with δέ (not "but"): "moreover, there did come upon them the wrath to the uttermost." It would be strange and incongruous to regard this verb as a prophetic aorist that amounts to "will come"; it is likewise not a timeless aorist. This is a historical aorist like "you obtained" in v. 13; "you were," "you suffered" in v. 14. The wrath is not waiting, and it is not coming timelessly — nothing arrives timelessly. The Jews ever filled up their sins, thus the wrath arrived. The two statements correspond; δέ shows that the second belongs to the first and is only somewhat different. The English would use the perfect (R. 842, etc.): "has arrived," φθάνω being understood in its later sense "to arrive" (we have the earlier sense in 4:15).

The adverbial phrase εἰς τέλος (no article) = *fuer immer, unablaessig, in Ewigkeit* (B.-P. 1299), or *vollstaendig, das ist bis zu dem Ziel hin, das in dem betreffenden Subjekt gegeben ist* (C.-K. 1045) = completely, with finality, for good and all. The comment that the phrase refers to the end of the world, or to the end which God makes (or will make) of the Jews, or to the end of the wrath itself when it has consumed the Jews, is not in keeping with the context. The Jews as a mass have been petrified (Rom. 11:7, 25, ἐπωρώθησαν, πώρωσις) and shall remain so until the last day. "The wrath" is terse and concentrated and needs no further modifier than the article. Long, long ago this punitive, retributive wrath arrived upon the Jews. Among the notable manifestations of this wrath is the deportation and the total disappearance of the ten tribes in the Assyrian captivity, also the Babylonian captivity of the other two tribes. Paul tells us why God did not abolish the Jews once for all in Rom. 9:22, etc., (see the exposition) and in a number of other places. The fact that God had rejected the Jews (save for a remnant) Isaiah already proclaimed, for he was sent for this very purpose (Isa. 6:1-13). Thus Isa. 64:1-12 with its heart-rending cry for the Jews and then the divine answer of doom for the Jews in Isa. 65:1-7 (see the author's *Eisenach Old Testament Selections,* 118, etc.).

Some critics refer this verse to the destruction of Jerusalem in the year 70 and thus deny that Paul wrote this epistle. Others suppose that this verse is a gloss or an interpolation by a later hand. But the wrath arrived long centuries before Paul wrote. It did so with finality because always the unbelieving nation filled up its sins, these awful sins to which Paul points. Other nations plunged into vice and corruption and were thus

simply wiped out; but the Jews, chosen as God's own
nation, spurned his covenant and gospel, killed his
prophets, finally God's own Son (their history as
sketched by Jesus in Matt. 21:33-46, to which add
23:34-39). Hence the wrath that made them "with
finality" what they are to this day and will be to the
end of time: the one outcast nation of the world, without country, capital, ruler, scattered over all the world,
yet never absorbed — they constitute a sign of the
wrath that is visible before the eyes of all the ages
until time shall cease.

Here we have no final conversion of the Jewish nation as we have no millennium. God, indeed, has great
plans for this nation, but only the plan of his wrath
εἰς τέλος, with finality. When this wrath would be done
with the unbelieving nation Paul does not say; ἔφθασε
reaches only into the distant past. Comment such as
that Paul expects the Parousia very soon is out of
place. The comment that Paul was angry when he
wrote this letter because the Jews at Corinth had opposed him makes the great apostle a petulant fellow
who is unable to control his temper. This epistle was
written *before* Acts 17:5, etc., occurred.

The Vain Endeavors to Return to Thessalonica

17) All that precedes in this chapter deals with
the time Paul spent in Thessalonica: v. 1-12 with the
kind of men he and his companions showed themselves
to be; v. 13-16 with the kind of a church the Thessalonians were. Then came the forced separation
(Acts 17:10). Now Paul speaks of the time following
this separation. This is the obvious connection of
thought. The motive for writing this chapter as well
as the next is one and the same and not a complex of
several motives. The kind of men Paul and his helpers
were while they were in Thessalonica, that kind of men
they were after they left; all insinuations of the oppo-

nents that were made to disturb the faith of the Thessalonian believers are thus shown to be false.

Wholly unselfish and solicitous only for the Thessalonians (v. 1-12) who from the start had to suffer like the very first churches in Judea (v. 13-16), the one thought of Paul and his helpers was to get back to Thessalonica (v. 17-20), and Timothy was sent back for a while (3:1-10), all three hoped to return (3:11-13). The reason for this strong desire is evidently the fact that Paul and Silvanus had been forced to leave Thessalonica after only a month's work, which was too short a time for all that Paul felt should be done in Thessalonica.

Two thoughts underlie these two chapters: 1) they answer the insinuations of the opponents and reassure the members of the congregation; 2) they tighten the bond between the apostles (1:6) and the newly founded church.

Δέ is continuative and not adversative; ἡμεῖς is without contrast. Paul passes on to the time after he and Silvanus had been compelled to leave and thus speaks of their desire to get back and hence uses ἡμεῖς. **Now we, brethren, orphaned from you for a period of time as regards face, not as regards heart, made more diligent effort to see your face in great desire, for we resolved to come to you, I, Paul, in particular both once and again, and Satan cut us off. For who is our hope or joy or crown of boasting; or are not also you in the presence of our Lord Jesus in connection with his Parousia? Indeed, you are our glory and (our) joy!**

The affectionate "brethren" is never inserted lightly even as it here marks the intimate character of what Paul is stating. One wants to get back to "brethren" with whom one is as closely connected as were Paul and the Thessalonians, Silvanus and Timothy likewise, who shared all Paul's feelings. It is a bit unfair to Paul to have "nurse" in v. 7 mean "mother" and to prefer the reading "babes" instead of "gentle" and thus to cause Paul to mix his figures so that he makes himself a babe, a mother, a father (v. 11), and now an orphan for the Thessalonians (R., *W. P.*). As far as the passive participle "orphaned from you" is concerned, this is also used with reference to a father or to parents who are separated from children. It thus occasionally has a non-literal sense. The more common χωρισθέντες means "separated from you in space"; "orphaned from you" connotes the love that is affected, the pain of the separation, the desire to get back.

We read together: "orphaned from you for a period of time as regards face, not as regards heart," for Paul cannot believe that this separation will be longer than a period of time, and even during this period it is only a matter of not seeing each other and not a matter of inward separation. He is still with the Thessalonians in heart. The two datives refer to relation. Only in this passage the two nouns are combined: πρὸς καιρὸν ὥρας; elsewhere we have either πρὸς καιρόν or πρὸς ὥραν; ὥρα does not mean "hour" but is to be understood in the wider sense of "time."

"A period of time" says nothing about its length, whether immediately after the separation or after a longer wait diligent efforts were made to see the Thessalonians again. The aorist participle refers only to the fact that the separation preceded the efforts to get back. The passive states that the separation was a forced one as Acts 17:5-10 describe, the Thessalonians themselves sending Paul and Silvanus away. Paul and Silvanus yielded for the time being. The fact that this was a longer period of time goes without saying, for they could not hope to go back immediately; in due time, when they thought it safe, they made repeated efforts.

Paul tells the Thessalonians this: "We made more diligent effort to see your face in great desire." If Paul had not written the comparative περισσοτέρως he would have spared the commentators some trouble. We need not review the different interpretations. R. 664, etc., is right in holding to the comparative idea, which must be drawn from the context. Here this is furnished by the passive participle: they used diligence "more abundantly" because the separation was enforced, because Paul and Silvanus felt orphaned, i. e., driven away from their charges in untimely haste when they felt that they were still greatly needed. Hence also we have the phrase that they made efforts to get back "in great desire," the desire to do for the Thessalonians what they still needed. Ἐπιθυμία, often used with regard to sinful desire, is here to be taken in the good sense. The second πρόσωπον seems due to the first; Paul might have written "to see you."

The kind of men that Paul and his helpers were when they worked in Thessalonica the Thessalonians know (1:5); they remained that kind of men after they were forced to leave, a fact which the Thessalonians must also know. Paul and Silvanus would encounter danger by returning to Thessalonica, nevertheless, disregarding such danger to themselves and thinking only of their beloved brethren in the great city and what might yet be done for them, they sought to return. The imperfect might have been used here because the efforts did not succeed; instead of expressing this thought the aorist is used to express the fact: "we did use diligence to see your face." Who frustrated these efforts is stated in a moment.

18) Διότι has the force of ὅτι the German *denn* (B.-P. 310), our "for." The Thessalonians, of course, know that Paul and Silvanus did not return to their city, that only Timothy was sent to them to strengthen them and then to return in order to report to Paul.

Thus they also know what has just been said, namely that Paul and Silvanus themselves wanted very much to come and made diligent effort to do so. What is written here and in 3:1, etc., is not new information to the Thessalonians but is similar to what the writers say about themselves in 1:5-2:12, a reminder of the kind of men the writers are, men who were prompted only by unselfish love and zeal for their converts, let opponents say what they will. We were diligent to see you with much desire, "for we resolved to come to you, I, Paul, in particular both once and again, and (the only reason this resolution was not carried out was that) Satan cut us off." The verb means "we willed," i. e., we had the plans made; "would (A. V.) and "would fain" (R. V.) are too potential; the idea is: "we actually resolved," we had it all arranged.

"I, Paul, in particular, both once and again" says that the plan resolved on twice included Paul. We know that no more could be carried out than to let Timothy go alone for a brief stay (3:1, etc.). We conclude that their other plans were to have Silvanus and Timothy go, perhaps also Silvanus alone. But twice the plan was made so that all three were to go, including Paul in particular (the idea was not, of course, that he should go alone).

Here there is a beautiful instance of μέν *solitarium.* Μέν is construed with ἐγώ and is pointedly restrictive (as Robertson puts it) : "I in particular, Paul." Paul has been using the plural "we"; the Thessalonians know that Timothy came alone (3:1, etc.) and also that Silvanus was Paul's assistant in Thessalonica. The relation of the three men, the fact that all three united in sending this epistle (1:1), is perfectly plain to the Thessalonians. The main personage of the three is Paul whose return to Thessalonica was desired most of all. The parenthetical insertion: "I in particular,

Paul," thus lifts Paul out of the "we" subject of the verb, a common practice with all writers. Yet R., *W. P.*, thinks that we here have a clear example of the literary plural, i. e., that Paul speaks of himself as "we." Robertson's grammar offers more of these editorial or majestic plurals from the pen of Paul. Yet Paul never uses "we" when he is referring to himself.

Καὶ ἅπαξ καὶ δίς (Phil. 4:16) = "both once and again" and draws attention to each of the two times the resolve was made. When the first plan went by the board, the matter was not dropped; plans were made a second time, and these two plans could not be carried out. The second clause: "and Satan cut us off," also depends on διότι so that καί does not add an adversative thought as it sometimes does (A. V. "but"). It completes the explanation made by "for." The supposition that the Jews blamed everything of an adversative character onto Satan, and that Paul adopts this Jewish view, really implies that Satan was not to blame, that circumstances alone frustrated the plans. Paul never adopts mistaken Jewish views. Satan was back of the riotous proceeding that drove Paul and Silvanus out of Thessalonica, and he was also back of the hindrances that frustrated the two plans to return to Thessalonica.

This by no means excludes divine providence which rules in the midst of our enemies. Satan entered the heart of Judas so that he made plans to betray Jesus, and God permitted the betrayal for his own divine and blessed ends. So Satan succeeded in frustrating Paul's two plans to return to Thessalonica, but only because this accorded with God's own plans regarding the work Paul was to do. Satan has brought many a martyr to his death, and God permitted it. The death of these martyrs was more blessed for them and for the cause of the gospel than their life would have been. It is ever so with Satan's successes. No thanks to Satan! His guilt is the greater. It was due to Satan that the

Thessalonians suffered just as the original churches in Judea had to suffer (v. 14) although God permitted this suffering. Here Paul touches only Satan's activity and does not need to say more, for the Thessalonians understand. The verb means that Satan "cut in on us," i. e., stopped us. "Us" means "us" and not "me" (literary plural). All three planned to go together to Thessalonica; they were prevented both times.

We do not know the details. Timothy (3:1, etc.) reported them to the Thessalonians so that Paul needs to say no more. Supposition leads to nothing definite: the supposition that Paul became ill and could not travel as planned, that stormy weather spoiled the plans, that troubles beset Paul and detained him, and Ramsay's idea that Jason's bond given to the Thessalonian authorities was still valid (Acts 17:9). Dobschuetz is right: When we do not know, it is scientific not to surmise but to confess that we do not know.

19) Opponents in Thessalonica may well have said that Paul and Silvanus were only too willing to be rushed away from Thessalonica when the riot took place (Acts 17:10), that the believers would not see them again, and that they were men who cared only for themselves, were like the religious deceivers that were so numerous in the entire empire. The answer to this statement is not only Paul's strenuous effort to return with his assistants but his effort combined with his motive, and that not merely the motive to do something for the Thessalonians in unselfish love but the still higher motive that the Thessalonians were everything to Paul and to his companions. These insinuations are met, not indirectly, but head on, directly. The charge: "These men are self-seekers!" is made a boomerang: "We *are* self-seekers — you Thessalonians are everything to us!" Paul states it in dramatic question-and-answer form: "For who is our hope or joy

or crown of boasting; are not also you in the presence
of our Lord Jesus in connection with his Parousia?"
All the hope that we have as ministers of Christ, all our
joy, all our crown of boasting, i. e., all that means success to us in our work when we at last stand in Christ's
glorious presence at the last day centers in *you Thessalonians!* In whom else could it center?

"Who," not "what," because persons constitute the
hope, the joy, and the crown. Christ's apostles (v. 6)
must win souls; for that purpose they are sent out
and not for anything less than that. "Our hope" is
placed first and thus makes the joy and the crown likewise reach forward to the last day: our hope for the
day of Christ's Parousia. You Thessalonians constitute "our hope" means that all we hope for at that
great day when the Lord will reward his ministers as
he has promised in Luke 19:12-19 is that we may present you Thessalonians to him as people who have been
won for the gospel (II Cor. 11:2). All of the "or" are
conjunctive and not disjunctive: call it our hope, *or*
call it our joy, *or* call it our crown of boasting, which-
ever way you look at it, the hope we now have regarding what shall be at the last day, or the joy we now
anticipate regarding that final joy, or the crown of
which we boast as being ours already now and to be
placed upon our heads at that day. Who is any one,
yea, all three of these?

"Or are not also you," etc., repeats the question in
an alternative form. Instead of repeating "who" it
advances and asks directly: "Are not also you?" The
criticism that this extension of the dramatic question is
stoerend and "a confused construction" does not note
the effective thing Paul is doing, does not note that
"or" means: "or to put it directly about *you*." "Also
(*καί*) you" includes the other churches that had been
founded by Paul and his assistants. Οὐχί (the strong
form of οὐ) implies a decided affirmative answer.

If the alternative question is reduced to the words "or not also you" and then made a parenthesis, it would be an awkward insert and a break in the thought. But no ordinary reader would note such a parenthesis. Nor is there a reason for referring the two final phrases across these words so as to join them to the first question. "Or are not also you?" means all that the preceding contains: "Are not also you our hope," etc.?

"In the presence of our Lord Jesus in connection with his Parousia" conveys one thought: the great day when Paul and his fellow workers shall stand in the glorious presence of the Lord Jesus at his return to judgment. He and his assistants did all of their work in the light of that day. They taught all their converts to do the same: "to await the Son of God from the heavens. . . . Jesus, the One who saves us from the wrath to come" (1:10). They had but one interest, namely at that day to stand crowned before the all-glorious Lord.

Much may be said about Παρουσία αὐτοῦ, "his Parousia" or "Presence." Deissmann, *Light from the Ancient East*, 372, etc., finds that in the papyri the word denotes the arrival and the visit of the Roman emperor in some city, the inhabitants dating a new era from such a parousia. He leaves the impression that the readers of Paul's epistles had this Hellenistic use of the term in mind, that Paul also adopted the word from this its pagan use. M.-M. 497 also adopts this view. But the apostles use "thine own Parousia and the completion of the eon" even before Christ's death, cf., Matt. 24:3, where Christ also describes his Parousia at length. C.-K. 406, etc., is right when he states that the Biblical use of the word does not go back to paganism but to the Old Testament. Its synonym is ἡ ἀποκάλυψις τοῦ Κυρίου Ἰησοῦ ἀπ' οὐρανοῦ (II Thess. 1:7), "the revelation," etc. In the Scriptures Christ's Parousia is not the date for a *new era* but the consummation of the *old* (Matt. 24:3, "the completion of the eon"). We speak of the Second Advent and of Christ's Return; C.-K. points out that Parousia is not *Wiederkunft* or return but the supreme apocalyptic presence, the climax of all Christian faith and certainty. There are not two Parousiai but only one: *the* Parousia. The coming of Christ in the flesh is not the consummation. "Our Lord Jesus" is probably usesd in view of Acts 1:11: "this same Jesus" and "Christ" is not added.

20) We regard γάρ as confirmatory: "Indeed, you are our glory and (our) joy!" That is why we labored as we did in Thessalonica, that is why we are so determined to return. In the question "our hope, joy, and crown of boasting" are subjective; in the answer "our glory" is objective and thus is an advance while "our joy" summarizes the subjective feature of what the Thessalonians are for Paul and for his assistants. One has joy in his heart when he has glory for his head. "Our glory" is not the same as "our crown of boasting," i. e., the acme of our boasting, in which not "crown" but "boasting" is the fundamental concept.

CHAPTER III

The Sending of Timothy

1) The Thessalonians know, of course, that Timothy had come to them and had returned to Paul. This paragraph contains nothing that is especially new to them. The idea that what Paul writes is intended to allay suspicions in the minds of the Thessalonians is untenable. The Thessalonians had no supicions. This paragraph is to be closely connected with the preceding (2:17-20); we should also note what follows (3:11-13).

Opponents in Thessalonica vilified Paul and tried to present him as a religious charlatan who looked out only for himself, of whom the believers in Thessalonica had seen the last. Paul has obtained this information from Timothy who had just returned from his mission to Thessalonica. While he was in Thessalonica, Timothy had certainly answered these vilifications. This letter from all three (Paul, Silvanus, and Timothy, 1:1) corroborates all that Paul had already told the Thessalonians, probably also says even more than Timothy had said while he was in Thessalonica. It reveals even the inmost feelings and motives that actuated the three. A few of the Thessalonian converts might give ear to the slanderers; this letter aims to make even that impossible. The kind of men the writers were when they were with the Thessalonians (1:5-2:12), that kind they still are and remain (2:17-3:13): wholly devoted to the Thessalonians.

All three intended to return to Thessalonica; when this plan was frustrated by Satan (2:18), at least Timothy was sent. **Wherefore, no longer standing it, we thought it best to be left alone in Athens and sent Timothy, our brother and God's minister**

in the gospel of Christ, to make you solid and
to encourage you in behalf of your faith that no
one let himself be fooled in these afflictions, for
you yourselves know that we are appointed for this
thing.

The previous plans had been frustrated (2:17, 18).
The writers could endure it no longer. Thus Timothy
was sent. The verb στέγω does not only mean, "to cover
up"; "no longer hiding our concern for you"; the verb
also means "to stand something," to endure. In μηκέτι
the μή is the regular negative with participles and not
οὐ. The present tense means: "no longer standing it
without doing something." It was a relief to act, to
dispatch at least Timothy.

Three persons were involved in the decision to act.
When they thus write: "We thought it best to be left
alone in Athens and to send Timothy, our brother," the
force of this "we" and of the plural μόνοι is plain. All
three agreed on the mission of Timothy to Thessalonica. Timothy was not a mere ὑπηρέτης such as Mark had
been when he was with Paul and Barnabas (Acts 13:5,
an "underling" or servant); Paul never calls him anything else than an assistant and associate like Silvanus,
Luke, and Titus. The reason for choosing Timothy was
not because of his inferior position but because Paul
and Silvanus had been driven out of Thessalonica while
Timothy had not been. Timothy would encounter
fewer difficulties. That the "we" who were left behind
were Paul and Silvanus needs no further proof. The
remark that Paul and Silvanus, both older men, could
well spare the much younger Timothy adds nothing of
value to an understanding of this passage.

A number of Bereans took Paul to Athens (Acts
17:15). Paul told them that when they got back to
Berea they should forthwith send Silvanus and Timothy to him in Athens, and Luke's aorists imply that
the two came to Athens as had been ordered. What

Paul did while he was waiting for them Acts 17:16, etc., records. Paul wanted to take both men with him as he advanced from Athens to Corinth. Acts 18:5 shows that he was able to take neither of them. Our passage shows that the anxiety about Thessalonica had grown so great that, when Silvanus and Timothy came to Athens, all agreed that Timothy should hurry back to Thessalonica. That left only Paul and Silvanus in Athens, and these two might well have gone on to Corinth together although Timothy, too, would be greatly needed for the work in Corinth. But Acts 18:5 shows that Paul did not even have Silvanus with him when he went to Corinth. We have no further information regarding Silvanus except that it was imperative for him to go back to Macedonia. To what congregation he went no one knows, it was probably to Philippi although this is only conjectural. We thus see what the writers mean by the statement that only two of them were left behind "alone" in Athens. How soon also Silvanus had to leave is unknown. Eventually Silvanus and Timothy rejoined Paul in Corinth. What is said in our passage is that somebody simply *had* to relieve the anxiety about Thessalonica, and Timothy was selected as the man for this.

2) Paul speaks of Timothy as "our brother and God's minister in the gospel of Christ," not (as Chrysostom states it) in order to honor Timothy, but rather in order to honor the Thessalonian congregation to which he was sent. Paul does not say *"your* brother" but places him into relation with himself and Silvanus as *"our* brother" because Timothy is to go to Thessalonica to ease the anxiety of Paul and Silvanus. At the same time Timothy is put into relation to God as "God's minister in the gospel of Christ" because he was to minister to the Thessalonians with the gospel of Christ: "to make you solid," etc. "God's minister" = one whom God appointed, not one whose ministration

benefits God. The benefit of the διακονία was to go entirely to the Thessalonians. The genitive in "the gospel of Christ" is similar: the gospel which is Christ's,
which he ordered preached; the genitive does not mean
that the gospel deals with Christ although this is true.
Note that God — Christ — we are involved in Timothy's mission: brotherly representation of Paul and
Silvanus in Thessalonica — service to the Thessalonians under God's appointment — gospel help under
Christ's command. The kind of men Paul and Silvanus had been when they were in Thessalonica (1:6)
Timothy was to be for the Thessalonians in this mission of his.

Εἰς τό with its two infinitives states the contemplated result which Timothy was to achieve: "to make
you solid (to fix or make steadfast) and to encourage
you in behalf of your faith," i. e., so that no opposition
should destroy this faith. Both aorists are effective.
Our versions have "to comfort" as a translation of
παρακαλέσαι. The word may mean this, or it may mean
to admonish, or to encourage, according to the context; we prefer the latter in the present connection.
The second infinitive supplements the first: the Thessalonians were to be made firm and solid by being
encouraged in regard to their faith. Ὑπέρ and περί are
often used without much distinction, here the phrase
states with what Timothy's work was to be concerned:
"concerning your faith," πίστις combining both what
the Thessalonians believed and their activity of believing, the *truth* in which they trusted and the *trust* in
that truth.

3) R. 1059 regards τὸ μηδένα σαίνεσθαι as an accusative of general reference, his *W. P.* adds that it is
epexegetical. Others construe differently. B.-D. 399, 3
says it is a negative purpose clause with ἵνα μή, "lest."
The meaning is plain: what Timothy is to achieve by
confirming and encouraging the Thessalonians in re-

gard to their faith is this: "that no one is to let himself be fooled in these tribulations." The previous infinitives are active effective aorists to indicate what Timothy is to do; now the infinitive is passive and present to indicate what, as a result of Timothy's work, the Thessalonians are not to let occur. We regard this passive as permissive: "that no one let himself be fooled," the present tense being descriptive and also matching the iterative idea in "no one," i. e., no one at any time, whether now or in the days to come. The writers do not want to lose a single sheep from the flock.

As the construction is debated, so also is the meaning of σαίνεσθαι and the phrase "in these afflictions." The text that has this infinitive is assured so that we discard the decidedly inferior variant σιαίνεσθαι, "to become disheartened," plus all other conjectural readings. The debate centers on the meaning of σαίνω which originally means to wag the tail, to fawn upon, to flatter, thus to fool with flattery. We see no reason for discarding this assured original meaning for the still more modified one "to move" (our versions), "to disturb, upset." Paul wants no one to allow himself to be wheedled away from the faith, to be fooled by persuasive talk amid these afflictions. What is wrong about the expressive figure of a dog wagging his tail and seeking to ingratiate himself? Paul is not speaking of persecutors who would come like a dog with his fangs exposed but of pagan friends of the Thessalonians who are sorry to see them cling to their faith and to suffer the consequent persecutions. These well-meaning friends are the worst kind of a temptation. We may think of Peter remonstrating with Jesus (Matt. 16:21-23).

Does "in these afflictions" refer to afflictions suffered by the Thessalonians or by Paul and his assistants? Those who think of the latter point to the following "we" forms and construct their arguments accordingly. *"These"* afflictions is simply deictic and points to all of them, no matter when they may occur. The afflictions of the Thessalonians themselves are included. It is incongruous to think that Timothy is to fortify the Thessalonians only against what Paul, Silvanus, and he had to endure. In 2:14 we see that the Thessalonians themselves suffered when their church was established, and that the original churches in Judea had suffered the same things, both of them from their own countrymen. What Paul says in the following applies to Christians generally.

Thus we have the explanatory statement: "For you yourselves know that we are appointed for this thing." Now Paul uses the comprehensive singular "this thing" which summarizes the plural "these afflictions." "This" and "these" are deictic and point to the affliction. Κείμεθα (used as the passive of τίθημι) = "we are set," i. e., appointed for this thing: God placed us in a position where we are bound to encounter affliction. The "we" suffix of the verb naturally refers to the writers and the Thessalonians. It is the first time in this epistle that the "we" is broadened in this way.

4) A second γάρ elucidates still further: **For also when we were with you we kept telling you in advance that we were** (the Greek retains the present tense of the direct discourse: "we are") **about to be afflicted** (compelled to suffer affliction) **even also as it occurred and you know.** Like Jesus, Paul and Silvanus warned their hearers in advance that affliction was impending. It came quickly as the Thessalonians well know and involved both the Thessalonians and Paul and Silvanus (2:14; Acts 17:5-10). We have no report as to what happened after Paul and Silvanus left the city, but we can be quite sure that the opposition continued to the distress of the Thessalonians.

5)   Reverting to v. 1 but now speaking of himself alone, Paul continues: **On account of this also I myself, no longer able to stand it, sent to know your faith lest in some way the tempter tempted you, and our toil got to be for nothing.**

"On account of this" refers back to the whole of v. 4, to Paul's advance warnings about coming afflictions as well as to what happened then. The warnings had not deterred the Thessalonians from believing; but it was quite another matter when the warnings came true, when afflictions actually set in; then the real test came. But Paul and Silvanus were forced to leave when the uproar occurred, and no further news had reached them save that the implacable Jews of Thessalonica followed Paul and Silvanus to Berea and tried to stir up a mob also there (Acts 17:13, 14). Judging from this act of the Thessalonian Jews, things must have gone hard with the Christians in Thessalonica. If these Jews pursued Paul to Berea, Paul could not but believe that they continued to harass the Christians in their own city. So in Athens, whither Paul had gone after being driven from Berea, having had no news at all from Thessalonica, Paul worried not a little. Although he had left Silvanus and Timothy in Berea for the sake of the Bereans he ordered them to come to him at once and then sent Timothy back to Thessalonica.

In v. 1 we learned that all three could endure the uncertainty no longer. When Paul now speaks of himself and uses the same participle: "also I myself no longer able to stand it," this individualization is entirely natural because Paul was the leader to whom Silvanus and Timothy looked and under whose direction they worked. Yet he writes κἀγώ, "also I myself," which, of course, refers to the other two (Silvanus and Timothy) but in a way that implies that, as he was the leader, even *he* could not resist the anxiety. The implication is that the other two might worry more easily, but that when also Paul himself could stand it no longer, something had to be done. So he now writes "I sent" whereas in v. 1 he stated "we sent," and the simple verb is enough. The idea that this "I sent" refers to a second sending, to some second messenger who is not named, who was dispatched by Paul alone after Timothy had gone and after Silvanus had also left, is scarcely worth noting.

The fact that Timothy was sent has already been stated, also what he was to do in Thessalonica (v. 2, 3). Now Paul adds what Timothy was to do for him personally: he was to bring him the news from Thessalonica without which Paul could stand it no longer. For we should note that Silvanus, too, left at this time, and that Timothy would thus in all probability return to Paul alone. It happened, however, that Timothy and Silvanus returned at the same time or nearly so, one can hardly decide (Acts 18:5); at least this epistle was sent by all three (1:1).

The aorist in εἰς τὸ γνῶναι = "so that I might get to know (ingressive) your faith." And γνῶναι means more than εἰδέναι; the latter would be used to indicate information only (like the οἴδατε occurring in v. 4, 5), the former implies Paul's concern in this information (see C.-K. 388 for the distinction). "Your faith" has the same force it had in v. 2.

Μή πως is construed with an indicative aorist and then with a subjunctive (the two are reversed in Gal. 2:2). This double construction is a source of worry to the grammarians. B.-D. 370, 2 supplies little; Moulton, *Einleitung* 318 regards it as an indirect question, but this is not convincing; R. 988 is most satisfactory. He says that the clause denotes purpose, and that in purely final sentences the ancient idiom used a past indicative to express a purpose that was not attained, and that this is precisely the case here and in Gal. 2:2.

In Gal. 2:2 Paul did not run in vain; in our passage the tempter did not succeed with his temptation. "It is thus unfulfilled purpose that Paul neatly expresses in accord with the Attic diction." Moulton rejects this view because the New Testament would have only two instances of this kind. But how many instances need occur in order to establish an idiom? One is enough. We may add that Paul had Timothy's report and that all three writers know that the tempter had not succeeded. The subjunctive γένηται needs no explanation. It is punctiliar (ingressive) and future in meaning, but a future dating from what Timothy would find in Thessalonica on his arrival: "lest our toil got to be (as Timothy might find) for nothing," εἰς κενόν, "for something empty" (a nut without a kernel).

"The tempter" agrees with the mention of Satan in 2:18, the greatest enemy of the gospel who is back of all opposition to its success; but the idea in temptation accords also with the σαίνεσθαι used in v. 3, the deception by which the Thessalonians were not to allow themselves to be fooled. In "our toil" we once more have the plural, the toil spent on the Thessalonians by Paul and Silvanus when they were founding the congregation, not excluding Timothy who was sent on this mission.

6) After having stated how all of them, in particular Paul, felt when they sent Timothy to Thessalonica, we now hear how they feel since Timothy has returned and has reached them in Corinth. It seems as though Silvanus had returned just a little before Timothy, but one cannot be sure (Acts 18:5).

But Timothy, having just come to us from you and having brought us good news of your faith and love, also that you always have good remembrance of us, longing to see us just as also we you, because

**of this we were comforted, brethren, over you in all
our distress and affliction by means of your faith,
seeing that now we live if you on your part keep
standing fast in the Lord.**

Instead of merely saying that Timothy has just
returned, Paul says that he has just come "to us from
you," as if to say that the bond which was broken by
the forced departure has now been knit again. Εὐαγγε-
λίζομαι is used in its ordinary sense of bringing good
news, here with the accusative and also with ὅτι. Paul
gives a condensed but rather complete report of the
news brought by Timothy: 1) about the faith and love
of the Thessalonians (see 1:3), i. e., about their spiritual state; 2) about their feeling for Paul and Silvanus, that this was as deep as ever: "also that you
always have good remembrance of us (the past), longing to see us" (in the future). "Remembrance" is a
vox media; one may have a bad remembrance of someone, hence "good" is added. The longing to see each
other was strong on both sides: you us as also we you.
The two points: the Thessalonian faith and love and
their feeling for Paul and his assistants really belong
together; lack in either would show in the other. To
say that Paul was most concerned about the latter is
incorrect, for Paul lists "your faith and love" first.

7) Διὰ τοῦτο, "for this reason or cause," resumes
all that Timothy reports. In good Greek fashion Paul
uses a phrase because the main verb is passive, the
sense is: all this comforted us. The address, "brethren," is expressive of the deep, fraternal feeling thus
strengthened. Παρεκλήθημεν here means, "we were comforted." The feeling of anxiety and concern that we
could not stand indefinitely had disappeared. The two
ἐπί phrases are alike in force, both mean "over"; yet
the one phrase tops the other: "over all our distress
and affliction" is covered by "over you." One article

combines "the distress and affliction," the two express one idea: ἀνάγκη, "necessity" that forces itself upon one, θλῖψις, "pressure" that crushes.

This does not refer to Paul's past worries about the Thessalonians, which were shared by Silvanus and Timothy, for these had now disappeared; these are the other troubles of Paul, and he calls them "great." They are not due to finances as some suppose (while he was in Corinth Paul had found employment with Aquila), nor to opposition from the Corinthian Jews (this came later, Acts 18:5-17), but to the situation in Galatia (Paul had just recently received a delegation from Galatia and had written his epistle to the Galatians) and to other exigencies and difficulties in his work, which are not further indicated here (II Cor. 11:28). Moreover, since he had come to Corinth he had been alone, even without the comfort of his companions. The good news from Thessalonica refreshed him like a cool drink does a weary man. He says *"our* distress," etc., but we know that Paul bore the brunt of it.

Paul does not often give us a glimpse into what oppressed him in his labors. We have such a glimpse here. When one sits in a comfortable study and reads this short phrase he may wonder at the fervor with which the apostle writes about the comfort the Thessalonian firmness and loyalty afforded him; if one could sit for a while in Aquila's shop where these lines were written he would rather wonder how Paul could write with so much restraint and would catch something of the mighty spirit throbbing in Paul's great heart.

"We were comforted . . . through (by means of) your faith" singles out the main point: the faith of the Thessalonians. For their faith produced their love and also their loyalty and their desire to see him and his helpers again. Their steadfast faith was Paul's greatest joy, faith that was unshaken by opposition, so young as yet and nevertheless so true. Διὰ τοῦτο (accusative) at the head and διὰ τῆς ὑμῶν πίστεως (genitive) at the end do not conflict, the one is the cause, the other the means, for the causal idea of the former is very slight, its main force is resumptive. But we see that "your faith" is mentioned twice; this was *the* feature that cheered Paul and his assistants.

8) We regard ὅτι as *consecutivum* and not as causal, not, "for" or "because" but "seeing that." The fact that the writers "now live" is not the cause which produced their comfort but the thing that followed the comfort and is the evidence for the value of the comfort. You can see, Paul says, how we are comforted and what this comfort means by observing that "we now live," etc. The figure is a strong one: before the good news came, there was deadness. We might picture it as a leaden weight, the heart seemed to have no life. Now, in consequence of the good news, there is once more life with all that this means to the writers in their arduous work. The implication is that, if the faith of the Thessalonians had failed, if the church had broken up, it would have been a deathblow to the writers. One must see the importance of the church at Thessalonica as Paul sketches the effect of its faithfulness for all Macedonia and Achaia in 1:7-10 (see the exposition). Unfaithfulness would have had an equal opposite effect.

Paul says: "we now live if you on your part keep standing fast in the Lord." Ἐάν looks to the future. Hence ζῶμεν also is durative: "we continue to live," i. e., our living thus depends on your continuous standing fast; ὑμεῖς is emphatic. The verb "stand" is like the one used in Eph. 6:13, 14, but we now have a later form στήκω, which is formed from ἕστηκα, the perfect of ἵστημι. To stand "in the Lord" means "in connection with him" by unshaken faith. The Koine admits the use of the indicative after ἐάν (R. 1010; Moulton, *Einleitung*

263) ; in modern Greek ἄν is used with either indicative
or subjunctive.

9)   The firm stand of the Thessalonians brought
a great benefit to the Thessalonians themselves, but
its influence went beyond them and became of the
greatest benefit to Paul and his assistants and to
their work in Macedonia and Achaia.   Paul, therefore, continues with a mention of the thanks which
he and his assistants owe to God for what the firm
stand of the Thessalonians has done for them.

**For what thanks are we able to give God in due
return concerning you in all the joy wherewith we
rejoice because of you before our God, the while
asking by night and day exceedingly that we may
see your face and may complete the backward things
of your faith?**

The force of the rhetorical question lies in the
thought that the writers are unable to return adequate
thanks to God for the joy God has given them in the
Thessalonians.   ʼΑντί in the verb = in return; ἀπό
refers to what is due "from" us: hence "to give in due
return."   Paul views everything as coming from God.
His first reaction is: "Thank God!"   But how can any
thanks be commensurate with the gift of joy he and
his assistants have received?

Enter into Paul's emotion.   What would have been
his distress of soul if, in addition to all the other loads
resting upon his heart, there had come the report that
the Thessalonian church had gone to pieces!   It would
have stunned his weary heart and left him as one dead.
Now there comes the report that the young Thessalonian church has not only survived but is standing firm.
What an emotional reversal for Paul's heart, which
causes him to reach the very heights of joy!   Oh, that
he could thank God as he ought!   The intensity of feeling is augmented by this reversal from a great depth
of depression to the loftiest height of jubilation.

'Eπί is used as it was in v. 7: "on (or upon or over)
all the joy with which we rejoice because of you before (or in the presence of) our God." Note the
cognate dative which emphasizes the idea of joy: "the
joy with which we rejoice." So also "concerning you"
and "because of you" double this; and a third time:
returning thanks "to God" and rejoicing "before our
God." As though standing in God's presence, Paul and
his helpers live and work; from God they receive this
as they do every other blessing; their hearts ever automatically turn to God.

10) The thanks expressed in 1:2 and 2:13 were
prompted by the auspicious beginning made in Thessalonica; the thanks voiced in 3:9 are due to what has
occurred in Thessalonica since Paul and Silvanus left
there. Paul continues with a present participle, which
means that what he now asks of God is subsidiary to
his efforts to thank God as he should and also that his
asking and his thanking are simultaneous, thanks and
petitions are mingled. The participle is temporal; v.
9 is a unit so that the nominative participle modifies
the subject and thus the entire unit: "the while asking," etc. "By night and day" has the same force as in
2:9 (time within which); it is our "day and night."
The Greek idiom places night first as we also do at
times. The fervor of Paul's feeling is made evident by
the strong complex adverb "exceedingly," (literally,
"more than out of abundance"). The joy God has
granted causes the new petitioning to go beyond all
the bounds that would otherwise apply. Answered
petitions produce still more earnest petitions.

Eἰs τό = ἵνα (non-final), B.-D. 402, 2, and states the
contents of the petitions (compare 2:12): "the object
of verbs of command or entreaty giving the content of
the verb" (R. 1072) in place of an unmodified infinitive
or of ἵνα or ὅπωs. What the writers ask of God is that
they may again see the face of the Thessalonians and

may again work among them in order to bring to completion the things in which the Thessalonians are behind in their faith.

'Ιδεῖν and καταρτίσαι are to be construed with the one article τό and thus form a unit: the seeing of the Thessalonians is desired not merely for the pleasure this affords but for the opportunity to supply any lack in the faith of the Thessalonians. This expression does not suggest the idea that Timothy has had to report some adverse things about the Thessalonians, or that Paul injects a gentle reminder to the effect that they must not think that, because Paul is so overjoyed concerning them, they have already reached the highest Christian perfection of faith. Such a suggestion might cause them to fall into dangerous pride. We must remember that Paul and Silvanus had worked approximately four weeks in Thessalonica. Even if all the members had had the benefit of all the work of these four weeks, the time was too short to give them all the instruction they needed and themselves knew that they needed. They longed to have the missionaries return for a much longer stay just as the missionaries longed to make this stay (v. 6).

The work that had been done in Thessalonica was incomplete. It is a wonder that so much thorough work had been accomplished with such permanent results. The last man to be satisfied to leave any lack (ὑστερήματα, "shortcomings") was Paul, and Silvanus and Timothy were like him in this respect. They burned with desire to make everything complete (καταρτίσαι, from which we have "artisan"), like good, skilled artisans to finish their task shipshape. Faith is the one thing mentioned (both in the objective and the subjective sense) just as in v. 5 and 7, the basis and ground of all that constitutes Christianity. This epistle itself is an effort to add at least a few additional incentives to the faith of the Thessalonians.

The Concluding Prayerful Wishes

11) The two wishes are presented in this form because they are being written to the Thessalonians; they are in reality the prayers which Paul, according to v. 10, addresses to God. So also this brief paragraph amplifies v. 10 and brings the first part of the epistle to its close. **Now may he, our God and Father and our Lord Jesus, direct our way unto you!** i. e., may he so guide the course of our missionary work that we may get to you Thessalonians to do the further work we have indicated. Like the two verbs used in v. 12, κατευθύναι is the third person singular aorist optative of wish (not the aorist infinitive or the aorist middle imperative, R. 940). The verb means to make a way straight toward a goal. Some, like our versions, consider αὐτός reflexive: "our God and Father himself." They support their view by the argument that, if the writers alone attempted to direct their way, Satan might cut them off as he had done hitherto (2:18). This argument overlooks several points, for hitherto the writers had never tried to direct their own way, nor had Satan for that reason been able to cut them off (see 2:18). Αὐτός is intensive: "*he*, our God and Father and our Lord Jesus," and is thus followed by the singular verb κατευθύναι, a plural would not be proper after αὐτός.

This means that αὐτός refers to the Father and to Jesus as one just as the singular verb does. The fact that the verb does this is generally recognized, but not so the fact that αὐτός also does this and really makes the use of the singular verb possible. Moreover, why should "himself" be added to "our God and Father" and not to "our Lord Jesus"? Why not αὐτοί so as to include both our Father and Jesus "themselves" with a plural verb? To treat the two divine persons as one as Paul does here is striking, but it offers no difficulty to those who recognize the deity of both, their unity of will and work. Paul's form of statement has precipitated a dogmatical debate with a sharp pro and con regarding the relation of the two persons to each other. The whole New Testament and even the Old Testament settle this question, which is more than enough. Second Thessalonians 2:16 does exactly what our passage does, but it places Jesus first and the Father second; add I Thess. 5:25, which has God alone.

Even this causes discussion as to whether "our" belongs to both "God" and "father" or only to the latter. One article combines the nouns, and "our" belongs to the combination. But ὁ Κύριος ἡμῶν Ἰησοῦς is "our Lord, Jesus," and "Jesus" is an apposition to "our Lord." The two "our" are confessions of faith even as the divine names are soteriological, indicative of the true knowledge of faith.

This wish and prayer was not fulfilled except that the writers did, indeed, revisit Thessalonica, but not for a period of intensive work such as v. 10 evidently contemplates. The Father and the Lord manage the church; they directed Paul and his workers: four weeks in Thessalonica, eighteen months in Corinth. The results were good. The wishes and prayers of Paul were uttered in submission to the divine will. Let us learn from him also in regard to our missionary work.

12) **And you may the Lord increase and make to abound with the love toward one another and toward all just as also we toward you so that he may stablish your hearts as blameless in holiness before our God and Father in connection with the Parousia of our Lord Jesus together with all his saints!**

The wish expressed in v. 11 pertains to the writers, to having their way directed to Thessalonica; the added wish pertains to the Thessalonians, and hence ὑμᾶς is placed emphatically forward. When Paul now writes only ὁ Κύριος, this should be understood in the same sense as it was in v. 11 where both divine persons are named; the fact that he has both persons in mind we see from v. 13 where both are again mentioned. "The Lord" thus means: this same person, "our Lord Jesus" who ever works as one with "our God and Father."

The prayerful wish for the writers themselves is expressed by only one verb and in a very brief form; the wish for the readers is expressed more intensively by two verbs and in a longer and thus a weightier form. "May increase and may make you abound" (both aorist optatives of wish) convey one idea. The verbs are synonyms; either one alone might be sufficient, but the doubling makes the wish stronger: πλεο-νάζω (here transitive), "to make more and more," περ-ισσεύω (also transitive), "to make abound," both are construed with the dative of the thing: "with the love toward one another and toward all (men)."

This is the same intelligent and purposeful love mentioned already in 1:3 and 3:6, but it is now named with its personal objects. Such love the Thessalonians already have; it is to increase in richest abundance, there is to be more and more of it, so much that it abounds and excels. This dative is to be construed with both verbs and not only with the second. "That you may increase" does not refer to an increase in numbers.

The question is asked as to why love and not faith is made prominent. The conclusion that love is more essential than faith is refuted by 1:3 and likewise by 3:2, 5, where faith alone is mentioned and by all that we know about the relation between these two. This love can increase and abound only as faith grows in power. Paul knows love only as the fruit of faith. He speaks of the great increase of love because it is the tangible evidence of faith and as such reacts so strongly, not only between the members themselves,

but even between them and other men; hence the two
εἰς phrases: "toward one another (in your own midst)
and toward all men," no matter who they are. The
fact that this includes also the opponents and persecutors goes without saying (Matt. 5:44-47). This
ἀγάπη will see the evil in men and will seek to overcome
and to free them from this evil. Love is the power
to destroy hate and persecution. It wins great victor-
ies even in the midst of Christ's enemies. Yet the
writers do not demand this love of the Thessalonians as
though they themselves are able to produce it; they
ask the Lord to bestow it even as he is the fount of this
love. Without him and the power of his love we are
able to do nothing.

"Just as also we toward you" is without a verb,
which fact causes a debate among the commentators
as to what verb is to be supplied. Shall we say: "just
as also we increase and abound with this love toward
you" and change the transitive verbs into intransitives
or: "just as also we have love for you," and supply a
verb *ad sensum?* Both have the same sense. We prefer the latter because the writers make the love they
have for the Thessalonians the model for the Thessalonians and scarcely the increasing abundance of their
love.

But why make themselves the model, why not Christ
and his supreme love, which is the model for us all:
"just as the Lord (loves) you"? Because the Lord is
here presented as the source of our love, and because
the Thessalonians have seen the love of Paul, Silvanus,
and Timothy, actual examples of the love produced by
the Lord in the hearts of his true followers. If the
Lord filled these three with such love, the Thessalonians will see that the Lord can do this also for them.
As the Thessalonians became imitators of these three
in the way in which they endured affliction (1:6), imi-

tators also of the first churches (2:14), so they will
want to imitate also the love of the writers since they
themselves had experienced the power and the sweetness of the love of these writers from the very first
day they began their work in Thessalonica.

13) Eἰς τό might denote purpose, but contemplated
result seems more in line with the thought of a prayerful wish: "so that he may stablish your hearts as
blameless in holiness," etc., make firm and solid (as
in v. 2). Paul writes "your hearts" and not merely
"you" because holiness pertains to the heart. The
adjective "blameless" is predicative, and "blameless
in holiness before our God and Father in connection
with the Parousia," etc., belong together. "Holiness"
is the quality of being holy, and when it is used with
reference to us, it, like the adjective "holy" or ἅγιος,
implies our separation from sin and our devotion to
God.

The Thessalonians were to be blameless or unblamable in holiness "in the presence of God in connection
with (or at) the Parousia of our Lord Jesus," i. e.,
before God's judgment bar at the time of Christ's arrival and presence to execute the judgment of the last
day (compare 2:19 on the Parousia). In Matt. 25:34-
40 Jesus has described how we are to stand blameless
in holiness at that day. This is not the total sanctification of perfectionism even as ἅγιοι, "saints," the common New Testament term for true Christians (see the
last phrase), never signifies persons who no longer sin.
Justified believers do live holy lives, and any stains
of sin they may acquire are removed daily by Christ's
blood. Thus they will stand "as blameless in holiness"
at the last day.

Compare the ἔμπροσθεν in 1:3 (God) and in 2:19
(Christ) and now again God; and note how God and
Christ are united in v. 11. The two are equal, yet three

times Paul writes "our Lord Jesus," the name "Jesus" referring to his human nature, Acts 1:11: "this same Jesus" who, as he went into heaven, shall so come again.

The debate centers on the last phrase: μετὰ πάντων τῶν ἁγίων αὐτοῦ. Does this mean "together with all his saints" in the sense of with his "holy ones," the angels, or with his "holy ones," both the saints and the angels? Does the phrase modify the main statement "establish you blameless in holiness . . . with all his saints," or the minor phrases: "in connection with his Parousia with all his saints"? As far as ἅγιοι is concerned, this is the standard New Testament word for "saints," and it does not once occur in the New Testament as the word for "angels" unless it would have that meaning in this passage. This fact is rather decisive. Add the fact that ἐν ἁγιωσύνη and μετὰ ἁγίων are undoubtedly to correspond: "in holiness" — "together with holy ones." We thus cannot escape the meaning: "*your* hearts blameless in holiness (before our God and Father at the Parousia of our Lord) together with *all* his saints," i. e., you holy ones together with all the other holy ones, you being in their great body.

We are told that Paul here alludes to Zech. 14:5 which the LXX render: καὶ ἥξει Κύριος ὁ Θεός μου καὶ πάντες οἱ ἅγιοι μετ᾽ αὐτοῦ. The Hebrew is: "And the Lord, my God, shall come, and all the saints with thee." We doubt that this is an allusion, the wording is quite different; the claim that Zech. 14:5 decides for the meaning angels in this passage is unwarranted. Jude 14 has: ἐν ἁγίαις μυριάσιν αὐτοῦ, "amid holy myriads," "holy ten thousands." To point out the fact that the LXX make ὅσιοι = saints and ἅγιοι = angels is beside the mark. In the first place, the latter is not true; when angels are referred to, ἄγγελοι is the regular term employed. The remarkable fact is that, while ὅσιοι is the standard term for *die Frommen* in the Old Testament, this word is rarely found in the New Testament where ἅγιοι is the standard designation for the godly. The reason that the New Testament could not follow the LXX in using ὅσιοι is sketched in C.-K. 53 and 824. Those who think our passage refers to angels find no support in the New Testament.

What influences some is the idea that Paul conceives all the Lord's ἅγιοι as *coming* with him at his Parousia. It is this conception that leads some to believe that these ἅγιοι consist of both angels and saints. We are thus referred to all the passages which describe Christ's coming for judgment with all his holy angels and told that their presence enhances his glory. Those who think of the saints also think of their coming out of heaven with the Lord and add that already here Paul anticipates and hints at what he says about the departed in 4:13, etc. But even when this μετά phrase is construed with the preceding ἐν phrase, Paul says nothing about a coming of either saints or angels in company with Christ; the Parousia is the Lord's *presence* and not his *coming* out of heaven.

This last phrase should, however, be separated by a comma, for its purpose appears to be, not to connect the Lord with these saints, but to connect the Thessalonians as blameless in their sainthood (holiness) with all the Lord's saints at his final presence. This is the great result the writers pray for, that on the last great day the Thessalonians may be found together with all the Lord's saints as belonging in their blessed company (μετά). How fitting and satisfactory this thought is here at the close of the first part of the letter we need hardly say. Important texts add "amen" as the seal of verity and assurance, which our versions omit.

CHAPTER IV

The Hortatory and Instructive Section
of the Epistle

Living a Clean and Respectable Life

1) The incision which marks a new section of the epistle after the prayerful wishes of 3:12, 13 is indicated by λοιπόν; we now have hortation and instruction which is based on the report Timothy brought back from Thessalonica. While the writers thank God for what had been accomplished (1:2, etc., plus other statements in the first three chapters) they are also intent on removing the moral faults and weaknesses that remain and on correcting wrong ideas that have begun to spread. We should remember that Paul and Silvanus had labored only about four weeks when they were founding the church. Then came Timothy's visit (3:1, etc.) which was also all too brief. Great things had, indeed, been accomplished, yet much remained to be added. The main things are now taken up.

As for the rest then, brethren, we request and admonish you in the Lord Jesus that, as you received from us how it is necessary for you to walk and to be pleasing to God as also you are walking, that you abound more and more.

Λοιπόν is the adverbial accusative and points to all that remains to be said. Thus the affectionate "brethren" is in place; this is matched by the two fraternal verbs, "we request and admonish you in the Lord," two verbs instead of just one in order to make a deeper impression. Paul uses the second verb παρακαλῶ, "to admonish," often; when he now adds ἐρωτῶ, *bitten*, "to ask or request," the idea of fraternal appeal is made prominent in the admonition. The writers speak as the dearest friends of the Thessalonians who have already shown their deepest love and affection (compare 2:7, 8) and have already heretofore admonished them as a father his own children (compare 2:11, 12).

The request and the admonition are made ἐν Κυρίῳ Ἰησοῦ, "in connection with the Lord Jesus." Both the writers and the readers acknowledge this Lord who has saved and made them his own and has sent out these apostles (1:5). His authority as well as his grace are back of this fraternal request and admonition. No statement that is made in the following comes only from men.

Nor is the present admonition new and strange; the Thessalonians have already received it from the writers, they have been told before how they must walk and be pleasing to God. Τό before the indirect question makes a noun of it; it is the object of "you received," and this is done in the fashion of the classics (R. 1046): "as to how it is necessary," etc. The one question for all followers of the Lord Jesus is: "How must we walk and please God?" All the ministers of the Lord must help the believers to answer this question even in detail. This the writers did for the Thessalonians in the very beginning, and they now repeat their instruction. Δεῖ may denote any type of necessity, it is like our "must"; here moral and spiritual necessity is referred to.

Paul coordinates: "that you walk and be pleasing to God," and stresses both verbs as though a question might be asked about each one: "How shall we walk? How shall we be pleasing to God?" Yet by combining them the two become one: "How shall all that we do in our daily life and walk be pleasing to God?" The thought is not only that we constantly test ourselves as to whether we are pleasing to God but in addition that we walk as constantly being under God's eyes.

The force of "pleasing to God" is sometimes overlooked. Paul has used this expression in 2:4 regarding himself and Silvanus and the way in which they speak God's gospel. To be pleasing to God appeals to the *gospel* motive for believers, their love for God in the Lord Jesus, and not to the motive of *law,* the fear of punishment. The verb includes the work of the Spirit who moves our hearts to please God by sincere obedience to God's will. The appeal is directed wholly to voluntary activity. Moreover, to be pleasing to *God* adds also the thought that he is above us; to please ourselves in sin is to turn from God, and this involves a serious calamity; the heathen do not even know God (v. 5), we do.

To the first καθώς clause a second is added: "as also you are walking." This excludes the implication that the Thessalonians have not as yet been walking as they ought to walk. It brings out the force of the aorist παρελάβετε: "you did receive effectively" what we taught you Thessalonians, you are, indeed, walking in a manner that pleases God. In this second clause the one verb is sufficient, there is no need to add "and are pleasing to God." For all that had been attained in the Thessalonians the writers thank God as they have already stated. Their admonition is: "that you may abound more and more," μᾶλλον meaning "more and more" or "still more." Non-final ἵνα is repeated because of what intervenes; it states the contents of the request and the admonition.

The Thessalonians already abound. When one compares how they once walked and how they now walk, the change is great indeed, thank God! Yet there is room for still more of this blessed abundance of holiness of life. The Thessalonians are to please God in a still higher degree. Not only is perfection still unattained, there are faults that are of a kind that ought to disappear completely. The Thessalonians have for the greater part come out of rank paganism and have not at once shaken off all pagan ideas and practices. They have succeeded in varying degrees, but some of them still have plain ὑστερήματα, things in which they are behind, and all of them should continue their blessed advance.

The opening statement of the admonition is psychologically perfect. It acknowledges all that the Thessalonians have hitherto achieved and makes this the ground for achieving still more. It in no wise discourages the Thessalonians, it encourages them in the strongest manner. Paul still deals with them as a nurse does with her own children (2:7), as a father with his own children (2:8). He directs his appeal to the highest motives and states it in the most effective way. There is no call, as far as the Thessalonians are concerned, to smite their sins with full apostolic authority, the Thessalonians are not rebellious but willing to heed and follow. Paul stimulates their willingness most strongly. We may well learn from him.

2) Explanatory γάρ adds "we gave to you" to the preceding "you received from us": **For you know what orders we gave to you through the Lord Jesus.** The admonitions now given are repetitions of the orders already given and received. The point that the orders are not new is thus emphasized. Those orders still stand. The Thessalonians know them, have begun to act on them, and have done well as far as they have gone; they are to go on still farther under these orders, to carry them out still more completely. While "we gave" is the other side of "you received," the whole thought is amplified. The Thessalonians "know," the orders need not be given anew, they have not been forgotten, and they, of course, still stand.

In place of the indirect question used in v. 1, "how it is necessary that you walk," etc., we now have "what orders," and this, too, is an indirect question. But these are really "orders," παραγγελίαι, the word to designate military commands passed along from the commander through his captains to the troops. The word thus points to divine authority. This does not turn from gospel to law, for Jesus himself speaks of his ἐντολαί, (John 15:10, 12, 17), the sum of which is that we love him and thus obey and also that we love each other (John 13:34; 15:12), all of which belongs to the gospel. The motive is ever gospel love.

The following states what orders Paul has especially in mind. They are and remain "orders" or "commands," for they come from "the Lord Jesus" who is our divine Lord, whom we are pledged to obey most fully because we love him as our Savior-Lord. Paul has used "the Lord Jesus" repeatedly; he has at times combined it with "our God and Father." But Paul seems to reverse things here: instead of saying that the Lord Jesus gave the orders through us he says we gave them through him. This does not, of course, mean that Paul, etc., issued the orders by their authority and conveyed them through the Lord as their subordinate agent.

Yet "through the Lord Jesus" puzzles the commentators who offer a number of inadequate explanations. The one that διά really = ἐν (v. 1, for instance) is linguistically untenable. Διά is used by Jesus himself in John 14:6; we meet it elsewhere even with reference to God, and it always means "through." Here the matter is quite simple: Paul means that we gave the orders, not "through our own selves" (δι' ἑαυτῶν), but wholly and altogether "through the Lord Jesus." For although *we* gave you the orders, and you saw and heard only us, they were really given to you "through the Lord."

We need not adopt the view of B.-D. 223, 2, who remark that the originator is at times spoken of as the mediator, for Paul and his helpers always transmitted all orders "through the Lord," i. e., let all orders come to their hearers through this divine channel, the Lord alone. That this is true because these orders originate with the Lord alone is not said by διά; it does not need to be. From whom else could they originate? In v. 1 of this very chapter and elsewhere Paul gives the orders "through the Lord Jesus," for he says: "we admonish you in connection with the Lord Jesus." He keeps this connection, and that is transmitting the orders "through the Lord."

3) Γάρ specifies. **For this is God's will, your sanctification, that you hold yourselves away from the fornication, that each of you know to acquire his own vessel in sanctification and honor, not in passion of lust like also the pagans who do not know God; etc.**

We decline to render: "For God's will is this, your sanctification," etc. Nothing is gained by this reversal, this making the subject the predicate, and the predicate the subject. Paul has spoken of what the Thessalonians have received and what makes them pleasing to God, of what commandments the Thessalonians know Paul, etc., have given them through the Lord. He now specifies (γάρ): "This is God's will," etc., τοῦτο points to what he says at length. The absence of the article marks the predicate as such: θέλημα τοῦ Θεοῦ, "God's will," the thing God wants. To say that what follows is "God's will" matches what has just been said about the Thessalonians' "pleasing God," in order to please him they must know and do his will. This correspondence in expression is all that is said here; nothing is to be inserted.

The apposition to the deictic τοῦτο is "your sanctification" plus the epexegetical infinitives. The word employed is not ἁγιωσύνη (3:13), the quality of "holiness," but ἁγιασμός, "sanctification," not, however, the

middle sense, that the Thessalonians sanctify themselves, but the passive sense: the condition brought
about when the Thessalonians are sanctified and set
apart by God (C.-K. 59) ; ὑμῶν is thus not the subjective
but the possessive genitive.

This word appears only in Biblical Greek.   There
is no stress on *"your* sanctification" as though this
were opposed to some pagan consecration to some god
who requires less than the true God does.   Paganism
offered nothing comparable to Christian sanctification.
The word is to be understood in the narrow sense:
sanctification of life and conduct.   It is not like ἅγιοι,
"saints," which is understood in the wider sense and
therefore includes also justification.   While ἁγιασμός is
in direct apposition to the subject τοῦτο, it is also in
apposition to the predicate θέλημα τοῦ Θεοῦ: this thing
that God wills is the condition of the Thessalonians
in which they are set wholly apart for God and are
separated in life and conduct from the world which is
not thus set apart and does not even know God.

ʽΑγιασμός covers this entire condition.   The epexegetical infinitives point out only two sides of the whole:
sexual purity and honesty in business, the opposites of
two common, ugly vices of paganism.   First: "that
you hold yourselves away from the fornication, that
each of you know to acquire his own vessel in sanctification and honor, not in passion of lust like also the
pagans who do not know God."   All of this belongs together.   The first infinitive is properly a durative present: "ever to stay aloof (to abstain) from the fornication."   Πορνεία is used in the widest sense to indicate
anything that can be called "fornication," hence we
have the Greek article, some texts offer "from all fornication."

Wohlenberg supplies a survey of the Greek terms
pertinent in this connection: πόρνη = *die Kaeufliche,
Feile,* the purchasable one (feminine), the whore in

this sense; πορνεύειν, the filthy business of making a living by prostitution; μοιχός, an adulterer, frequently one who has intercourse with a person who is married to another or with the daughter of an honorable family; ἑταῖραι, mistresses, intercourse with whom was allowed to unmarried young men as long as the daughters were not daughters of families that had full citizenship rights. To this list we may add the prostitutes who were kept at pagan temples for the men who came to worship the god or the goddess of the temple. "The fornication" covers all these types of whoredom.

4) The second infinitive is positive, is an epexegesis of the preceding negative infinitive: "that each of you know to acquire," etc.; εἰδέναι is a second perfect form used as a present tense, its object, κτᾶσθαι, is also present. Both tenses are iterative as also the subject "each one of you" indicates. Every man is to have his own wife, every woman her own husband as Paul says in so many words in I Cor. 7:2. Κτᾶσθαι means "to acquire" and not, as our versions translate it, "to possess." Nor is this acquisition sufficient: "acquire in sanctification and honor, not in passion of lust." Paul even adds: "like also the pagans (Gentiles) who do not know God." This last "know" (εἰδότα) explains the first "know" (εἰδέναι). It is God's will that every Christian is to know how to act in the matter of sex so as to be pleasing to God (v. 1). He is to know that God instituted marriage, that each man is to have his own wife, each woman her own husband (monogamy), that every type of fornication is excluded as being contrary to God's will. This is what pagans do not know, they do not even know God and thus run wild in all manner of sexual excess.

Εἰδέναι is not γινώσκω, "to know sexually," it is never used in this sense; the object is also an infinitive. "His own vessel" does not mean "his own body" or the male organ because neither can be acquired. It is plain that

the infinitive does not mean "to possess" save only as
this is implied in the perfect: "having acquired and
thus now possessing." The expression κτᾶσθαι γυναῖκα
occurs in Xenophon and elsewhere in the sense of acquiring a wife; I Pet. 3:7 uses σκεῦος in the sense of
wife. The present tense "to acquire" has already been
explained as a present iterative which matches "each
one of you" and thus is not durative. Paul speaks of
acquiring a wife, i. e., entering upon marriage, and
not of the conduct of marriage; when it is entered into
in the right way, marriage will be conducted in the
right way.

The objection that Paul's words would then apply
only to unmarried men, and that some of these might
not even need marriage, is pointless; for Paul is opposing all fornication by urging a legitimate monog-
amic marriage that is entered upon in the true Christian manner. His readers understand perfectly that
if marriage is purified at its inception, this purity is
not to be lost later on. Is it necessary that he add at
length what those should do who had married as pagans before their conversion? By writing τὸ ἑαυτοῦ
σκεῦος the reflexive pronoun is made emphatic, which
also indicates that "vessel" refers to the wife.

The main stress rests on the modifiers which are
thus also expanded, the positive being followed by an
even longer negative. "In sanctification and honor" =
in a condition of having been set apart for God so as to
please him (the same word that was used before) and
in a way that is accounted honorable or worthy of
honor among men. The one is wrought by God, the
other is bestowed by men, especially by Christians.

Von Hofmann's peculiar spiritualization misunderstands Paul's simple thought: by acquiring a wife
the Christian husband sanctifies the wife and the order
of nature created by God and honors the vessel that he
acquires. To acquire a wife "in sanctification" is to

go about the whole matter as a Christian should, who knows God's will and would in no way displease him. To do this "in honor" is to do it so that men see that it is done honorably, in a clean, commendable way, without the least cause for scandal.

Equally strange is the idea that Paul intends to oppose family interference in Christian marriages, betrothals in extreme youth, which also adds that later even Christian congregations felt that they must arrange the marriages. Is this the reason that Paul says, "That each one know to acquire his own vessel"? He does not intend to imply that each man is to be free to choose his own wife without family or other interference. This is not his point, in fact, parental advice and consent are most valuable to this day. The point is that Christians must go about the whole matter "in sanctification and in honor."

5) Therefore also "not in passion of lust as also the pagans who do not know God" and let passion alone guide them. Paul is not dependent on the Stoics for his use of πάθος. This was wider in force than ἐπιθυμία and included a variety of passions, among which ἐπιθυμία was only one. To Paul πάθος means sexual passion in the passive sense, an ungovernable desire like a fire that starts by itself; while ἐπιθυμία is "desire," active; it is not always used in the evil sense, it is like a fire that one encourages and feeds. Hence the combination: "in passion of lust," carried away by passion to which "desire" (here in the evil sense of "lust") eagerly consents.

The genitive is qualitative so that Luther translates *Lustseuche,* and the revised German Bible, *Brunst der Lust.* The doubling of terms matches the two positive terms. The objection that not all pagan marriages were prompted by lustful passion overlooks the fact that Paul knew at firsthand what paganism exhibited regarding marriage, it may be seen today even among our American pagans and pagan moralists. In their case passion governs, and when this ceases, the marriage is wrecked, or the passion finds another woman (or man).

When Paul points to the ἔθνη who do not know God, this is strong motivation, for the Thessalonians have left paganism and do, indeed, know God and his "orders" (v. 2) and how they should walk and be pleasing to God. No verb form is needed whether finite or infinitive. As "saints" who have experienced God's ἁγιασμός the Thessalonians are separated unto God, are his peculiar people (I Pet. 2:9) who do not run with the pagans (I Pet. 4:4) but ever follow God's guidance.

6) The writers continue: **that (he) do not go too far and overreach his brother in the matter of business because the Lord is an avenger in all these things even as also we told you in advance and testified.**

We side with the majority of the commentators who contend that in this verse Paul admonishes to honest and unselfish business dealing and does not continue the admonition against sexual sins. The commentators generally note that the infinitives are introduced by τό, but some do not note that this τό points to an appositional construction, and that this appositional connection is with ὁ ἁγιασμὸς ὑμῶν and is thus a second appositional specification of "your sanctification" and "God's will"; the first is abstaining from all fornication; the second, abstaining from all greed in business dealing. To mark this new sin the subject of the infinitives is not ὑμᾶς which is the subject of ἀπέχεσθαι but, as "*his* brother" indicates, a singular, either "he" understood or ἕκαστον ὑμῶν supplied from v. 4. It is scarcely necessary to remark that the two outstanding vices of paganism were sexual and commercial vileness and greed. It has been well said that Thessalonica was a great trade center which was busy with all sorts of mercantile dealings. The fact that Paul speaks of more than one kind of sin is indicated by the plural phrase περὶ πάντων τούτων, "concerning *all* these things."

Robertson, *W. P.*, is among those who find an admonition against the sin of adultery in this verse and thus construes the infinitives with τό as being final, probably meaning final to the εἰδέναι clause: "that each one of you know to acquire his own vessel . . . in order not to go too far and overreach," etc. But this purpose clause would not cover the purpose to be covered if Paul has purpose in mind. Is each one to marry only in order not to seduce a brother's wife? Has Paul not said much more already, namely that the Thessalonians are "to hold themselves away from all fornication"? Does that not include adultery with a brother's wife? Is there any reason for mentioning adultery separately at the end, and this only in a purpose clause? The real danger was the seduction of girls and not of wives. And why mention "his brother" when adultery would violate *the wife* and cause *her* to disrupt her marriage? Others who find a reference to adultery in this passage make the infinitives parallel to εἰδέναι and, like this infinitive, appositional to ἀπέχεσ-θαι; but this does not explain τό nor remove the other incongruities.

We do not regard ὑπερβαίνειν as transitive nor "his brother" as the object of the two infinitives instead of just the one. There is no need for a modified meaning, for ὑπέρ in the verb means "beyond," thus the sense is: "to go too far." This limit is at times indicated by an object accusative which makes the verb transitive: "to go beyond the law," etc.; a personal object is naturally rare. The τὸ μή does combine the infinitives but only as constituting their appositional relation as shown above and not, as some extend this relation, also the object, "his brother." For the second infinitive is ep-exegetical: going beyond is specified as overreaching his brother in the matter of business; it is this going too far that the writers have in mind.

Πλεονεκτεῖν has the same meaning as πλεονεξία, "covetousness": the act of coveting or being greedy. The marginal translation of our versions: "overreach," may be accepted, also "defraud" (A. V.); "to oppress" (A. V. margin) is a different verb just as is "to wrong" (R. V.), which would be ἀδικεῖν. Πράγμα is a regular commercial term: "business" or "matter of business." The article is the same as that in the phrase ἀπὸ τῆς πορνείας, generic and comprehensive: the whole matter of business, and not the enclitic "in some matter of business," nor the demonstrative "in this matter" (i. e., the one mentioned in v. 3, fornication).

Covetous greed is to be impossible for the Thessalonians in their business dealing. This applies not only to merchants, for the phrase is broader and includes any transaction in which one man may covetously get the advantage of the other. Honesty is referred to, and more than that, also fairness in dealing, concern for the profit and the interests of others. When Paul writes "his brother" he may have in mind Lev. 25:14, 17 where we have "neighbor" and "one another," and uses "his brother" as an equivalent. This does not make "brother" = fellow man; on the other hand, Paul is not advocating a double standard such as the Jews had who often still think that, while cheating a Jew is wrong, cheating a Gentile is quite in order. Paul's admonition is the same as when he bids us love the brethren, which never means *only* the brethren. All holy virtues that are exercised in regard to the brethren and commanded with reference to them cannot and do not stop there but reach out to all others in all such ways as are possible. Christian ethics treat a Christian brother as a clear example of how to treat other people and thus differ from all worldly ethics (Mohammedan,

Masonic, and other mere humanly arranged brother-hoods).

As an antidote against sin the Scriptures use the positive motive of love to God and Christ, which seeks ever to please God (v. 1) and thus shrinks from all sin; but also the negative motive of fear lest God punish us. Sin disregards God in two ways: it ignores his love, grace, and blessings by refusing to respond in grati-tude and obedience; it sets aside his warnings and threats by regarding them as idle words. Paul has appealed to the gospel motive in v. 1; he now adds the motive of law. For when the former fails to be effec-tive, the latter must always step in (Matt. 10:28). It does so here: "because the Lord is an avenger regard-ing all these things even as also we told you in advance and testified." The predicate is placed forward for the sake of emphasis: "an avenger the Lord," etc., nothing less, an ἔκδικος (also in the papyri), one who exacts legal justice from a culprit. Chrysostom re-marks: "God does not avenge the persons who have been wronged but himself," let us rather say his δίκη or norm of right.

This appeal to God's legal justice is supported by the conviction of the natural conscience as Acts 28:4 so plainly indicates: ἡ δίκη did not let him live. It is made much stronger by the knowledge of the true God, of his justice coupled with his omniscience. Κύριος, without the article, refers to Christ in his divine lord-ship; if God were referred to, we should have Θεός. Paul is not citing the Old Testament so that Κύριος might be regarded as = Jehovah. "All these things" implies at least two kinds of sins and then requires that we think of various transgressions, such repeti-tions showing that no repentance has set in.

"As we have told you before" = when we were with you founding the church. All that the writers state is elementary Christian instruction which is given to the converts at once. We need no πρό with the second verb. The addition "and testified" adds the note of solemnity to that of the telling, the compound is even stronger than the simplex occurring in 2:11. Impressively as well as with genuine testimony the Thessalonians had been warned of God's justice upon all these sins in which they had lived with unconcern before their conversion. The Thessalonians know it well but, as we today, need constant reminders. It would be uncharitable to conclude that Timothy had found that these sins were still rife among the Thessalonians. These admonitions intend to deepen their fear of God regarding the danger of viewing such sins lightly and thus perhaps yielding to temptation.

7) When the writers add: **For God called you not on the basis of uncleanness but in connection with sanctification,** this explains (γάρ) why these admonitions and reminders are necessary. Paul again sounds the full gospel note. The aorist "God called you" refers to the historical fact and, as always in the epistles, to the efficacious and successful call. The call is generally ascribed to God, but this in no wise excludes Christ. By stating it actively: "God called you," and not passively: "you were called," Paul emphasizes the new relation to God which brought the Thessalonians into blessed union with him; for in καλεῖν there lies the whole gospel of unmerited grace which drew the Thessalonians out of paganism and into God's blessed kingdom.

The force of the preposition is lost in the A. V.; these are not two εἰς, "unto." The R. V. misunderstands ἐπί by translating it "for" (the Greek for this would be εἰς). "Not on the basis of uncleanness" (ἐπί) = not with this understanding; "but in connection with sanctification" means in the connection indicated by the context, i. e., by the act that called the Thessalonians. It is true that "uncleanness" is the opposite of "sanctification," the one is as broad as the other, and "uncleanness" does not refer only to sexual sins just as "sanctification" includes far more than sexual purity. "Uncleanness" describes the whole former pagan life; "sanctification," the new Christian life.

More must be said, and this is also in line with the prepositions: "on the basis of uncleanness" describes a state or condition while "in connection with sanctification" describes an action, namely God's sanctifying action which separated the Thessalonians more and more from all sin and in all their life and activity drew them to him (see this meaning in v. 3). The word used is not ἁγιωσύνη (3:13), "holiness," the state or quality, which would be the formal opposite of ἀκαθαρσία and would permit the use of the same preposition with both nouns. Here the contrast is between the former filthy pagan *state* in which the pagan Thessalonians were and the new divine *work* which set in when the divine call won them, which they are constantly to experience in their hearts and their lives. God's call cannot possibly let the Thessalonians rest on the old unclean *basis;* that call at once connected them with God's sanctifying *action.* Prepositions and nouns are most exact.

8) With τοιγαροῦν (found only here and in Heb. 12:1), the re-enforced οὖν, the summary conclusion is drawn. **Therefore, he who sets aside, not man does he set aside but God, him who gives his Holy Spirit to you.** I Sam. 8:7; Matt. 10:40; Luke 10:16; John 13:20. Ἀθετέω == "to annul." "He who cancels" and thus sets aside as if the thing were finally disposed of and could be disregarded needs no object, for the reference is plain in its brevity: he who rejects this divine sanctification and thinks he may remain in his former unclean state. The present participle is qualitative and describes this man. With equal terseness Paul states what this man does: "he sets aside" (an-

nuls, rejects) ; Paul does not say: "let him know that he sets aside," nor does he use some longer expression. The present tense states the simple fact as is done in any general (often doctrinal) statement. "Not man but God" = not us but God; not a mere human being but no less a one than God himself. Compare 2:13. Here the entire emphasis is once again placed on God.

Yet the gospel note continues: "God, him who gives his Holy Spirit to you," τὸν διδόντα, again qualitative and an apposition. Now we hear how the sanctification which has been mentioned three times is wrought, namely by God's giving us τὸ Πνεῦμα αὐτοῦ τὸ Ἅγιον. Thus this paragraph presents all three divine persons. By placing the adjective after a second article and even after "his" this is made a kind of appositional climax (R. 776) : "his Spirit, the Holy One," who is called "holy" for the very reason that he sanctifies and makes us holy. To reject God who does this for us poor sinners is to remain in our uncleanness, to sink ever more deeply into it. "He who gives" contains all that God's grace means, and we should not overlook this precious participle. The A. V. has translated the inferior reading εἰς ἡμᾶς which should be ὑμᾶς; for "us" would mean "us writers," but Paul beyond question refers to the Thessalonians.

9) These verses (9-12) still belong to what the writers had taught the Thessalonians (v. 1) as the will of God, their sanctification (v. 3), transitional δέ introducing them. **Now concerning the brotherly love you have no need that (we) write you, for you yourselves are God-taught so that you love each other; indeed, you also do this toward all the brethren in all Macedonia.**

Timothy had brought the report, and the writers are informed about the brotherly love of the Thessalonians; περί introduces the subject and not an inquiry made by the Thessalonians. In the classics φιλαδελφία is

used to designate the love of relatives, in our literature
it expresses the love and affection of spiritual brethren.
Already in 1:3 this love has been acknowledged with
thanks to God; it is now acknowledged to the Thessalonians themselves: "you have no need that (we)
write you." When B.-D. 393, 5 finds the simple active
infinitive "incorrect," we think this is saying too much,
for it is evident that "we" is the implied subject.

It is saying a good deal to assert that there is no
need to dwell on this subject as far as the Thessalonians are concerned; but it is saying even more to claim
that the Thessalonians are God-taught so that they love
each other. Θεοδίδακτοί appears only here and in later
ecclesiastical writers, but the compound is quite regular, it is a passive verbal adjective (compare John
6:45). Εἰς τό denotes result and does not introduce an
object clause as it did in 3:10, nor is it epexegetical
(R. 1003, 1072). "God-taught" refers to v. 8: taught
by the Holy Spirit, yet not immediately by direct revelation but mediately through Paul and Silvanus and the
Word the Thessalonians had received from them. On
ἀγαπᾶν see the noun as used in 1:3. True teaching produces results, and the Thessalonians showed the results
as the writers are happy to say.

10) We regard γάρ as confirmatory: "yea" or "indeed" and not "for." The Thessalonians had not only
a parochial love but one that took in all the brethren
in the whole of Macedonia. Thessalonica was a great
seaport which carried on much trade with the entire
province. Believers from the other Macedonian cities
thus had cause to come to Thessalonica and there found
the Thessalonian brethren full of true love for them,
willing to lend them any assistance they needed. Some
think of charity sent to brethren in other cities, but we
have no hint of charity; v. 6 speaks of business with
brethren, and business is transacted by people with

means, and to have brethren full of love in a strange city where one transacts business is a great help.

Δέ is slightly adversative: **Yet we admonish you, brethren, to abound more and more** (the same expression found in v. 1). It has been asked why this subject is mentioned since the Thessalonians exercised true Christian love as they did. The answer is twofold: 1) such love deserves commendatory mention and receives it here; 2) when the writers are commending this love, these young believers are not to think that their love is already perfect, it is to increase and abound still more. It is to grow like a living plant and to bear still more fruit. The address "brethren" is proper because the admonition includes more than the one point of abounding in the love already manifested, and because the Thessalonians were treating other brethren as they should (in all Macedonia).

11) Instead of making a separate item of this second admonition Paul simply adds it to the brief one about abounding still more in love. This has been criticized as being laxity in expressing thought. But Paul's further admonition is entirely in line with this abounding in love toward the brethren near and far. Verse 12 makes this plain, for "those without" are to be considered alongside of "the brethren." These two hang together, "the brethren" and "those without." It is thus that Paul adds: **And to be ambitious to be quiet and to attend to your own business and to work with your hands even as we gave you orders that you should walk in seemly fashion toward those without and should have need of nothing.**

It is the last clause that makes this second admonition plain because it is a second one and yet is related to the first. Fervent love to the brethren cannot possibly disregard our conduct toward those without. The infinitive means "to seek honor in something," which needs an addition to explain how and in what the honor is sought; we have this explanation in the next infinitive: "to be quiet." But this is still incomplete, for it leaves the question as to what is meant by being quiet. The answer is found in the following infinitives plus the καθώς clause which includes also v. 12. We may translate καί "namely": "namely to attend to your own business and to work with your hands even as," etc.

Πράσσειν τὰ ἴδια, which is followed by ἐργάζεσθαι ταῖς χερσὶν ὑμῶν, refers to two groups of members, businessmen and ordinary laborers. We have heard of businessmen in v. 6; they are not to cheat in their business dealing. Here they are to attend to τὰ ἴδια, "their own affairs," business affairs. Those who depend on labor that is to be done with their own hands are to be satisfied with that. This is what being ambitious to be quiet means. This is again not a new thought but only what Paul and Silvanus ordered when they first brought the Thessalonians to faith (v. 2).

The usual view of this verse does not find a reference to two groups, businessmen and those who work with their own hands, it considers that τὰ ἴδια refers only to "one's own affairs," the opposite of mixing in with other people's affairs, being busybodies (II Thess. 3:11). This view regards "to work with your hands" as being explicative of "to attend to your own things." The fact that nearly all of the Thessalonians were manual toilers, dock workers, who did heavy work, cannot be established. They were businessmen as we see them today who sold things in Oriental bazaars and craftsmen who often work in little shops as we can see them to this day working by hand at their trades, many of which require great skill of hand. This is a truer picture as those know who have traveled in Oriental countries. The contrast here intended is not one of attending to public affairs in the state and city, and still less ambition to inaugurate a public program that is in line with unsound Christian eschatological ideas; nor the idea that common labor is the affair of slaves while free men should devote themselves to politics in the Agora, to public celebrations in the theatre, and to relaxation in the public baths.

We should not introduce II Thess. 3:6-15 as though this were a part of First Thessalonians. The neglect of business and labor is here considered only briefly and from the angle of its effect on those outside. This neglect was in its incipiency. Second Thessalonians sheds light on it only as being something that Timothy had reported as having begun and as causing comment among outsiders. The best we are able to say is that the ardent expectation of Christ's Parousia, which was regarded as being certain to occur in the near future, caused a few of the Thessalonians to give up their ordinary occupations and earnings. Examples of like fanatical expectations on a large scale have occurred at various times. See below on v. 13, etc. In First Thessalonians we have no more than a small beginning in this direction.

12) We regard the ἵνα clause as the object of παρηγγείλαμεν: "even as we gave you orders (παρά, passed the order along to you) that you should walk in seemly fashion toward those without and should have need of nothing." Our versions and the older commentators were not acquainted with this expanded use of ἵνα and thus regard this statement as a purpose clause; some of the later commentators still cling to this idea of purpose although the papyri have taught us a good deal on this subject. Paul's original instruction to the Thessalonians was: always to walk as regards those without εὐσχημόνως, in a manner that is *anstaendig*, "in good form" (not: "honestly" as in our versions), but so as to cause no offense. Those who regard this as a purpose clause make the original orders given to the Thes-

salonians the contents of at least the two preceding
infinitives. But this would mean that when Paul and
Silvanus were in Thessalonica the Thessalonians were
beginning to neglect business and labor, which was not
the case. This fault appeared later and was reported
by Timothy.

Paul adds: "and should have need of nothing"
(neuter, not masculine: "no man," A. V. margin), in
an applicatory way. By attending to business and
daily work in a quiet, sober, steady fashion each Christian would earn his own living and escape need so that
no outsider could point to him with slurring remarks.
Verse 6 takes care of honesty in business dealings.
Poorer members would soon get into need if they
stopped work.

Instruction regarding Those who Die before the Parousia

13) Δέ introduces a new subject. Efforts are made
to discover a close connection with something that precedes in v. 9-12 such as that the φιλαδελφία of v. 9 extended to the dead and caused this grief that Paul is
allaying. But this and other suggestions of a close
connection are not convincing. Of more merit is the
observation that this entire epistle has an eschatological tone (see 1:10; 2:12; 2:19; 3:13). The reason for
this is the fact that Paul intended to write these two
sections (4:13-18 and 5:1-11) to furnish the Thessalonians the instruction they needed according to the
reports Timothy had brought. Timothy had, no doubt,
done what he could to clear up this whole subject, but
now all three writers put the instruction down black on
white. These two paragraphs thus form the burden of
the second part of the epistle. The church has always
considered them of the greatest value. The first paragraph is closely allied to I Cor. 15:51, 52.

Now we do not want you to be ignorant, brethren, concerning those that fall asleep in order that you may not grieve as also the rest, those who have no hope.

The plural "we" refers to the three writers (1:1), and "we do not want you to be ignorant" (similar formulas are used a number of times by Paul himself) introduces additional information, here on the subject mentioned by περί, "those who fall asleep," (note περί in v. 9). "Brethren" helps to mark the new subject. The present participle: "those who fall asleep," is passive (it is far better attested than the perfect passive). Κοιμάω = "to put to sleep," the passive, "to be put to sleep," i. e., to fall asleep. In our literature we find only the passive (B.-P. 685). The question of the Thessalonians dealt not only with those who had already died but equally with any others who might die before the Parousia.

During the four weeks that Paul and Silvanus were founding the congregation this specific question had not arisen and hence had not been answered in a direct and specific way. Probably no deaths had occurred during those four weeks. A number of believers had died since that time, and the prospect was that more would die while the church was waiting earnestly for God's Son from the heavens (1:10). We know what disturbed the Thessalonians only from what is written here; we ought not to be influenced by those commentators who add material that is borrowed from Jewish and pagan sources. The negative purpose clause at once helps to show us what troubled the Thessalonians regarding these deaths. The instruction here offered is to stop them from grieving over these deaths as the rest grieve who have no hope. "The rest" are "those outside" (v. 12), pagans, who are devoid of hope. Their grief is not assuaged by hope; that of Christians is. The claim that the pagans have no hope (Eph.

2:12) is an objective statement that is made by the writers. There is only one hope for those who die, the hope based on the sure promises of God and Christ; all who do not have this hope are without hope whatever they may think of death and the hereafter, whatever hope or hopes they may manufacture for themselves.

Interesting collections have been made especially from pagan inscriptions which show what paganism thought about death, the hereafter, immortality, etc. See the works listed by Dobschuetz, *Thessalonicher-Brief*, 189. Deissmann, *Light from the Ancient East*, 164 presents the facsimile of a letter of condolence that was written by Irene, an Egyptian, to a family that has lost a son, which tells how everything that was fitting was done. "But, nevertheless, against such things one can do nothing. Therefore comfort ye one another. Fare ye well!" Nothing that is more bare of real hope and comfort can be imagined. See v. 18 of this chapter! Well may Deissmann exclaim in discussing this letter: "Poor Irene!"

Here we, however, see what troubled the Thessalonians: they were grieving over these deaths like those who have no hope, they thought that these dead were lost. Do you ask how this was possible? Was not the doctrine of the resurrection a part of the gospel, and had Paul and Silvanus not taught the blessed resurrection to the Thessalonians at the very start? Surely, but the Thessalonians were unable to apply this teaching to the deaths that had occurred. They were bginners, had come mostly from paganism, and constantly looked for the Son of God from heaven, the Deliverer from the wrath to come (1:10). They applied this deliverance only to the believers whom Christ would find alive at his coming. They failed to see that it applied to the dead believers as well. Hence their grieving without hope for these dead. The sad feature was not too much grieving on the part of the Thessalonians such as sometimes occurs in the case of Christians even today but grieving like pagans who have no hope although the Thessalonians had the one genuine hope but did not realize its great range.

It is quite true that also paganism called death a sleep. But when the Christian and the pagan use of the word are placed on the same level, or when the Christian use is said to have been drawn from the pagan, and both are called a euphemism, we offer objections. Behind this word sleep and sleeping the pagan sees nothing but his pagan conception of death, to him the word is a mere euphemism. Behind the Christian word lies all the Christian knowledge of the saving facts which actually make death a mere sleep. This is not altered by I Kings 22:40 where the Hebrew phrase "slept with his fathers" is used regarding wicked Ahab. When Paul uses the word he employs it as it is used in I Cor. 15:18; and it is not a mere pious homiletical idea that the word "to fall asleep" implies the awakening in the blessed resurrection.

This sleep applies only to the body of the dead believer and not to his soul. This, too, is correct, that the Scriptures say regarding Christ that he died and not that he fell asleep (Stephen, Acts 7:60). His death was a death that expiated our guilt and thus made our death a sweet sleep because all our deadly guilt had been expiated. This, too, is not mere homiletical language. The view which is widely held today is without foundation, that Paul's conception of death was that, on separating from the body, the soul "leads a shadowy existence in the chambers of *sheol,* which cannot be called life until the reawakening, i. e., the reunion with the (then glorified) body; and that this intermediate state of body and soul is here designated by κοιμᾶσθαι." We quote Dobschuetz as a sample of this idea of *sheol.* It is answered by Acts 7:59, by Phil.

1:23, by Luke 23:43, 44, by all that the Old Testament says regarding *sheol,* by all that the New Testament adds. No intermediate place between heaven and hell exists. In no sense do the souls of the dead "sleep." Were Abraham and Lazarus asleep in Luke 16:22, etc.? Lazarus lay on Abraham's bosom as John lay on the bosom of Jesus (John 13:25).

Similar to this idea of the soul's existing in a shadowy, sleeplike state in an intermediate (Romanistic) "realm of the dead" is the other that is built on the millennium. Some think that Paul taught the Thessalonians that there would be a millennium, and that they imagined that those who died before the Parousia would not enter this millennium. The further supposition of two resurrections is introduced, one that occurred at the beginning of the millennium, the other at its end. But this results in a difficulty; for millennialists usually believe that the former includes *all* believers so that the dead Thessalonian believers would, after all, enter the millennium. To obviate this we are told that the first resurrection applies to the martyrs only and not to those who die a natural death. Accordingly, these dead Thessalonians would have to wait for the second resurrection, and this caused all of their grieving.

This structure crumbles before the clause: "as the rest, those who have no hope." Waiting for the second resurrection cannot mean having no hope. The Scriptures know of only one resurrection; see John 5:28, 29 in *The Interpretation of St. John's Gospel,* 382, etc., also the author's *St. John,* 189; Rev. 20:6; also the complete exposition in *The Interpretation of Revelation.* The Scriptures know of no millennium. The Old Testament passages used in support of the millennium are treated in the author's *Eisenach Old Testament Selections.* The present passage is a fair sam-

ple of the method employed by chiliasts to find chiliasm
in certain passages.

14) "For" is expository. **For if we believe that
Jesus died and arose, thus also those who fell asleep
will God through this Jesus bring with him.**

The condition of reality: "if we believe," implies:
we do, indeed, believe. Here we have the second "we"
(compare 1:10) in which the writers combine themselves and their readers. What they jointly believe is
stated in the briefest form and is one great objective
fact: "that Jesus died and arose." The name "Jesus"
brings to mind the Savior as a man who was like unto
us men, who "died" as such, died as the Thessalonian
dead had died. Yet concerning Jesus the writers do
not say that he "fell asleep"; in a marked way they
say that Jesus "died," and they do that in a context
in which they twice say of believers that they fall
asleep. The difference is too marked to be accidental;
we have already stated what this difference implies.

Here, however, the fact that Jesus died is stated
only because it is involved in the fact that he "arose."
Only one who died can arise. The second verb calls
for the first. Paul does not say that Jesus "was raised"
(passive), that God raised him from the dead. Neither does he say that Jesus "was put to death" (passive). Such passives would make Jesus only the object upon whom others acted. This is proper in other
connections such as Acts 4:10 and 5:30 but not in this
connection in which the effective greatness of Jesus
is to stand out. It was *he* who stepped into death and
then stepped out of it again; *he* had power to lay down
his life and to take it up again (John 10:17). One
thought is expressed by two verbs which center on
what Jesus did, but because of its very terseness it
speaks volumes in regard to this Jesus who died for
our advantage and rose again to make this advantage

ours when we believe, when we embrace him in complete reliance by faith.

What is said of Jesus lends significance to the following phrases: διὰ τοῦ Ἰησοῦ and ἐν αὐτῷ. We should note well that τοῦ is the article of previous reference which is made distinct by Ἰησοῦς in the ὅτι clause which has no article, so that we translate: "through this Jesus," the one who died and arose, and "with him," the one who died and arose thus. Both phrases contain what is said of "the (this) Jesus." Commentators are divided regarding the first phrase and ask, "Does it belong to the substantivized participle or to the main verb?" Is it: "those who fell asleep through Jesus," or is it: "God will bring through Jesus"? It must be the latter. How anyone can fall asleep "through Jesus" has never been adequately explained.

This διά is not = ἐν in I Cor. 15:18 although some have thought so. It denotes mediation and not union as "in" does. We are pointed to v. 2 and similar expressions with διά, but none of them fit the intransitive idea which we have in falling asleep. Some point us to the martyrs as those who fell asleep "through Jesus"; but even with regard to martyrs the phrase to be used should be either "in Jesus" or "because of Jesus" (διά with the accusative). If martyrs are here referred to, the whole point would be lost. These dead Thessalonians were not martyrs, they had died a natural death. We have no trace of bloody martyrdom in the whole epistle, and still less can we assume that all who had died in Thessalonica were martyrs. It is urged that the main verb cannot have two phrases as modifiers, but, pray, why not?

Paul says: "through the Jesus (who died and rose again) God will bring those who fell asleep with him" (i. e., this Jesus), *with* him because *through* him, through his mediation, this *with* (associative σύν)

could not be without this *through* (saving mediation,
δια). The two phrases regarding Jesus get their full
meaning when it is remembered that both belong to
the verb. The mediation of Jesus did not stop when
these believers fell asleep, it continues and will continue until the Parousia when it will show itself in the
glorious association with this Jesus. In other words,
the power of Jesus' death and resurrection does not
stop when we fall asleep, its efficacy will show itself
in all its glory at the Parousia. These dead in Thessalonica only "fell asleep." Why should their sleeping
interfere with the mediation of Jesus? The aorist passive participle refers to those who had actually fallen
asleep; it is not like the present passive used in v. 13
which refers to any and to all who may yet fall asleep.
This aorist is intended especially for the bereaved in
Thessalonica who each think of the dear one whom
they have lost and not just in general of Christians
who die.

God will bring them with Jesus, through Jesus, this
Jesus who by his death and rising up wrought out our
eternal salvation. We have already seen in v. 1-8 how
everything is referred back to God, the living and genuine God, to whom the Thessalonians turned from their
idols (1:9). What is here said could, of course, be
worded so as to make Christ the great subject even as
Christ says in John 6:39, 40, 44: "I will raise him up
at the last day," in v. 44 even using the emphatic ἐγώ,
"I myself." But when God is made the subject, the mediation of Jesus in his death and rising again is made
to stand out so that the brief statement is greatly enriched. "God will bring or lead with him" puts all into
one statement, which is then expanded in the following
(v. 15-17) : the Lord will descend from heaven — the
dead will arise — the living will join them — together
they will meet the Lord — and thus we shall ever be
with the Lord. All this lies in ἄξει σὺν αὐτῷ, God will

bring with Jesus. Those who fell asleep refers to the bodies in the graves; these shall arise (v. 16) and be glorified, united with their souls, thus forever to be "with him" who died and arose for their eternal salvation.

Commentators wrestle with εἰ . . . οὕτω, and Winer alone among the grammarians seems to come to their rescue. "If . . . thus" really do not match, they are not intended to match. Οὕτω does not mean "then," nor εἰ "when." So also "if *we* believe" does not match what God will do with *other* people, i. e., with those who fell asleep in Thessalonica, those who are already dead. In order to match, the statement should read: "If *we* believe, God will do something for *us*." Οὕτω has nothing to do with εἰ, nor is it pleonastic (an older explanation); the adverb does not introduce the apodosis after a protasis as some think, nor is there "inexactness, a shift of thought" as others assume. "Thus" refers only to the ὅτι clause: thus as Jesus died and rose, thus God shall bring those who fell asleep through this Jesus with this Jesus. This, too, is why the verb in v. 16 is "shall rise" (like "he rose," Jesus) and not passive, "shall be raised." "Thus" = with Jesus dead and risen, the very thing involved in the act of bringing these sleepers along with Jesus.

15) "For" ushers in the explanation or elucidation. **For (in order that you may fully understand) this we tell you in connection with the Lord's Word that we, those that remain alive, those that are left for the Parousia of the Lord, shall in no way be ahead of those who fell asleep.**

So little is there a reason to grieve over those who have fallen asleep. Those who are alive at Christ's Parousia shall not even precede those who have died, to say nothing of the fear that there is no hope for them. The living and those who fell asleep shall together be joined in glory to the glorious Lord.

When the writers say "we" and add the appositions "those who remain alive, those who are left for the Parousia of the Lord," they do not assert that they and the Thessalonian readers will be alive, will not also fall asleep before the Parousia; 5:1, etc., is plain as to that. No one could know when the Parousia would occur, whether it would come in a short time or after a long delay; no one could know how few or how many would yet fall asleep just as we today do not know. Yet we now know that almost two millenniums have passed since Paul wrote, and thus our expectation of the last day has been greatly dulled. In Paul's day this expectation was keener.

We do not translate: "We tell you *by* the word of the Lord" (ἐν is not "by") but "in connection with the Lord's Word." This is not a quotation, nor the substance of a quotation, nor a reference to some single statement of the Lord's, whether this is recorded in the Gospels or not recorded, but a reference to all that the Lord said about his Parousia, all of it being to the effect that those who live at that time will in no way be ahead of those who died. Ἐν λόγῳ Κυρίου may well accord with I Cor. 15:51, 52 where Paul calls what he says about this matter "a mystery," from which fact it is generally concluded that Paul had received further specific revelation regarding the instantaneous transformation of the living without their first dying, and that this added revelation connected with all that the Lord had said regarding his Parousia in his discourses while he was on earth.

16) Our versions and others obtain a smooth translation by rendering this second ὅτι as the causal "for"; they regard it as giving the reason that the living shall not precede the dead. Yet, the more the writer looks at these verses, the more their contents appear to him as facts that are told the Thessalonians; this ὅτι is like the ὅτι of fact that occurs in v. 15.

These verses offer further information that is to enlighten and not reasons that are to convince the Thessalonians. The two ὅτι are alike, both are declarative after "we tell you": **That the Lord himself in connection with a command, in connection with an archangel's voice, and in connection with God's trumpet will descend from heaven; and the dead in Christ shall arise first, then we, those that remain alive, those that are left, shall together with them be snatched in clouds for meeting the Lord, into the air; and thus shall we be evermore with the Lord.**

Here the Thessalonians have an exact record of what shall happen; this removes all cause for grief regarding their dead. Not only is there hope, but they can have the greatest possible hope, one that is equal to the hope they have for those who will be alive at the Parousia.

"The Lord himself will come down from heaven" = 1:10: "to await God's Son out of the heavens, Jesus, the One saving us from the wrath to come." This verb means literally *herniederschreiten;* αὐτός fixes the entire attention upon him in this grand act; this word does not contrast him with others. "Lord" is to be taken in its full soteriological sense, the Lord who has made us his own, he who at his Parousia will receive all his own unto himself, John 12:26; 14:3; 17:24. Also these passages are parts of "the Lord's Word" (v. 15).

The ἐν phrases are placed forward for the sake of emphasis. They, of course, show the greatness of the Lord's descent from heaven, but they also elucidate the very point here at issue, namely what shall happen with regard to the dead at the Parousia: the Lord shall descend ἐν κελεύσματι, "in connection with an order." While it occurs only here in the New Testament this word is common to designate a loud military command, the shout of a charioteer to his horses, of a hunter to his hounds, of a shipmaster to the rowers. John 5:28: "All that are in the graves shall hear his voice," namely that of the Son of man. This is then the Lord's "command" to all the dead to arise and not the Father's command to Christ to descend, nor Christ's command to his angel host. "Shout" in our versions is inexact; the word means a shouted order or command.

The next two phrases are connected with καί. Some regard them as appositions to the first phrase, but this construction would make the command one that is issued through the voice of an archangel, which angel would use God's trumpet. John 5:28 shows that the command comes through the Lord's own voice; the Lord's command is not issued to the archangel to blow the grand signal with God's trumpet. The archangel's voice and God's trumpet are distinct; both shall sound forth in connection with (ἐν) the Lord's command.

Note the absence of the article in the phrases, which stresses the quality of the nouns. Scripture mentions only one archangel, namely Michael (Jude 9; Rev. 12:7; compare Dan. 10:13, 21; 12:1). We take it that only this one exists. To talk about Gabriel's trumpet is unscriptural. The greatest of the angels shall sound the trumpet. It has been well said that when the Lord, the King, comes in all his glory with all his holy angels the greatest of them all shall sound forth his majesty.

Φωνή is not a second "command" that is uttered by the archangel but the sound this angel sends through "God's trumpet," I Cor. 15:22: "the last trumpet" (compare Matt. 24:31: "with a great voice, φωνή, of a trumpet"). Here καί connects φωνή and σάλπιγξ, sound (or voice) and trumpet. This is also "God's trumpet," the blast of which comes with God's power and penetrates to all the dead. It is idle to ask why there will be this trumpet blast in addition to the

Lord's command. All of us will know when we hear both.

As to the last day, all that we can do is to combine what the Scriptures say regarding it and to remember that all of it is beyond human imagination. This record is intended for our hope and our comfort and not for speculation and rationalization. It is folly to introduce our conceptions of time and of space; for then time shall cease (Rev. 10:6), a thought no human mind can conceive, and we may add that the same will be true regarding space as we know it (the two always go together).

Here the writers are concerned only with what shall occur with regard to the dead and the living saints at the Parousia for the hope and the comfort of the Thessalonians. Nothing is, therefore, said about the wicked, about the judgment, or about other details that some of us would like to know.

Καί may be translated "and so," i. e., as indicating the result, "the dead in Christ shall arise first," the active voice of this verb was explained in v. 14. Here νεκροί is used but with "in Christ" (I Cor. 15:18: "those fallen asleep in Christ"), they are called "the dead" in I Cor. 15:52. On Christ and "them that are his" compare I Cor. 15:23. Because of the thought "in Christ" cannot be construed with the verb. Πρῶτον is placed last in order to abut it with ἔπειτα: "first" what shall happen with regard to the dead saints, "thereupon" what shall happen with regard to the saints still living. "First" refers to "thereupon" as "thereupon" refers to "first."

This is so plain that one is surprised to note that a man like Wohlenberg finds an indication of two resurrections: first, that of the saints only; then, after 1,000 years, that of the wicked. To quote John 5:28, 29 in support of two widely separated resurrections is to misunderstand Jesus' words: *"All* that are in their graves shall hear his voice," the command of which Paul speaks, all shall hear when it is uttered in that "coming hour"; "and shall come forth" — all of them — "they that have done good unto the resurrection of life, and they that have done evil unto the resurrection of damnation." This is also "the *last* trumpet" (1 Cor. 15:52) as this is *"the last day"* (John 6:39, 40, 44, 54; 11:24) when time shall be no more. In the face of all this chiliasts add 1,000 years and a second resurrection.

"Shall arise" = John 5:28, the *bodies* shall come forth out of their graves. There is no such thing as a resurrection of souls, the very idea is impossible. In Rev. 20:6 the word resurrection is used symbolically. First Corinthians 15:12, etc., also v. 23, speak of the dead body of Christ and of the dead bodies of believers which are raised by the resurrection. To deny the bodily resurrection is to reject Scripture. We need scarcely add that the bodies are glorified in the resurrection (Phil. 3:20, 21), and that all of this is an incomprehensible miracle.

The claim is often advanced that the idea of a resurrection is only a late Jewish conception which was adopted by Paul who developed it and also changed his own ideas about it. But what about Jesus ("the Lord's Word")? Did he, too, pick up an idea of late Judaism? "The Word of God they shall let stand, nor any thanks have for it." Luther.

17) Now regarding the living that are left (the same terms that were used in v. 15): "together with them (σύν associative: with the risen dead) they shall be snatched in clouds (the Lord's chariots on which he himself shall come in glory, Matt. 24:30; Mark 13:26; Rev. 1:7) for meeting the Lord, into the air." The main point is the union of the dead and the living believers who form one joint host that is lifted in a divine

raptus to meet their heavenly Lord as he descends. First Corinthians 15:51, 52 supplies the thought that the living will be changed without passing through death, in the twinkling of an eye. Glorified in body and soul like the risen dead, they will be swept up "into the air" and thus rise to meet the Lord at his descent. We take this to mean that they will meet the Lord in welcome and will descend to the earth with him and all his angels for the purpose of judgment.

"Snatched into the air" does not mean into heaven. The Lord will descend to the earth (Job 19:25; Acts 1:11) where the judgment shall take place. It shall not take place in the air; nor shall the wicked, after being raised, be taken into the air. Revelation 21:1, 2 unites the new heaven and the new earth with the holy city; and the judgment will exclude the wicked from it. We read nowhere that the Lord will return to heaven after the Parousia, but rather that heaven and earth shall be one. Εἰς ἀπάντησιν is an idiom (it is also found in the papyri) that always occurs in this form and is like a compound preposition with the genitive, it is the German *entgegen*.

"And thus shall we be evermore with the Lord"; the adverb is emphatic, the "we" suffix refers to the writers and their readers; this "we" includes also those Thessalonian Christians who are already dead. Regardless of the fact whether they shall live until the Parousia or not they shall all "thus" (in the way described) be with (in association with) the Lord (the same phrase that is used in Phil. 1:23). This is the hope the Thessalonians have with regard to their dead, they have the same hope for themselves. This is the answer that removes all the grief that their doubts and their questions about the dead had caused them. This paragraph is of inestimable value to all Christians when they stand beside their dead.

18) So the writers close: **Wherefore comfort one another with these words.** Ὥστε = "and so" (R. 999), it is inferential also in paratactic sentences. The context gives the imperative the meaning "comfort" (cheer, encourage) rather than "admonish" or "exhort" (R. V. margin) although the verb itself may have either meaning. "One another" is stronger than the reflexive "yourselves." The grief (v. 13) naturally affected the bereaved Thessalonians most of all; the others would want to comfort them. They have genuine comfort to offer which is not one like the comfortless comfort of the Egyptian Irene quoted in connection with v. 13. The Christian faith is the one faith which has the true facts that overflow with real hope and thus comfort.

CHAPTER V

Instruction regarding the Times and the Seasons

1) This paragraph is the companion piece to 4:13-18. Paul could not be content to tell the Thessalonians to be comforted and not to grieve about their dead but would add to this that they should be ready for the Parousia of the Lord. So the two paragraphs form a unit. We see this when we note that Paul concludes the first one: "Comfort one another!" (4:18), and the second one: "Comfort one another and build up one the other!" (5:11). Thus 5:1-11 adds upbuilding to the comfort found especially in 4:13-18.

Now concerning the times and the seasons, brethren, you have no need to be written to, for you yourselves know accurately that the Lord's day so comes as a thief at night.

Δέ indicates a new subject which is again introduced by περί (as in 4:9, 13) and again followed (4:10, 13) by the address "brethren." "The times and the seasons" are the subject now considered by the writers themselves in order to add to 4:13-18 instructions as to how the Thessalonians should live in view of the Parousia. To say only: "Be comforted and do not grieve for your dead!" is not enough, for this refers only to the dead. What about the Thessalonians themselves and their thoughts regarding themselves? A word regarding themselves is in place. There is no indication that they had asked about themselves either through Timothy or in writing; why should they have written when Timothy had just been with them?

"The times and the seasons" repeat Acts 1:7 and imply that the writers were acquainted with this word

(339)

of Jesus'. "The times" simply denote stretches of time while "the seasons" (καιροί) refer to periods that are marked by what occurs in them. The former is a general expression to indicate the mere passing of the years, to which the second is added as being explicative of the years which include this and that that happened in them. We must include the days of the last tribulation, which Jesus mentioned especially as those which would precede his Parousia (Matt. 24:22; Mark 13:20). We cannot agree with those who say that this double plural is only a general formula, for it is nowhere used as a common expression. The plurals are especially worth noting in view of II Thess. 2 and the charge that Paul himself had overdone things in I Thess. and had to tone them down in II Thess. The disorderly actions rebuked in II Thess. 3:6, etc., cannot be charged to Paul as though he had pictured the Parousia as an event that was certain to come in a year or two. He was acquainted with Acts 1:7 and never pretends to know more than Jesus himself said on this subject. The extravagant ideas of the Thessalonians were in no way traceable to Paul. Such ideas have appeared in far later times and will probably appear again, all that Jesus has said and all that Paul has written to the contrary notwithstanding.

Paul acknowledges that nothing needs to be written to the Thessalonians about the times and the seasons; now he uses the passive γράφεσθαι whereas in 4:9 he has used the active γράφειν since the matter may be expressed in either way. In connection with both infinitives the subject need not be expressed since the active in 4:9 itself suggests the writers and this passive in 5:1 suggests the readers, and the Greek mind needs no more.

2) From previous instruction on the part of Paul and Silvanus the Thessalonians know accurately (the same adverb that occurs in Luke 1:3) what is the main

thing to be known "concerning the times and the seasons," namely "that the Lord's day so comes as a thief at night." The years may pass on, one period after another may bring this or that, no one can be sure when the Lord's day will arrive. Ἡμέρα Κυρίου needs no article, for there is only one such day, and the omission of the articles makes the expression a standard one although the articles could also have been added.

The writers know the contents of Matt. 24:43 and Luke 12:39 just as did Peter (II Pet. 3:10; compare Rev. 3:3; 16:15). They had undoubtedly told the Thessalonians what Jesus had said when he used this illustration of the thief. "As — thus" make the comparison a strong one. To say that the day comes thus is the same as saying that the Lord comes thus; and the present tense "comes" is not used in the sense of the future "will come" but is the present tense that is found in doctrinal statements. The ancients thought that "at night" indicates that Christ would literally return during the night, but "at night" is suggested by the illustration of a thief. The Lord's day and its arrival are described by Jesus in Matt. 24:29-31. The *tertium comparationis* in the illustration of a thief is unexpectedness coupled with unpreparedness, which are very clear in Matt. 24:43.

3) This is made plain by the literal statement which thus needs no connective: **When they are saying, Peace and safety! then sudden destruction comes upon them just as the travail upon the woman with child, and they shall in no wise escape.**

The indefinite λέγωσιν (the subjunctive after ὅταν which refers to the expected future time) is made definite by its contrast with "you, brethren," in v. 4: all those who do not know as the Thessalonians know. They will go on saying, "Peace and safety!" and will conduct themselves accordingly, will act as if everything is still as peaceful and safe as it was during the

days past (Matt. 24:37, etc.; Luke 17:26, etc.). Some
will even scoff at the promise of the Lord's coming because they are certain that all things will go on as they
have ever gone (II Pet. 3:3-10). The blind world will
remain blind to the last despite the great procession of
signs during the course of the years, that advertise the
Lord's day as the advertising signs do along our public
roads. Rationalists will use scientific learning to prove
that the prophecies of Scripture are false.

Then, like lightning, the bolt will fall (Matt.
24:27): "sudden destruction will come upon them."
The Greek can place the adjective far forward and
thus give it a powerful emphasis; the subject is placed
last and is thereby made equally emphatic; subject
and predicate are reversed, and this construction also
emphasizes the latter; it is impossible to duplicate this
in English. "Sudden" what? We must wait in suspense until after the verb has been written and we read
the terrible word "destruction." The present tense
ἐφίσταται is the same as ἔρχεται in v. 2. This is the significant verb which is often used with reference to the
sudden appearance of angels and of other manifestations and thus matches the adjective. Consternation
will smite the world of worldlings.

The illustration of the woman caught in travail and
rendered helpless is used repeatedly in the Old Testament (Exod. 15:14; Isa. 13:8; Jer. 13:21; Hos.
13:13). We have the same *tertium* of helpless pain in
our passage. Jesus used it with a different *tertium* in
John 16:21, 22: birthpains which end in joy and thus
illustrated what the disciples and not their enemies
shall pass through. Isa. 26:17, 18 use this illustration
in a still different way. Ὠδίν is nominative, and "she
having in belly" is the Greek idiom for a pregnant
woman. No illustration should be extended beyond the
one point to elucidate which it is used. Here we are
not to introduce the thought that a pregnant woman

knows about when the time of her giving birth is due
to arrive. That feature would illustrate something else
just as in John 16:21, 22 the pregnant woman's pain
and her child thus born illustrate still another matter.
Many a pregnant woman is *suddenly* seized by birthpains, all at once stricken with *helplessness*. That is
the sole point here.

We see this in the literal addition: "and they shall
in no wise escape" (ἐκ, flee and get "out of," aorist),
the futuristic subjunctive in a main sentence (R. 928,
etc.), hence also οὐ is added to μή to express the negation. Then the terrible words "Too late!" will seal
the tragedy of all these people.

4) In sharp contrast with these it is stated:
**But you, brethren, you are not in darkness so that
that day** (article of previous reference) **will catch
you as a thief, for all you are sons of light and
sons of day; we do not belong to night nor to darkness.**

"Brethren" helps to emphasize "you" in contrast
with other men. The rest are "in darkness," in unbelief, in ignorance of the light of the Word, but not *you*.
Ἵνα is consecutive: "so that," although our versions
have it denote purpose. The Lord's day will *not* catch
the believers as a thief catches the sleeping owner of a
house. Καταλαμβάνω means to catch or capture. Believers know all about "the day" and how it will come and
thus keep themselves in perfect readiness. All this is
said about the Thessalonians (v. 5 includes also the
writers) just as we say it regarding ourselves because
neither they nor we know when "the day" will come.

5) The negative statement is re-enforced by the
positive; the negation can be made only because of the
affirmation, and hence we have γάρ. Paul likes to add
something when he writes such corresponding statements; here he adds *"all* you," no believer in Thessalonica is excepted. The predication, too, is double and

is the reverse of the one found in v. 4. To be "in darkness" is merely to be surrounded by it, to be helpless victims of darkness; but to be "sons of light and sons of day" is more than being surrounded by the light of day; this means to have the nature of light and of day. R. 651 would make the genitives adjectival, but they are evidently more, call them ethical or possessive as in compound terms: *Lichtsoehne, Tagessoehne.*

In Eph. 5:8 we have both more and less, for there Paul writes: "You were at one time darkness but now are light in the Lord" (which is more) ; then he calls the Ephesians "children of light" (which is less than "sons of light"). The difference is that existing between "children" who are born as what they are and "sons" who are in the full standing of what they are. "Sons" connotes maturity, full conscious dignity; "children," only native condition. "Sons of darkness" is never used, neither "children of the darkness," but only "sons of the disobedience," Eph. 2:2, and "children of wrath," because darkness can neither bear children nor have sons because it is full of death and not like light which is full of life. The doubling "sons of light and sons of day" produces an emphasis, but we do not think that "of day" alludes to "the Lord's day"; both "light" and "day" are opposites of "night" used in v. 4.

Paul makes this emphatic contrast still more pronounced. The negative sets the affirmative into the boldest relief by being placed both before and after it. What is said of the Thessalonians must also be said of the writers; therefore we now have the first person: "we are." The double positive is now matched by a double negative. "In night" (v. 2) and "in darkness" (v. 4) are not enough; we now have: "We are not of night nor of darkness," which is the idom for: "do not belong to night, to darkness," i. e., are not owned by either, for how can night and darkness control sons of light and sons of day? A tone of victorious exultation

fills these terse assertions. Read the verse aloud in
this tone. Feel how it stiffens and strengthens you.
These writers know of no twilight zone or condition.

6) Now there follow two brief hortations, one
negative and positive, the other positive (v. 8), both
are supported by instruction. One reason for the
"we" used in v. 5 is the "we" occurring in these
hortations. This does not, indeed, imply that they
are to soften the hortations but to say that the
writers do, indeed, apply them also to themselves as
being persons who live in constant expectation of
"the Day." **Accordingly, then, let us not be sleeping like the rest, but let us be watching and be
sober!**

Ἄρα οὖν is a favorite combination of Paul's which
introduces what is involved in some presentation. Sons
of light, sons of day cannot be sleeping "like the rest"
who belong to night and darkness. The deduction is
simplicity itself. To be sleeping is to lie secure in
night and darkness so that no faculty is aroused or
awake to be on guard, so that no light of the Word
opens our eyes. Note v. 3: "Peace and security!" The
subjunctive is hortative.

The two opposites are allied and yet different: "but
let us be watching and be sober," i. e., awake, aroused
by the light of the Word, by the impending day of the
Lord, and in addition to this sober, the opposite of
drunken drowsiness and sleep (v. 7) which dull the
senses (see the synonyms under ἀγρυπνέω in Thayer).
All the tenses are present to express enduring conditions. Christians must be warned in order not to drop
back into their former state.

7) "For" establishes. **For those sleeping sleep
at night** (genitive of time within which), **and those
drunken are drunken at night.** Sleep and a drunken
condition belong to the time of night. We fail to
see that being drunken refers to an exaltation that

is caused by extravagant ideas about the Parousia and its possible nearness. Since it is here combined with sleeping, which denotes complete spiritual insensibility, being drunken adds the soddenness of vice which intensifies this insensibility. This is not tipsiness, the taking of a drink or two that makes a man gay. Of course, drunkenness may also occur in daytime just as one may sleep during the day, but to this day the night is the time for carousing. Both genitives are placed emphatically forward: "at night they sleep, at night they are drunk." The terrible factor is "night" and thus what goes with spiritual night.

Because "at night" is a natural designation of time, this does not imply that this verse is devoid of spiritual significance and refers only to what happens during literal nights. Such an idea ignores the spiritual context with its significant mention of "night," "darkness," and "day" and "night." Μεθύσκω == to make drunk; μεθύω == to be drunk; the participle is a middle: "those making themselves drunk, at night they are drunk."

8) The fact that v. 7 has a spiritual content is seen when "of day" is now opposed to "at night," and being sober to being drunk. **But let us, because we belong to daytime, continue to be sober, as having put on the breastplate of faith and love and as helmet hope of salvation.**

As in v. 5, the Greek "being of day" is our "belonging to day"; the participle is causal in the present connection: since we no longer belong to pagan night but to the light of day in Christ, let us ever keep sober; this verb which is second and last in v. 6 is enough in the repetition.

We regard the second participle as an expounding of ἡμέρας ὄντες: as belonging to day and not to night we did put on faith, love, and hope, which made us sons of light, sons of day (v. 5). All three are produced in us by God, and it is thus that we put them on. The military figures of a thorax or breastplate and of a helmet do not denote mere clothing for the sons of day as though those who are drunk at night lie around naked. In Eph. 6:13, etc., Paul describes the entire panoply or armor of the Christian, which is necessary for victory against all satanic attacks, because the picture is that of a decisive battle. Here there is only a contrast between men who are living in sodden drunkenness in constant night and Christians who are living in continuous light and day, awake and sober. The sober are not to fight the drunken, hence no sword or offensive weapon is mentioned. The *tertium* in "thorax" and "helmet" does not extend beyond conservation and preservation.

Faith, love, hope occur in this order in 1:3. "Faith's and love's breastplate" has appositional genitives, and genitives always make the governing noun definite even when they are not appositional; here no other breastplate exists except faith and love. No objects of faith and love are mentioned, for these concepts are regarded as being complete in themselves and as including their well-known objects. So also these two are a unit as the breastplate, for neither is ever without the other, and both in their conjunction, like a breastplate, cover the heart.

Breastplate and helmet are of a similar nature, the one graces and conserves the heart, the other the head. We might have had just the one word "hope"; but since "faith and love" are two, and since the third in a series is often given greatest fulness, we here have "hope of salvation," the genitive being objective: hope for the final rescue and state of safety. Thus, too, "hope" is not again a genitive like "faith and love" but the object accusative with "as helmet" as its predicative accusative, a beautiful rhetorical variation.

Conscious of our separation from "the rest" and of
the new state into which faith, love, and hope have
placed us, these three will ever control us.

9) ῞Οτι states the reason for the whole of v. 8,
and this reason is the act and the intent of God regarding us: **Because God did not appoint us unto
wrath but unto possession of salvation through our
Lord Jesus Christ, him who died in our behalf, so
that, whether we are watching or sleeping, we shall
live together with him.**

Our own faith, love, and hope should ever keep us
sober as being men belonging to the day, and they
should do this for the greatest reason of all: God
himself has set or appointed us not for wrath but for
the opposite, for salvation and everlasting life. Some
would place the aorist ἔθετο back into eternity, but we
should then expect πρό or some equivalent expression
with this aorist. True, all God's acts and purposes are
eternal, yet they are not always so presented. It is
sufficient to make the action of this aorist contempor-
ary with the action of the preceding participle ἐνδυσάμενοι: the divine appointment and our putting on
faith, etc., occur at the same time.

The main thought concerns itself with the final
result, i. e., the consummation at the Parousia, which
the writers treat in 4:13-5:11. God did not appoint us
"for wrath," i. e., "the wrath to come" (1:10) from
which Jesus saved us. "On the contrary (ἀλλά), for
salvation's possession" by means of this Savior, περιποί-
ησις, "possession" (our versions, "obtaining"). God
wants us to enjoy eternal salvation, σωτηρία as in v. 8.
Διά names the Mediator and does so with his full soteriological title and name: "our Lord Jesus Christ." To
this is added the apposition: "he who died in our behalf." His resurrection has been mentioned in 1:10,
and there, too, in connection with his rescuing us from
the wrath to come. It is typical of Paul to name the

death; in naming the resurrection the death is not forgotten, and the double reference to the wrath connects the two. But that is only one point.

10) Another is that Christ's death bought our eternal salvation which God wants us to have; ὑπὲρ ἡμῶν makes this so plain that one wonders why certain commentators seemingly go out of their way to deny it. To be sure, the brevity here used does not explain how Christ's death operates in securing our final salvation; this the Thessalonians knew, but "died for us" certainly = II Cor. 5:14, 15; Rom. 5:6; 8:32, not to mention other passages regarding Christ's atoning death.

The reading varies between περὶ ἡμῶν and ὑπὲρ ἡμῶν, "concerning us" and "in our behalf"; this is also the case in a few other similar passages. While the former would not directly state that Christ died as our substitute, it does so indirectly, because if he did not die as our substitute, his death cannot be the means for bestowing eternal salvation upon us. We note that Dobschuetz seems to think that ἀντί is necessary to express the idea "instead of," and that ὑπέρ means less. To settle this point reread Robertson, *The Minister and his Greek New Testament*, chapter 3; ὑπέρ is *the* preposition for substitution throughout the Koine. We are linguistically correct when we translate: "he who died in our stead." If we are content with "in our behalf," this by no means loses the substitution just as περί does not lose it. Christ died only one death, which, however we may speak of it, avails nothing for our salvation if it was not died in our stead.

The older supposition that ἵνα can denote only purpose still leads some expositors to prefer the idea of purpose wherever it is at all possible. It will probably take time to overcome this and to recognize that ἵνα has expanded its force in the Koine. We think that it expresses result here: "so that we shall live with him," the result God had in mind when he appointed us for salvation. Just as εἰς περιποίησιν σωτηρίας, *"for* possession of salvation," undoubtedly indicates a result, so does this clause which says that this salvation is our living with him who died in our stead. See the paradox which is beautifully Pauline: with him who *died* we shall *live.* But see the solution: died *in our stead,* together *with him* we shall live. His efficacious death makes possible this life with him. "I am he that liveth and was dead; and, behold, I am alive for evermore, amen; and have the keys of hell and of death," Rev. 1:18, with him shall we live. The adverb ἅμα intensifies associative σύν: "together with."

Here we have εἴτε — εἴτε, two εἰ with subjunctives instead of indicatives just as though we had ἐάν. We do not accept the explanation that this is due to the fact that the double clause is inserted into a ἵνα clause which has its natural subjunctive. R. 1017 points to the classics and to later examples of the Koine, plus others in the New Testament. But is there not a reason for using εἰ instead of ἐάν? The latter expresses an expectation, the former advances this to an expectation (hence still subjunctives) which shall, indeed, become a reality (hence εἰ). Some *will* be awake and watching at the Parousia, some *will* be sleeping in their graves.

Γρηγορῶμεν is the same verb that was used in v. 6, yet the R. V. translates the latter "watch," the former "wake" (margin "watch"). Both should be translated alike, "watch"; for of those who are alive at the Parousia only such as watch will live together with him. But the second verb καθεύδωμεν is the same verb that was used in v. 7 with reference to the pagan sleepers and drunkards; it is not a form of κοιμάω as in 4:13, 14 with reference to the godly dead. This change of verbs with reference to the godly dead arrests attention. Those who translate: "whether we are awake or asleep," get rid of all difficulty, "awake" means to be alive, "asleep" to be dead. But the first verb is "watching," the sec-

ond means done with watching and "asleep." It seems
that Paul purposely did not use the verb he employed
in 4:13, 14 but the one employed in 5:7 in order to
make us think of the two kinds of sleep: the one that
of the ungodly while they are yet alive, and, in contrast
with it, the other that of the godly when they lie down
in peace and sleep in death.

This double "whether" clause undoubtedly reverts
to 4:13-17 and to the answer there given regarding
the Thessalonian dead. This means that the two sections 4:13-18 and 5:1-11 belong together and are the
real burden of the second part of the epistle.

11) This certainty is increased by the closing
admonition which plainly recalls 4:18 although an
addition is now made: **Therefore, comfort one another and build up one the one even as also you are
doing.** The first clause is so plainly an exact repetition of 4:18 that we cannot translate: "Exhort one
another" (R. V. and A. V. margin); this is the less
possible since "build up" follows. No; comfort is
also proper in 5:1-10, and this is what the Thessalonians needed first of all.

When Paul repeats he usually adds something; he
does so here: "and build up one the other one," etc.
This is Biblical edification, namely increase in knowledge, assurance, spiritual strength. It is this upbuilding which will produce comfort. Instead of a second
ἀλλήλους, or instead of omitting this and allowing it to
be supplied, we have εἰς τὸν ἕνα, "the one the one," one
Christian another one. B.-D. calls this a Hebraism;
R. 692 does better when he calls this a distributive
explaining the reciprocal ἀλλήλους and in *W. P.* points
to I Cor. 4:6. Wohlenberg cites an example from the
classics that duplicates Paul's expression. Individual
is to build up individual; this goes beyond reciprocity,
for he who has shall supply him who yet lacks.

"Even as also you are doing" is commendation. This was the practice followed among the Thessalonians in regard to all other Christian matters; it was to be the practice also in regard to this important matter. So all unnecessary grieving would cease, all the bereaved would be comforted by being built up in clear, sound knowledge and blessed conviction.

Admonitions regarding Congregational Matters

12) The hortations given in 4:1-12 pertain to the individual lives of the members; the hortations found in 5:12-22 deal with the membership as a whole. The admonitions are intended for the congregation. They are the reaction to information brought by Timothy. We may call them fitting; yet not as though they are correcting glaring faults but only as helping the Thessalonians "to abound more and more" (4:1). A simple transitional δέ introduces them.

Now we request you, brethren, to know those toiling among you and superintending you in the Lord and remonstrating with you and to consider them very much on account of their work.

"We request" is used as it was in 4:1 without again adding "we admonish." It is a fruitless effort to prove that Paul is not speaking of the presbyters of the Thessalonian church but only of voluntary workers which the church is to hold in esteem. Was the church still unorganized? If it was still unorganized when Paul and Silvanus had to leave, had not Timothy attended to proper organization? If, however, the church had presbyters, would they be passed by and the church be told to honor only voluntary workers?

The Thessalonians are "to know" their spiritual leaders because of the blessed work they are doing and, knowing them as such workers, they are ever "to consider" them "very much" (literally, "exceedingly") for their work's sake. In Rev. 2:2 Jesus, too, uses οἶδα: "I know thy works." Simple knowledge is referred to, for the effect of this knowledge upon those who know is expressed by the second infinitive, and hence γινώσκειν is not used. The second perfect εἰδέναι is used in the sense of the present.

The writers give great credit to the Thessalonian elders when they describe these elders as "those toiling among you and superintending you in the Lord and training you," the one article denotes one group and not three. These elders toil, preside, train. No work is too hard and ardous for them; they take the forefront and preside or superintend; they also train and discipline the Thessalonians. M.-M. 541 and others argue that because "preside over you" occurs in the second place, and because this word is used in so many connections, therefore it does not mean "official" presiding, i. e., that it does not refer to elders.

So much is true, official position is not the point of these participles, the Thessalonians are not asked to esteem these men because of the high office for which they have been chosen. It is because of *what they do* for the Thessalonians that they are to be considered; but that fact in no way implies that, when they are doing this, they cannot be elders but must be only energetic volunteer workers. Like all verbs of ruling, the second participle governs the genitive, and "in the Lord" means that their taking the lead is done in a truly Christian way.

Trench has νουθετέω = to train by word, "by the word of encouragement when no more than this is wanted, but also by the word of remonstrance, of reproof, of blame, where these may be required." "The word indicates much more than a mere Eli-remonstrance: 'Nay, my sons, for it is no good report that I hear' (I Sam. 2:24); indeed, of Eli it is expressly recorded, as regarding his sons: οὐκ ἐνουθέτει αὐτούς

(3:13)." Consider the three descriptive participles together; they certainly describe what we to this day would call good pastors.

13) "To consider them very much in love on account of their work" implies appreciation, esteem, and thus willingness to be led and trained. Intelligent Christian love is to be the inward motive for this consideration, and the work these faithful men do is to be the outward motive. "Their work" sums it up in one word. Wherever we have faithful pastors such as these and appreciative members the right condition obtains for spiritual success and progress in the work of the church.

Note that no request is made of the Thessalonian elders, which says a good deal in regard to their faithful work. Also, only a request is made of the membership to continue to esteem the elders, which means that the good condition already existing is to continue. The two durative infinitives say a great deal. In line with them is the durative present imperative: "Continue to be at peace among your own selves." This implies that they are at peace and is thus a commendation. But when a congregation has beautiful peace in its midst, the devil likes to stir up trouble. He likes to destroy the lovely garden. Let him not do this! "Among your own selves" includes elders and members jointly.

14) Commendation underlies v. 12, 13 as we have seen; the present imperatives which now follow likewise tell the Thessalonians to continue and thus in a way also commend them because they ask for no new courses of action. But now faulty members are named; the Thessalonians had some, which is no surprise seeing that all had been pagans not so long ago, that all faults could not be sloughed off at once by all, and that new converts were constantly coming into the congregation. Παρακαλοῦμεν is now in

place, and the repetition of "brethren" indicates a new line of admonition.

Now we admonish you, brethren, keep remonstrating with the disorderly, keep encouraging the fainthearted, keep supporting the weak, keep being longsuffering toward all.

The imperatives are *oratio recta*, which is stronger than the infinitives used in v. 12, 13 and stronger than ἵνα found in 4:1. Note that Paul is flexible in the use of his language. Some have thought that these imperatives are intended for the elders, especially also since νουθετεῖτε repeats the participle used in v. 12 regarding the elders. Correcting faults in members is, however, the duty of the whole congregation; the elders would certainly also do their part.

The ἄτακτοι are those out of line, they are like the careless soldier who is too far forward or too far back and thus needs a sharp word of rebuke. The ones who are out of order are usually thought to be the members who stopped work in view of the nearness of the Parousia; 4:11 is referred to and II Thess. 3:6 where ἀτάκτως appears. But we know as little about this lack of Christian order as we know about the form the "weakness" took. All the statements are so brief, there are four of them in rapid succession; accordingly, none of them could have been grave. Disorderliness could have been of various kinds just as weakness was.

The fainthearted (literally, "small-souled") are thought to be those who grieved for their dead (4:13, etc.), but we doubt this, for the grieving was done by the members in general, and twice (4:18 and 5:11) we see that they are to be comforted while they are here to be encouraged. These small-souled members are perhaps those who had small courage to face the afflictions that were caused them by hostile outsiders.

The weak are not the physically sick but those who were spiritually and morally weak, who thus need to be supported; ἀντέχω is used in the New Testament only in the middle and means "to hold to" and thus governs the genitive. They are not to be let go and to be abandoned as persons who amount to little but are to be held to and to be supported.

Longsuffering toward all means not only toward all in the three groups mentioned but toward all, including even outsiders, who may be very trying at times because of their hostile actions. The verb means to hold out long before taking action; God himself is longsuffering toward us.

15) Thus the next admonition is in line with the thought: **See that no one renders meanness for meanness, but always keep pursuing the thing that is good** (in the sense of beneficial) **in regard to one another and in regard to all.**

The whole congregation is to see to it that none of its members gives way to revengeful actions. There was provocation enough, for 2:14 states that the Thessalonians had suffered because of persecution. The old feeling to pay back some persecutor when the opportunity offered itself could easily arise in young Christians. Κακόν = "meanness," baseness; and ἀπό in the verb = to give back "in full" (as ἀπέχω, Matt. 6:2, 5, 16, to have all that is due, receipted in full). The absence of the article means "anything bad in exchange for anything bad," tit for tat.

"On the contrary" (ἀλλά), the Thessalonians must ever keep on pursuing the thing that is good (now we have the article, not just something that is good but *the* thing that is good and beneficial to others, friend or foe) in regard to one another (in the congregation) and in regard to all (even those outside). One wonders whether the Greek readers felt the double sense in which they used διώκειν, "to pursue or chase" and "to persecute," that, whereas someone persecuted them, they were not to persecute in turn but were to pursue and to get for their persecutors the thing that was beneficial for them. But this applies also to fellow members who may on occasion serve us a mean turn. Take it with longsuffering and, when an opportunity offers itself, do them the best thing in return.

These are the astonishing ethics of Jesus, Luke 6:27, etc.; Matt. 5:39, etc.; 44, etc., which are constantly inculcated by the apostles, I Pet. 3:9; Rom. 12:14, etc.; I Cor. 4:12, etc.; 6:7, etc. What a contrast to the world's ethics! Yet how sensible, for when I receive a slap and slap in return I only provoke a second slap to my own hurt and thus slap after slap, hurt after hurt to myself; but when I reward a slap with a favor I make it hard for the man to slap me again, he will soon cease, and I gain less harm to myself and may very likely win the man himself as my friend. Yet we persist in being resentful and vengeful.

16) From actions toward other persons the admonition turns to actions that are spiritual in themselves. **Always rejoice!** The adverb is placed forward for the sake of emphasis; this is also done in the next admonition, and in the third the phrase is placed forward. This helps to show that the trio belongs together: joy — prayer — thanks, these three are well called *die Grundstimmung des Christen.* No special connection with what precedes is necessary: Rejoice in spite of meanness and persecution. The joy of the Christians is the product of the whole gospel and of the salvation that is theirs in Christ. Earthly joys fade after a brief moment; our joy of salvation never fades. Yet we need to be told ever to rejoice, for we let so many little adversities lessen and even darken our joyfulness. The Christian life is the only truly joyful and happy life even as it merges into eternal joy. II Cor. 6:10.

17) **Ceaselessly pray!** Eph. 6:18, "at every season"; Rom. 12:12, "continuing steadfastly"; Luke 18:1, "always." All these have the same meaning. Paul himself did not constantly murmur and utter prayers so that his mind was occupied with nothing else. "Ceaselessly" does not mean that our regular custom of praying in the morning, the evening, at meals, in church, is not to be broken. The "always" of Jesus and this "ceaselessly" = that we are always to be fit and ready for an approach to God in worshipful praying. This verb is never used with reference to praying to men; it is used only in the full sacred sense of turning to God in worshipful forms. The heart which is ever attuned to God as being his child turns to God as well in its secret thoughts as in its many utterances.

18) **In everything giving thanks!** Ἐν παντί is not ἐν παντὶ καιρῷ (Eph. 6:18), "on every occasion," but "in connection with everything." The explanation of this πᾶν is found in the πάντα, "all things," of Rom. 8:28, all of which cooperate for good to God's children and thus call forth our thanks to God.

We need to learn this secret of the happy Christian life — thankfulness. If everything actually conspires to do us good, how can we do otherwise than always rejoice? What if we do not always at once see and feel the good, is there not joy in anticipating the sight? The Christmas tree is already being decorated although the doors are still closed, yet how the little hearts beat with expectant joy!

For this (is) **God's will in Christ in regard to you.** What is? The three just mentioned and surely not only the last. God wants us to rejoice always, to pray ceaselessly, to give thanks in everything. If it is all his will, we certainly must not frustrate that will with our folly. Θέλημα is the thing God wants in regard to us (εἰς). This is his sweet gospel will "in connection with Christ," in connection with all that is embodied in the Anointed One. To what a new, high, blessed plane these injunctions lift us!

19) The γάρ clause separates the trio of imperatives from the new group which now follows. Formally, the first two are negatives with μή, the others positive, although the last ("hold yourselves away from") is negative in thought. Really, we have but three admonitions; the third about testing everything is only expounded by the last two. **The Spirit do not extinguish!** The present imperative indicates a course of action. In all five injunctions the imperative is placed last, thus both object and verb are emphatic, all is striking brevity.

This is scarcely "the spirit" of the new life in the Thessalonians but the Holy Spirit who moves their hearts. The writers of this epistle are not referring to the special miraculous charismata such as speaking with tongues, inspired prophetic utterances, healings, and the like. They are writing about the ordinary and regular work of the Spirit and not about his extraordinuary, miraculous manifestations. All that v. 12-18 contain, and all that follows in v. 20-22 deals with nothing exceptional. All of the Thessalonians are addressed, all of them are to let the Holy Spirit guide and prompt them, and none are to squelch these holy promptings.

They must not "extinguish" the Spirit, quench the holy fire and ardor he kindles in their hearts. The expression "to extinguish the Spirit" is concentrated, the Spirit being identified with what he produces; "extinguish" is figurative for putting out the holy fire upon the altar of the heart. Such quenching occurs when the fervor that the Spirit kindles in us is greatly lessened or put out altogether by fleshly, worldly objections. Many a noble, generous, godly impulse dies without producing fruit in action or brings only a fraction of what it might produce. Who has not seen many a good suggestion, plan, appeal, which certainly came from the Spirit, literally extinguished in whole or in part by unspiritual objections of ignorant or hostile brethren? So often some refuse to respond to the Spirit's promptings and yield to the flesh. These are worthy of blame. This occurs both in the individual, in the inner circle of his own motives and impulses, as well as in meetings where united efforts for some plan or work are to be set going.

20) **Prophesyings do not set at nought!** Because prophesyings are mentioned, some commentators regard this as a reference to the extraordinary charismata. They overlook the fact that two gifts of prophecy are clearly distinguished in the apostolic church: one was the reception of immediate revelation, the other the acquisition of mediate revelation and the ability to transmit this acquired revelation to others. The former was miraculous, highly exceptional, and could not be acquired. Paul received such revelations but not Silvanus and Timothy, the other writers of this epistle; Agabus received minor revelations. Yet Silvanus and Timothy prophesied by transmitting revelation that had already been given in the Word (Old Testament) and in the apostolic teaching. In I Cor. 14 all the Corinthians are urged to seek this gift and ability. In Rom. 12:7 this kind of prophecy stands at the head of the list of gifts, none of which are miraculous.

This kind of prophesying is certainly suggested in v. 12, for elders were chosen for their ability along this line. In no way does this foster the "clerical idea," for in the apostolic church, even more than in ours today, this ability to deal with the Word was cultivated by the members in general. That is one reason for the rapid spread of the church; that, too, is the reason that Paul could write the letters he wrote, which often have so many quotations from the Old Testament, quotations which our people, including preachers, can scarcely find in the Old Testament without the aid of printed references.

Such prophesyings (note the plural) might be "set at nought," regarded as being worth little or nothing. Some made light of the instruction and admonition thus offered and made derogatory, unspiritual, or even flippant objections, especially when the prophesyings were offered by fellow members and not by the elders themselves. Against this sort of thing the writers warn the Thessalonians: let it never occur (durative present imperative).

21) **All things, however, test!** Adversative δέ is fully supported. Instead of setting prophesyings at nought, the Thessalonians ought to test everything, not only prophesyings but "everything" (πάντα) that might affect their religious life. For the idea of testing prophesyings compare I Cor. 14:29. Some had a special gift for this, I Cor. 12:10. The rule to be applied is indicated in Rom. 12:7, the Analogy of Faith. See the author's interpretation of this passage. Everything in the church was to be tried and tested by means of the Word. Δοκιμάζω is a favorite word of Paul's: to test as coins or metals are tested in order to see whether they are genuine and of full weight. This figurative meaning lay back of the common use of this word.

A true test may have one of two results: the thing tested may prove to be genuine or may prove to be spurious. Paul does not, however, stop with what the thing itself may prove to be, he advances at once to what the Thessalonians ought to do with the thing, whatever way the tests may result. **The excellent thing hold fast! From every form of what is wicked hold off!**

These two commands complete the order to test everything. Note the verbal correspondence in κατέχετε and ἀπέχεσθε; both mean "to hold," but the active means "to hold the excellent *thing fast*," the middle "to hold *oneself* away from the wicked thing." Τὸ καλόν is generic, "the excellent thing" that you have found so by applying the real test, no matter what this thing may be. This word has a fine flavor in the Greek and means excellent, fair, and beautiful, something that is an honor and a grace to the possessor. Κατά in the verb is perfective and lends it energy: hold firmly fast. Since prophecies have been mentioned, we think especially of the excellent doctrines, individual truths, spiritual principles and precepts that are often offered in a most effective way by such prophecy. This epistle is full of such καλά. Hold to them!

22) On the other hand: "from every form of what is wicked hold yourselves off." Since τὸ καλόν is a substantive, its opposite, πονηροῦ, must also be. The point to be noted is that τὸ καλὸν is definite while πονηροῦ is not; for the opposite of "the excellent thing" is not merely πονηροῦ but the entire expression: παντὸς εἴδους πονηροῦ, "every form of what is wicked." This "every" is both definite and comprehensive, and πονηροῦ must thus be anarthrous: "what is wicked" (qualitative).

Trench and C.-K. make a distinction between μορφή and σχῆμα, "form" and "fashion" inherent in the object irrespective of the fact whether it is seen by others or not, and εἶδος, "form" as seen. Yet the latter is not a mere appearance without a corresponding substance as Luther has translated it: *allen boesen Schein;* which is also the translation of the A. V.: "all appearance of evil." The latter would mean that we are to avoid everything that *looks* wicked to those who happen to see it although it *may not be* wicked at all. What is said by Paul is that wickedness has many forms, every one of which *is really* wickedness and also appears so to men, and we are to keep away from every form that wickedness may assume.

Πονηρός is always to be understood in the active sense as denoting something malignant, working mischief, hurting all with whom it comes into contact. Who, then, would want to have contact with such a thing in any form? It blasts, poisons, kills. Keep away from it entirely. We should not restrict this command to the field of morals. The worst forms of wickedness consist of perversions of the truth, of spiritual lies, although today many look upon these forms with indifference and regard them rather harmless. The fact that moral perversions are included is self-evident; these also work to destroy the spiritual life and appear in many forms. Only he will be "without blame at the coming of our Lord Jesus Christ" who follows the Spirit, obeys his Word as true prophesyings bring it to him, holds to the good, and rejects every form of what is wicked.

The Conclusion

23) As the first part of the epistle closes with a prayer-wish (3:11-13), so also does this second part. **Now he, the God of the peace, may he sanctify you wholly, and your spirit entire and (your) soul and (your) body, may they blamelessly, in connection with the Parousia of our Lord Jesus Christ, be preserved!**

The synonymous adjectives ὁλοτελεῖς, predicate accusative to ὑμᾶς, and ὁλόκληρον, predicative nominative, are placed so closely together, one at the end, the other at the beginning of its clause, in order to obtain an emphasis for each. They resemble one another very much in sound, in sense they are synonymous. God is to sanctify *vos totos*; Luther: *euch durch und durch*; R., *W. P.*: "the whole of each of you, every part of you." In English we should use an adverb "totally" or "wholly." To what extent this is to occur is added by specifying still more closely: spirit, soul, body, each "as entire," is to be preserved blamelessly.

Αὐτός is not in contrast to anyone else; it merely intensifies the subject: "Now *he*, the God of the peace." He is named according to the divine peace he bestows (see "peace" in 1:1). "The peace" is articulated because there is only one of this kind which, through Christ, repairs the rupture caused by sin. The genitive characterizes. Paul does not refer to strife among the Thessalonians; he is not trying to overcome such strife. He would not strike at a new fault in a closing wish. The God of the peace who has bestowed all his saving peace upon us, Paul says, may he finish his work by sanctifying you each in totality, i. e., set you apart for himself *in toto*. Some think the adjective denotes quality, but the thought is evidently one of extent: sanctify your complete being.

No nook nor corner of your life is to be left where the peace of God does not penetrate; it is to reign undisturbed in every province of your being. Many are satisfied with a partial Christianity, some parts of their life are still worldly. The apostolic admonitions constantly prod into all the corners of our nature so that none may escape purification. Here sanctification refers to the whole work of God, which follows the kindling of faith in our hearts. The aorist optative of wish ἁγιάσαι is constative. The sanctification is not wrought in one instant, as many perfectionists imagine, but is a steady development (II Pet. 3:18; Eph. 4:15).

Καί is explicative. The wish is stated in another way and also with more fulness. Instead of the simple pronoun "you" we now have what "you" means: "your spirit and soul and body." Instead of the predicate adjective ὁλοτελεῖς we have the allied ὁλόκληρον, which is neuter only because the first noun τὸ πνεῦμα is neuter, but is to be construed with all three nouns just as is ὑμῶν. Instead of "sanctify" we now have "be preserved," τηρηθείη, another constative optative of wish which sums up the whole preservation just as the first aorist sums up the whole sanctification. When God sanctifies us, our spirit, soul, and body are to be preserved. This sanctification preserves and keeps us.

But we have two necessary additions, an adverb and a phrase. These are necessary because, while "may sanctify" is a complete concept, "may be preserved," when it is used with reference to the spirit, soul, and body as "entire," is incomplete, the more so since this might mean that no constituent of our spirit or of our soul or of our body is to be lost, which is, of course, not what is meant. So we have: "may they be blamelessly preserved." The adverb is used for the simple reason that a predicative adjective precedes, and the use of another predicative adjective: "preserved as blameless," would not be good rhetoric. To think that the adverb is "hard" (really meaning that it is out of place) is unfair to Paul because the subject is not God but "your spirit," etc., because the verb of this subject is passive, and because any adverbial modification of this verb, like the verb itself, automatically pertains to the subject. What undergoes a blameless preservation is blameless. The kind of act governs the kind of result.

The ἐν phrase does not state the date of this being preserved, for the preservation occurs in this life and not "*at* the Parousia of our Lord Jesus Christ." This ἐν is exactly like the one occurring in Rom. 2:16 (on which see the author). The conscience of the pagans does not accuse and at times excuse them *on* judgment day but here and now in this life "*in connection with* a day when God shall judge the hidden things of men." Conscience would not judge as it does if no such day were impending. So here our being preserved now is "in connection with" Christ's Parousia. If there were no Parousia, this preservation would be pointless. The context in which ἐν is used always indicates what connection is had in mind. In Rom. 2:16 it is the connection of conscience facing the coming judgment; in the present passage it is the connection of what is done for our spirit, soul, and body in view of the Parousia of our Lord.

Trench defines ὁλόκληρος as retaining all that was at first allotted (ὅλος plus κλῆρος), entire in all its parts, nothing that is necessary to completeness being lacking. An unhewn stone has as yet lost nothing through the shaping process. The word is used with reference to an entire week, a whole skin. A Levitical priest, a sacrifice, dare not be maimed. Some apply the idea of sacrifice in our passage, but this is only one use of this word. It is the Latin *integer* and *integritas* and came to be used with reference to mental and moral entireness. One is spiritually ὁλόκληρος when no grace is missing, but τέλειος when grace has not merely made a beginning but has produced a mature condition. Here "the spirit, the soul, the body," each entire = unmaimed, *unversehrt* (C.-K. 605); if they are unpreserved they will be maimed. This thought is involved in passages such as II Cor. 11:2; Eph. 5:27; Col. 1:22, 28.

Delitzsch, *Biblische Psychologie*, 84, etc., offers information on the various views of trichotomists and dichotomists. The question is simple: "Is man composed of two or of three parts?" In other words, can spirit and soul be divided as soul and body can? A reference to Heb. 4:12 does not establish the affirmative. Man's material part can be separated from his immaterial part, but the immaterial part cannot be divided; it is not a duality of spirit and soul. Where, as here, spirit and soul are distinguished, the spirit

designates our immaterial part as it is related to God,
as being capable of receiving the operations of the
Spirit of God and of his Word; while soul (ψυχή) designates this same immaterial part in its function of
animating the body and also as receiving impressions
from the body it animates. Death is described as the
spirit's leaving the body and as the soul's leaving, for
it is the sundering of the immaterial from the material.

The spirit ought to rule supreme; wholly controlled
by God's Spirit, man ought to be πνευματικός. Sin enabled the ψυχή to control so that man became ψυχικός, his
bodily appetites having sway. The subject is extensive
and can only be touched here. Modern psychology disregards it despite its supreme importance. The view
that Paul was influenced by the pagan views of his day
is unwarranted; the whole Scriptural revelation knows
the constitution of man as it really is and speaks accordingly. We note one wrong opinion, that in our
passage πνεῦμα signifies the new heavenly life that is
kindled in us by God's Spirit. The word is at times
so used, but certainly not here where it is associated
with ψυχή and σῶμα.

When we study this subject we should bear in mind
that the English word "soul" is not a true equivalent
of the Greek ψυχή. While πνεῦμα and ψυχή are at times
used as being practically identical when the context
requires no specific distinction, in English we quite
generally speak of "the soul" as amounting to "the
spirit." This is different in the Greek. For ψυχή furnishes us the adjective ψυχικός while in English "soul"
supplies us no such adjective, and we are compelled to
translate this important Greek adjective with "carnal"
which is derived from the Latin *carnis* and not from
"soul."

The three are merely named side by side in our passage and should be left so and not be changed as though
the wording combines spirit and soul, or as though it

combines soul and body. Yet *"your"* is most significant and thus also the order of the nouns. These Thessalonians are Christians, whose spirit is controlled by
God's Spirit and is not like the helpless spirit of pagans.
Their soul (ψυχή) is thus also controlled by the spirit
(πνεῦμα) and is not like the soul of pagans, which runs
away with the spirit and gives rein to the body. Their
body is thus also with the animating soul submissive
to the spirit and not like the body of pagans which is
urged on by its own low desires. Of *your* spirit, soul,
and body it can be said that they are preserved in a
blameless way, the passive implying the divine Spirit
as the agent.

24) This doubled wish is sealed with the assurance of fulfillment for the writers who make the
wish and for the readers in regard to whom it is
made. **Faithful (is) he who calls you, who also will
do** (this) ! "Faithful" = we may trust him. That
is why he is here named "he who calls you," for
why this call if he is not faithful, if we cannot
depend upon him to do this, i. e., to sanctify and
preserve? Ὁ καλῶν simply characterizes, the participle is used irrespective of time, yet (as always in
the epistles) this calling is efficacious, successful,
having produced acceptance.

"He also will do this" is not absolute but like the
calling; this sanctifying and this preserving are
accomplished only through the Word and the Spirit's
grace. These are *sufficiens,* we can rely on them to the
utmost. The Christian knows: "With strength of
ours here nought is done" (Luther).

25) The writers give the readers first consideration, only in the second place do they think of themselves. **Brethren, keep praying for us!** Περί, "concerning," is the Greek idiom. This request is based
on the efficacy of prayer and at the same time on the

relationship of spiritual brotherhood. Paul seldom begins with "brethren"; this fact makes this construction effective when he employs it.

26) Now the salutation: **Salute all the brethren with a holy kiss!** This is the regular form and not "we salute you"; all the Thessalonians are to act for the writers in conveying to all of themselves the salutation sent. On doing this "in connection with a holy kiss" see Rom. 16:16. "All," not one is to be omitted.

27) The adjuration that follows is exceptional: **I adjure you by the Lord** (two accusatives) **that this letter be read to all the brethren!** We naturally wonder why Paul should use this strong final adjuration. In the first place, it demands that the letter be read to the congregation, for this is what "all the brethren" means; it was not to pass from hand to hand so that it would not reach some. That, too, is why the passive is used. In the second place, this letter was not carried to Thessalonica by Silvanus and Timothy (Coptic versions, note at the end) or by Timothy (Peshito), but by an ordinary messenger and would be handed to some Christian, perhaps not even to an elder, in Thessalonica. Thus, whoever receives and first reads it in a small circle is to see to it that it be read to all in the congregation. The supposition that, because Paul did not come in person, a mere letter would perhaps be regarded as amounting to little, does not seem warranted.

Paul uses the first person singular even as he is the one who is most responsible for the whole work in Thessalonica as also for the contents of this epistle. So it is he who is deeply concerned that the whole congregation with all its members shall get to hear these admonitions, instructions, and evidences of his love. If a special and peculiar reason existed in Thessalonica for an adjuration such as this, the epistle nowhere betrays that fact, and no one has yet successfully stated what it could have been.

28) The final benediction: **The grace of our Lord Jesus Christ with you!** is exclamatory and needs no verb to complete the thought. Other final greetings vary a little, the one in Col. 4:18 being the briefest. "The grace of our Lord Jesus Christ" with all its saving power and all its heavenly gifts summarizes everything. Let this be μετά, in company with you!

The note in the A. V.: "The first (epistle) unto the Thessalonians was written from Athens," is the opinion of the early collectors of the sacred manuscript copies. The letter was written from Corinth; the amanuensis is not known.

Soli Deo Gloria

St. Paul's Second Epistle
To the Thessalonians

CHAPTER I

THE GREETING

1) Paul and Silvanus and Timothy to the church of Thessalonians in connection with God our Father and the Lord Jesus Christ: grace to you and peace from God the Father and the Lord Jesus Christ!

See the discussion in I Thess. 1:1. The writers again use only their unmodified names. The church is addressed as it was in the first epistle save that ἡμῶν is added in the phrase attached. "Grace to you and peace" is amplified by the addition of the phrase "from God the Father and the Lord Jesus Christ." See the discussion of this phrase in the exposition of some of Paul's other letters. The point to be noted is the fact that the Thessalonians are addressed in the same way in both epistles, which means that the attitude of the writers toward the Thessalonians has not been altered by what had occurred in Thessalonica since the first letter was written and sent.

Paul and Silvanus had received the fullest information about Thessalonica from Timothy whom Paul had sent to bring a report (I Thess. 3:1-6). Second Thessalonians evidences the fact that it, too, rests on full information regarding what had occurred since Timothy's return and since the dispatching of First Thessalonians. How did this further information reach Corinth and the writers? Some assume that the Thessalonians had written a letter to Paul. But this epistle nowhere indicates that it is an answer to a letter received from Thessalonica. Still more convincing is the full and detailed information about Thessalonica presented in this epistle, plainly being information which no letter from Thessalonica could have contained — if

(373)

such a letter had been written and had prompted an answer on the part of Paul and his assistants. We know the fact that this information reached Paul, but we do not know how the information was carried.

The Preliminary Section of the Letter

Once More Gratitude to God for the State of the Thessalonians Combined with Prayer for Them

3) This is plainly *the introductory section* of the epistle. Several things are worthy of note. Here the thanksgiving ends with prayer for the Thessalonians; in First Thessalonians the thanksgiving stands alone, and the prayer-wishes are placed at the end of the two parts of the letter (I Thess. 3:11-13; 5:23, 24). A comparison of the two thanksgivings answers the question as to which epistle is first and which second. I Thess. 1:2-2:20 could not appear in a second letter, for it speaks of the beginnings in Thessalonica and, as chapter 3 shows, of the time of Timothy's visit and the reception of the information he brought. II Thess. 1:3, etc., cannot antedate First Thessalonians for this applies only to the later growth in Thessalonica. We note these and still further facts because some critics reverse the order of the two epistles.

Again we note that this second thanksgiving merges (v. 5-10), not merely into the great hope of the Parousia, but, as combined with this, into a reminder of the great final judgment with its terrors for those who disobey the gospel and with its glory for the true saints. The new note, struck with such force already in the opening paragraph of this second epistle, is that of damning judgment. This note is not found in First Thessalonians; it belongs in this second epistle which sketches the great Antichrist and his doom; it serves as a warning also for the Thessalonians, a few of whom were not following the gospel properly but were acting disorderly. This second epistle at once takes a firm, almost stern grip on the Thessalonians — at once reflecting and then fitting the situation in Thessalonica.

The Thanksgiving

We are obliged to give thanks to God always concerning you, brethren, even as it is worthy, that your faith grows exceedingly and the love of each single one of you increases toward one another so that we ourselves boast about you in the churches of God over your perseverance and faith in all your persecutions and the afflictions which you endure, an indication of the righteous judgment of God so that you are deemed worthy of the kingdom of God, in behalf of which you also suffer; etc.

Every commentator remarks that the writers do not say simply, "We give thanks to God always concerning you" (as in other epistles), but here and in 2:12, "We are obliged to give thanks," etc. We need not take note of all the explanations. To call this statement un-Pauline, a mark of spuriousness, implies that a writer must always use the same expression no matter what the circumstances and what his thought may be. To attribute the insertion of obligation to someone who wrote this letter and only submitted it to Paul for his signature is to overdo the explanation. To find "a full-toned liturgical formula," commonly used in later devotional language, and thus to deny the Pauline authorship of this letter, is to misread the meaning of Paul's wording and what the later phraseology intends. In our Communion liturgy the minister still says: "Let us give thanks unto our Lord God," the congregation responds: "It is meet and right so to do," and the minister continues: "It is truly meet, right, and salutary, that we should . . . give thanks," etc. Later forms of language did not produce either Paul's wording or the thought it intends to convey.

The feeling that the expression "we are obliged to thank" (are morally compelled) seems to indicate a reluctance is correct; the wording is intended to make that impression. But instead of being weaker than the simple "we thank," it is stronger. We use similar expressions, for instance: "We (or: you) cannot help but say," etc., implying fullest readiness to say because of facts which are all too plain. So here "we are obliged" means: "we cannot help it, you Thessalonians with your faith and love amid all your persecutions simply make us thank God concerning you." The idea is: if we writers should ever want to hold back our thanks regarding you we just could not. The writers remember I Thess. 1:2 and now say still more. They cannot help it in view of what has transpired since the first letter was written. Πάντοτε has the same force it had in I Thess. 1:2. The placement of "brethren" so far back is also viewed critically, which would have caused Paul to wonder. Why must *he* place every address farther forward? In I Thess. 1:2 he has none!

True, this placement makes the first clause a kind of unit by itself but scarcely so that it separates the next so that we must read: "even as it is worthy because," etc., ὅτι depending on this clause and not on "we are obliged to give thanks." Ὅτι states that for which thanks is being given (*dafuer, dass*, B.-P. 572; "for that," R. V.). Does that, then, make "even as it is worthy" rather superfluous since it is already contained in "we are obliged"? On the contrary, it brings out the very point intended by "we are obliged." Of course, καθώς does not express degree but comparison. It is a *worthy* thing to feel an *obligation to thank God* and *to meet* this obligation, especially when the object imposing the obligation for thanksgiving is so weighty. In ἄξιον there is the idea of weight, one that balances the scales; here the meeting of this obligation and the worthiness of doing so are to be balanced.

This thanksgiving to God concerns the faith and the love of the Thessalonians despite the persecutions that have continued since the visit of Timothy and the sending of the first letter. These persecutions did not upset the faith of the Thessalonians; instead, their faith "grows exceedingly," they cling more intensely to Christ. The supposition that ὑπέρ in the verb implies that their faith grows "beyond" proper sober bounds and thus refers to the disorders mentioned in 3:6, etc., is not supported by the context. The faith is growing "beyond" what it was at the time when the first letter was written. Perhaps even this is too specific; the verb may indicate only a very strong growth, one that is wholly praiseworthy, for who can have too much faith? So also their love is increasing. In I Thess. 3:12 "abound" is added; its absence here is of no particular significance. Persecution drew the members most closely together: "the love of each single one of you all for one another," which is stronger than ὑμῶν εἰς ἀλλήλους, "your love for one another."

In I Thess. 1:3 hope is added to faith and love as an object of thanksgiving. In this epistle hope is not mentioned, and, as we gather from the rest of the letter, this is due to the fact that in Thessalonica some were misconstruing this hope and thus also were changing their conduct. Paul praises what is good and true without the least discount; but he does not praise, he corrects what is faulty and wrong. He does so here. The two letters are misunderstood when the Thessalonian fault, which is revealed in the second letter, is found mentioned in the first. If that were true, I Thess. 1:3 would not speak of the Thessalonian faith, love, and hope with equal gratitude to God, as it does, but would deal with the fault regarding hope.

This fault has developed since the first letter was written. Did it develop as a result of that first letter? Of course, not as a legitimate deduction but due to misunderstanding?   Such an opinion is not justified, whether it is expressed in language that is derogatory to Paul or is toned down to milder language. I Thess. 1:10 speaks of the waiting for Christ as this was reported by Paul prior to the first letter, a waiting with which no fault could be found. I Thess. 5:1, etc., states that the Thessalonians "know" about the times and the seasons and only repeats the main facts of this knowledge. The admonitions to soberness (I Thess. 5:6, 8) are elaborated in such a way that they exclude the conclusion that some were already losing their balance. Finally, Second Thessalonians makes no correction regarding a misunderstanding of anything said in First Thessalonians.

The point of I Thess. 4:13-5:11 is the grieving for the members who had already died.   Second Thessalonians says nothing further about this grieving.   The legitimate conclusion to be drawn is that the comfort offered in First Thessalonians (4:18; 5:11) had been effective — the grieving ceased. What, then, caused the disorderliness that had developed since that time? All that we can say is, the pressure of persecution; and this we say chiefly on the basis of later experiences in the church when calamitous times led many to imagine that Christ would come immediately.

It would be unfair to think that all the Thessalonians or even a majority of them had become unbalanced regarding the Parousia. This was true regarding only comparatively few. But incipient errors must be promptly checked, and it is this that is now done for the Thessalonians. In 3:6, etc., plus v. 14, 15 we see that the church had kept its soberness and thus is ordered to deal with the few who have gone off on a wrong tangent.

4) Ὥστε states the result which the growing faith
and the increasing love of the Thessalonians has: "so
that we ourselves (like others who hear about you)
boast about you in the churches of God over your perseverance and faith in all the persecutions," etc. Ὑμᾶς
αὐτούς is not reflexive but intensive (R. 687) like αὐτός
in I Thess. 5:23; the persons about whom the boasting
is done are indicated by ἐν, which is quite regular even
when the verb is the simplex (it is not a Hebraism).
Where this boasting is done is also stated by ἐν although
this might be a dative stating to whom the boasting is
made. The infinitive is durative. The compound verb,
which is used also by other writers, is proper with the
two ἐν phrases.

Rather much is inferred from the plural "in the
churches of God" when these are thought to be a number of churches that had been newly founded in Achaia,
sufficient time having elapsed since the writing of the
first letter to permit the founding of so many churches
in this new territory. We do not know where the
churches referred to by the writers are located. The
phrase does not necessarily mean that the writers are
present in each church when they boast. It is natural
to think of all the churches with which the writers
from time to time keep making contact through visit-
ors, oral messages, etc. Some of these churches may
have been located in distant places. The word ἐκκλησία,
"assembly," still needs a modifier to show that a Christian assembly is referred to, hence we have "the
churches of God"; the unmodified *ecclesia*, like our
word "church," soon became sufficient.

We recall I Thess. 1:8 where the writers are happy
to say that reports about the Thessalonians have gone
out far and wide so that the writers find the churches
informed about the Thessalonians and need not tell
the news themselves. In II Cor. 8:1, etc.; 9:2, etc., we
see that Paul loves to boast to others about the faith-

fulness and the zeal of one church or of a number of churches. This delights his heart. Who would not a thousand times rather boast than lament and complain?

This boasting is never self-glorification which says what the *churches* are doing while meaning what *Paul himself* has done. The credit is given wholly where it belongs. And the aim is always to encourage and strengthen those to whom the boast is made, to stimulate their consciousness that they are not a lone handful standing by themselves but are bound together with so many others in other cities and provinces. Paul ever has in mind "the Communion of Saints." To this date we boast of one church to another, and it is right so to do. In those early days, when the church was first being planted, it was still more proper to do so. The firm stand of the Thessalonians meant much to the churches who heard of it; and the thought of how much it meant stimulated the Thessalonians, too, to stand ever more firmly and faithfully.

Ἐν indicates the personal, ὑπέρ the impersonal object of the boasting (in II Cor. 10:8 it is περί) : "over your perseverance and faith in all your persecutions," etc., the whole of which should be read as a unit. One article combines the two nouns, ὑμῶν and also the entire phrase belong to both. The fact that love is not again named does not imply that it is disregarded, for it is ever the fruit of faith. It is not stressed in this connection. The stress is on the perseverance, ὑπομονή, "the remaining under," "the brave patience," as Trench calls it, with which the manly Christian holds out. It accompanies genuine faith. The perseverance is named first simply because it is stressed; it is so also in Rev. 13:10 and similarly "thy love and faith" in Philemon 5. We need not regard this double expression as a hendiadys as the older commentators do: persevering faith or faithful persevering, yet the two are closely connected; nor does πίστις mean "faithfulness," it is the same "faith" that was mentioned in v. 3, it is confidence in Christ.

The reason that perseverance and faith are thus combined appears from the phrase "in all your persecutions and the afflictions which you endure." So "the persecutions" have continued, apparently in repeated outbreaks; "all" may reach back and take in those also that occurred prior to the time of the first letter. "Afflictions" is a wider term and includes the painful effects of the persecutions, many of which persist long after the persecution dies down. The view that the article in the expression ταῖς θλίψεσιν prevents ὑμῶν from being construed with this noun is not supported by grammar. The relative clause is added because the Thessalonians are still enduring the painful results.

In the New Testament ἀνέχω always occurs in the middle and is construed with the genitive (B.-D. 176, 1), so we assume that αἷς is an attraction to the case of the antecedent. This verb may govern the accusative, and even a dative of means is at times found. The writers are proud and happy to tell all the churches that the Thessalonians bravely hold out in their faith in spite of all their persecutions and consequent sufferings. Regarding the earlier sufferings see I Thess. 2:14. Therefore the greater is the pity that a church so brave, etc., should have members that have wild, disorderly notions in another direction.

5) We regard the next statement as a simple nominative apposition: "an indication of the righteous judgment of God so that you are counted worthy of the kingdom of God, in behalf of which you also suffer." What is such an "indication," ἔνδειγμα, "a thing pointed out" (ἔνδειξις is the act)? Suffering these afflictions as the Thessalonians suffer them with perseverance and faith. Suffering persecution would not yet be such an indication. When we are construing the apposition we

cannot stop with the minor relative clause "which you endure" but must include the main concepts plus the minor one: "your perseverance and faith in the midst of all your persecutions," etc. But this is not an indication offered by the Thessalonians but one that Paul now points out to them, one that the Thessalonians may not have noted but should note for their comfort. To endure persecution and painful affliction in perseverance and faith may seem like a hardship, often like a needless hardship for the believers. Viewed in its true light, it is "an indication of the righteous judgment of God."

Some expositors regard this judgment as a present judgment of God, others warn us against accepting this idea as though Paul is speaking of "an advance indication of the judgment God will render at the last day." They point to what follows as substantiating this idea; but this only follows and is not yet said in v. 5. Nor does the article "the righteous judgment" compel one to think of the "the final judgment." This is God's judgment on the persevering faith of the Thessalonians right here and now. The thought often occurs to true Christians that God is unrighteous when he lets them suffer severe persecution. This is the problem with which Ps. 73 deals. It is ever a righteous and thus most blessed judgment, and we are to see the indication to that effect.

Hence also εἰς τό does not denote purpose as those suppose who think of the final judgment. This infinitive phrase states the outcome or result of God's righteous judgment: "so that you are deemed worthy of the kingdom of God," namely in this judgment of his which is indicated by the perseverance and faith with which you suffer. The genitive indicates to what the ἔνδειγμα refers; the infinitive clause states to what the κρίσις refers. "To be accounted worthy of the kingdom of God" is almost the verdict now pronounced upon the

Thessalonians; yet one may debate a little as to whether εἰς τό is meant in that sense, for every act of judging (κρίσις) involves a verdict. The infinitive rather at once states the outcome or result of the act of judging. The idea that εἰς τό expresses purpose is not tenable. A righteous verdict has no further purpose than to be what it is, a righteous act. But a verdict always has a result, and that is the main thought here. For this reason, too, the infinitive is an aorist.

Here we again have the idea of weight in ἄξιος (as in the adjective in v. 3). The ungodly are like chaff which the wind drives away, they cannot stand in the judgment now or ever (Ps. 1:4, 5); but perseverance and faith which are tried by persecution and affliction have weight in God's judgment. This weight of worthiness does not lie in our suffering but in Christ who fills our faith. The infinitive, too, does not mean "to be made worthy," least of all by what we suffer, but "to be deemed or accounted worthy" and thus matches the idea of a "judgment," God's pronouncing a verdict. Here "the kingdom of God" is the kingdom of glory. "To be accounted worthy of this kingdom" = to be considered fit for entering this kingdom at the final consummation.

It was a tremendous encouragement to the Thessalonians to be told that their unshaken faith in all their persecutions constituted an ἔνδειγμα or indication that God judged them to be worthy of eternal blessedness, that his judgment pointed to this outcome and result.

6) The point to be noted is the fact that this judgment of God which results in regarding the Thessalonians worthy of God's kingdom is absolutely *righteous*. Hence the substantiation: **if, indeed, it is righteous with God duly to give in return affliction to those afflicting you and (thus) to you that are afflicted surcease in company with us in connection with the revelation of the Lord Jesus from heaven**

in company with his power of angels in flaming fire, etc.

Εἴπερ is the strengthened εἰ and is used in a condition of undisputed reality that is fully assured for the reader as well as for the writer, here: "if, indeed, it is righteous as it most certainly is in your judgment as well as in ours."

The Scriptures emphasize the absolute righteousness of God in the final judgment. In this public judgment before the whole universe of men and angels all will acclaim that God is righteous in acquitting the believers and equally righteous in damning the ungodly and unbelievers. Both verdicts will rest on absolute justice. The damned themselves will not dream of challenging or even questioning the verdict that sends them to their doom. Those who appear in God's judgment with the righteousness of God bestowed upon them by the gospel through faith (Rom. 1:16, 17) *must* be declared righteous by a righteous God; those who appear in the unrighteousness of their sin and unbelief (Rom. 1:18) *must* be damned by a righteous God. In the full light of the last day all the fallacies that today darken men's judgment will disappear. The fact that God is and must be righteous is axiomatic; a God who is unrighteous in the least cannot exist.

Ἀπό has the force of "duly"; ἀντί, "in return for," hence "duly to give in return" and in this sense "to recompense"; aorist to denote the complete final act. The justice of giving "affliction to those afflicting you" is beyond question (Matt. 7:2). This is what they demand of God by their actions, demand again and again, and God would not be righteous if he did not meet this demand upon his righteousness. The proposition is axiomatic even as far as all ordinary sense of human right and justice is concerned.

7) Καί has consecutive force: "and thus." The self-evident nature of the first proposition carries with

it the self-evidence of the second, that in righteousness God must then duly give "to you that are being afflicted" by these afflicters "surcease" from affliction "in company with us," the writers, who now endure the same unjust affliction. Ἄνεσις is relief or rest and is exactly the proper opposite to affliction. The righteous hand of God must interpose: as it crushes forever the afflicters of the righteous, so it must free the afflicted and place them into his kingdom. Their affliction was permitted only to test and try the genuineness of their justifying faith. The end must be eternal rest in the kingdom to which they clung by faith in the Savior-King.

The idea that their suffering affliction merits this reward is the very opposite of all that the Scripture teaches and of the justice here set forth, for the acts of afflicting God's people are only the public evidences of ungodliness and unbelief, i. e., of the rejection of God and Christ, while the perseverance under such afflictions belongs to the public evidence of faith in God and Christ, in the grace and the salvation they bestow. The final public judgment deals with the open evidence as establishing what it evidences in the hearts of the one class as well as in the hearts of the other. It is this fact that publicly displays the absolute righteousness of God's judgment.

Paul is the last man to fail to include himself and his assistants with his readers. The Thessalonians saw how the storm of persecution broke over him and Silvanus when they worked in Thessalonica, which involved also Jason (Acts 17:5, etc.). Verily, they were in company with each other (μετά) in the matter of this significant affliction for Christ's sake and the gospel's (Mark 10:29). What Paul writes to the Thessalonians in the way of assured comfort is what is his own deepest assurance and comfort. He also ever has in mind the fellowship of all believers in the *Una Sancta*.

The world hates all of them because Jesus has taken them out of the world (John 15:18, etc.) ; every evidence the world supplies for this fact is so much assurance and comfort that the righteous God deems the believers worthy of his kingdom and will duly grant them rest in that kingdom.

God often deals with those who afflict the believers now and grants to the latter seasons of refreshing (Acts 3:19). But all this is only preliminary and only partially reveals the justice of God. Not of this does Paul speak here but of the last day and of the final judgment: "in connection with (or: at) the revelation of the Lord Jesus from heaven in company with his power of angels," etc. This is the Parousia (I Thess. 2:19; 3:13; 4:15; 5:23; II Thess. 2:1, 8) which is called "the revelation" because the Lord Jesus will then be revealed visibly in all his glory, majesty, and power so that every eye shall see him, also they that pierced him (Rev. 1:7).

In these two letters the expression "the Lord Jesus" occurs a number of times. When Paul attributes the final judgment to God he does so in the sense of what John 5:27 and Acts 17:31 state, and what the phrase "in connection with the revelation of the Lord Jesus" conveys — ἐν being more than temporal. "From heaven" ("out of the heavens," I Thess. 1:10; Acts 1:11) means visible descent in glory. "With his power of angels" is not a genitive of quality: "with his mighty angels" (A. V., but the margin is correct). Μετά governs δυνάμεως αὐτοῦ. Then ἀγγέλων is regarded as an appositional qualitative genitive since μετά is evidently chosen because of the mention of angels: "in company with his power as exhibited in angels" who will accompany him. Next to Christ are angels; all Christ's power is visibly displayed in them at his Parousia.

8) The reader automatically continues with the next phrase: "in flaming fire." He would not halt at

the end of v. 7 and connect this phrase with the following participle, and still less would he halt before αὐτοῦ and connect this with the participle and thus obtain a genitive absolute: "he with flaming fire giving due justice," etc. This is not a genitive absolute, for the genitive participle modifies τοῦ Κυρίου Ἰησοῦ, who will execute the judgment for God. We construe: "in company with his power of angels in flaming fire." This is an allusion to Ps. 104:4 (Heb. 1:7): "who makes his ministers a flaming fire." Those who consider only Isa. 66:15 and 29:6 think that the Lord himself appears as flaming fire; it is his power as displayed in his angels that flames like fire.

The Scriptures use both "in fire of flame" and "in flame of fire" so that the readings vary in our passage. The expression goes back to Exod. 3:2 although Paul's wording has its source in Ps. 104:4. "A fire of flame" = a flaming fire (characterizing genitive). Some of the early commentators understand δύναμις, "power," in the sense of "army": "his army of angels" (the abstract for the concrete); but the word is not used in this way.

The picture presented is most tremendous. While the description pertains to the angels — the Lord's power exhibited in them, their innumerable host being a vast fire descending with shooting flames — it leaves us to imagine the unimaginable power and glory of him who descends in the center of this host, whose power and glory in this revelation human words cannot describe.

Διδόντος ἐκδίκησιν is also Old Testament phraseology (Isa. 66:15): **giving justice to those who do not know God and to those who are disobedient to the gospel of our Lord Jesus,** etc. The present participle is descriptive; the expression is used regarding the guilty: "rendering vengence," it is used with this verb only here in the New Testament. The two articles point to two classes: "those who do not know God" (pagans without contact with the gospel) — "those who obey not the gospel of our Lord Jesus" (Jews and pagans who reject the gospel). The two substantivized participles are present tenses and are descriptive of condition (εἰδόσι is a second perfect and is always used as a present). This not knowing God is the wilful, guilty ignorance described in Rom. 1:18-32 and further explained in Rom. 2:14-16. Not obeying the gospel is to refuse it the faith which it would create.

9) Οἵτινες is both qualitative and causal: **such (and because they are such) as shall suffer as justice destruction eternal away from the face of the Lord and from the glory of his might when he comes to be glorified among his saints and to be marvelled at among all those that believed, for our testimony to you was believed in connection with that day.**

"Such," as v. 8 states they are, and as such the justice they shall suffer is no less than "destruction eternal away from," etc., where there is only outer darkness, weeping, and gnashing of teeth, Matt. 22:13. Δίκην is the predicate accusative. No man can describe all that ὄλεθρος and its synonym ἀπώλεια contain. Those who think that Paul does not dwell on the horrors of hell because he does not describe its details may note that he uses these most powerful terms. Nothing can go beyond paying as a just penalty "destruction (ruin, devastation) eternal."

The view that this consists in being "away from the Lord's face," etc., is untenable. "Destruction" itself states in what it consists, for it is a descriptive term. Those who find annihilation in it would thereby abolish hell, others misunderstand αἰώνιος and reduce it to a long term which, however, eventually ends. There is no time beyond the last day, either short or long, but only timelessness, eternity, "the eon to come"; this is what the adjective means, which is true of the ζωή or "life" of the blessed as it is true of the "destruction" of the damned. This destruction occurs "away from the Lord's face" and thus in the outer darkness. They loved the darkness rather than the light (John 3:19) during their earthly life when they might have walked in the light; they thus brought upon themselves damnation, destruction where the face of the Lord sheds no light, which is already description enough.

"And from the glory of his strength" rounds out the description of the destruction. Ἰσχύς means the might or strength that the Lord possesses whether he exhibits it or not; compare δύναμις in v. 7. But "the glory" of it is its blessed and thus glorious manifestation. So the Lord does let his might shine forth, namely in his glory-reign in heaven, far away from which glory the damned lie wrecked in an eternal wreck.

10) "When he comes" (or "shall come") ; ὅταν, "whenever," once more points to the unknown date of the Lord's Parousia. Two infinitives of purpose follow, they are aorist passives, effective constatives (not descriptive presents) : "to be glorified among his saints and to be marvelled at among all who believed." Some have at least the first ἐν mean: *an seinen Heiligen,* so that the glorification really goes out from the Lord and glorifies his saints; but the two ἐν are exactly alike, and the second will not permit such a modification. Both prepositions mean "among." The saints will surround their Lord with praise, honor, and glory; his believers will marvel at his glory "in that day" when their bodily eyes shall see him as he is (I John 3:2). The verbs are passive and not middle as some would render them: glorify himself, have himself marvelled at.

In v. 9 the damned are removed from the glory that shines in Christ; in v. 10 the saints surround Christ and not only see his glory but also glorify him in response. They are rightly named saints, for sinners must ever flee from the face of Christ's glory. The language has an Old Testament flavor. Various passages may be cited that have similar expressions. We have even a kind of *parallelismus membrorum* in the correspondence of the second infinitive: "and to be treated with wonder among all his believers." Wonder or marvelling is only a second term for glorifying — glorifying going out toward him in praise, marvelling keeping ourselves filled with wonder. "Among all his believers" (aorist: that did believe) fits this wonderment. At one time they walked by faith, by trusting this unseen Lord Jesus; now at his Parousia they see him. This is far beyond all that they had ever conceived, and wonder overwhelms them.

Here we have the same order of terms: saints — believers, that occurs elsewhere (Eph. 1:1); the former is more comprehensive and is also passive; those upon whom all the Spirit's sanctifying work has been done, all his work in setting them apart for God; the latter indicates the central part of this work and is expressed actively, the response of trust and confidence. Αὐτοῦ does not need to be repeated. The aorist participle conveys the idea that their faith has now turned to sight. The duplication in the second infinitive clause emphasizes and magnifies the effect of the Lord's appearance among the blessed; in fact, it cannot be adequately stated because it will be so great.

It is characteristic of Paul's style to add something when such an expression is duplicated; here it is the word "all." This "all" conveys the idea that at the Parousia the multitude of believers will be great. The Thessalonians are not to think that the ones who believed will be only a little flock. When all of them are at last assembled they will be a glorious host. "All" also conveys the thought that everyone who believed will be there to marvel. Beyond this we need not go; the thought of the *Una Sancta* is enough. The fact that "all" includes the Thessalonian believers is stated in the next clause; the fact that those already dead will also be there (I Thess. 4:14, 15) is certainly true although the difference between the living and the dead is here not touched upon in any special way. The resurrection is implied. The supposition that *after* "that day" still more will be brought to faith and become believers is excluded by the very idea of the Parousia itself.

The fact that a parenthesis should be inserted at this point in Paul's grandiose description has been called an anticlimax, a weak ending. In the first place, we question that we have a parenthesis. It rests on the supposition that $\dot{\epsilon}\nu$ = "at," and that the last phrase is to be construed with $\dot{\epsilon}\lambda\theta\eta$: "whenever he shall come . . . at that day." This is, however, not tenable because $\dot{o}\tau a\nu$ is *indefinite* and cannot be modified by a phrase that indicates a *definite* date; we cannot properly say: "*whenever* he comes . . . at *that* day." The clause: "whenever he comes" is complete in itself. To construe as has been done would require $\dot{o}\tau\epsilon$ in place of $\dot{o}\tau a\nu$. To escape this conclusion we cannot attach the phrase to the two infinitives because they are already dated by being construed with the main verb, and thus their date likewise comes under the indefinite "whenever." The last phrase belongs to the $\dot{o}\tau\iota$ clause where Paul placed it and where the common reader would naturally leave it. This $\dot{\epsilon}\nu$ is not the temporal "at" but the connective $\dot{\epsilon}\nu$: "in connection with." We have it in Rom. 2:16: the accusing and excusing of pagan consciences is "in connection with" the coming judgment day; these actions would not at all take place if that day were not expected. See the same $\dot{\epsilon}\nu$ in I Thess. 5:23: God keeps us *now*, this keeping is ever as "in connection with" the Parousia and certainly not "at."

Since there is no parenthesis, we note the full weight of this important clause with explanatory $\dot{o}\tau\iota$: "for believed was our testimony to you in connection with that day." The presentation is wholly objective since v. 6; it is now given a strong subjective, personal turn. Paul would do that: the Thessalonians are to apply all the objective truth to themselves. *They* believed the testimony which Paul and Silvanus brought to *them* (ἐπί, literally, "upon you," note the accusative), believed it "in connection with that day." Their whole faith connected it with that day of final judgment. The aorist designates the fact.

The fact that the gospel testimony itself dealt with that day is self-evident. See a sample of it in Acts 17:30, 31; God wants all men everywhere to repent *now* because he has appointed *a day* in which he will judge the world through Christ. This is "testimony." Paul and Silvanus and Timothy themselves believe it and hence testify. This testimony "was believed" by the Thessalonians "in connection with that day." They believed it in order that by their faith they might appear at that day among "all those that did believe" and would thus be accepted by the Lord Jesus. It was the connection with that day that was important for the Thessalonians. In I Thess. 2:19 the writers declare that the Thessalonians are their hope, joy, and crown "in the presence of our Lord Jesus Christ in connection with his Parousia." It is always that day and the Parousia in connection with which everything culminates. Note that ἐπιστεύθη links right into ἐν πᾶσι τοῖς πιστεύσασιν and places the Thessalonian believers among all the believers.

Here there is presented what "the revelation of the Lord Jesus" will bring upon all those who did not believe and upon those who did believe, the Thessalonians being among the latter. The righteousness and justice of it all are stressed just as they are in Acts 17:31 and elsewhere. God and the Lord Jesus could not possibly judge save in absolute righteousness.

But the whole impact of this presentation appears in the stupendousness of the Parousia at that day. It exceeds all imagination. The point of it all is directed against those who do not know God and those who do not obey the Lord's gospel, whom the eternal righteousness will bring to just and eternal destruction. The believers are introduced only in the "whenever" clause and are not paralleled with the godless and the disobedient but are only glorifying and marvelling.

Why a description of this kind? Its silent aim for the Thessalonians is to impress them with the terrors of "that day." When that day comes, the universe will know it. The supposition that only believers will know it (2:2) is completely removed. The supposition that it has already come and is here (2:2) is equally destroyed. The godless and disobedient in the whole world will know it as their day of doom. Let the Thessalonians remember all the descriptions of that day which Paul and his assistants have given them by their testimony, which is here once more pointedly summarized for them.

A second, silent aim underlies this passage. Woe to those who disregard the testimony given to the Thessalonians! A few of them have recently done so by acting contrary to the tradition which they received from Paul and the apostles (3:6). Let them think of "that day"! The fact that the Lord's day will come as a thief comes at night they have already been told (I Thess. 5:2) and know. What if that day comes upon them while they are engaged in their disorderliness?

The Prayer

11) It is perfectly in order for Paul to continue with a relative instead of beginning a new sentence. Continuous connection, sometimes in long chains, is the Greek way of linking thought. It is so here: **in regard to which we are also praying always for you**

that our God may count you worthy of the (your) calling and may (thus) fulfill every good pleasure of goodness and (every) work of faith with power in order that there may be glorified the Name of our Lord Jesus in you, and you in it according to the grace of our God and Lord Jesus Christ.

The A. V.'s "wherefore" as a translation of εἰς ὅ is more correct than the R. V.'s "to which end." "In regard to which" is the proper rendering, and the neuter relative refers to what the previous verses state. Ἀξιώσῃ harks back as far as καταξιωθῆναι in v. 5 so that we need not hesitate in regard to making the relative refer to all of v. 5-10 and need not confine it only to what v. 10 states about the saints and believers, for the Thessalonians are to escape the righteous judgment of the godless and disobedient and are thus to be among those glorifying the Lord when he comes. "Also" adds the praying to the thanksgiving (v. 3); on "always" see I Thess. 1:2. Περὶ ὑμῶν has the same force it had in v. 3; we say "for you." Non-final ἵνα states the substance of these prayers for the Thessalonians.

Subject and predicate are reversed in order to obtain an emphasis on both; the object ὑμᾶς is placed before both for the same reason. It is impossible to reproduce this in our non-flexible English. In v. 5 it is being counted worthy of admission into the kingdom of glory (κατά in the verb is perfective); here the verb means to count worthy of the calling we have already received and in which we now live. Κλῆσις has the same meaning it has in other passages: the effective gospel call. The thought is the same as that expressed in I Thess. 2:12: "walking worthy of the God who called you for his kingdom and glory," or in Eph. 4:1: "to walk worthy of the calling wherewith you were called." The only difference is the fact that "our God" is named as the one who judges in regard to our worthiness, whether we walk as our calling intends that we should walk or not. The writers pray that God may deem us worthy and not reject us as unworthy and as unfaithful to the calling he has bestowed upon us. The verb is thus properly the effective aorist.

The counting worthy in v. 11 is the same as that mentioned in v. 5 save that v. 5 looks to the final goal, worthiness for heavenly glory, while v. 11 looks at what intervenes, at our present calling and how we measure up to that. He who is worthy of his present calling is thereby worthy of the kingdom of glory; he who is worthy of that kingdom must be worthy of God's calling. We posit no new meaning for κλῆσις such as a call that is yet to come at the last day, that call then bidding us to enter heaven.

We keep together: "that our God may count you worthy of the (the article in the sense of his or your) calling and may (thus) fulfill every good pleasure of goodness and (every) work of faith with power." This fulfilling is to be the result of God's deeming worthy. Whom our God regards worthy of his calling, to him he will grant this fulfillment. Him who is called and then proves himself unworthy of that gospel call our God cannot bless with this fulfillment but must abandon to his unworthiness and unfaithfulness. "May fulfill" is again properly the effective aorist.

Both genitives are subjective: "every (or "all") good pleasure of goodness," and: "(every or all) work of faith." This is the good pleasure which our goodness puts forth, the work which our faith produces (on the latter compare I Thess. 1:3). Ἀγαθωσύνη is our *bonitas*, the "goodness" which God's call has wrought in us; "faith" is the heart and center of it and is likewise produced in us by God's gospel call. When a Christian proves worthy of his calling, the goodness in his heart and soul will produce all manner of εὐδοκία, good determination of his own free will, and the faith

in his heart will produce all manner of work. Our God
will bring these to fulfillment; the good pleasure will
be carried out, the work completed and not left abor-
tive, half-done. C.-K. 354. God will do this ἐν δυνάμει,
"with power," not with omnipotence, but with the
power of his gospel grace. "All" is not repeated with
"work" but, despite the difference in gender, is intended as a modifier of both nouns: "all good pleasure"
— "all work."

The A. V. translates: "all the good pleasure of his
(God's) goodness." While εὐδοκία is often used with
reference to God, this cannot be the case here because
the two objects cannot be diverse: the good pleasure
of *God's* goodness, the work of *our* faith. C.-K. 354.
Both must be ours: the one the free determination to
which our goodness moves us, the other the good work
to which our faith impels us. The power of grace will
bring both to fulfillment so that God finds us worthy of
his calling. The point to be noted is that we cannot
by our own unaided strength attain this fulfillment
and retain this worthiness. God must do it. Hence
the writers ever pray to him, and the Thessalonians
will follow their example. Another point is that some
of us may lose this worthiness; 3:6, 11 refer to those
in Thessalonica who are in such danger. By losing
this worthiness they would lose also that mentioned in
v. 5. We need scarcely add that in neither passage
the worthiness of work-righteousness is implied; such
false righteousness is the opposite of worthiness in
God's judgment.

12) Ὅπως denotes purpose and is used here because
ἵνα has already been used to introduce the substance of
the prayers, and if it were again used, this would make
the impression that this substance is being continued.
God's purpose in granting us the indicated fulfillment
is "that there may be glorified the Name of our Lord
Jesus in you, and you in it according, etc.," the subject

and the verb are transposed in order to make both emphatic. The relation of this glorification to that mentioned in v. 10 is the same as the counting worthy in v. 11 to that mentioned in v. 5. Already in this life the glorification (like the counting worthy) is to take place, and thus at the last day the final glorification of Christ in us (like the final counting worthy).

Paul does not write that "our Lord Jesus" may be glorified in you but that "the Name of our Lord Jesus" may be glorified (again the effective aorist). We often find τὸ ὄνομα inserted thus: "in the Name of the Lord (Jesus, Christ)" is a frequently occurring phrase. The comment that this Name is a designation like "the Lord" or "the Lord Jesus," etc., is inadequate. "The Name" = the revelation. By the Name he reveals himself to us, and by this revelation of himself we are able to apprehend him. The Name is the link: all by which he makes known to us his person and his work for our saving apprehension. This is to shine forth in glory ἐν ὑμῖν, "in connection with you," so that men may see it. The connection referred to is stated in v. 11: the fulfillment of all the good determination (εὐδοκία) and the work of faith in the Thessalonians. "In you" does not mean secretly, within the recesses of your hearts, for the verb refers to a splendor that is to shine forth so that others may see it (Matt. 5:16); ἐν ὑμῖν means "in connection with you."

Paul also adds strikingly: "and you in connection with it." One may argue as to whether ἐν αὐτῷ means "in connection with him" or "with it" (the Name). In itself this makes little difference, but as it is the Name that receives glory, so it should be the Name that bestows glory. In this life the glory which the Name displays in us believers is wholly spiritual: we appear as blessed (Matt. 5:3, etc.), as God's children and sons, etc. The world, indeed, scorns this spiritual glory, yet many others see it, especially our fellow believers. It was so in the case of Jesus; John says: "We beheld his glory" (John 1:14); the world shuts its eyes against it.

This double glorification is to take place "according to the grace of our God and Lord Jesus Christ." In v. 11 it is "power," here it is "grace." These are not two separate items, for we have defined this power as being spiritual (Rom. 1:16: the gospel is the power of God unto salvation). It is proper to stress the power of grace in the fulfillment of our good determination and of our work and to stress the undeserved favor of God (χάρις) in the reciprocal glorification as the purpose of that fulfillment. It is pure grace and undeserved by us sinners that in connection with us Christ's Name is glorified and we in connection with it. So also ἐν and κατά are proper, the one merely marking the connection that the power has with the fulfillment of our good intent and work, the other doing more by indicating the norm for the double glorification. For this ever follows one norm or rule and keeps to that course, namely the grace of Christ. The moment this grace is abandoned, neither the Name nor we are glorified, the opposite ensues.

The genitive τοῦ Θεοῦ ἡμῶν καὶ Κυρίου Ἰησοῦ Χριστοῦ raises an interesting question: "Is this one person or two?" Our versions translate it as being two by inserting "the" ("the Lord," etc.). Those who think that two persons are referred to, God and Christ, are sometimes governed by dogmatical interests, namely by their claim that Christ is never called God, at least not in such a direct way. For us no dogmatical interest is involved; it makes no difference whether Christ is here called God or not, elsewhere he is called God and is shown to be God. We thus have only a linguistic interest, and this is strongly in favor of one person, for one article (τοῦ) unites both nouns.

Moulton, *Einleitung* 134 (R. 786) quotes examples from the papyri which show that the early Christians called Jesus "our great God and Savior." Robertson says, "Moulton's conclusion is clear enough to close the matter," and then quotes Moulton: "Familiarity with the everlasting apotheosis that flaunts itself in the papyri and inscriptions of the Ptolemaic and Imperial times lends strong support to Wendland's contention that Christians, from the latter part of 1 A. D. onward, deliberately annexed for their divine Master the phraseology that was impiously arrogated to themselves by some of the worst of men" (meaning the Roman emperors). The only thread on which objection could be hung is the fact that Κύριος without the article is often used as a proper name, and this thread is rather weak.

This matter is important for the critics, for they make genuineness of the epistle depend on the answer to this question; if only one person is here referred to, they claim that this epistle cannot be written by Paul.

We note furthermore that Paul loves to bring his thoughts to a unified conclusion and does not conclude at random or with a duality. This he does here by stating that the grace comes to us from one person and not from two. The position of ἡμῶν has nothing to do with the question. The reason that the designation of "Jesus Christ" is here made so weighty by the addition of "our God" to "Lord" is seen when one considers what precedes, especially the glory and the power described in v. 7-10. His revelation we await whose grace now operates in us, God's Son (I Thess. 1:10), "our God and Lord."

CHAPTER II

The Burden of the Letter

The Great Apostasy and the Revelation of the Antichrist Precede the Parousia

1) Δέ passes on to the new subject which ὑπέρ (very much like περί) names: "concerning the Parousia of our Lord Jesus Christ and our gathering together unto him." Now, however, the point is the one that recently became acute in Thessalonica where some imagined ὅτι ἐνέστηκεν ἡ ἡμέρα, "that the day of the Lord is present," and sought to support this strange idea by supposed testimony of Paul's and his assistants' themselves. The writers inform the Thessalonians that all such alleged testimony is false, and that two dreadful things must precede the coming of the Lord, the great apostasy and the great Antichrist. We see why in 1:7, etc., "the revelation of the Lord Jesus" is described as bringing the final judgment upon the godless and disobedient — the Antichrist is the climax of this opposition. The first two chapters of this epistle plainly stand in the closest connection to each other. The supposition that 2:1-12 is an interpolation is not borne out by the facts.

We see still more. In I Thess. 4:13-5:12 the writers *comfort* the Thessalonians with the thought of the Parousia by showing what the Parousia means for them and for their beloved dead; now the writers *correct* those of the Thessalonians who were erring in regard to the date of the day of the Lord and were drawing dangerous conclusions from this error regarding their lives. Thus our passage supplements First Thessalonians. What First Thessalonians says about

(400)

the godly at the time of the Parousia is again summarized in II Thess. 1:10; in fact, I Thess. 4:15-17 is
summarized in a particular way in the first verse of the
present section where the subject is not merely "the
Parousia" but also "our gathering together unto him,"
i. e., when all the blessed shall meet the Lord in the
air.   All this shows the connection between these two
letters as well as their chronological order.

**Now we request you, brethren, in regard to the
Parousia of our Lord Jesus Christ and our gathering together unto him that you be not easily
shaken from your mind nor be troubled either by
spirit or by word or by letter as** (claiming to
come) **through us, that the day of the Lord is**
(already) **present.   Do not let anyone deceive you
in any way!**

'Ερωτῶμεν is used as it was in I Thess. 4:1: "we request" (not "beseech"); it is at once dignified and
kindly, the address "brethren" helps to bring out the
kindly spirit of this request, and, like the address in
1:3, helps to introduce a particular section of the letter.   This request deals with the Lord's Parousia (see
I Thess. 2:19), in particular with the great moment
when we shall be gathered together unto him as has
already been set forth in I Thess. 4:17.   There is no
need to stress the force of "our" so as to make it mean
that the writers and the readers would live to see the
Parousia; we have discussed this matter in connection
with I Thess. 4:17.   Whoever lives and whoever has
died will be in this ἐπισυναγωγή at the time of the Parousia.   If the writers were writing today they could use
this same pronoun "our."

The matter to be noted in regard to this subject is
taken up after 1:5-10.   In I Thess. 4:13-5:11 the fate
of the wicked at the time of the Parousia is touched
upon only briefly (in 5:3); in order to understand the
great apostasy and the great Antichrist, the judgment

upon the wicked at the Parousia must be fully understood, for this judgment will destroy also the Antichrist; hence II Thess. 1:8, 9 properly precedes. We
shall be received by the Lord, the rest shall be damned,
the apostasy and the Antichrist together with them.
All that Paul says about their fate accords with what
Jesus himself said so clearly in Matthew 24 and elsewhere.

2) The εἰς τό states the contents of the request.
The writers ask their readers to keep their mental balance (εἰς τό introduces an object clause just as it does
in I Thess. 2:12 and 3:10). The aorist infinitive σαλευ-
θῆναι, which is followed by the present infinitive θροεῖσθαι,
is graphic, the first expresses the momentary shock
to the mind, the second the agitation that results and
continues. The first suggests the impact of a blast
or of a wave, the second the dangerous disturbance
that follows. When the Thessalonians first heard the
cry that the day of the Lord is already present, this
came as a shock to the mind and then left them in the
greatest mental agitation. Note that Christians are
to keep their heads against error and fanatic notions;
they are to use their νοῦς or "mind." The truth of God
is sane and never unbalances the mind. In Matt. 24:4-6
Jesus himself says: "See to it, let no one deceive you,"
and uses the same verb θροεῖσθαι: "See to it lest you be
shaken!" It seems fair to conclude that Paul is practically quoting Jesus.

The means that cause this shock and this disturbance are named by the three διά phrases (R. 582 makes
them agents — agencies would be better): "spirit —
— word — letter," any or all of these "as δι' ἡμῶν," coming through us. Some interpreters refer to I Thess.
5:19; but there we have τὸ Πνεῦμα, "the Holy Spirit,"
here only πνεῦμα, "spirit." The idea is expressed that
this word refers to ecstatic utterances that were made
by somebody among the Thessalonians themselves who

had the spirit of prophecy. This first phrase is said to be complete in itself, and "through us" is applied only to one or to both of the other phrases. We deem this unsatisfactory. Μήτε διὰ πνεύματος is no more complete in itself than μήτε διὰ λόγου or μήτε δι᾽ ἐπιστολῆς; all three leave unsaid *whose* spirit, word, and letter are referred to. Moreover, the three form a gradation: spirit is the ultimate means — word or statement the intermediate — letter the direct means. All are referred to "us" as being the personal means, yet this means is only alleged (ὡς). Somebody in Thessalonica had spread the news that one or the other of the writers (Paul, Silvanus, Timothy) had made the assertion "that the day of the Lord is already present," made it "by spirit," as a divine communication received from God by his spirit, made it by a statement to someone, yea, made it by a letter to someone. The thought is that the news had been derived only *at thirdhand*, had, perhaps, traveled through even more hands — we, however, Paul, Silvanus, Timothy, our spirit, word, or letter being the supposedly original medium. Those who believed this report very likely made use of all three expressions, some using one, others the other.

We reject the view that Paul himself was not a prophet whose spirit could receive divine communications, and that Silvanus was such a prophet, from whom Paul received prophecies at secondhand. There is no record that a prophecy was revealed directly to Silvanus, but regarding Paul we have Gal. 1:12 and a number of other direct revelations made to him by the Lord.

The charisma of prophecy is often not properly understood. It did not come as a sudden seizure that threw the recipient into an ecstatic state and made him utter direct revelations. *All* Christians were to seek the charisma of prophecy as the highest of all charismatic gifts (I Cor. 14:1); in the congregation they were to exercise this gift in decent order (I Cor. 14:26, 29-35) and "according to the analogy of faith" (Rom. 12:6). This charisma consisted only in properly transmitting the Word of God as this had been learned from the Old Testament and from the apostles. The transmission was never made while the speaker was in an ecstatic state. The apostles were prophets in a higher sense: they received *direct* revelations from the Lord. When they uttered them they, too, spoke naturally and not in ecstasy. A few others, like Agabus, received minor direct revelations; in Acts 21:10, etc., we see how they delivered them.

"Letter" cannot refer to First Thessalonians, for there is nothing in First Thessalonians that can be construed so as to mean that the day of the Lord is already present. Moreover, the Thessalonians have this letter and can see for themselves that it contains no statement of this kind. This is a supposed letter, one that someone was supposed to have received or was supposed only to have seen or to have heard about.

In the Koine ὡς ὅτι = ὅτι (R. 1033), and we may regard it so here (compare II Cor. 11:21). Yet here it follows a ὡς that denotes unwarranted allegation. We thus may translate: "*as if* through us, *as if* the day of the Lord is already present." Both are unfounded allegations, both are here denied as being wholly untrue. B.-D. 425, 4; 396, Vulgate *quasi*. Note how both the verb and the subject become emphatic by being transposed. The perfect of ἵστημι is always used in the sense of the present. But does ἐνέστηκεν mean "is at hand" (A. V.), "is imminent" (Lightfoot and others), or "is present" (R. V.)? There is no question as to the meaning of the verb: it means the latter (see B.-P. 414: ever since Xenophon, in Polybius, in the inscriptions, and in the papyri).

The question as to the meaning of the word is raised by the commentators because of the context.

They think that the Thessalonians could not mean that the day of the Lord "is present," could mean only "is imminent," "is at hand" (A. V.), i. e., is very near. So these commentators say that the verb has another meaning here and thus change all that follows and regard Paul as saying that the day of the Lord is *not* near — a thing he could not say because he did not know.

Compare Rom. 8:38; I Cor. 3:22; Gal. 1:4; I Cor. 7:26. When ἐνεστῶτα is used with μέλλοντα, "present things — future things," "the present eon — the future eon," it is μέλλω that designates what impends, what is about to arrive. If the Thessalonians meant that the day is *nearly* present they could have used this verb μέλλω or some adverb like ἐγγύς but not the verb ἐνέστηκεν, especially not this strong compound with ἐν. The commentators seem to assume that "the day of the Lord" and "the Parousia" are practically identical, which is not the case. The false allegation in Thessalonica was not "that the Parousia of the Lord is present" (Παρουσία and ἐνέστηκεν, "Presence" and "is present," cannot be combined: the Presence is present), but "that the day of the Lord is present" — "the day" is a wider term. When the apostle describes this day he does not mean a day of twenty-four hours but a timeless day when the clock of time has ceased to run, when time is no more.

One ought not to think of the judgment as taking place in twenty-four hours, nor to think of a period. "The day" is a human word, the best that human language affords. Matt. 24:29, etc., should correct our thinking of that day as being a day that is composed of twenty-four hours or of time in any sense. When the allegation about "the day" was made in Thessalonica, it was half-right and half-wrong, right in *not* thinking of a day of twenty-four hours, wrong in still thinking of time. How long these people imagined "the day" to be we can only guess, they probably thought of a few

weeks or a few months at the end of which the Parousia
would occur.

Here is the place to remember that the Lord himself was detaining Paul in Corinth (Acts 18:9-11) by
a direct revelation, which the Lord could not have done
if "the day" (as this Thessalonian allegation claimed)
were already present. Moreover, in Paul's answer to
the Thessalonians he says nothing about "the day" but
confines his answer to "the Parousia" alone (v. 1).

3) "Do not let anyone deceive you in any way!"
re-echoes Jesus' warning given in Matt. 24:4. It
brands the allegation as a "deception," and "in any
way" refers to the three forms of the allegation already
indicated as well as to any other forms that may yet
appear. The idea that the subjunctive with μή is less
peremptory is not grammatically justifiable; negative
commands with the aorist regularly use the subjunctive.
And why should this warning be toned down and be
made less peremptory?

'Οτι substantiates the warning: **because . . .
except there first come the apostasy, and there be revealed the man of the lawlessness, the son of the perdition, the one opposing and exalting himself against
everyone called God or** (every) **object of worship, so
that he seats himself in the sanctuary of God, showing
himself off that he is God.**

We have an ellipsis; the apodosis of the ἐὰν μή protasis is omitted because it is unnecessary for the
Greek mind. Those expositors who call this an anacoluthon (a break in construction) confuse anacoluthon
and ellipsis; and when it is said that Paul "forgot" to
write the apodosis, his forgetting is overrated and the
fact is overlooked that Paul's scribe and Paul, too, read
the letter before it was sent. Many think that it is
essential to supply the omitted apodosis and generally
supply: οὐκ ἐνέστηκεν ἡ ἡμέρα τ. Κ. But the omission implies that the apodosis is immaterial to the Greek mind,

and that the whole thought deals with the protasis. It is only because the English mind is more pedantic that our versions feel it necessary to supply something, it being quite immaterial what they supply.

The first thing on the program is the arrival of the apostasy and the revelation of the man of the lawlessness. The article designates these two as being the only ones of their kind, and v. 5 indicates that Paul and Silvanus had mentioned this apostasy and this man of the lawlessness when they first worked in Thessalonica. Πρῶτον is to be construed with both verbs as the thought also indicates: these two events precede. The verbs are placed before their subjects, not in Hebrew, but in good Greek fashion, which makes them emphatic; this is also done because they are aorists. The fact that this apostasy will occur in the Christian Church is beyond question; it would otherwise not be an "apostasy." The man of the lawlessness will be its head. Yet some have thought of a Jewish apostasy, the Jewish national rejection of Christ, and also of the Jewish political apostasy from imperial Rome. Others think of a general moral falling away from such standards of morality as existed in the pagan world or of an anarchical apostasy from the established governments of the world. None of these interpretations are satisfactory.

While ἔλθῃ suffices to describe the apostasy, ἀποκαλυφθῇ applies to the man of the lawlessness: "he shall be revealed," this verb recalls the noun used in 1:7, "the revelation of the Lord Jesus." This man does not merely "come" as does the apostasy. While he at first remains hidden, he at last gets "to be revealed" as what he really is. These two revelations are undoubtedly opposites, for which reason we may speak of Christ and of Antichrist although the latter term does not occur in this epistle. The readings vary between the more precise ἀνομίας and the broader ἁμαρτίας: "of the lawlessness" — "of the sin"; there is not much difference in substance between them, the former is probably textually correct. The genitive is qualitative: the man marked by the lawlessness; both articles are most definite: there is no other man, no other lawlessness like this. For "the lawlessness" is not lawlessness in general but the special, unprecedented lawlessness that marks this man and accompanies this apostasy.

The same is true with regard to the apposition: "the son of the perdition"; perdition marks him from the start, and there is only one such perdition. This is exactly what Jesus called Judas in John 17:12; he, too, was an apostate in an eminent sense. The Antichrist is thus the antitype of Judas. To say that "the son" of the perdition means no more than "the man" and is no more than a Hebraism, is to undervalue the term "son." When it is used in Hebraic literature, "son" means even more than "child" in connections like this, for a child only belongs and still develops ("children of wrath," Eph. 2:3), a son is fully developed and has a standing accordingly. So "the son of the perdition," than whom there is no other. These first two epithets evidently belong together just as "the lawlessness" tends toward "the perdition." Ὁ ἄνθρωπος states that the Antichrist is not Satan but a human being and thus ὁ υἱός, "the son of the perdition."

4) The next apposition, two middle present participles substantivized by one article and modified by the final phrase, describes this man and son still farther: "the one opposing and exalting himself against everyone called God or (every) object of worship," etc. This is "the lawlessness" that connects him with "the perdition." We at once see that no lawlessness such as this has ever existed in the world. Pharaoh was not like this; Antiochus Epiphanes (the Illustrious, whom the Jews called Epimanes, the Raving) was only this Antichrist's type, Dan. 11:36. The ἐπί phrase modifies both

participles, otherwise we should have ὑπέρ to match the
last one (ὑπεραιρόμενος) ; thus it does not mean "above"
(A. V.), which would not be true, but "against" (R.
V.), which is suitable with both participles.

Those who translate ἐπί "above" put a limit upon
"every God called so and (every) object of worship"
by excepting the true God since no one could exalt himself above this God. So they refer λεγόμενον to pagan
deities who are only "said" to be gods while they are
in reality nothing. But why should opposition and
exaltation above every merely "so-called" god and every
merely "so-called" object of worship (σέβασμα) be the
pinnacle of lawlessness that deserves utter perdition
when these are only "said" to be what they are not
in fact? Instead of minimizing by leaving out the true
God, this participle particularly includes him as also
the next clause shows which twice names the true God.
This preposition means "against." The phrase points
out what the extreme of lawlessness is: opposition and
self-exaltation *against* no less than every God "said"
to be God plus every reverenced object "said" to be
reverenced. Πάντα and λεγόμενον are masculine because
of Θεόν, but both words are likewise construed *ad sensum*
with the neuter σέβασμα.

By saying "everyone called God," etc., the Antichrist's lawlessness is described as being worse than
that of the worst pagans. Pharaohs and Roman
emperors were deified and claimed divine honors, but
never for one moment did they do this "against" any
of their pagan gods, temples, altars, etc. Antiochus
desecrated the Jewish Temple, but he did it by erecting
an altar to Zeus. About thirteen years before the writing of this epistle Caligula, the Roman emperor, did the
same by trying to have his own statue erected in the
Jewish Temple, but even he was in no way opposing
and exalting himself *against* the Roman gods and objects of worship; quite the contrary. The very nature

of polytheism permitted the addition of new gods and of deified human rulers. But the Antichrist shall be worse, much worse, than these deified rulers. The very point of this description is broken off when ἐπί is understood in the sense of "over" and not "against" and the true God is excepted.

The result clause introduced with ὥστε should be regarded as a part of the participial apposition, the whole being a unified thought, for it states what the Antichrist actually does when he opposes and exalts himself against every God and every object of worship that are said to be such: "so that he seats himself into the sanctuary of God as showing himself off that he is God." Εἰς indicates that he is depositing himself "into" this sanctuary; ναός is not "temple" but "sanctuary." In pagan temples this sanctuary was the place reserved for the god's statue, in the Jewish Temple it was the building made up of the Holy and the Holy of Holies. The ἱερόν was the entire Temple complex with all its buildings and courts.

The emphasis is on the phrase "into the sanctuary of God." The aorist καθίσαι is to indicate the one act: "he seats himself" (intransitive), but it has the idea of permanency. The thought is still incomplete although we already perceive that the sanctuary of God is intended to have God and God alone as its permanent occupant. Yet God does not *sit* in his sanctuary. In the Holy of Holies of the Tabernacle of Moses and of the Temple of Solomon God was in the glory-cloud between the cherubim of the Shekinah. The lid of the ark of the covenant should not be conceived as a seat because of our English word "mercy seat"; this is a translation of ἱλαστήριον (see Rom. 3:25). This infinitive is *pagan* and thus is suitable to the Antichrist, his is a pagan act. Many statues of pagan gods represent the god in a sitting posture. Even when the figure of the god is in an upright position, the statue is said to sit in the pagan sanctuary.

The thought is thus completed by the addition of the predicative participle "showing himself off that he is God." Those who refer the previous phrase ἐπὶ πάντα λεγόμενον Θεόν only to so-called pagan gods encounter insuperable difficulties in their efforts to interpret this result clause, for they can think only of the Antichrist's sitting in a pagan god's sanctuary, exhibiting himself as a pagan god. The whole action would thus transpire in the world of paganism. And since there is a large number of pagan sanctuaries, the Antichrist would occupy only one of them and would dwindle down to one figure in the pagan pantheon.

Θεός is without the article only because it is the predicate as in John 1:1: Θεὸς ἦν ὁ λόγος. To add the article would change the meaning, for it would make the subject and the predicate identical and interchangeable (R. 768) so that the meaning would be: the Antichrist is the one true God beside whom none is God. Ὅτι ἐστὶ Θεός, without the article, does not mean this. To say that Θεός is a proper name and thus may or may not have the article stresses one point of Greek diction in order to remove another, namely that the presence or the absence of the article with predicates does make a difference. Thus with τὸν ναόν we have τοῦ Θεοῦ but not with this predicate Θεός; yet both mean "God" in the Christian and not in the pagan sense.

The sense is plain to the ordinary reader whether he be Greek or English. This Antichrist reveals himself as the Antichrist by this *pagan* act of seating himself in the *true* God's own sanctuary. He does not deny the true God, he is neither atheist nor agnostic; in fact, he worships the true God. But he does it by this pagan act, the climax of all anti-Christianity. He sits in God's own place as if he, too, were God and shows and exhibits himself to all Christendom with the claim "that he is God," that no less than deity belongs also to him. The very idea of extending deity in this way is utterly pagan. The great apostasy accepts this claim and honors this Antichrist with divine honor. That is what constitutes this apostasy. When Paul wrote, the people of God had never seen an apostasy and an Antichrist like this; nor has there been another who is comparable to this one since that time.

5) **Do you not remember that while I was still with you I kept telling you these things?** Paul is merely refreshing the memory of the Thessalonians. He had told them "these things" when he and Silvanus first worked in Thessalonica; this letter merely recalls these things. He employs the singular in the verb ἔλεγον, but it is without the ἐγώ used I Thess. 2:18 and 3:5; in a perfectly natural way he thus refers to his own former teaching. As far as Silvanus is concerned, he, too, had received these facts from Paul and taught them, for they are facts that were made known to the apostle by direct revelation.

We do not find "impatience" in this question. This question is a reminder just as one often says, "Do you not remember?" We often let matters become dim that should remain bright and effective. Some of the Thessalonians had allowed a good part of Paul's teaching on the Antichrist to fade from their minds and were entertaining the foolish supposition that the day of the Lord was already here. There is a tinge of reproof in this question. Do the Thessalonians not know that the first event to be expected is the revelation of the Antichrist? If any forget this, should not the rest remind them?

Some of the newer commentators have a new way of interpreting this whole section, but they have discarded the doctrine of inspiration. But this section offers no problem in inspiration; it is a matter of revelation. The question is: "Where did Paul get this information about the Antichrist?" He undoubtedly got it by direct revelation from God. These commentators deny this. They state that Paul remolded and reworked old Jewish apocalyptic ideas, some of which appear in the Old Testament prophets, for instance, Isa. 14:13, etc., Ezek. 28:2, perhaps also Daniel. The origin of these ideas is said to be lost in the dim prehistoric past, for these prophets, too, could not have spoken by divine revelation. These apocalyptic, eschatological ideas originated spontaneously, nobody knows just how. Paul elaborated them, taught them as being vital to the gospel, and developed them more and more as occasion required.

But the test of the matter, we are told, is the fact that these prophecies of Paul's "were never fulfilled and could never be fulfilled." In plain language, Paul is a false prophet, one who foretold what has never happened, what can never happen. We may then ask: "Why do these commentators write their books and waste their learning on these words of Paul's?" If Paul offers nothing but supposition in this chapter, why bother with it? And if Paul is, indeed, a false, self-deluded prophet who predicted something that has not come and can never come to pass, can the rest of his writings be taken seriously? According to their own logic these commentators have nothing worth-while left to comment on; they themselves have destroyed the value of this material.

Since Paul's words are not divinely revealed, these commentators treat them in the scientific way, namely *zeitgeschichtlich*, in the light of what men thought at that time. Paul was a child of his time. We therefore search through the old apocalyptic writings to discover the sources of his ideas. The pagan world had some of these ideas, but they are found especially in the Jewish world where they may be traced back to a few of the Old Testament prophets, back of whom lies the prehistoric source.

The results are rather strange. "The sanctuary of God" is the Jewish Temple in Jerusalem. This Antichrist is Caligula and his unsuccessful attempt to erect his statue in the Jewish Temple. Similarly, Antiochus Epiphanes and his desecration of the Jewish Temple are referred to. This monster was to return "from the realm of the dead" in order to repeat and to exceed his former desecration. The commentators who deny that Paul wrote this epistle and ascribe it to a late forger secure still other material for their *zeitgeschichtliche* exposition. First, the notion that the Jewish Temple which had been destroyed by the Romans would be rebuilt so that Paul's Antichrist might seat himself in it as God. Again, the monster Nero may be this Antichrist; he, too, will return from "the realm of the dead."

Of course, *such* a prediction never was and never could be fulfilled. These commentators present it as such a preposterous prediction that no one will today take it seriously, no one will even attempt to find its fulfillment. The fulfillment that *has* come to pass is thus regarded as something that Paul could not possibly have foreseen inasmuch as he was both without revelation and without inspiration.

We see what this makes of Paul, of Christ, and of the Old Testament prophets. We see what an absurd thing Paul did by writing these untrue prophecies to the Gentile Thessalonians. He tried to correct one error by another that was equally extravagant. He may have meant well but blundered nevertheless.

Paul has written about "the ναός or sanctuary of God" a number of times. "Do you not know that you are God's ναός (sanctuary), and that the Spirit of God dwells in you? If anyone destroys the ναός of God, him shall God destroy; for the ναός of God is holy, since of

such kind are you," I Cor. 3:17. "Or do you not know
that your body is a *ναός* of the Holy Spirit in you, whom
you have from God?" I Cor. 6:19. This is "a holy *ναός*
in the Lord," Eph. 2:21, 22. "We on our part are the
living God's *ναός*; even as God said: 'I will dwell in
them, and will walk about in them, and will be their
God, and they shall be my people,'" II Cor. 6:16. This
statement refers to Lev. 26:11, 12; Ezek. 27:27; Hos.
2:23; Jer. 24:7; 30:32; 31:33; 32:38; etc. Compare
also I Pet. 2:5: "a spiritual house." Scripture is expounded by Scripture, historically by considering Paul's
own words about this *ναός* and not *zeitgeschichtlich* according to what Jews and pagans thought in early
times. This *ναός* or sanctuary of God is his church,
which is sacred to him as his dwelling. God and his
Spirit do not *sit* in it, God *dwells* there as the *living*
God; only pagan idols *sit* in their temples.

Thus it is plain what the Antichrist would do, he
would seat himself in the church like a pagan god and
show himself off that he is God. He does not say that
God and Christ are no longer God, that this "sanctuary" is no longer theirs, but that he, this man, has the
right to sit there as a divine being. Anti-Christianity
can go no farther. The history of the church during
these hundreds of years presents only *one* phenomenon
of this type, the papacy.

What Daniel foretold about Antiochus presents him
as a type of the Antichrist; every antitype exceeds its
type. In Matthew 24 Jesus does not mention the Antichrist, and while Paul's revelation goes farther, it
agrees *in toto* with that of Jesus. So does I John 2:18:
"Little children, it is the last time, and as you heard
that *Antichrist is coming,* even now there have come to
be many antichrists; whence we know that it is the last
time." John had received the same revelation that
Paul had; he even distinguishes between what we have
come to call the little antichrists, of whom there were

many already in John's day, and the great Antichrist who also in John's day was yet to come. The whole question as to whether this would be a pagan or a Jew is beside the point; also his political claims and power are not the real point but his depositing himself in God's sanctuary as God.

6) **And the thing now holding up you know, so that he is revealed in his season, for the mystery of this lawlessness is already operating only until the one holding (it) up now shall get out of the way. And then shall be revealed the lawless one whom the Lord Jesus shall make away with by the breath of his mouth and shall abolish by the epiphany of his Parousia.**

The debate regarding νῦν, as to whether it modifies the participle or the verb, is settled by B.-D. 474, 5: it is to be construed with the participle; examples show that such a modifier may be placed before, after, or between the article and the participle with practically no difference in emphasis. The Thessalonians know the thing now holding up the revelation of the Antichrist. Paul had pointed out to them what this κατέχον (neuter participle) is. The idea that the Thessalonians themselves know this thing so that they need not be told about it is not suggested, especially since v. 5 precedes. The Thessalonians know because Paul had told them long before this time.

The εἰς τό is generally regarded as introducing a purpose clause; it is so regarded in our versions: "in order that he may be revealed in his season," i. e., according to God's purpose. But we deem a result clause more in order after "you know," "so that he is revealed in his season." There is no need for debate. There is no question about the sense, for the words are quite simple: something is now holding up the revelation of the Antichrist so that this revelation will occur in its proper season. This answers the idea which was

spread in Thessalonica to the effect that the day of the
Lord is already present. The revelation of the Antichrist (v. 3) comes first, and not until then the Lord's
day; and this revelation of the Antichrist has not yet
occurred.

Three times we have the passive ἀποκαλυφθῆναι (v. 3,
6, 8); in 1:7 we have the noun ἀποκάλυψις which indicates an action and refers to the Lord; both shall be
revelations, that of the Antichrist being forced upon
him by God, that of the Lord being effected by himself.
As regards "the times and the seasons" (καιροί) or even
any one of them, these the Father has placed in his own
authority (Acts 1:7), nor has Paul a further revelation on this point. Things may move so rapidly that he
may live to see this "season," the seasons may move
slowly so that Paul will be dead before the season of
the Antichrist arrives. Paul does not know, does not
pretend to know.

7) This thought lies in the explanation introduced
by γάρ: the mystery of this lawlessness is now already
(ἤδη) operative. How rapidly it is operating Paul does
not know or pretend to say. Again we say that Paul
does not present this fact as a deduction of his own
reason or as a mere opinion of his own or as a speculation based on Jewish apocalyptic ideas but as a piece of
divine revelation. This "lawlessness" (the ἀνομία of v.
3) is still veiled in mystery, no one is as yet able to see
it because something is holding it up. The term "mystery" matches "shall be revealed." The damnable thing
is not merely dormant but is already operative (ἐνεργεῖται) although as yet unseen. It is like a viper in its
shell that will presently crawl out and then be blasted.

This revelation is exactly like the great Old Testament prophecies; it offers a succession of events, but
the intervals of time are omitted. The whole is one
view that is flat and without perspective. We have a
plain example in the case of the Baptist (Matt. 3:7-12)

who saw the grace of Christ and his final judgment as one. We even have the Baptist's puzzlement regarding it when he saw only the grace in Jesus and as yet nothing of the terrible judgment (Matt. 11:2-6); the great interval between these two was not revealed to him. We have a similar situation here with regard to Paul and the Antichrist. He did not see whether ten or ten thousand years were involved.

In the μόνον ἕως clause the subject is placed before the conjunction as in Gal. 2:10 it is placed before ἵνα: "only the one holding (it) up until (this one) shall get out of the way" (out from between). As the flexible Greek can separate "the mystery . . . of the lawlessness," a noun and its genitive, each thereby receiving an emphasis, so it may transpose the subject and the conjunction and give the subject an emphasis. Our versions supply something and make two clauses of the thought, but this is not necessary; nor is there a "letting" (A. V.). The Koine does not need an ἄν; the subjunctive is also perfectly regular (even classic) when ἕως refers to the future (R. 976), this subjunctive does not present a thought of wish ("must," Luther) or of condition. The aorist marks a point of time: "get out of the way."

The neuter τὸ κατέχον is now replaced by the masculine ὁ κατέχων. These terms are, however, not parallel to "the apostasy" and "the man of the lawlessness" mentioned in v. 3. For "the apostasy" is an abstract term and refers to *the many* who turn away from the true gospel while "the man of the lawlessness" is *one* and refers to the leader in the lawless apostasy. Nor does Paul write "the man of the apostasy." The case of τὸ κατέχον and ὁ κατέχων is different, we merely have a change in gender in the word: "the *thing* that holds up — the *one* that holds up" (we say "up," the Greek κατά, "down"). This thing and this one are evidently a unit, a certain power (thus neuter), a certain person exer-

cising this power (thus masculine). R. 409 remarks
that the neuter leaves the person involved concealed.
R. 411 adds: "The neuter singular in the collective or
general sense to represent persons is not peculiar to the
New Testament." Robertson means that the collective
or general sense of the neuter (here τὸ κατέχον) refers
to all the elements or powers in the hands of the persons involved who are here named by the masculine
ὁ κατέχων. This explains the use of the two genders.

Those who search the Jewish apocalytic literature
for the source of Paul's statements are disappointed:
no κατέχον or κατέχων, neuter or masculine, appears anywhere in this literature. It should, therefore, be evident that Paul does not use such sources but presents
the Lord's direct revelation. Some men are, of
course, not ready to admit the patent fact that Paul
was a true prophet of God. We are told that, while
Paul's sources were these Jewish apocalyptic writings,
he was the man to *"create"* this κατέχον and κατέχων, in
other words, Paul was the man to invent this thing and
this man that were holding up the apostasy and the
revelation of the Antichrist. But no true apostle of
Christ could be carried away by such apocalyptic tradition, nor would he himself add to it.

Γάρ explains. It adds by way of explanation that
"the mystery of this lawlessness is already operating,"
ἐνεργεῖται, is already actively at work. It is compelled
to work under cover; this lawlessness is still held down,
its cover has not yet been stripped away by the Lord.
The latter will not happen until he who holds this evil
force down gets out of the way. The reason that ὁ
κατέχων, the subject of the clause, is placed before ἄρτι
ἕως has been explained above.

It should be noted that "this lawlessness" with its
article of previous reference repeats "the lawlessness"
mentioned in v. 3. At the time of Paul's writing it was
still "the mystery of this lawlessness" and had not yet

come to an open head in "the man of the lawlessness."
The Antichrist had not yet appeared, but the lawlessness he would represent was already active. In due
season it would develop a personal head, the one described in v. 3, 4.

8) "And then (when that καιρός or season arrives)
shall be revealed (the same verb that was used in v. 6)
the lawless one," ὁ ἄνομος, who is called "the man of the
lawlessness" in v. 3. The three expressions ὁ ἄνθρωπος
τῆς ἀνομίας — τὸ μυστήριον τῆς ἀνομίας — ὁ ἄνομος undoubtedly
refer to the same lawlessness which marks the apostasy
and thus the Antichrist. It is now, at the time of Paul's
writing, working in secret because it is still being held
down; but the restraining power and its agent will
eventually be removed, but Paul does not know how
soon this will occur. And then, when this season arrives, the secret lawlessness will be revealed together
with its head, "the man of this lawlessness," the
Antichrist.

What Paul writes is not new to the Thessalonians.
He is merely recapitulating his former teaching, note
v. 5 and also "you know" in v. 6. This explains his
brevity and conciseness. While we may wish that Paul
had written with greater fulness for our sakes we have
an advantage which the Thessalonians did not have,
namely the long history of the church, which has
brought the first great fulfillment of Paul's prophecy,
we see the mystery of the lawlessness unveiled, the
restraining power removed, "the man of this lawlessness," "the lawless one," revealed. The fulfillment
which we have the Thessalonians had only in the form
of prophecy.

Paul could not date τότε: "*then* shall be revealed the
lawless one." The agent of this passive verb ἀποκα-
λυφθήσεται, "shall be revealed," is the same as the one
of the passive infinitive occurring in v. 6; it is the
Lord. Paul indicates how he will end the mystery

surrounding the lawlessness: the one holding up the full development of this lawlessness will get out of the way, i. e., will cease to hold up. Ἐκ μέσου γένηται does not mean "be taken out of the way" (passive, our versions) but "get out of the way." He will no longer be in the way in order to continue the holding up. The decisive restraint will be removed, the lawlessness will have free course to develop and to show itself. It will then produce "the man of the lawlessness," "the lawless one will be revealed." We need not be told that all this will occur under divine providence; "be taken out of the way" may pass as being substantially correct.

The relative clause: "whom the Lord Jesus (the better reading has Jesus) shall make away with . . . and shall abolish," should not lead us to think that the moment the lawless one is revealed he will also at once be destroyed. This clause states only the final fate of the Antichrist. We have no dates but only a succession; the intervals of time, as we have already indicated, are wanting. Paul does not say how long it will be until the Antichrist is revealed. He does not say how long after he has been revealed the Antichrist will be allowed to remain until the Lord Jesus strikes him with the breath of his mouth. Paul does not even say that there will be an interval, nor does he state how long a period of time there will be between the making away with the Antichrist and the abolishing of him. Paul did not know whether he might or might not live to see this, it might come to pass with great swiftness. We now know that it is a matter of centuries, and that the end of this development has not even now been reached. We stand where Paul stood. The final end may come swiftly, yet it, too, may still be a long time off (Acts 1:7).

In these two letters Paul repeatedly uses "the Lord Jesus" and does so here. Ἀνελεῖ is the future of ἀναιρέω; the readings vary, and some (like the A. V.) prefer ἀναλώσει (from ἀναλόω = ἀναλίσκω), "shall consume." We prefer ἀνελεῖ and note that "to make away with" is the verb so often used to designate murder (Luke 22:2; Acts 2:23; 5:33; 7:28; 9:23, 29; 22:20; 23:15, 21; 25:3). The dative of means is here added: "shall make away with by means of the breath of his mouth." Because of the genitive τοῦ στόματος αὐτοῦ we do not take πνεῦμα in the sense of "spirit" (A. V.); the word is used in its first sense: "the breath of his mouth." The breath of the Lord's mouth is his Word. This explains "make away with." The Lord will not go to war against the Antichrist with great armament, he will merely blow his breath upon this lawless one, that will blast him. The Word is poison to the Antichrist.

There are evidently two acts because the two verbs have two different datives of means attached: 1) the Lord shall make away with the Antichrist by means of the breath of his mouth (his Word); 2) the Lord shall abolish the Antichrist by means of the epiphany of his Parousia. One might think that these two acts may come in quick succession like two blows that are almost simultaneous. The fact that there shall be two acts is plain; also that, since this is prophecy, no reference to an interval of time, whether this be short or long, is found. This the fulfillment shall reveal.

Καταργεῖν is one of Paul's favorite words: "to abolish," "to put out of commission," and the various connections show just what is meant. Here *vertilgen, beseitigen,* complete abolition is meant (B.-P. 652). This is indicated by the mighty dative which is vastly greater than the preceding "breath of his mouth": "by the epiphany of his Parousia." On the Parousia see I Thess. 2:19; it is the Presence at the last day for the purpose of the final judgment. Here this term is enhanced by the ἡ ἐπιφανεία which is more than "the manifestation" (R. V.), more also than "the brightness" (A. V.). Some refer to the Hellenistic "appearance of

the gods"; some think of the first burst of glory in the
Parousia or of "the sign of the Son of man" mentioned
in Matt. 24:20; Deissmann (*Light*, etc., 374, note 4, and
378) refers to pagan sources (but see C.-K. 1111); the
ancients thought of the overwhelming glory of the
Parousia. This word "epiphany" goes back to the Old
Testament manifestations of God.

It is in contrast with "the breath of his mouth"
(the Word). While the Word blasts the lawless one,
"the epiphany of the Parousia," the actual appearance
of the Lord himself, will abolish him completely. "The
epiphany" is vastly more than "the breath" or Word.
On the last day the Lord himself will appear in his
Presence (Parousia) for the judgment. The idea of
"epiphany" is added to the Lord's Parousia because
the lawless one also has a parousia (v. 9). It is described in v. 4, but only as "a showing off" (ἀποδεικνύντα
ἑαυτόν), a display of pretense of being God; the description is completed in v. 9, 10; it will be a "parousia" or
"presence" in accord with Satan's working in connection with all power and signs and wonders of lying and
in all deceit of unrighteousness, etc. We might call all
this the epiphany of the parousia of the lawless one.
When the epiphany of the Parousia of the Lord descends upon this lawless one it will, indeed, destroy
him forever.

Paul writes about the Antichrist's ἀνομία, "lawlessness" (v. 3, 7) three times, the third time he plainly
calls him ὁ ἄνομος, "the lawless one." We at once note
the stress that is laid upon this term. We do not accept the reference to the Gentiles as being ἄνομοι, people without the law of Moses, with only the moral law
engraved in their hearts. The Antichrist is not classed
with the Gentiles as also being "lawless." In the whole
history of the church there is to be only *one* who bears
the designation "the lawless one." His description as
here given shows him to be not merely *without* the law,

as the Gentiles did not have the law of the Mosaic code, and not merely without the *moral* law in general as this is written in the hearts. The *nomos* here referred to is "the Law" in the sense of the Word; and "lawlessness," "the lawless one" are intensive: not merely without but contrary to the Law or Word. While v. 4 might lead us to think of the First Commandment of the Mosaic law, namely of idolatry, and certainly this is a part of the divine Word, Paul's description of "the lawless one" evidently goes much farther and includes the height of opposition to the gospel: deceit of unrighteousness — not receiving the love of the truth that saves — working of error to believe the lie — not believing the truth — pleasure in unrighteousness (v. 10-12). All this constitutes "the lawlessness." All this shall proudly exalt itself, not *outside of* the sanctuary of God in the world, but *in* the sanctuary, *in* the church, the head of it all displaying himself as himself being God (v. 4).

No wonder the breath of the Lord's mouth (his Word) smites this lawless one who is enthroned in opposition to the Word; and no wonder the epiphany of the Parousia of the Lord annihilates and ends forever the parousia of this lawless one and all his contradiction of the Word.

9)   Paul continues with a relative clause, but this is introduced by one of those demonstrative relatives (Rom. 2:29; 3:8, 30; plus others) and is exceedingly weighty and has causal force: because this lawless one is lawless in the way now described he shall receive the doom just indicated. Our versions are correct in translating: "even him, whose," etc. (A. V.); "even he, whose," etc. (R. V.): **he the one whose parousia is according to Satan's working in connection with all power and signs and wonders of a lie and in connection with all deceit of unrighteousness for those perishing because**

they received not the love of the truth that they be saved.

Oὗ, like ὅν in v. 8, has ὁ ἄνομος as its antecedent so that we translate: "he (not : him) whose," etc. It is plain that παρουσία does not mean "coming" (our versions) but "presence" (A. V. margin) although the duration of this presence is not indicated. How long the parousia or presence of the Antichrist will be endured by the Lord depends on the Lord. By ascribing a parousia to the Antichrist a parallel is drawn between him and Christ. But when a second parallel is drawn between the revelation of Christ and the revelation of the Antichrist, we should note the difference: Christ's revelation is active (1:7), made by himself, the Antichrist's is passive (2:3, 6, 8), one that is made by the Lord. The Antichrist's revelation is an exposure.

When Paul writes "is" and not "shall be" he merely states the fact without reference to the time when this fact will take place. The three predicative phrases are not coordinate, for the two introduced with ἐν specify what the one beginning with κατά contains, and hence no καί follows the first phrase: "is according to . . . in connection with . . . and in connection with." To say that ἐστίν ἐν is Hebraistic is to overlook the extensive and the varied uses of this preposition in the Greek.

The parousia of the lawless one is "in accord with Satan's working" or operation; it is normated by Satan's way of working. What is this norm? Lying, deception, error, and their result, eternal destruction (John 8:44). The whole parousia of the Antichrist is defined by this norm (κατά). We see it in the deception of Eve and in the story of the fall. The climax appears in the Antichrist, beyond whom the lie and the destruction cannot go.

Two specifications follow: 1) the means employed; 2) the inner motive followed. "In connection with all power and signs and wonders of a lie (or lying)." Some regard the three terms as a reference to miracles; but in Acts 2:22; II Cor. 12:12; Heb. 2:4 all three are plurals while here "all power" is singular, and only "signs and wonders" are plurals. The difference is material. When miracles are called δυνάμεις, "powers" in the sense of "power works," they are designated as works of divine omnipotence. Such works are beyond Satan and the Antichrist who follows Satan's norm. Satan has power, and his power works with this greatest tool of his, but his power is not omnipotence, nor can it perform δυνάμεις, genuine "power works," genuine miracles. So many are ready to attribute real miracles to Satan and to his agents; the Scriptures never do. In accord with Satan's working the Antichrist operates with all kinds of power, but that is all; this is creative power and no more. This triad: "all power and signs and wonders" is diverse. Such limited power as Satan has the Antichrist uses for his signs and miracles.

These are also limited by the genitive which we regard as a modifier of the two plurals "(all) signs and wonders"; these two terms are so often combined. Our versions make the genitive adjectival and construe it only with "wonders": "lying wonders." But Paul means: "lie-signs and lie-wonders." The genitive is qualitative and stronger than an adjective. It does not denote source: "derived from what is lie"; nor effect: "producing what is lie"; or a combination of these two ideas. These signs and wonders are themselves, in their own quality, "lie." Nothing is more deadly and damnable than what is "lie"; nothing more satanic than to make men believe that lie is truth. We may translate: "pseudo-signs and pseudo-wonders." All the destructive power of Satan and of his agents lies in this "lie," a pretense of reality, a sham of truth and

genuineness. Note that "all deceit of unrighteousness" follows. This explains Matt. 24:24: "pseudo-Christs and pseudo-prophets (none of them real) and they shall give great signs and wonders so as to deceive," etc.; none of these great signs and wonders are real, all of them are deception only, or, as Paul qualifies: "lie-signs and wonders." This is the extent of Satan's power.

"Sign" is the higher word and is thus also used alone. A sign points beyond itself, it signifies something. But a lie-sign tries to signify something as being real and true that is neither; it thus deceives and wrecks. "Wonder" is the lesser word and is never used alone in the New Testament, for the pagan world also had wonders or portents, the word meaning something that astonishes and dumfounds. Not all signs are also wonders although real miracles are both. Here the two words apply equally to the Antichrist's pretended miracles. The papal apostasy is full of lie-signs and wonders. This mark alone is sufficient to identify the papacy as being the great Antichrist.

10) The second phrase: "and in connection with all deceit of unrighteousness for those perishing," reveals the inwardness of the Antichrist's parousia (presence) in its accord with Satan's working. Anything that accords with Satan's working is full of "deceit" or "deception" ("deceivableness," A. V., less good), and the presence of the Antichrist who is governed by Satan is most certainly so. Ἀδικία = unrighteousness, *Unrecht*, as having the norm of right and the right judgment of God against it (C.-K. 338), here it is used in the full religious sense. But this genitive cannot be qualitative or adjectival: "unrighteous deceit," for all deceit is unrighteous, there is no other kind of deceit. Some think of effect: "deceit that leads to unrighteousness," a kind of objective genitive. But neither this nor a genitive of source is adequate. This is the pos-

sessive genitive: *alle Taeuschungskuenste, wie sie der Ungerechte ersinnt* (B.-P. 26), all the different kinds of deception which unrighteousness employs. Nor is this the common unrighteousness of men generally as it is delineated in Rom. 1:18, etc., coupled with their "ungodliness." This is the unrighteousness already described in v. 4, which opposes self and exalts self against everyone called God, or against what is sacred, to the extent of sitting in God's own sanctuary and showing off as God. This is the pinnacle of all unrighteousness which is satanic in the highest degree and successful only in connection with proportionate deceit.

The thought is that by means of all this deceit this unrighteousness palms itself off as righteousness. As all this power, these signs and wonders are necessary, so all this deceit is necessary to make the Antichrist appear as the true exponent of Christ, rightfully sitting in the sanctuary of God. Yet Paul adds the *dativus commodi aut incommodi* "for those perishing," i. e., for those of the great apostasy (v. 3) and thus not for the true part of Christendom (Matt. 24:24). The present participle is timeless and merely describes these people according to what is happening to them. The present participle is often used in this way. The ἀπολλύμενοι are the opposite of the σωζόμενοι, those being saved.

'Ανθ' ὧν = "because" in the sense of "in return for these things," i. e., the things involved in the power, in the signs and wonders, and in the deception of unrighteousness. We say simply, "Because they did not receive the love of the truth that they be saved." This is the reason for their perishing. The aorist presents their fate as having occurred in the past; this is often done in prophecy when the prophet contemplates the fulfillment as being already accomplished. Not to receive "the love of the truth" says more than not to receive "the truth," for it adds the subjective idea of "the love," which always accompanies the reception of "the truth." Note the articles, not love in general for truth in general, but this definite love for this definite truth that saves, i. e., the gospel. The apostasy (v. 3) consists in the loss of the love of the saving gospel truth. Hence the perishing. Compare John 3:19. We decline to accept the older interpretation which refers this love to God's or Christ's love which appeared in the gospel truth. Some regard this as a characterizing genitive: they did not receive "the true love" (God's love in Christ Jesus). We do not find a rhetorical correspondence between "all deceit of unrighteousness" and "the love of the truth," for in the one expression the articles are absent, in the other they are used; besides, the genitives also differ, the one is possessive, the other objective.

The thought is that the saving gospel truth was brought to them so that they might see and love it and might thus accept it. This they would not do. They perish because of their own guilt. The infinitive clause is not "epexegetical purpose of 'the truth' if they had heeded it" (R., *W. P.*); it denotes simple result: "that they be saved." Receiving the love of the truth effects salvation; not to receive this love loses this result.

Note well that this is applicable to the papacy and Romanism, for the papacy ever repudiates the truth and the love of the truth. The decrees of the Council of Trent word the truth with great exactness in doctrine after doctrine and then append to this truth the awful anathema. Travel in the Holy Land and view the so-called sacred sites — fakes upon fakes; the relics in great papal churches — fakes; the story of saint after saint — faked tales, faked wonders. The love of historical truth disappears when it is thought that lies, deception, shams may serve the pope.

11) **And because of this God sends them error's working so that they believe the lie in order that**

they all may be judged who did not believe the truth but had good pleasure in the (i. e., this) **unrighteousness.**

These plurals point to the Antichrist and to his apostate following. First Paul states the guilt (v. 9, 10) and then the judgment and the penalty for that guilt. The two match as they must in the righteousness of a just God. Whereby men sin, thereby they are punished. "Because of this" refers to v. 9, 10, namely to all that is said about the guilt of the lawless one and the guilt of those perishing. They did not receive the love of the gospel truth but preferred the lie. As a judgment "God sends them error's working so that they believe the lie." The present tense is like that used in v. 9, it is a statement of fact without regard to time. In v. 10 we have the aorist. Prophecy may use all three tenses, present, aorist, future, when it is describing coming events. This sending of error's working is not a mere permission, an allowing error to work in the Antichrist's apostasy; on the other hand, it is not a production of error by God. The working of Satan (v. 9) produces ever new errors, for Satan is the father of lies (John 8:44). When these errors are, however, produced by Satan they do not work merely when Satan pleases. It is God who rules. He sends them where he wills. He uses them when he is executing his righteous judgments upon those who scorn his saving truth.

It is significant that Paul does not say that God sends merely error or errors but "error's working," compare "Satan's working" in v. 9. Error works, and its working always destroys souls. The idea that error is harmless is deceptive. Many have their pet errors; but every one of them is dangerous. The result clause states what error does by its working: "so that they believe the lie" (effective aorist), so that they definitely put their trust in what is not true as if it is true. "The

lie" with its article is the opposite of "the truth" occurring v. 10 although some think that the article indicates previous reference ("of lie" in v. 9). Πιστεύειν
with the dative means to believe what the lie says. The
lie of the Antichrist says many things, all of them are
not true. All the false doctrines of the papacy are
referred to. The A. V. translates "error's working" as
"strong delusion," as if ἐνέργειαν were adjectival; but the
governing noun is never adjectival, only the genitive
may be, thus here the meaning is not "energetic error"
("strong delusion") but "erroneous energy." This
will, however, not do, for the sense is evidently the
energy or working that belongs to error (possessive
genitive). On "error" compare Eph. 4:14.

12) The fact that God's purpose is judgment upon
the anti-Christian apostasy the ἵνα clause states in so
many words: "in order that they may all be judged,
they that did not believe the truth but had good pleasure in the unrighteousness." The A. V. translates
"might be damned," which is substantially correct
although κρίνειν is a *vox media* and means "to judge";
κατακρίνειν = "to judge adversely," "to damn." "All" is
added so as to include all who are in this apostasy, in
fact, this "all" seems to extend farther so as to include
any and all who may belong to the church outwardly
and who do what is here stated.

The apposition: "they that did not believe the
truth," etc., justifies God's judgment. He sent them
his saving gospel truth; these people did not believe
what this truth told them, they treated it as though it
were a lie and not true. The papacy has branded the
saving facts of the gospel truth with its "anathema,"
than which nothing more anti-Christian can be done.
The dative is to be understood in the same sense as the
one used in the infinitive clause. "But had good pleasure in the unrighteousness" increases the charge
against this apostasy by adding the positive guilt to

the negative. This is the same "unrighteousness" as
that mentioned in v. 9 (which see), love for what is
said about the Antichrist in v. 3, 4 and for what is
added in v. 9. In v. 9 "all deceit of unrighteousness"
might lead us to think of poor victims who were drawn
into unrighteousness by deceit; but here we see that
these people had the truth and refused to believe it,
and that they not only accepted the Antichrist's unrighteousness but made it their good pleasure. The
apostasy of the papacy boasts of its error and its unrighteousness. The two participles are aorists, not to
express past action, but to indicate the simple fact.

*   *   *

Many commentators offer a survey of the interpretations of this famous portion of Second Thessalonians
and begin with those of the early church fathers and
come down to recent efforts. We deem it needless to
offer a new survey. We have already sufficiently indicated what the latest commentators have to say. The
writer offers the following:

(1) Paul and his associates utter a prophecy.

(2) They have received this prophecy by divine
revelation.

(3) The fulfillment down to the very letter is
beyond question.

We are today in a position that is similar to that of
the Jews who had the Old Testament prophecies regarding the first coming of Christ and clung to their
own apostasy. Those prophecies were literally fulfilled; Christ came, the Jews became apostate, Jerusalem fell, their nation was abolished and made a sign
of God's judgment for all time. The scribes had this
mass of Old Testament prophecy; they refused to believe, refused most obdurately, especially when the
fulfillment came to its culmination. Prophecy and ful-

fillment agreed to the letter. They would not see it. The Jewish doom has continued during all these centuries; the Jews still refuse to see.

The period of this fulfillment was brief. From Bethlehem to Christ's ascension was a period of thirty-three years; Jerusalem fell in the year 70. We have already pointed to the Baptist who saw Christ's work of grace and his work of judgment in one view, the interval of time being omitted. So Paul saw the Antichrist and his apostasy; revelation withheld the καιροί (Acts 1:7). The course of this prophecy might have been as rapid as that regarding Christ's first coming and the apostasy of the Jews. The time was not revealed to Paul. We who live today know that nearly nineteen centuries have passed, and the Parousia has not yet become a reality. But much of the fulfillment has occurred.

This is an apostasy (v. 3). It is, therefore, to be sought *in* the church visible and not *outside* of the church, not in the pagan world, in the general pagan moral decline, in Mohammedanism, in the French Revolution, in the rise and spread of Masonry, in soviet Russia, or in lesser phenomena. We should not confuse the little antichrists with the great Antichrist, the antichrists *outside* of the visible church with the great Antichrist *inside* of it.

The secret beginnings were actively stirring in Paul's own time (v. 7). We may debate as to what or who still held these beginnings down at that time (τὸ κατέχον — ὁ κατέχων). In the writer's opinion the best view is that this was the Roman imperium, a force (neuter), and this force was represented in the person (masculine) of the pagan emperors. This got out of the way (v. 7) when Constantine, the first Christian emperor, came to the throne. Only then did the papacy become possible. The great apostasy is Romanism, its head is the papal succession, which is called "Antichrist" in I John 2:18 in distinction from "many anti-christs," the lesser anti-Christian powers.

All that Paul says agrees with the papacy and Romanism down to the present day. We need not repeat the details. The pope's divine self-exaltation in God's own sanctuary appears not only in arrogating to himself divine titles but also in handing down his false doctrines and decisions as though this were done with divine authority and anathematizing all who will not submit. We are pointed to "good" popes, but these, too, held to the papal authority, to the false Romish doctrines, to the false Romish worship. These things constitute the ἀνομία whether a pope is personally moral in the Romish sense or not. As the papacy emerged and the Romish system developed, the Antichrist's par-ousia and revelation occurred. During nineteen centuries no greater apostasy has ever appeared in the visible church. Nor *can* a still greater one appear. The climax has been reached in the papal system.

What causes some to deny that the pope is the Antichrist is the fact that they have not themselves experienced that justification by faith alone is the soul and center of all that is true Christianity. All other true doctrines have their roots in this one. We quote Franz Pieper: "It is true, the open unbelievers are raging enemies of the church. But what Christians are to think of pronounced unbelievers they know. By these they are not deceived. How does it then come about that men are today disinclined to recognize the pope as the Antichrist? Whence this strange and deplorable fact that nearly all late 'believing' theologians hunt about for the Antichrist while he does his great and mighty work in the church right before their eyes? *They are not established in the living knowledge of the doctrine of justification and in the importance of this doctrine for the church.* From my own experience I must confess that in my own conscience I was not vitally convinced that the pope is the Antichrist until, on the one hand, I realized what the doctrine of justification is and what its significance is for the church, and, on the other hand, that the papacy has its real essence in denying and cursing the doctrine of justification and by its show of piety and its claim to be the only saving church binds to itself men's consciences." *Christliche Dogmatik* II, 669, etc.

Beyond the curse pronounced by the Council of Trent, *sessio 6, canon 11,* nothing can go in the way of anti-Christianity in the official church: *Si quis dixerit, homines justificari vel sola imputatione justitiae Christi, vel sola peccatorum remissione, exclusa gratia et caritate quae in cordibus eorum per Spiritum Sanctum diffundatur atque illis inhaerit, aut gratiam qua justificamur esse tantum favorem Dei, anathema sit.* The same curse is pronounced in the same official way and with the same finality upon one doctrine after another that radiates from and rests on justification by faith alone.

The confessional statement of the Smalcald Articles II, Article IV, 10-11 (*C. Tr.* 475) is true: "This teaching shows forcefully that the pope is the very Antichrist who has exalted himself above and opposed himself against Christ because he will not permit Christians to be saved without his power, which, nevertheless, is nothing and is neither ordained nor commanded by God. This is, properly speaking, to 'exalt himself above all that is called God' as Paul says, II Thess. 2:4. Even the Turks or the Tartars, great enemies of Christians as they are, do not do this; but they permit whoever wishes to believe in Christ and take bodily tribute and obedience from Christians. The pope, however, prohibits this faith, saying that to be saved a person must obey him." Read all the rest.

Paul's prophecy does not point to a double Antichrist, one being Oriental (Turkish), the other Occidental (papal). The debate as to whether the Antichrist is to be of Jewish or of Gentile origin is pointless. Will the papacy produce a superpope, the final one, the Antichrist in the eminent sense of the word and as such to be struck down at the last day by the Lord's Parousia? An affirmative answer cannot be based on the fact that Paul uses the singular in v. 3, 4, 8 as little as on the claim that ὁ κατέχων in v. 7 refers to only one individual. As the succession of pagan Roman emperors held up the great apostasy and the actual appearance of the papacy, so "the man of the lawlessness" and "the lawless one" denotes a succession of popes.

The "Scarlet Woman" of Revelation, "Babylon the Great, the Mother of the Whores," is not the great Antichrist, the Roman papacy, but the symbolized anti-Christian seduction of the entire world in all the departments of life and not only in the church although it also includes this domain. See the author's *Interpretation of Revelation.*

Let me venture to state my personal opinion regarding v. 8: the papacy received its mortal blow by "the breath of the Lord's mouth" (the Lord's Word) during the Reformation and has shown the effects ever since without prospect of recovery. Until the time of the Reformation the papacy ruled practically the entire church with its fearful deceit; this is not true since that time. The Reformation cast a blight upon the papal rule, a blight that has continued unchecked during the past four hundred years. Who is able to say what the future, prior to the Parousia, will bring as a further fulfillment of Paul's prophecy? We cannot go beyond Matt. 24:12 and Luke 18:8. I look for no superpope at the end, for no pope who shall wield supreme secular power over the world's states and governments.

What about the Thessalonians as regards These Coming Events?

13) The writers thank God for the state of the
Thessalonians (v. 13, 14), urge them to maintain it
(v. 15), and pray for them (v. 16, 17). The third section of the letter does not begin at this point as some
have thought. The prayerful wish expressed in v. 16,
17 marks the end of the second section of the letter just
as does the prayerful wish in I Thess. 3:11-13 and
another prayerful wish at the end of the last section in
I Thess. (5:23, 24). The third section begins at 3:4.

Although some have tried to agitate the Thessalonians by telling them on the basis of fake authority
that the day of the Lord is already here (1:2), Paul
and his associates are not worried about them. They
once more point out to the Thessalonians that the apostasy and the Antichrist will precede that day and the
Lord's Parousia; this will settle whatever disturbing
thoughts the Thessalonians may have on the whole subject. As far as the writers are concerned, they can
only thank God for the blessed state of their readers,
admonish them to stand fast, and pray that God may
encourage and establish them. These verses round out
the renewed instruction (v. 3-12) in the most appropriate and natural way.

**Now we on our part are obliged to thank God con-
cerning you, brethren beloved of the Lord, that God
chose you from the beginning unto salvation in connection with sanctification of spirit and faith in truth,
for which he called you by means of our gospel for obtaining our Lord Jesus Christ's glory.**

Δέ is transitional and not adversative. "We on our
part" is emphatic, but only in the sense of "as far as
we writers are concerned because of our special relation to you Thessalonians." We have already explained
why "we are obliged" is inserted (see 1:3). The writ-

ers cannot but thank God as regards the Thessalonians;
God has done too much for the Thessalonians so that
Paul and his associates should let anything prevent
them from expressing the most fervent thanks to him.
The wording is purposely the same as in 1:3, the
thanksgiving with which the first section of the letter
begins is to be the same as that with which the second
section ends. Like two arms these two thanksgivings
embrace all that they encircle and hold it all up to God
in deep gratitude.

In 1:3 "brethren" suffices; but now the much richer
address "brethren beloved of the Lord" is in place,
"having been loved by the Lord" and thus still being
loved by him. How far back this love reaches is not
stated. Time does not limit the Lord; the next clause
takes us back to the world's beginning. The Lord's
love for his own goes back to eternity. See how he
speaks of his "other sheep" in John 10:16, all those
of future ages, some of them having as yet not even
been born. As "brethren" the Thessalonians belong
with the three writers, all of them being embraced by
this love. This is the love of full comprehension and
corresponding blessed purpose.

The answer to the question as to why the Lord thus
loves lies in the nature of the Lord's own being; his love
is the infinite attribute which is to be blessed for his
loved ones, ever to be worshipped and adored by them,
but beyond their fathoming. "Lord" is Christ, the second person, and not God, the first. Many note this and
also that "God" precedes and follows; but they do not
note that in the word "Lord" there lies not only Christ's
deity but also all his saving work by which he has purchased and won us and made himself our Lord and us
his own.

῞Οτι states the object of the thanksgiving and not
the cause (A. V.): "that God chose you from the beginning unto salvation," etc. Only the middle of αἱρέω

is used in the New Testament (Phil. 1:22; Heb. 11:25) and only the simplex. The sense is much the same as though Paul had used ἐκλέγεσθαι or προορίζειν although each verb has its own connotation. Here εἵλετο means no more than that God "took you for himself," took you for his own, in that sense "chose you."

"From the beginning" (no article is needed in such phrases in the Greek) dates this act of God's, but not *at* the beginning when time began; ἀπό, "from the beginning," dates from that extreme point of time (the Greek always thinks forward from the farther point) because beyond that no point of time exists. The sense is thus the same as "before the foundation of the world" (Eph. 1:4), in eternity. God created time but is not bound by time; all that exists in time from the first moment until the last lay before him in the timelessness of eternity, save that eternity has no past tense like "lay." The matter is really inconceivable to our finite minds which are chained to terms denoting time. The same is true regarding Eph. 1:4. By stressing ideas of time we only misconceive this and other divine acts, note Rev. 13:8. The variant reading ἀπαρχήν, "as first fruits" is not authenticated.

The whole clause expresses one thought: "God chose you from the beginning unto salvation in connection with sanctification of spirit and faith in truth." There is no other choice or election save this one for salvation in connection with sanctification and faith. Some think only of final salvation (heaven), i. e., of the "glory" mentioned in v. 14; but sanctification and faith point to "salvation" both here and hereafter. In connection with I Thess. 4:3 (see also 4:4, 7) we have already explained ἁγιασμός as being an activity on God's part and thus not the state expressed by ἁγιωσύνη. The salvation to which God chose the Thessalonians is wholly "in connection with God's sanctifying work" and thus also "in connection with the Thessalonians' faith." The fact that this sanctification signifies the whole work of setting the Thessalonians apart for God is self-evident. Καί is explicative. After naming God's activity it adds the main factor in our reception of that activity, which is "faith." So also Christians are called "saints (whom God sanctifies) and believers" (who by faith receive this sanctification), Eph. 1:1. The idea is the same.

We differ with our versions and with all those commentators who regard the genitive as the subjective genitive: "sanctification of the Spirit." Both datives have objective genitives. The fact that God, i. e., his Spirit, does the sanctifying need not be stated, for this lies in the word "sanctification" which is itself a term that expresses action. It is our "spirit" that God sanctifies just as it is "truth" that our faith trusts. It should not be said that πνεῦμα always means the Holy Spirit. In Gal. 5:16, 17, 18, 22, 25 (twice); 6:8 (twice) our "spirit" is referred to. To be sure, Πνεῦμα does not always need the article in order to refer to God's "Spirit"; the question is not linguistic, it is exegetical, the thought and the context decide.

Nothing especial is at stake here, for in any case it is the Spirit that sanctifies, and it is our spirit that is sanctified. Yet where two datives have genitives, the assumption is that the genitives are not diverse but alike. In v. 10 and 12 "the truth" has the article; here all four nouns are without the article in order to stress their quality. This also helps to make the two objects of ἐν alike even as the one preposition treats them as being only one object. The fact that this "truth" is the same as "the truth" mentioned in v. 10 and 12, namely the gospel, need scarcely be said. What Paul prophesies concerning the Lord's Parousia is a part of this "truth." Note the chiasm: "sanctification (God's) of spirit (ours) — faith (ours) in truth (God's)."

The ἐν phrase modifies all that precedes it in this clause and not merely the verb. This ἐν is not instrumental, for choosing requires no instrument. Ἐν does not mean *in der Weise und dadurch dass;* "through" in the A. V. is incorrect, for the Greek word for this would be διά. Ἐν does not mean "in view of" or "in the foreknowledge of." It does not mean "unto," the Greek for which would be εἰς. Ἐν has its first and original meaning: "in connection with sanctification and faith." None were chosen by God without this connection. F. Pieper says well that sanctification and faith belong to the *act* of choosing and not merely to the *execution* of the act as Calvinists teach (*Christliche Dogmatik* III, 538). Grammatically stated, ἐν modifies "God chose you from the beginning unto salvation" and states no separate thought.

We note that the choice was not abstract or general but concrete and definite: "God chose *you*." The idea that, when this choice was made, "you" were "unbelievers" is excluded by the ἐν phrase. We usually say that the choice is not absolute; also that it is not conditional. It is ordinate: "in connection with," etc. This is as near as our finite minds can approach God's timeless act. For in no way does time limit God as it always does our minds. As God saw "you" in the act, so he saw the whole "salvation" to which he chose "you" and also the "sanctification of spirit" and the "faith in truth." There is no limit at which God halted unless we in some way bind God as we ourselves are bound to succession in time, which we should never do. This statement pertains to all the timeless acts of God as we poor mortals now attempt to rethink them; all of them are beyond us, and we may easily go astray.

14) Εἰς ὅ makes the next clause subordinate: "for which he called you by means of our gospel for obtaining our Lord Jesus Christ's glory." Καί would coordinate and place the choice and the call side by side; but

the latter is already involved in the "salvation, sanctification, and faith" mentioned in v. 13. We remember that εἰς ὅ is the equivalent of a particle: *dazu* or *wozu, warum* (B.-P. 356), it is much like διό or δι' ὅ. It is thus not necessary to search for an antecedent (one or the other of the preceding nouns, a combination of them, or the whole preceding statement, R. 714). What God did for the Thessalonians in time rests on his timeless act: if no choice, then no call, etc. "Wherefore he called you" refers to the successful call; the verb and the noun are always used thus in the epistles.

"By means of our gospel" does not refer to a peculiar form of the gospel that was preached by Paul and by his assistants; it refers to these men only as being the ones who preached the gospel to the Thessalonians, who brought the Thessalonians to faith by God's gospel grace. Those who regard εἰς ὅ as a relative with an antecedent consider εἰς περιποίησιν epexegetical: "unto which he called you, namely unto obtaining," etc. They justify the epexegesis by saying that in v. 13 only salvation in general is mentioned while now its consummation is introduced, the final glory. But what ordinary reader would connect the two εἰς phrases in this manner? We cancel the comma in our versions and read the whole clause as one thought. Our call through the gospel is for one purpose only: "for obtaining our Lord Jesus Christ's glory" (Phil. 3:21). "Obtaining" is better than "possessing" or "possession." The genitive is objective: we are to obtain Christ's glory. Luther strangely makes "glory" the adjectival and "our Lord," etc., the subjective genitive: *zum herrlichen Eigentum unseres Herrn,* etc., the Thessalonians are called to be "Christ's glorious possession." Paul now repeatedly uses the full title "our Lord Jesus Christ" and not "Lord Jesus."

15) An admonition is added to this thanksgiving: **Accordingly, then, brethren, keep standing**

fast and holding fast the traditions which you were taught, whether by means of our discourse or by means of our letter!

On Paul's favorite double connective ἄρα οὖν see Rom. 5:18. In accord with all that v. 13, 14 state regarding the blessed state and the prospect of the Thessalonians, and in the light of all that the Thessalonians know about the Lord's Parousia and about the apostasy and the Antichrist that will precede the Lord (v. 1-12), the one thing the Thessalonians themselves must do is ever to keep standing fast and holding fast to what they have been taught. Both imperatives are present tenses and thus durative. Courageous, manly standing, combined with masterful, strong holding, both of which are wrought by the grace received, constitute the response of the Thessalonians, there is to be no letting themselves be shaken or disturbed (v. 2). This is the same standing fast which I Thess. 3:8 expects.

The use of παραδόσεις does not contain something rabbinic, for this term is used in the Gospels and also by Paul in Gal. 1:14 and Col. 2:8 to denote Jewish and human "traditions." Here and in 3:6 and in I Cor. 11:2 the word = the gospel teachings, "truth" (v. 13), "the truth" (v. 10, 12), the plural to indicate the different parts of the gospel truth. The word itself points only to transmission: the things given or handed over from teacher to pupil. Romanists have appropriated it and refer it to teachings handed down in the church and not recorded in the Scriptures; but this late Romish use has nothing to do with Paul's use. In I Cor. 11:2 Paul also has the corresponding verb.

Εἴτε — εἴτε is not disjunctive but conjunctive, and ἡμῶν is to be construed with both "discourse" and "letter," the oral teaching of Paul, Silvanus, and Timothy, and the letter the three had sent (First Thessalonians). The latter is especially mentioned because of an alleged other letter which purported to teach contrary things

(2:2). The Thessalonians are to cling to the things they have personally heard from the lips of Paul, Silvanus, and Timothy, and have personally received in the authentic letter sent by these three.

The admonition is properly brief and fits exactly all that precedes in this chapter.

16) Thanks to God, admonition to the Thessalonians, and now prayer for them, intercessory prayer, a prayer-wish because it is written to the Thessalonians and thus couched in the third person; recall I Thess. 3:11-13. **Now may he, our Lord Jesus Christ, and God, our Father, he who did love us and did give (us) eternal encouragement and good hope in grace, encourage your hearts and stablish (them) in every good deed and word!**

Here ends the main burden of the letter, the rest is supplementary. As was the case in I Thess. 3:11 and 5:23, αὐτός is not reflexive ("himself") but merely emphatic. Both divine persons are named in the full liturgical and solemn way. The two "our" are confessional and include both the writers and the readers. In two other instances, Gal. 1:1 and II Cor. 13:14, Paul names Christ first for no special reason. By naming the two persons together he places them on an equality. Αὐτός applies also to "God, our Father," and thus justifies the singular verb. The same is true with regard to the apposition: "he who did love us," etc. The two divine persons act as one, which causes no difficulty for those who know John 10:30; 12:45; 14:9.

There is no need to debate about the punctiliar force of the aorist participles and to date them so as to apply to some special act of love and giving; let them be constative, summarizing what both of these persons have done in loving and in giving. Compare v. 13 on love. The giving is the product of the loving. Παράκλησις = *Zuspruch*; the following verb = *zusprechen*; this may be admonitory, encouraging, or com-

forting as the context may require. The noun and
the verb ought to have the same meaning; one may
debate as to whether to choose: "gave us eternal comfort — or eternal encouragement; may comfort — or
may encourage your hearts." If this were I Thess.
4:13-5:11, "comfort" would be correct. Since they are
here joined with hope, we prefer "encouragement"
and "encourage." Both are, however, not subjective
states in us but objective gifts: encouragement spoken
and given to us; hope, that for which we are to hope.
This explains the added adjectives which also lend
fulness to the expression: "eternal encouragement" =
the effect of which is eternal; "good hope" = the realization of which will prove it valuable. "In grace"
does not name a third gift of love but brings to mind
the fact that the love which prompts these gifts is
wholly the undeserved favor of God (1:2). All this
giving and these gifts are "in connection with grace"
and with grace alone.

17) The participial apposition brings the past up
to the present; the two optatives of wish reach into
the future. This double wish (the aorists are again
constative) asks for nothing new. For "may encourage your hearts" refers to the same "encouragement"
that was mentioned in v. 16, the two words are the
same. The same is true with regard to the hope and
the wish: "may stablish your hearts," for one must be
firm and solid in clinging to this hope (objective). This
will show itself "in every good deed and word," in all
that we do and say, in all our daily activity of life. We
will act as though our life belongs to heaven. "Word"
does not here mean "doctrine." A few texts transpose:
"word and deed" (A. V.), which is the more regular
order.

CHAPTER III

Request for the Prayers of the Thessalonians

1) This request belongs to the foregoing. The third chapter should begin with v. 4. As the writers pray for the Thessalonians in 2:16, 17, so they now ask the Thessalonians to pray for them. This request is like the one found in I Thess. 5:25, but it is more extensive. Τὸ λοιπόν should not mislead us on this point, for it applies only to v. 1-3 and not to the body of this chapter which consists of v. 4-15. **As regards the rest, keep praying, brethren, for us that the Word of the Lord may keep on running and be glorified even also as with you, and that we may be rescued from perverse and wicked men, for the faith does not belong to all.** "As for the rest" joins this request to the thanksgiving (2:12-14), the admonition (2:15), and the prayer-wish (2:16, 17), and completes the group of thoughts contained in 2:12-3:3.

The effectual, fervent prayers of the righteous avail much, and thus, as these writers pray for others, so they ask the prayers of others for themselves, and thereby express the unity of the *Una Sancta*. The imperative is durative, and περί is used as it is in I Thess. 5:26; ἵνα introduces the substance of the prayers, and its tenses are durative. "That the Word of the Lord may keep on running and be glorified" is graphic. We do not think that this running refers to the stadium and the running of races, because the Word scarcely runs in such a race, nor does the second verb "be crowned" refer to the crown and the prize that are mentioned in I Cor. 9:24, 25 where we have the figure of a race track. The Word of the Lord runs when its proclamation spreads; it is glorified when men believe and prize it. As far as the writers are concerned, the Word cannot run too fast and too far and receive too much glory in the hearts of men.

The added clause: "even as also with you" ($\pi\rho\delta s$ as in I Thess. 3:4) applies to both verbs; there is no reason to restrict it to the running. This is commendation: the Thessalonians were concerned to have the Word run and be glorified in their own city and territory. Yet Paul means more: since the Thessalonians are so concerned they will desire to have the Word run and be glorified also elsewhere, especially where the men who first brought them the Word are seeking to spread the Word. They will, therefore, pray earnestly as requested.

2) A second $\dddot{\iota}\nu\alpha$ follows and introduces the prayer that the writers may be rescued from perverse and wicked men who are set on stopping the free course (A. V.) of the Word by silencing the voice of the preachers. The verb is the same as that used in I Thess. 1:10; here it is an aorist to express effective rescuing. $^{*}A\tau o\pi os$ = "out of place" and thus applies to anything that is improper. The men who seek to silence and stop the Word are "out of place." The idea is not complete, hence the second adjective is added which completes the description; "wicked" is always to be understood in the active sense of viciously wicked. These men might themselves refuse to accept the Word and still permit those who will to believe it; but no, the devil rouses them to make efforts to destroy the preaching of the Word and the very preachers themselves. This clause vividly recalled to the mind of the readers how God had rescued Paul and Silvanus in their own city (Acts 17:5-10).

Luther translates this word *unartig*, our versions translate it "unreasonable" although there is no reference to reason in the word. The main adjective is "wicked." When Paul explains: "for the faith does not belong to all" — the Greek idiom: "is not of all" (possessive genitive) — he does not minimize the guilt of these wicked men as if to say that they cannot avoid what they are doing. He points to the real source of their guilt. If the word of anyone deserves to be received by faith, the Lord's Word should be so received. When this Word comes to men and does not become theirs, this is due to the fact that they reject it. After that one may expect anything from such men. The statement implies that there will always be such men: "the faith not theirs." "The faith" (with the article) is usually regarded as being subjective faith, and C.-K. asserts that this word is always used in the subjective sense in the New Testament. In a number of passages it is certainly used in an objective sense. Here, we submit, it seems to be used in both senses.

Does this clause reflect Paul's situation in Corinth? Was he in danger at the moment? Some think so. But this is a precarious opinion. The best view is that this letter was written before the events recorded in Acts 18:12, etc., occurred. It is sufficient to think of Paul's past career, of Acts 13:50, etc.; 14:19, etc.; 16:19, etc.; 17:5, etc., 13, etc. We should think of what this clause meant to the Thessalonians when they heard it read; this letter has no reference to persecutions that were being suffered at the moment in Corinth.

3) While the writers ask for their own rescue from every danger that may come to them in the course of their work they are mainly concerned about their readers and thus revert to them. **Yet faithful is the Lord who will stablish you and guard you from the wicked one.** To the prayerful wish for the Thessalonians found in 2:16, 17 there is now added this word of assurance; note that "will stablish you" repeats the "may stablish your hearts" found in 2:17

but is now amplified by the addition "will guard you."
The one refers to inward rooting and grounding, the
other to protection from outward assaults. We recall
I Thess. 5:24 which is also an assurance regarding
God's being "faithful," but here it is "the Lord"
(Christ) who is faithful.

Because πίστις and πιστός are juxtaposed, some assume that we have a play on the words: many have
not "the faith, yet faithful" is the Lord. There is
merely a similarity in sound, therefore the juxtaposition seems to be merely incidental. Does the final
phrase mean "from the evil" (A. V.) or "from the evil
one" (R. V.)? True, there is no material difference,
yet Paul intended to write either the neuter or the
masculine and not both. A look at Matt. 13:19; Eph.
6:16; I John 2:13, 14; 5:18 would argue for accepting the masculine form in our passage. When we also
note that in 2:9 Satan is placed back of the apostasy
and the Antichrist, it is not difficult to believe that
here, too, Paul would put "the wicked one" back of
"the wicked men." Add to this the fact that it would
seem strange for Paul suddenly to use the abstract
"guarding from the wickedness" when he has thus far
consistently written in a personal and a concrete way.
Therefore "guarding from the wicked one" continues
this personal and concrete method of presentation.

The Complementary Section of the Letter

Directions regarding Disciplining the Disorderly

4) Some call chapter 3 "the parenetic part" of the
letter. But it does not contain a series of exhortations
as I Thess. 5:12-22 and other letters do. Verses 4-15
are the complementary section of this letter. They
complete the main section, 2:1-12, by telling the Thessalonians what to do about members who may cling to
their extravagant notions that the day of the Lord is

already here (2:2) and may thus continue to walk
disorderly and not in accord with the gospel teaching
they have received. The question as to what to do
about such members was bound to arise, and thus the
writers complete their instruction by giving a full and
an explicit answer. This section may also be said to
give instruction just as the main section does, yet it
is naturally cast into the form of command which tells
the Thessalonians what to do. The fact that the Thessalonian membership will accept the information given
in 2:1-12 is not questioned by the writers; they are
also certain that the church will act in accord with
these complementary instructions.

This is stated in so many words. **Now we are confident in the Lord regarding you that what things we
are commanding, you are also doing and will do.
Moreover, may the Lord direct your hearts into the
love of God and into the patience of Christ!**

A transitional δέ introduces this preamble which
ought to begin a new paragraph and not be made a
part of v. 1-3 as is done in the R. V. The present force
of the second perfect tense with ἐπί (instead of the
dative) is seen from the translation: "we have come to
place this confidence on you." As they are about to
send them orders as to what to do (v. 6, etc.) the writers are confident in the Lord, in connection with whom
they have done all their work in Thessalonica and
brought the Thessalonians to their present state, that
they will earnestly follow these orders. This is one
compliment to the Thessalonians; it is joined with a
second, namely that they are already doing what the
writers are now telling them to do. Timothy had evidently directed them during his visit and had reported
to Paul and to Silvanus when he returned to them in
Corinth that he had found some disorderly and that the
Thessalonians were following his directions in dealing
with them.

If it be asked why, then, this repetition of what Paul had already attended to, the answer is, to give greater assurance to the Thessalonians in this matter. After all, Timothy was only an assistant of Paul's; to receive these written orders from all three, Paul, Silvanus, and Timothy, gave greater certainty, especially to so young a congregation. Paul's voice in the matter they would prize especially and also the fact that what Timothy directed them to do is thus corroborated and not altered by Paul and Silvanus. On παραγγέλλομεν see I Thess. 4:11. Καί — καί may be translated "also — and" or "both — and."

5) Δέ adds another point in the form of a prayerful wish: "Moreover, may the Lord direct your hearts into the love of God," etc. See the verb in I Thess. 3:11 where it is used in the literal sense: "direct our way to you," while here it pertains to "your hearts." The fact that this is the optative of wish is assured by the nominative subject (R. 1092). The Thessalonians will need the Lord's direction in this whole matter of discipline. The supposition that the writers are not quite sure of the Thessalonians despite what they say in v. 4 is not fair to the readers; the best of us need the Lord's help. Two things are needed for applying discipline to erring church members, namely love and patience, such love as God has for all of us and such patience as Christ exercised while he was on earth. Both genitives are subjective. Discipline which is exercised by us in such love and with such patience that do not readily give up the erring one will be true Christian discipline and will be crowned with the greatest success in winning back the erring ones.

Some commentators combine these verses into one paragraph with v. 1-3 as the R. V. does and interpret them without regard to what follows despite the fact that the παραγγέλλομεν of v. 4 is repeated in v. 6 and in a different tense in v. 10. They generalize these two verses as though they referred to any and to all the apostolic commands, and some introduce the *Heils-gewissheit* of the Thessalonians which rests on God's love for them and their patient waiting for Christ's Parousia. Thus also there is a difference of view regarding the genitives "the love of God — the patience of Christ" (they are regarded as being objective or indicating source, some making them diverse). Even when they are regarded as being subjective they are generalized and are not applied to the matter of discipline. Some of the remarks of these commentators might be in place if these verses constituted the conclusion of a series of commands; but all that the preceding contains is 2:15 which is not a command but a fraternal admonition. Ὑπομονή is referred to persecutions which the Thessalonians are to endure with "patience wrought by Christ" (genitive of the agent) although this would take us back as far as 1:4 and would seem out of place here in 3:5.

God had sinners to deal with and used his love to win them, the love of full comprehension and corresponding purpose; we are still sinners, and he treats us with this love in order to correct us. Christ walked among sinners and treated them, especially his friends, with his wondrous patience (see the author's chapter: "Have I been so long time with you?" in *His Footsteps* 229, etc.). See how he dealt with Peter. Into this love of God for sinners, into this patience of Christ with the weak and the erring the Thessalonians must be conducted in order to succeed in what they are now told to do. These two verses occur in the proper place, with the disciplinary directions. Because a pronoun could not be used in the last phrase we have τοῦ Χριστοῦ, which is different from ὁ Κύριος, the subject, although it refers to the same person. As "the Christ" (the article making the noun appellative) the Thessalonian Christians are to use his "patience," his brave perseverance (Trench).

If you wish, regard v. 4, 5 as a little preliminary paragraph or combine v. 4-15 into one paragraph.

6) **Now we command you, brethren, in the name of the Lord Jesus Christ that you withdraw yourselves from every brother walking disorderly and not according to the tradition which they received from us.**

Like the δέ in v. 4, this δέ is also transitional; it turns to the particular matter to be discussed. We now hear about the things to which v. 4 refers, wherefore also the verb "we command" is the same. Its meaning is better understood when we note that it signifies "to pass a military order along," one that comes from a superior commander, hence we have the addition "in the name of our Lord Jesus Christ," the full solemn designation.

This frequently found phrase is often misunderstood as though it means "on the authority of Christ" (thus also R. 649 and *W. P.*). But see ὄνομα, for example, in Matt. 6:9; John 1:12; Acts 2:21, 38; 3:6, to mention only these: "the name" always means "the revelation." So here it means "in connection with the revelation of our Lord Jesus Christ." In most connections the idea is not that of authority; here the note of authority in connection with "the name" does not lie in "the name" but in the verb: "we pass along the order," and this order is in connection with (ἐν) the whole of Christ's revelation. The whole expression is one of dignified formality as befits such an order.

"You, brethren," addresses the congregation; the writers transmit an order, but it comes from a higher source than themselves, and thus, as far as the writers are concerned, from brethren who themselves have received this order to other brethren whom they serve.

This is nothing hierarchical. The discipline to be exercised in the Thessalonian church belongs to the Thessalonians yet is not to be exercised as they may or may not please but as their Lord directs "in connection with his name or revelation." In connection with the terrible case referred to in I Cor. 5 Paul does not use his authority to expel the man but sends the congregation the resolution to be adopted (v. 3-5, see the author's *Interpretation*). It is the congregation's function to discipline and, if necessary, to expel, all papal claims to the contrary notwithstanding. The clergy act as brethren and use their office as such.

The cases that occurred in Thessalonica cannot have been numerous since "from every brother walking disorderly" refers to only one here and there. They also were not grave, for the writers retain the word "brother" and point only to withdrawal and not to expulsion and excommunication as is done in I Cor. 5:3-5. These cases were also of such a nature that they would soon come to an end, for trying to live without work in a city like Thessalonica would soon cure most of those who tried it once their means gave out.

When we here read: "That you withdraw yourselves" (middle voice) we should not forget that the Thessalonians have already been told to deal with the disorderly in I Thess. 5:14, that the writers themselves have sent them admonition in I Thess. 4:11, 12 and are repeating this here in v. 11, 12, and that these two letters are intended to remove any foolish thoughts that might produce disorderly living without working. The point is this: only when all such admonition and correction proves in vain, when in spite of it all a brother continues to walk disorderly, the next step that the congregation is to take is to withdraw from such a brother.

This word is carefully chosen, for it is not "expel" or "excommunicate." It is a preliminary step, the effect of which is calculated to make unnecessary the final step. Fortunately, v. 14, 15 state quite clearly what withdrawal means. Its purpose is to make the disorderly brother ashamed so that he will forsake his wrong action. Withdrawal from him calls his brotherly standing into question so that, if he persists, he will compel the congregation to separate itself completely from him, i. e., to expel him. Withdrawal also means that the congregation protects itself and its members against this disorderly man's conduct and its spread in their midst. Finally, withdrawal means that the congregation does not allow itself to become guilty of any part of this man's sin.

This man will be refused participation in the agape of the congregation and thus also in the Lord's Supper. These were the great rites in which the congregational spiritual brotherhood expressed itself. All the early congregations also met in assemblies for the purpose of elections and for other business; from these, too, the disorderly were to be excluded. In fact, v. 4 states that the Thessalonians were already doing what is here enjoined, most probably under the instructions given by Timothy on his visit (I Thess. 3:1, 2) although Timothy needed only to make effective what had already been taught the Thessalonians regarding Christian discipline (Matt. 18:15, etc.) when Paul and Silvanus first worked in Thessalonica.

Regarding ἀτάκτως, "not in line," see the adjective which is explained in I Thess. 5:14. The brief admonition: "Train the disorderly," which is embedded among other brief admonitions in I Thess. 5, shows that at the time of the writing of the first epistle the disorderliness had only begun. When a whole paragraph is now devoted to the subject, we see that the evil had spread. Hence we now also have the order to take disciplinary steps so as definitely to check the evil.

We decline to transfer into I Thess. 5:14 all the developed disorderliness of our present paragraph. Then this paragraph of Second Thessalonians ought to have been placed into First Thessalonians. No; the news that Timothy brought at the time of the composition of the first epistle made it appear that a dose of νουθετεῖν, administered by the congregation, would squelch the beginnings; but the news that prompted the writing of the second epistle made it plain that the stronger medicine of στέλλεσθαι was now called for.

In I Thess. 5:14 the unmodified noun "those disorderly" is sufficient; but in Second Thessalonians these disorderly ones are described since their conduct had come fully to light in greater development and also in wider extent. True, the lone reference to the ἄτακτοι in I Thess. 5:14 might refer to any kind of irregular conduct; but in II Thess. 3:6, 8, 11 the same word is used, ἀτάκτως twice and the verb ἠτακτήσαμεν (we gospel ministers "did not act disorderly among you"). The only fair deduction is that we have a reference to the same kind of disorderliness as that mentioned in I Thess. 5:14. At that time it was incipient, now it is more developed.

What walking disorderly means the addition: "and not according to the tradition which they received from us," indicates. We have explained παράδοσις in 2:15: the doctrine and the principles of the Word transmitted to others. To disregard and to forsake this teaching is to walk "out of line," disorderly. A soldier who does not keep in line naturally first gets a reprimand (I Thess. 5:14); but when he continues it and induces a few others also to get out of line, sharper measures must be applied (those now indicated).

The military flavor of ἀτάκτως is the same as that of παραγγέλλομεν. The form παρελάβοσαν with its -οσαν suffix is textually correct (it is thus written in the LXX, the papyri, and inscriptions, R. 335, etc.; B.-D. 84, 2). This third person plural is plainly a *constructio ad sensum*, for "every brother" suggests a number. The texts vary and have forms that show as many as five different endings. The only important variant is: "which *you* received" (R. V. margin), but this seeks only to get rid of the third person plural; "he received" (A. V.) is textually inferior.

7) *Verba docent, exempla trahunt.* The doctrine Paul, Silvanus, and Timothy preach they themselves follow. **For you yourselves know how you ought to imitate us because we did not act disorderly among you nor ate bread gratis at anyone's hand but with toil and hardship, working by night and by day, so as not to be a burden upon any of you.**

Explanatory γάρ can be regarded as offering a reason that the Thessalonians should do what is here ordered only by those who mislocate v. 4, 5, where the writers say that the Thessalonians are already following the orders. It is unconvincing to say that it is now being intimated that they ought to have withdrawn from the disorderly and ought not to have waited until now when they are being told. The Thessalonians were withdrawing. They had rightly understood the original teaching ("tradition") they had received from Paul, Silvanus, and Timothy. In First Thessalonians these writers thought that no more was required on the part of the congregation than a good rebuke to the disorderly ones. When this had not availed, the congregation went farther, for which action v. 4 commends them.

In v. 6 the Thessalonians receive formal orders that tell them for their still greater assurance to go on as they are doing. These disorderly members are not following the Christian teaching; withdrawing from them is the proper course to follow in order to bring them to their senses. These disorderly members are not only turning from what the Thessalonians have been taught but equally from the example the Thessalonians have seen in the writers who have lived what they taught. Γάρ adds this example in corroboration of the teaching ("tradition") in order to assure the Thessalonians still more that the withdrawing they have begun is beyond question the proper procedure. They themselves know how they must imitate their teachers. "How" says more than declarative "that," for it adds the thought of manner. Both in fact and in manner the disorderly members were no longer imitating Paul, Silvanus, and Timothy. Δεῖ expresses any kind of a necessity, here the moral necessity of joining their teachers in obeying the doctrine.

There is no manifestation of pride behind the statement that the Thessalonians must be imitators of the writers but quite the opposite: teachers and pupils, preachers and members are placed on the same level, under the same obedience to the doctrine. Note that I Thess. 1:6 and 2:14 speak of imitating suffering, and our passage of imitating "toil and hardship"; neither are commonly deemed enviable experiences. These disorderly members wanted to remain acknowledged members although they walked disorderly, an intolerable presumption although it is often advanced today. By their disorderly action they had begun to sunder themselves from both their teachers and their fellow members, which raised the question whether the separation soon would be complete. Withdrawal from the disorderly was thus forced upon the true members for their own sakes as well as for a warning to those from whom they were withdrawing.

῞Οτι is "because"; it states the reason for saying that the Thessalonians know: they had seen the conduct of the writers: "we did not act disorderly among you." Note the repetition of this distinctive word.

8) "Neither" speaks of the particular as though it were distinct from the general, for one might admit a broad denial as being true and yet hold to some particular charge. It is the particular that is here essential: "we did not eat bread gratuitously at anyone's hand," δωρεάν, "for nothing." When they were in Thessalonica, Paul and his helpers did not accept the invitation of any of their converts to lodge with them and to share their table free of charge, "as a gift" (adverbial accusative). Despite all their arduous work of preaching to establish a church they earned their own support: "with toil and hardship, working by night and by day, so as not to be a burden upon anyone of you." These are the identical words that are used in I Thess. 2:9 (on which see the details). This example is the more effective because the writers had the calling and the work to preach the gospel, which alone was enough to require the full strength of any man; yet they added the work of supporting themselves; no wonder it extended their labor into even the night. But these disorderly members in Thessalonica just stopped working altogether.

This is the place to recall 2:2, the plea that the Lord's day is already here, that Paul, Silvanus, and Timothy had in some way or other themselves said so. On this basis the disorderly Thessalonians justified their stopping of work. The writers had not taught such errors while they were in Thessalonica as 2:3-12 states, nor had they acted upon such doctrine as the Thessalonians know. They had taught and acted to the very contrary. Note 2:5 on the teaching and I Thess. 4:11, 12 on the conduct according with this teaching, conduct which Paul, Silvanus, and Timothy had most decisively exemplified. As these disorderly Thessalonians were repudiating the teaching ("tradition"), so they were also repudiating this strong apostolic example.

All this is set down here, not because the firm
members in Thessalonica had any doubt about it, but
to reassure them, to stop all propaganda on the part
of those who were walking disorderly, and to bring
these themselves to their senses.

9) Yet this example of the writers is not to be
misunderstood so as to imply that preachers are not to
receive support. I Cor. 9:13, 14 is true although it was
written much later. **Not that we do not have authority
but in order to offer our own selves as an example to
you so that you imitate us.**

Οὐχ ὅτι — ἀλλά is a common form of elliptical or
abbreviated statement also in English; it is so stereotyped that no verbs need to be supplied; ὅτι is not
"because" (our versions) but declarative. Here we
see the great character of the example furnished to
the Thessalonians. Paul and his helpers had the right
to accept full support from their converts but did not
use this right as Paul states regarding himself in
I Cor. 9:12, 18. Jesus gave them that right in Luke
10:7, 8, nor can it ever be abrogated. But to have
the right and to use it are two different matters. Paul
did not personally use it for three reasons. The gravest is stated in I Cor. 9:16 (on which see the author's
exposition). The other reason appears in I Thess.
2:9: no one was to charge Paul with preaching for
profit and to put him into the same class with the
charlatans who infested the Roman Empire at that
time. Thirdly, he, together with his assistants, wanted
to give an example to his converts — as is here stated
— of unselfish love and devotion, being a burden to
no one.

These three reasons do not contradict each other.
When one is advanced, the others are not contradicted.
One may do a thing for several reasons and may as
occasion requires advance one or the other without self-contradiction. From τύπος, example or pat-

tern, we have "type" and the compound ὑποτύπωσις as in I Tim. 1:16. "To imitate" does not necessarily mean to copy but to be like in a general way. The Thessalonians were not apostles, not all of them were teachers, and yet they could imitate their unselfish teachers by working steadily at their business or trade instead of being disorderly and following fanatical notions.

10) The γάρ is confirmatory, but of the entire statement and not merely of "when we were with you." **And indeed, when we were with you, this we commanded you: If one does not want to work, neither let him eat!** This is the climax of the whole matter; hence we have γάρ, and καί connects with the foregoing. At the very start Paul and his assistants repeatedly gave this command to the Thessalonians. The imperative "neither let him eat" makes this statement a command to the Thessalonians. In the Koine οὐ is the negative in a protasis of reality; the negative with an imperative is regularly μή as here.

One may question whether this dictum is really a Jewish proverb, as some say, as long as the sayings collected and called proverbs are not after all the same. The same is also true regarding the general supposition that Gen. 3:19 is the source of this statement: "In the sweat of thy face shalt thou eat bread." Collections of pagan sayings are of the same character as when the ant says to the fly: *Nihil laboras ideo quum opus est nil habes.* In all such statements we have the idea that sloth does not pay, that laziness is condemned, which is rather commonplace truth even when it is aptly worded. Deissmann, (*Light, etc.,* 318) says that "Paul was probably borrowing a bit of good old workshop morality, a maxim coined perhaps by some industrious workman as he forbade his lazy apprentice to sit down to dinner." Yet his idea, too, is not altogether satisfactory. This, however, is true, that Paul's

word will mean a little more to us when we think of
him as a man whose hands are calloused because of
honest toil. It is also not correct to call this "a catechism truth" although it has the Jewish form of balanced sayings.

Bengel stresses the point of the saying: *nolle
vitium est*. "Non-willing is vice." In this statement
Paul is expressing the Lord's will. It is not apparent
why he should be borrowing from any source. It is
saying too little to claim that he is voicing the dignity
of labor; he is voicing the gospel which requires honest work from all who profess faith in the gospel,
which is a quite different and higher matter. The
church has therefore seen that this dictum abolishes all
false asceticism, all unchristian disinclination to work,
all fanatic exaltation above work, all self-inflicted pauperism. The ἐργάζεσθαι refers to the honorable work in
any Christian calling; be it ever so humble, it has
God's blessing. This word condemns not only the professed lazy Christian; it condemns also him who pro-
poses to live richly without making an honest return.

11) The point of this as well as of Paul's own example is obscured when "being burdensome to someone else" (v. 8) is made the chief point, the fear lest
the congregation be overloaded with objects of
charity. That is a minor point. The main thought
is the fact that such disorderly members are not
true to the gospel teaching, are following the fiction that the Lord's day is already here. "For"
explains. **For we hear some are walking among you
disorderly, not working at all but acting as busybodies.** The writers indicate how they had received
their information since the sending of the first epistle;
it was not through some letter but from travelers: "we
are hearing" implies repetition, several travelers had
told the same story. That is why no name is men-

tioned, none need be. That is also why the writers act
upon what they hear, the matter itself was public in
Thessalonica and the information about it was full and
continuous. The accusative with a participle is the
regular construction with ἀκούω.

Once more we hear the specific word: "some are
walking among you *disorderly.*" Only "some," but that
was bad enough. It has been well remarked: not
some "*of* you," but some "*among* you." The question
which their conduct was raising is whether they would
really remain "of" their brethren. Now we learn what
"disorderly" means: "working not at all (or: nothing) but acting as busybodies"; this is an effective
paronomasia in the Greek. The latter means to be
busy with what is none of their business. They gave
up their employment, spent their time in idleness, and
occupied their idle time by running around and agitating and bothering other people.

"Being busybodies" does not say with what they
busied themselves; but we are right in connecting this
with 2:2: agitating the claim that the Lord's day is
already here, that in some indirect way they have received this information from Paul, Silvanus, and Timothy themselves. We may picture them sitting around
for hours in the bazaars and little shops of the other
members, making a nuisance of themselves, and trying
to unsettle the stable members with their fanatical notions. It is well to note the sober restraint of this
brief negative and positive description of the disorderly, the word "disorderly" is itself rather mild. Neither the church itself nor its erring members are helped
when a fault is exaggerated by those who would correct it.

12) **Now such we command and admonish in the
Lord Jesus Christ that, working with quietness, they
eat their own bread. But you on your part, brethren,**

do not become discouraged in well-doing. Yet if anyone obeys not our word by means of this letter, him mark so as not to associate with him in order that he may be ashamed.

In Christian countries where Freemasons use the Bible in the meetings of their lodge they read this section from Second Thessalonians but omit the phrase "in the Lord Jesus Christ" and the one found in v. 6, "in the name of the Lord Jesus Christ," just as the Odd Fellows use the parable of the Good Samaritan in their ritual but fail to state that it is a parable spoken by Jesus. So the Sanhedrin avoided, wherever possible, to take the name "Jesus" on their lips.

"Such we command and admonish" is addressed to the Thessalonian congregation and thus only indirectly to the disorderly members. As was the case in v. 6, this command stands in connection with the Lord; "in the name" is not repeated for the sake of brevity. For the fourth time we have "we command" (v. 4, 6, 10). When "we exhort" is now added, this does not intend to soften or to tone down "we command." The verbs are coordinate; the second is not reduced to a modifier by being added in the form of a participle. This implies that the command is in the full sense of the term a command, and that what is commanded is at the same time made an admonition. If the command were intended only as an admonition, we should have only the second verb. Ἐν is to be taken in the same sense as it was in v. 6 and does not mean "on the authority of." Ἵνα, etc., is an object clause.

"That working (at their regular occupation) with quietness (the quietness mentioned in I Thess. 4:11) they eat their own bread" sums it all up briefly but precisely. These members are to work; they are to stop running around, agitating, and spreading their false ideas; they are to earn their living by working "with quietness"; they are to eat their own bread

(note v. 11) and not to inflict themselves on others.
This has always been the Christian ideal and desire;
hence we pray for the government "that we may lead a
tranquil and quiet life in all godliness and gravity."
Compare I Tim. 2:2, 3.

The main point is not work in place of idleness, or
eating one's own earned bread instead of unearned
bread; for the emphasis rests on the phrase μετὰ ἡσυχίας.
This phrase is placed forward for the sake of emphasis
just as in I Thess. 4:11 ἡσυχάζειν is placed forward for
the same reason. The old, the weak, and sick cannot work and earn something but they, too, can keep
tranquil and quiet. Unbalanced notions about the day
of the Lord started the stopping of work and the busybody's running around to spread false notions. This
bad fountain is rightly to be dried up. Hence 2:3-12
precedes; it is to effect the proper quietness when also
sensible working will follow. Such activity will keep
the mind away from fanatic notions, will also furnish
one's own bread for his eating. The importance of the
μετά phrase must be noted otherwise we shall think
that only pauperism is to be avoided.

13) Some commentators understand this verse to
mean: "Yet do not grow weary in exercising charity"
where charity is in place, where members are in need
without fault on their part. But καλοποιοῦντες does not
mean "extending charity." It means what I Thess.
4:11 states after the injunction to be quiet; the καλόν or
"excellent thing" the Thessalonians are to do is "to
attend to their business" (if they are merchants), "to
work with their hands" (if they are craftsmen or
laborers). Nothing is to unsettle them when they are
doing this "excellent thing." Compare II Cor. 13:7;
Gal. 6:9; Rom. 7:21, on the meaning of this word.
Some confuse καλόν and ἀγαθόν, but the former means
what is excellent and is accounted so by those who see
it. In I Thess. 4:11 the outsiders are included; they

are to see that the Christians are conducting themselves εὐσχημόνως, namely by working quietly at their business or trade. The other adjective means to do good to others, something that benefits them although even this will be charity only where the context so requires.

This aorist is ingressive: "do not get discouraged" (aorist negative commands use the subjunctive), it is a compound of κακός in the sense of inferior, thus: "do not become weary," "do not let down." See the explanations given in II Cor. 4:1, 16; Gal. 6:9. Note that "you on your part, brethren," differentiates the sober Thessalonians from the few flighty ones. It is correct to say that in v. 6 "brother" is used also with reference to the latter. But who does not feel the difference between that faint "brother" and the strong, hearty "brethren" of the present verse, which is used in contrast to the disorderly and is intended to be so used? Undisturbed they are to go on in their excellent way, undiscouraged by what others may do. This is not a broad, general, and thus disconnected admonition as those regard it who find only a reference to the practice of charity. It is entirely to the point since only brethren who are undiscouraged in doing what is excellent can, by keeping so, do the proper thing in correcting the flighty ones and again bringing them to earth.

14) This is their task for which they are now offered more specific direction. In v. 6 "withdraw" summed it up. We see what this means: "In case anyone does not obey our word by this letter (namely the order of v. 12), note this man so as not to associate with him in order that he may be ashamed" and may mend his ways. The condition of reality contemplates an actual case. As was the case in v. 6, the singular indicates that probably there will be few such cases.

Christian obedience is referred to as also all that is commanded is to be done in connection with the Lord.

"Our word through the (this) letter" expresses one thought and refers to v. 12. We cannot construe: "through the letter this one signify," i. e., signify or report to us in Corinth. This construction places a wrong emphasis on the phrase, calls for the active imperative, and goes counter to the principle that discipline belongs to the congregation. "Him note" has the middle voice: "note for yourselves." The reason is at once added. This does not imply that the congregation had a blackboard on which it wrote the names of its black sheep. What is to be done is to be done by united action on the part of the congregation; not some but all are to do the disciplining, for only in this way will it have its maximum wholesome effect.

The negative infinitive expresses contemplated result: "so as not to associate with him," it is really passive, "not to be associated." As v. 15 shows, this does not mean breaking off all intercourse with him but it does mean breaking off all association with him in the congregational church life, a serious questioning as to whether such a man is still a brother. R. 1047, 1170 make this an imperative infinitive although in 944 Robertson admits that purpose is possible. A variant reading has the imperative. But it would be strange to place together a regular imperative and an imperative infinitive; nor is purpose the best construction, it is plain result. This is the more the case since ἵνα introduces the purpose: "in order that he may be ashamed," a second aorist passive subjunctive, ingressive: "may get to be put to shame" by this action on the part of the congregation, ashamed of his folly. The purpose of church discipline is always to bring the sinner to this repentant shame and thus to win him back. Some point out the fact that Paul says nothing about expulsion. But this withdrawal of the congregation (v. 6), this refusal of association leaves only one door open for a return, namely repentant shame; the sinner who refuses to make use of this door is certainly to be permanently expelled.

15) **And do not consider him an enemy but remonstrate with him as a brother.** Καί adds something and is not adversative. Paul is not returning to mildness after he has been rather severe. Paul keeps his balance. Such a disorderly person certainly harms the congregation; he does so by his busybody efforts to affect other members with his folly and in the eyes of those without (I Thess. 4:12). That fact might lead at least some of the members to regard him as an enemy since even most outsiders do less harm. But such conduct would at once close the door against the disorderly sinner. That door is to remain open as long as repentant shame may yet be brought about. So the members are to remonstrate with the disorderly one as they would with a brother. See Gal. 6:1.

The word Paul uses is not "consider" or "treat him as a brother." The Thessalonians are to consider him ἄτακτος, as nothing less than disorderly; as to treatment, they are to withdraw, to refuse fraternal association until shame results. But they are not to turn their back upon him and at once to abandon him as being hopeless. Their part is to be remonstrance, see this word as it is explained in I Thess. 5:12 and used regarding the disorderly in I Thess. 5:14. His sin and folly are to be held up to him in a brotherly way and with brotherly intent. To call this a difficult proceeding is not warranted; it is the one Christian and even natural thing to do. What if this remonstrance proves in vain? The answer to that question need not be explicitly stated, it can readily be supplied: the sinner drops out of the congregation.

The Conclusion

16)   A prayerful wish closes the first section of the first letter (3:11-13) and also its second section and the entire letter (5:23) ; a similar wish closes the main section of this letter (2:16, 17) and now its final section and the letter itself (the present verse) ; all these sections have optatives. **Now may he, the Lord of peace, give you this peace at all times and in all ways! The Lord with you all!**

Αὐτός is to be understood as it was in I Thess. 3:11; 5:25, and in II Thess. 2:16. "He, the Lord of the peace," is like I Thess. 5:23; "the God of the peace," the article with "peace" is used for the same reason. Εἰρήνη is "peace" in the objective sense as it is used in the epistolary greetings. Hence it is bestowed as a gift by Christ and recalls John 14:27. It is the condition that obtains when all is well between God (Christ) and us. From this flows the subjective feeling of peace in our hearts which, though it sinks at times, always arises anew out of the objective condition since this remains unchanged.

The repetition of the noun "peace" gives it an emphasis, the article with the second noun is the article of previous mention or = "his." Διαπαντός may be written as one word or as two; it = "always" (Rom. 11:10; Acts 2:25). The next phrase with παντί = "in every way"; the two are a neat rhetorical combination. The Lord's peace is where the Lord himself is. Thus the brief wish: "The Lord (be) with you all!" completes what we may call the prayer. Note πάντων: all time — all way —all you. Μετά = in your company.

The thought that peace is the closing wish has been connected with the foregoing directions about discipline, "peace" being contrasted with "enemy" occurring in v. 15. But the keyword of the foregoing is not strife but "disorderly"; this closing wish also does not close only chapter 3 but the entire letter. So we should not stress the idea of peace among the members. While the Lord's Parousia is delayed, although the apostasy and the Antichrist come, the Lord's peace keeps us, and, having it, we shall live as we should, and our remonstrance will correct any who act disorderly. This is the force of the closing wish.

17) **The salutation with my own hand, Paul's, which is a sign in every letter; so I am writing.** Paul, Silvanus, and Timothy are sending this letter, and all three might have signed it. Even then it would be Paul who did the dictating, his would be the signature that is vital for this reason as well as because of his position as an apostle. But this letter is really Paul's, and so, after he has finished the dictation, he takes the pen and himself writes the last few words. "The salutation with my own hand, Paul's" is identical with Col. 4:18 and I Cor. 16:21. The genitive belongs where it is; our versions transpose it. There is no ground for believing that Timothy is the writer, and that by his signature Paul merely adopts what Timothy has written.

The exceptional feature is the addition: "which is a sign in every letter; thus I am writing." This is added because of 2:2, some supposed letter from Paul. Thus this letter is especially indicated as being genuine by this special addition. In I Thess. 5:27 Paul found it necessary to make certain that that letter should be read to all the brethren; here he finds it necessary to attest the genuineness of this letter. He does not merely sign: "Paul," but writes all of v. 17, 18 as "a sign," which also includes his name.

18) **The grace of our Lord Jesus Christ with all of you.** The final wish is like that found in I Thess. 5:28, save that Paul adds "all."

Soli Deo Gloria

St. Paul's First and Second Epistles
To Timothy and that to Titus

TO ALL

THE PRESIDENTS AND THE DISTRICT PRESIDENTS

IN THE

AMERICAN LUTHERAN CHURCH BODIES

INTRODUCTION

The so-called Pastoral Letters were written *after* Paul's first imprisonment in Rome. It is unnecessary, as far as our purpose of interpreting these letters is concerned, to review the strong evidence for this acknowledged fact.

To date the death of Paul at the close of his two years of imprisonment in Rome, Acts 28:30, implies casting doubt on the genuineness of these three letters. If their genuineness is admitted, it is a hopeless task to find a place for them somewhere in the life of Paul as this is depicted in Acts. Only a few would today attempt this task. They would also be obliged to ignore the volume of ancient tradition which establishes the fact that Paul carried out his long-cherished plan of doing work in Spain (Rom. 15:28).

Paul was acquitted and freed from his first imprisonment in Rome in the spring of the year 63; some think that this occurred during the summer of that year. It is well to remember that Paul was a prisoner of state, a Roman citizen who had appealed his case to the emperor, and that he was detained in Rome only until such a time that the imperial court could act on his appeal. No actual charge was filed against him; in fact, this circumstance made his case irregular as Acts 25:26, 27; 26:31, 32 indicate. Festus did not know what to write to the emperor, and Paul's defense before Agrippa resulted in the admission of his innocence, which left only Paul's own appeal to Caesar as the reason for sending him to Caesar's court. Paul's second arrest was an entirely different matter.

The burning of Rome (July 19-24, 64) which was followed by new fires several days later after a time was charged against the Christians, many of whom

(473)

were killed in consequence. At first Nero tried every other means to avert from himself the suspicion of having fired the city, and not until these attempts failed did he charge the Christians with this crime, thus, as Zahn thinks, "not before October, 64." This frightful persecution brought about the martyrdom of Peter who was crucified in the fall of 64.

Paul was at this time in far-off Spain and so was not involved. But the whole situation was now changed. Christianity had become a *religio illicita,* and especially its propagation became a crime against the state. Not long after Paul's return from Spain he was arrested. Now he would be charged with a crime; Paul was, therefore, thrown into a dungeon as a felon. After some delay he was tried and executed. Tradition asserts that he perished under Nero who died June 9, 68. The details of his martyrdom are not known. He must have been condemned to death for spreading a *religio illicita.*

* * *

The problem that confronts the student is the task of arranging the data mentioned in these three letters within the interval between Paul's release in the spring of 63 and his execution late in 65 or early in 66. We shall also have to note Phil. 1:24; Philemon 22; and Acts 20:25. These three letters resemble many old letters in which places and journeys are mentioned: the persons addressed fully understand while those who read them in afteryears have difficulty in piecing the items together, are often able only to guess, and sometimes are unable to do even that. One thing lies almost on the surface: no forger would be able to insert into his forgeries data such as the ones contained in these three letters, at least no known forger or romancer has ever done so. This is one of the hurdles

which those critics must clear who deny that Paul
wrote these letters.

The value of these letters to the church does not
depend on the solution of the problem here indicated.
The value lies in the substance — naturally so. Yet
all inspired documents are so precious that earnest
students are always willing to spend much time and
much effort in ironing out every little historical wrinkle
they may find. In the present instance we are not surprised to find divergent views among the best students. There is no way in which any man now living
can determine with full certainty how to fit together
all the data concerned and do this in such a way as
fully to satisfy himself. We are really dealing with no
more than probabilities, in part with even less.

We have the accepted tradition that Paul did go to
Spain as he had planned as early as when he wrote
Rom. 15:28.

We next have the fact that First Timothy and Titus
were written first with at most but a brief interval
between their composition, while Second Timothy was
written soon after Paul's arrest. We cannot determine the exact extent of the interval occurring between this last letter and the other two. The letters
of Paul that have been preserved in our New Testament are not arranged in chronological order but
according to length so that Philemon comes last (not
after Colossians) and Second Timothy before Titus
and not after.

The three letters state nothing about Paul's work
in Spain although the fact that he labored there is
assured by tradition; this is in harmony with Rom.
15:28.

Four items referred to in First Timothy and Titus
should be properly arranged:

1) While he was proceeding on his way into Macedonia Paul urged Timothy to remain in Ephesus and

do the work with which this letter to him also deals; Paul intends to return to Timothy in Ephesus (I Tim. 1:3; 4:13).

2) Paul delivered Hymenæus and Alexander over to Satan and thus seems to have remained in Ephesus for some time (I Tim. 1:20) after he and Timothy returned there.

3) Paul visited Crete where he left Titus to do a work similar to that for which he left Timothy in Asia and thus urges and instructs Titus just as he does Timothy (Tit. 1:5).

4) Paul intends to spend the winter at Nicopolis in Epirus (Tit. 3:12).

These four items belong together. Did Paul go to Spain soon after his release from confinement before the first two of these letters were written, before these four items occurred? Zahn thinks so. We do not agree with him.

In the first place, confidently expecting his release, Paul promises the Philippians that as soon as he sees how he will fare at his trial he will dispatch Timothy to them and even states why he selects Timothy; he also trusts that he himself will shortly be able to go to Philippi. Paul was acquitted and released and we have no doubt that he promptly sent Timothy to Philippi as he had promised. One reason for sending Timothy was that through him Paul might learn of the state of the Philippians. Did Paul wait in Rome until Timothy returned and then go on to Spain? We do not think so. When Phil. 2:19-24 was written, Paul and Timothy planned that upon Paul's release Timothy should hurry to Philippi with this news while Paul went from Rome to Ephesus and Colosse. Timothy was to join him at Ephesus and deliver a report about the state of the Philippians. The probabilities lie in this direction.

Secondly, some time prior to the composition of Philippians Paul wrote Colossians and Philemon. Already at that time the prospect for his release was brightening. Thus he invites himself to the home of Philemon in advance (Philemon 22). Was also this visit postponed until after the journey to Spain? We do not think so. From Rome, Paul went to Ephesus, then the short distance to Colosse where he visited Philemon and the congregation and returned to Ephesus where Timothy, coming from Philippi, met him. In Ephesus, Paul attended to all important matters that needed attention. Timothy was to remain in Ephesus and after Paul's departure was to have the general supervision of the churches in this province (I Tim. 1:3). Immediately on his arrival and before Timothy came Paul most likely attended to the expulsion of Hymenæus and Alexander (I Tim. 1:20). After Timothy arrived, Paul proceeds on to Macedonia to visit the Philippians as indicated in Phil. 1:24.

Does Acts 20:25 present a flaw in this sequence, namely the fact that Paul never expected to see the Ephesians again? If Acts 20:25 were a prophecy that was uttered by revelation, it would be a fatal flaw to *any* sketch of events that include a return of Paul to Ephesus. But Acts 20:25 is not a prophecy, it is only a statement of what Paul thought at the time, a sad conclusion *he himself* drew from the Spirit's warnings, that imprisonment awaited him in Jerusalem. Imprisonment came as the Spirit said, but Paul returned to Ephesus, for the Spirit never said that he would not return.

Thirdly, if Paul went to Spain immediately after his release from prison in Rome, First Timothy and Titus were written after the return from Spain. Then, however, the four items we noted in First Timothy and Titus must be combined with the items found in Second Timothy in some consequence. No combination that is plausible has been made; we are free to say, none can be made, see these items in the consideration of Second Timothy below.

But what about Crete and about Paul's leaving Titus on this island (Tit. 1:5)? When Paul went from Rome to Ephesus and then to Macedonia (thus redeeming the promises made in Philemon 22 and in Phil. 2:24) he stopped at Crete on the way from Rome to Ephesus or went from Ephesus to Macedonia by the way of Crete. The former is the more probable. Titus, it would seem, had worked in Crete before Paul arrived there, had founded congregations there, and in the letter to him Paul does just what he does also in First Timothy: he repeats to Titus how he is to organize the congregations thus gathered.

At the same time Paul summons Titus to meet him in Nicopolis where Paul intends to spend the winter (Tit. 3:12). We thus get this sequence from First Timothy and Titus: from Rome — via Crete — to Ephesus, to Colosse, and back to Ephesus — to Macedonia — to Nicopolis. This covers about one year, from the release in 63 to the end of the next winter early in 64. The fact that Paul visited also other congregations along the indicated route we need scarcely state. The character of the letters shows why no more places are named in them.

First Timothy and Titus were thus written in the year 63 after Paul had left for Macedonia and before he went to Nicopolis, probably in Macedonia or in Greece (Corinth?).

*   *   *

Our opinion is that Paul went to Spain in the spring of 64. What route he took from Nicopolis, perhaps through Dalmatia and Gaul (see II Tim. 4:10), who can say? Judging from the ancient tradition, he returned after more than a year; we have no details whatever.

This leaves the items mentioned in Second Timothy in a group by themselves; and they should probably be placed subsequent to the work done in Spain.

1) Leaving Trophimus sick at Miletus (II Tim. 4:20).

2) Leaving the cloak and the parchments at Troas (II Tim. 4:13).

3) The reference to Corinth (II Tim. 4:20).

4) To which add the fact that Paul writes this last letter of his when he is a prisoner in Rome a second time with death in prospect.

Miletus — Troas — Corinth — Rome form a natural line of travel. Ending as this does with the fatal imprisonment, it belongs after the work done in Spain. Where Paul stopped first on leaving Spain no one knows, nor at what place he stopped last before reaching Miletus. Since Miletus was the harbor town of Ephesus, we conclude that Paul reached it by sea, and since he left Trophimus there when he went on, we take it that Paul again took ship in order to go on to Troas. The rest is conjecture. We think that he again visited Ephesus, for why would he land at Miletus and again leave from this port? Did he visit any other cities in the neighborhood such as Laodicea and Colosse? We do not know.

We do not know how he came to leave some of his belongings at Troas. He did; that is all we know. In II Tim. 4:13 he asks Timothy to bring them along and in 4:21 to come before winter. It is unwarranted to assume that Paul's cloak, etc., had been left in Troas during the entire time since he had visited Macedonia (I Tim. 1:3); they were left in Troas when Paul came up from Miletus (II Tim. 4:20) and then passed on to Corinth and Rome; no other supposition seems tenable.

Now as to the probable dates. If Paul went from Nicopolis to Spain in the spring of 64, how long did he remain in Spain? It is assumed that he did not remain there a long time and that he left in the fall. If this is true, then it would seem that he reached Miletus, Troas, Corinth, and Rome before the winter of 64 set in, and that he was executed during that winter, late in 64 or early in 65. Peter was executed in 64. The tradition that Peter and Paul were executed at the same time is due to a late error as Zahn has shown rather conclusively.

We submit that Paul's long-cherished desire to work in Spain (Rom. 15:24) could scarcely be served by a summer's work in this large territory, which also required so long a journey to reach it and a still longer journey to return to Miletus, Troas, and then Rome before winter. Compare the previous year (63), all of it was consumed by visiting Crete, Asia Minor, etc., and spending the winter at Nicopolis. We submit that Paul remained in Spain from the time he reached it in 64 until some time in 65, that he then returned to the places named in Second Timothy. He was arrested in Rome in 65 and wrote to Timothy to come before winter; his execution followed before the year was over, or when 66 began. We confess that we cannot find a probability for the supposition that he returned from Spain in 64 and then spent over a year in the Orient (Zahn would extend this another year).

One question remains. Where was Timothy when Second Timothy was written? The place is not named (as it is in I Tim. 1:3), but the contents of the letter point to Ephesus. Our assumption is according.

*　　　*　　　*

Do these three letters show that Paul is aging? Do they lack the virility of the other letters or the perfection of Philemon in particular? Are they less well arranged? To give an affirmative answer to these questions is in our judgment going too far. The purpose and the subjects treated are different; the mastery with which they are handled is the same as we find in the other letters. Paul's mental powers are undiminished. His last letter (Second Timothy) has been well called his "swan song."

The term "Pastoral Epistles" dates from the year 1753 and has become current; yet it is not exact, for it leaves the impression that Paul is coaching Timothy and Titus as "pastors" of a congregation. This is not the case. Timothy and Titus were not "pastors," either in the present sense of the word (one pastor to a congregation) or in the older sense of elders (each congregation having a number of them). Nor were Timothy and Titus "head pastors," each being a chief of the group of elders in the congregation as James was among the elders in the church at Jerusalem. They were also not bishops with episcopal jurisdiction over a diocese, this was a far later office. Timothy and Titus were representatives of Paul for the guidance of the churches, the one being Paul's agent in Asia Minor, the other Paul's agent in Crete. Through them Paul exercised his apostolic care and oversight; his directions are according: to do what Paul would do if he were present and could do the work himself.

The idea that these letters reflect a far later time, namely the second century when a later type of church organization and government were current, cannot be maintained. The church in Jerusalem already had deacons and already had a widow problem (Acts 6:1, etc.). The congregation at Cenchreæ near Corinth had a deaconess (Rom. 16:1). These three letters cannot be regarded as second-century forgeries on the basis of the type of church organization which they reflect.

Second Timothy differs from the other two epistles. These deal with the work that was to be done at that particular time in Ephesus by Timothy and in Crete by Titus. Moreover, Titus will soon have completed this work in Crete and is to join Paul at Nicopolis and in the spring is to go with him from Nicopolis, as we may conclude, to Spain. Second Timothy is not a sort of continuation or amplification of First Timothy. It has been well called Paul's "last will and testament to Timothy." Written in the certain expectation of death when Paul will have no further personal representatives to place over groups of his churches, this letter treats of Timothy's ministry and work in general and points out to him that he is to carry it on in the spirit of his spiritual father, whose son as well as whose assistant he had been for so long a time.

This last letter is full of restrained emotion and is the nobler because of the restraint. This should be felt by the present readers, otherwise the letter will not be properly appreciated. We have so much cold and matter-of-fact comment on the New Testament on passages where deep emotion throbs. The longing expressed in II Tim. 4:21 is that of a dying father for his son, compare Phil. 2:20-23. Almost the whole of chapter 4 throbs with most powerful feeling. Did Timothy read it without a sob in his throat? When he wrote, Paul was not sure that Timothy would be able to arrive before the end came to Paul. Remember that if he did arrive in time he saw the execution of his beloved master with his own eyes.

* * *

Although they were addressed to Timothy and Titus, these letters were of utmost value also to the churches, both because they came from the apostle's own hand and because they dealt with the work to be done for them at that time and in later years. No wonder they were placed into the canon without question.

That place was never questioned until the last century. These recurrent attacks upon the genuineness of these letters, whether of one or of all three, whether leaving some residuum from lost letters of Paul or not are unwarranted and have been of no service to the church which has these letters in her canon. Forgery is posited because First Timothy and Titus are said to present a development of church organization and a view of the ecclesiastical office which are far beyond those of Paul's time and of the New Testament generally; secondly, because all three letters are said to combat later errors, namely Gnosticism. The forger's motive, we are told, is to secure the authority of the great apostle for the later episcopal form of church government and against the late type of errors. It is tacitly taken for granted that the church was easily deceived and universally accepted these forgeries as genuine letters of Paul.

The fact that these claims are indefensible has been proved at length so often that we need not again go over this ground. Those interested may consult Zahn, *Introduction* II, 85, etc., the extensive chapter on the genuineness, in fact, the whole of II, 1-133. Add the fact that Timothy and also Titus lived for many years after Paul wrote these letters to them and thus for years attested their genuineness with the result that they were placed into the canon.

The linguistic character of the letters has been emphasized in order to prove their later origin. These linguistics have aptly been called "the last refuge of so-called criticism." No forger would write greetings like those that are found in these letters; he would copy those of Paul's other letters. Let this serve as a sample. Word lists have been compiled to show the number of words and expressions that are not found in other letters of Paul. But this can be and has been done by comparing also the other Pauline letters with each other; and every letter has peculiar words, etc., of its own.

The contents of each letter call for the words that it contains. Now the contents of these three letters are quite distinctive. Even Second Timothy differs from First Timothy and Titus and thus has words and turns of phrase of its own. One claim only may be supported by the appeal to their linguistic character, namely the fact that these three letters were, indeed, written late in Paul's life and with no long intervals between their composition.

It is worth noting that the Vaticanus is incomplete and breaks off in the middle of a word in Heb. 9:14; it does not contain these three letters nor Philemon nor the Apocalypse. Some of the other uncials are fragmentary as regards these three letters. Wohlenberg, *Pastoralbriefe* 75, etc., presents the textual data in detail together with a paragraph on textual values.

St. Paul's First Epistle
To Timothy

CHAPTER I

THE GREETING

1) Each of the three stereotyped members of the greeting: "Paul (nominative) — to Timothy (dative) — grace, etc. (nominatives)," is amplified, and these amplifications reflect and harmonize with the contents of the letter just as is done in other letters of Paul. **Paul, apostle of Christ Jesus by order of God, our Savior, and of Christ Jesus, our hope, to Timothy, genuine child in faith: grace, mercy, peace, from God the Father and Christ Jesus, our Lord!**

In II Cor. 8:23, Titus and two other brethren are called "apostles of churches," representatives of the Macedonian churches; in Phil. 2:25, Epaphras is called the apostle of the Philippians, their representative. In Acts 14:4, 14, Paul and Barnabas are termed "apostles" in a higher yet in a broad sense: men sent on the gospel mission by the Holy Spirit. Here, however, "apostle of Christ Jesus," etc., is to be understood in the eminent sense and is to be confined to the Twelve plus Paul. These were called to go on their mission by Christ Jesus himself, and no others were ever called and sent out in the same way. Derived from ἀποστέλλω, the term means one sent on a mission. The genitive indicates who commissioned Paul. The more important question is why, in writing this letter to Timothy, Paul adds this important apposition. Certainly not as he did in Galatians in order to emphasize his authority; Timothy never forgets that. It is because of the contents of this letter. Timothy is to act for Paul in Ephesus; this letter contains the necessary instructions.

Timothy had long been Paul's assistant and knew what Paul wanted him to do. At various times Paul had sent him on important missions. Before leaving him at Ephesus, Paul had, no doubt, also given Timothy his instructions. Yet Timothy's task was by no means a light one. It was a great advantage for him to have full instructions in writing, not only for his own sake, but also when he was challenged by others. Here are the apostle's own words, set down by the apostle himself. They are both a written authorization that grant Timothy the right to act for Paul in this apostolic work and written directions about which no person could quibble.

For that reason this apposition is so extensive. "Apostle of Christ Jesus" is not enough; Paul adds: "by order of God, our Savior, and of Christ Jesus, our hope." Note this κατά phrase in Rom. 16:26; I Cor. 7:6; II Cor. 8:8. Here it expands what is already contained in the genitive "of Christ Jesus," namely that Paul's commission rests on a specific ἐπιταγή or "order" given by God and by Christ. Instead of using this phrase, Paul generally writes διὰ θελήματος Θεοῦ, "through God's will" (what God willed). "By order of God" is more specific and fits the two genitives "order of God and Christ Jesus" as pointing to the appointment by which Jesus made him an apostle, Acts 26:16-18.

The naming of the two persons who ordered Paul's apostleship is by no means mere repetition. Note that in this greeting Paul and Timothy are named once, God twice, and Christ Jesus no less than thrice. This is not redundancy. In the work of Paul and of Timothy and in their own spiritual blessing everything comes to them through Christ Jesus whom God the Father sent. The repetition of these divine names is a confession that glories in all that these persons have done and still do. In "Christ Jesus" we have office and person combined much as in General Washington, President Lincoln, etc. The difference between this and "Jesus Christ" is slight.

The significance of the naming of these two persons in this order is brought out fully by the genitive appositions, both of which are enriched by the appropriative "our": God is "our Savior" — Christ Jesus is "our hope." The one is the fountain of our salvation; the other the embodiment of our hope. The idea of Σωτήρ is that of rescue from mortal danger, which places the rescued into complete safety. All of God's saving work is included in this title "Savior." Hence we do not refer it only to the past while "our hope" is contrasted with it as referring to the future. Still less can we say that God saved us "potentially," and that "our hope" (Christ) realizes this potentiality. The expression "our Savior" is a noun and thus has no tense which might refer to the past. We therefore do not say that the aorists used in II Tim. 1:9 and Tit. 3:5 have this effect on the noun. The verb itself does not only include the momentary act of rescue but in addition to that the effect of placing the rescued ones into permanent safety, which refers to the present and to the future.

Paul uses "Savior" with reference to God only here and in I Tim. 2:3; Tit. 1:3; 2:10; 3:4; with reference to Christ he uses it in II Tim. 1:10; Tit. 1:4; 2:13; Phil. 3:20; Eph. 5:23. This is regarded as a point in support of the claim that Paul did not write these letters. This claim advances an untenable criterion of authorship, namely that if at any period of your life you use a certain word oftener and with a wider range than you did at other periods, you cannot be the writer of what you have thus written, irrespective of the special reason you may have for thus using the word when you need the idea which it expresses.

We note that it is equally exceptional when **Paul** calls Christ Jesus "our hope" and uses an abstract term to designate a person.   Yet in Eph. 2:14 he similarly calls him "our peace." "Our hope" is plainly objective and highly concentrated. It is saying too little to claim that our subjective hope rests on Christ for its fulfillment, too little also to think only of the future. Christ is the actual embodiment of our hope, i. e., Christ as he is with all that he has done to be exalted as "Prince and Savior" (Acts 5:31).   So certainly is he "our hope" that he is this whether we actually hope in him or not although we most certainly do hope in him.

"Our Savior" and "our hope" are evidently companion terms, the "our" is used with each to indicate appropriation and confession of God as our Savior and of Christ as our hope. Yet "Savior" is a word that expressed an action so that "our" has the touch of an objective genitive: we are the ones God is saving, we are the σωζόμενοι (passive), the ones being saved by him; while "hope" is a term that indicates an object so that "our" has the flavor of a subjective genitive: we appropriate Christ as our hope. In this way the terms are combined and form a unit.

By their order the two persons thus designated made Paul the apostle who was to bring this salvation and this hope to men. Timothy is to regard what follows in the light of this fact, a fact that he has well known for many a year. For all that this letter will say about the errorists and about Timothy's opposing them means that as Paul's representative he is to stand as a rock against those who would rob the churches of this blessed "salvation" and of this "hope"; and all that this letter contains about Timothy's arranging the worship and the organization of the churches and about the conduct of his further work in these churches aims at this one thing, to preserve and to extend the fullest appropriation of this our God as our Savior and of Christ as our hope. The light of these focal terms illumines the whole letter. Unless this is appreciated, much will be lost as we read the epistle.

The pagan world of this time called Zeus the Σωτήρ or "Savior" and applied this title to other gods and to deified emperors and even called the latter "god and savior." This extension of the expression to great men came after the time of Alexander the Great. This pagan usage of the title "Savior" has led some to conclude that Paul's use of the term and also John's is derived from paganism. To justify this view the Christian sense of this word has been reduced so as to mean *Nothelfer*, "deliverer" in general. We are next referred to the derivation from the Greek mystery cults, but these cults flowered in the second century.

This pagan use of the title "Savior" is found on the low level of political and economic life and never rises to the spiritual and the eternal. The Christian use is derived from the Old Testament riches which are augmented by the New Testament light. C.-K. 1035 adds that the Christians probably used the title "Savior" the more emphatically because the paganism around them made its gods and emperors "saviors." That is about all one can say. Nor may we say that Paul here and elsewhere uses "Savior," "to save," etc., (whether with reference to God or with reference to Christ) just because he has this pagan contrast in mind. When he wrote and when Timothy read "God our Savior," both thought of the Old and the New Testament revelation which God had made of himself as Savior and probably not at all of a refutation of heathen saviorhood and a rejection of pagan "saviors."

2) When Timothy is addressed as "genuine child in faith," the word "child" carries with it the idea of tenderness and endearment. "Son" would touch upon Timothy's standing. Paul wants the former idea. Yet observe that neither here nor in II Tim. 1:1, Paul

writes *"my* child." We may believe that Paul converted Timothy and was thus the spiritual father of
this his child, but that is not the point here. On this
account passages such as Philemon 10; I Cor. 4:15;
Gal. 4:19 are not pertinent; they would, to say the least,
require: *"my* genuine child." By the very word "faith"
"genuine child in faith" relates Timothy to God and
to Christ Jesus even as "Savior — hope — faith" are
closely related terms. Timothy is here designated as a
"real" child of God, γνήσιος, and thus not a νόθος, a bas-
tard, misbegotten. The phrase does not depend on the
adjective: "a child genuine in faith," but on the noun
which needs this phrase as a complement to bring out
the fact that spiritual childhood is referred to: ἐν πίστει,
"in the sphere of faith."

We thus do not agree with the thought that Paul
is addressing Timothy as one of his numerous converts
as he addresses his converts in Gal. 4:19; I Cor. 4:15;
Philemon 10. This is not a letter to a mere convert. It
is not its burden to tell a convert how to live and to
act as a convert. It tells Timothy how to proceed as
the apostle's representative who has his headquarters
in Ephesus. We correlate "apostle of Christ Jesus by
order of God," etc., with "genuine child in faith." Instead of giving Timothy a title of office, one that might
name his office as being beneath that of Paul, Timothy
receives a more pertinent designation. This apostle,
appointed by God and by Christ, is using this "genuine
child" of God as his assistant for work connected with
their "Savior" and their "hope" and with his own
"faith." All that this letter asks of Timothy appeals
to him in this work to show himself "a genuine child
(of God) in faith." The perfection of this designation
is thus apparent.

With reference to himself Paul cannot say that he
is a "genuine child"; this designation would not be
enough, he must refer to God's "order" which made

Paul an apostle and established his office, in which Timothy is this apostle's representative. But while he is acting as such a representative, the coaching which Paul gives him in this letter is not that which a superior might give to a subaltern who is to please his chief, but that which befits Timothy as being God's child in faith, whose one object in the position the apostle has assigned him is to please his divine Father. As a willing and an obedient child in faith Timothy will want to do his Father's will. What that will is in regard to the Asian work Paul desires to place into Timothy's hand in writing. It is the will of God, their Savior, the will of Christ, their hope, which Timothy will carry out as "a genuine child in faith."

We regard "grace, mercy, peace," etc., as exclamatory, as thus needing no verb. Regarding "grace" and "peace" see the other letters of Paul, which contain only these two. Also consult these same letters regarding the added phrase in which "our" may be placed either after "Father" or, as here, after both names. "Our" is to be construed with both divine names: "from God (our) Father and Christ Jesus, our Lord."

The exceptional feature here and in II Tim. 1:2 is the insertion of "mercy." While "grace" is the undeserved favor of God, which is extended to the guilty and relieves him of guilt and of the punishment he deserves, "mercy" is the commiseration for the miserable and distressed, which frees him from his wretchedness. Grace is multiplied for God's children in a constant shower of undeserved gifts (John 1:16: "grace for grace"), and so mercy continues in ever-new deliverance out of trouble. "Peace" is the fruit of both, the blessed condition when all is well between me and God.

Right here the idea that this letter is forged breaks down. All the letters that Paul had written up to this time use only "grace and peace"; a forger would have copied this greeting, would not have even thought of risking the innovation: "grace, mercy, peace" — the effective asyndeton is also exceptional.

We are compelled to ask why Paul adds "mercy" in these two letters. To be sure, he might have used the triple form in all his letters or only the double form in these two, see the variety in James, Jude, and the three letters of John. Homiletical and devout remarks on grace, mercy, and peace are not an answer to this question. Oosterzee says: grace for the guilty — mercy for the suffering — peace for the fighting disciples. This is an undue limitation of "peace." Grace and mercy are related to God while peace would pertain only to men with whom we fight. All pertain to God.

We object to the assertion that it is *Spielerei* to "press" this greeting as though it applies to Timothy's special circumstances; we likewise object to interpreting this greeting as though Paul addresses it to all preachers everywhere and at all times. Whatever we may draw from it for ourselves, it was certainly written to Timothy personally; and all that Paul's letters contain, even down to the details and the implications, always fits the circumstances of the person or the persons addressed.

As this letter shows, Timothy's position in the Asian field was a trying one. He needed all the gifts of God's grace, apart even from all special worries and griefs and also God's peace in which to assure and to rest his soul; but in addition to these two, for all discouraging situations and painful experiences, God's mercy to sustain him. Even ordinary pastors need God's healing, comforting mercy, often in large measure. This word is not added inadvertently or for rhetorical fulness. It belongs where it is — for Timothy in his trying work.

Let us also say once more that Timothy was not a mere pastor in Ephesus. This church had its proper pastor-elders, among whom Timothy was not just another. He was Paul's representative for all the churches in this region with work according, directing, organizing, supervising, helping to eject errorists, etc., as Paul himself would do if he were on the ground. The work of Titus in Crete was of the same order.

How Timothy Is to Deal with Those Teaching Different Doctrine

3) The main sections of this letter stand out clearly in the chapter division of our versions. The different matters which Timothy is to look after are taken up in order, and the order is simple and apparent. The first deals with the disturbers of the faith; they must be stopped. This properly comes first.

As I urged thee to remain on in Ephesus when proceeding to Macedonia, so I still do, that thou charge certain ones not to teach differently, nor to devote their attention to endless myths and genealogies such as (and because they are such as) **furnish questionings rather than an administration of God, one in connection with faith.**

With R. 439 we find no anacoluthon here; this is a simple ellipsis. We disagree with the statement of B.-D. 467 that the construction runs out in a *reines Wirrsal* with its ceaseless insertions and additions. This view thinks that the ellipsis comes at the end of the entire sentence where it is also supplied by our versions. It comes where we have indicated it and thus allows Paul to add whatever he pleases. As far as the Greek reader is concerned, we should remember that, unlike the English and the German reader, he at once catches the ellipsis after καθώς: "so I still do," and does not need to have it written out as we do. This is another instance of the nimbleness of the Greek mind as compared with the slowness of our minds.

The moment Paul was released in Rome he sent Timothy to Philippi as he had promised in Phil. 2:19-23. Then Paul went from Rome to Ephesus, visited Colosse as he had promised in Philemon 22, and returned to Ephesus where he met Timothy who came to Ephesus from Philippi. See the introduction. When the two met and surveyed the situation in Ephesus and in the whole field of which this city was the center, Paul did what he says: he urged Timothy to stay in Ephesus while Paul himself proceeds to Macedonia in accord with his promise made in Phil. 2:24. A lot of work needs to be done in the churches of this region, apostolic work; this letter shows what it is. Paul turns it over to Timothy as his representative while he himself proceeds to Macedonia. We see a similar situation in Tit. 1:5, where Paul leaves Titus in Crete to serve in a like capacity.

It is possible that even before his release in Rome, when he wrote to the Philippians, Paul knew about the general situation in the Asian field and made the plans we have indicated, namely to have Timothy meet him in Ephesus. When, upon his arrival in Ephesus, he saw how things stood he felt that he himself did not need to remain, that Timothy could well take care of everything in his stead. So he turned the supervision of this work over to Timothy. He had previously used Timothy on important missions, note the one mentioned in I Cor. 16:10, etc., also Paul's confidence in Timothy as indicated in Phil. 2:20, etc. Timothy had had plenty of experience.

When Paul now says that he had urged Timothy to stay in Ephesus, this does not imply that Timothy did not want to stay or was afraid of the task. Paul uses the same word with regard to Titus (παράκλησις, the noun) when he sent him on a second mission to Cor-

inth, where there was also much to be done (II Cor.
8:17, see this passage and note also v. 23: "associate
of mine"). Παρεκάλεσα may well imply that, when Paul
and Timothy discussed matters, Timothy preferred to
have Paul himself stay in order to attend to all that
was needed, the two of them working together would
thus get through more quickly. Paul urged Timothy to
remain on (προσμεῖναι) while he himself proceeds to
Macedonia and thus extends their labors. The view
that Paul should have written προπορευόμενος because he
was going forward or ahead to Macedonia misunderstands the situation by thinking that Paul had been
no farther than Ephesus. We have seen that he visited
Philemon at Colosse and after returning from there
is "proceeding," πορευόμενος, on to Macedonia.

It is a misunderstanding to think that Timothy had
been working in Ephesus for some time, that he
wanted to be released from the hard task, and that
Paul urged, admonished, or encouraged him to stay
on. Timothy had just arrived, so had Paul, and the
work was yet to be done. Furthermore, the nominative πορευόμενος does not modify the accusative σε, nor
does ἐν Ἐφέσῳ modify παρεκάλεσα, so that the meaning
would be that at some earlier time Paul urged Timothy
to make his headquarters in Ephesus while he proceeded to Macedonia for checking errorists in that territory. This is done in an effort to find room in the
period covered by Acts for what is here said. But the
language will not permit this. The time of Acts lies
in the past.

Ἵνα indicates simple purpose or the contemplated
result of Timothy's staying on in Ephesus. He is to
charge (effective aorist) certain persons "not to teach
differently nor to devote their minds or attention
(προσέχειν) to endless myths and genealogies," etc. This
is to be the first duty to which Timothy is to attend.
As Paul had urged Timothy to stay on for this task

when he was leaving, so he again does. We have no more reason to think that Timothy is loth to do this work than that he is loth to do the other things mentioned in this letter. Paul repeats in writing what he had outlined orally for Timothy in order that Timothy might have it black on white and that he might present it as written evidence to those who objected to Timothy's activities: here are the apostle's own written instructions, repeated a second time and in deliberate written form. Former oral instructions, agreements, or advices are repeated for similar purposes in written form. This satisfies this situation.

"That thou charge" is the same verb that is used in 6:13, "I charge thee." Nothing of special note can be drawn from the absence of the so-called *Nominal-elenchus,* not naming the errorists. We find this often as in II Cor. 10:2; Gal. 1:7; II Thess. 3:11. The idea is not to spare them as some think. Scorn is at times thus conveyed. We cannot even say that Paul knows who the "certain ones are." He may have heard a few names mentioned while he was in Ephesus, but this is all. These "certain ones" were not located in Ephesus, for then Paul would have dealt with them right then and there. They were scattered here and there throughout the province, which by this time had been well planted with congregations. The indefinite pronoun "certain ones" means: whoever and wherever they are. The implication is that their number is not large and also that Paul thinks of them slightingly.

Timothy is to charge them "not to teach differently nor to devote their attention to endless myths and genealogies." In the direct discourse the infinitives would be imperatives, and since the present tenses are negatived, the imperatives would mean: "Stop teaching differently and stop devoting attention to myths and genealogies!" R. 851-2. These foolish persons are to stop their teaching other people and are at the same time to cease devoting their own minds to these trivial topics.

The use of the new compound ἑτεροδιδασκαλεῖν has been considered linguistic evidence that supports the claim that Paul did not write these letters. But writers freely form any number of new compound terms as they need and find them useful for their thought. Is Paul forbidden to do this? Paul coined this word, which is used here and in 6:3, because it designated exactly what these persons were doing. Nor need we puzzle about the first part of the compound as to whether it is the neuter plural ἕτερα, "different things," or the adverb ἑτέρως, "differently," for Paul himself tells us that these "certain ones" are teaching and devoting all their attention to endless myths and genealogies, which are ἕτερα, "different things."

As far as teaching them "differently" is concerned, in a manner that was very different from that employed by the true teachers, such things as myths and genealogies could not be taught in the *same* way as the certain truths of the gospel were taught. This verb does not say that they taught a "different gospel" as was the case in Gal. 1:8, 9, what we generally call "false doctrine" or heresy; Paul would then have said so as he does in Galatians 1. He would have added the refutation as he does in I Cor. 15:12, etc. No; their minds were taken up with a lot of unwholesome stuff on which they prided themselves (6:3, 4), Jewish myths (Tit. 1:14), foolish disputes (Tit. 3:9).

4) Προσέχειν, with or without νοῦν, means to turn the mind to something, to devote attention to something. They were not elders and called teachers of congregations but operated on their private account, "vain talkers and deceivers," especially of the circumcision, who subverted whole houses and did this for filthy lucre's sake (Tit. 1:10, 11).

We have every reason to believe that those who worked in Crete were of the same type as these in the Asian province. Their taking good pay for what they taught was the "different way" (ἑτέρως) that went with their teaching these "different things" (ἕτερα) as it naturally would. They crept into families and offered their superior silly goods for good pay.

The gospel and its sound teaching were relegated to the rear. Endless myths and genealogies were taught as being the important thing. The effect was bound to be disastrous. A plant that is smothered by rank, alien growths dies as surely as one that is torn up by the roots.

These μῦθοι were not pagan legends. They were fanciful Jewish fictional tales, the Haggadoth of the Midrash of that time, "which had germinated in a fungus growth over the whole body of the Mosaic institutions" (Farrar, *Life of Christ,* chapter 58). R., W. P., thinks that the "genealogies" denote "the Gnostic emphasis on eons," the lines of eons and emanations; but these were never called "genealogies" (C.-K. 240), and Gnosticism was of a later date. Paul refers to Jewish Old Testament genealogies; the Old Testament lists of ancestors were amplified, names of wives were invented, allegorical and additional tales were woven into them. In 4:7 they are called "profane and old wives' myths" (tales). Wohlenberg writes: "One needs only to cast a glance into the 'Book of Jubilees' to see what a role the Old Testament genealogies, the wives not named in the Old Testament, or the incompletely listed sons and daughters of the ancient fathers, played." He furnishes samples which substantiate this insignificance of "myths and genealogies." The two terms belong together, "endless" modifies both, properly so because there was no limit to such invention, there could never be.

Ἁἵτινες is both qualitative and causal and states of what sort these endless tales and genealogies are and intimates that, because they are such, teaching them and filling the mind with them must be stopped: "such as furnish (supply, afford occasion for) questionings (searching out and questing for more and more of these fancies spun from Scripture names and words) rather than (what Christians need) God's administration connected with faith." No wonder Paul calls them "endless": once an appetite for such pabulum is cultivated, it will try to find more and more of it, question every word, pry for new allegories, invent new fancies, and turn the golden Word of God into a mine for such pebbles.

The A. V. version translates the very inferior reading οἰκοδομίαν and makes Θεοῦ an adjectival genitive: "rather than godly edifying." But we prefer to read οἰκονομίαν and make Θεοῦ a subjective genitive: "God's administration," to which the article adds the phrase as a kind of apposition (R. 776), "the one in connection with faith." The sense is not difficult. God administers the universe, but here the administration of his grace and Word or gospel is indicated, which is the administration connected with saving faith. These men play with the Word; God's work is not carried forward by their teaching, nor do their fables have anything to do with saving faith. They fill the mind only with pure rubbish. We have discussed οἰκονομία in Eph. 1:10; 3:2, 9; Col. 1:25, in none of which it means "dispensation," a translation that would be peculiarly unsuitable here.

5) **Now the goal of the charge is love out of a clean heart and a conscience** (that is) **good and a faith** (that is) **unhypocritical.**

Δέ is not adversative, nor does it indicate anything parenthetical; it adds this important point about the τέλος, goal, aim, intended outcome of what this charge to Timothy really is, namely the purest and the truest kind of love. The charge itself as it comes from Paul's heart and goes out to Timothy flows from such love and thus, of course, aims to produce such love in these deluded people who are certainly unable to obtain it either for themselves or for their adherents through their sterile occupation with myths and genealogies. We may translate the article of previous reference deictically: "now the goal of *this* charge is love."

Stopping this kind of teaching and occupation of the mind, making people drop all these endless myths and genealogies and thus all the resultant questionings, and thereby giving God room for his administration, that blessed administration which is in connection with faith, can have only the blessed outcome of "love," ἀγάπη, the love of true intelligence and understanding combined with corresponding purpose in life. Paul says "love" and adds no limiting modifier except the one denoting its source. So we do not ask whether love to God, to Christ, to the brethren, or to men generally is referred to, for "love" is to be understood in its broadest sense. Those who restrict it to the love of the brethren also say that this love does not exclude love to God.

We do not understand why the article used with παραγγελίας should not point back to the verb παραγγείλῃς in which this noun is contained, why Paul should use this noun only in a general way to match the verb. How can the noun have a different meaning, not "the charge" to Timothy, but "the preaching of the gospel" in general? If we look at Acts 5:28; 16:24; I Thess. 4:2; I Tim. 1:18, we see what this noun regularly means: "charge, order, command." Our passage would be a strange exception, the more so since v. 18 follows.

"Faith" has just been mentioned in its connection with (ἐν) God's administration (the administration of

his grace and his gospel). "Love" follows, the fruit of
faith and its clear evidence. Operating with myths
and genealogies has no connection with such faith and
does not aim at such love. To make this plain over
against every empty claim of these foolish teachers
that they, too, produce true faith and love, Paul adds
the phrase regarding the one true source of this love:
"out of a clean heart and a conscience (that is) good
and a faith (that is) unhypocritical," the one preposition combines the three nouns as a unit.

Some think that the order is reversed, that Paul
says: clean heart — conscience good — faith unhypocritical but really means: faith unhypocritical produces a conscience that is good, and such a conscience
produces a clean heart. But why attribute such an
inversion to Paul: 2 preceding 1, and 3 preceding 2,
and thus 3 and 2 preceding 1? This inversion also disregards the context and generalizes: faith secures forgiveness and frees the conscience of guilt, and such a
conscience cleanses the heart. Yet Paul is dealing with
his specific charge to Timothy about certain men and
their foolish operations, which lead neither to faith
nor to love. It is this charge to Timothy which aims
at love out of a clean heart. By their whole work these
foolish teachers muddy the whole fountain of love.

We leave Paul's order as he has it: a clean heart
produces both a good conscience and an honest faith;
an unclean heart cannot have a conscience that is good
and a faith that is unhypocritical. The fact that this
is the meaning is indicated by the position of the adjectives: *clean* heart — conscience *good*, faith *unhypocritical*. In the Scriptures "heart" is by no means only
the seat of the emotions; the word for these latter is
σπλάγχνα, the nobler viscera. Heart is the seat of the
mind, the emotions, and the will, of the whole inner
consciousness of the heart regarding its moral condi-

tion but the heart or ego pronouncing verdicts upon
its thoughts, words, and deeds.

There is no reason to distinguish between the antecedent conscience, which judges contemplated actions,
and the subsequent conscience, which judges completed
actions, and to let Paul refer only to the latter. "Faith"
has the same meaning it had in v. 4, saving trust in
Christ and the gospel. The *clean* heart leaves the conscience *good* and the faith *unhypocritical;* and "out
of" these three flows love. But what is there in these
endless myths and genealogies that will lead to anything but ἐκζητήσεις, seeking out still more fables and
fancies? Only the charge to put away all this noxious
stuff will reopen the fount of love that flows from a
clean heart, etc.

Here is the motive that should prompt Timothy to
carry out this charge, to induce the churches to support him when doing so, to appeal to the foolish members themselves to drop their folly. Love is to bind
all of them together, love out of a clean heart and a
conscience that is good and a faith that is unhypocritical. Nourishing ourselves only with the gospel
produces all these, they are never produced by feeding
ourselves or any number among ourselves with myths
and genealogies even though these are spun from the
Pentateuch or from other parts of the Bible. Conscience is "good" when it functions as it should and
approves only what is good in God's sight. Faith is
"unhypocritical" (without a mask such as the ancient
show actors wore), "unfeigned" (our versions) when
it is not a mere lip faith but sincere trust and confidence of the heart.

6) Paul continues with a relative clause: **which
things some, having missed, turn off into vain talk,
wanting to be law teachers although not comprehending either what they say or concerning what they confidently affirm.** In English we might begin a new

sentence with coordinate verbs: "These things some have missed and have turned off." These things are the three mentioned in the preceding phrase. We cannot add "love" because this is not coordinated with the three. These "some" went wrong already regarding what forms the source of love. Like bad marksmen, they either never aimed at this right mark or shot so as to miss it altogether (on ὧν see R. 518). So, instead of reaching the "goal" (τέλος), they turned off into vain talk. Μάταιος in the compound = what does not lead to the goal; the word used is not κενός which means empty, without content. There is some content in what these people say, but it does not get anyone to the goal.

The three terms match beautifully: wrong aim — straying off — landing in vain talk. No wonder Paul charges Timothy to stop this sort of thing, this is motive enough for anybody.

7) Yet there is more: "wanting to be law teachers although not comprehending either what they declare or concerning what they make confident affirmation." Pitiful indeed! They want to be law teachers, pose as such with great pride; yet they do not themselves comprehend with their νοῦς or mind the things they say or the questions concerning which they make confident affirmation as though they know. The change from the relative ἅ to the interrogative περὶ τίνων is not a confusion of the two (R. 1045) but precision; they declare certain things without understanding "what" they declare, and pronounce with great confidence on what this and what that signifies without even understanding what these things are on which they make such sure pronouncements. Do you know people like this?

With νομοδιδάσκαλοι Paul is turning to the more important part of the assertions of these ignorant and foolish people. They spun their myths from the Old Testament and played pranks with genealogies found in the Pentateuch. A mere reference to these silly things is enough. Then they also found the law in the Pentateuch and went at that with silly ignorance, made useless assertions about this and that and even offered proof regarding what they did not as much as understand. It is bad enough to assert (λέγουσι) vain things that one does not comprehend; it is worse to add strong affirmations (διαβεβαιοῦνται) regarding questions that one does not even understand.

Since these people also tamper with the law, Paul points out a few fundamental things regarding the law, things which these ignorant and pretended "law teachers" have never understood. We may note that they were former Jews or pupils of such Jews (Tit. 1:10, 14). Yet they did not belong to the type of Judaizers found in Galatia, nor to the type of those found in Colosse. They were an ignorant, fantastic lot, and Paul's polemics are according and not like those employed in his letters to the Galatians and to the Colossians.

8) **Now we know that the law is excellent (Rom. 7:12) if one uses it lawfully, as knowing this that for a righteous person law is not established but for lawless and disobedient persons, for ungodly and sinful, for impious and profane ones, for father-smiters and mother-smiters, for man-killers, fornicators, pederasts, kidnapers, liars, perjurers, and if anything else opposes the healthy teaching, in accord with the gospel of the glory of the blessed God with which I on my part was entrusted.**

Δέ is scarcely adversative, it seems to be transitional: from ignorance to knowledge. This is the more true since no contrasting ἡμεῖς appears.

The statement is a simple assertion that the law is excellent if one uses it lawfully. This is not a concession. Teaching the law of God is not wrong, but

it is wrong to want to teach it and not to know how
but to abuse it in pitiful ignorance by saying things
about it which one does not himself comprehend, etc.
Thus this statement about what we know does not deal
with the law as such but with the law in its lawful use,
its excellence and its moral value which come to view
when it is employed as it itself demands. The proof
of its quality lies in its proper use. The opposite of
this statement is thus not that the law is base when
it is not used lawfully but that the law is abused when
it is used in an unlawful way. In itself and aside from
any use, whether lawful or unlawful, it remains what
it is, what God made it.

The play on "the law" and "lawfully" is keen; the
law itself, because it is law, dictates its lawful use
and condemns every abuse as being unlawful. All pretending law teachers stand condemned by the very law
they pretend to teach. Bengel finds approval for his
remark: *Hoc loco none de auditore legis sed de doc-
tore loquitur.* But using the law applies to both teacher and hearer. Verse 7 speaks of law teachers, but
v. 9-11 certainly of law hearers, of people upon whom
the law is used, lawfully used.

9) "As knowing this that," etc., is an explication
of the preceding clause and its τὶς, hence the participle
is singular. Any teacher, of course, uses the law lawfully when he knows and teaches that law is not established for a righteous person, etc.; κεῖται is a substitute
for the passive of τίθημι. But is teaching this the only
lawful use of the law? Is not our acting on this teaching equally a lawful use of the law? Those ignorant
teachers of the law are not blamed merely for their
teaching but equally for what their teaching leads to
in the case of themselves and of those who hear it
(relative clause in v. 4). One must not only have the
right teaching but the right conduct with it.

This is the place to read the Formula of Concord VI (*C. Tr.* 805, etc., 963, etc.) on the uses of the law. It has been put into three words: the law acts as *Riegel, Spiegel, Regel,* as a bar with its threats, as a mirror to reveal sin, as a rule and guide to point out the works that please God. *Spiegel* is used in the *C. Tr.* 969, 21. We also have the exposition (963, 5): "Although 'the law is not made for a righteous man,' as the apostle testifies I Tim. 1:9, but for the unrighteous, yet this is not to be understood in the bare meaning that the justified are to live without law. For the law of God has been written in their heart, and also to the first man immediately after his creation a law was given according to which he was to conduct himself. But the meaning of Paul is that the law cannot burden with its curse those who have been reconciled to God through Christ; nor must it vex the regenerate with its coercion, because they have pleasure in God's law after the inner man."

Those who think that νόμος and ὁ νόμος refer to the Mosaic law will receive clearness by a study of these two terms in Rom. 2:12-27. "Law" is used in the widest sense and has the meaning legal demands; "the law" is the Mosaic code and is as such included in "law." For this reason this code is largely followed in the following list of sinners as it certainly is the best code, especially when the relation of "law" to the gospel is touched upon as is done in v. 11. These facts do not support the conclusion of those who think that because δίκαιος = the justified man and not merely one whom the world calls just, therefore "law" must here mean "the law" (Mosaic). What Paul says is that nothing in the nature of law binds the justified Christian.

This does not refer only to the law of Moses. For among all codes and legal systems that of Moses is only supreme; and if the righteous man is free from

this, is he not then free from all that has the nature
of law? We are told that one *might* regard the whole
statement as abstract and general like that of Socrates: "Law would not be for good persons." Someone
else has stated it: "He who does no wrong needs no
law," ὁ μηδὲν ἀδικῶν οὐδενὸς δεῖται νόμου. But v. 11 *compels*
us to refer Paul's statement only to the "righteous"
whom God acquits by the forensic act of personal justification. Such a man is no longer ὑπὸ νόμον (no article: "under any law") but ὑπὸ χάριν, "under what is
grace" (Rom. 6:14, 15). See how often ἔργα νόμου is
used (Rom. 3:20, 28, etc.: "works of law," of anything that is law).

The foolish teachers in and about Ephesus were
applying their allegorical and other nonsense about
the Mosaic law to Christians, were bothering and confusing them in their understanding of this law, were
interfering with the healthy teaching that accords with
the gospel. They did not seem to know that this and
all other legitimate law, when it is used lawfully, is not
established for the righteous person in order to disturb
his faith, but for the wicked whom Paul now names at
length so that law may hold them in check with its
threats and its penalties (police function) and may
show them what they are (mirror) in order to crush
them in contrition and repentance. Paul omits the
third use of the law when it acts as "a cudgel of penalties and plagues" on "the old Adam, as an intractable,
recalcitrant ass," when it kills the flesh still left in us
(*C. Tr.* 969, 24, where several lines of the English type
have dropped out).

"A righteous person" is singular and thus indi-
vidualized; all the wicked are named in plurals, for
they are all an abominable mass. We have six in three
pairs; all are apparently condemned by the first table
of the law. Then eight under the second table of the
law. The first two of the eight are also paired by καί

and thus connected with the foregoing three pairs so that we have a rhetorical set of four pairs. Read them as pairs, and you have eight; read those of the second table, and you again have eight. Read those of the first table, and you have six; read those unconnected with "and," and you have six. This makes an interlocked chiasm. The significance of six (one short of seven) appears in Rev. 13:18. These last six are divided into two threes: "murderers — fornicators, sodomites"; next: "kidnapers, liars, perjurers." The list of the Ten Commandments is not exhausted; "anything else" takes care of any other class of sinners. Did Paul arrange this list consciously as we here trace it in sense, rhetorically, and in numbers? Say "no" if you will; but here is the list. Study his other lists, they are *all* arranged in this way. The grandest is found in II Cor. 6:4-10; compare my analysis. I confess that I have not seen such lists in secular writers, have you?

"Lawless and disobedient" evidently go together: they throw off law, they will not obey authority. They intend to act as *they* please. The second term occurs also in Tit. 1:6, 10. We may place both terms under the First Commandment, but they are broad enough to come under all ten. It is striking to hear that "law" is established for "lawless" people. Yet they are the very ones for whom law *is* established, so established that, although they mock at law and all authority that calls for obedience, law, nevertheless, brings them to account. None can escape the arm of law. Although God's law may at times grind slowly, in the end it grinds exceedingly fine. Ἄνομοι is used with reference to pagans who have never had the Mosaic code (including also the ceremonial elaboration) and thus means only "devoid of law"; here it is used in its severe sense: "opposed to law," and its companion term is "opposed to ranging oneself under" proper authority.

The ἀσεβεῖς, "ungodly" (the abstract "ungodliness" is used in Rom. 1:18) are not atheists but those who disregard God and God's will in their life and actions, whether by means of atheism or otherwise. Ἁμαρτωλοί is the proper companion term which is so often used to designate plain, open sinners. The former term refers to the First Commandment although both pertain to law in general.

The ἀνόσιοι are the impious to whom nothing is sacred, and their companions are the βέβηλοι, the profane, who walk over everything and make it as common as dirt. We think of the Second Commandment, of all profanation of God's name. Both terms occur only in these letters. Law will reckon with all such men. It goes without saying that each of the six terms is not exclusive; in a manner all are synonymous, especially those that are paired. All six refer to God and to what pertains directly to God and is thus most sacred.

"Father-smiters and mother-smiters" take us to the Fourth Commandmment, both are compounds of ἀλοιάω, "to smite" (Exod. 21:15). The reason for listing the grossest sins throughout the list is the same as that for the wording of the Ten Commandments. In Matt. 5:21, etc., Jesus explains that by forbidding the actual crimes, the law against murder, adultery, etc., also forbids everything that leads to these crimes, beginning with the faintest stirring in the heart. The worst must be named so as to include it; but naming the tree thereby names its roots, down to the smallest rootlets. Formal pairing with "and" ends here, but the fourth pair has reached the second table. "Man-killers" or murderers points to the Fifth Commandment (note Matt. 5:21); the extreme includes all that is less. While the two smiters and these killers are linked in thought, in form the killers belong with the next two, for no further "ands" follow.

10) The next two, "fornicators, pederasts," belong together (Sixth Commandment). Compare I Cor. 6:9; Rom. 1:27. *Knabenschaender* were prevalent in the highest social ranks; and there were open apologists of this vice.

"Kidnapers" (to catch a man by the foot) is also followed by an allied pair, "liars, perjurers," and thus makes another trio which is like the preceding one. With "kidnapers" — there were many in that day — we are referred to Exod. 21:16, and Deut. 24:7, which regard this the worst crime against the Seventh Commandment. "Liars, perjurers" take us to the Eighth Commandment, a third eight (two short of the ten).

Thus an *et cetera* follows: "and if anything else opposes the healthy (a participle used as an adjective) teaching," etc., τι ἕτερον occurs as it does in Attic Greek, at the close of an enumeration. By an implied contrast the teaching of the ignorant and fantastic "law teachers" (v. 7) is called unhealthy, diseased, morbid, and as such it "opposes" the healthy, sound teaching as everything unhealthy conflicts with health. Only in these Pastoral Letters does Paul use this figure in regard to teaching or doctrine. To assail the genuineness of these letters on this account is not warranted. For Paul had not hitherto encountered such fanciful teaching and had not had occasion to use words that so keenly punctured such bubbles. To speak of enlarging his vocabulary as time went on is pointless since the verb "to be healthy" was known to Paul since his boyhood.

11) The final phrase cannot be construed with anything in the preceding sentence; it modifies the whole of it from "we know" onward (v. 8-10). All that is said here is "in accord with the gospel of the glory of the blessed God with which I on my part was entrusted," we should say "have been entrusted," the

Greek merely marks the past fact. The fact that, as we know, the lawful use of the law is to apply it to all lawbreakers accords with the gospel; the right use of the law always does so. It cannot possibly oppose or even interfere with the gospel. Properly, i. e., lawfully, as it itself demands, used upon the wicked, it reveals their wickedness and aims to crush them in contrition so that they may be made "righteous" by the gospel. But to weave in allegories, myths, vain talk, and questings about the law is to deal unlawfully with the law itself and thus to frustrate its lawful purpose and use; "for by means of law (of what is law) is the knowledge (realization) of sin (of what is sin)," Rom. 3:20. "Gospel" is not used in the wide sense as including the law but in its regular sense, the glad news that we are justified and saved from all condemnations of law through Christ by faith.

"The gospel of the glory of the blessed God" is matched by II Cor. 4:4: "the gospel of the glory of Christ." Neither of these expressions is to be translated with a qualitative (adjectival) genitive: "the glorious gospel" (A. V.), because of the article: "of *the* glory," and because: "the glory of the blessed God" (in II Cor. 4:4, "of Christ") is a concept by itself. Some call it an objective genitive: "the gospel which brings or proclaims the glory of the blessed God"; but τὸ εὐαγγέλιον does not harmonize with such an object since it lacks action, nor does "the glory of God" fit as such an object. This is a possessive genitive: "the gospel which belongs to the glory of the blessed God."

God's δόξα is the sum of his attributes as they shine forth in effulgence. Here those attributes are especially to be thought of in which we see God's blessedness, the blessedness which he intends to have us share, for which the gospel is the one means since it alone has the power to cleanse and renew such sinners as have just been named in a list of fourteen groups. In accord, then, with this gospel and in no other way may the law be lawfully used.

ᵔΟ is the retained accusative with the passive and its nominative subject: "with which I on my part was entrusted" by this blessed God. Compare v. 1: "apostle of Christ Jesus by order of God, our Savior." Just as "our Savior" is there added to "God," so "blessed" is added here: blessed in his own being and glory, God intends to save us and sent "the gospel of his glory" with this object in view. Paul is one of the apostles who was especially entrusted by God with the gospel. This clause harks back to v. 3, to the charge which Paul in this capacity of his gave and now gives (v. 18) to Timothy. He would not be true to his trust if he should do less. Timothy knows that and will receive this renewed charge accordingly. Paul, however, writes this word about his trust (just as in v. 1 he started his letter with the order that made him an apostle) especially for all the Asian churches, so that they may see why he must charge Timothy as he does, and why this unhealthy, unlawful playing with the records of Moses and the law must be stopped in their midst.

"With which I was entrusted" is an essential clause. It should not, therefore, be dismissed with a few remarks and pious reflections such as that Paul often finds it necessary to emphasize his apostleship, that he did not seek it, that he shows his humility, defends it with warmth, and praises God with overflowing heart for his unmerited distinction.

* * *

12) Paul does not go off on a tangent in this paragraph because he was deflected by the last clause in v. 11, which clause is not in line with the preceding. This paragraph is an integral part of the charge to

Timothy and belongs right here between v. 3-11, the substance and the details of the charge, and v. 18, 19, the person to whom it is committed.

These pretended "law teachers" (v. 7) whom Timothy is to stop had no conception of how to use the excellent law in a lawful way, namely upon wicked sinners in accord with the gospel; they played with it in fanciful, rabbinical ways just as they played with the genealogies in Moses by spinning myths and fabulous tales around the ancient names mentioned in them. The very soul of Paul rebels against this ignorant folly when he thinks of himself, of his conversion and his apostleship. He had to take measures to stop it. As Stellhorn states it: "He would have had to deny his own most blessed experience, cast from himself all that made him happy and blessed, if he had acted otherwise," in fact, also give up his whole apostolic office and disown all that he had accomplished and also suffered in this office. He himself was the most outstanding example of what the right use of the law is able to accomplish when it is applied in accord with (κατά) the gospel of the glory of the blessed God (v. 11). Jesus had so applied the law to him (Acts 9:3-5) and had then sent him where he could find the gospel (v. 6), and it was thus that he had been entrusted with the apostolic office, the office rightly to apply the law so that the gospel may do its work. Stopping these silly law workers through Timothy is a part of Paul's great office and work.

The intensity of feeling expressed in this paragraph should not be lost in the cold type one reads or in the cool, dissecting comment to which the typed lines are subjected. Here speaks the very soul of Paul. Here is doctrine turned into life. Past experience burns undimmed, confession of sin, confession of faith, gratefulness burst into praise and doxology. This was not for himself but "for an example of those that were to believe on Christ unto life everlasting," to aid Timothy in his work of stopping the foolish teaching by true enlightenment.

Grateful am I to him that enabled me, to Christ Jesus, our Lord, that he considered me faithful, appointing me for service, formerly being a blasphemer and a persecutor and an insolent; but I was treated with mercy because, being ignorant, I acted in unbelief; moreover, exceedingly did abound the grace of our Lord accompanied by faith and love in connection with Christ Jesus.

The emphatic ἐγώ used in v. 11: "I on my part," inserts Paul's own person and soul into this dealing with the "law teachers" who so hurt the gospel by not knowing what the law was for. This was not a merely intellectual matter but one that struck at Paul's very spiritual existence and thus at the spiritual existence of every true Christian. Unless the evil was checked, the trust Paul had received in his apostleship could not be carried out, yea, his whole office would amount to nothing. He does not expand and say that the other apostles would also be in the same position although he might have done so (as he did in I Cor. 15:15 in the case of the Corinthian error); he lets his own concrete case suffice. His conversion and his appointment as an apostle (v. 1), while they are distinct, occurred at the same time. He naturally sees both involved here.

Χάριν ἔχω ("and" in the A. V. is the translation of an inferior reading) is not altogether the same as εὐχαριστῶ or χάρις τῷ Θεῷ which are otherwise used by Paul; it expresses his continuous thankfulness in the sense: "Grateful am I," the emphasis being on the Greek noun. His gratitude goes out "to him who enabled me, to Christ Jesus, our Lord," which names him according to his Messianic work and his exalted Lordship as our Savior (Acts 2:36).

It is best with Bengel to refer the aorist to Paul's *conversio et vocatio* and not to his later suffering, not to the miracles he was later on "enabled" to work, and not to his liberation from his Roman imprisonment. While it is true that in the next clause he speaks of his "ministry," we know from Acts how closely the enabling for this was connected with his conversion. In Phil. 4:13 the present participle is in place: "he who enables me," for this passage does not speak of the very first enabling but includes all that followed. In II Tim. 4:17: "the Lord stood by me and enabled me," we have an aorist because it refers to the Lord's help in the hour when he faced the imperial court.

The reason Paul's heart overflows with gratitude to the Lord is "that he considered me faithful, appointing me for service," meaning in the apostleship. There is a reason already in the designation "to him who enabled me." Paul might have coordinated: "Grateful am I to Christ Jesus, our Lord, that he enabled me *and* considered me faithful," etc. But the participle makes the enabling subsidiary to the act of considering; at the same time the substantivizing of the participle and the making it a designation for the Lord lifts it into great prominence: Paul's Enabler considered him faithful and gave him his office. The Lord made Paul something and considered what he made him out there before Damascus and thus gave him his appointment. All this aroused Paul's everlasting gratitude.

Πιστόν matches ἐπιστεύθην used in v. 11, for one entrusts only a person whom he considers trustworthy, especially one whom he himself has made so. Participles always express relation, and the context determines what this may be. The θέμενος has been made temporal: "when he appointed me." It seems to imply more, for the appointing of Paul to the apostleship is the evidence that the Lord considered him faithful and does not merely mark the time: literally, "placing me for himself (middle) for ministry," not specifying just what ministry is meant. The word does not, however, mean "ministry" that benefited the Lord but that benefited other people. Paul is now exercising such ministry through Timothy for the churches in and about Ephesus.

13) ·The climax of the sentence is the apposition to "me" which is delayed until this point is reached in order to be the more effective: me — "formerly (adverbial accusative whether with or without τό) being a blasphemer and a persecutor and an insolent." This is the astounding thing: a man with such a record, yet so appointed! Such a man enabled, considered faithful! Now we see why we have the long list of awful sinners in v. 9, 10; at one time this man not only belonged in that list but topped it. Here is an open and a full confession of sin, not one word is softened.

"A blasphemer" who blasphemed the Lord of the church by using the most wicked and hateful language against him and tried to force others to do the same, Acts 26:11. "A persecutor" (found only here in the New Testament) who chased the Lord's people as one chases wild animals, Acts 22:4, 7, who himself acted like a wild animal, Acts 9:1, who in this activity persecuted the Lord himself (Acts 9:4, 5).

"An insolent" (noun) who both outraged and insulted, see Trench, *Synonyms*. Each term is severer than the other, καί heaps one on the other. Can you imagine a worse sinner? Should he not have been struck down and made an example of the Lord's justice? The participle is generally regarded as being concessive: "although formerly being." In Luke 18:32 we have ὑβρισθήσεται to mark the insolent blows and insults that were to be heaped on Jesus in his mockery by the Sanhedrin and by the Roman soldiers.

But, wonder of wonders: "I was mercied," the Greek has just one word in the aorist passive: I was treated with compassion in my indescribably pitiful and wretched state; "grace," which is added in a moment, denotes the unmerited favor bestowed upon this man of blackest guilt. It is Pauline thus to vary the verb and the noun. The glory of gospel mercy and grace lay in changing such a monstrous sinner into a penitent believer and a mighty apostle of the Lord.

῞Οτι means "because" and offers an *Erklaerungs-grund*, not in order to lessen his guilt by an excuse, but to admit all of it (ἐποίησα, "I did it") and to bring out *how* he plunged into all of it: "being ignorant, I acted (did it) in unbelief." This was the same ignorance that is referred to in John 16:2: "Whosoever killeth you will think that he doeth God service" (Acts 26:9); the same ignorance that brought Jesus to the cross, Luke 23:34; Acts 3:17. The mercy with which Jesus prayed for his murderers (Luke 23:34) was the mercy that reached Paul near Damascus. Being ignorant does not mean having a mind that was utterly blank regarding Jesus; "in unbelief" excludes that thought. This is the ignorance that is always found in unbelief, that does not see what it ought to see: the deity and the Saviorhood of Christ. It is inadequate to say that the ignorance causes the unbelief, and that the ignorance is therefore placed first. No causal relation between the two is here indicated. The phrase and the participle could be reversed. See the author's exposition of Eph. 4:18.

No question should be raised regarding the guilt of Paul's ignorance; so also unbelief is always full of guilt. The main word is ἀγνοῶν, which is the reason it is placed forward and is thus made emphatic. There is an unbelief that acts against better knowledge, that plunges men into the sin against the Holy Spirit. In

Matt. 12:31, 32 (Mark 3:28; Luke 12:10) Jesus warns the Pharisees against going that far; in Heb. 6:4-6; 10:26-29 we see that Christians, too, need this warning.

However black Paul's guilt was, he did not go against better knowledge, did not oppose "wilfully" (ἑκουσίως, Heb. 10:26), "wilfully despise it (the Word), stop their ears and harden their hearts, and in this manner foreclose the ordinary way to the Holy Ghost, so that he cannot perform his work in them" (note "cannot," *C. Tr.* 835, 12); where "man . . . entirely resists the Word, there no conversion takes place, or can be" (note "can be," 913, 83). Thus it was that, when this ignorance was shattered by a burst of mighty knowledge, Paul says (Acts 26:19): "I was not disobedient unto the heavenly vision." When he realized the deity and the glory of Jesus, his unbelief was changed into belief.

14) This clause is not dependent on ὅτι, and δέ does not mark a balance with an omitted μέν, omitted because the use of μέν is on the decline in the Koine. The sinner's ignorance and the Lord's grace cannot be balanced in such a way. It is hazardous to supply a μέν where Paul has written none. The reference to Paul's acting ignorantly is properly found in a subordinate clause; the abounding of the Lord's grace, just like the extension of mercy, is properly mentioned in a coordinate main clause; δέ is either "and" (our versions) or, preferably, "moreover." Rom. 5:20: "Where sin abounded (ἐπλεόνασε), grace did much more abound (ὑπερεπερίσσευσεν)," here we have ὑπερεπλεόνασε.

"Grace" is the undeserved favor shown to the guilty sinner, here the favor of our Lord. Great and terrible as Paul's sin was with all the ignorance that went with it, the Lord's grace went ὑπέρ, "beyond" it with its abundance. This does not mean that it did so irresistibly, for grace is never irresistible. Some sinners yield to the slightest touch of grace, some need all its blessed power. The Lord's grace is not a variable quantity that comes now with small, now with large volume at the Lord's pleasure so that some to whom little grace comes are not converted although they would have been if they had experienced more grace. Jerusalem and Judas resisted all grace.

We should also not confuse the strength of grace with the Lord's appearance to Paul, for in that appearance the Lord crushed Paul with the law: "Saul, Saul, why art thou persecuting me?" In order to hear the gospel of grace Paul was directed to go to Damascus, Ananias preached the Lord's grace to him, the same grace that is preached everywhere. The visible appearance of Jesus was preparatory to Paul's apostleship, for an apostle had to be a witness who could testify that he had seen the risen Lord with his own eyes (Acts 1:8). This appearance placed Paul on an equality with the other apostles. Matthias who was chosen in the place of Judas met that requirement (Acts 1:22).

The fact that this grace of the Lord was successful in Paul's case is indicated by the phrase that is introduced with μετά: "accompanied by faith and love in connection with Christ Jesus." The preposition merely states that faith and love were "in company with" grace. It does not say how they came to be there although we know how: they were wrought by this grace. This brevity will be understood by Timothy. To be sure, grace comes from the Lord, and faith and love were in Paul's heart; but to combine these two with "the grace of our Lord" by means of μετά implies that both of them, faith and love, came into Paul's heart, grace kindled them. Both ἀγάπη and πίστις are feminine, hence, just as χάρις has its modifier "our Lord," so these two have their modifier τῆς ἐν Χριστῷ Ἰησοῦ, "in connection with Christ Jesus." What this connection is, is not further described. The supposition that this would entail a difference in the force of ἐν, the connection with faith not being the same as that with love, is untenable. It would be strange, indeed, to construe only "love" with Christ when both faith and love are mentioned in one breath and τῆς follows. So we also do not agree with the view that this is Christ's love and not love which is the fruit of faith.

We should note the pertinency of all this regarding Paul's own person for his charge to Timothy to stop the ἑτεροδιδάσκαλοι and νομοδιδάσκαλοι. What could their playing with myths and genealogies and their ignorant fancies about Moses' law do for a sinner like those named in v. 9, 10 or for one like Paul had once been? Absolutely nothing! They could work no contrition with such unhealthy teaching, nothing "in accord with the gospel of the blessed God (our Savior, v. 1)." Paul's order to Timothy is not due to what men today call a difference in doctrinal "views" but to the very life of faith and love in Paul's soul as connected with Christ Jesus and to the blessed apostleship and ministry with which God had entrusted and for which the Lord had enabled him. If Paul were not to stand on this order to Timothy, this would mean to be faithless to his office and trust, yea, to contradict his own faith and love. He significantly joins "love" to "faith," his whole διακονία, his whole ministry to men, was upborne by love.

15) All this, which is written with such intensity about himself, applies to Paul himself because it applies to all sinners (see the list in v. 9, 10); yea, in all this the Lord made Paul an example of his longsuffering for all future sinners who would be saved.

Faithful (is) the statement and of all acceptation worthy, that Christ Jesus came into the world to save

sinners, to whom I on my part belong as foremost; but for this reason I was treated with mercy that in me as a foremost one Jesus Christ may display all his long-suffering for a model of those who are about to believe on him for life eternal.

"Faithful (is) the statement" occurs only in these Pastoral Letters (3:1; II Tim. 2:11; Tit. 3:8), and in 4:9 "worthy of all acceptance" is also added. The sense of these words is "reliable," "trustworthy" and thus of such importance as to be accepted by all who hear them; ἄξιος means "worthy" with the idea of weight. The absence of a connective arrests the attention of the Greek reader and makes the assertion stand by itself, in an independent way. Ἀποδοχή is more than "approbation"; it denotes "acceptance." A statement that is πιστός deserves the acceptance of πίστις. That does not mean mere assent but a faith that appropriates the statement for one's own soul, spiritual apprehension. Ὁ λόγος denotes the contents of what is expressed by words. Another and a longer wording might be used, but the *logos* would be the same. "Worthy of all acceptance" = complete acceptation in every way, without reservation, without hesitation, without the least doubt.

The statement presents pure, objective fact: "that Christ Jesus came into the world to save sinners," the Greek reads: "sinners to save" (effective aorist), the verb and the object are transposed so as to emphasize both. "Came into the world" is restricted to the incarnation by some; but we may regard the aorist "came" as we do the aorist "to save," as a constative aorist which includes not merely the arrival alone but everything that occurred until the time of his departure from the world. Verses 9, 10 show what "sinners" Christ came to save. The idea that he came to save only *some* sinners by a limited atonement and left others to be doomed contradicts this *logos*. This is the gospel in brief; this is its very heart. It is a repetition of Matt. 18:11: "The Son of man is come to save that which was lost"; compare John 3:17; I John 3:5. This word of Jesus' was undoubtedly restated so many times that it is pointless to say that Paul quotes one of these restatements. There is no need to expand and to say from what Jesus came to save sinners, from their sins, their guilt, and the penalty of perdition. "Sinners" he came to save, not saints (Matt. 9:13).

Ὧν πρῶτός εἰμι ἐγώ, "of whom first or foremost am I on my part," has the Greek idiom "I am of," which = "I belong to." The adjective may be connected with the genitive: "whose first or foremost one I am"; but we prefer not to regard it as the predicate of the copula but as predicative to ἐγώ: "I as foremost." Its position is due solely to emphasis, ὧν εἰμι is itself a regular idiom so that one could say: "of whom I myself am," i. e., "to whom I belong." Those who think that Paul is humbling himself too severely may look at ἔκτρωμα in I Cor. 15:8, where he calls himself "an abortion," a vile, dead thing that ought hurriedly be buried from sight (see the writer on this passage).

Those who would make "first" absolute may note that Paul does not say: "of *all* whom I am first or *the* first," nor "of whom I am *the* first." In Acts 28:17, πρῶτοι is used in the plural: "foremost men of the Jews." What object is there in making Paul the worst possible of all sinners when we know about the one mentioned in II Thess. 2:3, 4? We certainly do not wish to reduce Paul's sinfulness, he would be foremost in stopping us. But we do refuse to say that every believer ought to confess, "I am the worst possible sinner," just because each one knows *his own* sins from personal experience and the sins of others only from what he sees and hears about them. Paul writes: "of whom I *am* foremost," not *was* foremost, but not because he vividly recalls only his past crimes but be-

cause he speaks of himself as a sinner, as one who
should be classed with sinners because of all his sins,
whether past or present.

16) In v. 12-14 Paul states what God did for him;
in v. 15, 16 what God thereby did for others. The conversion of one man often means much for others; this
was eminently the case with regard to Paul. But the
thought is not that by converting Paul, God would convert many others, through Paul's work; also not that
Paul's is an outstanding example of conversion which is
in this respect valuable for all future time, although
both those ideas are correct. Διὰ τοῦτο has the ἵνα clause
as an apposition. The reason that Paul was treated
with mercy although he was such a frightful sinner is
"that in me as foremost Jesus Christ may display all
his longsuffering for a model of those who are about
to believe on him," etc. The reason is not Paul or anything in Paul; the reason is Jesus, something in Jesus,
namely "all his longsuffering," μακροθυμία, holding out
long under provocation. Did any man provoke Jesus
more severely than did Saul? But instead of promptly
striking this blasphemous, persecuting insolent down
with the justice he deserved, as we might rightly have
expected, Jesus bore him and kept bearing him and
finally attained the most astonishing success by means
of his mercy (ἠλεήθην, the same verb was used in v. 13).

We should expect that after saying, "I was mercied," in v. 13 Paul would say that Jesus secured in
me a great example of his wonderful mercy, a sample
of that mercy which he would show toward all future
believers, which would certainly also state the fact.
But Paul sees much more in his own case. He certainly sees all the mercy of Jesus, for he writes twice,
"I was mercied," and both times he employs finite
verbs. But back of that mercy was the wondrous
"longsuffering" which held back judgment when it was
long overdue and thus enabled mercy to win its blessed

result.   Thereby Jesus provided a ὑποτύπωσις, an outstanding "model" (it is more than a τύπος or "example"), to set forth once for all as a display (ἐνδείξηται, aorist) as to how he would deal also with so many others who in future would believe on him.   Τῶν μελλόντων πιστεύειν is a periphrastic future: "those about to believe," i. e., future believers.   By using the present participle the iterative sense is made prominent, case after case would extend into the future.

It was the will of Jesus to use Paul's case as a display of "all his longsuffering."   This does not imply that there are not other cases.   Paul writes: that in me "as a foremost one" Jesus may display, etc.   With the first πρῶτος Paul says that "as foremost" he belonged to sinners; when πρώτῳ now follows so closely, it must again signify rank.   It cannot be a temporal designation and say that as "first" Paul antedated τῶν μελλόντων, the believers of the coming days.   Paul naturally deals only with a model of all the longsuffering of Jesus with reference to coming believers, whose cases, as far as Jesus' longsuffering is concerned, resemble this model, and not with unbelievers who, like Judas, despite all the longsuffering of Jesus persist in unbelief and do not end in mercy but in perdition.   We occasionally find "believe on Jesus" (ἐπί), to place confidence and trust "upon" him.   "For life eternal" adds the blessed result of believing.   This is ζωή in the spiritual sense which is now begotten in us by faith and extends to all eternity (see the fuller elaboration, *Interpretation of St. John's Gospel,* 249; compare Matt. 19:16).

How could the Jewish myths, the dabbling with the Mosaic genealogies, the ignorant playing with Mosaic law serve for the conversion of sinners, shed light on the Lord's mercy and on his longsuffering in enduring such sinners until mercy is able to bring them to faith and to salvation?   How would Paul have fared if there had been only such myths, etc.? What about all sinners in the future? Only when the law is lawfully used "in accord with the gospel of the glory of the blessed God," that gospel which is now entrusted to Paul (v. 11), could the longsuffering of Jesus at last bestow his mercy for faith and life eternal.

17) *Ex sensu gratiae fluit doxologia,* Bengel. This doxology is the outburst of a heart that is surcharged with feeling; it is induced not only by Paul's own experience but also by all that the Lord's longsuffering and mercy mean for all past and all future believers. He sees these fountains of his and of their salvation and this eternal life and salvation itself and, stirred thus, he exclaims: **Now to the King of the eons, imperishable, invisible, sole God, honor and glory for the eons of the eons! Amen.** He rules the eons, the vast eras that are marked by what transpires in them whether they are conceived as belonging to time or to eternity (see the following phrase).

This King is absolute. Note Luke 1:33 regarding the rule of Jesus "for the eons." Such a King is naturally "imperishable," "who only has immortality" (6:16). He is the Supreme Spirit over all, not the object of the senses, but of faith and hence "invisible," unseen. Yea, "sole God," there is none besides him. The order of these terms accords with their meaning. The King of the eons who rules them and all that is in them must be imperishable as being infinitely superior to them, must thus be Spirit, as such invisible because he is superior to all that is visible, must thus be sole and only God with no other God existing.

Paul has such a large number of doxologies, which are phrased in such varied forms that none of them follow a fixed formula but repeat precious Old Testament expressions in free appropriation. Thus we note Ps. 145:13. Because Paul uses two nouns, some would separate them: To the King of the eons — imperishable, invisible, only God (construing all the adjectives with "God"); but if this were to be done, the adjectives would usually be placed after "God." The variant readings need not detain us; one has been the basis of the A. V.'s translation: "the only *wise* God," which is adopted from Rom. 16:27.

We need no verb since this is an exclamation: to him "honor and glory for the eons of the eons!" Honor is the esteem and reverence, and glory is the ascription of our praise as we see and adore all his excellencies. "For the eons of the eons," plurals, adds the genitive in Hebrew fashion in order to indicate the superlative degree of duration, namely endlessness; it is our English idiom "forever and ever." Eternity is really timelessness and not in any sense duration, but human language has no words to express that idea since the human mind is able to form no adequate conception because in its finiteness it is bound to ideas of time.

"Amen" is the transliteration of the Hebrew word which (like hosanna and hallelujah) has passed unchanged into other languages. It means "truth" and, except in the Gospels, is placed at the end of a statement as a seal of verity. It is always emphatic and should be read so; it is a confessional affirmation that completely justifies what precedes and compels the reader to see and to recognize the fact.

18)   This charge I commit to thee, child Timothy, in accord with the prophecies proceeding in advance to thee, that thou war in connection with them the noble warfare as having faith and a good conscience which some, thrusting away, have made shipwreck as regards the faith, to whom belong Hymenaeus and Alexander, whom I have delivered over to Satan in order that they may be disciplined not to blaspheme.

"This charge," the one named in the verb in v. 3 and in the noun in v. 5 and elucidated in the whole of

v. 3-17. It is once more summed up in the ἵνα clause regarding warring the good warfare. Here at the end of this first part of the letter Paul commits this task of dealing with the ἑτεροδιδάσκαλοι to Timothy in a rather formal way. He has already urged Timothy (v. 3) to attend to these people; so that no one may question Timothy's authority in the matter Paul puts the commission into written form so that Timothy may produce it if necessary. Paul even points to his own summary action when he expelled two men during his brief stay at Ephesus (v. 20). Paul thus fortifies Timothy all around so that Timothy may act under Paul's own fullest authority.

The view that "this charge" = the gospel in general or something less definite interrupts the context and leaves these verses hanging in the air. "Child Timothy" recalls the endearing address used in v. 2. Those who refer the "charge" to the gospel think that Paul intends to commit the gospel to this child as an inheritance to be preserved; others think of Timothy's taking an admonition to heart. But the address "child" means that Timothy will carry out the charge of v. 3-17 in the spirit of Paul, "in accord with the prophecies proceeding in advance to thee."

Luther is puzzled about this phrase and confesses, "I do not know what he (Paul) means with this text," and wavers between the Old Testament prophecies and teachings and prophecies which were supposedly uttered with reference to Timothy when Paul in Lystra chose Timothy as his assistant. Most commentators decide for the latter, some refer to 4:14; 6:12; II Tim. 1:6; 2:2; others refer to Acts 16:2, the good reports of the brethren in Lystra and Iconium about Timothy although they wrestle with the following ἐν αὐταῖς, Timothy's warfare "in these prophecies."

Luther is evidently on the right track. These are, however, not Old Testament prophecies which preceded

Timothy by hundreds of years; why should their proceeding so far in advance be mentioned? These are the apostolic prophecies and teachings which are described with a present (not an aorist) participle as getting to Timothy in advance of this time when he is especially called upon to make his disciplinary measures accord with them (κατά) by conducting his good campaign "in connection with them." We have discussed prophecy in I Thess. 5:20; Rom. 12:6; I Cor. 14:3 (which see). This word may refer to immediate revelation, but it is also used with reference to all transmission of such revelation by those who have received it mediately, and I Cor. 14:1 urges all Christians to seek this gift and ability. This is the sense of "prophecies" in this passage.

Even now, in this letter, such prophecies are coming to Timothy in advance of his work in applying them to the flighty teachers in the province of Asia. Paul certainly includes the teaching he has presented in this chapter, and it agrees with what he told Timothy before he had left him (v. 3) and with all that Paul had taught him; "proceeding to you" is the correct word and the correct tense. It is well to note that ἐπὶ σέ does not = περί, "concerning thee." "Upon thee" means literally "to thee." Timothy is well fortified and equipped in advance. Προάγων even fits the idea of the next clause, that of waging a noble campaign. Like troops, these prophecies and true teachings come to Timothy in advance so as to enable him to make a good campaign in his new field. He is Paul's lieutenant-general who is re-enforced by his general--in-chief.

The ἵνα clause is an apposition to "this charge." This does not mean that "this charge" does not refer to the one mentioned ĩn v. 3 and 5, to silence those teaching something else; the ἵνα clause merely advances the ἵνα of v. 3, it merely says that what

v. 3 orders Timothy to do is a campaign, and that
it ought to be an excellent or a noble one, one that
is well conducted: "that thou campaign in connection with them the (i. e., thy) noble campaign" (cognate accusative). This is military language: Timothy is the στρατηγός — he has a στράτευμα — is engaged
in στρατεύειν — is to accomplish τὴν καλὴν στρατείαν. But
his forces are these "prophecies," his whole campaigning is a spiritual one. Paul's charge to Timothy does
not merely have this as its purpose; this *is* the charge
itself, this is what v. 3 means.

19) As he campaigns thus he is to have "faith
and a good conscience," not Christian faith in general
nor a good conscience in general; this is faith in the
prophecies he is to use as his victorious forces in this
campaign and thus a good conscience that is due to
relying only on these prophecies and apostolic teachings even as only "in connection with them" he is to do
the campaigning. Apart from them Timothy's conscience would be in a sad plight indeed.

That comment is not acceptable which says that
Timothy is to *add* to the prophecies "faith and a good
conscience." This comment misunderstands the force
of ἔχων which merely describes the subject of στρατεύῃ:
"that thou campaign *as having* faith," etc. We have
already said that this is not a purpose clause. Nor can
we accept any comment to the effect that Timothy is
not to lose his faith and a good conscience. Would
Paul appoint as his lieutenant a man regarding whom
he still had such fears? The point is that, when he is
correcting errors such as were found in the Asian field,
even a good man might resort to other means than
the prophecies, might not trust them sufficiently and
thus hurt his own conscience. We, too, who have so
many evils to contend with in the churches might well
note this fact.

The Greek permits Paul to continue with three consecutive relative clauses; in English we should use independent sentences. The first is to be construed with "a good conscience" and not also with "faith," for "the faith" appears in the relative clause: "which some by thrusting away (or: having thrust away) made shipwreck regarding the (their) faith." When they thrust aside their conscience which tried to hold them to the prophecies they had learned from faithful teachers they made shipwreck of their very faith. One cannot keep his faith while he plays fast and loose with the prophecies (Word). He will have to silence his conscience, make it cease crying out against such practice, and then his faith is wrecked whether he admits it or not. A new, graphic figure is added, but it agrees with the other figure. The one is the disturbance of war during a campaign, the other is the disturbance of a storm at sea. In both our one reliance is prophecy, the Word. It is a sad campaign, a sad wreck, if conscience is thrust aside and reliance is sought in something aside from or contrary to the prophecies or Word.

Paul says that "some" did make shipwreck of their faith and then names two who had already been expelled. The fact that these "some" are not identical with the "some" mentioned in v. 3 is apparent from what is said about each group. Both of the groups are mentioned in connection with the charge to Timothy and must thus belong to the same class from whose follies Timothy is to rid the churches. These "some" mentioned in our verse are the worst of the group mentioned in v. 3 and 7, the leaders in this business of myths and genealogies and fancies about the law that could not possibly help sinners in accord with the gospel. They got so far away from the apostolic prophecies that they did even what is here stated regarding their conscience and their faith. Paul himself had dealt with two of them, and when he held up to them the prophecies, i. e., the apostolic gospel teaching, and thereby tried to reach their conscience he found that they had actually thrust all good conscience away and had thereby lost their faith altogether. The true gospel teaching no longer made an impression on them, it had been smothered by their myths, etc.

Paul is not warning Timothy lest he, too, join their number and likewise be delivered over to Satan. One does not send as a lieutenant to smite such men with the apostolic teaching in a campaign a man whom he must warn not to go over to the enemy. These relative clauses point out the opposites: Timothy having the prophecies and thus faith and a good conscience — these men having neither; Timothy is thus to eject them as Paul has already ejected two of them.

20) "To whom belong" is the same kind of a genitive as that found in v. 16. There is reason for the construction with relatives, it ties everything together from the loss of faith to ultimate expulsion. We see no reason for thinking that this is not the Hymenæus mentioned in II Tim. 2:17. There he is an example of teaching that eats like a cancer; here an example of excommunication. Alexander is so common a name that we are not ready to identify him with the Jew Alexander mentioned in Acts 19:33. To think that this Jew became a Christian and then an apostate blasphemer whom Paul excommunicated, can be only a conjecture. Is he the "Alexander, the metalworker," mentioned in II Tim. 4:14? Why should he, then, be identified as "the metalworker" in the second letter and not in the first? Moreover, the two men referred to in this letter are residing in Ephesus or in one of the churches of the Ephesian group while the man mentioned in Second Timothy seems to be living in Rome. It is again conjecture to transfer him from Ephesus to Rome and then back again to Ephesus.

"Whom I gave over to Satan in order that they may be disciplined (see Trench on the word) not to blaspheme" reads so much like I Cor. 5:5 that the two acts are similar. Both of them were formal expulsions or excommunications, see the interpretation of the Corinthian passage. In I Cor. 5:3-5, Paul writes as though he himself were present at the meeting of the congregation in Corinth and were offering the formal resolution to expel the man (v. 4, 5), which was to be formally adopted by the congregation, "to deliver such a one over to Satan." The same words are here used. There the case was one of incest and impenitence, here it was one of blasphemy. In both instances excommunication must needs follow.

And that is the sense of "giving over to Satan." These two cases are like that of Judas whose heart Satan had filled. They are cases not merely of some false doctrine or other, whose proponent must also be expelled, but not by at once giving him over to Satan, for a doctrinal error may not mean that all faith has already been lost. Impenitence in the case of open sin, likewise blasphemy, does mean that. When Paul says "I gave over," in the light of I Cor. 5:3-5 this cannot mean that Paul did this alone, without the congregation, by his apostolic authority alone, but must be understood as it is in I Cor. 5:5. When the cases were brought before the congregation, Paul made the motion indicated, and the congregation adopted the motion. The New Testament knows of no hierarchical excommunication.

Some seem to think that I Cor. 5:5 implies that Satan is to punish the man given over to him by physical disease and the like; some say that he was to be punished by demoniacal possession, and such punishment was to bring the expelled man to repentance, as if repentance is ever produced by such means, as if

Satan would thus play into the hands of Christ! Such views are scarcely tenable.

The purpose clause: "that they be disciplined not to blaspheme," means that this congregational act of discipline may, as the church's final means, bring home to these blasphemers the enormity of their sin and guilt, and that they may be crushed in contrition by the law and come to repentance. Excommunication does not aim to bring about the sinner's damnation but his reclamation. Often the law does not strike through until it is applied to the limit. Even when it is so applied it does not always succeed; this is only the last expedient. The sinner may remain in Satan's hands.

Timothy knew these two cases. Whether he had already arrived from Philippi and was present at the double excommunication we are unable to say. That point is not material. If he came a bit later he heard all about what had been done. The point is that, when Paul left for Macedonia, all such discipline was placed into Timothy's hands, who was to direct and to supervise it in the entire province.

The conclusion is fully warranted that Paul found only these two, Hymenæus and Alexander, in Ephesus itself and thus under his own direction at once had the congregation deal with them. If there had been others of this type in Ephesus, Paul would have had them attended to just as promptly before he proceeded on his way. Thus Ephesus itself had been rid of such men before Paul left. The cases which Timothy would have to attend to would be found outside of Ephesus, scattered here and there in other congregations of the province. Paul's object in naming the two cases that occurred in Ephesus and in stating what he himself had done with them is to enable Timothy to show this letter wherever he may be questioned or op-

posed when he insists that effective measures be taken
in any congregation. Timothy has in writing what
Paul did in Ephesus; no less is to be done elsewhere
whenever it becomes necessary.

The word "blaspheme" sheds some light upon the
tenets of the men who taught ἕτερα, myths, genealogical
fancies, and ignorant legal notions in some of the Asian
congregations. Some of these men arrived at the point
where they actually blasphemed the true law of the
gospel teachings and endeavored to remove these in
order to make their myths, etc., the sole teaching. No
congregation could tolerate such men in its midst. Still
more light is offered by II Tim. 2:16, 17, the "profane
and vain babblings eating like a cancer," with malig-
nancy crowding out the teaching of the saving truth.
"Stop it!" (see v. 3) is Paul's charge to Timothy.

CHAPTER II

How Timothy Is to Regulate the Public Services and Offices

About Prayer in the Public Services

1) Paul treats two points when he considers the public services of the congregations: 1) who is to be included in the prayers; 2) the part women may take in the services. What Paul has seen and learned on his recent visit in the Ephesian field evidently led him to charge Timothy with the directions here given. Whether he had mentioned them to Timothy before he left Ephesus is not indicated.

I urge, then, first of all, that there be made petitions, prayers, approaches, thanksgivings in behalf of all men, in behalf of kings and all who are in eminence, so that we may lead a still and restful life in all godliness and gravity.

Οὖν merely makes the transition to something else; it is our "then." Since the subject of foolish teachers has been concluded, "then" takes us to the next subject. The efforts that regard this connective as basing what is now said on something special in the preceding are rather strained. John uses οὖν as Paul does here (B.-P. 945, also Kretzmann, *Pastoralbriefe*). When δέ is similarly used it is our "now" and not our "then." Paul is again urging (1:3), which is sufficient, for more than this is not needed in regard to this matter. "First of all" means that he has a number of other things that are likewise to be urged; we have them in the rest of this letter. The A. V. follows Luther and construes "first of all" with the infinitive; but no second and third infinitives or their equivalents follow.

"That there be made petitions," etc., is passive, which leaves the persons who are to make them (iterative present) unnamed. These persons are Timothy and the congregations; Timothy is to direct them, and the congregations are to follow his directions. Few commentators will entertain the thought that Paul's directions are intended only for individuals and not for congregations. Timothy should not be regarded as being the pastor of the church in Ephesus; the elders were the pastors, Timothy was Paul's representative who directed pastors and churches in the entire province; hence Paul also puts these directions into writing in case somebody raised objection.

We may now study a number of synonyms. First, there are four words for prayer: δεήσεις (δέομαι), "petitions" to fill needs; προσευχαί, the sacred word for "prayers," which is as broad as the English word and a reverent term; ἐντεύξεις (ἐντυγχάνω), found only here and in 4:5 in the New Testament, "free, familiar prayer such as boldly draws near to God" (Trench). These three belong together. Stellhorn, *Pastoralbriefe Pauli*, says that the first implies the humble feeling of our great need of the gifts and the blessings of God who alone is able to bestow what is good and wholesome; the second, coming to God with due reverence, recognizing him as the Lord, the great God of heaven and earth, before whom we must bow in the dust; the third, drawing nigh to him in childlike trust and freedom, making known our wishes, and knowing that he will, indeed, give us what is salutary. Congregational prayer, when one voice speaks for all, leaves many with idle, drifting minds, which is the opposite of what lies in Paul's words.

Εὐχαριστίαι, "thanksgivings," adds grateful acknowledgments for past mercies to humble, worshipful, trustful requests. These are never to be absent when we are praying, for however sad our condition may be, we always enjoy great and undeserved blessings. Trench writes about thanksgiving: "As such it may and will subsist in heaven (Rev. 4:9; 7:12); will indeed be larger, deeper, fuller there than here; for only there will the redeemed know how much they owe to their Lord; and this, while all other forms of prayer in the very nature of things will have ceased in the entire fruition of the things prayed for."

"For all men," ὑπέρ, "in their behalf," is world-wide and is not to be restricted in any way. No matter how far away men may be, the prayers of the church are able to reach them. Who can number all men? Yet these prayers omit none. "All men" transcends even national confines. "All men" means that, although millions do not pray or pray aright, the congregations of true believers who do know how to pray speak for them and leave none unprayed for. Paul does not seem to be afraid that a congregation may pray for too many or ask too much. If such praying were useless, the apostle would not write what he does write.

2) Prayer is international, cosmopolitan, and yet patriotic in the highest sense. "All men" and "kings and all who are in eminence" rightly go together. All men are divided into national and political groups under governmental heads who have lesser officials beneath them, each of whom has his own eminence. The welfare of each nation is bound up with its government so that Paul means that we are to pray for "all men" as men, as one great mass, and yet also for nations under their rulers and magistrates. We recall Rom. 13:1, etc. To pray for the latter is equally needful. When Paul refers to "kings" he is not endorsing monarchy as being the only rightful form of government. After writing "all men," "emperors" would have been too narrow a term, for although the Roman Empire was vast in extent it did not include all men and all nations. Some people had had other than royal

forms of government. "Kings" is the best term to use when supreme rulers in general are referred to. Some rulers, high and low, were evil; yet how many of "all men" were not also evil? The prayers of the church are not limited, in fact, especially evil men need prayers.

The church has followed Paul's directions. As a part of its main service it has what is called the General Prayer. We may ask why Paul urges this comprehensiveness of prayer for the public services in the Asian churches. He offers us no clew. During his recent visit he had perhaps noted a lack in this respect; the prayers offered in the churches were including only the church with its members or only the homeland.

We regard ἵνα as indicating contemplated result: "so that we may lead a still and restful life in all godliness and gravity." The statement that this clause after all asks the Christians in reality to pray only for themselves is an unfair remark. When Christians do pray for themselves, the blessings they receive are by no means confined to themselves; equally, when they pray for all men, their rulers, etc., "all men" not only includes all Christians but the many blessings secured by this prayer for the non-Christians, for rulers and people are again not confined to non-believers. One of the very great results will be the one here stated. Some specify what is to be prayed for. The best interpretation as to the contents of such a prayer is that embodied in our General Prayer: "Cause thy glory to dwell in our land, mercy and truth, righteousness and peace everywhere to prevail, etc. . . . Graciously defend us from all calamities by fire and water, from war and pestilence, from scarcity and famine," etc.

Stellhorn comments: "In the case of an individual mature Christian little or nothing for his own spiritual life may depend on the government of his country; the most wicked government may afford him opportunity to attest and to prove his faith in the most notable way. But for the weaker and younger Christians and thus for the congregation and the church, which as a rule consists for the greater part of such, 'a tranquil and quiet life' is necessary if it is to be at the same time a life of 'godliness and gravity.' . . . How disorder and wild, undisciplined conditions in a country, how especially cruel persecution harms the weaker members of the church and thus the church herself, experience has abundantly proved. Thousands, hundreds of thousands have permitted themselves to be drawn away from the Christian confession and life, have lost faith and salvation, no more living 'in all godliness and gravity.' "

Διάγω βίον is a current expression although it is found only here in the New Testament. Ἤρεμος and ἡσύχιος (the verb is found in I Thess. 5:11; the noun in II Thess. 3:12) are close synonyms: "still — restful," without inner fears or outward harassment. The two are combined in order to emphasize the idea. But "godliness and gravity" are not synonyms: the one = the right reverencing of God, inward and thus also outward — the other, dignified and worthy conduct toward our fellow men. "All" is to be construed with both nouns and means that both godliness and gravity are to be complete. Luther's *Ehrbarkeit* is a good translation of "gravity"; "honesty," the translation of the A. V., is to be understood in the older sense of honorableness.

3) **This (is) excellent and acceptable before our Savior God who wants all men to be saved and to come to realization of truth. For one (is) God; one also (is) Mediator for God and men, a man, Christ Jesus, the one who gave himself a ransom for all, this testimony for their own seasons, etc.**

Paul does not write this because Timothy and the people with whom he is to deal do not know it but be-

cause they do know it, and because this knowledge is
to be applied when they arrange their prayers for the
public services. The churches are to pray as stated,
not because Paul says so, not because Timothy tells
them to do so, but because this is excellent and accep-
able in God's sight as being the one who wants all men
to be saved, etc. Paul states these facts in order to be
helpful to Timothy and to the churches so that they
may act intelligently and from conviction and not me-
chanically. It is one thing to know and another to use
that knowledge aright.

Believers and the *Una Sancta* are to be separate
from the world, from all other men in many respects,
for they have been called out of the world, and the
world hates them (John 15:18, 19) ; but in the matter
of prayer this holding aloof from the world does not
apply for the reasons here stated. Who would pray
for the world if the churches did not do so? When
Jesus says, "I pray not for the world" (John 17:9),
this refers to what we call his special intercession in
which he asks for what can be bestowed only on believers, that God sanctify them in the truth so that they
may all be one. This special intercession does not
exclude Christ's general intercession, Isa. 53:12: He
"made intercession for the transgressors," even for his
murderers (Luke 23:34), his blood speaks better
things than that of Abel (Heb. 12:24).

Τοῦτο refers to the infinitive clause, to the making
of prayers for all men. The phrase "before our Savior
God" is to be construed with both "excellent and acceptable." When these prayers come before God on
his heavenly throne, his judgment pronounces them
morally and spiritually "excellent," a true expression
of the Christian spirit of his people, and thus God receives these prayers as being "acceptable," to be
answered in his goodness and his grace. In English it
is better to say: "of God, our Savior," but Paul writes:

"of our Savior God." The apposition is "God" and not, as in 1:1, "our Savior." The reason for adding the exceptional title "Savior" is the same as that advanced in interpreting 1:1. God's Word is to be applied to sinners (1:8, etc.) in order to save them as by it this great sinner Paul was saved, it is not to be played with and turned into fancies. It is the Word of our Savior God.

4) "Our" Savior cannot be limited to Paul and to Timothy: "thy Savior and mine," or only to Christians in general; the next clause removes such a limitation. "Our" means that God has already saved us, but none of us would be thus saved if it were not God's will that "all men be saved and come to truth's realization." "All men" is placed forward for the sake of emphasis. This is the important term, it is repeated from v. 1 and is followed by the general word "men" and by "for all" in v. 5, 6.

It is a severe indictment when in his Commentary Calvin says regarding this passage that all who use it to oppose his doctrine of absolute predestination "are subject to puerile hallucination," that Paul means that no people or class of men are excluded from salvation (*apostolus simpliciter intelligit, nullum mundi vel populum, vel ordinem a salute excludit*), that Paul is speaking only of the different races of men and not of individuals as such, and that he also wishes the class of kings and rulers to be included. But this is a universal statement of the Scriptures.

Our dogmaticians call this the antecedent will of God, which is stated so often in Scripture, as in Ezek. 33:11; John 3:16; II Pet. 3:9. The truth that God wants all men to be saved is corroborated by the fact that Christ "gave himself a ransom *for all*" (v. 6), and that God provides the efficacious means of grace and salvation for all. The passive "to be saved" certainly does not mean to be saved by somebody else than "our Savior God." The reason the active is not used: "who wants to save all men," is that the passive implies the means for being saved even as "to come to realization of truth" states the means. This second infinitive still refers to the antecedent will which applies equally to all men. When men reject this blessed universal will which also includes them (Matt. 23:37), the subsequent will sends them to judgment and to perdition: Matt. 23:38; Mark 16:16. The dogmaticians do not divide the will of God nor assert that God has two wills; they divide only the objects with which God's will deals as the Scriptures themselves do. See Franz Pieper, *Dogmatik* I, 558, etc.

Εἰς ἐπίγνωσιν ἀληθείας omits the articles and thereby merely stresses the quality of the nouns. Ἐπίγνωσις is more intense than γνῶσις, *Erkenntnis* over against *Kenntnis*. The English has no such companion terms, and we try to convey what the former means by translating it "realization," a knowledge which affects the religious life, *eine die persoenliche Teilnahme in Anspruch nehmende und auf die Person einwirkende Erkenntnis,* one which engrosses the personal religious interest and has its full effect on the person. There may be a false γνῶσις but never a false ἐπίγνωσις. "Of truth" is the objective genitive, meaning "saving truth" or the gospel in its substance as divine reality. Its embodiment is Jesus in his person and his work (John 14:6). "Truth" and "the truth" are regularly used in the New Testament as terms for the gospel, God's objective means for salvation. "Realization of truth" = saving apprehension of and faith in the gospel, the subjective and the objective means combined.

It is an undue limitation to say that "to be saved" is eschatological, for in the case of each person salvation begins when he comes to realization of truth. It is a distinction without a difference to say that the infinitives should be transposed since one is saved by coming to this realization. Here the will of God is expressed, and that will wants the result (salvation) and thus the one means by which this result is attained. The passive idea might have been retained: be saved and be brought to realization. The active removes the idea of compulsion and irresistibility when God *ex nolentibus facit volentes*. No one can possibly in the least degree come by his own efforts; the Father draws him (John 6:44) by his grace and his truth; it is given to him to come (v. 6), and so he comes. Jesus, the Truth, calls, "Follow me!" and, being thus drawn, we come unto him. But some set and harden their hearts against God and so do not come. The mystery as to why so many do this does not lie in God or in the truth but in themselves. In the writer's opinion an explanation of this phenomenon would require that we furnish a reasonable explanation for an unreasonable act, which is an impossibility. The Scriptures do not offer an explanation.

The fact that God, our Savior, wants all men to be saved and come to realization of truth is the reason that our praying for all men is excellent and acceptable in his sight. Ὅς thus has causal force: "because he is the one who," etc.

5) Γάρ elucidates by adding two great facts. Here are mighty facts that are in perfect agreement: the one, that God wants all men to be saved, etc.; then these two, that one and one only is God, and that one and one only is Mediator for God and men, etc. It is inaccurate to speak of proof; when we are shown the facts, they elucidate each other, we see each one with greater clearness. But let us understand the Greek correctly. It cannot be translated: "There is one God, one Mediator also" (R. V.), the numerals modifying the nouns; nor: "God is one, God's and men's Mediator is one," the nouns as subjects, the numerals as predicates. The numerals are the subjects, the nouns the

predicates (hence they are minus the article) : "One
(is) God," not two or more; "One also (is) Mediator
for God and men," not several. Nor should these two
facts be separated, for they have been joined in v. 3,
where "our Savior God" joins them; and they are again
joined here, not merely by καί ("also"), but by this
Mediator who is "Mediator for this one, namely for
God and *men*."

See how perfectly the facts harmonize : Our Savior
God is pleased to have us pray for all men and not
only for ourselves — our Savior God wants all men to
be saved and thus also us and not just us and some
with us — he and also the one who is Mediator is one,
he as Savior God and Christ Jesus as Mediator in the
one, identical relation to all men. Seeing all this, let
us confidently proceed to pray for all men, among them
being those men (kings, etc.) under whom all other
men are placed, whose management is so important
for themselves and for all others.

We cannot refer to Gal. 3:19, 20 in order to obtain
the sense of "Mediator for God and men" (objective
genitives), for Moses was a mediator only in the sense
of an *Uebermittler* who represented the many of Israel
in conveying God's law to them (see this passage).
The same is true regarding Heb. 8:6; 9:15; 12:14,
where Christ is presented as originating and transmitting a better testament and relation between God and
his people than the ones Moses brought to Israel. In
our passage two parties are mentioned so that the
rendering of our versions is substantially correct:
"Mediator between God and men," although "between"
is not in the text. We keep close to the context when
we say that Christ mediates the will (θέλει) of our
Savior God for him and by this realizes the σωθῆναι for
men, so that through him there is salvation for them.
For we must always remember that God and not men,
not even men in conjunction with God accom-

plished this mediation. What Christ did to effect this mediation is stated in v. 6. Christ is the Mediator "of men," of course, of all men.

In the apposition to "Mediator": "a man Christ Jesus," we have the name itself as an apposition to "a man." The emphasis is: *"One* also (is) Mediator for God and men, *a man* Christ Jesus." The fact that this one Mediator is "a man," just "a man," and not one who belongs to a certain class or kind of men, makes his mediation pertain to men as such, ἄνθρωποι, to human beings, none being excepted who are such. Paul is stating only the fact that the one Mediator is "a man"; he states this fact together with the others that God wants all men to be saved and that one is God, one also Mediator, and he Mediator for God and men. Thus as this fact of his being "man" gets its light from the associated facts, so it sheds its light on them, all men, human beings as human beings are involved. "Christ Jesus" is his blessed name, his official, mediatorial title: "Christ," Messiah, Anointed (Matt. 3:16, 17), and his personal name "Jesus," Savior, which was given him by God himself before he was born as man (Matt. 1:21).

6) Another apposition brings forward the main act by which he realized this universal mediatorship: "the one who gave himself a ransom for all," which should be read in one breath with the preceding. This refers to Christ's act in Gethsemane when he literally "gave himself" into the hands of his enemies, to die as he had foretold. This was a voluntary act; he laid down his life, no man could take it from him even also as he took it again, John 10:18. His voluntary sacrifice reveals all the greatness and the nobility of his love and settles once for all the charge of injustice on the part of God, that he should have unjustly punished the innocent instead of the guilty. Jesus gave himself **willingly**, assumed all our guilt and penalty, and God

accepted his all-sufficient sacrifice as "a sweet-smelling savor" (Eph. 5:2).

The substitutionary act of Jesus is here attested in a threefold way: twice by ἀντίλυτρον (by λύτρον which itself means "ransom" and by ἀντί which in this compound has the meaning "instead") and a third time by ὑπέρ, "in behalf of," which the ransom could not be unless it be "instead of." On the latter R. 631 says that in these passages this preposition "has the resultant notion of 'instead,' and only violence to the context can get rid of it." On the former R. 573, etc., says: "In λύτρον ἀντὶ πολλῶν (Matt. 20:28; Mark 10:45) the parallel is more exact. These important doctrinal passages teach the substitutionary conception of Christ's death, not because ἀντί of itself means 'instead,' which is not true, but because the context renders any other resultant idea out of the question. Compare also ἀντίλυτρον ὑπὲρ πάντων by Paul, where both ἀντί and ὑπέρ combine with λύτρον in expressing this idea." See also the whole chapter in Robertson's *The Minister and his Greek New Testament*, 35-42: the papyri evidence on ὑπέρ places the whole matter of substitution beyond all caviling rationalistic question as far as linguistics are concerned. Only one course is open to the objector, namely to refuse to believe what the Scriptures say in plain words. B.-P. 1341: ὑπέρ, *anstelle von, anstatt, in Stellvertretung;* 115, the whole article on ἀντί.

While Paul writes "Mediator for God and *men,*" we now have "himself a ransom for *all*" ("a ransom" is the predicative accusative) ; "men" = "all" even as v. 1 and 4 have "all men." Meyer combines the following passages: The entire human race lay bound in the power of darkness, Col. 1:13, and could not free itself, Matt. 16:26; then Christ came and paid the necessary ἀντίλυτρον, even himself, his own life, Matt. 20:28, and so obtained for us all the priceless σωτηρία. Other passages may be similarly combined. From λύτρον in Matt. 20:28

and Mark 10:45, plus ἀντίλυτρον in Paul we have ἀπολύτρωσις, "ransoming"; this English term is better than
the usual rendering "redemption."

The remark is true enough that Jesus had to be both
man and God in order to mediate between the two as he
did; yet that is not what Paul brings out by "a man
Christ Jesus." Again it is true that Jesus had to be
man in order to die for us; yet this is not what Paul
stresses here. We correlate "a man" with "for men"
in connection with what precedes as we have indicated
above. Docetism appeared later, became connected
with Gnosticism, and toward the end of the second century appeared as the heretical sect of the Docetæ, I John
4:3. To speak of "the representative man" is to misunderstand Paul who writes ἄνθρωπος, "a man," in the
sense of the R. V.: "One (is) Mediator, (himself) man,
Christ Jesus." Subordinationism finds no support in
this statement. The fact of Christ's being man in no
way contradicts his being God. In the work of pro-
viding salvation for all men the ransoming was assumed by the second person. Paul states the mighty
facts; theologians have devised their theories about
the atonement because they were not satisfied with the
facts as they stand.

Grammatically it makes no difference whether τὸ
μαρτύριον καιροῖς ἰδίοις is made an apposition to all that
precedes in v. 5, 6 or an accusative absolute. To restrict it to the last apposition ὁ δούς κτλ., is untenable
since this is itself an apposition; thus also the sense
cannot be that Christ's act of giving himself a ransom
for all is the testimony in act, the testifying to men,
however the following relative clause (v. 7) is then
understood. "This testimony for their own seasons"
is that of the gospel. The "witnesses" bearing it are
the apostles (Acts 1:8) who could, indeed, testify at
firsthand. Their testimony stands for all time. Paul
was added to the Twelve and was qualified as an apostle

by the fact that Jesus appeared to him on the road to Damascus.

We may regard the dative as temporal: "in their own times," or as *commodi:* "for their own times," these denoting the καιροί or "seasons" of the New Testament, from the time the ransom was paid until the last day. Before this, in the "seasons" of the Old Testament, there were and could be, strictly speaking, only promises and prophecies about the will of God for all men and about this Mediator for all of them. Now there is "this testimony" that all the promises and prophecies are fulfilled.

7) So Paul is able to add: **for which** (testimony) **I on my part was appointed a herald and an apostle — I am speaking truth, not lying — a teacher of Gentiles in faith and truth.**

This relative clause adds the final item to all that has been said about "all men" and having the churches pray for all of them. Since this is a relative clause it brings the secondary item; the primary ones are God's will that all men be saved, that one is God, one is Mediator, and that this is he who gave himself a ransom for all. Paul's appointment to teach such as are Gentiles (ἐθνῶν, qualitative, no article) is in line with these facts yet is secondary. To put this into a relative clause which is attached to "the testimony" is also proper because Paul completes the thought of v. 4: "and come to realization of truth." The bulk of humanity consisted of Gentiles, and in order to help to reach this vast bulk with salvation so that Gentiles as well as Jews might come to realization of truth, Paul was especially appointed an apostle of the Gentiles. We thus see that this clause rounds out the presentation concerning "all men."

It is rather unkind to say that Paul again obtrudes himself, his office and his authority. Nor is it correct to say that he was always beset by enemies who challenged his authority and then to find some of these enemies in chapter 1. In chapter 1 he is not fighting enemies and is not vindicating his authority. Those to whom he refers were foolish teachers and nothing more. In this second chapter Paul has no more to say about them and takes up the public worship of the churches, which is something that is entirely different. A reference to passages in other letters that speak about enemies is irrelevant.

"For which (testimony) appointed was I on my part a herald and an apostle," ἐγώ, I in particular, to help to spread this testimony which was intended for all men. "Herald" = one who makes a loud, public announcement as he is ordered by a superior; paired with this word is "apostle" which = one sent forth on a commission by a superior. The two convey one general idea, both as a herald and as an apostle one would be "appointed." Instead of at once adding to both nouns the apposition "a teacher of Gentiles in faith and truth," Paul prefixes the assurance: "I am speaking truth, not lying." We see that he does the same in Rom. 9:1.

This parenthesis is misunderstood when it is applied to "a herald and apostle"; it looks forward. Twelve others had also been appointed heralds and apostles; ἐγώ, "I on my part," points to something distinctive beyond that: *Paul's* appointment as herald and apostle was to the effect that *he* should be this as a "teacher of Gentiles." It is this point of being *their* teacher that is sealed with the assurance: "I am speaking truth, not lying." "Teacher" does not intend to add a third function. Paul is not speaking regarding different functions, for "apostle" expresses no function that is comparable to heralding and to teaching. No "and" joins "teacher" to herald and apostle, for "teacher" is an apposition to both "herald and apostle" and states the real point: "a teacher of Gentiles." Yet not "of *the* Gentiles," for Jesus sent out the Twelve to "all nations" (Matt. 28:19) ; Paul alone, however, was sent to Gentiles in a most specific way (Acts 9:15; 26:17, 18).

That explains the assurance that he is telling the truth; *he* was specifically the Lord's herald and apostle as a teacher of pagans. Paul does not think that Timothy might perhaps doubt this. Had Timothy not been Paul's assistant among these Gentiles for many a year? Once again let us remember that, while this letter instructs Timothy as to what he is to do in the Asian churches and states these instructions in written form, it at the same time certifies Timothy as Paul's representative and also certifies these instructions for all these churches so that no one may question them or Timothy's authority. Paul always uses such assurances when he is able to appeal to no other witnesses, when something is only in his own heart or conscience, and he does so here where he can bring no witnesses for the type of appointment the Lord had given him. The point is essential here because it brings out the fact that God wants "all men" to come to realization of truth. The great host of men were Gentiles; God made adequate provision to have the truth of the gospel brought also to *them*.

The closing phrase has been variously interpreted. Let us at once say that we do not accept the interpretation which regards it as adding two personal attributes to Paul as a "teacher": "in faithfulness and truthfulness," *treulich und wahrheitlich*; or the view that it is a hendiadys, "in true faithfulness"; or the view that one is a quality in Paul: his own faith, while the other is the object of his teaching, the truth or doctrine he taught. After naming the personal objects of διδάσκαλος with the objective genitive ἐθνῶν, Paul could not add the impersonal objects with two additional objective genitives; so he chooses ἐν which has so wide a range in Greek and writes: "a teacher of Gentiles in connection with faith and truth." Anarthrous "truth" is the same truth that was mentioned in v. 4, the gospel truth. The statement that Paul should then have placed "faith" in second place is not warranted; for both is done by good logical writers, they at times have: cause — effect; at other times: effect — then its cause.

Stellhorn states that the sphere (ἐν) in which Paul operated as a teacher was not worldly science or art, attainments of human knowledge and ability, new political and social ideas and ideals, but "faith and truth," truth as the contents of faith. "The basic error of our own religiously muddled, in the worst sense unionistic times that everything depends on faith as a general confidence of the heart in a Higher Being and little or nothing on the contents of this faith, surely has no support in Paul as little as in Christ or in general in the New Testament . . . What relates to faith and truth, to faith as the saving confidence of the heart and to truth as the contents and ground of this faith, to preach and to teach that, to expound and to inculcate that is his (the preacher's) office, this he must take into the pulpit, this he must make the all-controlling object of his study and work, and nothing else. All else dare serve only this one thing." Incidentally, this expositon explains why Paul places "truth" in the second place. As far as the construction with ἐν is concerned, we still have it in English: teacher in music, in Latin, etc.

*   *   *

Men and Women in the Public Services

8) As was the case in v. 1, οὖν turns to the new subject and is not inferential. **I intend, then, the men to do the praying in every place, lifting up holy hands without wrath and wrong consideration.**

Βούλομαι is synonymous with θέλω. Thayer's discussion of these two words is rather disappointing; C.-K. 224 is to the point: the former is wider, "to have in mind, to intend"; the latter means "to be energetically resolved," to have the will for the deed. Here "I will" (A. V.) is too nearly like the latter, and "I desire" (R. V.) is too weak, nor is "I wish" correct. As far as βούλομαι and παρακαλῶ in v. 1 are concerned, they are of equal force. Both simply direct Timothy, the latter urging him in regard to what is to be done in the public services, the former stating who is to do this. While either might be used in either place, to urge *what* is to be done fits exactly, and to say *who* is to do this again fits in the same way.

Προσεύχεσθαι, "to pray" or "to do the praying" is the broader term, which includes all that is implied in the four nouns used in v. 1. In v. 1 "petitions, prayers," etc., are properly without articles; now "the men" properly has the generic article. In v. 1 the four nouns imply no contrast with four opposites; here "the men" are in contrast with all who are women (v. 9). This difference is not felt in English as witness the way in which our two versions translate; but in the Greek this is plain. The men only and no women whatever are to do the praying in the public worship of the congregations. "In every place" = in every city or town where there is a congregation, where public worship is held. Timothy is Paul's representative in the whole Asian territory and not merely in the one congregation in Ephesus. "In every place" has no reference to private worship, that of one or of a few individuals at home.

The public worship and the entire management of it in each congregation were in the hands of the elders (5:17 refers to them). There was as yet no individual who was sole pastor. One or the other of these elders led the congregation in prayer; one or the other of them read from Scripture; one or the other likewise taught ("in word and teaching," 5:17) and prophesied (I Cor. 14), i. e., restated parts of the divine revelation. But all this was not restricted to the elders. Other members who had the proper ability were allowed to do the same things in and for the congregation.

All of this was inherited from the synagogue, even the arrangement to have such elders was borrowed from this institution. We know that in the synagogues the Jewish elders called upon Paul and Barnabas to speak, Acts 13:14-16, etc., because they were regarded as men who had the proper ability. In this way Paul and his assistants obtained the privilege to present the gospel in synagogue after synagogue. In I Cor. 14:29-33 Paul directs that all speaking be done in due order, each man who has something to offer is to await his turn. The same is true with regard to the public praying referred to here. Under direction of the called elders in every congregation only men are to lead in public prayer and not women, now one man, now another as the service offered occasion. The word Paul uses is οἱ ἄνδρες, "the men" (males), *Maenner*, not, as in v. 1, 4, 5, ἄνθρωποι, human beings, *Menschen*.

Paul's presentation affords no basis for assuming that a feminist or "woman's rights" movement was becoming evident in these churches. There were comparatively few Jews among the converts, who were acquainted with the synagogue and the Old Testament regarding women and the public services. These congregations were new, a number of them had only recently been established. Questions such as this one regarding women would arise. When they did, here was the proper answer, which is given in much the same way as it is in I Cor. 14:34, 35. In the rest of the letter other questions are similarly answered.

"Lifting up holy hands," etc., is only an incidental addition regarding the proper outer and inner attitude of the men who lead the congregations in prayer. To stand expresses honor to God, and to raise the hands is the attitude of one who is beseeching. One stands in the presence of superiors; one stretches out the hands when pleading, and since God is always above us, the hands are lifted up. The Scriptures also mention other attitudes. They are by no means immaterial, for they reflect the corresponding attitude of the mind and the heart. When one man voices the prayers, petitions, etc., of a whole congregation, his outward attitude is the more important, for all those present see it. Our ministers and our congregations stand.

We now fold the hands, which expresses the thought that, when we turn to God, we fold up and put away all that our hands are busy with in life so that none of these things distract our thoughts while we pray. Prostration, kneeling, bowing the head have their very proper significance and are to be used when they are in place. When Paul writes "the men" he means: "only men and not women"; when he uses the participle "lifting up hands" he does not mean: "only so," as though no other proper position of the hands were acceptable to God. Jesus did not always lift up his hands, he sometimes lifted up his eyes.

The important feature is "holy" hands, "without wrath and wrong considerations." Ὅσιος is used only a few times in the New Testament and is best explained by Trench as being the opposite of "polluted." "Holy hands" are such as have not been polluted by our previous actions, for if we raised polluted hands we should insult God by raising such hands to him, he would see the pollution and turn away. Ἅγιος would express separation and devotion to God and is used much more frequently. Trench refers to the case of Joseph in bringing out the difference: by reverencing the sanctities of marriage, which he could not violate without pollution, Joseph was ὅσιος; by keeping aloof from the temptress and being devoted to God he was ἅγιος. Since ὅσιος was frequently regarded as a word that had endings for only two genders, its construction with "hands" (and not with the participle) is assured.

"Without wrath" refers to men. If there is anger in the heart, no matter against whom, such a heart is rendered unfit for all worship (Eph. 4:31; Col. 3:8). Wrath is so prominently mentioned here because of the way in which it is put forward by Jesus in Matt. 5:22. To find wrath mentioned together with praying reminds one of Matt. 6:14, 15, where forgiving is mentioned in connection with prayer.

Wrath is, however, only a sample of sin in the heart; it is here combined with διαλογισμός, "wrong thought" of any kind. The best definition of this word is given by C.-K. 683: "In the New Testament only with evil connotation regarding reprehensible thoughts and considerations." This is exactly to the point here, for it covers all kinds of wrong thoughts regarding our fellow men or regarding God. This definition is also appropriate in Luke 24:38, and Rom. 14:1. We thus do not accept the rendering "disputing" (R. V.) and "doubting" (A. V. and R. V. margin) and the applicatory remarks based on these renderings. All wrong thought of any kind must be repentantly removed from the heart when we pray. The fact that this applies to those who are being led in prayer as well as to those who lead is self-evident.

9) **Likewise (I intend) that women adorn themselves in adorning dress with modesty and sobriety, not in braids and gold or pearls or expensive clothing but — what befits women professing godly piety — by means of good works.**

We supply only the main verb "I intend" from v. 8. Those who supply also the infinitive: "Likewise I intend that women pray," have difficulty with the infinitive κοσμεῖν which they then construe as epexegetical or as consecutive, but praying is *not* adorning themselves. This adorning takes place *before* they go to church and is not a result of this churchgoing. Just as we have an infinitive with "the men," so we have an infinitive with "women"; the infinitives are even placed chiastically. This answers the question as to how all the modifying phrases are to be construed: all three are to be construed with the one infinitive. It would be rather strange to understand Paul to say: "that women (pray) in adorning attire and (then epexegetically) adorn themselves with modesty," etc.; or consecutively: "so as to adorn themselves," etc. This construction is grammatically untenable on account of μετά, "in company with," which does not modify the infinitive; it modifies the ἐν phrase so that the phrases "in adorning attire with modesty and sensibleness" form a unit.

"Women," without the article = women as women; in v. 8 "the men" = these as distinguished from women. The fact that Paul is still speaking of public worship, of how women ought to appear there, ought not to be questioned, for in v. 11, 12 he continues to speak about public worship. This is, however, true, that "to adorn themselves" means to do this *prior* to attending public worship, and not *during* worship. The fact that, if women dress heart and body for church as here described, they will dress in no contrary way at any other time, does not need to be said. The holy hands without wrath, etc., are not a parallel to the phrases used regarding women.

There is a neat play on words in κοσμίῳ and κοσμεῖν which we seek to imitate: "in adorning attire — adorn themselves." Luther sensed this when he translated *in zierlichem Kleide sich schmuecken* although he has been faulted for using *zierlich*. Let some say what they will about Paul, he here states that women are to dress in good taste when they prepare to attend church. "Adorn" means to adorn, and the adjective "adorning" emphasizes this point. Καταστολή (found only here in the New Testament) is not *wuerdige Haltung* (B.-P. 655) but "dress" (literally, something let down), "habit," even as the simplex στολή always = a flowing garment or robe.

But this fair outward dress must ever be "in company with modesty and sobriety," which are inward. Αἰδώς = *Scheu, Scham, Ehrfurcht*, the negative side of the moral sensibility which shrinks from transgressing the limits of propriety; we may say "modesty," "shamefastness" (R. V. and Trench; not the corrupted word "shamefacedness" of our A. V.). The companion word σωφροσύνη = "sobriety," in Acts 26:25 it is like our "saneness" (our versions "soberness"). It is often translated "self-control" and is then uually referred to sexual passions in our passage despite Acts 26:25. Because these two words are here referred to women they should not be unduly restricted to sex. Vanity, pride, and other improprieties are here also excluded. Extravagant dress is generally worn for mere display with the secret desire to produce envy.

Isa. 3:18-24 names some of the extravagant female ornaments. Paul says: "not braids and gold or pearls or expensive clothes." I Pet. 3:3 writes: "not the outward adorning of plaiting of hair and of wearing things of gold or putting on apparel." This is the vanity of personal display in order to attract general attention, in particular to fill other women with envy, to outshine rivals. These are "braids" or "plaits" of the hair, the putting it up in a showy, unusual fashion so as to become conspicuous, and not just common and customary braids.

Paul does not say where the gold or the pearls are worn, whether in the braided hair, or in chains about the neck, or in pins, etc., on the dress. Display of jewelry is referred to. Aside from religion good taste forbids such display. The two "or" are not disjunctive so that, when gold is worn, pearls would not be; but conjunctive, which is a common use of "or" that draws attention to each item separately, to the gold for one thing, to the pearls for another, and also to the expensive clothes. The fact that flashy jewelry would be displayed with costly ἱματισμός or "clothing" is apparent. Such a woman wants to make a stunning impression. Her mind is entirely on herself; she is unfit for worship.

This verse does not refer merely to sex attraction. How many women who are past that age are given to the silly vanity of dress? Paul is not insisting on drab dress. Even this may be worn with vanity; the very drabness may be made a display. Each according to her station in life: the queen not being the same as her lady in waiting, the latter not the same as her noble mistress. Each with due propriety as modesty and propriety will indicate to her both when attending divine services and when appearing in public elsewhere.

10) When Paul now turns to the positive he does not become redundant as some think, for to the inner virtues of modesty and sobriety as shown in attire he adds the adornment of corresponding "good works" which are lovely in the eyes of God and of man, far beyond jewels and costly clothing: "but — what befits women professing godly piety — by means of good works." We accept this simple construction. The parenthetical clause "what befits" = ὅ, this thing of adorning themselves by means of good works, the relative means neither "in which" nor "according to which." Supply: "but (that women adorn themselves) by means of good works" — the thing "which befits

women professing godly piety" (this noun is found only here, the adjective is found in John 9:31).

Κοσμεῖν is not transitive, it is reflexive as in v. 9: "adorn themselves," and thus can be construed with either prepositions or with both: "adorn themselves in" (v. 9) and "by means of" (διά, v. 10). Women are to use "good works" as their adornment. Any and all of such works are referred to, we do not restrict them. We do not ask: "How about men?" The whole subject of adornment belongs peculiarly to woman — ever will. There is no need to say more. Here and in 6:21 ἐπαγγέλλομαι is to be understood in its modified meaning; it originally meant "to promise" but here means "to profess." The parenthesis should not be unduly extended: "professing by means of good works."

11) The asyndeton indicates a new point. Attention is arrested by the absence of a connective. The second point regarding women is thus indicated. **A woman, in quietness let her be learning in all subjection.** This = I Cor. 14:34, 35, which is a fuller statement: "The women are to keep silent in the assemblies, for it is not permitted to them to speak; on the contrary, they are to be in subjection even as also the law declares. Moreover, if they want to learn anything (on some special point) they are to inquire of their own men (men folks and not just husbands) at home." Paul does not state why he adds this. The view that Timothy had asked him about it in a letter is not satisfactory, for Paul would then have indicated this. To think that women were seeking to teach in public is also stating too much; there is no hint in the text to this effect. This is also true with regard to I Cor. 14. Timothy knew what Paul had written to the Corinthians; he also knew about the apostolic arrangement in all the congregations. He would meet this as well as other questions; Paul fortifies him in writing as he

does in regard to these other matters. The gospel brought a new freedom. What did this imply in regard to this subject? This question would certainly be asked.

In v. 9 Paul has written the plural: "that women are to adorn themselves," etc. It is characteristic of Paul now to use the individualizing singular. He might have reversed the two. As the plural refers to "women" as a class, all of them, so the singular refers to "a woman" as such, any and every woman — certainly not just to "a wife." The word used in v. 8 is not "husbands." "In quietness" she is to be learning and not to be assisting in the conduct of the services as qualified men are. The imperative "is to be learning" means by the teaching of others, that of the elders and of qualified men whom they approve. "In quietness" = "without herself talking, without placing herself on an equality with the men conducting the service and doing the teaching," Stellhorn. The imperative is placed between the two phrases, which means that "in all subjection" modifies "in quietness let her be learning" and not "in quietness" only. This quiet learning is to be done "in all subjection," ὑποταγή, ranging herself under, not putting herself forward, not in self-assertion, not making herself heard. "All" is not intensive but extensive. The reference to Tit. 2:5 is irrelevant, for our passage does not refer to subjection to husbands.

The position and the spheres assigned to the sexes in their concreated natures is not altered by Christianity; they are rather sanctified by it. The fact that women may teach each other is stated in Tit. 2:3, 4; that they may teach their children in private is stated in 3:15. Nor does Acts 18:26, the fact that Aquila and his wife instructed Apollos in their home, constitute an exception to what Paul says here and in I Cor. 14. Ellicott exclaims: "What grave arguments these few verses supply us with against some of the unnatural and unscriptural theories of modern times!"

12) Δέ is not adversative but only specifies more closely. **Now to teach I do not permit to woman, nor to exercise authority over a man, but to be in quietness.** The fact that a woman may not lead the congregation in prayer is settled by v. 8; the fact that she may not teach in the public assembly is now added. "I do not permit" = "it is not permitted," I Cor. 14:34. The verb means to turn something over to someone. This is not an autocratic ruling of Paul's; *he* does not permit because *the law* does not do so (I Cor. 14:34), namely the νόμος or Torah, i. e., Genesis, in the section which deals with the creation and the fall. If Paul would permit this he would be like those who set aside the Torah and decree as they please. If this statement were positive it would be followed by an explicative καί; since it is negative, we have explicative οὐδέ, for "neither to exercise authority over a man" states the point involved in the forbidding "to teach." To teach is to act as an αὐθέντης over all those taught, as a self-doer, a master or — to put it strongly — an autocrat. The verb appears here for the first time in the Greek, it is a vernacular term, αὐτοδικεῖν being the literary term. Verbs of ruling govern the genitive.

The opposite helps to bring out the meaning: "but to be in quietness." Those who are taught sit in quietness and learn; the one who teaches acts as the master who is to be heard, heeded, and obeyed. Because of its very nature his is the dominant position and function; the rest are there quietly to receive and to be directed. Nor is Paul speaking of ordinary schoolroom teaching, where secular knowledge is imparted by one who is authority enough in some branch of learning to sit at the teacher's desk. A learned woman may discourse to a whole class of men.

Paul refers to teaching *Scripture* and not to impart-ing intellectual secular information to the mind. The public teacher of God's people does not only tell others what they need to know, but in the capacity of such a teacher he stands before his audience to rule and gov-ern it with the Word. That position and that αὐθεντεῖν the Word itself accords to the man and withholds from the woman, and no woman may step into the place of the man without violating the very Word she would try to teach to both women and men. Her effort to do so would be self-contradictory in God's eyes despite what the world may say. Paul is bound as much in this as we all are. God and his Word have not "turned over" to him or to anybody else a right to say anything on this relation of the sexes in the church that is dif-ferent from what Paul says.

How all this affects other questions such as wom-an's right to vote in congregational meetings, her pro-tests of conscience in matters of doctrine and of prac-tice in the church, important work that is especially assigned to women, etc., we have indicated in expound-ing I Cor. 14:34. See at length Loy, *The Rights of Women in the Church;* also, *The Christian Church,* 292, etc.; in brief, my own, *The Active Church Mem-ber,* 91, etc. "But to be in quietness" after "I permit" is an instance of brachylogy.

13) Why Paul cannot permit this is elucidated by γάρ. **For Adam was formed as the first, then Eve; and Adam was not beguiled, but the woman, having been completely beguiled, has come to be in trans-gression.**

These are the facts, all of them are stated by aor-ists. These facts are what the νόμος, the Torah, records in Genesis 2 and 3. These facts are valid for all time in the church; the gospel does not alter them. These facts debar women from any position in the church by which she would become the head. There are two facts, and the greater is stated first although the second, too, is very decisive.

Adam and Eve were not created at the same time. Paul's brief statement is to the point. He uses the word ἐπλάσθη; the verb πλάσσω means to form or mold and refers to the bodies of the first pair because Genesis says nothing about the derivation of Eve's soul. Πρῶτος is the predicate adjective and not the adverb. Adam was created as "the first." He existed for some time before Eve was formed. That certainly reveals God's intention that Eve was not to direct, rule, supervise him, that she was not to be the head, but he. It is said truly that priority in creation includes dignity, I Cor. 11:3. God could have created both at the same time; he did not do this. The whole race was to be of *one* blood (Acts 17:26), was to have *one* head. Adam's creation is recorded in Gen. 2:7, and Eve's is not recorded until Gen. 2:21, 22. The facts pertaining to their position and their relation antedate the entrance of sin; Adam's creation precedes even the planting of Eden (Gen. 2:8). The fact that Adam was at once created as a male, and that thus Eve's creation was already in the mind of God, changes nothing as to priority and headship. Jesus refers to this fact that Adam was at once created as a male as being the foundation of marriage (Matt. 19:4); yet this only the more makes Adam and the husband the head.

"Then Eve." This brief adverb "then" = Gen. 2:18: "It is not good that the man should be alone; I will make a help meet for him" in the sense of I Cor. 11:8, 9. "The man is *not* of the woman, but the woman *of* the man; *neither* was the man created *for* the woman, but the woman *for* the man." "Then" also = Gen. 2:22-24, Eve was taken from the body of man, formed from a rib of his side (not from his head, his hand, his foot), brought to Adam (not he to her), "bone of my bones, and flesh of my flesh, called Woman (*Isha*), because she was taken out of Man (*Ish*)," her name stating her relation and her origin. Both are derived and thus second and secondary and not first and primary.

Can these things that were done by God ever be changed? But is this "rib-story" not just an ancient myth? The use of the word "myth" does not remove from the New Testament the use that Jesus and Paul have made of this record in Genesis. To wipe out the account in Genesis wipes out the truth of Jesus and of the New Testament. If these are mythical as to the very origin of man, can anything be true and trustworthy regarding the redemption and salvation of man? If Genesis is a "myth," what was the original fact? An animal origin, an animal evolution? Does this hypothesis change the nature of man and of woman as we now see this nature? Does it destroy the natural relation of the two?

"There are effeminate, long-haired men who claim the rights of women, and masculine short-haired women who claim the rights of men, and, in virtue of the good sense with which the Creator has endowed humanity, they become the laughingstock of the sober-minded in both sexes. But when such men, shouting liberty and equality, assert their right to be women and set up a lugubrious whine because all nature and all social instincts are against them, they become not only ridiculous, but simply contemptible. And when such women claim the rights of men, what then? Why, they are not men, and all their crying and clamoring and puling and whining will not make them men or secure for them the right to be men. How could they have such right when God has unalterably made them women and destined them to be useful and happy in their womanhood?" Loy. God did not make even all the angels alike. He made both angels and

human beings. Who will undo and re-do his creative
work?

"The fact that all believers have the same spiritual
prerogatives in the church (which are those of children as well) never for one moment abolishes the
differences due to nature. Always the husband is the
head of the family — two heads make a monstrosity.
As woman has her own divinely appointed sphere, into
which man intrudes only when he is a fool, so man has
his divinely appointed sphere, into which it is folly for
a woman to intrude. As in a normal family the husband and father leads and directs, and the sons gradually rise to the same duty, so in the larger family of
the congregation the mature men have the duty to lead
and direct. God's people gladly follow God's order,
and recognize that any wisdom of their own, dictating
a different course, is only pretense." *The Active Church
Member* (Lenski).

14) Καί adds the second fact to the first. This
is not done because a second is needed; yet Paul lets
two witnesses speak. "Adam was not beguiled, but
the woman, by being completely beguiled, has come to
be in transgression." This fact is not complimentary
to woman. By taking the leadership into her own
hands without warrant the fatal sin was committed.
Paul uses the simplex "was not deceived" when speaking of Adam and the compound with ἐκ when speaking
of the woman, she was "completely deceived." The
point to be noted is the fact that the completeness of
the happening (perfective ἐκ) deserves notice. "The
woman" is certainly Eve, yet the use of "the woman"
in place of her personal name emphasizes her sex so
that in v. 15 Paul may continue with the generaliza-
tion "she shall be saved," which applies to any and to
every woman, and after that with the plural "if they
remain in faith," etc.

But this is only formal. By saying "the woman" Paul means that she who as the woman was to be Adam's helpmeet, she was the one who also induced him to sin. The aorist participle states the fact: "completely beguiled." The perfect γέγονε = came to be in transgression and remained there. We discard the older "pregnant" idea of ἐν; it involves no εἰς: "got *into* and so was *in*." Nor is παράβασις a mild term for Eve's sin. Not inadvertently did she "step aside"; she "stepped aside" with God's plain command and threat on her own lips (Gen. 3:2, 3). This word is used in the New Testament with reference to a fatal stepping aside, for the Greek παρά means "aside" whereas the English (Latin) employs *trans,* "across": transgression. Both words mark the fullest guilt.

Despite all his brevity Paul regards the account of the fall as historical fact. Yet some of the comment on this passage is scarcely acceptable. Thus when it is said that Satan attacked Eve because she was the weaker vessel. Is this not confusing the physical with the moral? Eve was surely as perfect and as strong morally as was Adam. Again it is said that Satan promised himself an easier victory in the case of Eve because she was subordinate. But is it not true that our race did not sin when Eve fell, that it sinned only when the head, Adam, fell? "By *one man* (ἀνήρ, not ἄνθρωπος) sin entered into the world," Rom. 5:12. The victory over Eve alone would have been barren; Satan's aim was Adam. But this comment is true, that both Eve and Adam had to violate not only the command of God not to eat but also their respective positions toward each other in order to effect the fall: Eve her position of subordination, Adam his headship; she gave him to eat, and he did eat (Gen. 3:6, 12). God confronts both of them, but Adam first and then Eve. Eve usurped the headship in the fall; Adam, who was the head, became the feet and followed Eve in the παρ-άβασις, in the stepping aside.

Not much is usually said about the two statements that Adam "was not beguiled" while Eve was "completely beguiled." In Gen. 3:13 Eve says that the serpent beguiled her, ἠπάτησεν, the LXX rendering, the simplex; in II Cor. 11:3 Paul says that the serpent beguiled her, ἐξηπάτησεν, the compound verb as in our passage. It will not do to erase the difference. The simplex is here used with reference to Adam, the compound with reference to Eve. When Paul *denies* the deception of Adam, the simplex suffices; when he *asserts* the deception of Eve, the compound (perfective) is in place. But the latter does not mean that Eve did not know what she was doing. She had both God's command and Satan's lies before her; she accepted the latter and set aside the former, in this way she was deceived. Note the passive which implies one who did the deceiving. Eve let the lying promise of the serpent move her to disregard the threat of God. To accept, to believe, and to act on a lie in place of the truth is to be deceived indeed. An excellent presentation can be found in Meusel, *Kirchliches Handlexikon: Suendenfall.*

Paul writes: "Adam was not deceived." To explain that he was not the *first* to be deceived alters the sense. To say that he was deceived *indirectly* while Eve was deceived *directly*, does the same. To say that the serpent deceived the woman, but the woman did not deceive the man but *persuaded* him (Bengel, and others), is not in accord with the facts; for the serpent did as much persuading as Eve. Deception works by means of persuasion. Let us venture to say only this: "Adam followed Eve and was thus not deceived. She had sinned, and Adam had her before him when she came to him with the forbidden fruit. Thus he was not deceived. Yet when she came with the forbidden fruit, 'he did eat' (Gen. 3:6, 8)." You ask how he could do this. The only answer is: "Both Eve's act and Adam's are irrational." To ask how either could be done is to ask for a rational explanation of an irrational act. No man can give that.

May we say: "Paul's point is that the woman demonstrated her inability to lead the man, and that thus Christian women must not try to lead men?" I do not think that this explanation is adequate. Then Adam certainly demonstrated the same thing regarding himself. We can also certainly say that now, since sin is here, whenever a man is ignorant or when he goes wrong, a woman should lead him aright, but should do this in her divinely appointed position. Acts 18:24-26 is one example; Pilate's wife is another although she was unsuccessful (Matt. 27:19).

Paul's point is the divinely appointed relation between man and woman. In that relation each must keep his and her place. To point to ability in leadership deflects the thought. Paul does not here speak of the terrible disobedience to God's command not to eat. Moses does this. Paul first (v. 13) makes plain the two positions of the sexes, secondly (v. 14) the fact that Eve deserted her position. There is no need to say more, namely that Adam then also deserted his. Verses 9-15 deal with women and their position in the church in relation to men. Let the women remain in their subordinate position. Paul himself states what he wants men to do.

The question regarding queens, whether they are Christian or not, who rule earthly kingdoms, does not belong here where churches are discussed. Church and state are separate.

A word should be said regarding the charisma of prophecy which was bestowed also upon women. But first let us see what this charisma is, I Thess. 5:20; Rom. 12:6; I Cor. 14:3. Then let us consider Loy's remarks. "It is certainly gratuitous to assume that the silence of women in the public assemblies of the church, because they must not usurp authority over men, is inconsistent with the bestowal of prophetic gifts upon them. The Lord who bestows them offers ample opportunities to use them without violating his ordinance. It is not necessary that they should appear as teachers in the public assemblies of the church; they can do their work in private, for which they are much better adapted. It is not necessary that they should immodestly present themselves in public before the gaze of men in the attempt to usurp authority over them by presuming to be their teachers when there is plenty of work to be done among their own sex and among the children. The thought that woman is wronged when she is limited to her own sphere as woman, and when her claim to be a man and to do a man's work in the church is not admitted, is as irrational as it is impious. There is plenty of room for the exercise of her gifts in the place which God has assigned her." Let us add the fact that in the very chapter in which Paul deals at length with the use of this gift, I Cor. 14, he writes (v. 34): "Let your women keep silence in the churches! For it is not permitted unto them to speak, but to be under obedience, as also saith the law." Some take the charisma of prophecy to be a reception of direct and immediate revelation. They thus speak of "exceptions" from Paul's v. 11 and think that God makes them.

In the entire Old Testament but five women are called "prophetess": Miriam, Exod. 15:20, etc., only because she led the women of Israel in a great hymn of praise; Deborah, Judges 4:4, etc., only because she delivered a direct revelation to Barak; Huldah, II Kings 22:14, etc.; II Chron. 34:22, etc., only because she, too, had a direct revelation to convey; Noadiah, Neh. 6:14, a false prophetess; Isaiah's wife in Isa. 8:3, only because she was his wife. There is little material here for the advocates of woman preachers in the Christian Church.

15) When Paul continues: **saved, however, shall she be by way of childbearing if they remain in faith and love and sanctification together with sobriety,** the change of tense from the preceding aorists to the future shows that "the woman," which refers to Eve in v. 14, is now extended so as to refer to woman in general. We do not regard the mild δέ as a strong ἀλλά, "but" (R. V.). It merely adds this further statement in regard to the status of woman in the church. How she is to be outwardly and inwardly adorned when attending church; how she is there to learn and not to teach or to exert authority over the men because God did not intend that she should do this when he created her, and because by going contrary to this intention of God she brought on the fall: all this Paul has just said. Now this is completed by indicating in a few words her status in general as a Christian woman, namely her great sphere of motherhood in the family, a motherhood full of the essentials of the Christian salvation and life. This also ends the subject for the supervision Timothy is to exercise.

"Saved shall she be" states this supreme thing first. By not being permitted to engage in the public work of teaching, by letting men attend to that work, woman is not in the least curtailed as far as her being saved is concerned. No one is saved by teaching; all are saved by learning (v. 11), by remaining in faith, etc. Such learning will include a knowledge of what position and sphere God assigns to his children in the church and will produce thankfulness for the allotment he has made. Because of the διά phrase some alter the sense of "shall be saved" so that it means less than obtaining eternal salvation. This verb has its full soteriological meaning.

It seems rather out of place to think that Paul makes "childbearing" a means of salvation for woman, διά with the genitive does not, however, invariably denote means. Here and elsewhere it denotes *Art und Weise* (B.-P. 281), which is often called the accompanying circumstance. The great natural function of woman is childbearing, motherhood, with all that this implies for a saved woman. If our overrefined ears seem too delicate for "childbearing," it may be well to remember that each of us still has his "birthday," that we all joyfully celebrate Jesus' birthday, that the whole subject of birth is as openly mentioned in our day, if not more so, than in any other age, that motherhood (= childbearing) is today glorified with more sentimentality than ever.

"Childbearing" includes the rearing of the children, which means Christian rearing to every Christian woman. Paul has in mind what we read in his other letters: the Christian family and home, the mother surrounded by her children, happy in these outlets for her love and affection, in this enrichment for herself and for them, Eph. 6:1, etc.; Col. 3:20. "By way of childbearing" speaks of the highest ideal of Christian (and even secular) womanhood. Nothing shall erase or even dim that for us. Yet the subject is "the woman," which includes also women of all ages, also girls who die before maturity, and women who may never marry, and those who are married but remain childless. God's providence in individual lives in no way destroys his creative purposes. But when a woman deliberately contravenes his purposes and, although a mother bore her, will not herself bear a child in her marriage, God will reckon with her, the more severely if she professes godliness (v. 10).

Some would connect this childbearing with "the seed of the woman" (Gen. 3:15), with God's Son "made of a woman" (γενόμενον ἐκ γυναικός). They feel that διά must express means; that childbirth was the means of bringing the Savior into the world. They stress the article: by means of "the" childbirth. Then follow their arguments: this childbearing which was laid upon the woman as a penalty by means of God's wonderful plan was to bring the salvation into the world: she who caused the man to sin and to bring damnation into the world, she by the penalty laid on her was to help bring salvation for herself and for all. This argument can easily be met. Childbearing goes back to Gen. 1:28 and to Paradise. Childbearing was never the curse. The pain added to it because of the fall, this alone constituted the curse; and from this curse of pain the Savior did not come. Dropping this strange reference to the curse of birthpains, the fact that the Son of God was conceived and born of the Virgin Mary by God's miraculous act means no more than that God used this one woman for his saving purpose. Nor does this effect women as a class more than men as a class, or, stated in a different way, all have the Savior alike. It is idealizing to see either all mothers or all womanhood in the Virgin. So we might idealize all crosses and all tombs by way of Christ's cross and tomb.

"She shall be saved" speaks only about woman and does not generalize. "By way of the childbearing" is not "by means of," and "the" refers to the well-known childbearing, common motherhood by way of common fatherhood, and not to *the* miraculous birth from the Virgin.

The plural "if they remain" is used *ad sensum*. Moreover, Paul quite regularly concentrates and individualizes with the singular and then expands with the plural, he sees every subject in all its relations. The aorist = definitely remain. Faith secures salvation on the instant, but definite remaining in faith retains salvation and attains its consummation. The condition with ἐάν is that of expectancy.

When Paul writes: remain "in faith and love and sanctification together with sobriety," this is comprehensive, these four do not stand in the same relation to salvation. Faith apprehends it; love to God and to man is the invariable fruit of faith; sanctification (I Thess. 4:3, 7; II Thess. 2:13) is the result, which is here to be understood in the narrow sense of having the life sanctified. Μετά makes soberness (see v. 9) the accompaniment of sanctification. All four apply to all men and thus also to women; theirs is no peculiar way to salvation. The repetition of "soberness" from v. 9 and its attachment by means of μετά are pointed for the specific purpose here in hand, namely that women keep their proper place in the services. Christian sensibleness and balance will easily achieve that and will readily accompany faith, love, and sanctification, for they are really a product of the latter.

CHAPTER III

Qualifications for Offices in the Congregation

1) This chapter should not be entitled *die Gemein-deverfassung*, the congregational organization. Paul is not telling Timothy to arrange for these offices and to define their functions and their scope; such offices were already established and in use, and Timothy is merely to see to it that only properly qualified persons fill them. When Paul left Ephesus after founding this congregation, it had elders whom a year later he summoned to meet him at Miletus when he stopped there on his way to Jerusalem (Acts 20:17).

This chapter begins without a connective, and we first have the general statement: **Faithful (is) the statement: If one aspires to overseership he desires an excellent task.** Zahn rejects the reading πιστός although it is overwhelmingly attested and prefers ἀνθρώπινος which is but weakly attested (it is found only in D and in some Latin versions). He cannot understand how the latter could have been substituted for the former while he thinks the reverse might easily have been done since 1:15; 4:9; II Tim. 2:11; Tit. 3:8 have Πιστὸς ὁ λόγος. Zahn's subjective canon is unsafe, it is beyond our ability to explain many a variant. The other four instances where this expression occurs in these letters lead us to expect that in our passage πιστός would again be used and not a strange adjective. Yet a few of the fathers have the Latin *humanus* in 1:15 in the sense of *benignus,* and thus, by way of the Latin, D may have come to write its variant: "Human," i. e., benignant, is the statement.

Zahn's contention, however, is that ἀνθρώπινος means that this is a "human" saying in the sense of a *locus*

(576)

communis, a current expression of the day among pagans, that whoever aspires to an ἐπισκοπή desires an excellent task. Yet Zahn does not mention an instance in pagan literature, where such an expression was used. Besides, this word ἐπισκοπή is found nowhere in common Greek save once in Lucian's Dialogs, and there in the entirely different sense of "visit," *Besuch,* looking in upon someone (B.-P. 465; C.-K. 1000), and once in a Lycaonian inscription (R., *W. P.*). What a trivial preamble it would be to say that it is *allgemeine menschliche Rede* (Wohlenberg, following Zahn) that to aspire to an overseership is to seek an excellent task! It is a different matter and one very much to the point when Paul says that it is a *"faithful"* statement, reliable because it is true, a statement that he as an apostle makes about the holy office and its high desirability, the qualifications for which he intends to list. For if important qualifications are needed, the office must be valuable and desirable accordingly.

'Επισκοπή = the office of an ἐπίσκοπος, of one who oversees, from which we have "episcopal" and thus "bishop" and "bishopric." But in the New Testament ἐπίσκοπος and πρεσβύτερος, "overseer" and "elder," are titles for the same office and the same officeholder; he is called "overseer" in consideration of the work to be done, "elder" in consideration of the dignity. The latter word was borrowed from the synagogue which also had its "elders." The Jews also called them ἄρχοντες, "rulers," a term that was not adopted by the Christians since these Jewish elders had judicial authority and could try cases, which was not the function of the elders in Christian congregations.

The synagogue elders were usually older men who were dignified because of their age. The New Testament lays no stress on the age although in the first Christian churches older men would naturally be chosen. While Timothy was no longer young and was not an elder in a congregation but Paul's representative in the whole Asian territory he was still considered to have youth (4:12). Bishops, as officers distinct from men in the pastorate in the sense of superintendents over a diocese, do not appear until the second century. The suggestion that in these letters of Paul traces of a distinction between *episkopoi* and *presbyteroi* are apparent is, in our estimation, too difficult to prove.

On the basis of 5:17, where the elders are divided into two groups: those who teach and those who only preside or manage, Kretzmann concludes that the latter were διάκονοι while the former were ἐπίσκοποι, both being termed πρεσβύτεροι. He also thinks that in small congregations one ἐπίσκοπος may have sufficed and that for this reason Paul probably uses the singular in v. 2. That idea is interesting, but it would be difficult to substantiate it. Paul does have plurals in v. 8, 11, 12 and does require aptness to teach only of the ἐπίσκοπος (v. 2); but is that enough? If so, we should have pretty much our present arrangement of preacher-pastor and church council. A great deal has been written on the whole subject, which the student may investigate. The apostolic church had nothing resembling a hierarchy in its ministry; in fact, the term *episkopos* indicated only the labor while *presbyteros* connoted the dignity and the honor. Deacons were never called *presbyteroi*.

"If one aspires to . . . he desires" varies the verbs and makes the expression most exact. Paul commends the aspiration and thus encourages it. It is thus that he continues by setting down the essential qualifications which all aspirants must meet. It is not said that they would at once then be placed into the office; as is the case now, that depended on the needs of the congregations. One gains the impression, however, that there was plenty of opportunity for those who qualified.

Such an aspirant desires καλοῦ ἔργον, "an excellent work or task"; we have two genitives after verbs of emotion, R. 508. "Excellent" = noble in itself and also noble in the eyes of others who know how to appreciate this quality; ἀγαθοῦ would mean beneficial to those served as it does in Eph. 4:12. The emphasis is on "excellent." The fact that the office is a *negotium, non otium* (Bengel), a "task" that calls for all of the man's energy and not a mere honor to be enjoyed, is taken for granted even as it is already indicated in the title: *Episcopus est nomen operis, non honoris* (Augustine), which all theological students and all ministers may well note.

2) It is necessary, then, that an overseer be irreproachable, one wife's husband, temperate, soberminded, orderly, hospitable, apt to teach, etc.

In Tit. 1:6, etc., these requirements are made of an elder. This rather excludes the idea that only some elders taught and were thus called "overseers" while non-teaching elders were called "deacons." Δεῖ is used to indicate all kinds of necessity, here the necessity inherent in the office named. The word ἐπίσκοπος is far more frequently used in the Greek than ἐπισκοπή.

The first group of requirements consists of seven which may be divided into 1 + 4 + 2 or into 1 + 1 + 3 + 2; the number seven is intentional. "Irreproachable" is general: "not to be taken hold of," i. e., of such a character that no one can rightfully take hold of the person with a charge of unfitness, the following items list the points that need to be considered. It has been remarked that all of these save the ability to teach and that of not being a novice or beginner in Christianity are requirements that apply to all Christians, which is quite true and shows that, as far as morals are concerned, the New Testament has only one standard for both clergy and laity and not two. Yet we may note that in the case of the members of the congregation faults may be borne with which cannot be tolerated in ministers, for they are to be examples of the flock (Phil. 3:17; II Thess. 3:9; I Pet. 5:3). A man who aspires to the ministry must be of proved character.

Four personal qualities are then mentioned: "one wife's husband — temperate — sober-minded — orderly." The emphasis is on *one* wife's husband, and the sense is that he have nothing to do with any other woman. He must be a man who cannot be taken hold of on the score of sexual promiscuity or laxity. It is plain that Paul does not say that none but married men may enter the ministry, that every pastor must be married. Since the days of Origen the question has been raised as to whether a widowed pastor is here forbidden to remarry. The fact that Origen stoutly affirms this is not strange when we remember that he castrated himself; his exegesis is dominated by his peculiar asceticism. Others conclude that remarriage is here forbidden because they think that "one husband's wife" which occurs in 5:9 refers to a widow who had never had more than one husband. But the two passages are identical in wording, their sense is entirely the same so that we are able to get nothing out of the one that is not already contained in the other. We need not review the protracted discussion of this item, the non-exegetical arguments, the church legislation, etc.

Paul had a reason for beginning with *"one* wife's husband."` In those days mature men were chosen for the eldership, who, as a rule, were married and had families; there were no seminary graduates who were awaiting calls. The bulk of the membership from which the elders had to be chosen had come from paganism. What this means as to sexual vices is written large in the New Testament and in the moral records of the day. Even the early apostolic conference in Jerusalem warns against "fornication" and uses this wide term to cover all the prevalent pagan sexual excesses (Acts 15:29). The epistles fairly din the word into their readers' ears. There was the regular institution of the hierodouloi, pagan temple prostitutes; the common custom of having *hetaerae* ("companions," see Liddell and Scott ἑταῖρος), girls from noncitizen families who were used by unmarried and by married men; and thus, besides these standard practices, all the rest of the vileness that formed the soil from which these grew. Converts to the gospel did not at once step into perfect sexual purity. Hence this proviso regarding the "overseers": to begin with, a man who is not strictly faithful to his one wife is debarred.

It would be strange, indeed, if this first specific item implied that remarried widowers were to be refused. Were the woods so full of men who had second wives that a bar had to be put up lest they crowd the ranks of the ministry? Was remarriage such a sin that, of all sexual requirements, it alone is here singled out? Where in all Scripture is remarriage for a widower or a widow either prohibited or regarded as being a reflection on a person's morality? As far as 5:9 is concerned, would Paul advise young widows to marry again (5:14) if they would thereby forfeit the right which is offered to widows in 5:9? It is Paul who wrote I Cor. 7:9, 39 on this subject (also Rom. 7:2, 3). To point to I Cor. 7:2, 8, 27, or to 7:38, 40 is to misunderstand the very reason for which Paul writes this advice, which he himself states in I Cor. 7:26: "the present distress," and v. 28: "I am sparing you" (see *The Interpretation of First Corinthians*). Heb. 13:4 stands: "Marriage is honorable *in all.*" Paul does not in any way come under his own condemnation of those "forbidding to marry" (4:3). It is asked why, if he had in mind sexual purity, he did not use a wording that prohibited πορνεία and μοιχεία. Because in this group of four he has four positive qualifications, and because "one wife's husband" states the positive qualification with great exactness. The commentators of the early church misunderstood Paul because of their un-Pauline asceticism and not because his words are not clear.

"Temperate," or sober (compare the verb in I Thess. 5:6, 8), is like II Tim. 4:5: "temperate in all things," not only in regard to intoxicants, but also in regard to the mind, "spiritually temperate," not carried away by teachings such as those indicated in 1:4, etc. "Sober-minded" is added (the noun is used in 2:9, 15), soundness and balance in judgment, not flighty, unstable, and the like. A leader in the church who lacks these qualities would be dangerous, even a member who lacks them would be a liability.

We see from 1:3, etc., and from others of Paul's letters how all sorts of follies and errors tried to gain a foothold in the churches; in 4:1, etc., Paul warns regarding the future (Acts 20:28, etc., may well be recalled). Leaders of a temperate and sober mind were needed. They are needed today. Kretzmann points to modern results of science and of Bible criticism. Besides these we have all the religious fads, fancies, and fictions of unstable minds. We need pastors who will conduct their own persons and then also their congregations with a sane, safe, and steady mind in all matters of life and of faith.

The fourth requirement is κόσμιον (the adjective and the verb are found in 2:9), "orderly," but here it is to be understood in its broadest sense as denoting a quality of character. This has been regarded rather superficially when it is taken to mean "the refined, courteous, polite gentleman . . . of good breeding." Is this word ever used thus? The Greek calls the gentleman καλός not κόσμιος. Like the two preceding adjectives, this one also denotes a quality of mind and character which will then naturally manifest itself in the life. Bengel notes the relation to the preceding: *Quod σώφρων est intus, id κόσμως est extra;* but has the relation wrong, both refer *intus* to the character. A pastor's whole make-up should be "orderly," spiritually, mentally, and in his habits. Being tidy and courteous is only one of the outward marks, but this is by no means all that Paul requires. We said above that we may group together: "temperate, sober-minded, orderly." That would be an inadequate grouping if the latter means only "not slovenly in appearance or rough and boorish in his manners."

While these three are marks of character, "hospitable, apt to teach" again belong together and refer to imparting something to others. Christian hospitality is mentioned in Rom. 12:13; Heb. 13:2; I Pet. 2:9. It does not mean to entertain and to feast friends or even the poor but to take in Christian strangers or acquaintances when these are traveling, or when they are fleeing from persecutions and often are without means of any kind.

The very word conjures up the conditions of that day. There was much travel everywhere in the empire, which helped the spread of the gospel immensely. Christian travelers would want to lodge with Christians and to receive their trustworthy aid in whatever business they had. Christian hospitality was a great blessing to them. Persecution made fugitives who were often in great need. Then other cases such as poverty, sickness, the need of some widow and some orphan would afford opportunity for hospitality. The elders in the church, to whom all these cases would generally come first, did what they could and then appealed to others. A man who was ever ready with his own hospitality had one quality for being made an elder.

Διδακτικός does not mean "willing to teach" because of II Tim. 2:24, for in both passages as well as in Philo who alone uses this word it means "apt or able to teach." "Are all teachers?" I Cor. 12:29. No, not all. Those who still need much teaching and are themselves incompetent to impart knowledge should not be given an office in which some proficiency in teaching is needed. When we read in 5:17 that honor is to be accorded "especially to those laboring in the Word and teaching," we take it that the elders divided the work among themselves, and those who were most able to teach attended to most of the teaching and the preaching. This does not imply that the others could not teach at all. The fact that the latter were really "deacons" while the teachers were "overseers," and that both classes were called "elders," will be difficult to prove, the more so since ἐπίσκοπος does not connote teaching as little as διάκονος does. We have division of labor in our church councils today, yet our deacons do not act as our trustees although they could; also vice versa. Ability to teach means not merely a fair natural aptitude but the qualification of having been taught. Kretzmann: the διδακτικός must be a διδακτός, II Tim. 3:14; 2:2. The more a faithful teacher teaches, the more will he feel the need of acquiring more and more knowledge of the blessed truth he is to teach.

3) The first seven are followed by another seven, namely two with μή, three that are opposites, and two (a positive and a negative) that are elaborated. The six adjectives used in v. 2 remain adjectives because they may be so used with εἶναι; but the five terms used in v. 3 contain the noun πλήκτης so that we may regard the adjectives as being substantivized: **not one** (sitting long) **beside wine, not a striker; on the contrary** (ἀλλά), **one yielding, not fighting, not silverloving, etc.**

A πάροινος is one who lingers long beside his wine, a winebibber, a tippler. A striker is one who is quick-tempered, carries a chip on his shoulder, is ready with his fists. On the opposite side we have the ἐπιεικής, one who is *gelinde* (Luther), gentle, yielding. This is a beautiful Greek word which has no exact equivalent in Latin or in English. See the author on Phil. 4:5 where this word is treated at length. An ἄμαχον is one who never fights, who is not of the fighting kind. Lastly, one who is not a lover of money, not mercenary, not stingy. Note that the one positive term which names a virtue stands in the middle, on the one side are two negatives with μή, on the other two with a *privativum,* which arrangement is not accidental, not in the case of Paul as we know him. Also note that ἀλλά puts only ἐπιεικῆ and not the two following terms into contrast.

4) The construction with the accusative predicates after εἶναι continues with the participles: **superintending his own house well as having children in subjection with all dignity; if now one does not know to superintend his own house, how will he take care of God's church?**

The participle means "to superintend," to be first or at the head of his own house (household); "to rule" is less exact. In 5:17 the participle of this verb is used with reference to the church work of the elders. Any Christian man should be able to function well as the head of his own home; one who fails in so simple a requirement is not fit to be elevated to the ministry. Unfortunately, this test cannot now be applied for entrance into the ministry when unmarried or newly married seminary graduates are called. Note that the objects of both participles have an emphasis because they are placed forward; this is also true with regard to "God's church" in v. 5. Verbs of ruling govern the genitive.

This excellent superintendence is most evident in the case of such children as one may have, hence "having children" is not coordinate with "superintending" but subordinate to it. The requirement is not that an "overseer" *must* have children, that a childless man could not be chosen, but that, when he has a family as most men have, any children, whatever their age (τέκνα is thus anarthrous), be "in subjection with all dignity," "subjection" as in 2:11. There is no need to separate the two phrases as some do for fear that otherwise the dignity will have to mean the dignity of the children, and little ones cannot be expected to act dignified. The sense is: "in subjection to the father, with dignity on his part." "Subjection" has the passive sense and implies the father as the subject. We may translate: "holding such children as he has (anarthrous) in subjection (imposed by him) with all dignity." He acts in a dignified way when he secures due obedience.

5) Ill-trained, bad children reflect on any pastor, not merely because they are hurtful examples to the children of the members of the church, but still more because they show that the father is incompetent for his office. There is no parenthesis, δέ only specifies this point in a rhetorical question, εἰ with the indicative assumes such a case as real, οὐ is thus the regular negative. Credit the mind of Paul with making a comparison on two points, where most writers would stop with only one: 1) the objects: "his own house — God's church"; 2) the activities: "superintend — take care of."

This expresses a third thought that Paul wants to indicate: God's church is not to be conceived as being the overseer's family. In this church God and not the overseer is the Father; the overseer is only the *episcopos*. In order to make this evident Paul may have already in v. 2 chosen this title instead of "elder," in the Orient the old father-patriarch who has all his sons and his sons' families around and under him. When Paul speaks of his fatherhood in I Cor. 4:15, this refers to him as being the apostolic founder of the church at Corinth; in Gal. 4:19 Paul speaks of his motherhood. In our passage the "overseer" assumes a position in a congregation that is already established.

This is elementary logic, concluding from the less to the greater: one who does not know how to superintend (the effective aorist) "his own house," how will he handle the great responsibility of caring for "God's church"? If one cannot even "superintend" his little family, how will he attend to the far greater task of "caring for" all those in God's assembly (ἐκκλησία is here used with reference to a single congregation)? Δέ says that this is the point of the requirement presented in v. 4.

6) The last item, like the previous one with its exposition, remains in the same construction (accusative predicate of εἶναι, v. 2) : **not a novice lest, having become conceited, he fall into the devil's judgment.**

The adjective is here substantivized and = newly planted = "novice," a recent convert. To elevate such a man into the episcopate is to place him into a position that is entirely too dangerous for him; Timothy, as well as the congregations, are not to be guilty of placing a hopeful beginner who has the other qualities but not the one of maturity in the faith into office. Novice is not to be taken in the physical sense as referring to too young a man but in the spiritual sense. In Tit. 1:6, etc., this point is not included. The reason is that when the gospel was newly introduced in a territory — Crete was new territory — only novices could be placed in charge of the newly gathered flocks because no others were available; and because in the case of such novices there was no danger of falling into conceit, "the leaders of a forlorn hope." Where, however, the church was already fully established, where prominent elders were already in honored positions, there to elevate a novice might easily fill him with conceit and bring about his downfall.

Τυφόω, from τῦφος, "smoke" = to wrap in smoke; the aorist passive participle means "besmoked." But here the word is used in the metaphorical sense, "made conceited," although in the sense of obnubilation, the pride of conceit enfolding him as in a smoky fog. The final outcome might easily be that "he fall into the devil's judgment." In exegesis we must follow the analogy of Scripture as the safe guide. Now in the whole New Testament and also in the Old Testament LXX ὁ διάβολος with the article = the devil; it is the Hebrew *hasatan* save in Esther 7:4 and 8:1 where a different Hebrew word is used and refers to Haman. This analogy of Scripture has been set aside, and Paul is thought to speak of "the (human) slanderer who has his delight in calumny." But we have the word again in v. 7 and in II Tim. 2:26 where it undoubtedly means the devil. It is too radical a departure to translate II Tim. 2:26, "the devil's snare" and I Tim. 3:7, "the slanderer's snare." Κρῖμα is always a *vox media* and should be left so in translation; when an adverse "judgment" is meant, the context indicates this sufficiently.

But is this an objective genitive: the judgment which God rendered regarding the devil; or a subjective genitive: the judgment which the devil renders? C.-K. 188 and a few others modify this: the judgment which the devil is permitted to execute. This is done largely in view of the genitive found in v. 7 (II Tim. 2:26): "the devil's snare" (subjective), i. e., which the devil lays. The view that κρῖμα always has the subjective genitive as in Rom. 2:2, 3; 11:33 is answered by examples where it has the objective genitive as in Rom. 3:8; Rev. 17:1. It would be peculiar, indeed, if such a word as this, which denotes the result of an action, whose verb form admits both a subject and an object, should be construed only with a subjective genitive.

Judgment, moreover, is never ascribed to the devil: *God* judges. The very word means the judicial announcement of a verdict or the verdict as it stands. Where did Satan ever sit on the throne of judgment and render a verdict? "Judgment" and "the devil" *can* be combined in only one way: God's judgment pronounced *on* the devil (objective). The claim that this thought would require τὸ κρῖμα is untenable because every genitive already limits and makes definite its governing noun just as in the English "the devil's judgment." The very word "snare," cunningly laid to catch a victim, suggests "of the devil" and is a subjective genitive.

The devil's judgment is specific: God's judgment on his pride. Into that very judgment which has long ago been pronounced upon the devil the conceited novice might easily fall in his pride. This aorist refers to a fatal fall (just as it does in v. 7) and not only, as some who regard it as a subjective genitive suppose, a fall into temporal ills and punishments, the devil being allowed to inflict them. The view that a fatal fall would be too severe a punishment for a novice in the faith overlooks the fact that by his conceit this novice would smother his young faith and would thus plunge into what the devil plunged into. Unholy pride may, indeed, carry its victim that far.

7) Verses 2-6 are but one sentence, νεόφυτον still being dependent on εἶναι. This means that δέ now introduces what may be termed the conclusion of the whole. It thus reverts to the very first predicate that an overseer in a congregation must be "irreproachable," he must be that, as we are now told, even as far as outsiders are concerned. **Moreover, it is neces-**

sary also that he have excellent testimony from those without lest he fall into reproaching and the devil's snare.

Δεῖ takes us back to v. 2 where ἀνεπίληπτον is negative: "nothing left on his doorstep against him"; now we have the positive: "excellent testimony from those outside," from non-Christians. This, then, closes the whole presentation regarding the kind of men that are to be made overseers in the church.

Only here and in Tit. 1:13 Paul uses the word μαρτυρία; he has used the neuter in 2:6. Yet each form is quite in place; here the word means "excellent testimony in general." This refers to testimony concerning his life since his conversion. The kind of a pagan or the kind of a Jew the convert who is now aspiring to office in the church had been could not be considered. On this basis Paul himself would have been excluded. The testimony that Paul refers to is such as Timothy and the congregation could really take into consideration. Rabid haters of all Christians would vilify all of these, but decent outsiders would acknowledge Christians of good Christian character. Paul properly uses the plural "from those without," for some personal outside enemy would not be considered.

The negative purpose clause causes some discussion among commentators: "lest he fall into reproaching and the devil's snare." The verb is the same one that was used in v. 6 and is in a similar unemphatic position. The two ἵνα clauses thus resemble each other; yet this does not parallel the two requirements themselves as we have already shown, "not a novice" is not paired even in form with: "Moreover, it is necessary," etc. The Greek is so flexible that the use of ἐμπέσῃ in both ἵνα clauses (v. 6 and 7) may have no significance in regard to the words which are construed with each of these verbs although it may be possible that in v. 6 the verb means that we are to construe: "judgment (verb) upon the devil"; and v. 7: "into reproaching (verb) and the devil's snare."

Be this as it may, although only one εἰς is used with the two nouns, in the latter clause the genitive cannot be construed with both, i. e., the "reproaching" and the "snare" cannot be predicated of the devil. The use of but one preposition does not decide the matter as some claim; it is decided by the nouns themselves. The one is literal and indicates an activity; the other is figurative and does not indicate an activity but an object. That also means that "snare" is not an explication of "reproaching" so that the reproaching forms a snare for the man in question. What the devil's reproaching might mean has yet to be discovered. He certainly is the last one to reproach a faulty Christian for his faults. All twinges of conscience come from God and tend to repentance and never are a devil's snare into which a Christian falls with fatal results (effective aorist). Even if we translate "reviling" (Matt. 5:11: the verb; but see Matt. 11:20: Jesus "upbraids," "reproaches"), to attribute this to the devil is incongruous.

This reproaching is usually taken to be that of the outsiders just mentioned. But why restrict it to them? Would not the Christians likewise engage in reproaching and rather openly when such a man is a disgrace to them in his sacred and high office? Ὀνειδισμός is in this case justified reproaching; in Rom. 15:3 it is unjustified. The one preposition indicates that falling "into reproaching" is not a separate item, and falling "into the devil's snare" another item. That would be the meaning if two prepositions were employed; but here the reproaching of men and the devil's snare go together. The reproaching, especially of the Christians, removes him from them, and so the devil lays his snare for him, once more to catch him as his victim.

On "snare" in Rom. 11:9 (Ps. 69:22) see that passage. Here, in 6:9, and in II Tim. 2:26 no special interpretation of "snare" is given although some supply this and go into descriptive details. The figure interprets itself: to fall into the devil's snare = into his deadly power like an animal that is caught and then killed. A novice may lose his soul if he is made a minister; so, in a different way, may a man who bears no good reputation although he has been a member of the congregation for a long time.

*   *   *

8) All that we know about deacons as they were found in Paul's day is contained in this passage and in Rom. 16:1; Phil. 1:11. The διακονία used in Rom. 12:7 and the διακονεῖν used in I Pet. 4:1 point to the office of deacons although both passages refer to all who have the charisma of ministering to others. This is true also regarding the ἀντιλήψεις or "helps" mentioned in I Cor. 12:28. We must, therefore, be content with the little information that we have. The fact that two offices are referred to by "overseers" and "deacons" is assured by our passage and by Phil. 1:1. The fact that deacons held the minor office and did not teach is also certain. What the deacons actually did is nowhere stated in detail. To say that they performed the same work as the *episcopoi* with the exception of the teaching is not provable. They were not the overseers, did not act as pastors and spiritual leaders of the flock. The best we can say is that they assisted the overseers by performing the minor services and attending to incidental matters such as collecting and distributing alms, looking after the physical needs of the sick, keeping the place of worship in order, etc. Thus there were also women deacons (v. 11); Phœbe was one of these, and she is referred to as early as Rom. 16:1. We note the errand she performed for Paul.

Voluntary *diakonia* was plentiful. The regular choice and appointment of deacons in all probability grew out of this voluntary service. The fact that these deacons were called "elders," and that together with the *episcopoi* they formed the πρεσβυτήριον or "presbytery," is nowhere indicated. If we may use the word "clergy" with reference to the officers of this early period, the deacons were not considered as belonging to the clergy. The "overseers" oversaw also the deacons.

As far as Acts 6 is concerned, the seven men appointed in the mother church were not called deacons, yet the work for which they were chosen by the church was evidently that of deacons, attending to aid for the many widows when the mother church had grown to a membership of thousands, estimated at 20,000 to 25,-000. This example seems to have prompted Paul's congregations to appoint men for similar purposes and then to call them deacons. Stephen's other activities such as doing miracles and testifying mightily in the synagogues were not a part of the work to which he and the six others were appointed. But all this was discontinued when Stephen was stoned and the mother church was widely scattered because of the first great persecution. It was then that we read of Philip doing evangelistic work in Samaria and elsewhere. His office in the mother church had ended. The scattered Christians, too, started congregations in the places to which they had fled.

With this background which has been gleaned from the records we read Paul's directions about the kind of men to be used as regular deacons in the churches. **Deacons in like manner dignified, not double-tongued, not devoting themselves to much wine, not out for shameful gain, possessing the mystery of the faith in a clean conscience.**

This statement is still to be construed with the δεῖ εἶναι used in v. 2; not with δεῖ ἔχειν occurring in v. 7. This means that v. 2-7 are a unit and that v. 8 begins another unit. It is scarcely accidental that Paul speaks of the high office of the *episcopos* in the singular and of the lower offices of men and of women in the diaconate in the plural. "In like manner" simply means that, as of the former, so of the latter, certain requirements must be made; δεῖ = necessitated by the very nature of the office in question. Nothing need be said about aspiring to the lower office; the fact that aspirants were found for this as well as for the higher office is implied.

Paul divides the enumeration of the requirements for deacons by inserting those for women deacons in v. 11, between v. 8-10 and v. 12. His intention is to place together and on a par the personal moral requirements of men and of women deacons. In the case of the men v. 12 adds also the requirement about family life. We note that while this requirement is divided with reference to the overseer ("one wife's husband" in v. 2, the rest in v. 4, 5), it is combined with reference to deacons in v. 12. No such requirement is listed for women deacons because mothers with children found their duties in their homes and not in the diaconate.

"Dignified" (our versions, "grave") is the adjective corresponding to the noun σεμνότης which was used in v. 4; it is Luther's *ehrbar*, of serious bearing because being of serious mind and character. Because they had to deal with all classes, all ages, all types of people in their work sensible, steady men were needed.

Three disqualifications follow although these extend beyond what "dignified" implies in a positive way. "Not double-tongued," saying one thing to one person and a conflicting thing to another so that, on comparing notes, the discrepancy becomes apparent. This is bad in any person; it would be especially bad in an officer of the church, who had constant rounds of visitation to make and would talk with many members.

"Not devoting themselves to much wine" (προσέχω with τὸν νοῦν understood) does not forbid the use of wine, the common drink of the day, but the love of too much of it. "Not out for shameful gain" (Tit. 1:7; adverb, I Pet. 5:2) = like pilfering Judas. The point is the disgracefulness of such an act whether it be by embezzlement of the alms entrusted for distribution or by otherwise currying favors for mercenary ends (G. K. 190).

9) "Possessing the mystery of the faith in a clean conscience" is the direct opposite of the preceding three. But instead of merely saying that in all their work the deacons must preserve "a clean conscience" Paul adds to this what is greater than conscience, what is to enlighten and thus to govern and to hold the conscience true, and thus to keep it clean. Even in 1:19 "a good conscience" is not sufficient for Paul.

Many commentators consider "the mystery of the faith by itself" and then ask what this is and puzzle about the genitive. In addition, not a few say that "the faith" means *fides qua creditur* and either deny or do not consider that it may mean *fides quae creditur*. Thus we get various explanations, the best one being that the faith found in the hearts of the deacons is to believe the mystery. This view overlooks the participle ἔχοντας and does not note the kind of a qualifier τὸ μυστήριον should have. "Possessing" the mystery already includes the faith which believes and thereby "possesses" the mystery, namely personal faith, *qua creditur*. The feature that needs to be added is *what* mystery is referred to, a defining modifier is required. We have it: this is "the mystery of the faith."

This is also true in all those many cases where τὸ μυστήριον and its defining genitive appear: the mystery

of God — of Christ — of the kingdom of God — of
the will of God — of the gospel — of the lawlessness
(II Thess. 2:7) — of the godliness (I Tim. 3:16) —
and now: of the faith. All these are alike, all are defin-
itive genitives because "the mystery" leaves us with a
question mark, and the genitive supplies the answer.
It makes little difference what you call these genitives,
whether objective: "the mystery that deals with these
persons and objects"; or possessive: "which belongs
to this and that"; or something else. The point is that
these genitives are *alike* and are *not subjective*. In
other words, "the faith" and in v. 16 "the godliness"
are objective like "the lawlessness — the kingdom —
the will," etc.

The only question that remains is whether this
mystery treats about our personal believing and objec-
tifies it, or about the Christian faith as such, which is
considered as something to believe. This question
really answers itself. Some have said that a man's
believing, both the fact and the whole act, appear as a
great mystery when the man examines himself. But
my believing is not a mystery. The fact that I should
have faith in Christ, my Savior, is the most natural
thing in the world because he is so deserving of every
sinner's trust, and only by the most unnatural and
unreasonable resistance can any man remain without
the faith that his love and his grace would always
instill.

Lietzmann has stated it well in a number of places:
"the faith" is a synonym for "Christianity." Here
"the mystery of the faith" = "the mystery of Christianity"; deacons must possess this, must hold it "in a
clean conscience." C.-K. 893 denies this objective use
of ἡ πίστις by saying that the word never means *doctrina
fidei*. The objective use is not disposed of by narrow-
ing it down to the idea of doctrine or a set of doctrines

although ἡ πίστις does at times refer to the doctrinal contents of what we Christians believe.

"The faith" in the objective sense is always the substance, the contents of what we are to embrace in living trust, "the Way" (Acts 9:22; 19:9, 23; 24:22), the truth, etc. Μυστήριον always means, not something that is to remain hidden, but something that is to be known only through revelation. It would be strange, indeed, if a term like πίστις, which is derived from πιστεύω, did not admit of both the subjective and the objective use when a large number of similar words do this. Like ourself, many others find the objective use in quite a number of passages, compare 4:1; 6:10, 12, 21. "Mystery" is objective and thus also "the mystery of the faith."

Any man who is not careful of the truth, or who is enamored of wine, or who allows money to stick to his fingers, cannot hold to Christianity, to this blessed mystery of the faith, "in connection with a clean conscience," and is certainly not the man to be made a deacon in the congregation.

10) In order to be safe when deacons are to be chosen Paul adds: **These, too, moreover, let them first be tested, then let them minister as being men unaccused.** "And" in our versions translates δέ, "also" is the translation of καί. The former adds this point as one that is somewhat different from the preceding. The fact that such a testing was to be applied also to overseers is so self-evident from the nature of the requirements laid down in v. 2-8 that καί now refers to it. Lest one should think that such testing is unnecessary in case of the lesser office of deacon, Paul states that it is likewise quite necessary. He uses his favorite word for testing, which is employed regarding coins, metals, etc., but he does not use the aorist imperative to express a formal and a set test

but the present imperative which indicates a testing that covers some time.

This does not indicate a period of probation, that men were tried out in the office before permanent appointment was made, but a constant testing so that, when deacons are later needed, such men may be nominated as candidates. In Acts 6:3 we see that such men were sought out. The plural imperatives do not imply that Timothy alone is to do this testing and then let the men serve. This is the business of each congregation, Timothy guides and supervises it in place of Paul.

The participle is not conditional: "then let them minister if they be blameless" (R. V.) but predicative: "as being (men) unaccused," *unbeschuldigt*. Having been such before this time, the congregations may expect them to continue as such. Paul does not advocate what some would do, namely appoint to a place on the church council men who have hitherto been careless in their Christian lives in the hope that the being placed in office will improve them; that is not what church offices are for. To set aside good available men for poor timber always produces a bad general effect.

11) Women in like manner dignified, not slanderers, temperate, faithful in all things. First: "Deacons in like manner dignified," and now: "Women in like manner dignified." The wording is exactly the same. The idea that all women are referred to is untenable. All women as women are considered in 2:9, etc. That the wives of deacons are referred to (A. V.) is strongly argued especially by B. Weiss. Yet if deaconesses are referred to, why did Paul not write τὰς διακόνους, "feminine deacons"; the word διακόνισσα was not yet in use. He could not use the article in v. 2 when he was speaking of the "overseer" or in v. 8 and 12 with reference to deacons; the article would make the words refer to persons who were already in office while Paul speaks only of those who are eligible for office.

The plea that the deacons' wives are mentioned because these wives would help their husbands in their office while the wives of overseers could not do so because of the nature of this office, cannot be granted, for then the congregation would after all elect women deacons save that it would elect deacons' wives, mothers with families (v. 12). It would certainly be the sensible thing to elect unattached women. Paul would be the last one to select both husband and wife for an office and assign to the wife duties that would take her away from home and her children. The view that v. 11 speaks of the deacon's wife and v. 12 of his children has already been met in v. 8; it is just because lone women and not deacons' wives were considered for the office of deaconess that their personal qualifications follow v. 10, where the personal qualifications of men deacons are listed. Then, because these men alone have families, the qualifications in regard to this point follow in v. 12.

"In like manner" connects the qualifications for deaconesses with those required of the deacons; compare the adverb in v. 8. All three sets of officers must meet certain requirements *in the same way* and cannot be chosen without them. Deaconesses must be "dignified" just as deacons are (v. 8). "Not slanderous" is certainly to the point, for in their gossip many women like to tell others anything bad they have found out, and a deaconess would get around widely in a congregation. Here we have only the adjective which is not substantivized by the article: "slanderous." "Temperate" has the same force it has in v. 2. "Faithful in all things" = trustworthy in all respects. The opinion that the phrase is too indefinite unless deacons' wives and the things in which they assist their husbands in the office are referred to is inconclusive, for what about trustworthiness in other things? "In all respects" means just that: only all-around trustworthy women were fit for the office. Paul, for instance, entrusted his letter to the Romans to Phoebe, and she herself was a deaconess and not merely some deacon's wife.

12) **Let deacons be husbands of one wife, excellently superintending children and their own homes.** We need not repeat what has already been said about this requirement in v. 4, 5. "Husbands of one wife," with the singular, is the common individualizing singular with plurals.

Δεῖ εἶναι in v. 2 governs the construction of διακόνους in v. 8 and of γυναῖκας in v. 11: "an overseer — deacons — women must be," etc. The very construction indicates three offices. If Paul had continued this construction in v. 12, clarity would be lost; it would seem that Paul is adding a fourth office, which, of course, he is not. This he avoids by using the imperative just as in v. 10 he uses the imperative, there and here again adding only another point to offices already indicated.

13) The discussion of the requirements for the offices is concluded. A certain necessity for all of them has been stressed (δεῖ in v. 2 and v. 7, which is to be supplied in v. 8 and v. 11; imperatives in v. 10 and v. 12), a necessity that is due to the offices themselves. When Paul now closes with "for," this is not *begruendend;* here and in scores of instances γάρ is neither causal nor illative, it is explanatory, and the precise relation which it indicates is to be determined from the context (R. 1190, etc.). Here it introduces a result which is to act as an incentive to those who have obtained these offices and is to move them to fill these offices καλῶς, in an excellent way. The sense of "for" is: these are the requirements and qualifications; all of them are necessary, "for" these offices are not merely

to be filled somehow or other but so that those who fill them may gain for themselves an excellent standing as a result and a reward. As their very names indicate, all these offices are to serve others; hence the qualifications are such as will insure true service in advance. It is thus that those who do well in these offices thereby acquire a noble place for their own selves.

For they who ministered excellently are acquiring for themselves excellent standing, a great boldness in faith in Christ Jesus.

Who are referred to? All those mentioned in v. 1-12, overseers, men deacons, women deacons. Our versions render οἱ διακονήσαντες as though only deacons are referred to; some refer the word only to male deacons. This verb is, however, not technical: "to serve as deacons." The nouns ἐπίσκοπος and διάκονος are beginning to become technical but are only beginning to become such, the latter is also used with reference to deaconesses, Rom. 16:1. Πρεσβύτερος was used in a technical sense already in the synagogue.

Paul loves to call himself a *diakonos,* he applies this term also to his assistants; see Eph. 3:7; Col. 1:23; I Cor. 3:5; II Cor. 3:6; 6:4; 11:23; I Tim. 4:6. The verb διακονεῖν is still used in a general sense and means to do service for others; so also διακονία refers to any type of service. How could Paul hold out an incentive for male deacons only and not for excellent women deacons? How could he say that only deacons were to have a reward for their office and not the overseers or pastors? These questions are left unanswered by those who refer this verse to male deacons only. Moreover, it is well to note that Paul always has his whole paragraph in mind when he comes to the close of it. This promise pertains to all the servants of the congregation who minister excellently in their various offices.

Out of their very excellent work there ever springs for them an excellent reward.

Note the tenses: "they who did minister (aorist) are acquiring for themselves (present, durative)." Yes, they have already ministered, they have been doing a lot of excellent work. It is thus that they are acquiring something. We speak in the very same way; we say a person *has* done well and *is* thus getting somewhere. The aorist must not mean that the ministering is ended, that these persons are no longer in office. Reflexive middles may also have the reflexive pronouns in order to emphasize the reflexive idea; the pronoun may even be placed forward as is done in this instance. Καλῶς — καλόν is a play on these two words; they are placed chiastically: "*excellently* having ministered — a standing *excellent*," etc. To be sure, working excellently produces excellent standing as a result and a reward.

Βαθμός is derived from βαίνω. In the LXX it is used in a literal sense to designate a step before a door, in the plural to designate steps of a stairs; in the inscriptions it is used metaphorically in the sense of a foothold, a standing, a rank. By having ministered excellently all church officers are obtaining "a standing that is excellent," noble, fine. The thought is complete. Some think that a genitive, a phrase, or something should be added and state to what this step refers. They have in mind quite a different "step" from the one to which Paul is referring; he speaks of a step or a standing that is excellent in the ministering in which the congregational officers have been engaged (διακονήσαντες, aorist). He is dealing with nothing else. Because those who have served are still in office he says that they "are acquiring" (present) such an excellent standing and not that they have already ended it. Why Paul should have used the comparative "more excellent," as some think he should have done, is not apparent. This is not a comparison between a standing which they had prior to their offices or at the time when these persons were chosen and a standing to which they attained later on. "A standing that is excellent" in that persons have served excellently is at the same time a reward and an incentive.

This answers the thought of an excellent standing in the matter of personal salvation or of a high degree of glory in heaven. Paul is speaking of neither of these. Still less is he speaking of a standing of male deacons which places them in line for promotion from their diaconate to pastorates. We have already shown that οἱ διακονήσαντες = all the officers, the women, the overseers, or pastors, as well as the male deacons. The fact that pastors were often chosen from the ranks of male deacons may be true, but Paul says nothing about it in v. 2-7 when he speaks about the kind of men that are to be chosen as overseers. To what would the women deacons aspire, to what the overseers? Or is this reward and incentive intended only for male deacons? Paul is not presenting the diaconate of men as an apprenticeship for the pastorate. The ethics of such a procedure has been rightly questioned. The application has even been made that pastors who are stationed in small congregations ought to serve well in order to be called to larger congregations. Is that why they should serve well? What if they are not advanced and remain disappointed?

The verb separates "excellent standing" from the second object: "great boldness in faith in Christ Jesus." The two objects are thus distinct: "excellent standing" is one item to which another is added, "great boldness." Paul does not intimate that the standing has reference to men, to church membership, and the boldness to God, either now or on judgment day. Both standing and boldness refer to the offices of which Paul speaks, the excellent position one acquires when service has been excellently done, plus the free, open, assured feeling (παρρησία) for the work yet to be done. This is, of course, "great boldness in faith," the faith that rests "in Christ Jesus" (the phrase being added by the article). Here, too, "great" is proper and not the comparative "greater." All these offices — certainly not only that of the male deacons — are to be exercised "in faith"; all these persons serve as earnest believers. To have served excellently for some time places one beyond any timidity or hesitation and makes him act with boldness and assurance. The acquisition of such boldness in faith, the blessed faith that rests in Christ Jesus, is the most satisfying reward and the incentive to proceed on this tried course.

Paul's last sentence rounds out his instructions to Timothy and to the churches regarding these various offices in the most effective manner.

14) Just as Paul writes a personal word to Timothy at the end of the orders about the fanatical teachers in the churches (1:18-20), so at the end of the orders about men and women in the church and about the qualifications for church offices (2:1-3:13) he again writes a personal word to Timothy, (v. 14-16). As 1:18-20 concludes chapter 1, so 3:14-16 concludes chapters 2 and 3. This is so plain that we do not begin the third section of the epistle with v. 14.

These things I am writing to thee, hoping to come shortly; yet in case I am slow, that thou mayest know how it is necessary to behave thyself in God's house, which is the living God's church, pillar and foundation of the truth, etc.

If v. 14-16 conclude 2:1-3:13, "these things" = those mentioned in 2:1-3:13 and not those written in the entire letter, not those stated in the two preceding parts, and by no means those yet to be discussed in the part that follows, 4:1, etc. Paul is giving these things to Timothy in writing because, while he is hoping to come shortly (4:13), he rather expects (ἐάν, v. 15) to be slow. Did Paul return to Timothy in Ephesus? We have no means of knowing. He wrote to Titus about this same time and told Titus to come to Nicopolis for the winter (Tit. 3:14). This was his plan for the coming winter, which was probably a few months hence, so that before going to Nicopolis Paul hoped to visit Timothy in Ephesus.

15) The instructions here given in writing would guide Timothy in his superintendence of the Asian churches and let him know how to conduct himself as Paul's representative when he was arranging the worship and the offices "in God's house" where God dwells with his gracious presence, where everything must be as God wants it and not as various foolish men may wish to have things. The infinitive is a present middle: "to be conducting thyself," and here refers, not to ordinary Christian conduct like that of other godly church members, but to official conduct in supervision. Εἰδῇς is the second perfect which is always used in the sense of the present tense. The indirect question introduced with "how" is deliberative. Timothy will ask: "How must I act in this, in that matter?" Paul has here told him how. The directions are so important because Timothy is managing things "in God's house." This is not Timothy's own house nor the house of the church members; it belongs to God.

The gender of ἥτις is attracted to the predicative ἐκκλησία and, as is the case so often, this relative has a bit of causal force: "it being the living God's church." This is the sense in which it is God's house. The noun οἶκος often = family, cf., v. 4, 5, 12; some would give it that sense here by thinking of Eph. 2:19, but this is not exact, nor does the term "house" occur in Eph. 2:19. Even physically a father dwelling in a house

and dwelling in a family are not the same, he has his
family about him in the house but he is literally *in* the
house itself. Spiritually, with reference to God, this is
far more the case. Οἶκος = ἐκκλησία = not the family
in a house but the "assembly," the church members
themselves. They are this "house," which is called
"house" because God dwells in them. This is one of
the many beautiful expressions for the *unio mystica*,
in this case it is collective with reference to the church.

Paul says only "God's house," but when he adds
the relative he says "living God's church"; this adjectival participle is emphatic. Some expositors are content with remarks about God being the author and
source of life, who through Christ and his Spirit regenerates us and gives us life, etc. "God living" is the
tremendous opposite of dead idols. They are placed in
a temple, a house made of dead material. What more
can there be? But God is living, his very being is life.
His "house" are we ourselves, we the "church," in all
our being, as assembled and called to be God's own
spiritually. Wonderful and blessed indeed! And here
Timothy is appointed to direct how things ought to be
"in God's house." "In God's house" so plainly fits
2:1-3:13 and not 4:1, etc., that this little paragraph
belongs to all of chapters 2 and 3.

Continuing the implication of responsibility, Paul
adds the double apposition: "pillar and foundation of
the truth." A pillar supports the roof structure, and
an ἑδραίωμα (that which forms the seat), the real foundation (Luther: *Grundfeste*), supports the pillar. The
figure of the "pillar" is intensified by the figure of the
"foundation"; it is like saying: "The living God's
church is the pillar, yea more, even the foundation of
the truth." We do not translate "*a* pillar, *a* foundation" as if there were others; the church is the only
one; the absence of the articles stresses the qualitative
force of the nouns.

The gospel = "the truth." As ἀλήθεια, "reality," this truth exists independently and is dependent on no pillar, foundation, or other kind of support. Every reality and, above all this eternal one, is simply *there*, and that is all. Yet this gospel truth which God sent into the world is not just to be *there*, i. e., in existence; it is to save men, and thus the men it has saved, the living God's church, bear it as a pillar, yea as a foundation bears its superstructure. The church thus bears God's saving truth for all the world.

This is the living God's church, and as sure as he lives, his church will stand as "pillar and foundation of the truth." The gates of hell shall not prevail against the church. By means of the church, which the living God made his truth's pillar and foundation, this truth shines in the world and draws men unto itself, to be joined to those who are its pillar and foundation. In this church Timothy is to perform his work in Paul's place. A responsible, an inspiring, a blessed task! "God's house" and "the living God's church" direct Timothy's heart to God while he is engaged in the work of the church; "pillar and foundation of the truth" direct his heart to the supreme function of the church in the world, with which his task is concerned.

16) The substance of this truth is now summarily stated in a most effective form. While it is true that we cannot prove it, we, too, take it that Paul is quoting a Christian hymn or rather a psalm. We print accordingly: **And confessedly great is the mystery of the godliness:**

> **Who was manifested in flesh,**
> **Was justified in spirit,**
> **Was seen by angels,**
> **Was preached in nations,**
> **Was believed in the world,**
> **Was received up in glory.**

"Confessedly" refers to these lines. Since they were used in a hymn or a chant in the congregations themselves they express "in an acknowledged way" that "the mystery of godliness," the saving truth which the living God's church upholds as pillar and foundation, "is great." Because of its brevity and its restraint the mere word "great" is effective. Look at this truth, the mystery of the godliness, Christ he who (ὅς) is described in these hymn lines — "great," nothing less than "great." To be "confessedly" so refers only to the church, for she alone knows "the mystery of the godliness." What v. 9 calls "the mystery of the faith" is here termed "the mystery of the godliness," but here the hymn lines state just what is meant. We express our faith and our godliness, both of which are objective, in these lines: "Who was manifested," etc.

This is the substance of what we believe, the content of our godliness. We have explained this term in v. 9, which see. "The mystery" is the proper word and is often used by Paul to indicate the gospel content. The world does not know it, this mystery must be revealed or "preached" to it. "Of the godliness," however, takes us a step farther than "of the faith." What constitutes the one constitutes the other when both are looked at objectively; but "the faith" regards this mystery as the object intended for trust, "the godliness" presents it as the inwardness of all that forms real godliness, man's blessed relation to God.

One text and a few versions have divided the adverb into two words (ὁμολογοῦμεν ὡς): "We confess: 'How great is the mystery of the godliness!'" This is attractive but altogether too weak textually. "Confessedly" conveys substantially the same thought. Equally weak textually is ὅ for ὅς, the neuter being a mere accommodation to τὸ μυστήριον. While this makes a smoother connection with the antecedent, it weakens the connection with all the following verbs, the real subject of which is not the neuter "which" but the masculine "who," namely Christ. "The mystery of the godliness" = Christ "who," etc. Since the "who" clauses are a quotation, the change in gender is quite immaterial; similar changes are not infrequent when exact quotations are introduced. Some texts have "God" in place of "who" (A. V.): "God was manifested in flesh," which would make this quotation a *dictum probans* for the deity of Christ. One may hesitate regarding the reading; yet not because we need one more proof for Christ's deity, we have a rich abundance. The textual evidence is in favor of the relative.

Six terse statements, all with aorist passives, all with the verbs placed emphatically forward, all statements of fact, of ἀλήθεια, "truth," reality, that cannot possibly be annulled or even modified. Six tremendous facts, heaped one upon the other, all soteriological, all infinitely blessed. They are like the facts stated in the second article of the Apostolic Creed. Five have ἐν phrases; only the third has a dative. The form is striking indeed and also beautifully rhythmic.

"In flesh" and "in spirit" form a pair. "Angels" and "nations" are counterparts; so also are "in (the) world" and "in glory." The verbs "was preached" and "was believed" are correlative. "Angels — nations — world — glory" from a chiasm: the angels and the glory are placed first and last, nations and world in the middle, a plural and a singular in each. It seems that others besides Paul used the beauties of rhetorical form. Paul chose these lines as a quotation because he fully appreciated their form. They are to this day one of the high points of this letter. They were sung by Timothy and by the churches he was supervising, and Paul's use of them in these directions for the services (chapter 2) and for the church offices (chapter 3) is like drawing away the curtain from the inner sanctuary and revealing "the mystery" of blessedness it holds, Christ in all his saving acts.

These acts take us from heaven to earth and then from earth back to heaven, and both earth and heaven are ever after changed for us. The order is really chronological, for the preaching to the nations and the consequent believing in the world, which were due to Christ's great commission to the apostles and the church (Matt. 28:16-20; Mark 16:15, 16; Luke 24:47, 48) are properly placed before the ascension.

Christ "was manifested in flesh," was made to appear to men on earth "in fashion as man" (Phil. 2:8). "The Word became flesh and tented among us," John 1:14. Christ "took part of flesh and blood," Heb. 2:14. Each expression illumines the others. Each prevents undue stressing of the rest. Thus "was manifested" is not a mere appearance in flesh without having real flesh (Docetism). "Flesh" is the "flesh and blood" used in Hebrews, yet it is not only the physical body but all that belongs to our human nature, the body animated by soul and spirit. This is the incarnation: he who was manifested in flesh existed before that (John 1:1). Those who claim that Paul says nothing about the Virgin birth which is recorded in detail by Matthew and by Luke ignore statements such as this in our passage, in Rom. 1:3; Gal. 4:4, and elsewhere. Here there is more, however, than the mere moment of the incarnation; here there is the whole manifestation in flesh during Jesus' earthly life.

It is claimed that if we regard this verse as a quotation we must make the first clause the subject of all the following verbs: "Who was manifested in flesh was justified, seen, preached," etc. But why would a quotation need to be read thus? In any case, ὅς is the subject of *all* these passives, all of them aorist passives. Only this is true, these coordinate, asyndetic clauses are cumulative; they let us see this ὅς from his incarnation to his ascension. Each step upward rests on the preceding one. The first clause is not the subject of the other five.

"Was justified in spirit" = was forensically declared just and righteous. The forensic sense cannot be eliminated. Even if we translate *erwiesen*, it must be forensic: *als gerecht erwiesen*. This is the place to look at "the Righteous One," ὁ δίκαιος, who was declared righteous by God, Acts 7:52; "the Holy and Righteous One," Acts 3:14, both being titles of the Messiah. "God hath made that same Jesus, whom ye have crucified, both Lord and Christ," Acts 2:36, "Prince and Savior," Acts 5:31. Add "Jesus Christ, the Righteous," I John 2:1; "he is righteous," I John 2:29; "that Righteous One," Acts 22:14. Finally, "Thou art righteous, O Lord, who art, and wast, and shalt be," Rev. 16:5.

When and how was Jesus declared righteous by God? In and by the act of raising him from the dead. Men had nailed him to the cross, condemned him to the cross as one accursed of God, for to be hung on wood meant to be declared accursed of God; *him* God raised from the dead, *him* God thereby declared righteous. God's forensic judgment was analytic: Jesus himself was declared righteous; it was not synthetic: another's righteousness was not imputed to him. On Christ's sinlessness note John 8:46; Heb. 10:7, 9; 7:26; 4:15. Why this signal act of declaring Jesus righteous? He is made "unto *us* righteousness," I Cor. 1:30; "he was raised for *our* righteousness," Rom. 4:21; "that *we* might be made the righteousness of God in him," I Cor. 5:21; Rom. 10:4.

The phrases match the verbs; a person would not be manifested "in spirit," the manifestation would be "in flesh," for when "flesh" is used to designate the whole human nature, as it is here, it includes body, soul, and spirit and thus the whole visible, bodily life that is manifest to other men and manifesting the kind of person one is. So Christ was manifested "in flesh," and John 1:14 says, "we beheld his glory," etc. But one is not justified or declared righteous "in flesh" but "in spirit," for one's spirit is judged when a justification occurs; here it was Christ's spirit of holy obedience unto the death on the accursed cross. This explains Rom. 1:4 in which "spirit of holiness" is sometimes misunderstood, as is also I Pet. 3:18 and its dative πνεύματι: "made alive by spirit," Christ's spirit that returned to his body in the tomb. "Flesh" = the whole human nature of Jesus assumed at the incarnation = body, soul, and spirit, the material and the immaterial part; "spirit" = his human spirit as this was joined to his body, in which the ἐγώ was that of the eternal Son. That is the only contrast there is in these two parallel phrases. To assume a different contrast, one in which "spirit" is something else, is to go beyond Paul's intention.

The A. V. does this when it translates "in Spirit" and thinks of the Holy Spirit and prints as parallel references Matt. 3:16; John 1:32, 33; 15:26; 16:8, 9. How Jesus could be declared righteous "in the Holy Spirit" is inconceivable. At his baptism the Holy Spirit was *bestowed* upon Jesus for his great work; that was all that happened as far as the Holy Spirit was concerned. The declaration: "This is my beloved Son, in whom I was well pleased" (aorist), refers to the human spirit of Jesus who came to the baptism in holy obedience to fulfill all righteousness (Matt. 3:15).

As the A. V. has "spirit" = the Holy Spirit, so some have "spirit" = the divine nature, the deity of Jesus. They argue that, if "flesh" = the human nature of Jesus, then "spirit" must = his divine nature. Thus they get a wrong contrast. Since this is wrong, it matters little where they find the justification, whether at his baptism, or in his whole earthly life, or at his resurrection from the dead. It is unthinkable that Jesus should be justified in his deity just as it is unthinkable that he was justified "in the Holy Spirit." In order to uphold their view they give justification a meaning that is different from the one we have advanced above. It was not God's declaration that Jesus is "the Righteous One," "the Holy and Righteous One" (Acts 7:52; 3:14, plus the verdicts in all the other passages quoted above), it was not a verdict on his holy Messianic, substitutionary obedience, the perfect obedience of his whole life, the obedience unto death, even the accursed death on the cross (Phil. 2:8) which was rendered according to his human nature, in his spirit which directed his soul as well as his body — all this that is so plain in Scripture, even in Isa. 53:11: "my *righteous Servant*," is overlooked, and Paul is thought to say that "over against his enemies and accusers Jesus was proven to be what he claimed to be, God's Son and Savior of the world." Thus "spirit" is referred to Christ's deity. Δικαιοῦν, which always means to pronounce a verdict on character, conduct, deeds as to whether these are righteous or not, is taken in the sense of *erwiesen*, of *proving* the nature, the deity of Jesus.

Since it occurs in a series of six passives, ὤφθη should not be understood in the middle sense: "appeared to angels," but as a true passive with the dative of the agent: "was seen by angels." But when and where? When they answer these questions some refer to heaven and say this occurred when Jesus ascended to glory; but this virtually repeats the last clause: "was received up in glory." Some refer to hell and to the evil angels. They do this on the supposition that, if Jesus was declared righteous by being raised from the dead, this reference to his resurrection should be followed by a reference to his descent into hell. The analogy of Scripture shows that the unmodified word ἄγγελοι is never used to designate demons.

Some take the word to mean "messengers" and find these messengers in the apostles, to whom the risen Savior appeared during the forty days. This brings us close to the truth. Some include all the angels who saw Jesus while he was here on earth. "Was seen by angels" = in his resurrection. The Obedient, Righteous One whom God justified by raising him from the dead was seen in his glorified human nature by angels; these were the beings who first saw him thus.

"By angels," without the article, is not by "the angels," i. e., by all of them, the entire class. Angels saw him. Why does Paul not speak of the human witnesses as he does in I Cor. 15:5-8? Angels are greater; Paul is here not proving the reality of the resurrection as he is in I Cor. 15. This hymn dwells on the great saving features that appear in Jesus. That is why two points are mentioned in these hymn lines in regard to the resurrection; for in all the apostolic preaching the resurrection of Jesus is made to stand out most highly: God declared him righteous — angels saw him risen indeed. Whatever balance or parallel may be observed between "angels" and "nations," the main balance seems to lie in the verbs, all the verbs are placed emphatically forward.

"Was preached in nations," heralded in their midst, refers to Matt. 28:16-20 as explained above. "Was believed in the world" (no article is needed, there being only one world) goes with the preaching among the nations. Both phrases are general and do not distinguish between Jews and Gentiles. We might think that the last line: "was received up in glory," should precede the preaching and the believing, and so it might. In Acts 2:31-36 the resurrection and the ascension are preached, but as explaining the sending of the Holy Spirit at Pentecost. In Acts 4:2 it is the preaching of the resurrection (compare Acts 4:8-12; 5:31, 32). The order of this hymn is according. The point itself is of minor importance. Jesus ordered the preaching before his ascension; it was, of course, actually done after. Take the chronology as you wish. "Was received up" is the verb used in Mark 16:19 and Acts 1:4; "borne up" in Luke 24:51, and "taken up" in Acts 1:9, all mean the same thing, all are passives.

"In glory" is not, as the older grammarians supposed, a pregnant use of ἐν: motion "into" and thus rest "in." It is only a variation of this older view to say that "in glory" describes the condition that followed the receiving up. The act and its subject Jesus were "in glory," i. e., the glorious and glorified Jesus was gloriously received up. To say that the whole heavenly life of Jesus in glory is included in the verb is to extend unduly the force of the aorist which denotes one act. Of course, having been received up "in glory," Jesus is in heaven and in glory, but the verb does not extend beyond the reception. Some speak of a progression in glory, that Jesus grew in glory already during the forty days and then reached the pinnacle of glory when he entered heaven. But the Scriptures do not speak of such a process or progression.

Two trilogies are noted by those who think of the "angels" as being in heaven. Three pairs are noted by others; they get these by pairing the modifiers: 1) flesh — spirit; 2) angels — nations; 3) world — glory. Yet the verbs are the important words, and these do not form three pairs. Two threes are thought to denote: 1) Christ's person and work: incarnation — resurrection — ascension (this is the "seen by angels" in heaven); 2) the church militant and triumphant: preaching — believing — kingdom of glory. But the ascension is not number three, it is number six. And this is the ascension of Jesus, not *our* transfer to glory. These are neither pairs nor trios. There is only an interlocking in some of the verbs, also in some of the phrases, a beauty of thought and a wording that are of a rare kind.

CHAPTER IV

How Timothy Is to Be Prepared to Meet the
Apostasy Foretold by the Spirit

1) A reading of this chapter will convince one
that it is a unit: Timothy is to be prepared to meet
the apostasy foretold by the Holy Spirit. The particle
δέ is merely transitional and is inserted because Timothy is to warn also the churches and their officers
against the coming danger (v. 6).

**Now the Spirit states expressly that in later sea-
sons some will apostatize from the faith, giving heed
to deceitful spirits and doctrines of demons, in hypocrisy of lie-speakers, such as have been seared as to
their own conscience, such as forbid to marry, to abstain from foods, which things God created for reception with thanksgiving for the believers and those who
have realized the truth.**

This is the substance of what the Spirit "states expressly"; and it is stated in actual and not in symbolical terms. The question of prophecy is usually introduced at this place; see the subject under I Thess.
5:20; Rom. 12:6; I Cor. 14:3. There is no reason to
think of prophecy as being anything but direct revelations to Paul himself, to other apostles, and possibly
to the very few others who are known as recipients
of direct revelation (of the type of Agabus). A different type of prophecy is spoken of in I Cor. 14. Timothy had heard all about this prophecy; he was a fellow writer of II Thess. 2:1-12. He knew that Paul had
received this prophecy from the Spirit. It is here put
into indirect instead of into direct discourse because
several apostles had in all probability received the

Spirit's warning, certainly not because Paul had received it from others.

"In later seasons" does not mean "in the last days." The latter = the whole time between the two advents of Jesus, the whole New Testament Era, beginning with Pentecost. "Later seasons" are certain short periods that simply follow earlier ones. Earlier ones had passed when Paul wrote, later ones would appear, and in one or the other or in more of them there would be apostasy. "Some will apostatize from the faith" contains the same word that was used in II Thess. 2:3; there it is the definite noun: "the apostasy," here the verb ἀφίστημι in the future middle, intransitive, is used.

One must certainly be struck by the resemblance between II Thess. 2 and Paul's present statements. There the whole great apostasy which is headed by the great Antichrist is revealed, and we are shown how it shall be blasted by the Word and shall finally be utterly destroyed by the Lord's Parousia. Here Paul warns Timothy only regarding some who will apostatize a little later. We recall I John 2:18 where we are told that the great Antichrist is coming and that many little antichrists are already present when John writes his letter. They seem to be advance guards of the great apostasy and the great Antichrist. The Spirit gave warning already in Paul's time, some twenty to thirty years before John wrote (Zahn).

The ablative genitive "from the faith" is objective (see the discussion in 3:9), *fides quae creditur*, for the apostasy of these persons consists in heeding "doctrines" or teachings that come from demons. We fail to understand how Luke 8:13 can be cited to the contrary. "Some" — apostasy always begins with "some." Timothy and the churches must be ready when "some" appear. These give heed to (hold their minds toward) "deceitful spirits and doctrines of demons." These "spirits" and these "demons" are not identical; why should Paul use these two words in one brief clause? The deceitful spirits are false teachers. They are called "spirits" in accord with what they represent and in accord with the spirit that speaks from them. So I John 4:1-3 speaks of "spirits," and John tells us to test them. Πλάνος ("wandering," from which we derive "planet") = "astray from the truth" and thus "deceitful"; the word is used regarding impostors. Whoever lends an ear to such men will be led to apostatize.

First the impostors, then, coupled with them, the doctrines they teach, and these Paul calls "doctrines of demons"; James 3:15 has the expression "wisdom demoniacal." This is the genitive of source: doctrines that emanate from demons, and not the objective genitive: doctrines about demons, the latter the Scriptures themselves contain. How Satan himself gets hold of a man's spirit we see in the case of Judas (Luke 22:3; John 13:27; compare 6:70). Satan is the father of lies, deception is his great work. His tools are his victims. We need not puzzle our minds about the occult activities of demons; the antichristian doctrines betray their origin all too plainly. We can also note the way in which these doctrines wreck men's souls. Satan also controls the great Antichrist (II Thess. 2:9). The great danger is that today false doctrines are not recognized as coming from demons unless they deny the faith *in toto,* as if the devil is not cunning enough to begin with little lies, as if only those that are as big as mountains come from him.

Some will apostatize means some who at first were good church members, believers of the truth. Let us who stand be warned. All false security is dangerous. Paul does not indicate where these "deceitful spirits" come from. Some came from Judaism, some from paganism, the Roman world was infested with religious charlatans; some apostates would develop into heretical teachers; this was the case with Marcion who was at one time a Christian.

2) Some construe as appositions: "of demons, of lie-speakers, of branded ones, of forbidders," etc. And they regard these "lie-speakers" as the false prophets who are governed by the demons. The genitives occurring in v. 2 are not appositions to δαιμονίων; these genitives refer to men and not to demons. The first of these genitives depends on the phrase "in hypocrisy of lie-speakers," and the two participial genitives are predicative modifiers of "lie-speakers" which describe them: "such as have been seared . . . such as forbid," etc.

On what does the ἐν phrase depend? It may depend on the main verb "shall apostatize," or on the modal participle "giving heed," or it may be a modification that is coordinate with "giving heed." The meaning remains the same in all of these constructions. Every adverbial modification *eo ipso* gravitates toward the main verb because the participle is modal for that verb; so vice versa, the participle being modal. By coordinating phrase and participle both are in this way referred to the main verb. Drive a pair or drive tandem, you pull the same wagon.

"In hypocrisy of lie-speakers" means that the whole thing is done in this way, namely "in connection with hypocrisy," the wearing of a mask like the ancient show actors of the stage; and this is a hypocrisy (no article) such as belongs to "lie-speakers" who must dissemble and be hypocrites in order to get their lies across. The fact that the "deceitful spirits" of v. 1 are men is plain. As far as hypocrites are concerned, these may be conscious or unconscious hypocrites, the latter have gone so far in lying and dissembling that the vice has become a second nature to them. The entire stress is on the phrase.

In order to show how far they have sunken Paul adds the predicative perfect passive participle; he chooses the perfect to describe the state into which they have come: "such as have been seared as to their own conscience," the accusative object being retained with the passive. The demons have seared their conscience. The R. V. translates "branded" and thinks of slaves and criminals who were marked as such by a branding iron. We fail to see how that idea applies here, for a brand of this sort was to be seen, was to mark the slave or the criminal as such for those who saw, yet the brand here spoken of would be hidden in the conscience and invisible, it would be seen only by the demons and by God. The translation of the A. V. is correct, "seared with a hot iron," the conscience has been cauterized so that it has lost all sensitiveness and fails to respond. Judas is an example: Satan entered into him, and to the very last every effort on the part of Jesus to reach his seared conscience proved unavailing, see John 13:18, etc., a tremendous effort; already John 6:70; and the final effort of Jesus in Matt. 26:50. These deceivers and hypocritical liars are beyond all deterrents of conscience.

This participle is passive and not middle: "they have branded themselves" — "they are marked for themselves . . . drive the iron in more deeply," etc. Those who regard the participle as a middle offer the following interpretation: "They live in sins which, like branding marks, stain their conscience and are thus themselves conscious of this sin because of the feeling of hellish pain while they put on before others the glitter of holy doing." But this interpretation is scarcely satisfactory. What they do is to perpetrate demon doctrines of deceit and lies while their own conscience is rendered incapable of feeling even a misgiving. Nothing is said about other sins. Nor is

Luther so far wrong: "they have an invented (*erdich-tetes*) and false conscience, one that is forced by violence and not natural and honest." That is how a seared conscience looks.

3) To their character is added their teaching: "such as forbid to marry, to abstain from foods, which," etc. The infinitives after "forbid" are a case of zeugma; some call it ellipsis and remove the zeugma by inserting the opposite of "forbid" (as our versions do). In a zeugma the first term fits exactly but the second does not although the sense is perfectly plain. Paul instances only two specimens of the future teaching, both of which are contrary to the nature which God himself created. These he calls "doctrines of demons," such as can be advocated only "in hypocrisy" by religious liars, by men whose conscience is seared against God's own Word. He mentions these two because they are so plain, because they refer to conduct and are thus seen at a glance. They rest on a mass of other falsity, without which they could not be advocated.

To point to the Essenes, a small sect of Judaism that never amounted to much, is of little help. Josephus, *Ant.* 13, 5, 9, speaks of them as early as 166 B. C. They lived in seclusion near the Dead Sea and never spread. All but one group of them never married. Since they had been in existence for over two centuries, Paul could not be thinking of them here when he is speaking of devilish doctrines that are soon to arise in the Christian Church.

To mention the Therapeutæ also offers little that is tangible. Did such a sect ever exist? Somebody, it seems, at the end of the third century wrote a book under Philo's name in which he idealized and thus supported Egyptian monasticism. In this book the author describes what he calls the Therapeutæ, *Gottesver-ehrer*. This writing was attached to one of Philo's own and purported to date back to his time. We may safely say that no sect that bore this name ever existed.

These words are prophecy pure and simple. It is unwarranted to say that, when such prophecy is written, it must already have facts on which it is based and to claim that what is prophesied must grow out of what is already present. How or from what beginnings devilish doctrines were to arise is not the point, but *that* they would arise and be promulgated by scienceless liars. "In later times" does not say how soon this will occur. It is not Paul's object to set a precise date. His object is to warn in advance of coming danger, to have all the churches fully fortified long before the actual danger arrives. The whole monastic system that developed, together with all the lying teachings from which it arose, appeared soon enough. It still flourishes in Rome and in all the rest of the false asceticism. Paul properly writes βρώματα, *Speisen*, "foods," this and that a Christian is not to eat, not to drink.

Some refer to Col. 2:16: "in eating and in drinking," but this epistle cannot be quoted in corroboration. A peculiar type of Judaizers had recently appeared in Colosse who advocated a peculiar doctrine to the effect that Christians must avoid certain earthly elements (στοιχεῖα) because demons did damage through them. Paul treated these silly Judaizers with disdain. See Col. 2:20-23, also 2:8. By his descent to hell Christ celebrated a glorious triumph over all the demons (Col. 2:15); it is farcical to put up ordinances such as those that are mentioned in Col. 2:21. But Paul is not speaking to Timothy about such Judaizers.

The neuter plural is usually referred only to "foods." Thus all that follows (v. 3-5) would be restricted to "foods." We are told that marriage is not referred to because its prohibition needs no refutation. We doubt this. Why should ἅ, "which things," not include both marriage and foods? God created both; to forbid either is to challenge his creative will. For reception (μετάληψιν, participation) = to have our share in them, i. e., not to be debarred from them. Yet "for reception with thanksgiving," recognizing that these are God's good gifts to us and thus participating in them with due thankfulness to God.

We have the dative of advantage: "for the believers and those who have realized the truth." Because but one article is used, the two terms are regarded as constituting but one class of individuals so that καί is epexegetical: believers are such as have realized. The perfect participle also includes their present state: having been brought to this realization of the blessed truth, they still continue in it. The fear of a "difficulty" in regard to this dative, since God created these things for all men, is groundless. The Scriptures regularly speak thus of believers when they, for instance, say that Christ died for them, which never means that he did not die for all men. Paul is writing for believers (v. 6), fortifying them, and hence states what God's creative intention is in regard to them. This dative certainly does not belong to v. 4.

Paul's words are often extended beyond their intent as when it is said that some of the Christians in the Asian churches were already affected by these erors, or that some among them were weak (introducing Rom. 14:1), or that some forgot the proper thanksgiving.

4) Paul continues: **Seeing that every creature of God (is) excellent, and nothing to be thrown away, being received with thanksgiving.**

This is the ὅτι *consecutivum* (R. 1001): "seeing that." Certainly not "because" every creature of God is excellent did he create these things; he created them, and in consequence, because of this, every one of them is excellent (Gen. 1:31). Ὅτι is not expository of "the

truth"; the latter includes much more than is stated
in v. 4. "And nothing to be thrown away (to be rejected), being received with thanksgiving," is the elaboration. R. 1022 makes the participle conditional: "if
(or: when) received with thanksgiving." Others make
it adjectival: "nothing to be rejected that is received
with thanksgiving." Either will do.

5) "For" explains what Christian thanksgiving
does: **for it is sanctified by means of God's Word and
prayer,** set apart as divinely intended, as a gift that is
being received with due gratitude from God's own
Creator hand. The means for so receiving marriage,
our daily food and drink, and all other blessings of
God (note "every creature," everything created by
God) is not twofold: God's Word and prayer, for these
two are regarded as one. God's Word is *his* connection
with us, our prayer is *our* conscious and deliberate
entrance into this connection. These two unite and
become one. Thus the prayers that are used in our
marriage ceremonies, at table, and on other occasions,
as far back as we are able to trace them, contain pertinent Scripture words and references and, besides that,
are Scriptural in thought and in spirit. Passages such
as Ps. 103:1-3; 106:1; 145:15, 16 are used as table
prayers. Ἔντευξις is most fitting, prayer as free speech
to God (Trench) ; we freely speak to God on the basis
of his Word and perhaps even use expressions and
statements that are taken from that Word.

Two things are plainly taught. 1) The devilish-
ness of all teaching that what God has created for
man's use is not "excellent," that marriage is only
carnal and spiritually lower than celibacy (Heb. 13:4),
that, for similar reasons, certain foods and drinks are
not to be touched (Col. 2:21), and the like. The
demons do like to contradict God. Liars accept their
lies. Gnosticism attributed the creation of the world
to intermediate beings and thus laid the foundation

for all its vicious asceticism. 2) The reception of God's good creatures with Christian prayer. Think how many Christians neglect table prayers, especially when they are alone or when they are eating in public places. "Whether therefore ye eat, or drink, or whatsoever ye do, do all to the glory of God," I Cor. 10:31. "Whatsoever ye do in word or deed, do all in the name of the Lord Jesus, giving thanks to God and the Father by him," Col. 3:17. "Christ calls marriage a divine union, Matt. 19:6: 'What God hath joined together, let not man put asunder.' Here Christ says that married people are joined together by God. Accordingly, it is a pure, holy, noble, praiseworthy work of God. And Paul says of marriage, of meats, and similar things, I Tim. 4:5. 'It is sanctified by the Word of God and prayer.'" *C. Tr.* 371, 30.

Our passage has been used as a directive for determining how the consecration of the earthly elements in the Lord's Supper must be performed: we use the Word, namely the Scripture words of the institution, and add the Lord's Prayer because it was given by the Lord himself. But Paul was not thinking of the Eucharist when he wrote v. 5.

6) This verse does not introduce a main section of the letter, one that deals with Timothy's personal conduct. Chapter 4 constitutes a main section of the epistle; 5:1-6:2 is another which contains further official directions for Timothy. To make a section of 3:14-4:5 is unfeasible although it has been attempted. We have already shown that 3:14-16 concludes the second main part of the letter (chapters 2 and 3) just as 1:18, 19 concludes the first main part (1:3-17). The third main part (4:1-16) deals with coming heresies and tells how Timothy is to be fortified and is to fortify the churches against them. In 4:1-5 we have the Spirit's prophecies about these heresies, their devilish

source, their contradiction of God's own creation. **This is objective.** Now comes the subjective fortification of Timothy who is to fight these coming heresies. Note v. 6, 11, 16.

To speak about Timothy as though he were the pastor of the one congregation in Ephesus and thus to interweave applicatory admonitions to present-day pastors, is to misunderstand the paragraph. Paul is not addressing the pastor of the Ephesian congregation; he is addressing his apostolic representative for the whole territory of which Ephesus is the center. He has left Timothy there to supervise all the congregations in this most important field. Dangerous times are ahead; Paul saw them coming when he spoke the words of Acts 20:29, 30. These dangers are now near. Timothy and the churches under his supervision must be ready to meet them.

By submitting these things to the brethren thou wilt be an excellent minister of Christ Jesus as being nourished by the words of the faith and of the excellent doctrine which thou hast been following.

As in 3:14 ταῦτα refers to the preceding, so "these things" refer to the contents of v. 1-5 and not to those of the three preceding chapters. Timothy is "to submit" them to the brethren, keep bringing them to their attention in order to fortify them in advance. This verb fits v. 1-5 exactly. When Paul addresses the members of one or of more congregations he uses "brethren"; he does so also here when he speaks of them to Timothy. By doing this Timothy will be "an excellent minister of Christ Jesus." This word is not used in its technical sense as in 3:8 and 12: "deacon," but in the broader sense of "ministrant" or "minister"; yet it is not used with the objective genitive: one who ministers to Christ, benefits him, but with the genitive of

origin or possession: appointed by or belonging to
Christ, the benefit of whose work accrues to the
brethren.

The participle states in what respect Timothy will
then be an excellent minister of Christ, namely "as
being nourished by the words of the faith and of the
excellent doctrine which thou hast been following," in
brief, as a sound, safe teacher of all the brethren under
his supervision. Οἱ λόγοι τῆς πίστεως = *die Glaubens-
lehren,* the statements that constitute what is to be
believed. The genitive of πίστις is just as objective as
is that of διδασκαλία. How the one can be subjective
faith and the other objective doctrine is difficult to
understand. "The words of the faith and of the doctrine" = the words which state what the Christian
faith and the doctrine is. Every good servant of
Christ is constantly "nourished" by them (durative
present passive, the dative of means). Since he is fed
on them he is the kind of man and of a minister that
he ought to be. The connotation of "nourished" is
strength and health. We note the repetition of "excellent" (similarly in 3:13, where "ministered excellently" occurs): "excellent doctrine" makes "an excellent minister of Christ Jesus," especially when
doctrinal dangers lie ahead as Paul has just warned
Timothy.

We decline to accept the view that this is the subjective genitive: "the words in which the faith of Timothy and of true Christians expresses itself." One does
not eat and is not nourished by one's own words. B.-P.
1063 (3) is correct against C.-K. 893. These words
of the faith and of the excellent doctrine express "the
truth" mentioned in v. 3; they are the same as the
Word of God. Lest someone draw the inference from
"will be" that Timothy was not as yet an excellent
minister, Paul adds the relative clause: "which thou
hast been following," the perfect stating that through-

out the past Timothy has adhered to the true doctrine of the faith and that he is now doing this.

This is high praise for Timothy. It shows what Paul thought of him, why Paul trusted him and made him his apostolic representative. This praise shows how Paul's admonitions to Timothy are to be understood. It is unfair to conclude from each admonition that Timothy suffered from a corresponding weakness. These are the words of an old leader to his tried and true representative in the work of leading where dangers lie ahead. Timothy was deeply grateful for them. They called out in a higher degree all that was true, "excellent," and noble in him.

7) **Now the profane and old-womanish myths disdain to be bothered with, but exercise thyself with respect to godliness. For the bodily exercise is profitable** (only) **with respect to little, but this godliness is profitable with respect to everything, having** (as it does) **promise for the present life and for the one to come.**

Our versions and some commentators regard δέ as adversative "but" because they consider only "the words of the faith and excellent doctrine" and "the profane and old-womanish myths," which appear as opposites. An adversative "but" would, however, contrast two main sentences and not two nouns in two sentences, the first of which occurs in a participial modifier. A contrast of sentences is not indicated here; for how may "thou wilt be an excellent minister" be in contrasted opposition to the imperative "disdain myths"? This δέ simply continues the admonition. Moreover, the imperative exhortation of v. 7 has its contrast in the imperative exhortation of v. 8, the former is a negative act, the latter its positive opposite.

We scarcely need to say that these "myths" are not the teachings of demons mentioned in v. 1; the latter

were to occur in the future; they were also by no
means "old-womanish." The article of previous reference and the word "myths" itself take us back to 1:4
where we have explained these wild inventions and fictions. With these Timothy must *now* deal; in due time
devilish doctrines will appear, and *then* Timothy must
be ready to fight them by now training himself by the
way in which he handles these myths of the present
time. For this reason Paul again refers to these myths.
In chapter 1 Timothy is directed to order those who
promulgate these myths to cease this and to put their
minds on the gospel; here Timothy is directed how to
treat these myths themselves when people come to
him with them. Not for one moment is he to treat
them seriously, discuss them, argue against them:
"Disdain to be bothered with" such profane and old-
womanish stuff. This is sound advice, is intended as
advice, intended to confirm Timothy in the attitude he
already held toward these fictions. To think for one
moment that Timothy was in danger, or that Paul
thought him in danger of believing these fables is doing Timothy or both Timothy and Paul a grave injustice.

Paul's advice is sound psychology. People who are
fanatical in regard to some silly religious matter desire
nothing more than to have you argue with them. To
do so is to leave the wrong impression as though the
matter is worth discussion and argument. That encourages their folly; they think they really have something. For that very reason they will cling to their
infatuation more obstinately than ever when one makes
the mistake of treating them seriously. The thing to
do is: Παραιτοῦ, "disdain to be bothered."

That is the force of this imperative; it is finely
chosen in every way; it is the German *sich etwas ver-
bitten*. The present tense of this middle is iterative
and indicates that every time someone comes with

these myths Timothy is firmly, politely, the more firmly because politely, to beg to be spared. Paul uses the same imperative in 5:11; II Tim. 2:23; Tit. 3:10; the sense is each time according to the object involved and is more or less severe, G. K. 195. The two adjectives are also full of disdain: "profane," with not a sacred thing about them, unworthy of a truly religious person's attention; "old-womanish," unworthy even of a sensible person's attention, fit only for senile, silly old crones to chatter about. False doctrine Paul meets with divine truth; religious follies with disdain.

Instead of allowing himself to be bothered with discussions about the myths that were filling some people's heads, Paul advises Timothy to "exercise himself with respect to godliness." Our versions coordinate this with v. 7a. It is claimed that παραιτοῦ and γύμναζε are not adverse enough to have "but" placed between them. We answered this above when we spoke regarding the connection of v. 7 with v. 6, single terms are not the points of contrast but the thoughts of the two sentences. So here: Disdain and do not take up thy time and effort with useless stuff *but* devote thyself to what really pertains to godliness.

This is advice to Timothy who is Paul's representative. Paul is not concerned merely for Timothy's spiritual welfare lest *he* be captivated by these myths. If there had been a danger of that kind, Paul would have made a mistake in using such a man as his apostolic agent in a great field. No; Timothy has far more valuable things to do than to argue with ignorant and shallow fanatics. His great concern is "godliness," godliness in the sense of complete devotion to the true religion, certainly for the sake of his own person but also when serving in his great office. He is to maintain and to increase godliness in the membership of all the churches and to keep out everything that conflicts with this godliness. The implication is not that Timothy might forget the interests of godliness. These are not aorist but present imperatives. "Keep on in exercising thyself (present tense) with respect to godliness" = keep on as thou art doing. The implication is encouragement in following a *right* line of conduct, following it with all confidence.

The three πρός phrases have the same force, and we should retain that. Our versions fail to do this. Thus the first phrase does not indicate an aim: "unto godliness." This might be the sense since the preposition is at times so used; but it cannot be the sense here where two more πρός follow which do *not* indicate an aim, an end, or a goal. All these phrases express relation: "with respect to godliness" — "with respect to little" — "with respect to everything." The fact that the godliness referred to is not merely Timothy's own personal godliness but the whole cause of godliness for which Timothy labored has already been stated. The athletic term "exercise thyself" as a gymnast does by gymnastic training and contests is metaphorical and is explained in v. 10 where Paul includes himself: "we toil and strain." All the ardent, strenuous efforts of Timothy are to be put forth with respect to godliness, he is to be interested in this cause alone.

8) "For" explains. But not by contrasting physical exercise, gymnastics, calisthenics, physical work, brisk walking, etc., with spiritual exercise in Christian virtues. This is not an admission of what everybody knows, that every person ought to take some exercise, and that, when he does, he will be profited "a little." The caution is in place that, when Paul says a simple thing, it is a mistake to seek some deep, hidden meaning in his words. "A little" cannot mean: as far as physical health is concerned, for physical exercise does a great deal in that respect. Some even extend this "little" and say that robust physical vigor is also an asset in the godly life. But the fact that good physical

specimens of humanity are better Christians than weak and sickly persons would be a new departure.

Nor is Paul voicing his concern for Timothy's health and advising him that he ought to take at least some physical exercise in order to be able to do his spiritual work well, to which the application is sometimes added that preachers in general ought to watch this point lest they soon play out. Πρὸς ὀλίγον and πρὸς πάντα do not lie on different planes but on the same plane, the spiritual plane. "The bodily exercise" Paul refers to is the true Christian training of the body. The body is the temple of the Holy Spirit (I Cor. 6:19) ; its appetites must be kept in control, if necessary, by giving it a black eye as in a boxing bout (this is the word used in I Cor. 9:27). This is legitimate Christian asceticism, sober temperance in all bodily matters.

This, Paul says, is "profitable with respect to little," namely as far as true and complete godliness is concerned. Paul does not mean: This amounts to nothing; the phrase is not *wegwerfend,* for it is here paired with the other, "with respect to everything." Keeping the body with all its bodily desires well trained in the godly life is worth something, we must even say that it is a part of true godliness. Yet it is not the whole thing nor even the main feature; it is only "little" when it is compared with all that real godliness comprises. The base of godliness is in the spirit, its great field lies in the spiritual virtues, only a part of the territory lies in the body and the bodily members, in these physical instruments (ὅπλα, Rom. 6:13) of the godly spirit, which are to be slaves (δοῦλα, Rom. 6:19) of righteousness.

There is undoubtedly a reason that prompts Paul to say this. While in v. 7 "myths" refers back to the fables and genealogies mentioned in 1:4, the reference to "the bodily exercise" harks back to 1:7, to the ig-

norant use of the law by the pretended "law teachers."
The great use of the law in bringing sinners to contrition as it had brought the blasphemer and persecutor and insolent Paul himself to the Lord's feet was
a closed book to them. Their spurious godliness consisted in bodily exercises, in a false use of the law for
producing such exercises. This is the background of
Paul's present statement and not v. 2, 3 which lie in
the future. True godliness is acquainted with bodily
training and the degree of profit involved. This godliness is not derived from profane and old-womanish
myths or fables but from "the truth" (v. 3), from
"the words of the faith and of the excellent doctrine
which Timothy has been following" (v. 6), from the
pure gospel. These ignorant "law teachers" do not
even know what this godliness is. All of Timothy's
exercising himself (which will deal with far more
than a few bodily matters) will be "with respect to
godliness," for it is "this godliness" (article of previous reference) that "is profitable with respect to
everything," its fruit, profit, benefit literally extend
so far.

Paul does not say: "The bodily exercise is profitable with respect to (only) little, but the spiritual
exercise is profitable with respect to everything." That
would be a double falsity. There are not two kinds
of exercises: one that is altogether bodily, the other
altogether spiritual. The Christian's bodily exercise
is the body's obedience to his spirit; it is the spiritual
control of the body.

Secondly, this false parallel would lead to a false
conclusion; for if spiritual exercise profits in *all* respects, then the little profit of bodily exercise would be
included in this "all"; why, then, be concerned about
the body at all? No; the supreme thing, the product of
true gospel teaching, is true Christian godliness in
spirit, soul, heart, life; in faith, love, and all Christian

virtues. To exercise this godliness, to keep it constantly active in every way, is to have profit beyond compare. This exercise extends also to the body and includes also that small portion of profit; it is not lost. The great danger is to make it our chief concern.

The participle states the reason that godliness is so rich in profit: "having (as it does) promise for the present life and for the one to come." Since godliness is itself the spiritual life, we cannot agree with those who regard the genitive as the objective genitive, namely that godliness is promised life, the less so since this is "life now and to come," the two articles making these two expressions distinct and coordinate. An epexegetical genitive would yield the same sense: "promise, namely life now and to come," this double life constituting what "promise" contains.

A direct objective genitive ought to have the article, it would here be ἐπαγγελίαν τῆς ζωῆς. The anarthrous ζωῆς is the broader objective genitive: "having promise *for* life, *for* the one (τῆς) now, and *for* the one (τῆς) about to come." But would this not leave unsaid what is promised to godliness, and is "promise" ever used in such an unmodified way? C.-K. 29 supplies the answer: "promise" is never used as = the thing promised, this sense of the word is due to the context. So in this context after πρὸς πάντα profit in respect to everything *is* the promise godliness has. Let us add: no promise in regard to anything is what ungodliness and godlessness have.

Life now and life to come are illumined by the word "promise," not by a certain promise or other, but by a promise that covers everything. Throughout Scripture "promise" is written about, signed, and sealed *for* godliness. "With respect to everything" = "for life now" as well as "for life to come." That surely covers "everything," πάντα. As regards "everything" for this life note, for instance, Rom. 8:28. But the stream of "promise" does not stop at the grave, it flows on into eternity. Paul does not attempt to name all that "promise" contains; the sweet word itself is enough.

"Promise" connotes grace and does not imply that godliness earns and merits so much. Born of grace, godliness now and to all eternity walks in the golden garden of promise where it plucks endless profit. Many Christians foolishly imagine that godliness forfeits so much in this life. So they forsake it occasionally in order to snatch some of these things; but these things are only apples of Sodom. Some permanently forsake godliness for what the world promises. But look at the lying promise Satan made to Eve.

To cultivate godliness in all the Asian churches by means of the true gospel was Timothy's task. That, of course, meant that godliness would be richly cultivated in himself. Note Timothy's incentives; they could not be stronger and richer. Promise for life here and hereafter beckons him on in his work. Note that doctrine (in v. 6, 7) is connected with godliness (in v. 8, 9). Every sacrifice and every loss of the former entail the same for the latter. No godliness ever grew on error although some imagine that it does. They even estimate how large an error must be before it hurts godliness. So they also fail to distinguish between genuine godliness and many of its current imitations. When the truth fails to produce godliness the truth has not entered the heart.

9) **Faithful (is) the statement and of all acceptation worthy.** This dictum is identical with that occurring in 1:15 and does not seal what follows but what precedes, namely what is said regarding godliness and its promise. In 3:1 the wording is briefer. The ὅτι clause of v. 10 cannot be construed with v. 9: "Faithful is the statement, etc., . . . that we have set our hope on God," etc. There is no law that would compel a writer to use a confirmatory dictum in only one way.

Paul's seal: "Reliable, in every way worth accepting!" is as objective in form as is what he says about true godliness and its blessed promise. Trust this λόγος or not, it is and remains trustworthy; accept it or not, it is and remains "worthy of all acceptation." Verse 10 adds the subjective elaboration.

10) **Yea, for this thing we are toiling and straining because we have set our hope on God as living, he who is Savior of all men, especially of believers.**

This γάρ does not state a reason for the preceding. Subjective actions cannot prove or establish objective facts, i. e., the fact that godliness is what it is stands whether we toil and agonize about it or not. Nor does this γάρ suggest that Paul is here offering "another *reason* that should move Timothy to execute his office faithfully and diligently," the reason being that Timothy himself is one of those who are toiling and striving. Yet his doing this certainly cannot constitute a reason for his doing it.

This γάρ is *folgernd* and not *begruendend*. It does not state a reason but a consequence and is often used with exclamatory force. This is the German *ja*, the English "yea" or "hence." This statement is so trustworthy; hence thou, Timothy, and I, Paul, toil, etc., as we do. Εἰς τοῦτο does not mean "for this λόγος or statement" (the neuter τοῦτο does not refer to the masculine λόγος). "This thing" = what Paul is speaking about, this thing of true godliness. "We are toiling and straining as athletes" refers to Timothy and to Paul in their offices, to their strenuous exertions to spread true godliness among men and to maintain it against present errors (v. 7) and future attacks (v. 1, 2). As one who is full of this godliness Timothy is to work and is already working in the Asian field. Paul is, of course, doing the same wherever he is working. The "we" of these verb suffixes is not indefinite: "we apostles," leaving out Timothy, or: "we Christians." This "we" = "thou and I," Timothy and Paul. To combine himself thus with Timothy is beautiful on Paul's part, for it makes his advice to Timothy (v. 6-8a, especially 8a) apply also to Paul himself.

'Αγωνιζόμεθα has the variant ὀνειδιζόμεθα, "we suffer reproach," which the A. V. translates; it also places a καί before the first verb: "we both labor and suffer reproach." This reading, however, has less textual support. To adopt it because we cannot today see how it could displace the other reading is a precarious canon to follow. The fact that "suffer reproach" was changed into "strain" in order to make the thought easier, and that the alteration was suggested by Col. 1:29, is not apparent. It is worth noting that ἀγωνίζομαι is figurative: the gymnast carefully trains, the contestant strains every muscle.

We do not construe εἰς τοῦτο . . . ὅτι because of the tense and the sense of the verb "we have been setting our hope." This clause states the reason for all of the present toiling and straining of Paul and of Timothy: "because we have been placing our hope on God as living." This hoping started with Paul's and Timothy's conversion and continues. Hoping matches "promise" used in v. 8, so does God "as living," for only a living God is able to keep his promise; dead idols cannot even promise, to say nothing about redeeming a promise. Both Paul and Timothy have already experienced the fulfillment of God's promise to godliness in the life that now is, which is a sure evidence of the fulfillment that awaits them in the life to come. They have seen this fufillment in richest measure also in other godly believers. "To hope" may be construed in various ways; it is here construed with ἐπί, and the great ultimate basis of hope is indicated, the living God himself.

Toiling and straining means working and contending for others in the offices which Paul and Timothy occupied. The hope they set on the living God is not merely a hope regarding the promise for their own personal godliness but equally for that of all who can be brought to true godliness. Hence we have the relative clause, in which the relative is quite emphatic: "he who is Savior of all men, especially of believers." Compare the relative found in 2:3; both are far stronger than an apposition would be.

God is indeed "living," but he is also full of saving grace. All that we have said regarding "Savior" in 1:1 and 2:3 might be repeated here. He wants all men to be saved (2:3) and is thus called "Savior of all men." We know why so many are not saved (Matt. 23:37). Therefore Paul adds: "especially of believers" just as in 1:1 he says "our Savior," and in 2:3: "he wants all men to come to realization of truth." This does not mean that his will to save some men is stronger than his will to save others, or that there is a duality in God's antecedent will (Calvin). Μάλιστα, "especially," pertains to "believers" because God's good and gracious saving will is being accomplished in them and is not frustrated by obdurate unbelief. Paul is thinking not only of the believers already brought to a realization of the saving gospel truth, to godliness and to its sure and certain promise, but also of all believers of the future. The hope that rests on this Savior God is both sure and an inspiration to go on toiling and straining in teaching "the excellent doctrine" (v. 6), in fighting all error (v. 7), in preparing to fight all coming error (v. 1, etc.).

11) So Paul exhorts Timothy, his representative: **Order these things and teach them!** They are written to Timothy for the very reason that he may order and teach them in the Asian churches. Every personal word directed to Timothy is not just personal but is

directed to him because he is also Paul's personal agent in the work assigned to him.

What are "these things"? Some look at παράγγελλε and, because this often means "to pass an order or a command along," restrict "these things" to what may be regarded as commands in the foregoing. But here and elsewhere (1:3) the verb often means *einschaerfen* (C.-K. 30; B.-P. 978), "to pound in," and, according to the context, "to give notice" in regard to something (see on the papyri, M.-M. 481), perhaps in a formal, authoritative manner, formally to instruct someone, etc. The point is that the verb is used to express much more than merely conveying commands. "These things" refer to all that Paul says in v. 6-10. Timothy is to order, announce, pound them in in an authoritative manner as Paul's representative.

"And teach them," for they are fundamentally διδασκαλία (v. 6), doctrine, which, of course, governs conduct. To teach is to explain so that these things will be understood, assimilated, taken to heart (note "nourished" in v. 6). The two imperatives are closely united; both are durative: Timothy is to keep on in this work. These are his original directions from Paul, they are repeated here so that Timothy may show them also to others wherever it is necessary. It was an advantage to him to have them in writing; it is still an advantage in the case of officials who have congregations to supervise.

12) When he is attending to these things with due authority Timothy is to let no one question that authority on the score of his youth. **Let no one despise thy youth but continue to be an example for believers in word, in conduct, in love, in faith, in pureness.** We can only estimate Timothy's age; he was probably between 35 and 40 years of age. The Jew regarded a man as a νεανίας until he reached 40. Yet here age does not mean age in general but age with

reference to Timothy's position and office as Paul's representative. The "elders" of the congregations were commonly older men, often men of years. Timothy would also have to deal with all of them, and in case of a disagreement some of them might affect to despise Timothy because of his "youth." It has been well said that in the case of a captain in the army 40 is old, in the case of an Anglican bishop young, in the case of an English prime minister very young, in fact, too young. A college president, a synodical president, who is 40 years old or less, would be very young and would invite the charge of immaturity even in America. Age does count in high positions. Paul did not think Timothy too young; he says so here and will let no one contradict this estimate of his representative.

The conclusion has been drawn that Timothy was timid because of his years and that Paul is here offering an antidote for this timidity. But this may be an injustice to Timothy. Paul could not use a timid man as his representative in the Asian churches, nor could he hope to stiffen such a man's courage at a distance by means of a single sentence. Paul's remark is intended for any man who might try to oppose Timothy in his work and might thus pass a remark regarding Timothy's "youth" in order to influence the congregation; hence we have the wording: "let no one," etc.

The use of γίνου in no way implies that Timothy has as yet not been an example for the believers and is now to become one; it signifies that he has been and is such an example and that he is to continue as such as a full and sufficient answer to any man who presumes to reflect on his youth. Paul is not fearing indiscretion on Timothy's part; he is indicating the type of character and conduct that will hush every adverse remark about his youth.

Paul uses neither four (minor rhetorical completeness) nor seven (sacred number) nor ten specifications (major completeness) but five (incompleteness) and thereby indicates that he is not exhausting the subject. This appears also in the listing: two pairs and one additional point as though Paul breaks off instead of completing the list.

"In word and in conduct" = outward demeanor in speech and in general action. "Word" includes teaching and all other forms of speaking. "In love and faith," love being apparent in word and in conduct, faith being the root of love. "In pureness" adds this one Christian virtue, to which others might be joined: *Tadellosigkeit* (G. K. 124) — not only sexual purity. In the LXX the word is used to indicate ritual purity; here and also in 5:2 moral cleanness and spotlessness is meant.

13) **While I am traveling, pay close attention to the reading, to the exhortation, to the teaching!** Ἔως with the present tense means "while" (R. 975, also *W. P.*) although many translate it "till" (also B.-D. 383, 1). They misunderstand the situation. "While" Paul is away, (ἔρχομαι does not mean "coming" but "journeying," "traveling" from place to place) Timothy is to watch things in the churches. The usual understanding of this passage is that Timothy is stationed only in the congregation at Ephesus, and that he is there to read the Scripture lections in the services, exhort the congregation, and act as the teacher. If that were the situation, it would be strange, indeed, that Paul would here ask him to do these things. Did Paul not tell him to teach in v. 11? Some note that "the exhortation" precedes "the teaching" and feel that this is a bit strange; Timothy ought first to teach and then to exhort. A few say that "the reading" includes diligent private Scripture study on Timothy's part. But the articles used with the three nouns may suggest the proper interpretation.

Timothy has a number of congregations under his care; how can he conduct the services in all of them? Is he to displace the elders? Would that be proper? Verse 11 directs him to inculcate everywhere what in the preceding Paul has stated as being necessary. And now Timothy is directed to pay close attention to "the reading" in the churches, i. e., to what lections are being read at the services. Not *that* lections be read, still less that Timothy is to read them, but *what* lections are being read. From their very beginning all the congregations read the LXX Old Testament in their services just as was done in the synagogues. Now the present danger was that here and there some of the cranks and fanatics (1:4) and the foolish law teachers (1:7) might read or ask to have read as lections the Old Testament genealogies, to which to pin their myths, and lections from the Levitical laws, to be interpreted for their ignorant purposes. This Timothy was not to allow. It was not necessary for him to be present at every service in every church; it was easy to find out and to keep track of what was going on, to learn where suspicious lections were being read and where such as helped true godliness were being read.

The same was true with regard to "the exhortation." This is properly placed next. We know from statements by Justin Martyr that after the Scripture reading by the lector a presbyter or some other person admonished and exhorted the people to take to heart what had been read. At times there was also "the teaching," not necessarily of the lection read but on this or that subject. So Paul taught the gospel of Christ in the synagogues and did this without basing it on the *haphtarah* or the *parashah* that happened to be the lections of the day. How easy it would be for some of the ἑτεροδιδάσκαλοι to inflict some of their myths or some of their ignorant notions of the law on a congregation! In v. 1, 4 we see what damage this might do. Timothy must "give heed" to what is going on, "to the lection, to the exhortation, to the teaching." The articles are, indeed, material to the sense. The fact that Timothy is to stop this kind of thing 1:4 has already stated.

Unless we understand Timothy's office and situation as they were, this verse will be misunderstood. Wohlenberg has interpreted it correctly but treats it all too briefly and does not mention the δίδασκε of v. 11 and the fact that two orders to Timothy to teach personally can scarcely follow each other so closely.

14) Be not careless about the charisma in thee, which was given to thee by means of prophecy together with laying on of the hands of the presbytery!

What "charisma" is this? The one indicated in v. 13. Not all the charismata of apostolic times were miraculous or at least bestowed in a miraculous manner. The whole series of charismata mentioned in Rom. 12:6, etc., lists such as were non-miraculous both in character and in manner of acquisition. In I Cor. 12:8 the two main charismata are of the same character. In I Cor. 14:1, etc., all members are urged to acquire and to use with diligence the charisma of prophecy, regarding which see the exposition of I Cor. 14:3; Rom. 12:6; I Thess. 5:20. Timothy's charisma was his ability to understand the true gospel teaching over against spurious and false teachings. He had the gift of prophecy (Rom. 12:6; I Cor. 12:10) and of discerning of spirits (I Cor. 12:10), i. e., seeing through all false teaching. He could properly transmit the true Word of God, could also teach and expound it, and could detect what deviated from it. This great charisma he is to exercise as v. 11 and 13 state. "Be not careless" is a litotes which states negatively

what is meant positively: "Keep attending to diligently," "constantly care for." There is no thought of a
gift that has been miraculously bestowed on him. Also
no thought of a certain talent that Timothy is to develop by private reading and study and by efforts of
exercising such a talent.

How did Timothy get this charisma? The relative
clause answers: "Which was given to thee by means
of prophecy." God gave Timothy this charisma, not
by a miraculous gift from heaven, but "by means of
prophecy," by a communication of the Word to him,
and did that under the tutelage of one of the most
capable prophets this Word ever had, namely Paul himself. "Prophecy" was the means that enabled Timothy. Here, however, not the mere ability of Timothy
is referred to but along with it the office for using that
ability, which is the reason for mentioning the "laying
on of hands." Timothy had not received his charisma
as the church members referred to in I Cor. 14:1, etc.,
had, all of whom were to seek the charisma of prophecy
in order to use it merely in their capacity as church
members and as private persons. None of these had
hands laid on them.

Timothy was not even to be only an elder in some
congregation, who had received that kind of an office
as a part of the gift bestowed on him. His charisma
was the ability which he was to exercise as Paul's
assistant and representative for many congregations.
Thus "hands of the presbytery" were laid on him.
Μετά adds this act as the accompanying feature; the
imposition of hands accompanied the training in
prophecy. From II Tim. 1:6 we see that this included
also the imposition of Paul's hands. There is no reason for thinking of two impositions of hands, one occurring at Lystra when Paul first took Timothy into
the work, the other at Ephesus when Paul placed him
in special charge of the extensive Asian field. One

imposition is referred to, namely the one that occurred when Timothy was set aside for the latter office.

Timothy was not appointed as Paul's representative by an act of Paul alone but by a joint act of Paul and of the mother church of the Asian territory. That is why its presbytery joined Paul in setting Timothy apart for his important work and office. Paul was not a hierarch who acted alone in this matter. He mentions "the presbytery" in this letter and at this place because all that precedes deals with Timothy's work in the Asian churches, with his relation to them. Paul mentions himself in II Tim. 1:6 because in the opening section of that letter he deals with Timothy's relation to himself. See that passage. Paul writes μετά in our passage, διά in II Tim. 1:6, not because the laying on of hands by the presbytery differed from the laying on of his own hands. Μετά avoids the repeating of διά in our passage; moreover, the laying on of hands may be viewed in two ways: "given to thee *by means of prophecy* (διά) *in company* with laying on of hands" (μετά) — the charisma of God, "which is in thee *by means of* (διά) laying on of hands." "The presbytery" is a collective term for "the elders" or presbyters of a congregation, each congregation having several; Kretzmann wants "the deacons" included, a view which we have already answered in 3:1, 8.

We are somewhat surprised to note some of the interpretations of this passage. We note the following especially. Διὰ προφητείας is regarded as an accusative plural: *infolge von Weissagungen,* "in consequence of predictions." The view that προφητείας may be a singular is rejected on the plea that such a phrase could not express the mediate cause but only the immediate cause and that "*a* prediction" could not be this cause. Now διά with the genitive never expresses cause, it names the means. Paul is *not* speaking of prediction, whether of one or of more. The defenders of this view think that at Lystra a number of prophets made predictions regarding Timothy's future career, that the elders there then ordained him, and that this produced in Timothy an "enthusiastic state" — does that mean an ecstasy? — in which he received his charisma in a supernatural way. But one might well ask: "Whence came those inspired prophets in the young congregation at Lystra?"

15) **These things continue to care for, in these things ever be, so that thy advancement may be manifest to all! Continue to take heed to thyself and to the teaching! Keep remaining in them, for by doing this both thyself shalt thou save and those hearing thee!**

Μελέτα = μὴ ἀμέλει in v. 14; it places the positive beside the negative. The verbs are somewhat different in force, yet they are opposites: not to be careless about — to be careful about. The A. V. translates "meditate upon," apparently because of the use which the LXX makes of this word and because of the quotation found in Acts 4:25. The New Testament has this verb only in this place. Its regular meaning is well in place here, and there is no reason that continued meditation is a better meaning. All continued care for something involves abundant thought, and it is possible that one may do much meditating and little work.

"These things" on which Timothy is to spend his care, in which he is to be, are the ones Paul is speaking of in this paragraph and not merely his charisma in particular. "In them continue to be" is not as unusual an expression as some suppose; R., *W. P.*, reports that Plutarch says of Caesar that he was ἐν τούτοις, and Robertson explains this by using our "up to his ears." "Be wrapped up in them," Moulton. The repetition of the thought is to secure an emphasis. But the durative tenses should be noted, for they ask Timothy only to continue on the course he is already following.

Ἵνα expresses purpose or contemplated result. On "advancement" see Phil. 1:12, 25: a blow that moves forward. The usual interpretation is that Timothy will make such advancement in his field of work that everybody will see it, and that no one will then think of his being rather young for his position. We do not agree with this interpretation. What about the time that intervenes until this progress comes to the attention of men? No, Paul is not speaking of an advancement that is yet to be made but of one that has already been made a long time before Timothy's present task and position were assigned to him. Many years before this time, when the congregation in the city was first organized, Timothy had been with Paul in Ephesus. Since at that time he had been younger than he now was, he had not held so responsible a position. Since Timothy was ever steady and true in his present work, all would at once see the advancement that he had made since the years that intervened, and that Paul's now putting him in full charge was not a mistake, either as far as his age or as far as his qualifications were concerned. Although he would be watched a little at first, even this would soon cease.

The pastoral applications commonly made on the basis of this verse are rather inept, namely that every young minister ought to study hard at his sermons, his catechisations, etc., attend zealously to all pastoral duties, etc., so that all his people will see that he is developing into a good minister. Timothy was in a position that was similar to that of the president of a synodical district, which is a different story. People knew him as he had been in former years. As they now observed Timothy, they would all see that he was, indeed, the man for his high position. Draw some applications for synodical presidents if you wish, but scarcely, except perhaps at long range, for seminary graduates who are just starting in the regular ministry.

16) These present imperatives have the same implications as the preceding ones: not to *start* taking heed and to *begin* remaining but to *keep on* as hitherto. Πρόσεχε in v. 13 = to put the mind toward something; ἔπεχε to put it upon something. Here we have the mind, thought, and "meditation." "Continue to take heed to thyself" means to thyself in thy responsible position, to all that thou shouldst be therein. This includes much more than Timothy's personal godliness. A very godly man may nevertheless be a poor head of a church body. Not for naught did Paul write v. 14 regarding Timothy's charisma. So here, too, he at once adds: "and to the teaching." The R. V. translates "*thy* teaching." But the article is the same as that used in v. 13, and this dative means "all the teaching" that is done, no matter by whom, in the churches under Timothy's care. In v. 13 three items are to receive Timothy's attention; here "to thyself and to the teaching" combines the official and the fundamental part of the work under his supervision. Since "the teaching" in all the churches is the basis of everything else, it is enough to mention this here. Paul has no occasion to speak to Timothy about Timothy's personal teaching.

"Keep remaining in them" means "in these things" (v. 15). Αὐτοῖς is not masculine so that Paul tells Timothy to remain with the people; this would leave the pronoun without an antecedent, "without visible means of support" (Graebner regarding such pronouns). Here we have the verb which, not only in its tense, but also in its sense, shows that throughout Paul is asking Timothy to continue as he has already been doing, that the previous imperatives contain no fears on Paul's part. To think otherwise is to do Timothy an injustice.

Τοῦτο sums it all up in a singular; plurals and singulars are often used thus by Paul. Here at the end the singular is fitting because it brings everything to a focus. By doing this, Timothy will save both himself and those hearing him. Γάρ points to the great incentive for Timothy. God alone saves (v. 10). Yet he saves by means (2:4), and it is thus that one who uses and applies these means can very properly be said to save both himself and others. Hence also Paul does not say merely "others" but "those hearing thee" (Rom. 10:13-15.) Timothy is the mouthpiece for the Word, for all these churches regarding all their doctrine and their practice, and he saves others only as God's instrument. In order to be such an instrument Timothy first applies the Word to himself. R., *W. P.,* calls "will save" an effective future; like others, also he is thinking of final salvation. But why restrict this word to the moment of death? Our saving is an extended act, and the durative "doing this" includes all of it: "wilt be saving." This is the logical future which tells what effect will be consequent to Timothy's doing what Paul once more tells him to do.

Men are now trying to prevent this whole work of saving (v. 7), and devilish spirits will try to do this still more in days to come (v. 1, etc.). Regarding many men in pulpits and at the head of church bodies it may be said that they are saving neither themselves nor those who hear them. Even to head a church body or a congregation in the orthodox churches does not *eo ipso* assure a person's salvation. Peculiar dangers beset such a man. Let us read Paul's letters to Timothy frequently. Some years ago a searching book appeared under the title, *Kann auch ein Pastor selig werden?* Blessed is the man, church officer or pastor, whose ministry is saving himself and those who hear him!

CHAPTER V

How Timothy Is to Direct the Treatment
of Certain Individual Cases and of
Certain Classes of Members

1) Some think that chapter 4 brings the letter to a close, and that chapters 5 and 6 contain only afterthoughts. This view includes the supposition that the last two chapters are very loosely put together and are a jumble of minor subjects.

The first four chapters by no means conclude the directions given Timothy. As Paul's representative in all the Asian congregations Timothy will have to supervise the handling of certain individual cases as well as the general treatment of various groups in the membership of the churches under his care. Note the singular alternating with the plurals in chapters 5 and 6. Here we have Paul's suggestions for this important part of Timothy's work. These chapters are misunderstood when it is supposed that Timothy shall do all this in his own person, and when it is thought that all these cases and all these classes of people appear only in the one congregation at Ephesus. Timothy is supervising many churches, and it is his duty to show the elders in all these churches and the congregations themselves how to act and what attitude to take in regard to this or that person or this or that class of persons.

Now the items included in this final section of the letter are indeed quite diverse, we may say even heterogeneous. Paul speaks of elders and slaves, widows and rich men. Yet these items are not merely jumbled together. Matters that are so diverse are yet arranged in a natural order by Paul. Our mind might prefer a different order, which might also be good; but it is our business to follow Paul's mind, to appreciate his arrangement of the materials, which we shall do with much profit to ourselves.

Admonishing Individual Members, 1, 2

An older man do not assault but proceed to admonish as a father; younger ones as brothers, older women as mothers, younger ones as sisters, in all purity.

Among the various subjects which Paul wishes to take up for Timothy's detailed consideration this one is properly treated first because of its wide application. Admonition will ever be needed, and it will have to be given to men as well as to women, to old as well as to young. This first subject calls for no long elaboration, a few pointers are enough. We are, however, not to think that Timothy is personally to do all of this admonishing in all the congregations under his supervision. Elders have this obligation because of their office; yea, also Christians generally have it. What Paul addresses to Timothy in the second person is, indeed, to be observed by Timothy, but in such a way that he may direct all others in the churches to observe it likewise. Timothy could not possibly do all of the admonishing necessary in all these congregations, nor does Paul expect him to do this. We note 4:11, especially also 4:12: "continue thou to be an example to the believers," etc. We note similar statements in the following paragraphs. Timothy is to show his people how to proceed when they are admonishing those who may need it.

When the persons to be admonished are older, their age must be kept in mind by the person admonishing them; when both are of the same age, or when one is younger, they are to be treated as brethren or as sisters in Christ. When one old man admonishes another, one old lady another, they will, of course, treat each other as equals in age. There is no need to enter into all the details.

"Do not go at an older man roughshod!" The verb means to assault or strike with blows, but it is here used in the metaphorical sense of pounding with words. We shall see that even younger persons are not to be treated in that way. Our versions have translated: "Rebuke not an elder," but this leads us to think of the technical term "elder" (v. 17), of a man in that office, which the following shows to be incorrect. It also leads us to think that "rebuke" is improper, yet in II Tim. 4:2 both of our versions let Paul tell Timothy to "rebuke." Age does not make admonition unnecessary: *Alter schuetzt vor Torheit nicht;* but when a younger person is obliged to deal with an older one, riding roughshod over him or over her is peculiarly out of place because of the difference in age. The aorist means: "Do nothing of the kind!"

The present imperative is iterative and refers to all cases that may occur: "proceed to admonish (him) as a father," admonish, not assault, and do that as one would admonish a father who may in some way be at fault. In 4:13 Paul uses the noun that is derived from this verb παρακαλῶ, to call to one's side or to call aside; according to the context the verb means "to exhort," "to admonish," "to encourage," "to comfort," sometimes "to entreat." "Admonish" is the proper word here; it also refers to all the others, old women, young men, and young women. One would be very considerate when admonishing one's father, likewise one's mother. That is the cue for all admonition of older persons by younger ones. Lev. 19:32: "Thou shalt rise up before the hoary head, and honor the face of the old man." See Prov. 16:32; 20:29.

2) When Paul says "the younger as brothers, the older women as mothers, the younger ones as sisters,"

we have the picture of a whole family in which each
one is properly considerate of the others also when one
is obliged to admonish. The naming of these ages and
these sexes indicates that the faults here contemplated
as needing admonition for their correction are the
common ones to which old and young, men and women
are liable, and that errors of doctrine are not considered even as Paul has a separate section for such people (6:3, etc.) and in Tit. 3:10 uses quite a different
verb and orders a different kind of procedure.

The last phrase, ἐν ἁγνείᾳ, which has the same noun
that was used in 4:12: "in all purity," is commonly
understood to mean that Timothy is to watch his sexual nature when he is admonishing younger women
because he is still a younger man (4:12). This phrase
is to be construed with the verb. It does not modify
"younger women" or "as sisters," for then this "purity" would characterize *them* and not the act of admonishing. The noun does not mean *Keuschheit*, compare 4:12, because it modifies the verb and applies to
all four objects of that verb. This is "purity" in the
sense of *Tadellosigkeit* (G. K.): all admonishing is
itself to be without flaw or fault, for nothing spoils
admonition more than when it is done in a way that
lays the one who is admonishing open to counter-
admonition.

Widows, Their Support, Their Marrying again, 3-16

3) Paul devotes so much consideration to this
subject because it has several angles and because the
keeping of lists of old widows was a new matter. It
may be possible that this plan had been recently introduced and had not as yet been established in all the
churches; perhaps also the details had not as yet been
permanently fixed. Paul says nothing about orphans.
This is not to be a section on charity in general nor

even on charity to any and to all needy widows. It deals with all widows and thus also with the support of widows.

There are widows and widows. **As widows honor those genuinely widows.** Χήρας, without the article, is predicative to τὰς ὄντως χήρας. We do not think that τίμα means "honor with support." When this meaning is given to this word by an appeal to what follows, we answer that no reader can anticipate that this will follow. Two kinds of widows are not genuine widows, namely such as have relatives and such as plunge into a gay life. In one respect they are widows, for they have lost their husbands. In another respect they are not widows, they have not been entirely deprived. We get Paul's meaning when we note the significant predicate accusative "as widows." Χήρα is derived from χῆρος: "robbed," and thus means a woman robbed of her husband. Paul means: "As robbed ones honor only those who have really been robbed," i. e., those who have actually been left alone. Those who are in the midst of relatives still have these relatives; those who plunge into pleasures — well, they are dead while living (v. 6).

One might expect Paul to say: "Sympathize with real widows!" He says "honor." This is the word that is used concerning the regard children are to have for parents, cf., Eph. 6:2; Exod. 20:12. He is not thinking of age, for there are also young widows, and he himself speaks of such. Paul has the Old Testament views. Like orphans, widows are in a special way under the protection of God. To hurt them is listed among the great crimes. Exod. 22:22, 23; Deut. 14:29; 24:17, 19; 26:12; 27:19; Job 24:3; Ps. 68:5; Prov. 15:25. This applies not only to Timothy but also to all the congregations as v. 7 shows.

4) We now get the answer to the question as to who are "genuine widows." **But if any widow has**

children or grandchildren, let them be learning as the first thing to be dutiful to their own family and duly render requital to their parents, for this is acceptable in the sight of God. The genuine widow, however, namely (the one) **having been left alone, has set her hope** (only) **on God and remains on in her petitions and her prayers by night and by day. But the one luxuriating, though living, has died.**

Not a few widows have grown children, even grown grandchildren; these should be learning to take care of their mother or their grandmother, namely by constantly doing so (present imperative). Ἔκγονα and πρόγονα match, and the latter is aptly used here as a designation for either a mother or a grandmother of these children or these grandchildren. When the A. V. translates "nephews" it is perfectly correct, for in the English of 1611 this word was used in the meaning grandchildren (the Standard Dictionary lists this use as obsolete).

Paul states the proposition in its full breadth: the very first thing to learn is that such children or such grandchildren must be dutiful to their own οἶκος, "house" or "family," which includes *all* the members of the family. Εὐσεβεῖν, like the noun in 4:7, etc., is used with reference to dutifulness toward God and toward one's country or one's family, including parents, grandparents, and other relatives. When the object is God and what pertains to God, we translate "to be godly"; here we translate so as to fit "their own house." Epexegetic καί adds what the broad infinitive covers in particular: "and duly to render (ἀπό = duly, it is often used in this sense with διδόναι, to give) requital to their parents" (here = living ancestors and includes a father and a grandfather as well as a mother or a grandmother). Ἀμοιβή, a common word, means "requital"; our versions translate the verb and the noun together: "to requite." Requital may be used in the evil sense; here it is used in the good sense of returning the good which children and grandchildren have received in childhood from their parents.

"This is acceptable in the sight of God." This is true beyond question. No child can ever make full requital. Godly children should delight in making all the requital they can. Yet it has been well said that one father is able to keep and provide for ten children while ten children often cannot see their way clear to take care of one old father. Godly children will welcome the opportunity and will delight the more in embracing it because it meets with God's approval. The proposition is general and thus includes a widowed mother or a grandmother. Paul has these alone in mind in this paragraph.

This is the obligation of the church, namely to teach all children and all grandchildren what God wants them to do so that they may do it in every case and do it in the right spirit. This is, however, only one phase of the subject, namely where a widow has grown children or grandchildren. The consideration of widows with small children, of widows with other relatives who could take care of them is postponed until v. 16; Paul is not forgetting them. This problem of widows was more serious in ancient days than it is today because at that time widows and lone women could find far less opportunity for earning a living.

We now begin to see what Paul means by "genuine widows" and by "honoring" them. He is not disparaging widows who have children and grandchildren to provide for them, they are not left utterly alone. The widowhood Paul has in mind is a far sadder matter. Paul is not excluding from congregational help every widow with grown children and grandchildren lest the congregation be unduly burdened. Paul's words imply that *all* needy widows

are to be provided for; the church has the obligation
to see to that and to teach it to the members, in particular to children and to grandchildren who have
needy parents. What the congregation is to do when
children disregard this teaching need not be said; the
church will take proper measures and will not abandon
a widow who has heartless children.

Μανθανέτω, the singular: let the widow who has children or grandchildren learn, is textually worthless but
indicates how Paul was misunderstood by a few copyists who thought that Paul was saying that the *widow*
is to do the learning. The Vulgate, Chrysostom, Pel-
agius, and a few late writers retain the plural μανθα-
νέτωσαν: let them be learning, but think that Paul refers
to these widows. It is claimed that Paul has a similar
construction in 2:11; Rom. 3:2; I Cor. 7:36, and that
such a change in number is also made in Matt. 8:4;
Luke 23:50, 51. But neither Paul nor any other writer
has such a construction.

Just as decisive is the sense that would result,
namely that *these widows* are to learn first of all to
attend to their own household — when some of them
already have grandchildren! Are we to suppose that
widows who have reached this age did not do this εὐσεβεῖν while their husbands were still alive, and that now,
at an age when they have grandchildren, they are
"first to learn" this dutiful care of their homes? Are
we to suppose that these widowed mothers and grand-
mothers are for the first time to learn to requite their
dead ancestors for what these ancestors did for them?
The subject implied in the plural "let them learn" is
indicated in the previous clause: the children or the
grandchildren are to learn, now that their mother or
their grandmother has become widowed, that their first
great duty is to take care of their own house, which
includes requiting such a widow, taking proper care
of her.

5) Paul is not speaking of a widow who has children or grandchildren that have divine obligations toward her. It is the duty of the congregation to point such children, etc., to this divine obligation so that they may learn it. In case they are remiss in doing their duty, v. 1, 2 indicate that proper admonition should be applied. Δέ states the kind of a widow Paul *does* have in mind: "The genuine widow, however, namely (the one) that has been left alone (μόνος, solitary, the perfect indicating the continuing condition), has set her hope (only) on God and continues on with her petitions and her prayers by night and by day" (genitives of time within; "by night" is generally placed first). This describes a "real" widow, one who is completely widowed. Καί is epexegetical to ὄντως: one who is left all "alone" and in that sense is "desolate" (the word that is used in our versions). While we pity all women who have lost their husbands, our hearts go out most of all to one who is left totally alone. Lone aged widows are pitiful cases, but the worst cases are widows who are left with little children, half-orphans. The case is not so bad when there are children or grandchildren who are old enough for the εὐσεβεῖν (v. 4) that is so pleasing to God; but when the children are small, they burden the lonely widow's heart the more.

With tender tact Paul only *describes* this kind of a Christian widow. He says, "she has set her hope on God," on him who has made so many promises to just such sadly bereft widows and has raised so many protections around them in his Word. Paul states how this widow sets her constant hope on God (specifying καί): by ever continuing with her petitions, by laying all her needs before God, and by her prayers (the wider word which includes all types of praying), at night on her pillow, by day when worry would assail her about this or that. Paul does *not command* this widow so to set her hope, etc., nor *order* the church to ask her to learn to do this. This description, since it is only a description, is more effective than such a command or order would be. It implies that, before anybody can bid her do this, she has already complied. For the children and the grandchildren of the other widow Paul writes an imperative (v. 4) but not for this widow. Even the two tenses are significant: "has set her hope" from the start of her lone widowhood and "continues on" night by night, day by day. I greatly admire Paul for writing this verse as he did.

Include also the fact that he says not a word about the obligation of the congregation to help support this kind of a widow who surely needs such support if any widow does. Here we have the same tact. Is there a true Christian church that will *not* support such a widow, that must still be commanded and told to do so? The effectiveness of the description of a truly lone Christian widow is as great for the church in regard to what the church must do as for herself in regard to what her trust in God should be. In one little sentence Paul is able to touch both her heart and that of the church.

6) There is, however, another kind of widow who is not genuine — the worst kind of all: "But the one luxuriating, though living, has died." The impact made by this brevity is strong. Paul does not even use the word "widow" when he is speaking of her, she does not deserve it. The substantivized feminine durative participle is enough: "the one luxuriating." It is out of the question to supply ὄντως καὶ μεμονωμένη as though this kind of a widow could be "a genuine and lonely one"; yet this has been done. Σπαταλᾶν (see also James 5:5) = to luxuriate. She blossoms out in beautiful dress in order to enjoy her new freedom, is a rather fast lady (as White puts it), "the merry widow," and admirers give her "a good time." The word is exactly

proper. It does not say that she is sensual but somewhat suggests that. She is full of gay pleasure and enjoys the money spent on her. It is the German *schwelgen, ueppig leben.*

The oxymoron is devastating: "while alive, she has died." Or, since this perfect generally means that when one "has died" he "is dead": "is dead while she liveth" (our versions). She is both at the same time: physically "alive," spiritually dead. There have been two deaths, two funerals: her husband died, and the spiritual life in her died. He is a corpse, she a living one, her state is far worse than his.

Again we have only *description,* no word of command, no apostolic order for anyone. Why an order to her who is beyond reach of the Word? Why to the church and the ministry from whom she has separated? To tell us that Paul means that the church is *not* to support such a woman is to insult the apostle as well as Timothy and the church.

7) **And these things order in order that they may be irreproachable.** "And" makes this sentence a part of the foregoing. "These things" have been referred only to v. 5, 6 or only to v. 6 on the plea that widows alone are to be "irreproachable" (this term is used also in 3:2.) But how can v. 5, 6 be thus separated from v. 3. 4? Verse 8 restates v. 4 so that v. 3-8 really form a unit. Some things stated in this letter are simply to guide Timothy in his work of supervision; others he is "to announce" publicly in the churches and thus "to order"; everybody concerned is to be informed and is at the same time to comply. Note this verb in 1:4 and 3:11. The time to do this was not after cases had developed but far ahead of such development. The indefinite clause: "in order that they may be irreproachable," refers to any and to all whom the matters mentioned in v. 3-6 plus also v. 8 may concern when the time arrived.

While they are growing up, all children and all grandchildren are to learn what v. 4 contains so that they may requite their parents when the time and the opportunity arrive whether it be a father or a mother, a grandfather or a grandmother, who may be in need. Verse 8 states this in a still more comprehensive way since v. 4 names only a widowed mother or a grandmother and "parents." All maidens and all women are to learn what v. 5, 6 contain and not only after they have been married and become widowed. The roots of their irreproachableness reach far back. In other words, these matters belong to the life of the church. This should be remembered when the word "irreproachable" is considered. Reproach would descend upon a widow who is like that one mentioned in v. 6 as well as upon children and grandchildren who fail in what v. 4 states, reproach from outsiders and still more from true church members. But the whole church itself would incur grave reproach if what Paul here writes were not preached and ordered in her midst. Paul's ἵνα clause includes all of it.

8)   Some would separate v. 8 from the preceding and thus make δέ adversative or indicative of a new subject, one that has nothing to do with v. 7. The thought itself decides against this view. We note that connectives are used to join all the statements from v. 3 to v. 8. Not until we reach v. 9 do we come to a break in the thought; there we have an asyndeton. But does v. 7 with its command to Timothy not close the subject? If not, should not v. 8 precede v. 7? The matter is cleared up when we note that v. 8 concludes the subject that has been elaborated thus far; v. 8 states the sum of it all in the most general form. This matter regarding widows is not something that concerns widows alone as if they were an exceptional class; they, together with all other dependents, belong to a family, for all of whom the head of the house

must provide and not cast off or abandon a single one
to shift for himself or herself or to be cared for by the
congregation. It is thus that Paul says with a simple
δέ that adds something that is somewhat different
from the preceding (offering the whole principle):
**Now if anyone does not provide for his own and espe-
cially his family members he denies the faith and is
worse than an unbeliever.**

This is stated in the strongest form. Hence, unlike v. 4, the protasis is negative; it is characteristic
of Paul to state a thought positively and negatively
(or vice versa). In v. 4 it is: "Let them learn!" here
the sense is: "If one will not learn, this is the verdict
to be pronounced on him." But in v. 4 we have the case
of only one widow; here it is a question of any and of
all dependents. The reference of "anyone" is perfectly plain: it is the person who has a household,
whose business it is to provide for the members of this
household. The verb means "to think beforehand"
and thus (intensified) to carry out this thinking, i. e.,
"to provide." Paul states it in the most comprehensive way: "provide for his own and especially his family members." The preferred reading has only one
article, for Paul does not refer to two distinct groups.
Οἱ ἴδιοι, "his own," are all who belong to the head of the
house, servants and members of the family; οἰκεῖοι refers to the latter only; "especially" is used exactly as it
was in 4:10. Here is a strong argument regarding the
support of a widowed mother or grandmother: one
ought to provide for even his servants, how much more
then for one's own mother or grandmother. But all
dependents are included: father and mother, if these
are dependent, wife and children, also other relatives
such as orphaned nephews and nieces.

This is the Christian teaching. Now he who will
not live up to that, "the faith (placed forward for the
sake of emphasis, nothing less) he denies," etc. Here

we again have "the faith" (articulated). This does not refer to personal faith in the heart, the subjective *fides qua creditur;* it is the objective faith and doctrine that is held by the church, *fides quae creditur.* By his act this man denies, says "no" to what the church believes, namely the Fourth Commandment and all its teaching regarding the Christian obligations of the head of the house. One *denies* teaching, doctrine, principles, objective things; one *loses* something that is subjective. Paul does not say that he *has lost* his faith. Paul does not judge the heart. Paul judges actions, and these we *are* to judge. When by his action and course of action a man openly "denies the faith," repudiates and disowns the Christian teaching, what has he to cling to inwardly with his heart, with his subjective faith? He may cling to something, but since it is not the Christian teaching, it is a lie of some kind. Even if we translate τήν "his"; "he denies *his* faith," πίστιν remains objective: the thing that he ought to believe he denies and rejects.

In order to make plain the enormity of such an action Paul adds in an explicative way: "and is worse than an unbeliever," one who never believed and never professed to believe. The thought is not that an unbeliever would always provide for the members of his family and his servants — many do not; but when an unbeliever does not do so, bad as he is, bad as his action is, it is not as bad as having the true teaching and then flagrantly denying it. What the congregation should do with a member of this kind does not need to be added. His verdict is written here.

As a matter of record let us add von Hofmann's and his disciple Wohlenberg's interpretation of this verse: "It pertains to the housefather who during his lifetime did not fulfill the duty to provide in such a way for his own and in particular for his wife and children that after his death they suffer no need."

Again: "Verse 8 is to prevent the eventuality that a widow should survive penniless and needlessly become a burden to the congregation through the fault of him who should have provided for her."

9) There is no connective; hence, as in v. 3, we have a new topic. Paul is still speaking about widows, but what is the reason for entering them in a list — none below sixty — every one only when she is also otherwise duly qualified? Everybody would like to know more about this listing, but we have only this one sentence (v. 9, 10). The qualifications enumerated recall those that were stipulated for women deacons (3:11), but they are not identical with them. Did these aged women have official duties? Paul's statement regarding them does not appear in the section that deals with the various congregational offices. The fact that the congregations supported only widows of this age cannot be assumed, and the qualifications required for listing are of such a kind that only those women could meet them who during their married life had commanded means and had used them in good works also during their widowhood until they reached the age of sixty. This should be well noted, for it answers the assumption that these sixty-year-old widows were enrolled for the purpose of receiving support, either complete support or partial regular support.

Zahn regards these "widows" as being wholly supported by the church and regularly matriculated for that reason, as being without homes, home obligations, and home inclinations, as under a vow not to marry again — all these points, in Zahn's estimation, point to the fact that only the neediest women "enjoyed" the benefit of this institution. One notes that Zahn adds to the qualifications which Paul lists: 1) a vow (*Geluebde*), which we cannot accept; 2) extreme poverty, which does not agree with Paul's set of qualifications; 3) total disinclination to house and home duties, which does not agree with the motherhood Paul mentions (are all the children to be regarded as being dead?) and the previous free hospitality toward strangers and ·saints.   If Zahn's limitations and requirements are added, how many such widows who were fit to be enrolled would be found in a congregation?

To what extent the post-Apostolic institution of Honor Widows was a continuation of what we find in Paul's time is uncertain.   This we regard as being true: 1) these widows were not congregational officers such as elders, deacons, and deaconesses were; 2) they either had no special duties at all or none that were similar to those of the deaconesses; 3) they were not poor and destitute of means, at least not all were in such poverty; 4) they were not all childless and thus without home ties.   These are negative points and thus cast little light on the positive position of these enrolled widows and on the purpose of formally enrolling them.

As widow let there be enrolled such a one as has come to be not less than sixty years.   This is the Greek; our versions make it more English.   In order to be entered on the congregational list a widow must have attained the age of at least sixty years. Those who were below that age were ineligible already on that score.   The obvious reason for this age limit is the fact that widows of sixty and over would not be likely to be sought for a second marriage; but that is all that we are safe in saying.   The fact that they were required to make a pledge or a vow, or that they did this of their own accord, is not said or implied.   The fact that remarriage was forbidden these enrolled widows is also *not* in the text; it is only the natural expectation because of their age.   The verb means "to be elected" and thus "to be enrolled" or entered on a list.   The one would imply the other; a record or list of those elected would be kept.   We get the impression that the congregation took a vote and that the elders made a record.

Χήρα is the predicate nominative, the participle and
its negative modifier are the subject. The participle
cannot thus be construed with the following, for this
would leave the imperative without a subject. The
proposal to regard "as widow" to mean "as a genuine
widow" (supplying ὄντως from v. 3 and 5) we consider
untenable 1) because many a widow would be a genuine one in Paul's sense of the word before she reached
the age of sixty and 2) because the definition of this
genuineness has been given already in v. 5, and what
is now added pertains to the listing and is thus quite
distinct. The absence of a connective has brought us
to a new subject. Timothy and the churches knew
what entering names on the list meant; unfortunately,
we do not know. The genitive depends on the adverb:
"not less than sixty years"; and the negatived adverb
depends on the perfect participle "having come to be."

One husband's wife is an apposition to the subject-
participle; the A. V. construes the participle with this
apposition, which is not correct. The sense is the
same as that of 1:2, 12, "one wife's husband." None
of these three expressions means that the person must
have been married only once; all three mean that the
person must have been true and faithful to one married spouse. This subject has been much discussed,
principally, it seems, because in the present passage
γεγονυῖα was construed with γυνή. Even if such a construction were made, the sense would not be that the
widow to be placed on the list must have been married
only once and not twice. A widow who had lived as
"one husband's wife" should live was eligible.

10) The second apposition is a participle like
the subject itself: **attested in good works,** i. e., to
whom Christians lend testimony in connection with
(ἐν) excellent works. The form of thought is Greek
and neatly concise. The qualifications are two and
only two. Both refer to past conduct and thus to the

woman's reputation: faithfulness to her husband during his life, diligence in good works. The congregation could easily and very properly judge regarding
both points.

The clauses introduced by εἰ are indirect questions
and represent such questions as would be asked when
inquiry was made about the kind of good works the
woman had done. Paul has five such questions; we
have explained this five in 4:12; what we said there
applies also here. These five questions enter into a
part of the domain in which the woman may have testimony of good works. It is for this reason that the
last question opens a wide and no longer a specific
sphere: "whether she followed after every kind of
beneficial work."

The idea is not that, in order to be eligible, the
widow must have distinguished herself in *every one* of
these five fields of womanly work, for look at the fifth
field which is limitless, which might also include the four
other fields. In one or in the other, in several, perhaps
even in all four specific fields here touched upon and in
some not here touched upon her fellow members will be
ready to accord her the praise of good testimony. Thus,
**whether she brought up children, whether she washed
saints' feet, whether she relieved afflicted ones,
whether she followed after every kind of beneficial
work.**

Some suppose that these questions mean: whether
she is qualified for leadership. They think that her
enrollment indicates an office, and that these questions
indicate the work of this office: whether in the past
she has shown willingness and aptitude for the work
she is now to do officially. But this view cannot be
sustained when these questions are examined.

"Whether she brought up children" is naturally the
first question, for good motherhood is woman's great
province. Here the idea that Paul has in mind a lone

widow breaks down, for one cannot think that only sixty-year-old widows, all of whose children had died, were
eligible. How many widows of this kind would there
be? Women who were sixty years or more old would
not be proper persons to be made official caretakers of
orphans in the congregation. However, to say of an
old widow that in her younger years she was a good
mother in the home is noble praise. One may from
already this one item draw the most pertinent applications for the women of today.

"Whether she exercised hospitality" is explained in
3:2; here the wife's part in this hospitality is referred
to. The husband receives the guests, but the wife must
cook, see to the beds, and do the work generally. An
office is not reflected here: these old widows were certainly not to be the congregation's official dispensers
of hospitality. Poverty and destitution are ruled out,
for when hospitality was needed, guests would not be
directed to poor homes by the elders when there were
well-to-do homes to welcome the guests. The suggestion that these women who were now widows became
poverty-stricken since their widowhood, is untenable.
But generous hospitality that was exercised in the past
remains worthy of praise in later days.

Closely allied are the next two questions: "whether
she washed saints' feet, whether she relieved afflicted
ones." We think of John 13:15 and Luke 7:44. Travelers and guests who were received into the house had
their sandals untied and their feet laved. This was
the task of lowly servants, and when guests were to
be honored, the host attended to it. But the matter of
hospitality has already been named, and this new question cannot refer to one feature of that hospitality, to
its cordiality as some think. Nor would the housewife
of the Orient wash a guest's feet unless it be a woman
guest's. The expression is figurative for rendering
menial service, being not too proud to stoop. So also

these "saints" are not house guests but fellow Christians in the congregation who need lowly service and assistance. Thus hospitality in the woman's own home and then helpful lowly service in the homes of destitute fellow Christians are referred to.

So we come to relieving those who were afflicted, those who were in sad or dire straits, perhaps because of persecution. Here are four great fields in which a Christian woman could have distinguished herself during her married life and also after that. But the whole field is far wider, and Paul adds the question about "every kind of beneficial work," ἀγαθός, good and helpful toward others, (C.-K. 4), καλός in the first question means beautiful, excellent in the judgment of Christians and of God.

With this we shall have to leave the question unanswered as to what this enrollment of widows who were sixty years old and over really means. To mention a Widows' Honor Guild, a sort of widows' society, is supposition.

11, 12) **Now younger widows decline to be bothered with, for whenever they act high and mighty against Christ they want to marry, having a judgment** (resting on them) **because they set aside the first faith. Moreover, at the same time also they learn** (how to be) **idle, wandering around to the houses, and not only idle but also tattlers and busybodies, talking the things they ought not. Accordingly I intend younger ones to marry, to bear children, to rule the house, and** (thus) **to offer not even a single occasion to the adversary as far as reviling is concerned. For already some did turn off after Satan.**

One interpretation is: Debar younger widows from admission to the Widows' Guild and from the congregational support which the widows of this guild receive, for they are too likely to abuse this support;

instead of devoting themselves to the office they thus assume, their strong sexual desire will make them break their vow of celibacy, and they will want to marry again and in the meantime will gad around from house to house, tattle and carry tales. Hence Paul wants them to marry in the first place, to raise a family, and to be homebodies, etc. Another interpretation is: Debar these younger widows because the congregational support will make them want to enjoy Christ in such a luxurious fashion that they will break their vow or word, will want to marry again, etc. Parry offers the suggestion that admission to the Widows' Guild was by means of an ordination like that of bishops and deacons.

Τὴν πρώτην πίστιν does not mean "the first vow" or — toned down — "the first given word or pledge" never to marry again. Πίστις never means either. This is not a "first vow or pledge" that is to be followed by a second, either in the case of sexagenarian or in the case of younger widows. This is not an apostolic beginning of monastic orders. Paul is not in one breath keeping widows from remarriage and in the next breath urging this very thing. No sexagenarian widow was by some form of vow kept from a late honorable marriage. There is no trace of such false asceticism here.

The same is also true with regard to poverty and congregational support. We have presented the evidence that the old widows as a class were not penniless and dependent on congregational support. Charity, both private and congregational, was ever practiced where it was needed. It is incredible that Paul is here arranging congregational support only for lone widows who were beyond sixty and is insisting that younger widows be supported by second husbands. His object is not to relieve the charity budget of congregations.

Paul's concern is the spiritual welfare of all younger widows. That is why he wrote v. 6 about the gay widow who is already dead while living. Hinrichs strikes the point: "As soon as they get the idea of marrying into their heads they forsake the Christian religion and marry a pagan." The two νεωτέρας γαμεῖν in v. 11 and 14 are the same, the contrast and the difference lie in the additions: 1) growing wanton against Christ — having a judgment because they set aside the first faith — learning how to be what v. 13 adds — turning off after Satan; 2) marrying so as to offer no single starting point for an opponent's reviling tongue. Could a contrast be stated more concretely, more strongly? Spiritual welfare is the point, remaining with Christ and not letting Satan draw one away. The loss of a husband puts a young widow into danger; suddenly being alone, she may plunge into the gay life of the world (v. 6) ; or if she wishes to remarry may disregard Christ and disown her first faith. Support is not the question, for on an average young widows are not left more penniless than old ones. Paul is not speaking of the paupers among them.

Now the details. Δέ is not wholly adversative as if the whole of v. 11-15 is set over against v. 10. We do not attribute to Paul the statement that all widows up to the age of sixty ought to marry as he says in v. 14. "Younger" refers to the youthful widows. Because of their youthfulness they are often inexperienced also regarding the Christian faith. It is quite correct when it is remarked that the comparative is here not much different from the positive and is used only because old widows are mentioned in v. 10. Paul says nothing about the widows who are of an age between sixty and that of these younger ones except that they must wait until they are sixty before they can be enrolled in the class about which we know only what v. 10 states.

Παραιτοῦ has the same force it had in 4:7 and has in II Tim. 2:23; Tit. 3:10. Timothy is to decline to be bothered with younger widows in regard to arranging anything special for them such as had recently been arranged for those who were past sixty; those who were older but not yet sixty had to wait. This enrolling seems to have been a new thing so that in Paul's judgment it was wise not at once to try out a lower age limit. Younger widows belonged to an entirely different category, one in which, because of a second marriage, they would be fully occupied with little children and with running their households. "For" begins his explanations about younger widows and introduces all that follows about them up to and including v. 15. Our versions, which translate "refuse," are inadequate, for they lead us to think that all the younger widows wanted to be enrolled with those who were over sixty; but what about the intermediate class?

῞Οταν = "whenever" and says no more than that cases of this kind may occur and may be expected and not that *all* younger widows will act as is here stated. The compound καταστρηνιάω (found only here and in Ignatius) receives some light from the simplex which is used in Rev. 18:7, 9. *Uebermuetig werden* (Stellhorn) is exactly to the point: to act high and mighty, to cast off restraint. Some refer this to wanton sexual vigor in these young widows; they point to their wanting to marry and say that in Rev. 18:7, 9 the simplex is synonymous with πορνεύειν. But in Rev. 18 the wanton disposition adds the idea of carrying on in a high, unrestrained manner to the fornication. In our passage wanting to marry is also a distinct desire. But let us keep the connection. In v. 14 Paul himself wants these widows to marry, wants them to want to marry, which is *a good thing*. Here in v. 11 wanting to marry is the result of becoming high and unrestrained toward Christ and thus the very opposite and *a bad thing*.

These young widows find themselves to be their own masters and are restrained only by Christ. They are widows who do not have little children to burden them. They become overbearing against Christ, cast off his restraint, and do as they please. This is the way in which they want to enter into marriage anew. Paul even tells us more: "having judgment (resting on them) because they did set aside the first faith." Their acting high and mighty against Christ = their setting aside their first faith. Their Christian faith no longer holds them; they have put it away as being something that interferes with their new freedom and desire. The thought is not that Christ and this faith forbid their marrying, for how could v. 14 then follow? Nor, on the other hand, that they become strumpets or harlots. Paul does not say this, and the usual facts do not say it. These widows are ready to enter into a pagan marriage without Christ, without their first faith; they become pagans again in order to suit a pagan husband. Plenty of cases such as that occur to this day.

R., *W. P.*, like M.-M. 593, quotes Souter with approval: "exercise youthful vigor against Christ" (genitive after κατά in the verb) ; but we think that he refers to sexual vigor, and Paul speaks of something worse. Von Hofmann spiritualizes and drops the idea of "against": "take spiritual delight in Christ." Wohlenberg follows this lead: *Christum schwelgerisch geniessen*, "luxuriate in Christ," and then tries to prove that the κατά in this verb cannot mean "against" when the examples he supplies prove this very thing. We translate ὅτι "because" since epexegetical "that" would require τὸ κρίμα: "the judgment that," etc. Κρίμα is "judgment," the context alone implies that it is adverse; "damnation" (A. V.) and "condemnation" (R.

V.) are only *ad sensum*, for the word for this idea is
κατάκριμα. "The first faith" is like "thy first love" in
Rev. 2;4. Here, too, πίστις is objective, for ἀθετέω has
only objective objects in all the examples cited in Ab-
bott-Smith, *Lexicon*: set aside, reject "me," "you,"
"the law," "the covenant," "the commandment," etc.
Here "*what* is believed" is set aside; this "first belief"
is thrown away for a second (false) one.

13) "Moreover, at the same time also" adds further evidence that, after their husbands are dead, the
restraint also of Christ is removed for these foolish
widows. "They learn how to be idle"; μανθάνω, with
εἶναι to be supplied (R., *W. P.*, mentions examples found
in Plato and in Chrysostom), and thus: "*how* to be
idle" (R. 1040), which is always the sense of this word
when it is used with an infinitive. They do as they
please. The other nominatives are best regarded as
predicative appositions to the subjects: "running
around to the houses" of other people, mostly pagan
houses; "and not only idle" but worse, "also tattlers
and busybodies, talking the things they ought not"
(that are not necessary, the participle of δεῖ). Περίεργος,
literally, "around the work," — busy with all the tri-
fling things and not with real work (R. 617). It has
been well said that Paul draws a picture from real life.

14) So then (οὖν) Paul wants "younger ones to
marry, to bear children, to rule the house, to give not
a single occasion to the adversary with regard to reviling." This is the program stated briefly yet com-
prehensively. On βούλομαι see 2:17. Timothy and the
churches will join in this intention. It makes for exactness to omit the article: "younger ones to marry,"
i. e., as a rule. Again, as in v. 10, Paul glorifies motherhood for Christian women and thus for widows of
corresponding ages; children complete the home and
home life. In 2:15 we have the noun τεκνογονία, here
the verb τεκνογονεῖν, in 5:3 and 4 ἔκγονος and πρόγονος; all

are compounds with γόνος (γένω, γίγνομαι). All Scripture condemns the refusal of married women to give birth to children. "To rule the house" means as the wife and mother in the home, to manage the household affairs. This is the domain and province of woman, in which no man can compete with her. Its greatness and its importance should ever be held up as woman's divinely intended sphere, in which all her womanly qualities and gifts find full play and happiest gratification.

In I Cor. 7:39 the remarriage of widows irrespective of age is specifically endorsed. What Paul has to say in that chapter regarding marrying and regarding the distress of the times in no way conflicts with what he says in v. 39 and thus in our passage and in 2:15; see the exposition of I Cor. 7.

The last infinitive has modifiers and thus in form indicates that it sums up in brief the purpose involved in the three preceding infinitives: "(thus) to give not a single occasion (place to start from) to the adversary as far as reviling is concerned" (χάριν, adverbial accusative used like a preposition with the genitive and may follow its case, R. 425), literally, "in favor of reviling." "The adversary," the one who "lies against" us in battle, because of the presence of the article = the devil, even as "Satan" follows in the next verse and names him. He, of course, uses wicked men as the channel for his reviling and vituperation of the church (the noun is found again in I Pet. 3:9). Nothing is gained by making "the adversary" only a human opponent. The devil is always looking for something in Christians from which to start vilification of the church.

15) The explanatory remark introduced with "for" means that Paul is not speaking theoretically or abstractly but on the basis of sad experience: "For already some did turn off (we should use the perfect tense) after Satan," whose very name signifies "the

adversary." The fact that this means casting off
Christ and his spiritual restraint, rejecting the first
faith (v. 11, 12), is beyond question. One way of
doing this deadly thing is mentioned in v. 6; other
ways in v. 11-13. Paul varies his form of expression:
in the companion verse (6) it is entirely subjective:
while living she is dead (also singular), while in the
present verse "turned off after Satan" mentions also
the objective side (it is also plural). Still more: to be
dead is negative: spiritual life has ceased; but to turn
off after Satan is positive: godless life has set in.
"Satan" is placed in opposition to "Christ" in v. 11,
both names have the article; all restraint of Christ is
willfully cast off in order to gain new liberty, which
means following Satan in a liberty that is slavery.

16) The final point is added without a connective because it merely supplies an item that is not specifically touched upon in v. 8. Both verses thus begin
with εἴ τις. In v. 8: "If anyone does not provide for his
own," etc., we naturally think of the Christian *man*
who is at the head of a house. But in some cases the
man was not a Christian but only his wife was, and in
other cases a widow herself had a family and managed a household — Lydia even conducted her
deceased husband's extensive business and insisted on
taking Paul and his assistants into her home. There
were many capable women of this type who had abundant means. So Paul writes: **If any woman believer
has widows, let her relieve them, and let not the
church be burdened in order that it may relieve the
genuine widows.**

We see that the poorly attested reading which inserts πιστὸς ἤ (followed by the A. V.) is only a correction of copyists who failed to understand what Paul
is saying. Others, who accept the correct reading, call
it the more difficult one and seek to explain it. Thus:
1) Paul has a special case in mind and thus writes

πιστή; 2) Paul writes πιστή (feminine) but thinks of a man or a woman believer, anybody who has a widow in the relationship, and, if necessary, the help of other relatives is to be employed; 3) Paul writes πιστή because the woman of the house had the real work to perform when lodging a widow; 4) "have widows" means employs them as help or as servants in the house. Add that Paul writes: "has widows," plural. Some writers take this plural to mean: any believing woman who has *several* widows under her care, and a few writers think that all of these were *young widows*.

But the reading πιστή is not difficult. Any woman believer, whose husband is not a believer, and also any woman believer, who is a widow that has means or who was never married and has means, is to aid any widow, old or young, of her own relationship, who may be left destitute, with no one else able or willing to aid her. Most properly Paul writes: "let her relieve them," the same verb that was used in v. 10. How the relief is to be extended need not be said, for a number of obvious ways at once suggest themselves: give a lone widow a home; give her work; give her financial support — the cases may differ in detail. Thus one widow with means may help another widow; or a married or a single woman with means may do the same for a widow. The plural "has widows" is used because τις is indefinite and general and includes all cases.

"And let not the church be burdened" means that this would be improper since this Christian woman has the first obligation. The idea is not that the congregation would not step in; it would step in even where children refuse to support their needy parents; but what a reproach this would be to any who profess Christianity and yet so flagrantly refuse to meet their Christian obligations!

"In order that it may relieve the genuine widows" refers to those who have been completely left alone

(v. 5), the congregation as such bearing first and perhaps sole obligation regarding them. Here we have
the ὄντως used in v. 3 and 5, Paul's elaboration returns
to the starting point, the circle is thus completed. No
angle of the matter is overlooked. This is an instance
of the apostle's masterly thought and presentation.
The fact that the congregation is ever ready to relieve
any of its needy members is assumed throughout. The
fact that this includes penniless widows, young or old,
is also assumed. The fact that the congregation *will*
step in where an obligated member wrongfully refuses
to do so, is also understood; but this should never become necessary. As far as Timothy is concerned, Paul
does not need to repeat v. 7.

Honoring, Correcting, Selecting
Elders, 17-25

17) The subject of widows begins with honoring
(v. 3) ; so does the subject of elders. It, too, may be
divided into minor sections. The absence of connectives is marked. **The excellently presiding elders, let
them be counted worthy of twofold honor, especially
those toiling in connection with Word and teaching.**

We have seen that the πρεσβύτεροι and the ἐπίσκοποι
are the same persons. At one time they are named
according to their age and their dignity, then according to their task of overseeing. Here the former designation, namely "elders," is in place because the
predicate deals with honor; in 3:1 "overseer" is in
place because the discussion revolves about qualifications for the work.

"The excellently presiding elders" are certainly
those who grace their office by doing their work well.
The fact that some elders were at fault we see from
v 20; we are also told what is to be done with them.
But this obvious interpretation meets objections. We

are told that "the elders" refers to the older men in the congregations, that because of their age they already deserve honor, and that those among them who had an office in the congregation and were "elders" in the official sense deserved double honor, which explains also the predicate. Καλῶς is inserted because the office itself is to be called excellent or "because the office honors the man only when it is properly administered." Besides, we are told that the Lord always asks for faithfulness on the part of those in office, and that the word used here is not "faithful elders"; and we are also told that it is hard to differentiate between degrees of faithfulness.

Paul is not speaking of two groups: old men in general and some of these old men who are good elders; he refers to one group only, the good elders. The other kind will be discussed in v. 20. The participle with its adverb is attributive and is placed between the article and the noun. This second perfect is always used in the sense of the present: presiding excellently now. Wreaths are not to be laid on their graves after they are dead; flowers are to be given to them now in order to cheer them in their work. The idea that this adverb "excellently" describes only the office itself as being an excellent one cannot be successfully defended; it modifies the attributive participle, the excellent presiding of these elders. Twofold honor is *not* due to the other kind of elders.

The participle means "to stand at the head" of the congregation and includes the position and the work of these elders. They were, indeed, the congregation's head and functioned as such. When this was excellently done, it deserved recognition and should not be taken as a mere matter of course. Many congregations are remiss in this respect; they have a pastor who fills his office excellently, but nobody has regard to what this means for the congregation, the work is accepted, and that is all. This text should wake up such congregations. "Let them be counted worthy," etc., means: by the congregation. Timothy is to stir up the congregations so that they will appreciate such elders.

There is a diversity of views regarding the "twofold honor": 1) "twofold" = "in greater measure"; 2) it means double pay; 3) honor plus pay; 4) twice the pay of the sixty-year-old widows or of the deacons; 5) double honor *ut fratribus et propositiis*, one honor as to brethren and another as to superiors; 6) one honor because of age, another because of office. As for τιμή, this word never means wages, pay, hire, which are μισθός; in certain contexts (I Cor. 6:20; 7:23) τιμή means "price." "Honorarium" is the word employed by Dibelius; and it occurs only in this one passage (B.-P. 1307). The papyri have only the two common meanings: "honor" and "price," the latter is admittedly not applicable here. Even τίμημα means only price as of wheat, as when πάντα, everything, is high, and thus refers also to payment ("price") for dancing girls (M.-M. 635). In our passage τίμα precedes (v. 3) and τιμή follows (6:1: "all honor"), both of which denote "honor." Μισθός also follows in the quotation found in v. 18, but this changes nothing as to the meaning of τιμή.

The context itself explains "twofold honor." How elders as such deserve honor is indicated in v. 19, for no charge against them is even to be entertained except on the basis of two or three witnesses. "Twofold" honor thus belongs to those elders who serve excellently, the extra honor is due to the excellency. The fact that no mathematical computation is referred to ought to be apparent.

"Especially those toiling in connection with Word and teaching" does not mean that some elders did not teach, for all were required to have (and thus to use) this ability (3:2). Naturally, however, some would manifest especial zeal in this part of the work, actually toil in it to the point of fatigue and weariness. These richly deserve the twofold honor. The combination "in Word and teaching" = in what is to be taught (Word) and in applying this (by teaching).

18) Paul substantiates this demand: **For the Scripture declares: A threshing ox thou shalt not muzzle and: Worthy the worker of his pay!** Our exposition of Paul's beautiful use of Deut. 25:4 in I Cor. 9:9-11 is too long to be repeated here; the student is asked to examine it in the *Interpretation of First Corinthians* where we show that Paul points to a great principle, one that is only illustrated by such an ox and is thus applicable in scores of other instances. "The Scripture declares" settles every matter as far as Christians are concerned.

The second statement appears verbatim in Luke 10:7 as a word of Jesus' and almost verbatim in Matt. 10:10. Paul evidently intends to place beside the Old Testament word another that is equal to it from the New Testament time and thus, as it were, to cite at least two witnesses (v. 19). He would also indicate that the point involved is valid in the New as well as in the Old Testament. Paul connects the two statements with a simple καί. So it is debated as to whether Luke's and Matthew's Gospels had possibly already been written, and whether Paul is quoting from them as canonical "Scripture"; or whether he is quoting from Matthew's *logia*, which were written in Hebrew; or whether he is quoting from the hypothetical **Q** (*Quelle*), the supposed source of the Synoptic Gospels. We need not enter into the isagogical question regarding the dates of the Synoptic Gospels, on which, if it is desired, see the author's introduction to each of them.

"And" adds the word of Jesus' as being of equal authority with the Old Testament. From the very

beginning the whole gospel story constituted the subject matter of the whole gospel preaching of all of
the apostles. All Paul's congregations were founded
on this preaching, knew how Jesus instituted the New
Testament ministry, and thus were also acquainted
with this word from his lips. As for Gal. 6:6, which is
often cited in connection with the present passage,
its correct interpretation should prevent this.

It is generally assumed that the elders were paid
for their services in the apostolic churches. We are
convinced that this assumption is not tenable. The
probability is that none of them were paid. The elders
of the synagogues were not paid or salaried. Each
synagogue had a number of elders, too many to have
a payroll that would be large enough to support them.
The apostolic congregations imitated the synagogue
in this respect. Our passage speaks of "twofold
honor," not of twofold financial pay or salary. Paul's
two quotations support the injunction relating to
according due honor to diligent elders; such honor is to
be their reward just as the ox treading out grain is
accorded the privilege of eating as he tramped along,
just as the worker is accorded his pay. The *tertium*
of the analogy lies in the worthiness and not in the
identity of what the three are worthy of: the elders
worthy of what naturally should go with their office —
honor; the ox worthy of what naturally goes with the
task for which he is employed — wisps of grain; the
workman worthy of what naturally goes with his work
— pay for his work.

19) An elder sometimes received the opposite of
honor. Ill will and personal hate might trump up
some charge against him. **Against an elder do not
receive an accusation except on the basis of two or
three witnesses; those that are sinning reprove in the
presence of all in order that also the rest may have
fear.**

Timothy is not to receive an accusation against an elder so as to take further steps about it, make an investigation, hear even the accused elder himself regarding the accusation, except on the basis of two or three witnesses. The honor due to the office demands this protection, for even a charge of which an elder is acquitted nevertheless damages his office and his work to some degree. Paul's purpose is to have no case taken up in which the verdict will after all have to be acquittal; also, and in the very first place, to prevent anybody from bringing up such a case. This is to be a special safeguard that is to be thrown around the good name of the office and its incumbents in the interest of the church itself. Ordinarily the witnesses are cited at the time of the trial; in the case of an elder they must be cited at the time the accusation is preferred, otherwise this accusation is not to be received.

Ἐπί is not = ἐπὶ στόματος as in the LXX of Deut. 19:15 and in II Cor. 13:1, but simply "on the basis of," "upon." Some think of the legal use of the preposition: "before two or three witnesses," i. e., men who are simply present to hear what the accusation is so that they can afterward testify that this is, indeed, the accusation that was made. But the preposition is so used only with regard to a judge: Mark 13:9; Acts 25:9, 10; 25:26; 26:2. It would be a strange proceeding to hear an accusation before witnesses who also only hear it as though accusations against other persons could be heard without extra witnesses being present. Would the accuser, perhaps, alter his accusation afterward; or would Timothy himself think of doing this?

Since Timothy had the supervision over the churches, every accusation against an elder would be brought to him. Accusations against ordinary church members were naturally referred to the elders and were thus brought before the congregation. The demand for at least two, preferably three, witnesses is found throughout the Scriptures (Deut. 19:15; Matt. 18:16; II Cor. 13:1; Rev. 11:3, etc.). Death could not be decreed without such witnesses (Num. 35:30; Deut. 17:6; Heb. 10:28). Jesus himself offered more than one witness (John 8:17, etc.), his own witness could not be legally accepted as being true and sufficient (John 5:31-38). When the penalty was stoning, the Jews required that the witnesses on whose testimony the penalty was decreed cast the first stones so that, if they had lied and perjured themselves, they would also be guilty of the further crime of murder (Acts 7:58). Ἐκτὸς εἰ μή = "except," it is a pleonasm (it is found three times in the New Testament).

20) But what if witnesses do substantiate an accusation as Paul here prescribes? Then "those sinning" (the sinners, the participle is merely descriptive) are not to have the further protection of being reproved only in private by Timothy, *unter vier Augen;* they are to receive reproof "in the presence of them all," i. e., of all the elders of the congregation. This is not conceived as a special punishment to the sinning elder but as a wholesome warning also to all his fellow elders, "that also the rest may have fear," namely godly fear of sinning. Paul is not thinking of those grave cases when elders sin so seriously as to require expulsion from their holy office, for such cases are to be brought before the congregation itself, which gave the office and which alone can again take it away. The present tenses of the participle and the imperative are iterative. They refer to cases that may occur. The participle does not mean, "those who steadily keep on sinning"; nor does ἁμαρτάνω refer to the gravest kind of sinning "like fornication, drunkenness, and the like." That such elders should be allowed to retain their office is rather incredible.

21)   In this disciplinary matter it was vital that
Timothy should ever act with utmost impartiality. **I
earnestly testify in the sight of God and Christ Jesus
and of the elect angels that thou observe these things
without prejudgment, doing nothing according to
partiality.**

It is said that Paul did not have perfect confidence
in the moral courage of Timothy and that he therefore
wrote this solemn preamble — some call it an oath or
an adjuration that is equal to an oath although it is
neither — and similar references to God, etc., in 6:13;
II Tim. 2:14; 4:1. But then Paul would not have
appointed Timothy to this position. The apostle moves
in a sphere in which we should move more fully,
namely "in the sight of God and Christ and of the angels." To him the office of the holy ministry was
one that was always administered and to be administered only in God's sight. As being in such an office
Timothy is to deal with its incumbents. The verb does
not mean "I charge" (our versions) but "I earnestly
testify" (διά is strengthening) and does not apply as
an affirmation to *what* is said but to *the person* to
whom something is said. It intends to impress that
person: both Paul and Timothy are standing, as it
were, in the presence of God, Christ, and the angels.

One article is used with the first of these two expressions, another article with the angels. This is
done because the first two are divine, the rest are only
creatures. This mention of angels should be combined
with all the other passages in which Paul indicates his
view of the world. To him the angels were spectators
of what happens in the church (I Cor. 4:9), ranged
under Christ (Eph. 1:21; Col. 2:10), present in the
services of the church (I Cor. 11:10). Paul does not
mention the souls of the departed saints, for not they
but God's angels are in intercourse with the church
on earth.

The word ἐκλεκτοί, which is here applied to angels, is certainly to be understood in the same sense as when it is applied to God's "elect" among men. It is plain that the angels who kept their own principality (Jude 6) are referred to. Like the elect among men, they are God's own forever. We find no other meaning for the word when it is applied to angels. To say that "elect" means "holy" does not satisfy, for then Paul would have written "holy." God's elect in the church on earth deal with each other in the presence of the God and Lord who elected them and in the presence of the blessed angels whom he also elected.

It has been suggested that the guardian angels appointed for the congregations are referred to. But the Scriptures know of no such special guardian angels (see Matt. 18:10; Acts 12:15). Some have thought of "throne" angels; but while there are ranks among the angels, this interpretation does not fit the word "elect." Finally, some think that in 3:16 the apostles are called ἄγγελοι, and thus the elders with whom Timothy is to deal are also regarded as ἄγγελοι, the heavenly ἄγγελοι are then differentiated from these earthly ones by being "elect." But 3:16 does not refer to apostles but to angels, and such a differentiation would be strange indeed.

Ἵνα is non-final and states what Paul urges so solemnly upon Timothy, namely that he is to observe these things (about dealing with elders in v. 19, 20) "without prejudgment, doing nothing according to partiality." Prejudgment is risky and blinds the eye to just judgment when it should be rendered. Πρόσκλισις is "leaning or inclining toward" somebody or something, hence "partiality." Timothy is usually thought of as being rather tender, some refer to his youth (4:12), and so "partiality" is taken to mean that he is warned against being tender and partial to accused elders. But the Greek means "leaning toward," either

toward the elder or toward the accuser, for nothing is
specified about the direction of the leaning. In a manner Timothy had to act as a judge in these cases, and
in all of them, in those to be flatly turned down, and in
those to be heard, his one course, for the good of all
the elders and of all the churches, was genuine impartiality, consciousness of the fact that he was acting in
God's sight.

22) **Lay hands hastily on no one, nor fellowship
other people's sins; keep thyself clean.** Timothy is
not to ordain a man as an elder too quickly. This entire section deals with elders, hence the laying on of
hands pertains to this act in connection with the
induction of an elder into his office by means of a public ceremony before the congregation. This does not
mean that Timothy alone is to be careful, and careful
not merely when he is personally taking part in the
ceremony, but that he must see to it that no unfit man
is ever to be chosen for the holy office and offered for
ordination. The man must have the qualifications
listed in 3:2, etc. Due time must be taken to verify
the fact that he has them. He may have all of them
but the teaching ability, namely a full grasp of the
Christian doctrines to be taught. "Wait," Paul says,
"until everything is duly and fully ascertained; wait
also until thou art sure that he will make a capable,
sound, well-informed teacher. Admit to the eldership
and ordain only such a man."

Laying on of the hands is an ancient ceremony
(Acts 6:6; 13:3; I Tim. 4:14; II Tim. 2:16) that
was used in various ways (as in Mark 10:16) in conducting a person into office. We have retained it to
this day in connection with baptism, in confirmation,
in our present form of ordination to the ministry, although not when installing a man in a new congregation. It is not charismatic but only symbolic; it con-
fers no divine power or gift but accompanies the prayer

of the church that God would bless the person with all that he needs for his Christian life or, in the case of the minister, for his holy office and work.

Paul does not write, "And do not fellowship other people's sins" and thus lead us to think that by hasty ordination Timothy would involve himself in the sins of such hastily ordained elders, sins they had committed before and sins they would continue to commit after becoming elders. "And do not," etc., would then confine this warning to such sins. Paul writes "nor fellowship," etc., and thereby broadens the warning so as to include also v. 20, the sins of elders who at any time may be properly accused and who ought to be disciplined as well as the sins of false accusers who ought to be refused. Timothy would "fellowship" such sins of other people if he did not reprove a sinning elder but refused to entertain accusation; again if he listened to unjustified accusation.

Note that ἁμαρτίαις repeats the ἁμαρτάνοντας used in v. 20 and thus indicates to what the ταῦτα used in v. 21 refers. Luther's *Halte dich selber keusch* is incorrect; ἁγνός is not "chaste," nor does it refer to sexual conduct; it means "pure," "clean" of fellowship with other men's sins as just stated. Compare the noun in 4:12 and 5:2 and our discussion. Yes, one may "fellowship other people's sins" and do that in various ways. Preachers and general officers of the church need Paul's warning as other Christians do (Eph. 5:7; II Cor. 6:17; II John 11). To fellowship a sin is to share its guilt and its punishment.

23) **No longer be a water-drinker but use a little wine because of thy stomach and frequent attacks of weakness.** This is not a disconnected medical prescription, the outcome of a discussion of Timothy's case with Luke, the physician. Timothy is to keep in good physical condition. The imperatives used in these verses are personally directed to Timothy. If he

is subject to attacks that are caused by a weak and deranged stomach he will without due examination say "yes" or "no" to not a few things and will thus not succeed in keeping himself above reproach in his own office, he who is to see to it that others in office are to be kept so and dealt with if they are not. It seems that Timothy was most careful and drank only water so that no one should point to him as a πάροινος (3:2), which was all very well in one way but not in another. In all these countries it is to this day risky to drink water or milk since they are so often contaminated. When the author traveled in the Orient he received constant warnings about the water and the milk. One must drink coffee, tea, and wine; the alcoholic content of the latter is valuable for the stomach.

R., *W. P.*, tells us that "a little" has the emphasis. But an occasional sip of wine would do "little" good in a case like Timothy's. "Little" is no more emphatic than is "much" in 3:8. In both passages the object, "much wine — little wine," is placed forward in good Greek fashion. Timothy is to discard the use of water and is to substitute wine; Paul has no fear that he would overindulge. Complete abstinence is not needed in Timothy's office nor in order that he may serve as an example to the elders. Such abstinence may bring on attacks of dysentery and may lead to other dangers to his "pure" administration of office. The point is not medicinal with wine as the medicine but dietetic, substituting what is safe and wholesome for what is not. The idea of πυκνός is coming "thick" and fast. When both gender and number are different as is the case here with regard to "stomach" and "weakness," each noun has the article, and "thy" belongs to both nouns (R. 789).

24) **Of some men the sins are entirely evident, going on in advance to judgment; but some (men) they also follow after. In like manner also the excel-**

lent works are entirely evident, but the ones that are otherwise cannot be hid.

Both propositions, that regarding sins and that regarding excellent works, are entirely general. They deal with any human judgment regarding men, hence also with such judgments as Timothy is obliged to render when he is accepting or rejecting applicants for the eldership (v. 22; "one who aspires to overseership," 3:1). As far as avoiding mistakes is concerned and thus possibly making the wrong man an elder, Timothy need not worry, for the difficulty as to judging is not great. This is said for Timothy's comfort.

The few who object to the obvious connection with v. 22 have little that is worth while to offer in its place. To connect it with v. 23 affords no tenable meaning; for v. 23 is merely incidental. Moreover, ἁμαρτίας all too plainly resumes the ἁμαρτάνοντας used in v. 20 and the ἁμαρτίαις occurring in v. 22, especially the latter. The connection with 6:1, etc., namely with slaves, although it has been latterly suggested, has not been convincingly defended.

When it comes to judging the fitness of some men for the ministry, there is really no question: "their sins are entirely evident (πρόδηλοι, πρό is not temporal but intensive), going on in advance (here πρό is temporal) to judgment," like heralds who proclaim in advance the unfitness of such sinful men. Timothy and, in fact, everybody else knows even before the day on which their application for office comes up for κρίσις or decision what the verdict must be. The thought that Paul refers to God's judgment is untenable because "entirely evident" cannot refer to God but only to men.

Timothy and the churches will need to consider only the question in regard to men whose sins are not so evident. Even in their case the difficulty disappears: the more hidden sins of these men follow close

on the heels of these men when their cases come up
for decision. Their sins march right into the meeting
behind them and refuse to be left outside. Thus Timothy will easily be able to refuse these men. "In exceptional cases of deception and hypocrisy, which only
one who is able to see the heart could detect, evidently
no sin can be charged against the conscientious judge
who has nevertheless been deceived." Stellhorn. In
such rare cases Timothy will *not* be fellowshiping the
sins of such men; he will still be pure (v. 22b).

25) The same is true regarding the excellent
works, τὰ καλά being made emphatic by the second
article. These works are "entirely evident" (πρόδηλα is
minus the article because it is used as the predicate,
the copula being understood). This reads like a reference to all of the excellent works. This form of expression is found often in the Greek because the very
next clause speaks of the non-evident good works:
"but the ones that are otherwise," i. e., that are not
openly, publicly evident. "They cannot be hid," aorist
infinitive: permanently hid. A little investigation
brings them to light. Sins men like to hide; but not
generally known excellent works no doer of such works
has any reason to hide. Thus a little inquiry soon
brings them to light. Therefore Timothy will not likely
be guilty of refusing a man who is really qualified for
the holy office.

This completes the paragraph regarding the elders.

CHAPTER VI

Slaves, 6:1, 2

1) Eph. 6:5-10 and Col. 3:22-4:1 deal with the Christian obligations of both slaves and masters since these letters were written directly to congregations; hence also the obligations of wives and husbands, children and parents are discussed. In this letter Paul writes to Timothy, his apostolic representative for all the churches in the Asian territory, repeats certain directions he had given to Timothy on matters regarding his work. One of these directions is in regard to slaves, some of whom had pagan masters, others of whom were fortunate in having Christian masters. The idea is not that Timothy did not know how to handle these different cases. Timothy had been with Paul a long time, and Paul had left him in Ephesus (1:3) for this work of properly regulating everything for the many congregations. This letter gives Timothy these instructions in writing to be used as needed in the churches. So he sets down what Timothy is to inculcate in regard to the two groups of church members who are slaves.

The Roman world was full of slaves. Many of them were high-class servants who were wholly unlike the Negro slaves in America. What the Christian Church has to say to them we see from Paul's epistle. **As many as are under yoke as slaves, let them consider their own masters worthy of all honor in order that the name of God and the doctrine may not be blasphemed.**

We do not think that "as many as are under yoke" refers to a larger class than those named in the predicative apposition "as slaves." Instead of saying merely "as many as are slaves," Paul inserts the phrase "under yoke" in order to bring out fully what their condition was. Oxen are under a yoke and are driven by the will of their owner. That, too, is why Paul does not use κύριος but δεσπότης to designate their master. Both terms intend to bring to mind the full oppressiveness of the state of slavery. Trench has a fine essay on the two synonyms: "lord" is one who exercises dominion, *"despotes"* (from which our "despot" is derived) one who exercises domination. See further in Trench.

Although they are "slaves" in the full sense of what this implies, their Christian religion requires of them that they consider their masters, i. e., each slave his "own," worthy of all honor. Because a slave is a Christian, a child of God and an heir of heaven, and because his pagan master is not, the slave dare not despise that master of his. The human relation between the two is not abrogated; it is only sanctified on the slave's part, who will now honor his human master for God's sake. It is this very spirit which is here instilled into the slave, elsewhere in Paul's letters also into the master, which finally wiped out the whole institution of slavery. It must be noted that the thread of "honor" runs through 5:3; 5:17; 6:1.

The motive for the Christian slave's attitude toward his pagan master, irrespective, of course, of how that master may treat him, is to be the very highest and therefore the most powerful: "in order that the name of God and the doctrine may not be blasphemed." "The name" is more than this or that designation of the Christian God; it is his entire revelation of himself, by which alone we are able to know him; it is God in his holy gospel. Thus also "the doctrine" may be combined with "the name" and mean what Christianity teaches. If a Christian slave dishonored his master in any way by disobedience, by acting disre-

spectfully, by speaking shamefully of his master, the
worst consequence would not be the beating he would
receive but the curses he would cause his master to
hurl at this miserable slave's God, his religion, and the
teaching he had embraced: "So that is what this new
religion teaches its converts!" Instead of bringing
honor to the true God and the gospel of his high and
holy Name, as every Christian should be anxious to do,
this slave would bring about the very opposite, to the
devil's delight.

2) **And those having believers as masters, let
them not despise them because they are brethren, but
let them the rather slave** (for them) **because they are
believers and beloved, they** (too) **taking hold of the
well-doing.**

Note the way in which the positive is used and then
the negative in a veiled chiasm: for the pagan masters — all honor; for the believing masters — no
despising (literally, thinking down upon) because they
are brethren. Note also the self-evident logic: If all
honor for pagan masters, then certainly not less honor
for believing masters; more honor could not be used
because all honor is already superlative. The human
mind often acts queerly. Because spiritually and in
the sight of God slaves and masters (Gal. 3:28) were
brethren in the church, both equally dear, equally high,
these slaves might despise these masters, might serve
them less well.

They ought to do the very opposite. True logic
would require that they slave the rather (μᾶλλον) for
such masters and thank God that they have believing
and not pagan masters. The two ὅτι clauses correspond, which means that both of them have the same
subject, namely the believing masters. What Christian slave would not prefer to render his slave-serv-
ice to a master who is himself πιστός, a true believer,
and thus also ἀγαπητός, one truly beloved by the Chris-

tian slave? Οἱ merely substantivizes the participle
and makes it an apposition to the two predicates πιστοὶ
καὶ ἀγαπητοί. The subject lies in εἰσί, namely "they," the
masters: "because they are believers and beloved
ones, they (too) taking hold of the well-doing." *"The
working well"* is the good activity in which the Christian slaves work for their masters, hence the article
is used. This good activity, this working well, the
Christian masters also take hold of, *sie befleissigen
sich dieses Wohltuns,* (B.-P. 116), *nehmen sich dieses
Wohltuns an* (C.-K. 658). There is a mutuality, a
reciprocity: masters and slaves are both Christian,
alike concerned in doing good, each to the other.

The Christian slaves should appreciate having
Christian masters and thus serve them μᾶλλον. One
may say that this is a hint also for Christians who
owned slaves. Some suppose that the article with the
participles makes these the subject of the clause; they
apply the rule that when a nominative has the article
and other nominatives do not, the former is the subject, the others the predicate. But a participle must
have the article in order to make it a substantive and
thus to use it as an apposition, otherwise it would be
only a predicative addition. So here πιστοί and ἀγαπητοί
are used as nouns in the predicate just as ἀδελφοί is in
the other ὅτι clause. Then comes the apposition which
shows why these masters are "beloved ones" to their
Christian slaves: they, too, taking hold of this well-
doing.

It is important to note this construction because
it helps us to avoid several wrong interpretations.
Some of these alter the meaning of the participle and
of its dependent noun. There is no idea of "partaking
of the benefit" (our versions), whether the idea is that
the Christian slaves receive the benefit of food, protection, etc., from their masters, or whether the masters
receive the benefit of good service from their slaves.

Untenable is the view that εὐεργεσία is "benefit" or *Wohltat* or *Wohltun* that comes from God. 'Αντιλαμβά- νεσθαι = *sich befleissigen* (neuter object) or *sich an- nehmen* (personal object) and governs the genitive; the object is neuter: these Christian masters diligently occupy themselves with the well-working.

These things keep teaching and keep urging! This is to be Timothy's part; compare the same injunction in 5:7. By his teaching and his urging Timothy is to make "these things" the established ethical doctrine concerning slaves in all the churches. The second im- perative may mean "urge" or "exhort" or "admonish" or "comfort" or "encourage" as the context may re- quire; "keep urging" is our choice of meaning.

Teachers of Different Doctrines, 3-5

3) The teaching of different doctrines in the churches under his supervision must be stopped by Timothy (1:3-20); the Spirit states that devilish doc- trines will be promulgated in the future, and Timothy is duly to warn and to fortify the churches in advance (4:1-16). Once more Paul reverts to those who teach different doctrines and now tells Timothy and the churches under his care what their judgment on such men must be. Paul certainly does not mince words. He does not handle men who teach differently with kid gloves. The modern indifference to different doctrine is unapostolic. Much more may be said on this Paul- ine chapter, especially when all that he writes in his other letters is combined with what is said here.

If anyone teaches different doctrine and does not come to healthy words, those of our Lord Jesus Christ, and to the doctrine in accord with godliness, he has been puffed up, understanding nothing, but being morbid regarding questionings and battles about words, out of which there keeps coming envy, strife, blasphemies, wicked suspicions, irritations, of men

having been corrupted as to the mind and having been bereft of the truth, supposing their godliness to be a means of gain.

This is enough. When Timothy inculcates this correct view of all who teach a different doctrine, none of the churches will tolerate such men. This passage cannot be connected with the little paragraph regarding slaves (v. 1, 2) so as to denounce those who teach slaves something different.

We have had ἑτεροδιδασκαλεῖν in 1:4; but there Paul refers to those who were then teaching myths, etc., in the churches, now he refers to "anyone" teaching any doctrine that differs from the true one. Zahn, *Introduction* II, 127, defines ἕτερος in the compound verb thus: "It may retain its primary significance of simple difference or divergence, whether from the standpoint of the speaker or from that of the person or the thing spoken of, but quite commonly also may denote more specifically divergence from what is correct." Strangely, he objects to the use of this word made by Ignatius in the sense of "to propound a false doctrine" as being inexact; but is Paul here denouncing only small divergencies of doctrine and passing by open falsities? Fortunately, the apostle adds full specifications so that we cannot exclude gross false doctrine.

Paul defines: "and does not come to healthy words," and then defines the "words" he refers to: "those of our Lord Jesus Christ" (source), and adds the further specification: "and to the doctrine in accord with godliness" (norm). Προσέχεται has too little manuscript authority to be considered; the reading is προσέρχεται. M.-M. 646; R., *W. P.*, and others think that the word has an exceptional meaning in this passage, namely "consent to," and thus seek for examples of this sense. The sense is quite normal, the Germans have no trouble understanding it: "and does not come to healthy words," von Hofmann adds: as to a pure fountain. It is not even metaphorical, for one may come to spiritual things as well as to physical.

Λόγοι are statements, words conveying thought. "Those of our Lord Jesus Christ" are those spoken by him; note "these my words" in Matt. 7:24, 26; "my words" in Luke 6:47; the singular in John 12:48; 17:14, 17. Jesus' "word" and "words" constitute the gospel, the singular, the gospel as a whole, the plural as so many doctrines. Whoever does not come to them, strays around elsewhere, no matter where, and teaches both ἑτέρως and ἕτερα, "differently" and "different things."

Paul significantly calls them "healthy" words, *sanus*, which is not the same as "wholesome" (A. V.), *saluber* (Zahn, *Introduction* II, 129). This thought of health and healthy runs through these last letters: 1:10; II Tim. 1:13; 4:3; Tit. 1:9, 13; 2:1, 2, 8. Who wants unhealthy, diseased words and teaching? Here we have the German *reine Lehre*, a term that is scoffed at by those who want something unclean in the way of doctrine; we recall the use of the expression "unclean spirits" in the Gospels. Paul first uses the plural "unhealthy words" and spreads them out in their variety and their number; then the compact singular of the mass: "the doctrine not in accord with godliness," and also changes from an adjective to a phrase — both are typically Pauline. Κατά indicates the norm, it should be godliness; it is *not* this but some totally different norm that the unhealthy teaching follows. Who wants teaching that does not accord with godliness; there is no intermediate step. On "godliness" see 4:7.

4) We catch the idea of τετύφωται when we note that, like τῦφος, it is used in the sense of being conceited (B.-P. 1328; M.-M. 646); the perfect indicates continuous condition: "is puffed up with conceit." Demosthenes used it in the sense of *dumm sein*, which is

scarcely the sense here since "understanding nothing" follows and adds this thought to blatant conceit. Conceitedness and silly ignorance so often go together. "The *Sonderlehrer* know nothing in the domain in which they pretend to know something, in which they pose as teachers. They have no knowledge, they possess no understanding of what they claim to know far better than the true teachers, of the way of justification and sanctification. By pretending to teach and also making many words they by no means prove their expert knowledge. . . . This is still the characteristic of sectarians." Kretzmann who points especially to Christian Science and Russellism. But there are also others of this type.

Paul adds another participle: "but being morbid regarding questionings and battles about words" (our "logomachies"). Such a man will not even approach healthy words, "being sick with a morbidity" for all kinds of investigations and disputes about things valueless, that lead to nothing but endless word-battles. What a true picture even today! So much for the *subject matter* taught by such a man.

5) Now the ungodly *effects* of his teaching such "different" things: "out of which there keeps coming (durative present, γίνεται: there keeps occurring) envy, strife, blasphemies, wicked suspicions, irritations," such fruits as these. Paul names five, the half of full completeness, which means that there are others of the same kind that may be added to the list. These miserable products, we should note, appear in these false teachers themselves. In their questions and word-battles one envies the other because of the proficiency which he develops; there is strife as they vie with and contradict each other; blasphemies result, namely denunciations couched in sacred words; also ὑπόνοιαι, "underthoughts," suspicions of motives and of intents; διαπαρατριβαί (correct reading) "irritations,"

mutual rubbing and friction. Chrysostom thought of infected sheep, rubbing and spreading their disease; but these irritations are mutual between men whose minds are diseased with errors.

Paul starts with "anyone," a singular in form, which is indefinite and thus leads us to think of a number; he now adds the plural with characterizing participles, the perfect tenses describing present conditions that reach far back: all these and similar vices "belonging to men corrupted as to the mind (the passive retaining the accusative of the active) and bereft of the truth" (the ablative genitive, R. 518). Paul's analysis is keen. This trouble is in the mind, here corruption has occurred. C.-K. 764 is right, νοῦς is the organ of *moral thinking* and comprehension, the intellectual organ of the *moral* impulse of man's being. It is the result of corruption of mind to be bereft of the truth, i. e., of the reality which constitutes the saving gospel. The soundest psychology underlies these two participles, a psychology of error that is little understood today and one that is not investigated by professional psychologists. Will someone not write The Psychology of Error?

Νοσῶν points to mental morbidity which already says much in regard to the pathology here described; διεφθαρμένων says still more. We see the evidences of morbid thinking in what this thinking loves to occupy itself with, ζητήσεις, λογομαχίαι. The diseased state of the mind consists in a corruption and a disintegration — the mental faculties no longer function normally in the moral and the spiritual field. They do not react normally to the truth. All reality and its presentation in verity ought to produce the reaction of acceptance, especially the saving divine gospel realities should have this effect; all lies, falsities, perversions ought to produce rejection, most of all those in the moral and the spiritual field. Jesus was compelled to say: "Because

I tell you the truth, ye believe me not," John 8:45; also 5:43. When it meets "the truth," the corrupted mind sees and seeks only objections; when it meets what differs from this truth, it sees and seeks reasons for accepting this difference. Jesus presents this psychology in John 3:19-21. A deeper truth underlies it, II Cor. 4:4. The psychological feature of it is exceedingly important. For one thing, it reveals the guilt involved.

Thus they "are bereft of the truth." "Bereft" is correct, for these are not men who have never come into contact with the truth; then "bereft" would not be the proper word. The truth was theirs at one time or could and should have been theirs; thus they now stand as "having been bereft." The question whether elders or laymen are referred to is unimportant. Far more important is the fact that such men do not go out among pagans and work on them but keep undermining the health of the church and raise the cry of intolerance when they are stopped.

The present participle: "supposing their godliness to be a means of gain," seems to have been added rather incidentally, for it forms a transition to the next section. Here "their godliness" is not to be understood in the objective sense of the true, genuine godliness as it is in v. 3 but in the subjective sense in which these men conceive of "their godliness" (the article has the force of the possessive pronoun). Paul touches the mercenary side of false teaching. Our times furnish some glaring examples. Luther mercilessly exposed the greed of the papacy. Religious charlatans infested the Roman world, attached themselves to men of power and wealth, their great object being gain. Paul and his assistants refused to take even their daily bread from their converts. Also in Corinth the Judaizers "devoured" with rank mercenariness.

On slender textual grounds the A. V. adds: "From such withdraw thyself!" which a few commentators would retain on the plea that the insertion cannot be explained. But why not? Does not a similar command appear in II Tim. 3:5? Somebody thought Paul's words incomplete and completed them. However, in no case are we obliged to accept a variant just because we cannot explain its insertion. Paul does not need to say what Timothy and the churches are to do after he has said what these false teachers are.

The Desire to Be Rich, 6-16

6) We make a paragraph at this point because Paul is discussing different groups. He has finished his discussion regarding those who are teaching differing doctrines; he still has two further groups about whom he deems it necessary to say something: those who intend to be rich (v. 6-16) and those who are rich (v. 17-19). Where the thought permits it Paul links together. In 5:3; 5:17; 6:1 the links are "honor"; in 6:3 no link is offered; here in v. 6 "godliness" and "means of gain" link with v. 5. Yet the class now discussed is a separate group, those who are bent on getting rich.

Now the godliness (I have in mind) together with contentment actually is a great means of gain. Ἔστι is placed forward, is accented, is emphatic: it *is*, and there is no doubt about it. Also the predicate is placed emphatically forward, which leaves the subject in last place and lends emphasis to it also. This is what the flexibility of the Greek is able to achieve. The article is pointed: not the godliness that the mercenary false teachers have in mind but "the godliness" which Paul has in mind. Part of it is "contentment," hence it is always μετά, "together with" or "accompanied by" contentment, αὐτάρκεια, the condition of being satisfied with what one has and not looking elsewhere — see the adjective in Phil. 4:11. This is not the Stoic virtue that goes under this name but is distinctively Christian, for it rests on God's provident care. The preposition is neither causal nor conditional: "because or if together with contentment." Nor is it limiting as if there were two kinds of godliness, one with and the other without contentment. It is explicative: contentment always goes together with the true godliness, hence it also has no article.

As this godliness is a different matter from that of the mercenary false teachers, so it is also "a means of gain" in a far different sense. For the true godliness is profitable for everything, having promise for the life now and for the one to come, 4:8. It is thus "a great means of gain." Paul indicates only the negative side of the gain: being lifted above all the vexations, temptations, dangers, and disappointments of mercenary, discontented men (v. 9, etc.). Then one rests serene and safe in God's care, who provides what we need. Then one has the happiness and inward joy which the world in its chase after earthly treasures cannot know.

7) The first question is one regarding the reading. There are five variants in the Greek manuscripts: γάρ — ὅτι — δῆλον ὅτι — ἀληθὲς ὅτι — and ἀλλ'; several in the Latin versions. When we study them we find that the first has the most weight textually, and that all the rest are due to efforts to adjust the text to a preconceived meaning. Some think that γάρ introduces reasons that the true godliness with contentment is so great a means of gain. Some list three such reasons: the perishableness of earthly goods — their dispensableness — the danger connected with them. This is homiletics rather than exegesis. Some list only two reasons. But when we look at these "reasons," they are not reasons that godliness with contentment is so

great a *means* of gain, nor are they reasons that it is
so great a *gain*. Paul does not say: Godliness, etc., will
gain you this, will gain you that; or will be a means
for gaining this, that, etc. But he would be obliged to
say something like this if γάρ were to offer reasons.

**For not a thing did we bring into the world be-
cause neither are we able to bring a thing out. Now
having nourishment and coverings, with these we will
be content.**

Γάρ elucidates and this time does so by means of an
amplified restatement in a different form which ends
with the very verb ἀρκεσθησόμεθα, the noun for which
ends v. 6, αὐταρκείας. Verse 6 states the fact abstractly,
v. 7, 8 state the main point of that fact concretely, personally (with three "we" verbs). Γάρ thus = "to make
this clearer let me put it this way." The stress is on
"contentment," the last word of v. 6; and again on "we
will be content," the last word of v. 8. What true
godliness perceives is woven into v. 7, and with
what it is content is inserted into the participial clause
of v. 8. Proof for "great means of gain" is not in
Paul's mind. "We will be content" is enough for us
who are godly. The persons who have this true contentment need no proof or reason as to why their state
is so great a means of gain. Paul is not arguing anybody into contentment; he is telling the godly, who are
content, what a blessed source of gain they possess.
Then in v. 9, etc., he compares with us who are going
to be content those who are discontented and intend
to get rich.

It is an honest fact, "not a thing (οὐδέν) did we
bring into the world," not even a bit of clothing. Yet
how many think of this fact? But why did we not
bring in a thing? "Because neither are we able to
bring a thing (τι) out." Thus there was no reason for
bringing in even a single thing. Are we not in a little
while going out without a thing? Now do not philos-

ophize and seek for some peculiar meaning hidden in these words or change the reading to secure some such meaning. Having arrived naked because we are going to leave that way and cannot possibly leave any other way, the few things we really need for our short stay are not going to disturb our minds as godly people; we are simply going to be content. That is our great source of spiritual gain. Those who do not perceive what Paul here says are to be pitied, especially if they try to make their false godliness a means of gain.

What is so striking is Paul's ὅτι and the thought it contains, that *because* we cannot bring anything away we brought nothing along when we arrived. Even early copyists changed this thought by changing the reading by substituting a thought that was less striking. The two second aorists are exact opposites: "did bring in — to bring out," or "did carry in — to carry out." Our versions lose this contrast when they translate: "brought — carry."

8) Δέ is not adversative ("but," R. V.). It merely resumes the main thought of v. 6, namely "contentment," and now states it personally: "we will be (are going to be) content." Δέ adds the whole statement as it is centered in this main verb; it does not connect only with the modifier ἔχοντες. "Now" we who, just because we are unable to bring anything out brought nothing in, "we," taking what we find in our short stay in the world, "having nourishments (*Lebensmittel*) and coverings (things that cover or shelter: clothes, a tent, a house), are going to be content with these" (τούτοις, emphatic) and are not going to be discontented like those are who make their short earthly lives in this world a chase after riches as if they could take them along.

This is the simple thought. There is no necessity to seek to find more in it. We see that the verb "we will be content" (volitive future, R. 889) resumes the noun of the phrase "together with contentment" which occurs in v. 6: we Christians, we who have the true godliness, we are going to be content with these things. The verb is properly future: whatever we were before, whatever we did before, this is what we are going to do from henceforth. The verb, too, means just this and should not be altered into something else, for then we should lose its real point.

9) With δέ Paul adds a comparison to indicate what happens to the other kind of people. **But they who intend to be rich keep falling into temptation and a snare and many thoughtless and hurtful lusts such as sink men in destruction and perdition.**

On βουλόμενοι see 2:8 (5:14) : "those intending to be rich" whether they succeed in their intention or not. They "keep falling," iterative present. The Greek word for "temptation" is itself neutral but gets its sinister meaning from the context. Since it is here followed by "snare," we have the picture of being lured into a snare and thus getting caught and falling. But one preposition governs the three nouns, and these follow in proper sequence: falling into "temptation," they become enmeshed in a "snare," and this snare holds them with the cords of "many thoughtless (devoid of sound reason) and hurtful lusts." There they hang entangled and caught like snared animals. The qualitative relative completes the tragic picture: "such as sink or plunge men into destruction and perdition," two terms are used to express an intensification.

Note the paronomasia between πορισμός (v. 5, 6) and πειρασμός, and the alliteration of π running through ἐμπίπτουσιν — πειρασμόν — παγίδα — ἐπιθυμίας πολλάς. It is wholly unsought and is therefore beautiful. The word for "lusts" is also a *vox media*; the context and the adjectives give it an evil meaning. These lusts are without reason and good sense and thus also hurt and damage. Men who are set on being rich snatch at the

tempting bait, are caught in the snare, are held by the
lusts. So shrewd they thought themselves, but see into
what they have fallen! They may get rich, may boast
of their wealth, their business acumen, their successful
deals. But look at the most successful among them —
their lusts are "reasonless," such as a reasonable man
must shun! They promise a satisfaction which they
never give. They soon show how "hurtful" they are.
How seldom are riches and happiness combined! A
big price is paid to achieve the intent, and when it is
achieved, how many would not gladly pay a bigger
price if the whole thing could only again be undone!

The relative clause pictures the climax. It is not
merely a fourth and a fifth noun, like the three preceding nouns, but a clause with corresponding emphasis. The climax must be added because some are eternally lost. Dives in the parable, Judas, Ananias and
Sapphira. This is the strongest part of the warning
for all of us. Through God's grace some may yet escape out of the snare of their folly before they are
drawn into the final plunge by their evil desires. The
verb now used is stronger; it is not merely "fall into"
but "sink or plunge into the deep"; its corresponding
noun βάθος means "depth." Here "into destruction and
perdition" is literal, hence we do not translate "drown."
One does not "drown" when he sinks into hell. There
is no thought of annihilation. The two abstract terms
indicate concrete conditions, especially the latter is
used in the New Testament to designate the condition
after death when the exclusion from salvation has become a final, irrevocable fact (C.-K. 789).

Kretzmann makes the application: "Our land, in
which 'the almighty dollar' rules, approaches this condition with giant strides. Luxury, indulgence, pride
in clothing increase from year to year in astonishing
manner, moral decay grows, marital bonds become ever
more lax. And they who offer these things to the peo-

ple, many owners of theatres and many film producers, restaurant and cabaret owners, especially in the great cities, allege as the reason that increasing wealth is to blame. People have the money to waste and by means of it want the satisfaction of the lusts of their flesh and their eyes." The great world depression is on while these lines are being written, the "distress of nations," but now there is mostly only complaint because plunging into perdition cannot go on as merrily as before. Men only long for a new era of wealth and "prosperity" in order to abuse it as they did before.

10) Paul elucidates still further. **For root of all the evils is the love of money which some aspiring to were made to wander away from the faith and did pierce themselves with many pains.**

The predicate naturally lacks the article so that we should not stress either *"a* root" or *"the* root." Money-love is "root of all the evils"; κακά is explained at some length with its New Testament synonyms and antonyms in C.-K. 556-7. All things that are "bad" may grow out of money-love as shoots grow out of a root; nothing good ever grows out of it. This shows what money-love really is. A root is hidden in the evil; what it is we see from the growth it sends up. R., *W. P.,* says: "Undoubtedly a proverb that Paul here quotes" and then refers to Bion and Democritus. But these call money-love a "metropolis" of all the evils, which is a quite different matter. Paul quotes no author. The fact that worldly men express themselves regarding the vice of loving money is to be expected; they also express themselves in regard to other vices. Sometimes they do it aptly, almost like Holy Writ. There is no thought of quoting a proverb.

There is no irregularity in the use of the relative "which" as though it does not refer to ἡ φιλαργυρία but to the "silver" (i. e., money) in this compound, or as though its antecedent is "root" — men do not aspire to

a root. On the participle see "aspire to" in 3:1. One
aspires to the love of something by cultivating that
love. It is ever Paul's way to penetrate beneath the
surface; here he does not name the physical silver or
money but the vice itself that wants money, aspires to
that. One aspires to something καλόν, excellent, noble;
so in 3:1 to the holy office of the ministry. That is a
normal aspiration. Here we have a striking paradox:
aspiring to what produces all manner of κακά, things
bad, base, evil. The height of abnormality, of unnat-
uralness. A prolific vice regarded as a most desirable
virtue. No wonder Paul uses ἀνόητος in v. 9, "devoid of
reason," "senseless." So Satan kindled Eve's ambition to grasp the evil as though it were a great good,
to eat death by calling it life.

The participle is not an aorist but a durative present: "in, while, or by aspiring" these two things happened to these people (now we have historical aorists),
which constitute them concrete warnings for us: "they
were made to wander away from the faith (passive:
by their unnatural aspiration) and pierced themselves
with many pains." The result was in a perfect line
with their abnormality. They obtained the "evils"
tha' grow from this root. Who normally wants to
wander away from the right course like a planet
thrown out of its appointed orbit? Still plainer: who
wants to pierce himself with many sharp pains?
"Some" did these very things. We might think that
Paul speaks only of what resulted for these men in this
life; but this is the end of his paragraph, and while
he sometimes at the end weaves in a loose thread that
was left hanging in the previous discussion, this is not
the case here, these "many pains" include those suffered in "perdition." Think of it, they pierced *themselves!*

Some list these "many pains": worries about
wealth, pains of conscience because of the way in which

wealth is acquired, etc. But such a list should be very long. Many a would-be-rich man's success was his failure and ruin; many a son of such a father broke that father's heart. The delectable fruit of wealth became apples of Sodom in the mouth. The worst, however, is the end and the hereafter. Here again (see 4:1) we should say that "the faith" is objective, *quae creditur*. One wanders away from a course that has been laid down objectively for him to follow. Off the right course means to be adrift. A derailed train is wrecked. Sometimes drifting goes on and on, but there can be no question as to how it will end. Bengel, thinking only of this life, adds: *Horum dolorum remidium fides.*

11) There are commentators who suppose that Timothy was inclined to love money and point out that his present office afforded him opportunity to gratify this love, and that Paul thus inserted this paragraph as a most personal warning to him. But this supposition is not borne out by the context. For the very first verse of this paragraph names six virtues that are to be pursued, and the next verse speaks of the whole contest for the faith, which cannot signify that Timothy was inclined toward a money-loving vice, to say nothing of drawing a plausible picture of his present office with opportunities and temptations to enrich himself with money. We have 4:6-11 to guide us. In 4:8 Paul uses the second person singular when addressing Timothy; but in 4:10 he uses the first person plural, in which Paul includes himself. In 4:6, 11 Timothy is told to preach and teach "these things" to the churches. In the light of these facts the present paragraph is to be understood. In v. 13, 14, to which v. 15, 16 are attached, we have a similar order to Timothy regarding his teaching, which is followed in v. 17 by an order regarding what he is to teach to those who *are* rich.

This paragraph, then, presents the entire positive side of the godliness which shuts out the love of money. Such a vice will be wholly smothered by all that is here presented. Paul follows the same procedure elsewhere. He bombards some single error with all the guns in his heavy battery and crushes some single vice with the whole avalanche of the virtues and the supreme aim of the Christian life. As was the case in 4:12, Timothy in person is to be both the example and the solemn teacher of all these things: "thou, O man of God" (example, v. 11) — "that thou guard the commandment" (as teacher, v. 14).

But thou, O man of God, flee these things! And pursue righteousness, godliness, faith, love, patience, meekness! Be a contestant in the noble contest for the faith! Lay hold of the eternal life, into which thou wast called and didst confess the noble confession in the presence of many witnesses!

This is the mighty opposite of sin and its consequences, which have been presented in v. 6-10. Some would go back as far as v. 3; but this is not necessary. Not until he reaches v. 20 does Paul write, "O Timothy." Here he says: "But thou, O man of God," and uses an epithet that can be applied to any true Christian as II Tim. 3:17 shows. In the Old Testament it is applied to great men of God and to prophets, but here it is not restricted to such characters, for also all that follows applies to every Christian. Paul addresses Timothy in words which Timothy may use without change when he calls upon others in his preaching. Never does Paul exclude himself or his assistants when he admonishes. He often inserts a "we" and an "us" beside the "you." All that the word contains is intended for him as it is for others. That is also true with regard to this "thou."

The Greek seldom uses "O" with its vocatives; when it is used, the effect is the greater. Ἄνθρωπε means only

"human being" and not "man," the male. The very
address: "man of God," a person who belongs to God,
separates him from those whose hearts are set on
money and on earthly riches. God is greater than
gold. Blessed everyone who may rightly be addressed:
"O man of God!"

Φεῦγε = "ever flee these things" like a pestilence,
like poisonous serpents, like the devil's snares. One
would cease to be a man of God if he did not so flee
these things, if he let them catch him. Alas, some
only pretend to flee. They often stay near and think
they are at a safe distance until they are overtaken
and caught. Continue to flee, do nothing but flee, the
margin of safety cannot be too great.

That is enough for the negative; sufficient is said
in v. 9, 10. Here we have a preamble of only two
words, for here the positive is to spread out: Δέ, "on
the other hand, pursue," etc. The two are one, two
sides of one course of conduct: when we are fleeing
we pursue; when pursuing we flee, a halt in flight is a
halt in pursuit, and vice versa.

Six virtues are named in three pairs; they form a
chain, and in each instance the second one depends on
the first one named. "Righteousness" is the *justitia
acquisita*, the righteousness of life, which thus also is
to be pursued. It is never entirely caught in this constant pursuit, but it is caught in ever greater measure.
This righteousness has degrees; the *justitia imputata*
has no degrees. The word is always, yes always, forensic, for it denotes the quality which is what it is
because God, the Judge, declares it so by his verdict of
acceptance. This righteousness includes all the Christian virtues and good works, but it names them from
the forensic side, from God's verdict upon them. "Godliness" is only another word for the same quality, but
this names it according to its quality in us, namely as
our piety and reverence toward God. We might think

of placing godliness first, righteousness second; Paul's order is correct, which is felt when εὐσέβεια is understood with its Greek connotation.

Secondly: keep pursuing "faith, love." Why is this pair placed second? Should "faith" not be first in the list? Some answer that "faith" is the source of righteousness and godliness. But is it not also the source of love, patience, and meekness? Then it should be placed first, or, since it is the source of the entire five, last. Since this pair is placed where it is, "faith" together with "love" are as great virtues as the first pair: constant believing and loving. Like these other virtues, "faith" is here not considered as their source but as a good work. Thus: all our believing in God and his doctrines as it proceeds day by day; all our loving God and man, these two walking arm in arm, the latter being the love of intelligent comprehension and of corresponding intelligent purpose.

Thirdly, keep pursuing "patience, meekness." The ὑπομονή refers to things, hence it is never used with reference to God as is μακροθυμία ("longsuffering"), brave patience that remains under privations and sufferings without complaining (Trench); πραϋπάθειαν (better reading than πραότητα although the meaning is the same), "meek feeling," making and enforcing no high claims, the very opposite of what pagan and worldly morality admires, its ideal being strong, self-assertive men. Jesus was meek; a beatitude was pronounced on the meek (Matt. 5:5).

12) Paul continues: "Be (ever) a contender in the noble contest for the faith!" We have the cognate accusative: "contend the contest." "Fight the fight" in our versions alters the figure into a battle or a personal clash; it is taken from the athletic arena and refers to striving for a prize in an athletic event: "Keep on straining every muscle and nerve in the noble straining for the faith!" See this same figure

amplified in II Tim. 4:7. In I Tim. 1:18 we have the general campaigning a noble campaign.

Some note that the genitive is objective: "the noble contest *for* the faith," but regard "the faith" as subjective: "Fight to maintain thy own faith in thy heart!" This is only formally different from the subjective genitive which others note here: "Fight faith's fight!" i. e., the fight faith always has to fight. We consider this genitive objective and "the faith" as objective just as in 4:1 and 6:10. "Contend the noble contest for the substance of the Christian faith!" Hold the banner of the faith high! Carry it to victory! Paul and Timothy were called for the defense of the gospel; so are all of us in whatever station in life we may be.

Those who set out to stalk riches fall into a snare. Ours is a noble contest, it is entirely in the interest of the gospel, "the faith," the things we believe. The love of money is a root of all κακά; ours is a contest that is καλόν. Ignoble — noble: what a contrast! See the motivation in καλόν. See the virility in these imperatives: Pursue — contend! Here is Christian manhood, red-blooded, strenuous. Here, too, is the highest cause in all the world: THE FAITH. To give one's life for that is noble (II Tim. 4:6). To wander away from The Faith (v. 10), to be caught in the devil's snare, pierced with a thousand pains caused by our own folly — how ignoble, what shame ("flee these things")!

The figure is not continued when Paul speaks of the reception of the prize (βραβεῖον). This sentence is altogether literal. Not only is "the eternal life" literal but also the verb "lay hold of" and also the participial clause. Those who think that "the eternal life" is the prize overlook the fact that in the Greek games the victor did not "lay hold of" the prize, the victor's wreath was only placed upon his head. This literal clause interprets the preceding figurative clause. Yet not by describing the ἀγών or contest itself but by taking us to the last supreme moment of this contest.

The contending in the contest is long, hence the durative present: "keep on contending"; the supreme moment at the end is only an instant, hence the punctiliar aorist: "lay hold of" (see also v. 19). This aorist is not constative so as to include all the contending, making all of it a laying hold of eternal life. Such an aorist would be possible, but it would not do here. For the present imperative is an open tense: we see the contending going on and on; we are held in suspense by this tense, waiting for the outcome and the end. This outcome the aorist mentions as it always does in the Greek after an open tense (present or imperfect). "Grasp eternal life!" All our life long we keep on contending for The Faith so that at the end we may grasp the eternal life.

This is the life of glory in heaven, the opposite of the "destruction and perdition" mentioned in v. 9. The ζωὴ αἰώνιος may signify "life eternal" as we now have it by faith (John 3:15, 16); but here we must know the final outcome of all this long contending, and that is "the eternal life" of glory in heaven: *"Henceforth* there is laid up for me the crown of righteousness," etc. (II Tim. 4:8). The article is due to the following relative: "the eternal life for which thou wast called," etc.

The final outcome is combined with the very beginning. God called us by the gospel; in that hour we entered the contest; the end is the hour when we grasp and hold life eternal as our possession. As is always the case in the epistles, this is the successful and effective κλῆσις or "call"; ever it holds out to us "the prize of the high calling of God in Christ Jesus" (Phil. 3:14). That inspires us during the whole straining of the contest. The acceptance of God's call is added: "and didst confess the noble confession in the presence of many witnesses." Combined, as this confession is, with the calling unto eternal life, it can signify only the confession made at the time of baptism and not what may have been confessed when Paul took Timothy as his assistant, or when he appointed him as his representative for the Asian churches.

We have another cognate accusative. By occurring together they are most effective: contending the noble contest — confessing the noble confession. Καλόν — καλήν impress this point of excellence and nobleness. We possess no formula of the confession which was made at the time of baptism at this early date; its substance we know, it was "The Faith" for which the baptized confessors contended. That was a public confession: "in the presence of many witnesses," among whom we think Paul also regarded the angels (5:21) and not only the members of the congregation. The motive here touched upon is scarcely that of fear as Bengel states it: *Coram multis testibus, qui contra te, si deficeres, testuari forent.* Not that all these witnesses will rise up and testify against the one who wanders away from the faith (v. 10); but the fact tl.at all these earthly and heavenly witnesses inspire the confessor to be ever faithful to the confession he has made — this is the motivation also in Heb. 12:1.

13) While verses 11, 12 are addressed to Timothy, they are worded in a form that fits any and every Christian. Verses 13, 14 recall 5:21 and include Timothy's official position. In v. 13-16 the solemnity of the apostle's injunction to Timothy rises to its greatest height. Glance through the epistle: at the end of 1:4 the verb of enjoining is only understood — in 1:18 we have the first direct injunction — in 2:1 simply "I urge," but in 4:11 a brief, direct order — in 5:7 another — then the solemn one in 5:21, followed by the brief one in 6:2. Now the climax, 6:13-16; and then the close in 6:20, 21. The climax is purposely not

placed at the end. All good homiletics teach us *not*
to make a sky-rocket finish. Rom. 16:25-27 is a grand
doxology and only as such and as a summarizing of the
entire epistle forms the appropriate conclusion.

**I am ordering thee in the sight of God, the One
generating life in everything, and Christ Jesus, the
One who witnessed before Pontius Pilate the noble
confession, that thou guard the commandment spotless, irreproachable, until the epiphany of our Lord
Jesus; etc.**

On παραγγέλλω see 1:3; 1:18 (noun); 4:11; 5:7.
This word runs through the entire epistle. Paul does
not say: "I am ordering thee in the name of God" (in
connection with his revelation), but more effectively:
"in the sight of God and Christ." Paul himself and
Timothy are standing in God's and Christ's presence;
their all-seeing eyes are resting upon Paul and Timothy. The two participles are appositions. Paul calls
God "the One generating life in all things" because he
has just mentioned "the eternal life." God gives that
highest life, for he fills with life all that has life in any
form. The participle is the descriptive present, hence
it is not to be translated with a past tense. The etymology points to the generation of life: *der alles Bele-
bende*, a designation that is so true that we need not
think of the possible alternative meaning offered in
the R. V. margin: "preserveth all things alive."

While this apposition leads us to think of the spiritual life generated in us by God, which is presently
to merge into the glorious life of heaven, the apposition attached to "Christ Jesus" leads us to think of
our own "noble confession," the first notable act in
our spiritual life. What we confessed and still confess is "The Faith" (v. 12), for which we also ever
contend. Paul does not say: "the One who *confessed*

before Pontius Pilate the noble confession," as if he were only our great example, and as if our confession were only a repetition and a continuation of his. Paul says: "the One who witnessed . . . the noble confession." Bengel is correct: *Testari confessionem est Domini, confiteri confessionem Timothei.* Jesus witnessed or attested the noble confession (objective: its substance), and we have already pointed out that the noble confession in v. 12 means "The Faith" (objective, *quae creditur*). *What* we believe, *what* we confess that we believe, this is *what* Jesus attested, confirmed with his testimony "before Pontius Pilate." Some regard ἐπί as equivalent to the Latin *sub* or to the German *unter;* but little is gained thereby, and ἐπί is the regular preposition used when the standing before a judge or a judgment seat is referred to (see the evidence in 5:19); it is the German *vor,* our "before," and not the temporal "at the time of."

Jesus is "the faithful Witness" (Rev. 1:5), "the Amen, the faithful and true Witness" (Rev. 3:14). The question is asked as to how much Paul includes in this testimony of Jesus. Some restrict it to his verbal testimony as reported in Matt. 27:11; John 18:33-38. This would refer to "the noble confession" that Jesus confessed and testified in regard to himself when he was stating who he was. The ancients went farther; they regarded the phrase "before Pontius Pilate" as including the death of Jesus as decreed by Pilate as we confess in the Apostolic Creed: "suffered under Pontius Pilate, was crucified, dead, and buried." We must say that, like Stellhorn, we agree with them. Jesus' testimony before Pontius Pilate was not merely verbal; it was not even only "in the face of death," but also a testimony with and by his actual suffering, death, and burial. We do not extend it so as to include Jesus' testimony throughout his ministry, which only culminated before Pilate "in the face of death." "Before Pontius Pilate" should be taken literally; Jesus voluntarily went into the death on the cross. This was the crown of his testimony.

It is generally understood that "to confess the noble confession" is not the same as "to witness the noble confession," the expressions are not synonymous. Yet it is said that the latter is "somewhat anomalous" or even "harsh." But this criticism considers the expression apart from its context. Then it would, indeed, be odd. But "the noble confession" which Jesus attested is "the noble confession," "The FAITH," which Timothy confessed at the time of his baptism, which we all confess today. C.-K. 690, etc., beclouds the issue by stressing the subjective action of ὁμολογία over against the substance, the truth, the realities that are confessed. To be sure, "The Faith" could not be "The Faith" if no one believed in it; *what* is believed gets its name from this activity, but its objectiveness remains, would remain even if no one believed. So there would be no "confession" if no one confessed; but that means only that we would then not have the word "confession"; the substance, truth, realities would nevertheless remain, for they are objective. In both verses "the noble confession" signifies this objective reality. Timothy confessed it, Jesus attested it. A stronger term than "witness" or "attest" could have been used, for Jesus' attestation was an actual fulfilling of the prophecies, an attestation by deed and not only by word.

The suggestion has also been made that we construe τὴν καλὴν ὁμολογίαν with τηρῆσαι and make it the object of this word, with τὴν ἐντολήν as an apposition. This removes the balance: "thou didst confess the noble confession — the One who witnessed the noble confession." It also creates an untenable apposition: "the noble confession" is not "the commandment."

14) In the sight of God and Christ Jesus (both persons equally producing our salvation) Paul orders Timothy: "That thou guard the commandment spotless, irreproachable," etc. There should be no difference of opinion as to what "guarding the commandment" means, nor about the dependence of the two adjectives. In Rom. 7:12 "the commandment" is called holy and righteous and good although only the law is referred to; "the commandment" in the higher gospel sense of 1:5, where it is also called ἡ παραγγελία, is no less. It is Timothy's official task to guard and to keep it so, namely "spotless, irreproachable." Jesus says the same in John 14:15, 21; 15:10; three times he uses τηρεῖν with ἐντολή although without the adjectives. In Matt. 28:20 it is τηρεῖν πάντα ὅσα ἐνετειλάμην, "to guard all things whatsoever I did command you," and here the relative clause = ἡ ἐντολή. The sense is that Timothy is to guard, protect, preserve all the teaching enjoined upon him so that it will ever remain as spotless and as faultless as when he received it. He is to keep the *reine Lehre rein.*

Some think that the Word is called "the commandment" because the gospel commands men to repent, believe, etc. But Matt. 28:20; John 14:15, 21; 15:10 show clearly that the gospel is called "the command" because its preaching, teaching, inculcation were enjoined upon the disciples. It is not correct to say that when τηρεῖν is used with τὴν ἐντολήν it always means "to observe," i. e., to obey, to do the commandment, and thus not "to guard" it. The meaning of the verb is "to watch over, guard, keep safe, preserve"; the noun τήρησις means "safekeeping," "ward" (prison). It is plain that no one "observes" or "obeys" the commandment unless he keeps it intact, prevents anyone from tampering with it, altering, reducing or adding to it. Only he who is so concerned about it will be concerned about really believing and "observing" it with me-

ticulous obedience. To drop the one part of the meaning of the verb is to slacken hold of the other part. He
who guards will obey; he who really obeys must guard.

As the passages in John's and in Matthew's Gospels
show, "the commandment" is Jesus' "Word" or his
"words," and no less is referred to by Paul. It is the
substance of "the noble confession," the substance of
"The Faith" (v. 12). The term thus needs no further
definition: it is all that Christ commands us to believe,
teach, confess, keep inviolate, guard against alteration,
obey, adhere to throughout our lives.

Here the predicative adjectives "to guard spotless
and irreproachable" clearly state that the commandment
is to be kept as Christ gave it to us. It is said that in
the New Testament these adjectives are always used
with reference to persons only and that this analogy
compels us to construe them with σέ and not with τὴν
ἐντολήν. The very position of the adjectives argues
against this construction. Clemens Romanus uses
"spotless" with reference to the seal; Thayer has an
example of a reference to a horse, another to a sheep;
B.-P. examples of a reference to a lamb. B.-P. 101 has
an example of the use of "irreproachable" with πολιτεία,
another with βίος. It would be strange, indeed, if these
adjectives were applied only to persons. Stains, spots,
blemishes may appear in anything, so that reproach,
adverse criticism, fault may be found with them.
Hence also we have this order of the two adjectives in
our verse.

"Until the epiphany of our Lord Jesus Christ" =
until the end of the world. This is exactly what Jesus
says in Matt. 28:20. "The epiphany" is the manifestation or appearing of the Lord at the last day. He
entrusted the commandment to us; he will call us to
account to ask whether we have duly guarded it. This
term appears also in II Thess. 2:8; II Tim. 4:1, 8;
Titus 2:13; compare Col. 3:3, 4, Christ made manifest

in his φανέρωσις. Examine II Thess. 2:8. Jesus shall
step forth out of his present invisibility, "and every
eye shall see him, and they also who pierced him," Rev.
1:7. It is not correct to assert that Paul is certain
that he and Timothy will live until this epiphany takes
place. Paul never pretends to know the date of the
final day, Acts 1:7. Because that day might come at
any time and overtake them, he speaks just as we often
do, who know just as little whether we shall live to see
that day or shall die before it arrives. The full soteriological name and title are certainly in place here.

15) With a simple relative the great sentence
merges into one of Paul's most glorious doxologies:
**which at its own season he will show, the blessed God
and only Potentate, the King of those reigning as
kings and Lord of those ruling as lords, the only One
having immortality, inhabiting light inapproachable,
whom not a single man has seen nor is able to see, he
to whom honor and strength eternal!   Amen.**

Already the relative clause shows that Paul does
not intend to glorify the ineffable majesty and power
of Christ but of God, for not the fact that Christ will
display his epiphany but that God will display it is the
statement. In reality the one amounts to the other, for
the *opera ad extra sunt indivisa.* Christ's majesty is
not reduced when God's majesty is magnified. Those
who are inclined toward subordinationism will naturally interpret in agreement with their view, especially
when Christ is named as the Son, yet our old teachers
have long ago perceived that the Scriptures make no
difference by the way in which they name Christ
(whether according to one or to the other nature) when
they predicate of him what is human, what is divine,
or what is both. No individual passage should be
stressed so as to conflict with all else or with anything
else that is revealed regarding the nature and the essence of the Son.

The fact that God will display Christ's epiphany is mentioned only incidentally, the supreme object being the doxological glorification and magnification of God. This object is served when it is stated that *he* will make this display. The verb and the object match: "will show (or display) the epiphany (visible shining forth or appearing) of our Lord Jesus Christ." On the dative as indicating a point of time: "at its own season," see R. 495; the plural is idiomatic in the Greek but is a true plural in 2:6 and Titus 1:3.

When we answer the question as to why Paul so magnifies God at this place, it is well to note that in his letters Paul's pen often flows over into a doxology. Note how in this short letter he names God in 1:11, and how he turns to a doxology in 1:17. He lived in the very presence of the Almighty; he wrote as being in his presence; he thinks of his reader and his readers as being in his presence. In our minds and hearts, I fear, this direct contact with God is felt far less. This is probably enough to explain why 1:15, 16 is followed by 1:17. In our passage the prompting is far stronger and the magnification according.

In v. 11, 12 Paul sets the whole of the godly life and the confession over against the sin mentioned in v. 9, 10. The whole of this is enjoined on Timothy as the commandment which he is to keep intact as the Faith and confession of the church, and thus twice in this sentence (v. 13-16) God and Christ are placed before Timothy, in v. 15, 16 God in all his majesty. Only the last relative clause of v. 16 is a direct doxology; the rest is magnification.

It is probably best not to make the tremendous nominatives the subjects of δείξει but appositions to the subject contained in this verb. "Potentate" is used only here in the New Testament with reference to God and with reference to men in Luke 1:52, and Acts 8:27 (the eunuch), but in the Old Testament Apocrypha it is several times used with reference to God. The stress is on the two adjectives "the blessed and only Potentate," combining "the blessed God," 1:11, with "the only God," 1:17, substituting "the Potentate" for the term "God." As the only Potentate he rules with omnipotence, and as such infinite blessedness is his. There is little reason to think that this designation as a whole or that the word "only" are intended to be in special opposition to pagan gods or emperors.

A second article sharply accents a different aspect (R. 785): "the King of those reigning as kings and Lord of those ruling as lords," both of these terms belong to the second article. Literally: "the King of those kinging and Lord of those lording." It is thus not quite the same as Rev. 17:14, where the Lamb is called "Lord of lords and King of kings." This second apposition elucidates the first. As King of all others who act as kings and as Lord of all others who act as lords this only Potentate is infinitely supreme. We think this is a superlative: "the King and Lord in the absolute sense," there is none greater conceivable.

16) We have three nouns, two participles, two relatives — seven terms in all, the sacred three plus the four of the world, for the designations refer to the world of men. Again one article is used with both participles: "the only One having immortality, inhabiting light unapproachable." Note "incorruptible" in 1:17. In him alone immortality, absolute deathlessness, exists, other immortals derive their immortality from him. The very word ἀθανασία is, however, derived from the negative human condition called death. He is the opposite to us. The more positive designation would be "life," but this in the absolute sense.

"Inhabiting light unapproachable" likewise refers to us: we cannot even approach, much less enter this light. If such infinite light is God's habitation, what must God himself be? "God is light, and in him is no

darkness at all," I John 1:5. Jesus said: "I am the
Light of the world," John 8:12. This unapproachable
light is uncreated, eternal, and not the light that was
called into being on the first day and intended for the
earthly universe.

There follows an explication with a relative clause:
"whom not one of men did see nor is able to see," fact
and possibility are equally denied. Note "invisible" in
1:17; John 6:46; 1:18; Exod. 33:20. What the *visio
Dei* is we shall know only when we attain it (Matt.
5:8).

We regard the final relative clause as exclamatory
and not as imperative: "to whom honor and strength
eternal!" Its form as well as its contents show that
it is the final clause. It is ascription and thus doxological. "Honor" is all esteem, reverence, worship,
adoration; the term is to be understood in the widest
sense. "Strength eternal" is κράτος, might that is exercised in acts and not merely possessed. The ascription
is acknowledgment: eternal honor and exercise of
might *are* his, belong to him; we so confess and mag-
nify God. Here, as in Rom. 2:29; 3:8; 3:30, and elsewhere, the relative pronouns have demonstrative force;
here they are like the preceding articles, continuations
of them: *"He,* the One whom no man has seen — *He,*
the One to whom honor," etc. "Amen" seals this,
see 1:17.

The Godly Who Are Rich, 17-19

17) Now and then a thought is merely suggested
near the beginning of a paragraph; but it is invariably
considered before the paragraph is closed. We have
such an instance here. When Paul says in v. 9, "they
who *intend* to be rich," we automatically think also of
some who actually *are* rich. We think also of such
that never "intend" to accumulate wealth with an intent such as Paul describes — perhaps they are rich

through an inheritance, because of natural prosperity
in business, or in some perfectly proper way. What
about these? No, they have not slipped Paul's mind,
he takes care of them before he closes, has intended to
do so all along, does so now.

To think that he could have closed with v. 13-16,
changed v. 20, 21 to conform, and placed v. 17-19 elsewhere, is a legitimate opinion; to fault Paul for choosing a different arrangement is another matter. We
are to see just what Paul *has* done, to understand as
fully as possible why he has done so. We notice that
Paul separates what he says about the would-be-rich
rather widely from what he says about those who are
actually rich by placing v. 11-16 between the two
classes. That is intentional, it is also wise. The treatment of the former must cast no shadow on what Paul
has to say to Timothy regarding the latter.

Because Paul uses no connective, the rich stand
entirely by themselves. **To those rich in the present
eon continue to give orders not to be high-minded nor
to put their hope on uncertain riches but on God, the
One who furnishes to us all things richly for enjoyment; to be working good, to be rich in excellent**
(noble) **works, to be sharing well, fellowshiping, laying up for themselves as treasure an excellent** (noble)
**stock for the future in order that they may take hold
of the genuine life.**

Paul considers only two classes: those (whether
they are actually poor or rich) whose intention it is to
be rich (v. 9) ; those who are actually rich. The latter
should not be thought of as people who have realized
their worldly intention but as people who are simply
rich in a perfectly legitimate and irreproachable way.
The word "rich" is not sufficient because Paul intends
to play on the term ("riches" — "richly" — "to be
rich") ; he also means "rich in earthly wealth," hence
he adds "in the present eon," αἰών indicating the era

"now" in progress. This term refers to time and to what marks it or transpires in it, so that we may translate "in the present (now) world." Their wealth is only of this kind, a fact that they and we should mark well (note v. 7). Even the most honorable and legitimate wealth constitutes a danger for the Christian although, on the other hand, it also constitutes a blessing; it is a means for all kinds of good works, a means that is not in the hands of the poor.

What are Paul's orders to Timothy for people of this kind? They are brief, but when we ponder them we find that they are perfect and all-complete, a gem of a little sermon for the rich. Could you, using only a like number of words, preach a better sermon to the rich?

The first danger that confronts any rich man, also a Christian rich man, is to become "high-minded," to think himself superior to poorer people, to put on lordly airs, to make poorer people bow to him, etc. The inner attitude of being thus minded is the worst feature of it. "Not to be high-minded" = to be lowly-minded (Phil. 2:3). "As ταπεινοφρονεῖν (to be lowly-minded) is a disgrace in the conception of the Hellenists, a virtue in the conception of Scripture, so ὑψηλοφρονεῖν (to be high-minded) is praise in the conception of the Hellenists, but in the conception of Scripture a vice" (von Hofmann). The world of the Greeks despised the humble, lowly mind, admired the self-assertive mind which imposed its will on other men. The Christian reversal of attitude is, however, more than a reversal, for it involves a new basis. The coward, the base fellow who cringes, the man without spirit, is not praised in the Scripture; its lowly-mindedness is true humility before God, loving helpfulness to men, both being learned from the spirit of Christ.

Secondly: "nor to put their hope on uncertain riches but on God, the One who furnishes us all things richly for enjoyment." The perfect infinitive is intensive, for past hoping has developed to the present and thus goes on. It is foolish to hope and expect on the basis of wealth's uncertainty. B.-D. 165 understands the genitive and the dative correctly: "on uncertain riches": the genitive is not adjectival, but the dative is. Ἀδηλότης is "uncertainty." On etymological grounds it has been understood in the sense of: *Unbemerktheit, Verborgenheit*: not to put their hope on the hiddenness of their riches, on having their riches well hidden; but this is a rather strange thought. Earthly riches may disappear overnight or may dwindle and melt away like snow in the sun. To predicate the uncertainty of the wealth rather than of its owner is exact language. Sure hope must have a sure and certain basis, and wealth is not such a basis.

This is so important that Paul adds the sure and certain basis: "but on God, the One furnishing to us all things richly for enjoyment," πάντα, all, whatever we have, whether much or little. Hope that is placed on God will never be disappointed. How "richly" he furnishes us all things! Paul plays on the word. Read Ps. 145:15, 16; Acts 14:17; James 1:17; Ps. 37:25. No man has a thing that God did not furnish him. The Christian sees that fact and hopes in him and not in things. The wealthy Christian regards his wealth as a gift from God. So much God provides even beyond our actual needs! His hand is lavish. When he withholds *he* does it and for *his* purposes. Ps. 73:23-26; Job 13:15.

"For enjoyment" is significant. God does not bestow wealth merely in order that we may hold it, live as beggars, as ascetics, but that as Christians we may use and enjoy it with all gratitude. Refusal to enjoy it is as much a sin as misuse, waste, or overindulgence. "He is a rich God and will and cannot hear that we lament that he has not to give or cannot nourish and provide for our poor maggot-bag." Luther.

18) Thirdly, "to be working good," what is beneficial to others. Riches furnish a rich man especial means for tasting this enjoyment. He can be in only one room at a time, wear only one suit of clothes, sit only in one chair, eat only one meal at mealtime; but with his wealth he can reach out in a thousand directions and work good.

Fourthly, "to be rich in excellent or noble works." This is another, a higher mode of being rich, which is open even to the poorest, the accumulation of good works (5:10; Titus 3:8; Luke 12:21). We may regard numbers three and four as companions: "working good" as the production, "being rich in noble works" as the possession. Although they are done for others, many of these works benefit us more than they benefit others. Earthly riches are means to be employed for attaining the true riches. Gold that is invested with men brings only other gold, all of which is transient; gold invested in ἔργα καλά is transmuted into wealth that abides, Rev. 14:13, "and their works do follow them."

Fifthly: "to be sharing well" or generously, εἶναι with the verbal. The verb = to share what one has with another who is without means; the adverb εὖ is drawn into the compound. Generous, liberal giving is referred to, but as a personal attribute and in the beautiful way of sharing good fortune. This is not throwing a coin to a beggar; it is more than just handing out alms. It is giving so that others may have "together" (μετά) with us.

Sixthly, "fellowshiping," not holding aloof, not being inaccessible. Many regard this as a synonym of the preceding. Thus R., W. P., says: "old adjective, ready to share, gracious, liberal again." Others find some difference and include in the giving also friendliness, inclination, and the like. We are pleased to note that Wohlenberg has presented a more accurate meaning of this word. The word means "fellowshiping," ready to fellowship and actually doing so. The adjective, the noun, and the verb have the same meaning. On κοινωνία see the exposition of II Cor. 9:13, where the idea of "contribution" cannot be accepted; see also Rom. 15:26, 27. The Christian rich man is to be in fellowship with all his Christian brethren, down to the poorest and the humblest, is to be wholly one with them just as if he had no wealth.

As far as giving in a friendly manner is concerned, this thought lies in εὐμεταδότους. How can one share together with another and do it well without true friendliness? In μετά, "together or in company with," there lies the idea of fellowship and fraternal communion; but κοινωνικοί states it outright and with the perfectly correct adjective. The fact that a rich man cannot have such communion without sharing his wealth with the poor is self-evident, in fact, it has already been said in the verbal. As to both the sharing and the fullest fellowship we have the beautiful example mentioned in Acts 2:42 ("fellowship") and v. 45 (sharing); Acts 4:34-37.

19) Seventh, "laying up for themselves as treasure an excellent stock for the future (τὸ μέλλον, substantivized neuter participle) in order that," etc. Not accidentally does Paul have seven items; we have observed this feature in his other listings. You may divide these items into three pairs, these six being climaxed by the seventh. The fact that this item is to end the list we see from the meaning of the number seven, from the purpose clause and its meaning, perhaps also from the fact that this last item is a participle. Some regard these as a mixing of figures: treasure — foundation. But Paul is too able a thinker and writer to mix his figures. Θεμέλιος = *Grundstock;*

it is so used by Philo (B.-P. 555) ; "a solid and stable possession" (Thayer) ; *ein Kapital,* a capital sum invested and thus laid up for the future (Wohlenberg). What future Paul has in mind we see in Matt. 25:34-40.

"That they may take hold of the genuine life" (effective aorist) means the life to come (note "the future"). It has been proposed to join this clause to all the infinitives; it modifies the participle. Yet the thought of this proposal is correct. For we lay up an excellent stock when we live up to these infinitives and what they say and thus get a firm hold of the genuine life, "genuine" is repeatedly used in this letter (1:2; 5:3, 5, 16, the adverb is used as an adjective). Paul no more teaches a salvation by works than does Jesus in Matt. 25:34, etc. Good works are the evidence of faith and justification and as such evidence assure us the genuine life now and also in the verdict that will be rendered at the time of the Lord's epiphany (v. 14).

Conclusion

20) **O Timothy, guard the deposit, turning away from the profane babblings and antitheses of the knowledge falsely so named, which some, by professing, missed the mark as regards the faith.**

In 1:18 the personal address is "child Timothy"; on the effectiveness of adding "O" to the vocative see 6:11. The earnestness that runs through the letter and comes to its full climax in v. 13-16 continues to the end. In v. 14 it is τηρῆσαι τὴν ἐντολήν; now the wording is τὴν παραθήκην φύλαξον, the two are the same in substance. The noun means "the deposit." It is a term used in banking to denote a sum deposited, for which the bank is responsible, which it thus guards most carefully since it must pay it back. Here we have only the general connotation. The imperative reminds of a φύλαξ, a guard posted to keep something safe. One may τηρεῖν by locking up safely and securely; but one φυλάσ- σειν by standing guard like a soldier. We have the iden- tical expression, the noun and the verb, in II Tim. 1:12, 14. Paul has appointed Timothy as his repre- sentative in all the churches in the Asian territory. He is to serve as the apostolic guard, and to his guarding he has entrusted "the deposit," the trust committed to him for his work.

Some think that this deposit refers to the orders given to Timothy in this letter (the verb παρατίθημι is found in 1:18) ; and the imperative is modified so as to refer only to Timothy's own observance and Chris- tian conduct. This view excludes guarding the gospel and the gospel teaching in the churches. But this is the main part of Timothy's work and is what is here referred to. All of these are the same in substance: ἡ παραθήκη, the deposit — ἡ ἐντολή, the commandment — ἡ καλὴ ὁμολογία, the noble confession — ἡ πίστις, the Faith (v. 12, 21), only the connotations differ; they present the gospel as that which is believed and to be believed, as that which is confessed and to be confessed, as that which is commanded and ever stands as commanded, as that which is deposited in the official care of Tim- othy for all these churches and should thus be guarded by him. To think only of a deposited order is unten- able, for the order deals with something; the fact that it is a deposit means guarding that something with care against attack, hurt, damage. That something is the true gospel, not, indeed, considered in the abstract, but as something to be applied by Timothy in his work here in these churches to purify them and to keep them true, godly, etc.

Hence we also have the present participle after the effective aorist imperative: complete, effective guard- ing involves — to mention only this point which is re- peated from 4:7a — continued turning away from the profane babblings and antitheses of the falsely so-named knowledge, from "the profane old wives' myths" or fables (4:7), the myths and genealogies circulated in the Asian churches (1:4), the ignorant, antithetical or opposing teaching of law (1:7) with which the churches were bothered.

Paul does not say: Guard the deposit by *refuting* these profane babblings and antitheses. There is nothing in them that needs to be refuted. How could one refute a myth, a fictional story made up on the basis of the Mosaic genealogies? It is nothing but a κενοφωνία, "an empty sound" as when one babbles unintelligibly. How can one refute the ignorant "law-teachers" and their ἀντιθέσεις when they themselves do not know what they are saying and affirming (1:7)? There is just one effective attitude toward them: turn away from them with disdain. Acts often speak louder than words. To treat them in any other way is to honor them as if there *is* something in them. Here Paul's psychology is again correct.

With these two terms, which are combined under one article, Paul refers to chapter 1; the end of the letter reverts to its beginning. As far as the rest of the letter is concerned, we may observe that, unless the churches are freed from these silly, pestiferous pseudo-teachings, all else that Paul directs Timothy to attend to will be made quite impossible. Beginning and end, we may say, encircle all else.

The subjective genitive "of the falsely so-called knowledge" ("of science falsely so-called," A. V.) is one of Paul's striking expressions which still rings with crushing vigor. The article points to the γνῶσις that paraded as such here and there in the Asian churches, but there has been and is to this day a large amount of "science," "knowledge," that is equally misnamed. It calls itself what it is not. Its very name is κενός, empty, like a nut without a kernel. There is no need to expand. Our natural sciences as well as many theologies offer as *gnosis* much that is fiction. The Germans call science *Wissenschaft*. It is well to note that in the Greek γνῶσις can be used to designate pretended knowledge, but ἐπίγνωσις cannot be so used. The supposition that Paul refers to the Gnostics and thus to Marcion's "antitheses" conflicts with the time of the composition of this epistle unless this letter is regarded as a late forgery.

21) The relative clause is a warning. It is not directed to Timothy as though he might lose the faith but is a warning that Timothy is to address to the membership of the churches. We have already discussed this point in connection with other warnings found in this letter. In 1:20 Paul has pointed Timothy to two apostates. In the classics ἐπαγγέλλομαι is used somewhat as we use "profession": 1) to profess, advocate, and confess, 2:10; 2) to do this professionally, to make a business of teaching the pseudonymous knowledge. The latter is the sense here; these are the ἑτερο-διδάσκαλοι mentioned in 1:3 and 6:3, and the ignorant νομοδιδάσκαλοι referred to in 1:7, to name some of the professionals found among them.

By their professing and profession "they missed the mark (the same verb that was used in 1:6) regarding the faith." Here again, as in 4:1; 6:10, 12, "the Faith" is objective, *fides quae creditur*. Pretending to teach what ought to be believed, they missed it with their falsely so-called gnosis. The fact that their own *fides qua creditur* was also lost need not be added; for when the true object of faith is lost, subjective faith in that object is impossible. The deplorable fact is that these "some" had not been teaching "The Faith" for which Paul bids Timothy contend the noble contest (v. 12). As for personal faith in their own hearts, the disappearance of that was sad enough, but far worse was the profession of robbing others of the true object of faith, substituting something else, and thus wrecking also their personal faith and trust. Here we have a letter which ends with a negative thought, ἡστόχησαν, "they did miss the mark." A warning is sometimes properly the last word.

The closing benediction is the briefest in all of Paul's letters: **The grace with you!** i. e., *favor Dei* which we all need as sinners, which flows out to us in a stream of unmerited gifts ever new (John 1:16), walking arm in arm with you (μετά), σύν would be associative to indicate help. The expression is exclamatory as in 1:2 and needs no verb form. "With thee" in the A. V. follows an inferior reading. Neither textually nor otherwise can the plural be dropped. The letter is not addressed to others besides Timothy, but Timothy was to use it when he was dealing with the churches under his care. "With you" is most proper.

The colophon: "The First to Timothy was written from Laodicea, which is the chiefest city of Phrygia Pacatiana" (A. V.) only proves that its author lived after the fourth century toward the close of which that name for Phrygia Prima came into use. Otherwise this note reveals the effort to find somewhere in the canon the lost epistle to the Laodiceans mentioned in Col. 4:16. A few texts append a note which dates the letter at Nicopolis (Titus 3:12) ; the Coptic and a few Arabic versions mention Athens. See the introduction.

Soli Deo Gloria

St. Paul's Second Epistle
To Timothy

CHAPTER I

Be Thou Not Ashamed!

For the last time in Holy Writ we meet the great apostle and his beloved assistant Timothy. With the last word of this brief letter both pass from our sight, save for the mention of Timothy in Heb. 13:23.

Timothy is still in the Asian churches and supervising them as Paul's representative. But Paul is in a Roman prison awaiting trial, certain that the verdict will be death. We take it that he writes immediately after his arrest and begs Timothy to hurry to his side. As far as we know, Timothy did so and remained with Paul and witnessed his execution.

The first letter to Timothy is full of directions and instructions which tell him how to proceed in the management of the churches. This second letter contains no such directions. It is Paul's last will and testament for Timothy, his great legacy for the rest of Timothy's life. In the shadow of death Paul lays the work into Timothy's hands so that he might carry it forward as his worthy successor in the field where God shall place this beloved assistant of his.

This letter is personal throughout. Tender, yet with the tenderness of a strong, heroic heart. It is far from being sentimental. Timothy may have read and reread it with tears blurring his eyes, but every line braced him with power to make him valiant to contend in the noble contest, to receive at his own death the crown laid up also for him.

After Paul's death Timothy labored on in the churches in Asia Minor, which had received him under

(739)

Paul's direction (I Tim. 1:3). The Apostle John made his headquarters in Ephesus some time during or shortly after the war in Palestine which brought an end to the Jews as a nation. We do not know what finally happened to Timothy.

The four chapters of this letter divide it into its natural parts. The sum of the first part may be read in v. 8: "Be thou not ashamed!" This injunction is re-enforced in v. 12: "I am not ashamed," vividly recalling Rom. 1:16: "I am not ashamed of the gospel of Christ."

The Greeting

1) Paul, apostle of Christ Jesus through God's will in accord with the promise of life in connection with Christ Jesus, to Timothy, child beloved: grace, mercy, peace from God, (our) Father, and Christ Jesus, our Lord!

This is like and yet unlike the greeting in First Timothy. Here, too, we three times have the name "Christ Jesus" and twice "God." Here, too, occur "apostle of Christ Jesus" and as a designation for Timothy: τέκνον, "child." Here, too, the triple greeting: "grace, mercy, peace (asyndeton) from," etc. Yet nothing is merely stereotyped, a formula of words that is merely to be read and dismissed.

Personal, indeed, is this letter, yet not personal in the sense that one friend is merely writing to another friend, an older to a younger. Paul writes to Timothy as "Christ Jesus' apostle," and he writes in the interest of his great apostleship, in which Timothy had for years labored as this apostle's assistant. He urges Timothy to labor on even after the apostle's death, to the end of his own life. On "apostle," on the genitive, and on the phrase "through God's will" see the other epistles where these expressions are used. In First Timothy the special "order of God" is in place since Paul is transmitting to Timothy a part of this order which consists in specific directions about the management of the churches under his care. In this letter Paul refers to the θέλημα of God as he does in four other letters, to what God willed when he made him an apostle of Christ Jesus. God's will was now bringing his apostleship to its fitting end.

In First Timothy Paul calls God "our Savior" because in that letter he dwells on the saving of all men. He also calls Christ "our hope" because of the hope of salvation embodied in him. Both expressions refer to the blessed work of bringing this hope of salvation to men and letting nothing spoil or darken it. Now Paul writes: through God's will "in accord with the promise of life in connection with Christ Jesus." The whole will of God, all that he willed when he made Paul an apostle, accorded with the great gospel promise in which he promised "life in connection with Christ Jesus."

We do not place a comma after God and do not refer the κατά phrase across the intervening words and connect it with ἀπόστολος; we do not agree that the phrase expresses aim and not norm or standard; nor that, if it belonged to "God's will," the article would be required. Hundreds of phrases follow their nouns without an article. The phrase belongs where Paul placed it. The κατά phrase occurring in Tit. 1:1 is of a different nature, both as to its object (subjective faith and knowledge and *not* objective promise of God) and as to its dependence. Those who construe the phrase with "apostle" insert what Paul did not insert: "an apostle with the view *of proclaiming* the promise," or, as R., *W. P.*, phrases it, "with a view *to the fulfillment* of the promise." What Paul says is, however, that God's will which made him an apostle accords with God's promise of life. It certainly did. It harmonized perfectly. If it were not for this promise of life God would need no apostles at all, would not have willed to make Paul one.

This is not "*a* promise of *a* life," for τῆς and the phrase make ζωῆς definite. The genitive is objective: God promised life, the one in connection with (ἐν) Christ Jesus who purchased and won it for us; and thus it becomes for us "The LIFE" (John 14:6), the one source and fount of spiritual, eternal life. He who is by faith connected with him has this life (John 3:15, 16). This "promise" = the gospel. We see that "our Savior" and "our hope" which occur in I Tim. 1:1 are the same in substance. Paul might have used these terms a second time, especially "our hope." Yet how appropriate it is under the shadow of a martyr's death to cling to the life in connection with Christ, the life which no temporal death is able to harm.

2) In I Tim. 1:2 "genuine child" is significant since the whole letter expects Timothy to show his genuineness as a dear child of God in the varied tasks allotted to him. Here "child beloved" strikes a different note: so beloved of the apostle, his spiritual father, so long in true love associated with him in this father's work. The verbal of ἀγαπᾶν indicates intelligent and purposeful love for Timothy; this binds the two together. Paul does not need to add "my" to "child beloved." The whole letter throbs with the love of a father for a beloved child. "Child" is far more tender than "son," a thought which the A. V. does not express. "Child" is so very fitting for this letter (v. 5; 3:14-17) and finds repetition in 2:1, "my child," as in I Tim. 1:18, "child Timothy."

The greeting itself is identical with the one found in First Timothy; both are unusual because "mercy" appears between "grace" and "peace" (see First Timothy).

* * *

Paul's Grateful Memories

3) Read 4:9-12, 14-17. Paul's first hearing has been held. Only Luke is at his side. The prospect is altogether dark. How the apostle, locked in his cell or dungeon (the writer was in what is shown in Rome as Paul's underground dungeon, a hole in the domed ceiling affording the only light and air), longed for his faithful Timothy (v. 4)! He hurries to write to him and begs him to hasten and to bring Mark with him. He does not complain, does not recite his woes. His letter does not begin: "I am in a sad plight." It is filled with thoughts for his child Timothy. It is parental, inspiring. Paul is approaching his end, and as he starts to write, sweet, blessed memories flood his heart; with these he begins.

Why should anyone coldly say that he follows his old habit of beginning with thanks to God? He does not so begin either First Timothy or Titus. In fact, he here begins with gratitude, not with "I give thanks" but with memories that make him feel grateful to God. The whole blessed past crowds in upon his soul, gratefulness lifts him above all sadness. No; this is not a stereotyped beginning; it is exceptional, individual, full of a surge of emotion that is moved by memories. When Timothy read these lines he, too, was moved in the same way. Here speaks a great heart and spirit; use your own heart and spirit to apprehend what is written.

Grateful am I to God, whom I serve from (my) forebears in clean conscience, as ceaselessly I have remembrance concerning thee in my petitions by night and by day, longing to see thee while remembering thy tears, in order that I may be filled with joy, having received a reminder of the unhypocritical faith in thee, of a kind that dwelt first in thy grandmother Lois and thy mother Eunice and I am persuaded that also in thee.

We do not agree with those who say that the structure of this extended sentence is not clear. Of course, if χάριν ἔχω is understood to mean: "I give thanks to God," then there is no epexegetical object clause which would state for what Paul gives thanks. But Paul writes: "Grateful am I" (see I Tim. 1:12) and needs no object. What makes Paul feel grateful is implied in all that follows, namely in all his memories of Timothy, in every reminder that recalls him. No formal statement is needed.

This long sentence should not be read with an English mind. We should make two or three sentences of it. The Greek loves extensive connection; his flexible participles that have gender, case, number, and tense help him to construct such passages. Paul is thinking in Greek and not in Hebrew or in English. If that still seems strange to us, all that can be said is that we must learn to enter more fully into the language as well as into Paul's mode of thought. To make the ὡς clause a parenthesis, or to speak of parenthetical thoughts will then not occur to us.

Paul writes as one who from his forebears (the same word is found in I Tim. 5:4) worships God with a clean conscience. In this respect he is like Timothy who also had his faith from his mother and his grandmother, thus at least two generations back on the mother's side. Paul names none of his own forebears but does name two of Timothy's, Lois and Eunice, surely because he himself had learned to know them so well in the days long ago when he won grandmother, mother, and son, three generations, for the gospel in faraway Lystra. We see how memory takes him back even to his first missionary journey through Galatia. All the old scenes live up once more during these days and nights when he sits in his lone, dim prison cell. Λατρεύω denotes the service and the worship of God that is obligatory upon all men while λειτουργῶ denotes the public service of an official such as a priest.

It is asked how, in view of I Tim. 1:13, Paul can say that from his forebears he serves God in clean conscience. The proposal to take "in clean conscience" out of the relative clause and to construe: "grateful am I in clean conscience," is grammatically unwarranted. And a distinction between a "clean conscience" and a "good" one is playing with words. Acts 23:1 is not pertinent because it deals only with that period in Paul's life which is an answer to the charges on which he is held.

Some interpreters hold that Paul's conscience was "clean" when he persecuted the church, "clean" because he thought he was serving God by these persecutions (John 16:2), and because he did what he did "ignorantly" (I Tim. 1:13). But Paul himself would be horrified to hear that he covers his crimes with the mantle of "a clean conscience." In Acts 6:13 false witnesses are suborned; in Acts 7:58 Paul guards their clothes while these perjurers start the stoning; in Acts 9:1 we are expressly told that Saul consented to Stephen's death. This is one clear case, for who will say that Saul knew nothing about the criminality to which he consented? In the entire trial and killing of Jesus, in all the persecutions of Saul, there was ignorance, indeed, but never "a clean conscience." Paul's "clean conscience" is often also said to be his having acted without hypocrisy. But that explanation is unsatisfactory.

Acts 24:14-16 is the parallel to our passage. There Paul uses the same verb and the same tense: λατρεύω τῷ πατρῴῳ Θεῷ, and with the adjective refers to his ancestry (II Cor. 11:22); he likewise speaks of his conscience: "to have a conscience void of offense," i. e., clean. Neither in Acts 24 nor in our passage does Paul say that from childhood onward he has served God "in clean conscience." In order to express this idea the Greek perfect tense should have been used in both passages. 'Aπò προγόνων is not temporal so as to cover the whole of Paul's lifetime since his birth. The preposition denotes derivation. The true God whom Paul is *now* serving (present tense) in clean conscience he learned to know from his forebears. Note that Paul is able to say more regarding Timothy. "In clean conscience" modifies the verb. "I am serving" is not: "I have ever been serving" from childhood onward. Ἔχω — λατρεύω — and the following ἔχω refer to the present time.

Those who translate: "I give thanks," ask: "For what?" Some thus think that ὡς = ὅτι and states for what Paul gives thanks. Yet ὡς is not = ὅτι even as it would be strange to give thanks for having Timothy in remembrance in petitions by night and by day. The connective means: "*as* (denoting correspondence) I ceaselessly have remembrance concerning thee in my petitions by night and by day." "Concerning thee" does not refer merely to Timothy's person but to the circumstances surrounding Timothy, which induce Paul to petition God to help Timothy in this and in that matter.

Δέησις = the act of begging something and may refer either to a begging from man or from God; here it is the latter. The genitive denotes time within which: "by night and by day"; the accusative would mean "all night and all day long." Some of Paul's prayers were offered at night, some in the daytime. Paul always arranges these two genitives in this order. We may think of the long, lonely nights and days spent in the dungeon, especially since only Luke could visit him now and then. God was his refuge and help, the God whom he had known from his forebears, whom he now served in clean conscience.

We now see why Paul speaks of his "clean conscience." It is scarcely true to the facts to say that the purity of his *thanks* had recently been questioned, that Timothy himself had questioned it. Paul had been arrested on a criminal, yea on a capital, charge and was confined in a dungeon. His first hearing had gone against him. The charge preferred against him must have been that of spreading a *religio illicita,* the penalty for which was death. Such a charge was not preferred against Paul when Festus sent him to Rome; at that time Paul was sent to Rome only because he himself had appealed to Caesar. He had a long wait, but Caesar's court set him free. Then, however, Rome was burned, for which act Nero finally cast the blame onto the Christians, hoping thereby to allay the suspicion that he himself was the real incendiary. Numbers of Christians were killed in horrible ways. In the eyes of the imperial court Christianity suddenly became an illegal religion of the worst type. Peter had been crucified. This was the situation when a year and more later hands were laid also on Paul, the great protagonist of this nefarious religion.

We see why "clean conscience" and "forebears" are mentioned together, and that in the very first sentence of the letter. This God, to whom Paul is so grateful, the worship of whom is now charged as a mortal crime against Paul, is not a new, strange, illegal god in the empire, who could thus be worshipped only with a bad conscience, but the true God, who was served already in Tarsus, one of the great Roman cities, by Paul's forebears and in the entire empire by the Jews, in a religion that was legally allowed by the emperors and the imperial authorities, served thus in all good conscience for generations. The charge against Paul and this new imprisonment were thus the height of illegality. Why had Paul's forebears and also Timothy's mother and grandmother not been arrested and condemned? Yea verily, Paul's conscience as a servant of this true God is "clean" and remains so despite what Rome is doing to him. The thought that Paul is defending himself in the eyes of Timothy is untenable. Paul touches this defense of his, the one he is now offering the authorities, because it includes also Timothy and Timothy's Jewish forebears, and because Paul now urges Timothy not to be ashamed of this true God, of the testimony that the Lord Jesus has made regarding him, and of Paul, the Lord's prisoner who is suffering disgrace for this testimony.

This little relative clause at once strikes the heart of the whole situation, a situation in which Timothy is also vitally involved. What Paul had feared when, during his first imprisonment, his case came to trial, what then, however, had by God's grace been wondrously warded off, that was now coming to pass: the cause of the gospel was under the dark cloud of imperial hostility. The blood of many martyrs had already flowed, and Paul's blood was next to be shed.

4) The present participle states what accompanies Paul's prayerful gratitude to the God thus described: "longing to see thee while remembering thy tears, in order that I may be filled with joy." Some, like the R. V., construe: "by night and by day longing." If this were the sense, the genitive of time could not precede the participles because that position would lend them an altogether disproportionate emphasis. If it be stated that the ὡς clause already has a modifier of time in "ceaselessly" and therefore cannot have another, the answer is that "ceaselessly" is defined by "by night and by day"; "ceaselessly" does not mean uninterruptedly but iteratively, every time Paul turns to God in his petitions. "Longing" needs no temporal modifier; the aorist infinitive = "get to see you."

This participle "longing" is itself modified by the perfect participle: "while remembering thy tears."

This perfect is always used in the present sense (B.-D. 341; B.-P. 823); the verb governs the genitive. These are not tears that were mentioned in a letter that Timothy wrote to Paul but tears that Paul saw Timothy shed when he parted from Timothy. This is not, however, the parting mentioned in I Tim. 1:3. Paul planned to return to Ephesus after writing First Timothy (see I Tim. 3:14; 4:13). We have good reason to think that he returned and that, when Paul left to spend the winter in Nicopolis and from there to go on to Spain — a long separation — Timothy shed many tears at parting.

This does not imply that Timothy was unmanly, womanish, soft; or that he was fearful because of the prospect of being left alone with his management of the Asian churches. What shall we then say about Paul's "many tears" shed in Ephesus (Acts 20:19, 31), the sore weeping of the Ephesian elders (Acts 20:37), Paul's other tears (II Cor. 2:4)? Were these, too, unmanly, cowardly, and fearful? Noble tears, flowing from deep affection, most loyal devotion to this spiritual father, who inspired profoundest attachment in all his assistants! As for courage and ability, Paul was not so foolish as to leave a man in a post which he could not fill.

The ἵνα clause depends on ἰδεῖν: "get to see thee . . . in order that I may get to be filled with joy." Supply the implication: Paul's memories afford him great joy as he sits in his dismal dungeon, but once more to get to see Timothy, his beloved Timothy, will fill Paul's cup of joy to the very brim. Gratitude is coupled with anticipated joy. On these heights moves the soul of Paul while he is in prison with the prospect of death!

5) An aorist participle follows: "having received a reminder of the unhypocritical faith in thee." The construction is the same as that which we predicated in the case of "longing," save that the tense indicates

some one special reminder that had come to Paul.
Ὑπόμνησις = a reminding Paul received through somebody or through something while ἀνάμνησις is a remembrance which a person himself recalls. "Call to remembrance" in the A. V. is incorrect. There is no
reference to a letter received from Timothy. Nor did
Paul receive his information from an accidental vis-
itor from Ephesus who praised Timothy or reported a
notable instance which displayed Timothy's sincere
faith. Something had occurred in Rome and under
Paul's eyes which vividly reminded him of Timothy
and of Timothy's unhypocritical faith, and had done
that to such a degree that it left a deep impression on
Paul. The apostle must have exclaimed: "Just like my
beloved Timothy's faith!" What a gracious thing to
write to Timothy! We see how Paul esteems Timothy's faith, considers it a model with which sincere'
acts of other men's faith are compared in Paul's mind.

"Unhypocritical" = in no way wearing a mask as
did the ancient stage actors when they represented
some character, compare the positive word "genuine"
in I Tim. 1:2. A hypocritical faith is one that will
sooner or later be unmasked as a mere faith of the
lips. The real importance of Paul's meaning lies in
the relative clause: "of a kind (ἥτις, qualitative) that
dwelt first in thy grandmother Lois and thy mother
Eunice, and I am persuaded that (it dwelt) also in
thee." Timothy is a parallel to Paul. The parallel is
even in favor of Timothy. Paul's forebears were
Pharisees (Acts 26:5; II Cor. 11:22); from them Paul
inherited the knowledge of the true God — in v. 3 he
says no more. Timothy's grandmother and his mother
were true Israelites; from them Timothy inherited the
true faith of Israel, which 3:14-17 corroborates. What
faith in the true God means Paul did not learn until
the time of his conversion; Timothy had learned it in

the true Old Testament way: from a child, which then became Christian New Testament faith when the gospel arrived in Lystra. Paul is not recording a contrast between himself and Timothy because the latter was only Jewish on the mother's side. Most plainly Paul writes only "God" in v. 3 but "faith" in v. 5.

The fact that Paul names "Lois," the grandmother, and "Eunice," the mother of Timothy, leads us to think that Paul knew both women well. In Acts 16:1 only the mother is mentioned together with Timothy; at that time both were already Christian believers. We are not told who had converted them to Christianity. We think that this was Paul himself from the way in which he speaks of Timothy as "my child." This conversion was probably brought about on Paul's first missionary journey (Acts 14:6, etc.). It is the general conviction that Timothy's Greek father was dead when Paul first came to Lystra. We deem it equally fair to assume that Timothy's grandmother lived with her daughter. These two truly believing Israelites reared Timothy in the true faith of Israel, and Paul and Barnabas advanced this faith to Christian faith. No one can say whether Lois was still living when the incident recorded in Acts 16:1 occurred; it seems likely. Πρῶτον refers to the Old Testament Israelitish faith of Lois and of Eunice; they had it "first," Timothy had it from them, Paul made it Christian faith. To think that Paul never met the grandmother would disagree with the way in which he names her together with the mother.

The main thing is, however, that Paul here combines himself with Timothy by way of their ancestors because now this true God of Paul's ancestors and this old true Israelitish faith of Timothy's mother and his grandmother, to which Paul and Timothy both held with the New Testament gospel faith, were being con-

demned in Rome as a *religio illicita.* Paul was facing
death on this charge. What would happen to Timothy,
to others, to the Christian churches everywhere if the
imperial authorities proceeded consistently along this
line? This explains the admonitions that follow in
this letter. Paul, the expectant martyr (3:6), is in
advance fortifying his child and through him the
churches under him.

Πέπεισμαι, perfect tense, "I have been persuaded,"
= I am now so persuaded. The Greek reader needs
no verb after ὅτι. Paul rightly says no more than that
he is persuaded that before he met Timothy and his
mother and his grandmother these two had made of
Timothy a true Israelitish believer in the coming Messiah. The clause does not speak of Timothy's present
faith.

I Put Thee in Remembrance — Be not Ashamed!

**6)   For which cause I am reminding thee to keep
fanning into live flame the charisma of God which is
in thee through the laying on of my hands. For not
did God give us a spirit of cowardice but of power and
love and being sensibly-minded.**

Here and in v. 12 Paul writes δι' ἣν αἰτίαν, which
means more than διὰ τοῦτο, for it presents the whole
"cause" or "case" pictured in the preceding verses as
the basis of what follows, and this introductory relative phrase, which is purposely the same and exceptional in both verses, connects most closely. For this
relative really continues the previous long sentence as
far as grammar is concerned although the thought itself plainly advances to admonition. The new thought
begins here. We divide here and not at v. 8; again we
make a division at v. 8 and do not combine v. 8-14. The
αἰτία or "cause" (case) on account of which Paul admonishes Timothy is found in all of v. 3-5 and not

mereiy in what Paul says about Timothy's faith in v.
5. Paul's ancestral God and Timothy's ancestral faith
which are now being condemned as a *religio illicita*
call forth Paul's admonitory appeal.

What v. 3-5 contain is sometimes inadequately
understood; hence the connection is likewise misunderstood and is thought to be "because Timothy has had
such advantages from his mother and his grandmother," "because Paul is persuaded Timothy has the
true faith." No; because Paul's God and Timothy's
faith, which for so long a time were permitted by the
imperial court as a legal religion over all the Roman
Empire but were now about to be branded as illegal
and criminal by adding Paul's execution to all the kill-
ings that have already occurred in Rome since Rome
was burned, therefore Paul calls on Timothy not to be
ashamed of this religion, etc. The reason is a mighty
one, indeed, the more mighty for Timothy since his
spiritual father Paul, his apostolic chief and leader in
the work of the gospel and in the great cause of
Christ, must soon lay his head on the executioner's
block.

From his own memories and the reminder he has
recently received about Timothy, Paul passes to a
reminding of Timothy as to what he is now called to
do more than ever before. See how beautifully the
expressions advance: "I have in remembrance — having received a reminder — I am reminding." See also
the gentleness: Timothy needs only reminding.

How pertinent is Paul's reminding him "to keep
fanning into live flame the charisma of God" which
God gave him, "which is in thee through the laying on
of my hands"! Let us note the expressive present
infinitive which says that Timothy *has* been making
his charisma flame up, *not* that he has been letting it
get cold. Hitherto, however, Timothy has had only
a task with such difficulties as gospel work had always

had since Paul and Timothy had entered upon it; now Rome was frowning upon this work, was bringing Paul to martyrdom. Instead of being only an assistant, Timothy would soon himself be the lone chief in his great Asian field. Instead of being distressed and allowing the flame to burn lower, he must ever keep it burning brightly as Paul is passing from the scene. There is no touch of censure. Paul does not say, "Make the flame burn hotter than ever." Timothy is as ardent as Paul can wish him to be, and all that Paul asks is that he continue in the same ardor.

Timothy is to keep the live fire bright, namely "the charisma of God which is in him through the laying on of Paul's hands." This has been explained in connection with I Tim. 4:14, where even more is said; please read it. All we need to say here is that, while in I Tim. 4 Paul mentions the laying on of hands by the elders because this gave Timothy the right to function officially in the churches, here Paul refers only to his own hands because Timothy was to be Paul's apostolic representative, and because Timothy would soon have to carry on his great office without Paul. The idea that Timothy's charisma was *not* his office is evidently not correct. Timothy's charisma was the ability to preach, to teach, to admonish, and to supervise such work in the churches, for which God gave him both the office and the field for the full exercise of this gift when, as we may put it, he was ordained or formally installed into his Asian work by the laying on of the hands of Paul and of the elders. This act of laying on the hands is symbolic as explained in I Tim. 4; it conveyed nothing supernatural or miraculous.

The reference to Timothy's office is necessary. The fire of his ardor in it must burn on and on although Christianity be declared an unlawful religion by Caesar's court, although the apostle, like Peter, be executed because of its promulgation.

7) Why this reminder regarding Timothy's charisma? Ah, "not did God (this true God mentioned in v. 3) give us (Timothy and Paul) a spirit of cowardice but of power and love and of being sensibly-minded." Πνεῦμα is not the Holy Spirit nor the immaterial part of man; the descriptive genitives show that the inner quality is referred to which was given us by God by being wrought and developed in us. Dangerous clouds are gathering, there are dangers that are far greater than ever before, not mere local hostility to the planting and the growth of the church but imperial hostility.

The provinces of the empire will imitate what Caesar's court is doing. But God has put nothing of the nature of δειλία, "fearfulness," "afraidness," "cowardice" into our hearts so that we should now cower, let the flame of ardor burn low, lest we be made to suffer. Remember where Paul is while he is writing this: the sword is hanging over his head. He who preaches on this text during ordinary times can do so only by letting the greater illumine the lesser. What is any little ill that we suffer for Christ's sake compared with having the whole Christian religion outlawed in the whole state?

No, ours is a spirit "of power." This is not mere "courage" or "bravery" in danger; it far exceeds that as it would in Paul's mind: power, the great word δύναμις, power to work on, to hold out, to endure all things, to suffer, to die — victorious, triumphant power, an unquenched flame of living fire.

At the same time ours is a spirit "of love." Let us get the significance of the combination. Ἀγάπη is the love of full understanding coupled with mighty corresponding purpose, the supreme fruit of faith which is called "the greatest thing in the world." God is love and because of this love sent his only-begotten Son to save the world. Here the thought is not that this love works a thousand good works but that it faces and conquers the world's hostility with its power. It burns on and on. It sees all the sin and woe, and its one purpose is that of Jesus, to seek and to save.

The trio is completed by σωφρονισμός (the suffix denoting action, R. 151) and by σωφροσύνη which is only a quality. This is the German *Besonnenheit*, the exercise of a sane, balanced mind. This guides our power, applies the intelligence and the purpose of our love, and, while it is needed at all times, is most needed in dangerous times. For then any foolish, ill-considered, hasty, fanatical action precipitates dire results, especially if the leadership is not "sensibly-minded." Because this word is found only here in the New Testament, the dictionaries vary in defining it. They offer the meaning *Besserung* and admonitions along that general line; "self-control" and "self-discipline" in M. M. 622 (note R. V.) ; "sobering" in the R. V. margin. "Of a sound mind" in the A. V. is more correct.

Paul writes this trio in keeping with the very situation in which he and Timothy now found themselves. One who sits in his quiet study would not write such a trio, would not mention the third point, and this must be remembered when Paul's words are being interpreted.

8) Luther strangely finds the main thought of this chapter in v. 6, and some interpreters agree with him. But Paul himself indicates the pivot: "be not ashamed — I am not ashamed. — Onesiphorus was not ashamed." This repetition is self-explanatory. The deep basis lies in v. 3-5; on this rest v. 6, 7, the broad reminder about Timothy's charisma and the spirit which he and Paul have received; and on this is placed the specific call not to be ashamed, no matter what the suffering, even as Paul in his dungeon is not ashamed, as Onesiphorus was not ashamed. All is most lucid, it is built like a pyramid.

Be not, then, ashamed of the testimony for our Lord nor of me, his prisoner, but join in suffering disgrace for the gospel in accord with God's power, his who saved us and called (us) to a holy calling, not in accord with our works, but in accord with his own purpose and grace, that given to us in Christ Jesus before eon-long times but published now through the epiphany of our Savior Christ Jesus by (his act of) abolishing the death and bringing to light life and incorruption by means of the gospel, for which I on my part was appointed herald and apostle and teacher.

In negative aoristic prohibitions the Greek uses the subjunctive and not the imperative. Some commentators misunderstand this command. We shall let one speak: "This passage, too, furnishes proof for the assumption that Timothy had grown slack in the execution of his office because he had become timid on account of the persecutions which descended upon the Christians, in particular on the preachers of the gospel like Paul, as though the Lord did not concern himself about them but abandoned them to their fate." Read Moulton, *Einleitung* 201, etc., as an answer to this. The answer to this aoristic injunction: "Be not ashamed!" is not: "I will quit it," but: "I will never once be!" White, *Expositor's Greek Testament,* is right when he points to two grammars and says that this aorist subjunctive "forbids the supposition that Timothy had actually done what Paul warns him against doing." We must say more: if Timothy is to stop being ashamed, the present imperative should have been used (R. 855, etc.). Can the aorist subjunctive used in Matt. 6:13 (Lord's Prayer) mean that God has hitherto been leading us into temptation?

The implications are these: "Be not ashamed!" — Timothy: "I will never be!" — Paul: "I know thou wilt not." Do you ask why, then, this call to Timothy? Thousands of such calls are uttered by one brave man to another, each having the same brave response implied and accepted. Every such call cheers, makes the task easier, the victory surer. The severer the ordeal, the more we appreciate such aoristic calls. In the positive clause the aorist imperative has the same valiant effect and response.

Be not ashamed "of the testimony of our Lord" does not speak of the testimony that the Lord made (subjective genitive); this genitive is objective: the testimony "*for* our Lord," made by us "about him" in all our preaching and teaching. "Be not ashamed of valiantly uttering this testimony even when doing so is called promulgating an unlawful religion!" "Our Lord" is the correct term, he to whom we belong body and soul. Significantly, touchingly Paul adds: "nor of me, his prisoner," who is now being treated as a criminal. The accusative is the regular case with passives. Disgrace had come upon Paul which automatically involved all his converts, his churches, and especially his assistants. "His" prisoner is more than one who is imprisoned for the Lord's sake, or one who only belongs to the Lord; in his providence the Lord had brought Paul into prison and was soon to glorify him by martyrdom.

The direct opposite is to be proud, to glory in the testimony and in the apostle's imprisonment. Paul says more, "But join me in suffering disgrace for the gospel in accord with God's power." The dative is not due to σύν in the verb: "suffer with the gospel" (R. V.), the gospel never suffers actively. This is the *dativus commodi*: "for, in the interest of, the gospel," σύν associating Timothy with Paul in joint suffering. Κακός lies in the verb and does not mean "hardship" (R. V.) nor "afflictions" (A. V.) but something bad or base so that we translate "jointly suffering disgrace." Compare the terms used in 2:9. The thought is not that future suffering and disgrace may come upon Timothy, but that without a touch of shame he shall accept the disgrace that has now come upon Paul, which also involves Timothy. See the motive in the dative: who would not share in disgrace suffered "for the gospel"? No man has ever suffered disgrace in a nobler, more honorable cause.

9) Read in one breath and disregard the verse division: "in accord with God's power, his who saved us and called (us) to a holy calling," etc. Timothy is to use "the spirit of power" (v. 7) which God has given him for suffering disgrace conjointly with Paul. By doing this he will be "in accord with" (κατά) the very power of God himself, of the God who saved us and besides that called us to a holy calling or profession, the calling in which we are now asked to suffer disgrace in this unholy world. The thought is not that Timothy is to vie with this power of God or to make it a pattern but that Timothy is so to use the spirit of power which God has given him, use it in this suffering, that it harmonizes with the source of Timothy's power, the blessed power of the God who saved him and by his call placed him into the holy Christian calling.

Κατά is *gemaess*. The source of power in our spirit is God and his power. The test of our power comes when we must suffer for the gospel. Then we must not disgrace the power of God's love and grace which has done so much for us by having saved us and called us to our holy calling. Κατά does not say that God's power will help Timothy to suffer and to bear the disgrace, that Timothy is to rely on God's power. Paul has already said that God has given him a spirit of power, and we now see that this occurred when Timothy was called to his calling as a Christian. That calling Timothy is now to exercise in suffering just as Paul himself is doing.

One article unites the two participles and makes them an apposition to Θεοῦ. The debate regarding "us" is unnecessary. Paul refers to Timothy and to himself. What is true of these two is naturally true of all true Christians. God had, indeed, saved Paul and Timothy and called them. In the epistles this always refers to the effective and successful call. There are not two calls (Calvinism), but many reject the one great call of grace (Matt. 23:37). The power in it is not omnipotence but saving love, mercy, and grace. Our versions regard the dative as cognate: "called with a holy calling," which would mean a calling by a Holy One or uttered in holy words. Κλῆσις is used here as it is in I Cor. 7:20; Eph. 3:20, and elsewhere: a holy profession, one which separates us from the world, one which we must keep unspotted, one of which we are never to be ashamed, one that is never to be disgraced. Think of the blessed power that has done so much for us and even made us spiritually powerful. Shall we then not stand the test of suffering for God's saving gospel?

In a magnificent panorama that reaches back even to eternity Paul now unrolls all that God's power has done in saving and calling us and touches even the immortality that carries us into eternal blessedness. All of it is written in one flow of thought, in flexible Greek, no pause is made until at the end of v. 11; and this means that we must take all of it in with one view just as it is one comprehensive thought that starts even with the κατά in v. 8. When we now view the details we should *not* disjoin them. This is not a corpse that is to be slashed and cut up but a living body that is to be left as it is while we look at its symmetrical members.

No, the whole work of saving and calling us could not be "in accord with our works"; not one of them,

nor the least part of one, has even a trace of holiness
that would fit us sinners for a holy calling. On the
contrary (ἀλλά), God had to proceed "in accord with
his own purpose and grace, that (grace) given to us in
Christ Jesus before eon-long times," "before the world
began" (A. V. interpretative rendering), less well rendered in the R. V.: "before eternal times." Sasse in
G. K., 209, regards χρόνοι αἰώνιοι as periphrastic for αἰῶνες
in the Greek formulas for eternity; but he forgets πρό.
These are the world's "eon-long times," and prior to
these God made his gift, prior to them lies nothing but
eternity.

There was nothing but God's own πρόθεσις to serve
as God's norm and directive, and that means nothing
but God's χάρις. The former is the act of setting something before himself or the thing that is thus set
before, to express which idea we use the word "purpose." Controversy has developed regarding this word,
and it is still regarded as being equal to predestination or election. See the fuller discussion of Rom.
8:28; compare 9:11; Eph. 1:9, 11. The purpose is
always gracious and universal. Since it is here combined with "grace," this is most clear, for grace is the
undeserved *favor Dei* which extended to the guilty to
cancel and remove their sin and guilt; it is always
universal, unlimited.

But as this statement begins with saved and called
"us" (Timothy and Paul), so it also ends: "the (grace)
given to us in connection with Christ Jesus before
ages-long times," i. e., given to us already in eternity.
We take it that τὴν δοθεῖσαν refers to χάριν since Paul so
often connects these two, "grace" and "given." The
only reason that we do not include πρόθεσιν is because
we cannot well see how it can be "given" to a sinner.
The fact that this gift of grace to Paul and to Timothy refers to their predestination and election in

eternity is beyond question although neither word is used here. In fact, we may call this clause a brief Biblical definition of our predestination or election.

Already before the world began Paul and Timothy stood before the eyes of God, not only because they were included in God's blessed, saving purpose and universal grace, in the love which gave the only-begotten Son to the lost world; but as recipients of this grace "in connection with (ἐν) Christ Jesus," recipients not by means of a mysterious decree pertaining only to them, but recipients by the gospel call, the one named in this verse, which is wickedly rejected by so many others who thereby exclude themselves when God would have included also them (Matt. 23:37: "How oft would I!"). Only imperfectly, haltingly are we able to state these things because our finite minds are unable to think in terms of infinite eternity. Let us never forget that and then act and speak as if the timelessness of eternity were only a long, long time, and thereby mislead ourselves.

10) Paul returns to time: this grace was given to us in eternity in connection with Christ "but published now through the epiphany of our Savior Christ Jesus by (his act of) abolishing the death and by (his act of) bringing to light life and incorruption by means of the gospel." All of this actually occurred in the fullness of time but existed in eternity as though it had already occurred (Rev. 13:8: "the Lamb slain from the foundation of the world"). We thus again helplessly speak in human words of timeless eternity. The idea of φανερόω is that of manifestation or of publishing and thereby making openly known to men. This was effected "through the epiphany of our Savior Christ Jesus," ἐπιφάνεια, his "appearing," shining forth so that men could see him as the one that he was, namely "our Savior," which harks back to the τοῦ σώσαντος used in v. 9. "Epiphany" refers to the saving

appearance of Jesus (so also does the verb in Titus 2:11; 3:4). In I Tim. 6:14; II Tim. 4:1, 8 "epiphany" refers to the appearance for judgment. Some would restrict the word in our passage to the incarnation, but this alone did not produce the publication; we must take in everything, including Jesus' exaltation, as also the participles show.

These lack the article and are thus not appositions but descriptions of "our Savior Christ Jesus" and bring out his great saving act. It is well to note that σώζειν and Σωτήρ mean not only to rescue out of mortal danger but in addition to place into safety and thus to keep safe. Hence we have the negative plus the positive, which are even balanced by μέν — δέ; our Savior, indeed: abolishing the death on the one hand, bringing to light life and incorruption on the other hand, two aorist, definite historical past acts of our Savior. May we say that this twofold act constitutes his saving epiphany?

Paul uses καταργέω often and the context always indicates what "putting out of commission" or "abolishing" means. When Jesus died and rose again he abolished the death. He went into death with all our sin, but death could not hold him, for his death expiated all our sin, and thus he rose again, his expiation having destroyed, put out of commission the death itself. "The death" is not a personification but "the well-known death" that had full power over men. Since it has been shattered and pierced, this death's grip is released; all its victims are free to escape, it cannot hold them. Only those who will not have life, who deliberately throw themselves into the arms of this death, are its victims.

When he adds the positive side of the saving act of Jesus, Paul, as he does so often, does not stop with the exact counterpart of the negative: "purchased and won life," he goes far beyond, for he is telling of the φανέρωσις or publication of grace, and this through the epiphany of the Savior. So he rises to the high level of these two terms: "bringing (having brought, in one act, aorist) to light life and incorruption by means of the gospel." The gospel shines with the light that reveals this life and this incorruption. It is the gospel for which Paul so gladly suffers disgrace and bids Timothy to join him in the suffering (v. 8). There could not, of course, be such a gospel with such a light if our Savior had not, when he abolished the death, brought forth for us life, etc., and then made the gospel the means for dispensing it to us. The winning of life for us who were dead in sin underlies this bringing of it to light through the gospel. Since that act (aorist) the gospel shines in the Egyptian darkness of the world and draws men from their death to life, from their death's corruption to life's incorruption. The very heart of this gospel is Christ, the Life and the Light (John 1:4; 14:6; other passages), and he ever calls and draws: "Come unto me!" And yet see John 3:19; 5:40.

The fact that Paul does not stop with "life" but adds "incorruption" undoubtedly brings out the thought that this life applies also to our bodies. Corruption, decay, rotting pertains to the body and not to the soul or the spirit. Here we have the resurrection of the body (I Cor. 15:53-57; Phil. 3:21). The delay until the day of resurrection does not alter the fact. The "life" itself, although we already have it, assures also our blessed bodily resurrection. "The death" was here, hence the article is used just as it was in Rom. 5:12; "life and incorruption" came as something new and hence need no articles. The dispute about what "the death" means, whether it is physical, spiritual, or eternal, is pointless, for the whole power of death is abolished. Although we Christians die physically we shall yet live (John 11:25) ; "I will raise him up at the last day" (John 6:44, 54).

Once more read all of this together (v. 8-10) and with the impact of it all upon your soul think of Paul, the apostle of the gospel, awaiting his death with all this light shining in his soul and leaving Timothy behind, unashamed, having the same light in his soul.

11) This verse is still a part of the grand whole, and the relative clause brings out the fact that Paul is not a mere ordinary Christian and as such a beneficiary of this precious gospel and of all for which it is the means; Paul is far more: "for which (gospel) I on my part was set or appointed herald and apostle and teacher." So high a place was given to Paul in connection with God's saving work (v. 8) and Jesus' Saviorhood (v. 10) ; he (emphatic ἐγώ) was placed into the very greatest office, that of bringing this whole saving gospel to other men. This high distinction Timothy shares, has long shared, for Timothy was Paul's great assistant. We at once see and still more as we read on, how necessary this clause is as a word from Paul to Timothy who is never to be ashamed of the testimony for the Lord and of Paul, the Lord's prisoner, who is to join Paul in suffering for the gospel any disgrace that may come from Paul's martyrdom.

We pass by various inadequate interpretations of this clause.

The three predicative nouns expand the thought of Paul's high office. So great an honor was bestowed upon him, not only that his own soul might believe and receive the gospel salvation, but also that he might bring it to many, many others. How could he possibly be ashamed or Timothy, his associate, who shared in this distinction?

It is well to note that "apostle" is placed between "herald" and "teacher." We take this to mean that

Paul is not stressing his office as one that is distinct and higher than Timothy's. Timothy is not to say: "Yes, thou art the great apostle, I am not!" In other words, "apostle" is here used as it is in I Thess. 2:6, where the plural places Paul, Timothy, and Silvanus on the same level as "apostles." So Timothy is also all three: "herald" publicly to proclaim the gospel, "apostle," commissioned to do so, "teacher," fully to inculcate every part of it. Ashamed — never! Willing to suffer — indeed!

I Am Not Ashamed

12) Δι' ἣν αἰτίαν repeats v. 6. The relative connects with the preceding just as it does in v. 6, nor may we separate the two sections. We divide at this point only in order to indicate that v. 12, 13 rest on the preceding great facts. First, what Paul is doing; secondly, what Timothy is to do.

For which cause also these things am I suffering, nevertheless I am not ashamed. For I know him whom I have been trusting and am persuaded (see v. 5) that he is able to guard the deposit of mine against that day.

The great "case or cause" presented to us in the preceding verses is more than ample reason that Paul gladly suffers also these things that have now come upon him. Ταῦτα needs no further specification, for Timothy knows what is happening to Paul. Καί touches the fact that Paul has before this suffered many things during his career, and that "these things" which he is now suffering are the worst. The negative statement that, nevertheless, he is not ashamed reveals how the positive is to be understood, namely that he suffers gladly. To be confined on a capital criminal charge with the prospect of being executed as being guilty under that charge, is certainly the height of disgrace. So Jesus had been given the worst criminal's death and was even crucified between two malefactors. Yet, although all the world cries shame, Paul is not ashamed. We recall Rom. 1:16 which was written when Paul was first planning to visit Rome; before all of Rome's grandeur he declared that he was not ashamed to be the herald of the gospel, for all that grandeur could not save one beggar's soul while Paul's gospel saved every believer among Jews as well as Greeks. With a γάρ, like that found in Rom. 1:16, Paul adds why he is now, indeed, not ashamed.

"For I know him whom I have been trusting," trusting all along, trusting still. Οἶδα indicates the relation of the object (Christ) to the subject (Paul) and thus appears to signify less than γινώσκω which expresses the relation of the subject (Paul) to the object (Christ), see John 10:14; C. K. 388. It does say less, but by that very fact says more. Merely to know Christ is all that Paul needs in order to trust him; Peter denied that he even knew the man (Matt. 26:72, 74). Many an understatement is stronger than a full statement. This is not τίνι with an indirect question: "whom I have been trusting" (our versions) ; but the relative: "him whom," which leaves no doubt as to this person's identity: "the Savior Christ Jesus who put the death out of commission and brought to light life and incorruption" (v. 10).

So with epexegetical καί Paul adds what this trusting means for him in the present connection: "and am persuaded that he is able to guard my deposit for (or against) that day." Three times we have παραθήκη combined with this verb: here, v. 14, I Tim. 6:20. The two latter are exactly alike: Timothy is to guard the deposit placed into his keeping, i. e., the gospel, his commission in reference to that gospel. Can the word now mean the deposit which Paul has placed with Christ? Is the addition of "my" sufficient for that? We do not think so (C.-K. 1072). What Paul says is that the gospel, for which he suffers and is not ashamed, is entirely safe; he knows the Christ whom he trusts and is persuaded that, despite his imprisonment and expected martyrdom, Christ is able to guard the gospel so that its work shall not be stopped, guard it against that day when this gospel's work will be wholly done. Taken out of Paul's hands at his death, this "my deposit" Christ will guard, place into other hands, ever keep safe. This interpretation keeps to the line of the thought. In v. 11 Paul says that he was appointed as the gospel's herald, apostle, teacher; then he says that for this cause he is now suffering. His concern is not for himself, it is entirely for the gospel, his deposit, held by him from the Lord. In v. 13 and 14 he calls upon Timothy to hold and to guard this same deposit.

Our versions take the other view, that of a deposit which Paul has placed into the Lord's keeping. But there is no unanimity as to what this deposit might be. We append some suggestions: Paul's soul; Paul's spirit; Paul's salvation; Paul's good works with their reward. But what about εἰς ἐκείνην τὴν ἡμέραν which fits none of these? for it does not mean *"until* that day." None of these deposits fits the context in which Paul speaks of the gospel and even uses "deposit" again in v. 14. There was a reason that prompted Paul to say that Christ is able to guard the gospel. Many Christians would cry out at the news of Paul's death: "Now all is lost!" Timothy himself would experience a devastating shock. Calmly, in advance Paul says: "Though I die, Christ will not fail to guard his gospel."

13) Christ will use human means, and Paul counts on Timothy as being one of them. So he urges him: **As a model of healthy words (ever) have what ones from me thou didst hear in faith and love in Christ Jesus. That noble deposit guard through the Holy Spirit, him who dwells in us.**

Fan into living flame thy charisma — be not ashamed — suffer disgrace with me — ever have my words as a model — guard this noble deposit! These are Paul's urgings. The first and the fourth are given in durative form (ἀναζωπυρεῖν, v. 6, and ἔχε). The two imperatives used in v. 13, 14 are a good illustration of the present and the aorist: ever "have" before your mind and thus ever use the words you have heard from me as a model — definitely, decisively guard this excellent deposit.

The anarthrous ὑποτύπωσιν is not the direct object (our versions) but the predicate object, the article being omitted on this account. The actual object is the relative clause in which the genitive relative is attracted to the case of its antecedent, for *what* one hears is expressed by the accusative. Some say that ὑποτύπωσις means only "outline," sketch," but B.-P. 1355 renders it *Urbild* in I Tim. 1:16 and *Vorbild* in our passage. The sense is evidently that Timothy is not only to cling to the substance of what Paul has taught him but, when he is stating that substance, is also to use the very form of expression which he learned from Paul, not indeed slavishly, in parrot fashion, but using it as a safe model.

Here is the place to pause and to ponder. Paul received what he taught "by the revelation of Jesus Christ"; he spoke not in words which man's wisdom teaches but which the Holy Spirit teaches, "combining spiritual things with spiritual words" (I Cor. 2:13, see our rendering and its exposition). So also Jesus speaks of his ῥήματα, "utterances" (John 15:7; 17:8; 12:48) and, of course, also of his λόγοι (Matt. 7:24, 26). All these "words" we have as Timothy had them, to be used as the ὑποτύπωσις in all our preaching and theology; nothing must deviate even in the least from the lines, tracings, design thus laid down for us. Why?

Because every deviation from these λόγοι or ῥήματα is like a stepping from truth into falsehood.

Here we have Paul's verdict on modernism with its claim that all these λόγοι are "outworn categories of thought," "old thought patterns" that we have long ago outgrown. They have only an antiquarian value; they are mental costumes that ancient Jewish and Hellenistic minds once wore and thought to be stylish. We must substitute categories and patterns of thought which the wisdom of our day produces, that are derived from our science, democracy, sociology, philosophy; although just what these new patterns are to be is as yet in process of determination. The one thing certain is that the old *logoi* can no longer be worn. Even before the day of modernism it was proposed to use "new ways of teaching old truths," and new ways were offered. But always these new vessels did *not* contain the old truths, these new categories and patterns of thought were *emptied* of the old thought substance. All these new proposals were "words of human wisdom." Think not that the same view was wanting in Paul's and in Timothy's time. Just because it was present even then, Paul writes this sentence about "healthy words" being the "model" and pattern that Timothy was ever to hold.

Mark the word "healthy" which means *sanus,* not *saluber* (Zahn, *Introduction,* II, 129), and how often this healthiness recurs: I Tim. 1:10; 6:3; II Tim. 4:3; Titus 1:9, 13; 2:1, 2, 8. All other *logoi* are unhealthy, diseased, every other "model" or thought pattern is full of infection. Need we say what a force of argument this participle (used as an adjective) contains? Some have thought that Paul had a sort of fixed catechism for his converts and a kind of established dogmatics for his assistants and elders. What Paul's *logoi* actually were his letters show. These are our teaching, our theological model today. Blessed is he who abides by Paul's ἔχε!

Note that "from me" is placed forward for the sake
of emphasis: "which *from me* thou didst hear." "In
faith and love," both of these as connected with Christ
Jesus, is best construed with the imperative: "ever
have (and thus use) in faith, etc., these *logoi* as a
model." Timothy's faith is to be centered in them,
never forsake them; Timothy's love (intelligent and
purposeful) is ever to use them in all his loving work
of teaching and guiding others. True love will never
offer anything unhealthy. Can it be love when it does?
The Scriptures know of no blind ἀγάπη (see John 3:16).

14) On this injunction compare I Tim. 6:20. The
Lord had deposited with Timothy the same gospel that
he had deposited with Paul (v. 12). Paul is now about
to return his deposit to the Lord, who will take care
of it against that day. The Lord is doing that in these
very Scriptures. Timothy's end is not yet in sight, so
he must guard his precious deposit as Paul has guarded
his, as Timothy has likewise done hitherto. Here Paul
calls it καλή, "noble, excellent." How noble it is we
see from v. 8-10. Yet he is to do this, not by his own
ability and watchfulness, which would never suffice,
but "through the Holy Spirit, him who dwells in us."
When διά is used with a personal object, it has the
force of mediation, sometimes even of agency, and beyond that almost a representative agency: *vertreten
durch* (B.-P. 281). Here the Spirit's mediation and
assistance are enough. His dwelling in us (*unio mystica*) enables him to work through us. We may ever
call him to our aid. "In us" = "in thee and me."
Because he dwells in all true believers Paul can say
"in us" to Timothy.

Onesiphorus Was Not Ashamed

15) These verses lend much clearness to Paul's
situation as well as to Timothy's. We thus see how
pertinent every line in v. 3-14 is, in particular "be not

ashamed" (v. 8) and "I am not ashamed" (v. 12).
**Thou dost know this that there were turned away
from me all those in Asia, to whom belong Phygelus
and Hermogenes.** May the Lord give mercy to the
house of Onesiphorus because he often refreshed me
and was not ashamed of my chain but, when he was
in Rome, he diligently sought and found me. May the
Lord give to him that he find mercy with the Lord in
that day! And in how many things he ministered in
Ephesus, thou on thy part realizest better (than I).

Paul means that Timothy knows the fact (see "I
know," v. 12). How he knows it is entirely plain, for
"all those in Asia" (the Roman province "Asia" with
its capital Ephesus) were men from Timothy's own
churches. Paul names two of them (ὧν ἐστι = to whom
belong) who were probably the two most outspoken ones.
These two names do not shine in honor. Timothy
knows so that Paul needs to say only "they were turned
away from me" (second aorist passive) ; who turned
them away need not be said. We recall John 6:66 and
Jesus' question to the Twelve. The story is this: when
Paul was arrested and charged with a capital crime
he appealed by letter or by messenger to notable Christian men to come to Rome and to testify in his favor.
"They all with one accord began to make excuse." The
journey, the risk to themselves, the hopeless outlook
for Paul even if they testified caused them to turn
away as Timothy knows only too well. Paul could, of
course, not ask Timothy to testify, for he was an
assistant who aided and abetted Paul in the alleged
crime. Paul could ask only such men who would have
a standing with the imperial court. We take it that
even elders would not do.

We thus discard the idea that "all the Christians
in Asia" had been turned away from Paul or from
the gospel; also the idea that "all these *in* Asia" might
mean Asians who were at that time in Rome. The

trial of Paul was not hurried. This very letter shows that Paul hoped to have Timothy reach him before its end. Here were notable men right in Ephesus and in the province of Asia who were ashamed of Paul, the Lord's prisoner (v. 8).

16) Onesiphorus was the very opposite. Between two prayer-wishes Paul records what this man did. It is striking that, like two arms, these wishes lay before Timothy and the Lord what this man did for Paul. "May the Lord give mercy to the house (the whole family) of Onesiphorus — may the Lord give to him that he find mercy with the Lord in that day!" Twice we have the word ἔλεος, "mercy," evidently because Onesiphorus showed "mercy" to Paul — mercy to the whole family now, "mercy" to Onesiphorus himself at the last day. In 4:19 Paul sends a greeting to the whole family.

De Wette thought that Onesiphorus had died just recently, and many have agreed with him. I must admit that I cannot share this opinion. See, for one, Smith, *Bible Dictionary*. Some are convinced that Onesiphorus was dead because Paul uses the word οἶκος. But look at I Cor. 16:15 where the head of that "house" was not dead, and where "house" is used because its head was not the only member who ministered. How did Onesiphorus get to Rome? Not by mere chance. May we not assume that when Paul's appeal reached Ephesus, when all to whom it was addressed turned away, the whole family of Onesiphorus gladly let him go to Rome to do what he could for Paul? Yes, Paul had to write "house" here and in 4:19.

Others rely only on v. 18a to support their opinion that Onesiphorus was dead. Strange, indeed, for then the two prayers should be reversed, the prayer for Onesiphorus himself should be first, the prayer for his bereaved family second. Moreover, if the father had died recently, "comfort" should be Paul's prayer for

the family and not just "mercy," some word from
Paul that reflects the bereavement. That word, too,
should be found in the prayer for the family (this to
be placed second) and not in a prayer for the dead
man. We have never seen Paul fail in a tender situation; he always knows just what to say and just where
and how to say it. If this man had just died, I for one
cannot conceive that Paul would write as he does. The
family evidently lived in Ephesus, for Paul sends
greetings through Timothy. Some think that, although he had left Rome when Paul wrote, it was
not to make a direct return home, but that is only a
surmise. In both prayers we have the aorist optative
of wish.

Paul reverses the order of Onesiphorus' acts and
does not consider them in the order in which they
occurred but in the order in which he learned of them.
Onesiphorus often "refreshed" Paul; all that lies in
this word remains unknown. "I was in prison, and ye
came unto me," Matt. 25:36. Onesiphorus did not
come empty-handed, this refreshment went beyond
that. Onesiphorus was "not ashamed of Paul's chain."
Here for the third time (v. 8 and 12) we have this key
word "not ashamed." If he had been ashamed, Onesiphorus would not have come. We have already
stated how great a disgrace rested on this prisoner.
"My chain" is not δεσμά, a word that is used only with
reference to confinement, imprisonment; Paul *was*
chained in his dungeon. There was no rented house
now, no free and easy access as in that first imprisonment when Paul could invite all the rabbis and the
leading men of the seven Roman synagogues to visit
him and to stay all day (Acts 28:17, 23). Paul's situation was now sadly different. "My chain" — all
the shame and disgrace that might repel even dear
friends lies in that one word.

17) Now there is mentioned the beginning of it all. When Onesiphorus got to Rome he diligently sought and then found Paul. Some texts read: "more diligently" because Onesiphorus was not ashamed whereas nearly all others were. Was it, then, so difficult to find Paul? Did the Roman Christians not know where he was confined? Remember the conflagration in Rome, because of which so many Christians were executed. Remember Peter's crucifixion. What Roman Christian dared even to inquire about what had become of Paul? Not that they were "ashamed" of this prisoner but that they would likely precipitate his death or would make his state worse besides bringing dire results on themselves. Cautiously but persistently Onesiphorus made his search. The aorist states that it was successful. When Paul adds "and found me," this means that at the end of his search Onesiphorus could not at once get into Paul's dungeon, but he managed it somehow. Some say with bribes, others that Paul would not have allowed this. Yes, Onesiphorus found ways and means to visit Paul often; Luke, no doubt, helped him. Now, as Paul writes, Onesiphorus had departed. Would that we knew the details!

18) Paul breathes another prayer. The prayer voiced in v. 16 is for the family irrespective of time, for Onesiphorus and for all who are his. The prayer which is now added is for Onesiphorus "at that day." We again recall Matt. 25:34-36; these words of Jesus justify Paul's prayer. Κύριος is necessarily repeated because one pronoun (αὐτῷ) has already been used, and another that would refer to the Lord would be ambiguous.

If Onesiphorus was dead, we should have an apostle praying for the dead. Some want this (Catholics); some treat it lightly — what of it? Some say that this is a wish and not really a prayer. The Analogy of Scripture is solidly against anything in the nature of prayers for the dead.

The prayer is not parenthetical, for the last sentence is complete in itself. It is not "an afterthought," for the thought of Paul keeps the order already indicated in v. 16, 17; Paul goes backward and now takes the last step, namely to the many services Onesiphorus had rendered already in Ephesus before he came to Rome and to Paul. These, Paul says, Timothy on his part (emphatic σύ) realizes better than Paul himself does, for they happened under Timothy's own eyes. Such a man would rise to the height already described. Now the word used is not οἶδας as in v. 15 but γινώσκεις, "thou realizest." Timothy not only has a knowledge of the facts (as in v. 15) but a knowledge that affected him personally as the superintendent of all the Asian churches. See οἶδα in v. 12.

CHAPTER II

Join in Suffering What Is Bad

The Child

1) In v. 1-7 we have what Paul asks his *child* to be and to do; in v. 8-13 Paul tells what he as this child's *father* does. We let the key words συγκακοπάθησον (v. 3) and κακοπαθῶ ὡς κακοῦργος (v. 9) guide us when we consider v. 1-13, the second part of the letter, just as in chapter one "being not ashamed" in v. 3, 12, and 16 forms the uniting key word. Yet Paul links this second part into the first, for συγκακοπάθησον occurs already in 1:8; it is now restated in 2:3 and elaborated and expanded in v. 9. On these two verbs used in v. 3 and 9 the whole is pivoted. Transitional οὖν introduces the new admonition.

Thou, then, my child, be thou (ever) **made strong in the grace that** (is) **in Christ Jesus!** The translation "therefore" has this admonition rest on something that precedes, yet nothing precedes on which to base this admonition. Since the admonitions given in 1:8-14 have been concluded, Paul proceeds to the next admonitions. All that we have said in 1:2 regarding "child" applies also here; the endearing address helps to mark a new section of the letter. The main chord is struck at once: "Be made strong!" durative: Let the Lord ever fill thee with δύναμις, power! It seems best to keep the passive "be made strong" instead of reducing it to an intransitive "be strong." The source of strength lies in God's grace. This is "grace" in its full sense: God's unmerited favor which is extended to the guilty in order to cancel all their guilt and to

(777)

those who have been freed of guilt in order to keep them so and to shower upon them all the gifts and the blessings they may need. Here Paul is thinking of the gift of power. This source is ever open to us in Christ. The two ἐν become clear when we translate "be made strong in connection with the grace that (is) in connection with Christ Jesus," the connection referred to being apparent from the imperative verb and from the objects of the preposition.

2) Paul is not thinking of Timothy as a mere believer but also as the representative of himself whom he had stationed in the province of Asia to supervise all the churches. Already in I Tim. 3:1-13 Paul had directed Timothy regarding the kind of persons to be put into office. Now Paul thinks of his own end and thus adds: **And what things thou didst hear from me, supported by many witnesses, these deposit with faithful persons, such as will be competent also to teach others.** Timothy, himself made strong for the great gospel work, is to insure a succession of competent teachers for the churches.

"What things thou didst hear from me" repeats this expression from 1:13, where Timothy is told to have these things as a model of healthy *logoi*; here he is told to deposit these things which he has heard with persons (ἄνθρωποι) competent (ἱκανοί) effectively to teach (aorist infinitive) others and thus to transmit this true teaching on and on. The second aorist middle imperative παράθου, "do thou deposit," continues the idea of παραθήκη, "deposit," mentioned in 1:12, 14: guarding the true gospel himself (1:14), Timothy is at the same time to place it as a deposit with true and faithful (πιστοί) and at the same time competent people.

This is the true apostolic succession of the ministry: not an uninterrupted line of hands laid on which extends back to the apostles themselves so that all ordina-

tions which are not in that line are null and void; but
a succession of true apostolic doctrine, the deposit of
what we still hear from Paul in his writings, this held
by us in faithful hearts with competency to teach
others these same things. The apostle did not evidently
expect the future teachers of the church to produce
new or different teaching. The gospel is changeless
in all ages.

In 1:13 the position of παρ' ἐμοῦ lends it an emphasis
which is not needed in 2:2, where the thought differs:
"heard from me (who received these things by revelation, Gal. 1:12) διά many witnesses." Plutarch has this
use of the preposition; it is apparently used as a legal
term (R., *W. P.*; B.-P. 281), "with the support of
many witnesses," re-enforced by their testimony. We
decline to think of a formal catechism or of a kind
of dogmatics which was used in preparing Timothy
for baptism and for ordination, at which many witnesses were present to testify that "the things" had
been properly transmitted to Timothy by Paul. Nor
are the "many witnesses" the Old Testament writers,
the corroborative witnesses of Paul's gospel teachings.
The aorist "which things thou hast heard" is constative:
"heard many, many times from Paul throughout
Timothy's connection with him." These "many witnesses" do not attest that Timothy so heard, but
all testify together with Paul that his was, indeed, the
gospel truth.

3) After this preamble (v. 1, 2) Paul comes to
the main admonition: **Join in suffering what is bad
as a noble soldier of Christ Jesus!** This carries forward the imperative used in 1:8; but, as the reference
to the soldier shows, with a new turn. In 1:8 the context "be not ashamed" makes κακόν in the verb mean
"something bad," of which one might be ashamed, i. e.,
something in the way of disgrace: "the testimony of our
Lord" as constituting an unlawful religion, "me, his

prisoner," a criminal guilty of a capital crime for advocating this unlawful religion in the empire. In the present connection, κακόν, the bad thing to be suffered, is all that a soldier has to undergo while serving in the army in which he has enlisted. Christ Jesus is the general; Timothy is to be one of his "noble" or excellent soldiers who is to endure jointly, namely with the whole army, notably with Paul and with all these witnesses. There is a strong incentive in σύν: Timothy is not alone, he is surrounded by many others, all being noble soldiers of Christ Jesus. Will Timothy be a coward among them, shrink from what in the very nature of their profession all must endure? Paul uses the figure of a campaign already in I Tim. 1: 18. Only one side of soldiering is here emphasized, that of suffering what is bad; the other side, the vicious enemies who are to be fought by Christ's army, is not stressed.

4) Paul develops: **Nobody soldiering entangles (involves) himself in the affairs of the** (common course of) **life in order that he may please him who enlisted him as soldier.** The truth of this statement is obvious. The man who enlists steps out of the common βίος or course of life. All its ordinary "affairs" no longer concern him. His enlistment assures him of support; it also takes him out of all other occupations. His one aim and object is to be a soldier καλός — this word is a quiet oxymoron with κακόν in the verb of v. 3 — which means to please and to earn the commendation of his enlister. In the case of Timothy this was Christ. The thought that Timothy is not to think of enriching himself in his office is not in the text but is inserted by some who seem to have the opinion that Timothy was avaricious.

5) Brave soldiers, who distinguish themselves, receive decoration and preferment. Paul does not use this extension of the figure, for only some are thus

honored and advanced. For the added thought he
has a better figure, one that is often used by him.
Moreover also, if one contends (in an athletic event)
**he is not crowned unless he finish the contest law-
fully,** according to the rules of the game. Δέ marks
the new thought of distinction, and καί adds it to v. 4:
"moreover also" — δὲ καί go together. Our versions
place the "also" so that it reads: if a soldier also goes
in as an athlete, as in our army and navy football
games. R., W. P., calls attention to the distinction between the present subjunctive ἀθλῇ and the aorist subjunctive ἀθλήσῃ; but we cannot agree with him when
he has the latter mean "engage in a particular contest."
Both verbs refer to a particular contest. The present
subjunctive = "if one engages in an athletic event";
this does not assure him the wreath or garland "unless
(now effective aorist subjunctive) he lawfully (as the
law of that event prescribes) completes the event."
From start to finish no infringement of the rules dare
occur. To this day this rule is observed in all real
athletic events.

This added illustration is finely drawn. But we
should not spoil it by thinking of athletic events *between*
contenders, in which one is necessarily defeated, loses
the crown, although he observed the rules as carefully
as the victor. Paul's *tertium* applies to athletic
events in which a lone athlete tries for a record, and
not only tries but achieves or exceeds the record. Even
then, and that is the point, he loses the crown if in
all things he does not finish in exact compliance with
the rules; an infringement would be fatal. Here Paul
has no opponent in mind just as in v. 4 he has no
enemy of the soldier in mind; for this reason he also
speaks only of one soldier and not of an army. The
application to Timothy is most exact, especially in the
light of 1:13. Strong with power from the Lord, Timothy is not only to use all this strength but also to

use it lawfully as the Lord prescribes, not infringing upon a single *logos,* not deviating from faith and love (1:13). Ah yes, how many run in record time and think they secure the crown, but here and there they run off the course of the *logoi,* run off the track of faith and love, and thus after all lose the crown. When we interpret the crown (wreath) we may perhaps use I Cor. 3:13-16.

6) This illustration is added without a connective because it belongs to the one mentioned in v. 5, which it completes. The crown is bestowed only at the conclusion of the athletic event (4:7, 8); note the aorist subjunctive in v. 5. But what about the time before the conclusion is reached? Here is the answer with a present, durative infinitive. Like the two previous illustrations (soldier, athlete), this third, too, is axiomatic. Some think that Paul's thought is stationary and merely sets forth what lies in "join in suffering what is bad" (v. 3, compare 1:8); hence they interpret the illustrations accordingly. But already v. 3 has mentioned the "noble soldier." Paul's thought moves on, each figure bringing great additions.

As v. 4 has no connective and is thus to be connected with v. 3, so v. 6 is to be considered with v. 5. The connective is found in v. 5. It joins two smaller sections, namely v. 3, 4 and v. 5, 6. 1) A good soldier joins his fellow soldiers in enduring what is bad, his one aim is to please the commander with whom he has enlisted. 2) But while there is bad which is to be suffered nobly, there is a crown at the end as the athlete proves when he contends lawfully, and as the farmer also proves. There are fruits to be enjoyed for the toil expended. As always, Paul completes the subject: certainly much to endure, but all of it to be rewarded with highest, surest compensation, "having promise for the life that now is and for that which is to come" (I Tim. 4:8).

Here is the promise for the life that now is. **The toiling farmer, it is necessary that he as first one take his share of the fruits.** A statement of fact is enough in v. 4, 5; in the case of the farmer there is a necessity. He could not possibly toil on if he did not first take his share of his produce. It is immaterial whether we regard πρῶτον as an adverb or as a predicate apposition; it has the emphasis. The fact that the farmer (generic article) toils lies in the nature of his profession. Those who emphasize "toiling" get the false contrast with a lazy farmer whom Paul does not have in mind.

Also the fact that he toils so that other people may have produce lies in the nature of the case. The whole world lives on the farmer's produce. The point that Paul wishes to make is the fact that the farmer himself must ever be the *first* "to take his share," durative present, i. e., of every crop, year in and year out, whether he does this by eating or by selling his share. A peasant or a renter may have to turn over a share to the owner, an independent owner of a farm must pay his taxes; but every farmer must first have his share, otherwise his farming ceases quite promptly.

The application lies on the surface. This is *not* the truth that Timothy and Paul and preachers generally must have *physical* sustenance to do their *spiritual* work, the farmer takes his share of the very produce he raises for others. So Timothy and Paul, who toil for spiritual fruit for others, must ever and ever, as the very first ones, take of this spiritual fruit for themselves. They toil by preaching and teaching the gospel (1:11), and this toil produces faith, love, godlines, etc., precious "fruits" indeed. But unless they are the first to appropriate their share of these fruits they soon cease to be the Lord's farmers to produce anything for anybody. Yet the point which Paul would here make is the value, the blessedness of the fruits, and the joy of having one's share in them. Also this truth: there must be farmers to sustain the life of the world; there must be preachers to sustain the life of the church. Since this is a necessity in fact, the preachers sit at the very fountain, their very profession compels them to be the first to partake.

7) Paul uses figures in v. 3-6, for these are briefer and more incisive than literal statements would be. But they must be correctly understood. **Be understanding what I am saying!** The present imperative is in place: "be applying your mind"; "consider" (our versions) would be a different verb. The idea is not that Paul's figures are dark and difficult; they are quite lucid. But so much is concentrated into them that one must pause and think to apprehend it all. The words are so brief, one might read them too hastily and not comprehend all that they contain. The texts vary between ὅ and ἄ, the meaning being quite the same. The Scriptures are intended for our νοῦς or mind, which God has given us so that we may use it. Preachers may often forget that fact when they are reading the inspired words. To be sure, these words are to be spiritually apprehended (I Cor. 2:14), but no man will so apprehend them if he is too lazy to use his mind.

Paul adds the promise: **For the Lord will give thee understanding in all respects.** Σύνεσις = bringing things together and thus understanding them. For all spiritual things our thinking abilities, however keen and sharp, are not sufficient. The Lord must control, guide, enlighten our "understanding." He is ever willing to give us "understanding" if we only let him give it, recognize his gift, and prize it. The Lord so gives by means of the very Word itself and never apart from that Word which is a lamp and a light, the source of

all true enlightenment. "Search the Scriptures," and
the Lord will give thee understanding; it does not come
to one through the air. *Ora et labora.*

The Lord, however, uses also his gracious providence
in manifold ways. Experience helps to make many a
passage clear. Teachers and fellow workers are placed
into our path to help us. The Lord lets us find the book
we need for this or for that purpose. He quickens our
faculties, our memory. Sometimes we must wait, but
δώσει stands: "he will give." Even the adverbial accusative τὰ πάντα, and still more the phrase ἐν πᾶσι, mean
only "in all respects" or "in every respect," and not
"in all things" (B.-P. 1012, translates *in jeder Hinsicht*). Paul does not say that Timothy is to understand "all things." "All respects" is the meaning
wherever this phrase occurs; see, for instance,
Eph. 1:23.

The Father

8) The expression, "my child," in verse 1 was
written by a father's pen. That father now also speaks
about himself (v. 9) and does this with the significant
verb κακοπαθῶ, which resumes the verb used in v. 3 (also
in 1:8): Paul is suffering what is bad, suffering as
one who had done what is bad, and thus he is asking
Timothy, his child, to join him (v. 3; 1:8). This is
not all. In v. 11-13 we have an expressive climax in
all the "we" verbs. Paul and Timothy are united, and
both are joined to Christ Jesus, both are joined to him
in suffering and in glory. See how well all this (v. 1-13)
is written; νόει, let your mind dwell on it, for it is precious indeed.

Verse 7 concludes the first paragraph (v. 1-7) ; v.
8 opens the new one and does so without a connective.
**Remember Jesus Christ as raised up from the dead,
from David's seed, in accord with my gospel, in con-**

**nection with which I am suffering what is bad to the
extent of imprisonment as one suffering what is bad,
but the Word of God is not imprisoned!**

Luther renders the durative present imperative
well: *Halt' im Gedächtnis,* "ever keep in memory Jesus
Christ." Now Paul places "Jesus" first and "Christ"
second in order to indicate that the Jesus who lived
on earth was the Christ. The perfect participle is
predicative: remember him "as having been raised up
from the dead," as ever being the one so raised up.
Because it is predicative the article is absent. Recall
1:10: "having abolished the death and having brought
to light life and incorruption." What is here said about
Christ's condition is said in anticipation of v. 12.

Some think that Paul is using an established
formula, but this is Paul's own, terse formulation
which indicates the central gospel facts on which all
preaching and all faith rest. When Paul names Jesus
as one "raised up from the dead," this involves his
suffering and his death, and this as being vicarious,
expiatory, sacrificial (see I Tim. 2:6) ; for the resurrection of Jesus is God's everlasting seal upon his expiation and attests its sufficiency and its acceptance
by God. That is why the participle is passive: God
raised him up. The phrase ἐκ νεκρῶν is discussed at
length in Matt. 17:10; Mark 9:9; Luke 9:7; John
2:22; Acts 3:16.

Ἐκ σπέρματος Δαβίδ is a second predication (hence
it has no article) ; it makes no difference whether we
supply γενόμενον or not: "as come from David's seed,"
the Greek does not need the copula when it intends
to be terse. This phrase is not to be construed with
"having been raised up." Nor is the predication "from
David's seed" purposely placed out of the natural
order. To be sure, Jesus' being from David's seed
according to his human nature antedates his resurrection from the dead, but chronology is not the deciding

factor here; it is qualification as prophecy already states (II Sam. 7:12; Ps. 132:11). He whom God raised from the dead had to be "from David's seed" otherwise he could not have been the Messiah.

In order to understand this predication and its immense importance we should note Matt. 22:41-46; Acts 13:29-37, and the golden cord that runs through the Gospels: "Son of David — Son of David," in passages like Matt. 9:27; 12:23; 15:22; 20:30, 31; 21:9, 15 to mention only Matthew. This is *the* Messianic qualification. Those who find only the human nature of Jesus in this predicate are answered by Matt. 22:41-46. Moreover, who but a human being could have been raised up from the dead?

"According to my gospel," with its mild enclitic μου, in no way differentiates Paul's gospel from others as though this alone contained these facts. Paul repeatedly writes "my" gospel (Rom. 2:16; 16:25) when he thinks of himself as one of the immediately called apostles who received the gospel by means of revelation (Gal. 1:12), from whom Timothy and all those in Asia had received it. Κατά does not here indicate the norm in accord with which these things were expressed, or in accord with which Timothy is to remember them as B.-P. 635 states it; it indicates the place where certain facts are declared. We still say: "according to Matthew's Gospel or Mark's"; "according to the Scriptures," and often, as Paul does here, place the phrase at the end.

Some connect Timothy's remembering with the previous section, with the figures of the soldier, etc., or with the admonitions to suffer what is bad. Barnes is one of these: "Think of the Savior, now raised up from the dead after all the sorrows of this life, and let this encourage you to bear *your* trials. There is nothing better fitted to enable us to endure the labors and trials of this life than to think of the Savior."

But this verse faces forward and not backward; nor does it mention Jesus' sufferings. The verbs that are compounded with σύν are yet to follow (v. 11). Paul is summing up the heart of his whole gospel in connection with which he is now suffering what is bad.

In 1:8 he asks Timothy to join in suffering what is bad *"for* the gospel." The thought is far higher than a comparing of our little suffering with that of Jesus, for our comfort. In 1:12 Paul says, "For this cause I am suffering." So Timothy is now to remember the great cause, the great object, this Jesus according to Paul's gospel, as set forth in his gospel. In v. 9 he is to remember "the Word of God" and then all the elect who are brought to glory by it. All this Timothy is to keep in mind as he looks at Paul, at Paul in his dungeon, a *Schandmensch,* κακοῦργος, "scoundrel," and facing execution as such. After thus remembering and looking at Paul, v. 11-13 will take care of Timothy and will complete the joining begun in 1:8 and continued in 2:3 in the grandest way.

Into the expression "raised up from the dead" von Hofmann inserts: "from the *Totenreich,*" his fictitious "realm of the dead." This fiction has spread. We are told that at the time of his death the soul of Jesus did not pass into his Father's hands, into heaven, but into an intermediate place between heaven and hell, whither all the souls of the dead go until judgment day (or until the millennium). There the soul of Jesus remained until it was brought back to his body. This fiction has been elaborated. Jesus preached the gospel when he was in this Roman Catholic sort of place; in fact, we are told by some that gospel preaching still goes on in this *Totenreich;* it is a sort of infernal mission work. We have discussed this subject elsewhere. Here we merely note the dying cry of Jesus (Luke 23:46), the place where Stephen's soul went (Acts

7:56-59), and the place where Paul's soul wished to go (Phil. 1:23).

9) In 1:8 Paul asks Timothy not to be ashamed of the Lord's testimony and of me, his prisoner; here in 2:8, 9 we again have the two connected, Timothy is to remember Jesus, the sum and substance of Paul's gospel, to remember that in connection with both Jesus and the gospel Paul is suffering what is bad. In 1:8 Paul says only: "me, his prisoner," and in 1:12, "I am suffering these things," and adds "my chain" in 1:16. Now we get the full statement as to what Paul's condition really is: "I am suffering what is *bad* to the extent (μέχρι) of imprisonment as one working what is *bad*."

In order properly to understand both κακοπαθῶ and κακοῦργος we should get the full force of κακόν, the badness. Ramsay says: "exactly the tone of the Neronian period . . . refers to the *flagitia,* for which the Christians were condemned under Nero, and for which they were no longer condemned in A. D. 112." *Flagitia* = *Schandtaten, Niedertraechtigkeiten;* Cicero used the word by metonomy for *Schandmenschen,* Sallust for *Boesewichter.* Thus Paul says that he suffers the utmost shame and disgrace as a criminal of the most shameful and disgraceful kind. See how this casts light on 1:8, 12, 16, not being ashamed, and on 1:8 and 2:3, suffering disgrace. Δέσμα and also the masculine plural are regularly used to designate "imprisonment" and themselves do not mean "chains" as the "bonds" of our versions might lead us to assume. The fact that Paul was chained 1:16 states. Like one who had committed the foulest crimes Paul was confined in a foul dungeon.

See the interlocking chiastic terms: "in connection with which *gospel* I am suffering *foul disgrace* to the extent of *imprisonment* as a *foul criminal* — but the *Word of God* has not been *imprisoned*." One chiasm is: in connection with which (my gospel) — I suffer

disgrace as a disgraceful actor — but the Word of God.
Tied into this are: "to the extent of imprisonment —
has not been imprisoned." This wording is masterly.
We are first led down to the lowest depth: my gospel
has brought me down, down to this deepest shame and
disgrace of foul imprisonment. Then with a triumphant bound we rise upward: but the Word of God,
which my gospel is, has *not* been imprisoned. For *my*
gospel men could do this to *me* but with *God* and *God's*
Word they can do nothing. *Me* men can silence, but
that is far, far from silencing *God*. The perfect δέδεται
has a strong present force (like the perfect participle
regarding Jesus in v. 8) : "has not been and thus is not
now imprisoned" (bound as I am). Who can stop the
glorious, triumphant Word of God? "The testimony
of our Lord" (1:8) no man can silence. The apostle's
living voice may be smothered in his own blood, what
his Lord speaks through him still resounds in the wide
world.

Ah, yes, let Timothy ever remember this Lord,
raised up and glorious, from David's seed as David's
Lord — his Word triumphs.

10) **For this reason I am enduring everything for
the sake of the elect in order that also they may obtain salvation, that** (which is) **in connection with
Christ Jesus in company with eternal glory.**

We do not construe: "but the Word of God is not
bound on this account (διὰ τοῦτο)," i. e., because I am
suffering as a bound criminal in prison. The phrase
διὰ τοῦτο regularly begins a new sentence, and it is natural to think that it does so here. Because the Word
of God is not bound, "I bravely endure, remain and
hold out under everything." Read Trench on ὑπομονή:
brave perseverance under suffering; the verb is used
in the same sense here and in v. 12. If the Word were
also fettered and silenced, it would be useless for Paul
to hold out as he does.

The Word is free and goes on winning souls for salvation. It is unusual that two διά phrases should be found so close together in one sentence, and yet this expresses Paul's thought clearly. The first phrase looks back to the Word which is not bound, the second looks forward to the elect who are saved by this Word. The thought thus advances even as the Word is never without the elect.

"The elect" are not such in the Calvinistic sense, a fixed number chosen by a mysterious, absolute decree, for whom Christ made his limited atonement, who alone receive the serious call, whom an irresistible grace then saves. In the Biblical sense they are the saints and believers chosen as such in Christ, all of whom must make their calling and election sure (II Pet. 1:10). When we consider election, the idea of eternity should not be stressed over against that of time, in which the elect live; or the reverse, time over against eternity. Eternity is timelessness and is wholly inconceivable to our finite minds. *C. Tr.* 1085, 66: "The entire Holy Trinity, God Father, Son, and Holy Ghost, directs all men to Christ, as the Book of Life, in whom they should seek the eternal election of the Father." "They should hear Christ, who is the Book of Life and God's eternal election of all God's children to eternal life: He testifies to all men without distinction that it is God's will 'that all men should come to him,' who labor and are heavy laden with sin, in order that he may give them rest and save them, Matt. 11:28" (70). The election of the elect must ever be viewed thus, in the connection in which II Thess. 2:13 places it.

Just because Paul's supreme interest for his own soul and for his office (1:11) is the conquering Word of God (v. 9), he "holds out valiantly under everything for God's elect that also they (like himself) may obtain (or attain to) salvation, this blessed salvation (note the article defining it) in connection with Christ

Jesus (how connected with him we know) accompanied
by (μετά) eternal glory." The purpose of God, Christ,
their Word and gospel has become Paul's life's purpose. No suffering is too great for him if it in any way
and to any degree supports this purpose, which includes his own salvation, but oh, also that of so many
others.

It is one of those useless questions to ask whether
Paul thought only of the elect who lived in his own
time or of the elect of all times. Although he is dead,
he still speaketh. The office of the apostles, although
as active bearers of it they have long ago died, still
operates through their Word which is God's own. Even
the severest endurance is brief, but salvation with
its accompanying glory is eternal.

11) Thou, "my child" (v. 1-7), I, thy father (v.
8-10), and now "we" jointly with Christ (σύν in the
verbs). This is perfect in connection and reaches its
conclusion in the great summation. Even this we
should note: a strong "thou" with reference to Timothy in v. 1, a strong ἐκεῖνος with reference to Christ
in v. 13, but no ἐγώ in v. 9, 10. **Faithful the statement:
If, indeed, we died with him we shall also live with
him; if we are enduring we shall also reign with him;
if we shall deny him, also he on his part will deny us;
if we are faithless, he on his part remains faithful, for
to deny himself he is not able.**

We regard γάρ as confirmatory: If, "indeed," we
died = if this actually be the fact. This frees us from
the vain search which looks for "the faithful or trustworthy *logos*" in the preceding verses and then finds
nothing that is satisfactory. The great reliable statement follows: "If, indeed, we died," etc. We see that
Paul is not quoting some ancient Christian hymn as
some think. They say that this explains the γάρ which
he retained when quoting. Although we have sym-
metry in the sentences, this is not poetry but Paul's
own prose.

Condition — conclusion: as sure as is the one, so sure is the other. All these are conditions of reality; in each the fact stated is considered as being true. Γάρ emphasizes the assumed reality, and while it is found only in the first condition likewise affects all the other conditions: if, indeed, we died — if, indeed, we endure, etc. Two conditions are positive; two are negative. Rhetorically one doubles in order to make a thought emphatic; one also places positive and negative together for complete clearness of thought. The last conclusion: "he on his part remains faithful," forms a sharp contrast and thus enables Paul to add the final statement which brings all the balanced clauses down to the final unit point, where in that unit: "deny himself he cannot" the whole elaboration ends.

"If, indeed, we died," aorist, past — "if we are enduring," present — "if we shall deny," future. Past occurrence — present state — future happening. These tenses are decisive in answer to those who think that "if, indeed, we died with him" refers to physical death, a martyr's death. Both γάρ and the aorist tense exclude this thought. Paul and Timothy had not as yet died physically either by martyrdom or otherwise. Why should Paul put such a death first and the continuous enduring second when the order of the two is always the reverse? The statement that the aorist "died" is used because such a death precedes "shall live" breaks down when we look at the other clauses in all of which the same precedence appears and no aorist is needed for its indication.

This is the death which occurs in baptism by contrition and repentance. It is expressed in mystical language: "we died together with him." See Rom. 6:4, etc., where this language is fully explained. It has nothing to do with mysticism or mysteriousness. In the mystical terms we have great concentration, but a concentration of facts: the one fact happened to Christ: he died on the cross; the other happened to us:

"we died" to sin. The interval of time between the two deaths is omitted. Because the one death caused the other, because the latter rests on the former, σύν combines them: "we died together with him." If we truly did so die, of which there is no doubt in the case of Paul and of Timothy, it is equally certain: "we shall live together with him." As he, risen from the dead (v. 8), lives to die no more, so by virtue of his life we "shall live together with him" in heaven forever. Here the distant extremes: joint death in the past — joint living in the heavenly future are connected. The two form a paradox: having died — future living.

"We" in the verbs = Paul and Timothy. The fact that what is true of them is true also of all other Christians is self-evident.

12) Between the two extremes, the death in the past and the life in the future, lies our present endurance: "if we are enduring we shall also reign together with him." We think that Paul might have used the mystical "are enduring together with him" just as he uses it in the conclusion: "we shall reign together with him." This is really his thought although Christ's enduring has been completed long since. His death and his enduring were expiatory, *for* us, ours are only confessional, *together with* him. The Greek does not need the pronoun with these verbs, the Greek understands without the use of "him." Some are called upon to resist even unto blood (Heb. 12:4), to endure a great fight of afflictions (Heb. 10:32), like Paul, not counting life dear in defense of the gospel (Acts 20:24). Here is where death by martyrdom is touched.

"Shall reign" exceeds "shall live." This second paradox is just as tremendous as the first. Here we "endure," literally, "remain under," others trample all over us; there we shall reign as royalties with no one above us save Christ, and we are actually associated with him: sitting with him in his throne as he

sits in his Father's (Rev. 3:21; 20:4, 6). Here belong
all those passages that speak of the crown such as 4:8;
James 1:12; I Pet. 5:4; Rev. 2:10. Human imagination fails to visualize this exaltation. Say "reign" or
"crown" like this, and the chiliast has no trouble in
conjuring up his millennium despite all Scripture to
the contrary notwithstanding.

These mighty promises have a reverse: "if we
shall deny him" (the English needs the pronoun), disown, as Peter once denied: "I do not know the man."
The condition still visualizes reality and is not changed
to potentiality: "if we should deny," even though Paul
refers to Timothy and to himself. The future tense is
in place because both are now nobly confessing. Paul
is almost quoting Jesus (Matt. 10:33). Permanent
denial is referred to; Peter repented of his denial. The
days soon came when the pagan authorities demanded
of the Christians the denial of Christ by sacrifice to a
pagan god or by sprinkling incense on an altar and
naming the emperor as god. Paul has no more restriction in the verb than Jesus has in Matt. 10:33: denial
is fatal whatever its form.

The two ἐκεῖνος are very emphatic: "also he on his
part will deny us" before his Father in heaven. In
Mark 8:38; Luke 9:26 Jesus used also the word "to
be ashamed of" (see it in 1:8, 12, 16). No retribu-
tion could be more just. Only one who has confessed
can turn about and deny. He who by denial now cuts
himself off from Christ and so faces him on the last
day must not expect that Christ will be equally false
and will then confess where he ought to deny.

13) This already trenches on the fourth statement: "if we are faithless" (R. V.), which is better
than: "if we believe not" (A. V.) because of the context: "he on his part remains faithful." Yet to be
faithless is to give up believing, to be "faithless" in
this fatal way. The present tense is used at the end
because in general propositions the present is the rule,

and this last statement is intended to be general. Though we are false, no matter when or where or how, "he on his part" remains ever absolutely faithful and true. This means more than that he keeps his word in promise and in threat; this speaks of his very character and nature.

The final clause is not a mere attached reason for the last two "if" propositions. It applies to all the statements and makes all of them a faithful logos. It thus forms the keystone which closes the arch: "for to deny himself he is not able." Christ cannot contradict himself, prove false to himself, in the end disown what he was before. We must ever deny our evil nature; and some may do the reverse, deny their new spiritual nature. Men expect Christ to act in the same way on judgment day: deny all his warning threats, give them and thus himself the lie, and let these his deniers enter heaven as do his faithful believers. Οὐ δύναται, "he is not able." Count on the changeless Christ to all eternity.

Present Thyself as a Workman That Needs Not to Be Ashamed

14) This half of the chapter is a unit. The connecting link is ἀνεπαίσχυντον (v. 15), "needing not to be ashamed," which continues the "not to be ashamed" occurring in 1:8, 12, 16, and the thought of shame and disgrace that lies in the κακόν found in the verbs "suffer disgrace" in 1:8; 2:3, 9. After being thus joined to what precedes, the admonition advances to Timothy's work, which he is to do so that he needs not to be ashamed.

Cutting the Word of Truth Straight

Of these things put them in remembrance, earnestly testifying in the sight of the Lord, not to be battling about words for no useful result, (only) for upsetting those hearing.

Timothy is at the head of all the Asian churches. After himself taking to heart "these things" which Paul is writing to him, he is ever to keep reminding all the churches of them. By "these things" Paul refers to all that he has thus far said. Here the "we" of v. 11-13 broadens out so as to include believers generally. The imperative needs no personal object; its tense, however, implies that Timothy has been doing what Paul urges him to continue to do, and that the churches have been hearing these things from Timothy.

"Earnestly testifying in the sight of the Lord" (see I Tim. 5:21) is modal, and Paul adds the negative side: "not to be battling about mere words," not to engage in logomachies (the noun that is used in I Tim. 6:4), quibbling about words. The two ἐπί phrases speak about the result: "for no useful result," "for nothing that is useful" as the outcome; to which is added what the only result would be: "(only) for upsetting those hearing" by such foolish discussions.

We see that Timothy still had to contend against people like those mentioned in I Tim. 6:3, etc.; this kind often still bothers the church. Abiding by the *ipsissima verba* of Scripture, letting no one tamper with them, is not engaging in battles about words but is guarding the Lord's *logoi* as he commands (John 14:23, 24), both the vessels of the sacred word and the divine truth they contain. B.-D. 389 changes the infinitive to the present imperative on inferior textual authority; μή is the proper negative with the infinitive while οὐδέν is proper in the phrase (R. 947).

15) The second admonition is still more comprehensive: **Be diligent to present thyself to God as one tested, a workman not needing to be ashamed, (ever) cutting straight the Word of the truth.**

The aorist imperative and its aorist infinitive are constative; the action, which is in reality durative, is viewed as a unit, the present participle at the end spreading it out in its progress. Thus the aorist imperative also comes with more force. When we present ourselves to men ("those hearing us," v. 14) as preachers of the Word we must ever be conscious of the fact that we are also presenting ourselves to God in everything that we say or do (doctrine and practice) in regard to his Word. How this thought ought to drive out even loose carelessness, to say nothing about arrogant opinions, following human authorities, popular errors and practices! One concern should possess us completely: to be diligent to present ourselves (aorists) to God "as tested" (predicative accusative), a favorite term of Paul's. We should be as coins that are tested for purity of metal and for adequate weight and are accepted only after such a test ("approved," our versions).

"As one tested" has an apposition: "as a workman not needing to be ashamed" in the eyes of God. We see at once how this repeats the note struck in 1:8, 12, 16 although it is now advanced to Timothy's work. Like δόκιμος, also ἀνεπαίσχυντος is passive; it does not merely mean "unashamed" but "not forced to be ashamed," namely by the fatal disapproval of God. Many are now proud, unashamed, challenging their faithful fellow workers to try to put them to shame, feeling very secure and laughing at their judgment; alas, when the eye of God at last examines them regarding their work, utter, eternal shame will overwhelm them.

A second apposition to the predicative "attested" carries the thought to completion: "(ever) cutting straight the Word of the truth." The participle means just this. Paul is not referring to the main things in the Word in contrast to the minor things. "The truth" is not cut into main and minor pieces with the idea that one may disregard the latter just so he properly cuts out the former. Some interpreters introduce the idea of "roads" that are laid out straight, and some debate as to whether the idea of "straight" or of "cutting" is the main idea. So we have the R. V. margin: "holding a straight course in the Word of the truth," which some modify and translate: "going straight to the main thing in the truth" and not bothering with minor things.

The A. V. follows Luther: "rightly dividing the Word of truth," which is often taken to mean properly dividing between law and gospel; the R. V. translates: "handling aright." One has thought of running a straight furrow, another of a mason cutting stones straight; to which R., *W. P.*, replies, why not let the tentmaker Paul think of cutting straight the camel-hair cloth for tents? and adds: "Certainly plenty of exegesis is crooked enough (crazy-quilt patterns) to call for careful cutting to set it straight." Robertson is close to the point.

Cut the Word of the truth (and the whole of it is "the truth," appositional genitive or genitive of substance) straight when you present it to others by preaching and teaching. That is what preachers and teachers are to do. When they do not cut the Word of the truth straight and true, the result is "nothing useful, only something that upsets those hearing" (v. 14). Such preachers abuse the Word, and their hearers suffer the terrible effect.

Oh, what maltreatment of the heavenly Word, and thus of immortal souls! And to think that such men call themselves experts, master-workmen in the Word! God's Word they cut and slash as if it were the word of men. The eternal truth they cut up as being so many "outworn categories of thought" to be made over into something that is thought to be modern, up-to-date, as if the sin and woe in the world today were not the same old sin and woe of all the ages. Cain's murder is as modern as any murder on today's front page.

16) Verse 15 states what Timothy's life business is to be. **But profane babblings** (see I Tim. 6:20)

turn thy back on! The middle of περιΐστημι = to turn around, which means to turn the back on something in contempt. "To shun," "to avoid," in our versions, "to give a wide berth to," are inexact and also lose the contempt that lies in this act. In I Tim. 6:20 the verb "turn away from" is slightly less expressive. Such stuff is unworthy of any consideration, certainly not of refutation. Contempt is the correct answer to it.

One reason for turning the back on these babblings is offered. **For they progress farther forward in ungodliness, and their word as gangrene will have pasture — to whom belong Hymeneus and Philetus, of a kind who missed the mark as regards the faith, declaring the resurrection already to have occurred and are overturning the faith of some.**

"They progress" has an indefinite subject; Paul scorns to name these babblers and mentions only two names in v. 17 and singles these out because they are notorious by having progressed entirely out of the faith. The fact that the indefinite "they" is, indeed, the subject the following αὐτῶν, "their," ὧν, "of whom," οἵτινες, "of what kind," show. "The babblings" (a nominative drawn from the accusative) cannot be regarded as the subject because "babblings" never "beat or hammer forward" (προκόπτω). True, ἐπὶ πλεῖον is usually used without a genitive (see the verb with the ἐπί phrases in 3:9, 13) whereas here the genitive follows: literally, "beat forward for more of ungodliness"; yet in later Greek this verb is always intransitive (M.-M. 542), and accordingly the proposal to make ἀσεβείας an accusative plural object lacks support.

17) These babblers will progress in ungodliness inwardly, and epexegetical καί states how: "their *logos*," with which they occupy themselves, "like (eating) gangrene will have pasture," to eat more and more ravenously. The figure is striking but only too true. The term is medical and denotes cancer, gangrene,

"canker" (A. V. = spreading ulceration). These people, Paul intends to say, are incurable; their disease "will eat" on and on, and the more one argues with them with the idea of curing them, the more their disease is caused to spread in their system.

"Of whom are" is the Greek idiom for "to whom belong," see I Tim. 1:20 where Hymeneus is mentioned. This was apparently the same man; he was one of the two whom Paul had to expel from the church. We have no further knowledge concerning Philetus. These two were notorious examples and are named as such in order to illustrate Paul's point.

18) The indefinite relative is qualitative and thus refers also to others besides the two that are named: "of a kind who missed (we say: have missed) the mark (this verb occurs in I Tim. 1:6; 6:21) as regards the faith" (objective, *quae creditur*, the Christian truth and doctrine which is believed by us, it is so used in I Tim. 4:1; 6:10, 12, 21); they made shipwreck (I Tim. 1:19). The participle states how this happened: "by declaring the resurrection already to have occured," namely in baptism and conversion. Some think of the later Gnostic teaching to this effect; but this does not extend back to Paul's time. The Apostles' Creed opposes it with its σαρκὸς ἀνάστασιν, "the resurrection of the flesh" (German *Auferstehung des Fleisches*), which is modified in our English form of the Creed: "the resurrection of the body." Zahn, *Introduction* II, 129.

To spiritualize the resurrection in this way subverts the faith. Any denial of the *physical* resurrection, as Paul has shown so fully in I Cor. 15:12-20, involves denial of Christ's physical resurrection and thus destroys the very basis of the faith. Rationalism and modernism do this today and thus place themselves beyond the pale of Christianity. It may be that from this we can gather what some of these babblings and logomachies were, namely quibblings about utterances of Paul's regarding our actual spiritual resurrection (Rom. 6:3, 4; Eph. 2:6; Col. 2:12), attempts to play off these words against what Paul taught about the physical resurrection (compare I Cor. 15; I Thess. 4:13-18; see Jesus' words in John 5:28, etc.).

The last clause has a finite verb, for it adds the fact that, besides missing the mark, as indicated, to their own damage these babblers "are overthrowing the faith of some" (objective, B.-P. 1063), upsetting the doctrine which some have hitherto held with all the churches, substituting their κενοφωνίαι ("empty talk," v. 16) in place of this doctrine. Here Paul refers to the outward spread of this heresy. The present tense may be conative: "trying to overturn" some. But in either case "some" does not read as if the success of these babblers was very great.

19) **Nevertheless,** although some miss the mark and turn away as did the two that are named, **the solid foundation of God stands, having this seal: The Lord did know those who are his; and: Stand off from unrighteousness, everyone naming the Lord's name!**

The masculine ὁ θεμέλιος is the only nominative singular of this word that occurs in the New Testament; Rev. 21:14 has the masculine plural accusative; the neuter plural appears in Acts 16:26, in the LXX, in Attic Greek. R. 262 and others are evidently mistaken when they regard ὁ θεμέλιος as an adjective, λίθος being understood, so that this = "the foundation stone." We have the noun: "the foundation," the one laid down by God. This foundation is variously understood: the promises of God — *fides Dei immota* — the Christian religion — the doctrine of the resurrection of the flesh — predestination (Calvin) — the doctrines of the Old and the New Testament — divine grace and truth — Christ crucified and risen — or leaving the term undetermined altogether.

The A. V. translates: "the foundation of God standeth sure," margin "steady"; but the adjective is attributive: "the solid foundation," not predicative. This foundation is named as a solid one and as one not to be overthrown because of the double seal which it bears: "those who are the Lord's" — then individualizing: "everyone naming the Lord's name. The solid foundation of God is the church. This observation is to the point: Paul uses the figure of "the foundation" because this contains the idea of solidity, immovableness. There is no contrast with a superstructure that is placed on this foundation. See these two figures in I Tim. 3:15: the church is a pillar and in the next breath the ἑδραίωμα, *Grundfeste*, each idea being complete in itself and not conflicting with the other. We still call something that is founded, permanently laid down: "such and such a person's foundation." This is *"God's* foundation," it is certainly "solid"; hell cannot overthrow it, nor can these babblers. It "stands," ἕστηκεν, perfect tense but always used as a present.

"As having this seal" does not mean having "this inscription" as though this were an allusion to the practice of painting inscriptions over a door or carving legends on foundations or on cornerstones. A seal is more than an inscription. The seal is used for various purposes, such as indicating ownership, inviolability, guarantee, certification, etc.; here the two legends constituting the seal lead us to think especially of guarantee. It should not be said that a foundation, in the sense here intended, can have no seal, that such an idea is incongruous. All the great foundations founded by wealthy men in our time and bearing their name stand under a legal documentary state seal, and this makes the foundation so permanent. So also God's foundation, the church, in its solidity stands under the special seal which fixes and guarantees this foundation beyond any alteration or possible dissolution. Yet in the case of a human foundation even the strongest

legal seal and documentation are bound to fail sooner
or later, and the foundation suffers dissolution. Not
so God's foundation under God's seal.

This seal reads for one thing: "The Lord knew
those who are his." Review the difference between
οἶδα and γινώσκω (v. 12 and 18) and then mark the aorist
tense. As is the case in Matt. 7:23 and John 10:14 and
elsewhere, the verb is here to be understood in its most
pregnant sense, which involves to the full the relation
of the subject to the object (the Lord to his own):
cognoscere cum affectu et effectu, "to know with appropriating affection and effect," the definition of the
Lutheran fathers, none better has as yet been produced.
R., *W. P.*, calls the aorist "timeless": "the Lord know-
eth" (irrespective of time). In a manner "timeless"
is correct, for this aorist is dated in eternity: "the
Lord *knew* those who are his" before time was, in all
eternity. Moulton, *Einleitung* 183, calls this aorist
constative, as "gathering into one perspective all the
successive moments of γινώσκωσι σέ in John 17:3"; but
this *present* subjunctive in John sheds no light on this
or on any other *aorist*, whether it be ingressive, constative, historical, or something else.

This is a seal which, *once* affixed to God's foundation, guarantees permanency, makes dissolution impossible. It was affixed in eternity and reads: Ἔγνω
Κύριος τοὺς ὄντας αὐτοῦ, i. e., in all eternity the Lord knew
with appropriating and effective love all that are his
in all the ages of time, from the first one who is his to
the last one at the last day. A tremendous seal! God
knew them, knew them in eternity, these who are his.
That settles the matter forever. "They that are his"
are the foundation of God, and God's knowing them
eternally is their seal. The fathers are right when they
quote II Tim. 2:19 together with John 10:28 (*C. Tr.*
1093, 89). Here is comfort, indeed, for all "who are
his," not the comfort of Calvin's absolute, mysterious
decree by which some were reprobated in all eternity,

but the comfort of God's effective knowledge which
saw us from birth to death and from the first instant
of faith to its triumph in the hour of death, embracing
us as his own. This seal stands with the foundation;
the ages of the world never change a single letter of it.

The whole power of this seal lies in the historical
aorist. To make this aorist constative or "timeless"
dissipates the very point that is essential for the seal.
This seal was affixed *once*, not progressively. Ἔγνω *is*
this seal. "The Lord knew"; that sealed "those who
are his," sealed them as God's foundation from eternity to eternity. This comfort is so great when we
now see some giving up the faith and falling away
(v. 18). There *are* unfaithful members; but the Lord
"never knew" them (Matt. 7:23); they never disturbed his eternal foundation. "Those who are his"
are otherwise called the elect, thus in v. 10 and in I Pet.
1:2, "elect according to foreknowledge of God the
Father in connection with sanctification of spirit for
obedience and sprinkling of Jesus Christ's blood";
II Thess. 2:13: "God hath chosen you from the beginning for salvation in connection with sanctification of
spirit and faith in truth."

As these two passages show, the words: "Stand off
from unrighteousness, everyone naming the Lord's
name!" are an integral part of the seal and not a mere
appendix. This dictum is often regarded as an admonition such as might appear anywhere in this letter.
"God's foundation" — "those who are *his"* bear as
their great seal the fact that "the Lord knew" them
as such. This is the invisible part and is even dated
in eternity, in the mind of God. They equally bear as
their great seal the effective command that everyone of them "stand away from unrighteousness."
This is the visible part which is dated in time and this
life. Look at them; this injunction marks and stamps
them, has ever been their unchanged and unchangeable
seal. One sees on "everyone" of them this seal, not as

an injunction yet to be obeyed, but as one that is ever effectively and once for all actually being obeyed. Their inward heart and character, together with their visible life, ever cry: "I do, I do stand away!" By "naming the Lord's name," by confessing the revelation which the Lord has made of himself, the revelation by which he "knows (γινώσκω, John 17:3) the only true God and Jesus Christ whom he has sent," by which knowing he savingly embraces God, everyone thereby stands off and away from unrighteousness, repudiates, has already repudiated it.

The Lord's ὄνομα is not merely some name for God but the revelation by which he makes himself known; by which in faith we embrace him; naming that *onoma* is confessing that revelation as held by faith. Isa. 26:13. To stand off from unrighteousness is unduly narrowed by Bengel who thinks the abstract "unrighteousness" = the concrete unrighteous men, like the profane babblers mentioned in v. 16, 17. All unrighteousness is referred to. Nobody can be "his," God's, who does not bear the mark of separation from unrighteousness.

How the two parts of this seal, the one part occurring in eternity, that he knew his own, and the other part in time, that in us is exhibited the command to stand off from unrighteousness — how these fit together and form one seal our finite minds cannot understand. We cannot even comprehend eternity and the workings of God's eternal mind, to say nothing more. See the remarks on v. 10, "the elect." On judgment day, as Matt. 25:34-40 show, all the world shall see the elect, whom God knew, stood off from unrighteousness, and how the rest did not.

Κύριος seems to signify God. Paul's two statements, which he calls "the seal" of God's foundation, are not quotations. The first is generally referred to Num. 16:5, LXX, which does not agree with the Hebrew; some think of John 10:14, which does not agree

in tense. For Paul's second sentence an allusion to
Num. 16:26 or to Isa. 52:11 is assumed. It is best
to assume that both of Paul's statements are his own
formulation which voice the two pertinent Scripture
thoughts.

Distinguishing the Different Utensils
in the Great House

20) Δέ is not adversative, for it does not introduce
a contrary thought; it is parenthetical and introduces
a preliminary thought that is preparatory to what follows. What follows still speaks about the master-
workman who is to present himself as one who needs
not be ashamed. In v. 14-19 he will cut the Word
straight and will deal accordingly with men like
Hymeneus and Philetus. In v. 20-26 he will also distinguish between the different utensils in the house
and will deal gently with church members who are in
danger of being misled. In v. 14-19 the consideration
is the *Una Sancta,* the church invisible, God's solid
foundation with its seal, those who are his, etc. In
v. 20-26 the consideration is the church visible which
has two general classes of members and differences
also among those in each class. Δέ introduces this as a
preliminary consideration.

**Now in a large house there are not only utensils of
gold and silver but also of wood and earthenware, and
some for honor, and some for dishonor.**

This is how the external, visible church appears,
namely the members who are regarded as belonging
to it. We see at once that we are to hear about these
varying utensils of a large house, large because it contains so many, and not about the house itself, its stones,
its walls, etc. The house is mentioned only because
it houses all these varied utensils. To connect this
with v. 19 by thinking that this indefinite "large house"
has been erected or is in process of erection on the very

definite foundation of God is not practicable. Paul is
not concerned with the house as a house; in fact, οἶκος
is used in its first meaning, "a dwelling," any large-
sized human habitation. In this verse we have only
the illustration. In the application nothing more is
said about the house; the application limits itself to
the utensils, σκεύη, which are not only dishes, pans, pots
but anything that is used in a great, rich house, from
things made of gold and of silver down to the cheap-
est and those that are of no particular value.

There are two classes of utensils but a variation
also in each of these. We recall I Cor. 3:12, where we
have the same variation in regard to durable and in-
durable building material. The gold and the silver
utensils are the true members of the church visible, and
their being "for honor" means that they will always
be prized and kept and never thrown away. Yet some
are of gold and most precious, the faith, love, work of
such members are of the highest value; some are of
silver, members that are less precious. Two words are
enough to illustrate this minor point of difference.

The utensils of wood and of earthenware are persons who are only outwardly members of the visible
church; they are "for dishonor," which does not mean
for dirty use but unprized, eventually discarded and
thrown on the junk heap. Nobody throws utensils that
are made of gold and of silver out with the junk. We
now see why the division is made between "gold and
silver" on the one hand, "wood and earthenware" on
the other, and why no other materials are mentioned,
for that would spoil the illustration, i. e., its *tertium
comparationis*. Paul's *tertium* is disregarded when we
introduce *all* the household utensils and convert his
simple illustration with its one point into an allegory
with many points. Even among the utensils that are
destined sooner or later to be junked there are differences, but these make no difference as to the fate of
these utensils.

"For honor" and "for dishonor" do not refer to the *use* that is made of these utensils, some being intended for noble, some for ignoble use. Nothing is said about their use, for this is not the point; the one and only point is preciousness, some utensils being so precious as never to be thrown away, some so cheap as to be readily thrown away.

21) **If, then, one keeps himself clean of these he will be a utensil for honor, sanctified, well serviceable for the Master, prepared for every good work.**

The condition is one of expectancy, for who would expect any person to turn himself from gold or silver into wood or earthenware? The application is left general: "if, then, anyone," for it applies to all true members of the church and not merely to Timothy. The illustration and the reality are interwoven so as to bring out the point. But this, of necessity, strains the illustration. In the case of lifeless household utensils it is the rule: once a thing of gold or of silver always a thing of gold or of silver, and this is, of course, also true with regard to things of wood or of earthenware. But that is not the case with regard to the living persons here illustrated. They may change from gold and silver to wood and earthenware, from genuine to mere outward church members. Illustrations must frequently be strained in this way: they only touch the reality, indicate it only in a weak way; they are on a poor, low plane, the reality on a far higher plane. We should, therefore, accept the strain and not force the reality down to the illustration or the illustration up to the reality.

So here: if a person keeps himself clean (reality), aorist, effectively clean from these (figure: these valueless utensils) he will be (reality) a utensil for honor (figure). We see without difficulty what "keep clean from these" means, the more so since "stand off from unrighteousness" precedes in v. 19. While no such action can be predicated of lifeless household utensils, this action can be and is here predicated of us who belong to the church. In our contact with merely outward members we may contaminate ourselves with their spirit and may thus become like them, change from gold or silver to wood or earthenware. "Keep yourself clean of these!" is the call we need. "Remain pure gold or at least silver!"

The construction is perfectly regular: ἐάν with the subjunctive (protasis), indicative future (apodosis). There is no need to philosophize about this future tense. It simply states that this person will be a utensil for honor, never to be thrown away, permanently to be prized and kept as being of the highest value. Three elucidating predications follow, two perfect participles to indicate lasting conditions and between them a descriptive adjective. "Having been and thus remaining sanctified" = set apart by the Lord for himself and thus emphasizing and explaining the keeping clean. One keeps himself clean in doctrine and in life and yet is kept clean, is sanctified by the Lord.

The adjective advances the thought since the picture is that of a utensil: "well serviceable for the Master," one that he can use well and will not throw away. One may think of the figure and thus translate δεσπότης "master"; the proposal to let this word mean "owner" alters the sense of the word. We think not of the figure but of the reality, for "sanctified" has passed on to the reality, and so we translate "Master," our Lord Jesus Christ. Yet δεσπότης is used because he is the one who determines regarding all the utensils.

Still another predicative participle enriches Paul's meaning: "having been (and thus remaining) prepared and ready for every good work." The figure used in v. 20 could not include the use; it remained with the idea of value. In the application Paul beautifully advances also to the use. The moment we look at this advance we see why it had to be omitted in the figure: our Master uses only sanctified utensils (those of gold or of silver) and not the unsanctified (those of wood, etc.), not those that contaminate. The works of the merely outward members are not good in his eyes; although they do many great and wonderful works, he rejects all of them (Matt. 7:22, 23).

22) Paul has stated his thought objectively so that it applies to "anyone" and to "every good work" in the broadest way (v. 20, 21). Now he makes a few particular and detailed applications for the sake of Timothy in his great office of superintending the churches when Paul himself will be gone. The three δέ indicate the specifications; they are alike, not adversative although the R. V. translates the first two "but."

Now the (well-known) **youthful lusts keep on fleeing, but keep on pursuing righteousness, faith, love, peace, in company with those calling upon the Lord from a clean heart!**

This is the first specification. Timothy is ever to be a golden vessel, for quality is all that is here brought out. The first two specifications (v. 22, 23) have the second person "thou," the third (v. 24) has the third person: "the Lord's slave." This means that, while the first two are addressed to Timothy, as the third indicates, the two are not intended exclusively for Timothy. At times Paul specifies by referring to himself as he here refers to Timothy, and yet in such instances Paul makes himself only an example.

We also see that the entire emphasis is put on the positive side, for this has four great items: "righteousness, faith," etc. This means that the brief negative is only the foil even as it contains only the summary, general term "youthful lusts." The arrangement of the verbs and the objects is chiastic and thus brings together the verbs which are strong opposites: "keep on fleeing, keep on pursuing." On "youthful" read the remarks regarding I Tim. 4:12. These are not the sinful desires of an immature youth but of one who is not yet old and a greybeard. Here again some think that Timothy was inclined to go wrong, and that, if we deny this implication, we are only trying to shield Timothy. The very tense of these two imperatives answers such an interpretation. "Keep on fleeing youthful lusts" means that Timothy has ever been doing this very thing; "keep on pursuing righteousness," etc., points to the same continuance. The two also ever go together and signify: "Ever keep on in the true and blessed course you have followed all these years!"

Why should suspicion be cast on a man when he is urged to keep on in a course which flees evil and pursues good? Why may we not encourage a good man to keep on doing so without the reflection that he after all has a secret bent to go wrong? Paul is writing his last letter to Timothy. He is like an old father who is soon leaving his son forever. Shall he not be permitted to say: "Child, ever keep on as thou hast been doing until thou, too, art called away"? We also repeat that Paul would have been foolish to place and to leave a man in so responsible a position if he had fears about this man's going wrong.

These admonitions the very best men among us ever need. In v. 21 the two participles are passives: we have been and are being sanctified, prepared for every good work. The Lord ever does this, does it in good part through admonitions just like these given by Paul. An exegete must also observe the Eighth Commandment. To skim over the text and to note neither tense nor voice nor the inner situation is not fair exegesis. Here this fault is especially prominent so that we ask permission to contribute what we can toward correcting it.

As their objects indicate, both imperatives refer to the heart. One does not run from lusts or run after virtues with his legs. This is stated in order to correct some remarks that are made regarding "flee." Because Paul uses "youthful," some stress or at least introduce sexual lusts and expand on these by telling us how young preachers must be careful in their contacts with the fair sex. But this reflection cast on Timothy is not fair to him. Read the exposition in 5:2. Ἐπιθυμίαι, so often used in an evil sense, points to no one wrong desire more than to another. Each age of life has its own desires. The emphasis rests on the whole object and not on the adjective, for this is in the attributive position. Moreover, the article speaks of these desires as "the" common, well-known ones, and thus in no way singles out Timothy by referring only to his age of life. All the good objects are without articles, which stresses the quality: whatever there is of righteousness, etc. Here, too, we have the full rhetorical four, an expansion that is in strong contrast to the one negative term.

In I Tim. 6:11 we have: "keep on pursuing righteousness . . . faith, love" and two more. See the interpretation of these three. Here the fourth is "peace," undisturbed harmony, without strife, contention, battles about words (v. 14; I Tim. 6:4). How Timothy, for one, is to pursue peace in his office v. 24 explains.

In all this Timothy is to join the company (μετά) "of those who call upon the Lord from a clean heart." This links into the preceding terms. These are the true and genuine members of the church, the *vere credentes* who "name the Lord's name" in true confession and so also call upon him in prayer and praise. "Out of a clean heart" = "sanctified" (v. 21) = standing off from unrighteousness (v. 19) = keep himself clean (v. 21). The advance is the thought that all this cleanness centers in the heart, which in the Greek denotes the whole inner personality. Timothy and all his true company are ever to stand and to work together. It is very easy for clean hearts to find each other.

23) The second specification, again with δέ, is quite narrow: **Now the (well-known) silly and uneducated questionings disdain to be bothered with** (see I Tim. 4:7, where the same imperative is used). There they are termed "profane, old grannies' myths" or fables. Here the characterization is equally scornful: "silly," without sense; "uneducated," betraying a lack of elementary Christian education (such as already a παῖς or boy ought to have). "Questionings" or "questings" means that these people busy themselves with all sorts of useless matters and then come to Timothy with their opinions with the hope of receiving some support from him. The psychology of disdaining to be bothered with them is discussed at length in connection with I Tim. 4:7.

Here the reason for this advice is stated: **having gotten to know that they beget** (present: continue to beget) **battles.** By means of the aorist participle Paul says that Timothy has long ago gotten to the point of knowing this; he is no longer "uneducated" even on this point. We should not say: "If Timothy knows, why still tell him?" We are told many things that we know in order to confirm us. Incidentally, such an acknowledgment on the part of a greater person is worth much to us in other ways. It is a fact that many questionings are silly and without elementary education about the things they seek to pry into. If these are taken up and discussed seriously they end in nothing but battles, empty, useless battles. The one cure for them is not even to listen; if that fails, the last remedy is exhausted. Make people drop such stuff and let them hear the things that will give them some true religious education. We see why "peace" is introduced in v. 22: it is opposed to these "battles."

24) The third specification with δέ, now objective, in the third person, and thus applying to Paul himself and to any man who holds the position of "a slave of the Lord," elaborates this refusal to enter battles. **Now a slave of the Lord must not be battling but (must) be gentle toward all, apt to teach, putting up with what is bad, in meekness educating those placing themselves in opposition, if, perhaps, God may get to give them repentance for realization of truth, and that they get back to soberness out of the devil's snare, having been** (and remaining) **captured alive by him** (God) **for that one's** (God's) **will.**

The fact that "a slave" works is implied in the word itself; the thing to be noted is the fact that "a slave" has no will of his own when he works, he is governed by the will of his Lord (v. 19: we are "his"). When Paul says that "a slave of the Lord must not be battling," he refers to a slave who follows this Lord, who did not wrangle or shout or make a scene in the streets (this is the sense of Matt. 12:19; Isa. 41:2). As to 4:7 and Paul, the imagery is that of athletics and not of fighting in brawls. How Jesus, the Prince of Peace, came to throw not peace but a sword upon earth is explained by the author under Matt. 10:34-36 and likewise has nothing to do with boisterous altercations. Note the present infinitive: "must not be engaging in battles." This negative is again only introductory (as in v. 22), a foil to four positive items.

On the contrary (ἀλλά), "gentle must he be" as Paul, Timothy, Silvanus say they were gentle with the Thessalonians (I Thess. 2:7); in fact, gentle "toward all," thus broadening out beyond the members of the church. The Lord's slave refers especially to the called ministers and leaders, all of whom are missionaries, their great work is that of the Lord himself, namely winning people for salvation. Fighting never won a convert or corrected a member of the church; but the very character of the Lord's slave is marked by the pursuit of peace (v. 22). With this harmonizes "apt to teach," to explain, instruct, make clear the Word, the same qualification that is stated in I Tim. 3:2.

The same is true with regard to the next term which is even stronger than patient: "putting up with what is bad" in those with whom he deals, for not a few will at first act badly enough. Finally, "in meekness (without pride or arrogant airs) educating (note 'uneducated' in v. 23) those placing themselves in opposition" and by this means winning them away from their hostility, whether they be foolish, misled church members or outsiders.

This is, indeed, a picture of a true slave of the Lord in all his work for the church. But one should not strain these words and make a soft jellyfish out of the Lord's slave, a man who could not preach Matt. 23:13-39 or any of the stern texts found in the prophets. To wield the law is to strike with a hammer and no less.

25) "If, perhaps, (μήποτε R. 988) God may get to give them repentance for realization of truth" — note the force of the aorist: "get to give" by the means thus employed. The thought is not that God ever withholds repentance, but that men so often refuse to accept it. On repentance see the verb in Matt. 3:2, and Acts 2:38, the noun in Luke 3:3. Although it is seldom found in Paul's letters, this is one of the great cardinal terms of the Scriptures, the inner change of the heart when turning from sin and guilt to cleansing and forgiveness in God's grace. "May give" is full of this grace. Here repentance is amplified by "for realization of truth," for true heart knowledge, for such realization is ever the attainment of repentance. See further in I Tim. 2:4.

Texts, texts critics and editors, grammarians, and then commentators differ as to whether to read the

aorist optative or the aorist subjunctive for "may get
to give." In our opinion, since the original uncials do
not indicate the iota subscript, it is useless to insist
on the optative despite the texts that place an iota
under ω and the few examples of a similar construction. The second verb (v. 26) is an unquestioned subjunctive, and although it is used with a different subject it has the identical construction.

26) "And they get back to soberness (the same
aoristic force) out of the devil's snare" adds to God's
act of giving the effect produced upon those receiving
the gift. There is no mixing of figures between sobering up and getting out of a snare. There is a most
telling combination: like blind drunkards these people
got caught in the devil's snare and then, of course,
drunk as they were, could never get out of it. But
repentance and a realization of the truth mean complete sobering up, and so this, indeed, takes them out
of the devil's snare. Comparing I Tim. 3:7, we take it
that these are people who, after becoming Christians,
got caught in the devil's snare by being misled as v.
18 indicates. Proper treatment and careful teaching
and education may rescue them.

If Paul had stopped at this point, much ink would
have been saved, but he added the perfect participle
and two pronouns αὐτοῦ and ἐκείνου, and this divides the
commentators into three groups: 1) caught alive by
the devil for the devil's will (A. V.); 2) caught alive
by God (or by the Lord's slave) for God's will; 3) captured alive by the devil — the last phrase: "for God's
will" is then thought to modify the whole clause: "so-
bered up again . . . for God's will."

For ourselves several points are decisive. First,
θέλημα is used *ueberwiegend von Gott (Christus), . . .
in der Regel vom Wollen Gottes (Christi)*, B.-P. 553.
The A. V.'s: "at his (the devil's) will," is wrong in
regard to both pronoun and preposition. We should

translate: "for that One's (God's) will." Secondly,
some think that "snare" and "being taken alive" naturally go together, for does a snare not capture alive?
So they regard ὑπ' αὐτοῦ = by the devil. But this disregards the perfect tense of the participle; it should
then be the aorist. Is this not one of Paul's striking
paradoxes, an oxymoron: "the devil's snare," and set
over against it "having been and remaining captured
alive by him" (God)? The devil's snare does *not* catch
alive, it always implies spiritual death; or, if you will,
when his net closes, the devil hits his victim on the
head. God catches alive so that *his* catch remains
alive. One should not disregard this perfect participle: a recent past being caught alive and so remaining caught and alive. Is that not what the gospel does?

So we see why αὐτοῦ, which refers to God, occurs in
the last phrase and is properly followed by ἐκείνου and
not merely by another αὐτοῦ. This last pronoun is very
emphatic because it repeats the first: "caught alive by
him (who alone ever so catches and holds men) for
that One's will (who alone so catches)." Yes, "if perhaps," such a result is achieved; out of the devil's
snare (negative) and caught alive to remain so by
God and for *his* will, it would be a blessed result. To
aid in this, by acting as Paul says, means that any
Lord's slave is no less than a golden instrument, well
serving the Master's use, prepared for every good
work, an instrument for honor, to be highly valued
(v. 20, 21).

CHAPTER III

Know What Is Coming and Remain in What Thou Hast Learned

Grievous Periods of Time Will Come

1) The prophecy presented here is the same as that written in I Tim. 4:1-3, but it is fuller in every way. In both passages, as in II Thess. 2:3, etc., Paul speaks by revelation and does not offer deductions of his own. Paul's prophecy agrees with that spoken by Jesus in Matt. 24:11, 12 and yet it is not a mere repetition. There has been repeated fulfillment, and it is now in progress of fulfillment.

Paul prepares and fortifies Timothy. Paul now knows that his own life shall end soon. How much Timothy may have to face is not revealed, nor how long "the last days" until the Lord's Parousia will continue. The one thing revealed is the grievousness of what is in store. During Paul's own time errorists had arisen in the churches of his founding, foolish fanatics were disturbing the Christians in the province of Asia where Timothy was stationed. Worse times are impending, within the church and without it. The revelations Paul has received are God's advance warnings to fortify his ministers and their churches. Paul, approaching his end, is passing these warnings on.

Paul proves himself a prophet and thus refutes the statement made by some that he did not possess the gift of prophecy. See I Tim. 4:1, also II Thess. 2:2.

Now this realize, that in the last days there shall be present grievous seasons. For there shall be men (who are) self-lovers, money-lovers, boasters, haughty, blasphemers, disobedient to parents, un-

(819)

grateful, impious, devoid of natural affection, held by no truce, slanderers, uncontrolled, untamed, no lovers of good, traitors, headstrong, puffed up, pleasure-lovers rather than God-lovers, having a formation of godliness but having denied the power thereof: and from these turn thyself away!

Δέ is merely transitional. Paul does not use the verb οἶδα which means to know intellectually but employs γινώσκω which means to know as something that affects Timothy and toward which he must assume a personal attitude; see 1:12, 18 regarding the difference. The present imperative bids Timothy ever to realize what Paul states here. Note that Paul says: "In the last days there shall be present seasons grievous," i. e., within the longer period denominated "the last days" (no article is needed in the Greek) various short periods (καιροί) shall occur, and these shall be "grievous" or hard to be endured. "The last days" refer to the whole time from the completion of Christ's redemptive work until his Parousia; that a part of these days was already past when Paul wrote is, of course, self-evident. Within the rest of these last days of the world the grievous seasons shall appear. The last days are not those few that occur immediately before the end. In I Tim. 4:1 "the later seasons" are quite the same as the grievous seasons of our passage. A καιρός always bears a special stamp, something that differentiates it as a "season." Here it is the grievousness, the painfulness for Christians. Ἐνίστημι means "to stand right there"; in II Thess. 2:2 this precise meaning is important, see the discussion.

2) The seasons will be so grievous because of "the people" that live in them, οἱ ἄνθρωποι; their presence causes all this grievousness. By calling them "human beings" Paul refers to the people generally; the world is full of these vicious people, the church is surrounded by them, often invaded by them, and has a hard time

of it because of them (note v. 6-8). The description
is couched in predicative terms throughout, yet it is
certainly not a jumble to resemble the motley mass, as
has been thought, but an orderly survey. Paul is not
dividing these people into so many groups, for these
groups would always run together like liquids. The
sins indicated appear in the men who are living during these seasons, in some men some of these sins are
outstanding, in others, others of these sins; it is so in
Rom. 1:29-31, which list is similar.

We count eighteen specifications, five at the beginning, three at the end, twelve (three fours) between.
One may debate about the division, yet we think that
"disobedient to parents" begins a new group, that the
first five thus belong together, and that the next twelve
may be divided into three fours, which leaves the last
three that evidently belong together. Rhetorically five
represents half of what might be said in the way of
entire completeness (ten). The floodgates then open
and three fours are poured out, each four being a
minor completeness; the final three (if we call them
three) are the climax of the whole list, which at the
end deals with God.

"Self-lovers" properly heads the list and is balanced at the end by "pleasure-lovers rather than God-
lovers." *Self — not God;* the whole chain swings between these two. "Self-lovers, silver (money)-lovers"
constitute a pair. Selfishness, which is evidenced by
love of money, the means for gratifying what self
wants, this is the mark of people, but it is developed
to huge proportions.

Thus "boasters" (noun), bragging about self, and,
companion to this, "haughty" (adjective), overbearing
toward others. These two pairs are topped by "blasphemers" (adjective), not "railers" (R. V.) against
men; they are so haughty as to rail against God and
against men. With this fifth item a sort of climax is
reached. These five are also broad characterizations

so that Paul halts and then continues with more specific terms.

Men start young to be "to parents disobedient" (Rom. 1:30), to parents, whom God has placed over their children, whose very flesh and blood the children are, from whom the children receive countless benefactions. This is the frightful signature of our present time. "Ungrateful" for kindness and benefits received pairs well with disobedience. Ἀνόσιοι are "impious," who respect and revere nothing that is sacred.

3) "Without natural affection" (Rom. 1:31). The Greek word is derived from "love" in the sense of natural attachment which is seen even in brutes. Even this has disappeared. Hence ἄσπονδοι, "making no truce" to end a state of war (Trench), thus "implacable." Five terms in a series, all with a *privativum*. Next in line in this viciousness are "slanderers" who spread evil reports and invent them: then "uncontrolled," nothing holding them in check; "untamed" and fierce like wild beasts, restrained by nothing; and a third *a* term: "non-lovers of good," without love of anything good (beneficial) to others. But this term introduces the third quartet although its form links it to the second.

4) Without love for anything beneficially good; we see also the extreme of this, namely "traitors," betrayers, who repeat the act of Judas. Next, "headstrong" (literally, such as fall forward), rash, plunging ahead without thought. "Puffed up" (perfect participle with present continuousness) as knowing it all (see I Tim. 3:6). This rounds out the quartet.

5) As was the case in v. 2, we now at the end have two "lover" terms, but they are not companions as they were in v. 2; these are opposites and thus form a unit as ending the list. The two are tied together: "pleasure-lovers rather than God-lovers," the participle stating what their religion is. "Rather" means that in place of a love and liking for God, a love and liking for

pleasure, their own pleasure as they want it, wholly control them. Beyond all question that is the mark of the world of men today. How it invades the membership of the church we see on every hand.

"Having the formation (μόρφωσις) of godliness," a formation that looks as though it corresponds to the essence, "but the power thereof having denied," concludes the picture of the people living during these periods. Some think that these people are Christians and thus refer the entire list to the people in the church despite the great difficulties that then ensue. For a church that is composed of such people would certainly be no church in any sense of the term. This is a description of people generally, but these strongly affect the church and contaminate its membership. Today we see this formation of godliness (an expression like that used in Rom. 2:20) in many churches, in Catholicism, modernism, the heretical sects like Christian Science, Russellism, etc. In so-called Christian lands the world, too, adopts many Christian forms in its lodgism, in having prayers offered on all sorts of occasions, in talking about God, religion, morality. But where is "the power thereof," the divine, spiritual, regenerating, renewing, saving power of Christ and the true gospel? Totally absent. And this emptiness of power threatens the true churches and their members on all sides. Note the perfect tense: "having denied" and still continuing their denial. "When the Son of man cometh shall he find faith on the earth?" Luke 18:8.

"And" links the imperative with the one used in v. 1: "Keep realizing . . . and keep turning away from these!" Constant turning away is the only course of safety but it must be coupled with the realization of what such people are and of what a danger they constitute for us.

6) "Keep turning away from these!" means when these appear in the future regarding which Paul is

warning Timothy. This injunction cannot be separated from v. 1, etc., which deals with the future, nor can v. 6, etc., and the particular kind of people here described be placed into the present as though they were already at work in the neighborhood of Timothy. Paul's prophetic description does not come to a conclusion immediately before this injunction, for this itself points back to "these," the ἄνθρωποι just described; and v. 6 adds a further description of some who belong to "these," namely the ones who are most dangerous for Christians in the time periods to come. And this description plainly marks them in advance for Timothy. "For" is frequently used to specify by introducing an example after a summary statement. In v. 2-5 we have all of them, now we have a particular kind. The astonishing thing is that to this day we see Paul's prophecy being fulfilled over and over again.

To these belong those sneaking into the houses and leading captive silly women heaped with sins, led by motley lusts, ever learning and never able to come to truth's realization; in what manner, moreover, Jannes and Jambres withstood Moses. Thus also these withstand on their part the truth, men corrupted as to their minds, not standing the test in regard to the faith.

"Of these are" is the Greek idiom for "to these belong," or "some of these are they who," etc. In Paul's time the Roman world was full of religious charlatans and quacks, but these attached themselves to prominent men and did not operate with a following of female dupes. Thus Elymas had duped Sergius Paulus (Acts 13:7); Simon had a large following in Samaria (Acts 8:9); we may, perhaps, also mention the sons of Sceva (Acts 19:13, 14). The future charlatans make women their specialty. "They insinuate themselves into houses and lead captive little women, γυναικάρια, *Weiblein*," the neuter diminutive being used in a contemptuous way, which is expressed in our versions by the addition of the word "silly."

Four descriptive participles picture this type of women: "having been heaped with sins" (this verb is found also in Rom. 12:20) and thus now being in this condition. We should not be hasty in accusing these women of sexual sins. These women are uneasy about many kinds of sins; they have a religious bent and are thus susceptible to quacks who come to them with their panacea. Nor are these Christian women. For the most part they are not Christian; some may be attached to Christian congregations, but these gentlemen browse in wide pastures. Women of this kind do not feel comfortable in churches where true repentance is preached as the cure for sins.

Moreover, these women are described as "being led by motley lusts," varicolored sinful desires from which they do not care to free themselves. Again we should not restrict this to sexual desires. Some of them are rich and prominent; they also run after these deceivers and lionize them. Paul says that they are literally being taken as war-captives, are being held in thrall. The fact that a certain class of men is also captured goes without saying, but the notable thing is that these charlatans secure silly women as their dupes.

7) Ever learning, they are yet never able to come to realization of truth. Although they meet with the real gospel truth they find it unpalatable. Yet they are avid for learning. The fancied wisdom of "new truth," odd and pretentious inner wisdom and all the stock-in-trade of spurious religionists, attract them. So they are ever learning and never learn anything real in the way of truth.

We quote Jerome: "Simon Magus founded his heresy aided by the help of the strumpet Helena; Nicolaus Antiochenus, founder of all impurities, led a feminine bevy; Marcion also sent a woman ahead for greater excess; Apelles had Philomone as a companion; Montanus corrupted Prisca and Maximilla at first with gold, then polluted them with heresy; Arius, when he deceived the world, first deceived the sister of the ruler; Donatus was aided by the resources of Lucilla; blind Agape led blind Elpidius; Priscillianus was joined by Galla." We are unable to say how much dependence can be placed on this rather startling list. It can be put into the shade by modern instances. R., W. P., points to only two: the notorious Schweinfurth of some forty years ago with his "heavenly harem" in Illinois and the "House of David" exposed in the courts of Michigan. He might have added Brigham Young with his Mormon polygamy.

These are, however, the extreme cases. Much more to the point are the "religious cults" that purvey East Indian and other mysterious mysteries of the mystic order that are so attractive to wealthy ladies who lionize their leaders, and the proselyting heretical sects who make a specialty of creeping especially into Christian houses to make converts chiefly among religiously inclined women and actually winning so many. Kretzmann pictures them as smooth, slick-talking religious agents with ingratiating, clinging methods, insidiously introducing themselves, often as fatherly confessor brothers with a high-grade spirituality and great sanctity, actually taking such women captive body and soul. Women are their special prey. Paul certainly prophesied truly. Such periods have come only too often.

8) In ὅν τρόπον, the adverbial accusative, the antecedent is combined with the relative: "in what manner," and δέ = "moreover." These two Egyptian charlatans are not mentioned because of their pretended miracles, nor because they, too, were surrounded with silly women but because of their "withstanding" Moses, the verb even being repeated: "they withstood Moses, thus also these withstand on their part (middle voice)

the truth"; it is the same verb that is used in Acts 13:8 when Elymas "withstood" Paul.

The fact that Paul mentions the names of these Egyptian sorcerers deflects some commentators into a discussion as to how Paul knew these names. The point is the fact that these two men illustrate the enormity of the crime that all these deceivers commit. Jannes and Jambres withstood God's own servant Moses when they helped to harden Pharaoh's heart against the voice of God; οὕτως καὶ οὗτοι, *"thus* also *these,"* in exactly the same way oppose themselves to the truth by hardening the hearts of their perverts against the blessed saving truth. For this reason all of these belong in the same class with these two Egyptians.

They do the same kind of *work,* and they are of the same *character*: "men corrupted as to the mind," etc. The perfect participle indicates that the corruption began in the past and extends into the present; the passive points to the devil as having corrupted them. We need not supplement Paul's psychology and let "the mind" include the heart; the mind is the one avenue through which the truth reaches the heart (the inner personality, the ἐγώ, the will). If that avenue is corrupted, the truth cannot get through, cannot even reach the heart to cleanse and to free it. Whoever has dealt with such minds knows that they react to the truth with the most pernicious objections to every part of it; they often also become blasphemous. The passive retains the accusative which was found in the active.

᾽Αδόκιμοι means that, when they are tested in regard to the faith, they are found to be coins of base metal that must be discarded. Here, too, "the faith" is objective, *quae creditur.* They pretend to bring the true doctrine, "the truth," claim that *they* have the pure gold to offer, that the church and its true ministers have falsified the doctrine. In this way they win adherents and prove dangerous to Christians. This is the great reason for Paul's prophetic warning.

Some regard this as a reference to subjective faith and say that this is absent from the hearts of these men. But the Lord has not called us to look into men's hearts, he has not supplied us with a touchstone that may be applied to their hearts. He has supplied us with his Word, thereby to test all that men offer as "the faith" or doctrine. When they oppose this truth and this true doctrine they stand ἀδόκιμοι, "rejected," which completely settles their case. It is easy to apply this test; every test of the heart is impossible and is based entirely on inference. When a man is unsound as to the doctrine, we need no further witness. The fact that he cannot in his own heart be a believer is evident; yet this judgment we are ever to leave with the Heart-knower (καρδιογνώστης, Acts 1:24; 15:8) who has reserved this matter for his own judgment.

Where did Paul get the names "Jannes and Jambres"? From Jewish tradition; from the same source from which Stephen had obtained certain items of his address. This tradition preserved a number of correct facts that were not embodied in the Old Testament record. Certain sections of the genealogies recorded in Matthew and in Luke were obtained from this source. This question presents no difficulty. But this should be added: the Holy Spirit governed the New Testament writers and Stephen (who was filled with the Holy Spirit, Acts 6:5, 8, 15) so that they took only facts from this source and no fictions.

Additional information is given about these sorcerers in Jewish tradition, but whether it is correct or not does not concern us, for Paul did not use it, he recorded only the names. This shows the working of divine inspiration. We should not confuse this with revelation and say that the Spirit gave these names to Paul by direct revelation. In thousands of matters (take the genealogies) the knowledge of these was obtained in the natural way, but inspiration controlled the amount of information to be used, the manner of using it, and guarded against using anything wrong or mistaken.

Linguists study these names in order to arrive at their possible Egyptian etymology, etc. Whether this can be traced or not is problematic; nothing worthwhile has thus far been discovered. We do not know whether Jannes and Jambres (the form in which Paul has these names) were native Egyptians or foreigners; if they were the latter, it is wholly unlikely that they were Israelites or bore Jewish names as some have conjectured.

9) **But they shall not proceed farther,** namely farther than the success already indicated by their insinuating themselves into the houses, etc. Their vogue lasts only for one of the grievous "seasons" mentioned in v. 1 although such seasons will follow each other "in the last days" (the New Testament times). Why these men have only their season and then play out is added: **For their folly shall be fully manifest** ($\check{\epsilon}\kappa\delta\eta\lambda o\varsigma$) **to all even also as that of those got to be,** namely that of Jannes and Jambres. They deceived Pharaoh and the Egyptians for a long time, but when Moses came, they were fully exposed. Elymas had deceived Sergius Paulus perhaps for years, then his deceit was exposed. Acts 8:11 mentions the "long time" during which Simon played his role in Samaria, but it, too, ended. They have their day. It is often only a brief one, at times it continues for a rather long time. Their ἄνοια, lack of mind and good sense, will sooner or later become apparent "to all" — which means not merely "to all who are especially concerned," namely true Christians, but to men generally even as the senselessness of Jannes and Jambres got

to be (historical aorist, ingressive) fully apparent, not only to the Israelites, but to the Egyptians as well.

Even the two future tenses show that this is prophecy. Why, then, advance the idea that Paul is speaking only about deceivers who were working at that time? The main object of this statement is not comfort for Timothy and the Christians. This exposure of folly exposes in advance, by prophecy, what these deceivers really are, namely men who deal only in folly. Many, often all, of their dupes will eventually see that they have allowed themselves to be fooled. Paul's chief object is to fortify in advance.

Timothy's Faithful Stand with Paul in the Past

10) Paul will soon be dead. In this testament of his to Timothy he thus reminds Timothy of the past. **Thou, however, thou didst follow my teaching, my conduct, my purpose, my faith, my long-suffering, my love, my perseverance, my persecutions, my sufferings; what kind of things occurred to me in Antioch, in Iconium, in Lystra; what kind of persecutions I bore (up) under — and out of them all the Lord rescued me.**

By no means let the profound feeling underlying these words escape the calm reader of today. The heart that wrote these lines, and the heart that first read them were stirred with repressed tears. Just a few lines, but oh, how much they call to mind! They present practically all of Paul's labor as an apostle and all that was intertwined with it, namely Timothy's labor and life as the apostle's disciple and more than a disciple. We are gripped when we read this today. Paul is a master in concentration, and here it is that of restraint; the effect is to grip as with one strong grasp.

Σὺ δέ, and again σὺ δέ in v. 14, are always emphatic,
and here they occur twice at the beginning of two sentences; "*Thou,* however, *thou* didst follow" in extreme
contrast to the people mentioned in v. 2-8. "Follow"
is the only proper word. Paul led, Timothy followed:
apostle and disciple — father and child beloved (1:1)
— leader and companion, associate, assistant — head
and guide to inspire, direct, and lend courage — example and friend with whom ever to clasp hands — foremost to bear the brunt and never flinching or uttering
complaint, ever noble, true, unconquered, and Timothy
ever at his side. Yes, "*thou,* thou didst follow!"

The aorist is the proper tense because it presents
the great historical past and that alone. Some texts
substitute the perfect because they think that the
present connotation should be added. All four aorists
look back to the past only even as Paul knows that he
is now close to the end. This is a constative aorist:
it includes *all* of Timothy's following during the *entire*
past and it stops with that as constituting one grand,
unalterable fact: "thou didst follow." Why should
anyone regard this as an ingressive aorist: "thou didst
start to follow"? Look at the nine dative objects
which cover the whole of Paul's career and not only
the first part of it. Credit and honor to Timothy, not
for making a beginning, but for his entire past noble
following.

The nine items are in proper order, each item just
where it belongs: teaching, conduct, purpose — faith,
longsuffering — love, perseverance — persecutions,
sufferings; two threes; the second three being a pair
each; the second three emphasizing the first three. On
the "teaching" rest Paul's "faith and longsuffering" —
on his "conduct" rest his "love and perseverance" —
on his "purpose" all that resulted from putting it into
effect, all the "persecutions and sufferings," and these
are necessarily plurals. All have their articles so that
"my" is to be repeated with each one in turn, so that

each one stands out by itself (this touch is lost in our versions).

"My teaching" is the basis and ground of all else for Paul and for Timothy. Teaching is done by word of mouth, hence next in order is "my conduct"; Timothy followed Paul's conduct in his own conduct. Basic in the case of both teaching and conduct is "my purpose" which Timothy also followed. In a way the purpose controlled, in another it crowned the teaching and the conduct.

"My teaching" was intended to engender faith in others, this being "my purpose"; but "my faith" refers to Paul's own faith in his own teaching. What he taught others to believe he himself believed, and Timothy followed him in this respect. In order to indicate that "my faith" is linked with "my teaching," "my faith" is paired with "my longsuffering," for this is the quality needed when teaching others to believe: the mind must hold out long until the fruit comes. Some foreign missionaries taught and taught for years until the ice was finally broken. In this, too, Timothy had followed Paul. So "my faith, my longsuffering" build on "my teaching."

"My love" builds on "my conduct," for intelligent, purposeful ἀγάπη animated all Paul's conduct. With it goes "my perseverance," ὑπομονή, the brave patience which "remains under" all difficulties undismayed, not giving up, making "love" so strong for gaining its object. These two accompanied Paul's "conduct," and Timothy followed both.

Equally "my persecution, my sufferings" rest on "my purpose," for the prosecution and attainment of Paul's apostolic "purpose" involved for him so much persecution, so much personal suffering, and, crown of nobility, Timothy followed also these. So on each of the first three are built a pair of the next three which are pairs. "Thou didst follow" credits all nine also to Pauls beloved Timothy.

11) Two qualitative clauses follow: "what kind of things occurred to me (again constative historical aorist) in Antioch, in Iconium, in Lystra," and specifying still more closely: "what kind of persecutions I bore (up) under." Read Acts 13:50; 14:5, 6; 14:19, 20. Neither the first nor the last nor the two clauses together are exclamatory. This is evident from their relation, for οἷα, "what kind of things occurred" is indefinite, and οἵους διωγμούς, "what kind of persecutions I bore up under" adds definiteness. Both clauses amplify "my persecutions, my sufferings" by first referring to definite places and then to the persecutions here endured. Yet the qualitative relatives convey the thought that these were "of a kind" with many others that followed elsewhere and later. Paul mentions these three places because they were located in Timothy's home province Galatia, Lystra being Timothy's home town. The masculine οἵους has this gender only because of διωγμούς. Because these two clauses *might* be questions if they stood alone is not sufficient reason to suppose that they are indirect questions; cf., R. 731. If they stood alone they *might* also be exclamatory. But they do not appear separate and alone, for they continue verse 10.

We do not regard καί as the "and" of contrast: "and yet." This "and" is richer: " — and (as normal, as was to be expected, as thus properly completing this kind of a thing) out of them all rescue me did the Lord." The subject and the predicate are transposed, and thus both are emphatic: *this* is what the Lord did, this is, indeed, what *he* did. Timothy saw and knew all of it at the time, and such things in Paul's past life and work he followed.

12) All this has not been strange and exceptional. **Also all, moreover, who intend to live godly in Christ Jesus shall be persecuted** even though they are not apostles or assistants of an apostle. See what Paul said to those in Lystra, Iconium, and Antioch im-

mediately after he had had these experiences, Acts
14:22. The emphasis is to be placed on "all" (not only
Paul and Timothy) and on the verb: "shall be persecuted." Θέλω is often used with reference to the will
which intends, βούλομαι even more so. Some regard the
adverb as being emphatic: "who will to live *godly* in
Christ Jesus," and refer to others who only persuade
themselves that they are living in Christ Jesus. This
emphasis is misplaced, and the implied contrast unlikely; for "to live godly in connection with Christ
Jesus" is one concept.

13) **Wicked men, however, and imposters shall
progress to the worse, deceiving and being deceived.**
There is a contrast in δέ. "Wicked men and imposters" are the opposite of "all those who intend to
live in a godly way in Christ Jesus," and while the latter are bound to be persecuted and in this way have
much to endure, the former are bound to progress to
what is worse than their wickedness, a million times
worse than that which the godly experience in the way
of persecution. "Wicked men" are those described in
v. 2-5, and "imposters" those described in v. 6-9. They
are aptly called γόητες, "sorceres," in allusion to Jannes
and Jambres who were both sorcerers and imposters.
Incidentally, we see that what they did before Pharaoh
was nothing supernatural. The Germans have retained the word *Goët* as a synonym for *Gaukler*.

In v. 9 the imposters *"shall not* proceed farther,"
i. e., get very far before they are exposed. There Paul
refers to the success of their methods. Now Paul says
they *"shall* proceed to the worse," but he means shall
proceed inwardly; they shall degenerate more and
more. To say that they shall succeed in getting an
ever greater following *"but"* to the worse, is to give
Paul's thought a direction that he did not intend. Wickedness grows and grows and ever tends toward the
worse; imposture, too, grows through what it feeds

upon and also tends to the worse. To the double subject: "wicked men and imposters," both of whom are
bound to progress toward the worse, a double predication is added: "deceiving and being deceived." This is
placed chiastically: on the outside "wicked men — being deceived"; on the inside "imposters — deceiving."
Because this rhetorical placement of the terms is overlooked some have difficulty in understanding what Paul
means.

The moment we understand this we shall see that
this verse completes the paragraph and we shall not
adopt the suggestion that v. 13 introduces the following paragraph.

Timothy's Future Stand Is to Be True to His Childhood Past

14) Once more, as in v. 10, Paul writes σὺ δέ, but
now not with an indicative aorist to indicate the
definite historical past but with a present imperative
that reaches from the present into the far future.
**Thou, however, do thou (ever) remain in the things
thou didst learn and wast assured of, knowing from
whom thou didst learn them, namely that from a babe
thou dost know sacred letters, those able to make
thee wise for salvation through faith, that in Christ
Jesus.**
Like one who is parting from his beloved disciple,
Paul says: "be remaining, be abiding in the things thou
didst learn," and didst not only learn so as to become
acquainted with — more than that: "and wast assured
of," wast made inwardly certain of. The English
would prefer to use perfect tenses; the Greek aorists
intend to state the past facts simply as facts: Timothy
did learn these things, he did become fully convinced
of the truth of these things. He was, of course,
brought to believe them and in them (πιστεύω); but
Paul uses the word πιστόω, "to make firm, trustworthy,"

and puts it into the passive: "in which things thou
didst get conviction and firm assurance as to their
being altogether true and reliable."

This second thought is the main point. One may
learn things and yet know that they are not really
true or that they are at least doubtful. Although they
have been studied and learned, one is not convinced in
regard to such things, is not brought to firm personal
assurance and certainty; he places a question mark
after them, does not build on them. Timothy was convinced, was certain of the truth of what he had
learned. The two aorists state historical past facts,
both are constative; they do not, however, state how
far back this constative force reaches and how much
past time it covers. These points are made clear by the
context which extends back to Timothy's earliest childhood and reaches to the present moment in which he
is asked ever to remain in these things since he knows
even at this moment from whom he received these
things. Timothy knows their source; this source has
produced his personal conviction and assurance in the
past. Since he knows this source now (εἰδώς, second
perfect participle, which is always used in the present
sense), Paul asks Timothy ever to abide in these things
with firm assurance.

The participle is causal: "since thou knowest"; it
is present and states the reason for the present imperative, for Timothy's ever remaining in these things.
What is meant by "these things" is stated fully in the
following. These things are themselves such as produce the firmest conviction as to their truth and their
reliability. Here this is not, however, yet touched
upon; here the main point is the fact that the source of
these things makes them reliable and assured. Where
did Timothy learn them? Does he know now, today,
that the source is wholly reliable? It certainly is.
Παρὰ τίνων ἔμαθες is an indirect question. Note the inter-
rogatory word τίνων; Paul does not write the relative ὧν.

A few texts have the singular παρὰ τίνος. This singular is an emendation that was made on the supposition that Timothy learned "these things" from Paul. How incorrect this is the very next clause shows which states that Timothy knows the source of these things from his early childhood. Nor is Paul repeating what he has already said in v. 10: "thou didst follow my teaching." Paul is advancing beyond that, to a time long before Timothy ever saw Paul.

If παρά with the genitive were not almost universally used with reference to persons, we should regard τίνων as the neuter plural interrogative pronoun, neuter because of the following neuter ἱερὰ γράμματα. But B.-D. 971 knows of only one instance where παρά is followed by a neuter. Timothy learned these things from his mother and his grandmother, but the next clause brings out the fact that not these beloved persons but "the sacred letters" were the authority that made Timothy so certain of "these things."

15) This is the inner reason that καὶ ὅτι is epexegetical and not causal. Some regard ὅτι as causal: "and because thou knowest." This makes the clause parallel to and coordinate with the causal εἰδώς clause, i. e., it is the second reason that Timothy should remain in these things which he did learn. It is usually said that Paul does not continue with a second participle because he wants to make this statement stronger. He does indeed, but in a different way. Timothy's remaining in what he has learned is by no means to be caused by his knowing that he learned these things from his mother and his grandmother and then secondly because he knows the Scriptures. Why were Timothy's mother and his grandmother such great authorities? Where does Paul ever make human beings the authority for our assurance? If Lois and Eunice are to be reduced to minor authorities, how does it come that a man like Paul gives the first, the major place to this participial minor authority? Children do

receive the Word from and on the authority of parents, but intelligent parents always lead their children to rest their faith independently upon the Word and not upon them as parents.

Our versions are correct. They correct Luther's *weil* and translate: "and that thou knowest," which is epexegetical: "namely that," etc. Timothy learned these things from his mother and his grandmother and knew who they were; but the main point is that from early childhood these dear persons led him to know sacred letters, the divine source of all spiritual wisdom.

No greater mistake can be made than to ground any child's faith on parents. Soon they grow up and reason: Jewish children are Jews only because they believe what their parents taught them; Mohammedans likewise; and so the world over — we, too. If we had had other parents, our faith would be according. For this reason so many Christian young people lose their childhood faith. Not so does Paul point to Timothy's mother and his grandmother. Not so does he ever point to his own person. Look at Acts 17:11, at the Bereans who go to the Scriptures to see whether the things Paul is offering them are true. "Namely that from a babe thou knowest (extensive present) sacred letters." In these Timothy was taught by Lois and by Eunice, in these his assurance was made to rest with all firmness. Well may Paul say: "Ever remain in the things thou hast thus learned from thy mother and thy grandmother."

As is well known, βρέφος denotes even a child in the womb (Luke 1:41, with plenty of examples in B.-P. 231); it next denotes a suckling (papyri, etc.) ; next, a tiny child; here, "from a babe or infant." The textual authority for and against the article with ἱερὰ γράμματα is about equal, and no inner reason decides either way. If it is allowed, the article makes the sacred letters definite; if it is omitted, their quality is stressed. The claim that the presence of the article assures us that only the canonical writings are referred to, cannot be upheld if it is thought that its omission would mean that the Old Testament apocrypha are also to be included. The current LXX included the apocrypha. But at this time Timothy was a little boy. He learned the main things, he did not master the whole Old Testament canon.

Purposely Paul does not say Ἅγιαι γραφαί, "Holy Scriptures," but γράμματα, "letters," "script." Little Timothy learned his ABC's from the Bible, learned to read from the Bible, and thus from earliest childhood spelled out "sacred letters." As he spelled out this and that word, mother and grandmother told the story. Soon he could read a little, ask questions, hear more. A lovely picture indeed! I like it better than our method of today which supplies secular matter for the primers and holds back the sacred letters until later years. *Gramma* is just a written character; the plural, many of them as they make written words and thus convey sense.

Paul makes them definite enough when he adds the article with the attributive participle: "those able to make thee wise for salvation through faith," and then adds another article: "that (faith which is) in connection with Christ Jesus," a connection we all know, namely faith's receiving Christ and then trustfully embracing him. Not because Jews as Jews considered these writings "sacred" does Paul praise what Timothy learned out of them from infancy; but because, apart from Jews, these writings as such contain the power to make one who knows them wise, etc. Note that the intellectual apprehension (οἶδα, see 1:12) is not already saving wisdom but the avenue to such wisdom, which is inner spiritual apprehension, saving knowledge put to saving use for actual salvation. Little Timothy was a half-Jew, but let us not forget John 5:39 and the fact that through the Scriptures the true Jewish believers believed in the promised Messiah and were thus

saved. On this subject see the remarks on 1:5. Paul
uses the New Testament wording: "for salvation
through faith, the (faith) in Christ Jesus" (we read
this as a unit), for he says "thou knowest" and speaks
to Timothy whose knowledge and whose faith have
been advanced by the New Testament gospel that revealed Jesus as the Messiah.

16) To the subjective statements that are appended to the admonition occurring in v. 15 Paul adds
an objective statement. Apart from Timothy and
what the Scriptures are able to do for him, as divinely
inspired writings they are also *eo ipso* profitable in all
spiritual directions. This is the objective fact that
underlies what is said with regard to Timothy's abiding in the Scripture knowledge for his salvation by
faith. Here we have another sample of how Paul always penetrates clear through with his thought. Many
a writer would have stopped at the end of v. 15; Paul
adds what is really the main thing.

**All Scripture inspired of God (is) also profitable
for teaching, for refutation, for restoration, for
education, the (education) in righteousness, so that
the man of God may be fit as having been fully fitted
for every good work.** We may, however, just as well
translate: **Every Scripture is inspired of God and
(is) profitable, etc.** The one is just as correct as
the other as far as the Greek is concerned; and the
meaning is exactly the same save for the insignificant
shifting of the copula. This is insignificant because
θεόπνευστος is predicative even when the copula is placed
after it. Wherever the copula is placed, the thought is
that, because the Scripture is God-inspired, therefore
it is profitable for all that is said. In v. 15 we have
only the making wise for salvation (effective aorist
infinitive) ; now all this wisdom is spread out in four
great phrases.

The Scripture is thus absolutely incomparable; no other book, library, or anything else in the world is able to make a lost sinner wise for salvation; no other Scripture, since it lacks inspiration of God whatever profit it may otherwise afford, is profitable for these ends: teaching us the true saving facts — refuting the lies and the delusions that deny these facts — restoring the sinner or fallen Christian to an upright position — educating, training, disciplining one in genuine righteousness. The character of the source (God-inspired) is matched by the profit produced; the profit attests the character of the source.

The assertion that the Greek compels us to translate πᾶσα γραφή "every Scripture" is untenable. The rule cited in support of this translation does not apply to abstract terms: "With the abstract word 'every' and 'all' amount practically to the same thing" (R. 772). Whatever difference the Greek felt is not expressed by our "every" and "all." If γραφή is not considered an abstract but a concrete term that denotes the well-known canon called "Scripture," then this singular is a collective, and we may translate πᾶσα either "every" or "all," the former indicating every single part of the whole, the latter just the whole as such. But expressions such as "whole or all Israel," "all or whole Jerusalem," etc., point rather to "all Scripture" (A. V.) and less to "every Scripture" (R. V.). One thing is true: this is not ἡ πᾶσα γραφή and cannot be translated "*the* whole Scripture." The New Testament uses "the Scriptures," "the Scripture," and just "Scripture" as we, too, use these three expressions.

The major question is one regarding the predicative θεόπνευστος, or call it the predicate if you prefer the translation "is inspired." Is this verbal adjective passive or is it active? So assured is the passive sense that Wohlenberg is right when he says that this needs no proof. B.-P. 556 devotes only four short lines to establish the undoubted meaning: *von Gott eingegeben, inspiriert.*

The claim is often made that θεόπνευστος is active, "breathing God," at least that it may be active and must not be passive. Why is this verbal passive beyond the shadow of a doubt? Stoeckhardt and Kretzmann collect examples of compound verbal adjectives in τος and think the passive is assured when the antepenult has the accent. Yet the passive form is not a matter of the accent. This proof is not conclusive. In such compounds the accent naturally shifts forward: τος is also naturally passive and is only a few times used with actives. We have much stronger evidence.

The proof lies in Θεός and in the verbs that are compounded with Θεός to form the verbals. Let the student take Liddell and Scott and examine the long list of "god" verbals in τος. Why are all these verbals plainly and necessarily passive? Because God alone can be *the agent!* In this multitude of verbals there appears θεόπνευστος, "God-inspired." We find only two in which God is *the object,* and even one of these is passive: θεοδήλητος, "by which the gods are injured." The other is active: θεοσύστατος, "praising God." These exceptions are not due to the accent, which is still on the antepenult; they are due to the meaning of the two verbs involved. One of these verbs still leaves us a passive verbal, and only the lone other an active.

The inspiration of the Scriptures is constantly denied, and thus efforts are made to eliminate from Scripture itself any linguistic claim to its own inspiration. Some follow the bold method: they let Paul say what he pleases, they do not believe what he says. Others that are not so bold tone down the idea of inspiration until nothing but the decorative word is left. They at least do not like to give up the word. They generally, however, speak with contempt of what they denominate "the verbal *theory* of inspiration." They propose a "theory" of a different kind, one that allows for more or less error in Holy Writ. Thus this passive verbal is made the point of attack: it cannot remain passive and mean *a Deo inspirata*, "God-inspired"; it can at most be only active and mean *Deum inspirans*, "breathing God." Human writings of godly men breathe God more or less; the Scriptures do no more.

The later German theologians especially advocate this view. For them inspiration *ist ein ueberwundener Standpunkt.* Take C.-K. 492-3, a great *Woerterbuch,* that is regarded as a real authority, yet note its claims in regard to θεόπνευστος. It first lists a number of pagan mantic and mystery terms and places θεόπνευστος among them although it is admitted that, unlike the pagan terms, it does not involve an ecstatic state. Nothing is said about the multitude of compounds with Θεός (several pages in Liddell and Scott), in particular about the verbals compounded with τος (a long array of these). Next follow citations in which passive meanings are acknowledged by C.-K.; but on the authority of Nonnus θεόπνευστος is, nevertheless, made active. Why? Because of the analogy of ἄπνευστος, "not breathing" (or "poorly breathing"), and εὔπνευστος, "well breathing," two verbals which belong to an entirely different class, two which are compounded with adverbs and not with Θεός. The final point in C.-K. is argument, namely the claim that the passive "inspired of God" does not fit γραφή, but that the active "breathing God" does fit. But this is a subjective judgment. It is met by the fact that, if breathing can be applied actively to γραφή ("Scripture"), it most certainly can be applied also passively.

The passive idea is found throughout the Scriptures. Ὑπὸ Πνεύματος Ἁγίου φερόμενοι ἐλάλησαν ἀπὸ Θεοῦ ἄνθρωποι: "No prophecy of Scripture is of one's own interpretation, for not by man's will was prophecy ever brought forth, on the contrary, *being borne along* by the Holy Spirit spoke from God (certain) men," II Pet.

1:21. As the wind wafts and bears a sailing vessel along on its course, so men spoke from God, borne along by the Holy Spirit — *passive* participle, the divine agent being expressed by the regular preposition with *passives*, ὑπό, intensified by ἀπό. Next consider the long list beginning with Matt. 1:22: "that uttered (passive) by the Lord (again ὑπό) through the prophet, saying." The Lord is the speaker, the prophet is his instrument or medium (διά). This διά recurs again and again, sometimes with the expression "the mouth of the prophet." The Old Testament reports how God communicated his messages, and how the prophets then announced them with, "thus saith the Lord" — this preamble occurring again and again. Here, in fact, is the concise Biblical definition of inspiration: *By God — through or by means of men,* first orally, then in written form. God is the full and complete agent; holy men of God are only his instruments. These are not two causes, two factors, like two horses pulling a wagon; there is one and only one moving power, the holy men *were* moved. Much more may be said. All of it, presented by Scripture, is unanimously to the same effect.

All of it presents and reveals *the fact* of inspiration, only the fact. There is no theory about it, can be none. A fact is simply to be seen as a fact and then treated as a fact and not to be dissolved into a theory. He who does the latter may lose the fact, many have already lost it.

"All Scripture" is "writing," γραφή. The pen traces words and combines these into sentences and paragraphs. These words convey the thought. Erase the words, and the thought disappears. These are not *Woerter*, vocables, but *Worte*, words expressing thoughts. This is *Verbal Inspiration*. It is before us on every written page of the Book. *There is no other divine inspiration.* The thought cannot be separated from the words which are its vehicles. To speak of an inspiration of thought that is *not* an inspiration of the words is to disregard what the Scriptures show us as a fact. Τὸ ῥηθὲν ὑπὸ τοῦ Κυρίου, "the thing that was uttered or spoken by the Lord" (Matt. 1:21), was uttered in words, Yahweh uttered them.

Were these utterances fallible, errant in any way, in any word or expression? Does Yahweh ever err? "Thy Word is truth," ἀλήθεια, John 17:17. "Which things also we speak, not in words (λόγοι) taught of human wisdom, but taught of the Spirit, combining spiritual things with spiritual words (πνευματικοῖς πνευμάτικα, *sc.* λόγοις)," I Cor. 2:13. The very *logoi* were taught by the Spirit by verbal inspiration, they are inerrant in every word unless we intend to charge the Lord and his Spirit with errancy, fallibility.

We hear the statement: That is a "theory," a "mechanical" conception which makes the writers "automatons." When did God ever have difficulty or use faulty means in conveying his thought to men? *"God-inspired"* means "breathed by God," the very word "breathed" referring to his *Pneuma.* Is that mechanical? Peter says: "borne along by the Holy *Pneuma"* like a vessel on its true course by the gentle wind. This is neither a theory nor something dead and mechanical. God made the mind and the heart of man, and his Spirit knows how to guide them. He does not move them about like blocks but fills them with light, guides them with light, guides them in word and in thought. The fathers express the simple fact: God is the *causa efficiens,* men the *causae instrumentales;* the act itself the *suggestio rerum et verborum.* Any improvement on this formulation as a correct statement of the fact that occurred we are ready to accept, but we care for no "theory" and no speculation. We who have never ourselves experienced this act of the Spirit cannot penetrate the mystery of it; we doubt whether the holy writers themselves did. God's mysteries fill the natural world, yet, while they defy penetration, we get along quite well with the undoubted facts and realities of our natural world.

The product attests its source; the effect proves its cause. The police mentioned in John 7:46 realized the deity of Jesus when they returned without arresting him and reported: "Never man spoke like this man!" So here: "Never scripture spoke like this Scripture!" The strange thing is that even those who deny its inspiration treat Holy Writ as they treat no other writing. These men still write commentaries, place every word on the *Goldwage,* write New Testament dictionaries, expend endless labors generation after generation. If we gave these men a book which they would accept as being verbally inspired, could they treat it with more minute care?

Paul sketches the tremendous effect of this God-breathed Scripture. Because it is God-inspired it is "profitable for teaching." Here there is found all that man needs to be taught and to learn to make him wise for salvation; here and nowhere else. Scripture has the whole divine truth, the entire ἀλήθεια or "reality" (John 17:17). It is profitable for ἐλεγμός, "for refutation" of every religious lie, falsehood, fiction; truth naturally destroys all these and frees from them (John 8:31, 36). Where is there another scripture that is able to do such a thing? Compare what other so-called sacred writings have done. Our versions have the word mean "reproof," and some texts, thinking of sinners who are to be convicted of sin, have ἔλεγχον: "for convicting one of his sinfulness." But this thought is expressed in the next phrase.

"For restoration," for restoring the sinner to an upright position from his fallen state, the believer who has fallen back into sin and guilt. The world is full of this profit of the God-breathed Scripture; those who have experienced this profit should see whence it came and that God inspired this Book.

Finally, "profitable for παιδεία, the education in righteousness," as a child is educated, trained, and disciplined in all righteous living. Note that δικαιοσύνη is forensic: that quality which has God's own verdict in its favor, which he as the Judge approves by his verdict (Matt. 25:34-40). Only the Scripture that is inspired of God is able to train and to educate so as to secure the favorable verdict of God. Is any other Scripture able to do this? Yes, the effect proves the cause.

17) The ἵνα clause denotes contemplated result and is to be construed with all four phrases and not merely with the last, for righteousness in life is not attained without the other three. While the four prepositions make the four phrases distinct and draw special attention to each other, their four objects are connected in the order in which they appear: teaching first — refutation of falsehood second — restoration to an upright position third — education in righteousness at the end; and thus all these "so that the man of God (I Tim. 6:11), he who belongs to God, may be fitted up as having been fully fitted for every good work" whether it be to teach, to refute, to raise up somebody, to educate. All these which are received by the man of God from the inspired Scripture and make him such a man he in turn dispenses to others; this is the meaning of "every good (beneficial) work."

Ἄρτιος = *in gehoerigem Stande,* "in fit shape or condition." This idea is emphasized by repetition and by the addition of the appositional perfect passive participle ἐξηρτισμένος which also has the perfective ἐκ: "as having been (and thus still being) fully fitted up (by all Scripture inspired of God)." "Perfect" (A. V.) is incorrect; "complete" (R. V.) is little better. The idea that lies in both the adjective and the participle is a fit, adequate condition "for every beneficial work," the preposition adding the idea "altogether fit."

There is nothing wanting in the Christian's outfit for work, in his equipment for what God expects him to do. There is no restriction to a man of God in some office. This is plain: "all Scripture, inspired of God," is intended for every man of God so as to make him fit and not for the clergy alone who are to dispense this or that to others.

The value of Paul's famous sentence is beyond question. It is a proof passage for verbal inspiration and for much more besides. As such a proof passage it is outstanding and yet forms only a part of the entire volume of proof and evidence for verbal inspiration. It is one of the peaks in the Rocky Mountain range that establishes "The Impregnable Rock of Holy Scripture" (Gladstone) as inspired.

The fact that "Scripture" = the whole Old Testament canon is beyond question. That the New Testament writings are included rests on the fact that Jesus promised his Spirit of inspiration to the New Testament writers. The first church, which fixed the New Testament canon, did so on the criterion that the writer of any document must be inspired by God, and that his writing must have the stamp of being thus inspired. When it made this decision the first church had the aid of the apostle John who lived beyond the year 100, decades after the inspired writings of all others were in the hands of the church. The fact that John's own writings were inspired was beyond question.

CHAPTER IV

Hear the Last Solemn Testifying of
Him Whose End Is Near!

I Am Earnestly Testifying

1) We cancel οὖν ἐγώ, which was found in the text used by the A. V. We have no connective. The climax of chapted 3 is reached, yet the climax stands out by itself and is not made a part of what precedes. While "continue to remain" in 3:14 looks to the future, the things in which Timothy is to remain lie in the past, they are what he learned at his mother's knee, the divinely inspired Word. In this climax the entire future is presented; there is only an incidental reference to the period of defection (v. 3; compare 3:1, etc.). Besides, Paul presents the impressiveness and the solemnity of the epiphany of Christ, his judgment of the living and the dead, and his kingdom. From Timothy's past at his mother's knee Paul turns to the crown that he himself has almost attained.

This is the end of the body of the letter, the last word. It is surcharged with the profoundest emotion. Paul's course is almost completed, the crown is almost won, and he calls upon Timothy to strive also to receive such a crown from the Judge's hand. Paul is not passing into the shadow but into the glory. His "beloved child" (1:1) is beckoned to follow him. He beckons all of us. Paul's life is closing as it should close.

I am earnestly testifying in the sight of God and of Christ Jesus, the one about to judge living and dead both by his epiphany and by his kingdom: Herald the Word; stand at hand in good season, in no

season; convict, chide, admonish in all longsuffering and doctrine!

The verb does not mean "I am charging" (our versions), nor "I am adjuring," but "I am earnestly testifying"; and because Paul is doing this "in the sight of God," etc., and to make the statement more solemn he adds the accusative which is regularly used with verbs of adjuration: "both by his epiphany and his kingdom." Paul has used the participle of this verb in 2:14, where it is construed with the infinitive; in I Tim. 5:21 it is construed with ἵνα. Here the verb appears with a series of terse imperatives: "I am earnestly testifying: Herald the Word," etc. For that reason, too, the accusatives of adjuration are in place; the imperative object clauses lend their adjuring touch to the verb.

The reading κατά has about as good authority as the καί before "the epiphany"; some prefer it and then construe: "he who will judge in accord with his epiphany," etc. To construe, "I am testifying . . . in accord with his epiphany," etc., sounds rather strange. Still less acceptable is the construction that Paul is testifying in the sight of God and Christ, the Judge, *to* the epiphany and kingdom of this Judge ; then the imperatives are disconnected from v. 1. Nor can we accept the thought that the epiphany and kingdom are being cited as Paul's witnesses to his act of commanding Timothy to herald the Word, etc.

This is Paul's last, most earnest, and solemn testimony to Timothy. He makes it "in the sight of God and of Christ Jesus"; this is an expression that he has used before. He now wants it to be stronger, as strong as he is able to make it; it is his last, it is to impress Timothy more deeply than ever. So Paul adds the apposition: "of the One about to judge living and dead." Μέλλω with the present infinitive is a periphrastic future. In the sight of this Judge who will soon judge living and dead, whom Paul expects to meet after a martyr's death that is near at hand, whom Timothy, too, must meet, Paul here lays his solemn testimony upon the heart of Timothy. "Living and dead" are without articles and express quality. The former are those who will be alive at the last day (I Thess. 4:17), the latter those that will be raised from the dead at that day. There is no room for nor thought of a millennium.

With this vision of the Judge of the universe before his eyes Paul intensifies his testimony to the utmost and testifies "both by his epiphany and by his kingdom," i. e., by reminding Timothy of both. This is the epiphany or glorious appearing of Christ for the purpose of judgment at the last day (I Tim. 6:14; Titus 2:13) ; this word is also used to designate Christ's first appearance (1:10) and the appearance of the Antichrist (II Thess. 2:8). What glory it will be for Timothy and for Paul to be acknowledged by Christ at his epiphany!

"His kingdom" is added, Christ's reign in eternal glory. We do not think of a king and of his subjects, for we shall all reign with Christ (2:12; Rev. 3:21; 22:5). Where this King reigns, there is his kingdom; in that glory kingdom he is crowned with eternal divine glory according to his human nature, we are crowned with him and share his reign as heirs of the kingdom (Matt. 25:34). The article and the possessive pronoun are used with each noun in order to make each stand out by itself. The epiphany is for all men alike, the kingdom is for the blessed alone. What glory it will be for Timothy and for Paul to reign with Christ as kings in that kingdom! See the author's *Kings and Priests* for a fuller elaboration of the kingdom.

2) This solemn and exalted preamble ushers in the peremptory aorist imperatives. They are not ingressive (contra R., *W. P.*) but constative. Being five in number, the half of greatest rhetorical completeness, they imply that others could be added, but that

these five are enough. "Herald the Word!" is properly put first, for this is Timothy's greatest work and function. This connects directly with 3:14-17, especially with "all Scripture God-inspired." This word is regularly translated "preach" and regards the preacher as a κῆρυξ or "herald," whose function is κηρύσσειν, to make a loud, public proclamation, one that has been given him by a superior. He must announce it in its completeness (Acts 20:27) and not alter it in any way, not add anything of his own or anything that is borrowed from another source, not subtract a particle. "Herald!" and not offer religious opinions, not philosophize, not argue. In view of the connotations of this imperative many a preacher, who should be a "herald" and is not what he should be or not all that he should be, must stammer and blush when he faces Christ's appearance and his kingdom.

"Stand at hand in good season, in no season!" This is the correct translation of ἐφίστημι, intransitive: to stand by, be at hand, "be instant" (our versions, the Vulgate *insta*) ; not *halte an* (Luther). The verb is often used with reference to the sudden appearance of a person, of an angel, etc. "Be right on the spot!" conveys the meaning and not R., *W. P.'s,* "carry on, stick to it." Timothy is to be right there, namely with the Word, to herald it "in good season," when things seem favorable, "in no season," when it does not seem seasonable at all. We have no connective; the paradoxical oxymoron is therefore all the sharper. The Word knows no difference as to καιροί or seasons; it is proper for all seasons, everlastingly in season; there is never a time in which it is not needed. With it we are "to buy out" any season, Eph. 5:16. By adding the two adverbs Paul indicates that the first two imperatives belong together.

Thus the next three form a group, the more so since none has a modifying addition, and since these are specific or specifications of the first two: "convict,

chide, admonish." "Convict!" There is no need to say
with what (the Word) or whom (sinners, who are
always in season). "Chide!" or censure, blame. Again
there is no need to say with what (the Word) or whom
(Christians who get into sin or error). "Admonish!"
or urge, encourage (here the meaning can scarcely be:
comfort), once more with the Word, to stimulate slow
and lagging Christians. Recall 3:16. We feel that
Paul could have added a number of other imperatives
and completed what Timothy is to do with the Word,
the entire inspired Scripture. These five suggest the
rest; five is used for this reason.

All five Timothy is to do "in all (all manner of)
longsuffering and doctrine" (διδαχή, not διδασκαλία,
"teaching," 3:10, 16). The former is subjective:
brave, steady remaining under all that this work with
the Word will entail; the latter is objective: the sum
of the entire doctrinal content of the Word which is
to be conveyed by "teaching." "Doctrine" has been
decried in our day as though this word meant dry,
sterile dogmas which are simply handed out so that
people may bow to them in unquestioning assent. This
view is used to justify the opposition of "doctrine and
life" and the supposition that "people in our day do not
want doctrine." But "doctrine" is any adequate statement of a divine fact; the statement may be long or
short, may have one or another form, but it must adequately present the divine fact or facts. No sensible
man will say that he does not want to have these facts
presented to him, that he wants something else instead.
Doctrine is the foundation and the fountain of all religious life, false doctrine of a false religious life, true
doctrine of genuine religious and truly Christian life.
All Scripture, which is full of religious facts, *is* doctrine; and this applies in the four ways indicated in
3:16, and in the five indicated in 4:2. To be without
this doctrine is to be left in darkness, Eph. 5:8, to be
tossed to and fro by every wind of false teaching like

a helpless vessel that is at the mercy of the waves, Eph.
4:14, a pitiful condition.

3)   Paul speaks of these people right here.   **For
there will be a season when they will not stand the
healthy teaching but, having an itch to get their
hearing tickled, will heap up for themselves teachers
in accord with their own lusts and will turn their
hearing away from the truth but will wrench it out
upon the myths.**

This is a prophecy that is on a level with II Thess.
2:3; I Tim. 4:1, etc.; II Tim. 3:1, etc.; but with the
singular καιρός Paul foretells "a season" that is near at
hand.   "For" thus offers this warning to Timothy to
fortify himself and the churches in advance by power-
fully inculcating the Word (v. 2).   The subject is left
indefinite: "they will not stand the healthy teaching."
"Healthy" is used repeatedly in these letters; it is the
opposite of diseased and is here combined with "teaching" (not "doctrine," v. 2), which means both the act
and the product of teaching.   The verb means "will
not have up for themselves," i. e., will not stand.

Paul is not speaking of a change in the temper of
the world in general but of a condition that will appear in the churches.   Some churches will do what he
here foretells; we have them today.   Good, healthy
Scripture teaching that is able to do what 3:16 says
and profitable for what 3:16, 17 unfolds, namely good
health and strength "for every good work," is distaste-
ful to them; they cannot stand this sweet, wholesome
manna.   So they heap up for themselves teachers who
will furnish them "teaching in accord with the (perverted) desires that are their own," who will satisfy
their tastes.   Paul is not referring to esthetic taste but
to hankering after what is unhealthy for the soul and
the life.   "Heap up for themselves" like haycocks refers to the number of elders which each congregation
had: these congregations will be set on filling their

presbytery with only such men and at every election
will turn down sound men.

The Greek is able to place the participle "having
an itch as to their hearing" at the end, for its case,
number, and gender show that it modifies the subject;
the A. V. scarcely avoids ambiguity by placing a comma after teachers; the R. V. properly transposes.
The present middle is descriptive: "having an itch for
scratching or tickling their hearing or for getting it
scratched or tickled" (our versions use "ears" in place
of hearing). There is no contrast with healthiness but
rather a concordance with their own peculiar "desires"
or "lusts" which, like an itch, want tickling gratification. Paul's diagnosis is perfect. Good law and gospel
crush and heal and do not scratch a little in order to
tickle. Law and gospel eradicate the flesh, the old
Adam, and build up the new man "for every good
work" (3:17); tickling itchy ears does not do this.
The law severely boxes those ears until the itch is
gone, and the *terrores conscientiae* make them burn;
the gospel pours in the power that pardons, regenerates, renews. There will be those, Paul says, who
want tickling instead.

4) So they turn their hearing (ears) "away from
the truth," from all the divine, spiritual reality, from
that which is fact; and will wrench (or twist) it out
(ἐκ) upon (ἐπί) the myths, fictions or fables, that are
not true, that are foolish human inventions (compare
I Tim. 1:4; 4:7; Titus 1:14; II Pet. 1:16). The definite article is generic; the whole class of teaching that
deals in human religious inventions and is empty and
useless; the term "myths" is full of Paul's disdain. The
second verb is stronger than the first; these people will
wrench or twist themselves out of their normal position in order to get their ears upon tickling fables.

5) **Thou, however, continue thou to be sober in
every respect; suffer what is bad, do the work of an
evangelist, fulfill thy ministry!**

Compare "thou, however," in 3:10, 14. Here we have opposition to the preceding and also emphatic co-ordination with ἐγώ, "I on my part," in v. 6. The contrast in the first imperative is not that of drunkenness; when it is used in ethical connections, "be sober" denotes the clarity of mind and of sound judgment that is not blinded and carried away by follies, fables, and morbid opinions. It denotes a clear eye, a balanced judgment. The difference of tense is often disregarded or inadequately understood. This present imperative = "continue thou to be sober." It acknowledges that Timothy has been sober, has not lacked in that respect, and asks that he continue thus "in all respects." Once more we have this common adverbial phrase in this sense (B.-P. 1012) and not with the meaning "in all things."

The three aorist imperatives belong together. They are constatives (like those used in v. 2) and include the whole future to which they refer; thus they are not parallels to continuance in being sober (which would require present tenses) but illustrative of the directions in which Timothy's soberness is to manifest itself during the entire future, which helps us to understand the difference between these three injunctions and the aorists used in v. 2. In this coming period there will be much bad to suffer and to endure. The aorist thinks only of this and disregards anything of this nature that may have occurred in the past. See this verb in 2:9 and the κακόν in the verb itself in 1:8 and 2:3. Such coming suffering is not to becloud Timothy's soberness.

He is to do the work of an evangelist whatever the bad that he must suffer may be, do it effectively, completely (aorist). This soberness is to attest itself in that respect. "Evangelist" is not used in the technical sense of "revivalist"; some think it denotes "missionary"; but, like εὐαγγελίζεσθαι, it is entirely general: a man who operates with the gospel of salvation be his capacity what it will. We have already described Timothy's position in Asia, yet the word is not restricted to that position. The object and the verb are transposed and both are stressed in the Greek.

So again: "thy ministry (service for others) fulfill," carry out to fulness; at any time in the future let nothing be lacking in thy service. The measure is always to be full. Paul is not referring merely to the end, for this imperative is again constative and asks this further evidence of Timothy's ever continuing in soberness. Ranged under the soberness which Timothy has always shown and is always to show, the three added injunctions are exemplifications somewhat as the last three in v. 2 exemplify the first two. But in v. 5 the device for this is the change in tense; in v. 2 the device is the use of paradoxical adverbs after the first two imperatives; "in all respects" serves similarly in v. 5.

My Whole Life Testifies

6) Γάρ is explanatory of this strong coordination: *thou — I on my part*. All that is urged upon Timothy is done in view of what is happening to Paul. **For I on my part am already being poured out as a drink offering, and the period of my own departure is present. The contest, the noble one, have I been contending in, the race have I been finishing, the faith have I been guarding. As for the rest, there has been laid up for me the victory wreath of the righteousness, which the Lord will duly give to me in that day, the righteous Judge; moreover, not alone to me but to all those who have been loving his epiphany.**

Noble words! The sun is setting blood-red but is shot through with golden glory. Indeed, so should this great life close! These words have left an indelible impression upon all future ages. Socrates' attitude toward the cup of hemlock has been admired; it is the best that paganism can offer. But how pitifully empty it is when it is placed beside these few words of Christian triumph, Christian assurance, which are looking up to the Lord, the righteous Judge, with all those who are loving his epiphany and awaiting their crowning! Lord, give me a death like this!

This ἐγώ is as devoid of all egotism as it is of all false humility. It is written in the face of death. The facts it states are facts, and Paul writes them for Timothy's sake in order to inspire him by the grace of God to duplicate them in his life with the same courage, assurance, and joy. They so inspire every Christian soul that reads them today. Paul is asking Timothy to do no more than he himself has already done and is now completing. The valiant runner who is close to the goal is beckoning the other on to win the laurel crown. The apostle, almost through with his work, about to obtain the reward, is placing the glorious task on his faithful assistant's shoulders to carry it forward to the same reward.

The English does not have a word that corresponds with σπένδομαι; we must paraphrase "to pour out a libation, a drink offering of wine." Paul does not say θύομαι, "I am already being sacrificed," as though he likened his anticipated martyrdom to a burnt offering that is going up in smoke. The figure he employs is much finer. His bloody death he compares only to the pouring out of a drink offering (Num. 15:1-10), the libation of wine which was added to the sacrifice proper and formed the last act of the sacrificial ceremony. We have the same figure and the same word in Phil. 2:17.

In connection with the Jewish sacrifices the wine was poured out beside the altar, in the case of pagan sacrifices upon the sacrifice itself. Since he is writing to Timothy, it is probable that Paul thought of the former. Rom. 15:16 shows that he regarded his entire ministry as an offering to God. This offering his bloody death is now completing. The present tense and the "already" imply that Paul's imprisonment and his first hearing are beginning his libation. Whether, in connection with libation, we think of the pouring out of Paul's blood or of his life makes no difference, for the life is in the blood.

The parallel statement is literal: "and the season of my own departure is present." Καιρός is correct, for the imprisonment which shall end with death covers some months, yet from the beginning it is marked by ἀνάλυσις, "departure" or "departing," which, like the German *Aufbruch*, has just about lost the figurative idea of loosening the tent cords when breaking camp or of loosening a ship's moorings when weighing anchor.

"My own," the possessive adjective, matches the emphasis of ἐγώ, "I on my part." The perfect ἐφέστηκε is always used in the present sense: "is present"; this period is not merely at hand, close by, but right here. That is why Paul writes to Timothy as he does. He is engaged in the preliminaries of departing. If you wish to retain the old figure: Paul is busy taking down his tent; he is casting off his ship's moorings. Or to employ another figure: he is writing his last will and testament for Timothy who, when he reads these words, may well do so through a film of tears.

7) Paul's thought at once grows greater. From the last short chapter of his life, this "season" of his departing, he turns to the whole book of Christian life and apostleship. Once more we have a balance of phrasing: first the figure, then literal reality. There is no regret, no sadness but only uplift, holy satisfaction, triumphant hope on the eve of final realization. The objects are placed forward for the sake of emphasis.

Our versions convey a wrong idea when they translate "fighting a good fight," they also overlook the durative feature of the perfect tenses. Paul is **not** thinking of a battle, not even of a gladiatorial combat; he has in mind "the noble ἀγών," an athletic contest, the energetic striving for a prize which can be secured only by straining every muscle in a masterly effort to the very last. There is no reference in the figure to competing with others, to defeated contestants. There is a reference only to an athlete making the record set for him, reaching a set standard. We do not speak of the devil, the world, and the flesh as the defeated enemies. Paul has used the figure of a soldier elsewhere but does not do so here; he has even used the figure of a great general to illustrate his apostleship and of a mighty campaign along a vast front (see the exposition of II Cor. 10:4-6), and of a grand Roman triumph (see the notes on II Cor. 2:14); but we have no such imagery here. We recall I Tim. 6:12: "Keep on contending in the noble contest for the faith!" where the prize is also mentioned.

The article should not be overlooked, for it points to "the noble contest" in which every Christian is engaged. Paul is in the foremost rank, but Timothy and all of us are with him. No contest is as καλός, noble, as this one. It is "the high calling of God in Christ Jesus" (Phil. 3:14), where, too, the goal and the prize are indicated; "the holy calling" (II Tim. 1:9), "a heavenly calling," in which we are "partakers" (Heb. 3:1). The perfect tense of the cognate verb does not mean that the contending is now ended, but that Paul has been engaged in it all along and is still engaged in it. The graph of this tense which R. 895 offers is not applicable here; it is not: ———• (the goal reached), but: •——— (the goal not quite reached). The context states how near the goal is in this case.

This is equally true regarding the next two perfect tenses. The ἀγών might be any athletic contest; but here Paul thinks especially of the δρόμος, the running and speed contests; yet he does not have in mind the out-

running of others as he does in I Cor. 9:24-26 but only
the making of the prescribed speed record. This running of his, like the contest in general, might refer
only to his career as an apostle (Acts 20:24; Gal. 2:2),
but v. 8 leads us to think of Paul's whole Christian
life in which "all who have been loving the Lord's
appearing" are joined with him. Every Christian,
wherever God places him, has his race to run; Paul has
reached the stage where he can say: "I have been
finishing" — he is now at the finishing.

Now there follows the literal statement (compare
v. 6) : "The faith have I been guarding" and am even
now guarding. It is generally agreed that this does
not mean that Paul has kept "his faithfulness," πίστις
in the sense of *Treue*. Quite general is the interpretation that Paul has been preserving the personal faith
of his own heart against temptation and doubt. Yet
it is strangely claimed that the three statements are
practically one so that we are pointed to I Tim. 6:12.
They are indeed one, and the latter passage corrects
the idea that Paul's personal faith is referred to, for
it bids Timothy: "Contend the noble contest for the
faith!" i. e., for the substance of the faith. See the
exposition of I Tim. 6:12. All three nouns are alike
objective, and only thus are these three statements one.
"The noble contest" is one that has been set for Paul;
"the race" is one that has been appointed for him; "the
faith" is one that has been deposited with him so that
he may ever guard it. It is objective, the *fides quae
creditur*. The fact that no one can guard the substance, the contents, the doctrine without personally
believing it is self-evident. Paul's subjective faith lies
in the verb "I have been guarding." We have frequently found articulated *pistis* = the objective faith;
note a few samples: I Tim. 4:1; 6:10, 12, 21 (these in
succession).

Yet we should not think that guarding the objective faith refers only to an office such as that of Paul,

of Timothy, and of preachers. The gospel is entrusted to all of us; we are all to guard "the faith," i. e., its blessed substance, for if that faith-substance is lost, none of us has anything to believe subjectively; if that is damaged and destroyed in part, we are all placed in danger. We have no hierarchy that keeps the faith-treasure; we all are its guards, and the Lord will call all of us to account. Correct the traditional exegesis which the writer followed in the *Eisenach Epistle Selections*. "Have been guarding" includes the idea that Paul is still guarding, but he has almost reached the end.

8) Since Paul considers how nearly through he is he speaks of what awaits him. Λοιπόν is practically an adverb although it still retains its accusative ending; its meaning is not "henceforth" (our versions), for the verb which Paul employs is one of several present tenses which are used as perfects in meaning, it means "as for the rest," as far as anything else is concerned regarding me, "there has been laid up for me the crown of righteousness," etc. It is not being laid up now, nor about to be laid up, but "has been laid up" long ago, ever since Paul stepped into the noble contest and race, ever since he guarded the faith. The thought of that crown has ever kept his courage high, his hope triumphant. Now he is so very near that crown.

We regard the genitive as the possessive genitive: "the victory wreath of the righteousness," i. e., which goes with and belongs to the righteousness, namely to the imputed righteousness which is ours by faith and also to the acquired righteousness which is manifested in our lives by good works (3:17). In view of Matt. 25:34-40 we decline to separate them.

Δικαιοσύνη is always forensic; it denotes that quality which is ours by virtue of a decree of the divine Judge which declares us to be δίκαιος or righteous according to his δίκη or norm of right. The genitive is not qualitative: "the wreath which has the quality of being righteous." This meaning would require the omission of the article and thus secure the qualitative force of the noun. Moreover, the quality of this wreath is not righteousness (righteous bestowal); its quality is glory. As far as its being justly bestowed is concerned, this thought is stated in the following relative clause in no uncertain terms.

R. 498 and others regard this as an appositional genitive: the crown consists of righteousness, namely of the Judge's decree at the last day which declares the victor righteous. This confuses the reward (the wreath) with what wins the reward (the righteousness). Stellhorn adds that it is not Biblical linguistic usage to say that either the imputed righteousness or our acquired righteousness are a reward of faith, but that our state of righteousness shall receive a reward. The Judge's decree at the last day is not the reward; it is only the public statement of what this Judge has long before that decreed regarding the believer. Yet the crown is not given until that final statement of the decree is made. The body must lie in the grave until the resurrection day.

This genitive is like that found in Gal. 5:5, ἐλπὶς δικαιοσύνης: hope which belongs to righteousness, which righteousness has the right to have; not hope that *is* righteousness, for hope is *not* righteousness. Pointing to "the crown of life" in James 1:12; Rev. 2:10, and to "the crown of glory" in I Pet. 5:4, as parallels is not convincing. These are appositional genitives, "life" and "glory" are the crown and the reward. But "righteousness" cannot be the same although the expressions read alike. The righteousness receives the crown; it is the righteousness described in v. 7. Στέφανος ἄφθαρτος, "an incorruptible crown" (I Cor. 9:25); ἀμαράντινος, "unwithering" (I Pet. 5:4).

Trench calls our attention to the fact that στέφανος = a victor's wreath, *Siegeskranz*, and that it is to be distinguished from διάδημα, the crown of royalty. The former is woven of oak, of ivy, of parsley, of myrtle, of olive leaves; and when it is not intended for a victor but for festal joy, it is made of flowers: violets or roses. The "diadem" was a linen band or fillet encircling the brow. The conclusion which Trench draws is that στέφανος never means royal crown and has nothing to do with kingship. He explains Matt. 27:29, where Jesus is certainly crowned as a king in mockery, by saying that *stephanos* is used because his crown was made of twigs of thorns and thus "diadem" would not really fit. M.-M. 589 doubts Trench's statement on this point.

Trench carries his conclusion as to the difference between the two words too far. "Diadem" is purely royal and brings out the exaltation, the glory, the majesty of a king before whom all must bow as being far beneath him. "Wreath," *stephanos,* connotes victory after a contest or, in the case of a general, (who may himself be the king) after a battle or a war. Trench fails to note, especially in the passages in Revelation, that the victors who receive the *stephanos* do not sit as those do who receive a wreath of flowers; these victors *reign,* sit on thrones to judge and to reign, even sit together with Christ in his throne (Rev. 3:21) ; "we shall reign jointly with him" (2:12). The diadem belongs to Christ who is King by nature and not to us who are only made kings. We come to reign by being victors, the diademed King makes the wreathed victors reign as kings with him. This is the distinction.

This victory wreath is the one "which the Lord will duly give (this is the sense of ἀπό in the verb) to me in or at that day (resurrection day: the body included), the righteous Judge," he who ever righteously rewards righteousness by his just and righteous judicial verdict. Throughout the Scriptures there runs this double idea: 1) that the righteous are pronounced righteous by a judicial verdict; 2) that the Judge himself must and will be declared righteous for his absolutely righteous verdicts upon both the righteous and the unrighteous, must and will be so declared by the whole universe of angels and of men and even by the damned themselves. On that day, when all things are absolutely revealed, *his* righteousness which is evidenced in all his judgments will appear convincingly as well as the righteousness of all true believers. Note that Paul knows nothing about a preferred class, one that is crowned in a so-called "first resurrection." He knows of only *one* day, of only *one* crowning, when *all* who have loved the Lord's epiphany will be judged and duly given the victor's wreath.

"Moreover (δέ), not alone to me, but to all who have been loving his epiphany," includes us and all other true believers. Paul has, therefore, not been speaking of his apostolic office but of his Christian faith and life, wherein we are with him in the great "contest and race" of guarding the gospel faith. He is not thinking of degrees of glory in heaven. Paul sees himself amid the throng of all the righteous at the last day. It is a master-stroke to designate them as "all those who have been loving his epiphany." Who does not feel the questions: "Are we thus loving his epiphany now? Do we contend, run, guard the faith as if we love his epiphany?" The perfect tense is like those found in v. 7. Even if it is reckoned from "that day," this tense reaches far back to the time when this loving began in all these believers; it includes that day when they shall see that epiphany, and who will say that this their having loved it will then end? They will carry that love into all eternity.

This is the proper verb and it has the correct object. It is the love of understanding and comprehension, the eyes are open to see and not blind; and with the understanding it realizes the corresponding purpose concerning the epiphany. In love they *knew* what the

promises of the Lord's epiphany meant; in love they
held to the *purpose* of having all the blessedness of
that epiphany conferred upon them. They, of course,
believed in that epiphany, and therefore they also ever
loved it.

Paul does not write: "All those who have been loving *him*," the righteous Judge; he says far more even
as his epiphany includes all the glory of his second
coming, all his righteous judgment at that day, all that
this shall duly give to us. Few will confuse this final
epiphany with that mentioned in 1:10, Christ's first
redemptive epiphany. In that epiphany Christ did not
come to judge the world (John 3:17); in this he will
come as "the righteous Judge." This word undoubtedly repeats "his epiphany" from v. 1 and with this
statement about loving it sheds a flood of light on what
v. 1 says about "Christ Jesus, the one about to judge
living and dead," and Paul's testifying to Timothy "by
his epiphany and by his kingdom." The mention of
the final epiphany at the beginning and at the end
binds this paragraph together (compare I Tim. 6:14;
Titus 2:13).

Addenda to the Body of the Letter

Paul Begs Timothy to Come

9) The body of the letter is complete. The last
clause speaks fittingly about "all who have been loving his epiphany," and the last word is "his (the
Lord's) epiphany." So near is Paul's martyrdom
that the light of that epiphany is already reflected
in his eyes. The rest of the letter consists of personal addenda, the last of these being the greetings.

Be diligent to come to me quickly!

The fact that Timothy had news of Paul's arrest
and danger the letter itself shows. The supposition

that Timothy had already sent word to Paul that he was coming to him, and that Paul is now only asking Timothy to hurry, is rather doubtful. The letter reads as though on the heels of the bad news that reached or was at about this time reaching Timothy this letter is to get into Timothy's hands. Paul wants, needs Timothy. The aorist imperative is urgent, and the adverb "quickly" asks for speed. Timothy is to conclude his work with dispatch and is to hurry to Paul's side, to get to him "before winter" (v. 21).

10) There is ample reason for this request. **For Demas abandoned me, having come to love the present eon, and went to Thessalonica; Crescens to Galatia, Titus to Dalmatia. Luke alone is with me.** Save for Luke, Paul is alone. These are the men who were with Paul in Rome. It is nowhere stated where he had been arrested. If this occurred outside of Rome, we are left with the problem as to how he was brought to Rome. Because of the nature of the charge against him another appeal to Caesar could not have brought him there. He was arrested in Rome, and the men here named were with him at that time. Onesiphorus came later and had left when Paul wrote this (see 2:16, etc.).

Demas, the onetime faithful assistant (Col. 4:14), had quickly abandoned Paul, the doomed man. "Abandoned me" is poignant; the aorist is content to state the fact and nothing more. It is a closed tense, final. Some suppose that the ingressive aorist: "having come to love the present eon or world" (see I Tim. 6:17) means only that he went into business and thus left for Thessalonica, his former home. While we are ready to think as well of Demas as we possibly can, this falling in love with the world admits of no such mitigation. For the participle is here evidently the opposite of loving the Lord's epiphany which is mentioned in v. 8. We are compelled to believe that Demas gave up the love of that coming epiphany for the love of this present world's course. This is what cut into Paul's heart most deeply.

All that we know about Crescens is what is here said. We take him to be another assistant of Paul's, one who had joined Paul during this latter period. He had left on a mission to Galatia just as Titus had left on one to Dalmatia (a part of Illyria on the east coast of the Adriatic), in the neighborhood of which Paul had preached (Rom. 15:19). The variant "Gallia" for "Galatia" does not mean "Gaul" but is only the later Greek name for "Galatia" and was substituted in later manuscripts for this reason. On what pressing errands Paul had to send these two faithful assistants we do not, of course, know.

11, 12) This, however, left Paul with no one but Luke. Him alone he had been able to retain; he was the only one through whom Paul could communicate with the outside world. Luke must have dispatched this letter for Paul. At this time Luke was Paul's only loyal, faithful stay in Rome. "Luke only" — so brief the words, yet so full of meaning. Where were all the Roman Christians, some of them even in Caesar's household? To avert suspicion from himself Nero had blamed the Christians for the burning of Rome in July, 64, and many had perished awful deaths the following October (see the introduction). The few greetings, only four names, in v. 21 tell their own tragic tale.

Pick up Mark and bring him along with thyself, for he is useful to me for ministry. The aorist participle with ἄγε is the Greek idiom. Here we have a most interesting glimpse of Mark. The participle, "having taken up Mark," implies that Mark is assisting Timothy in supervising the churches in the great Asian field. Mark will be away when Timothy receives the letter, so Timothy is to pick up Mark wherever he may be and bring him along. Now Col. 4:10, written

in the year 62 toward the end of Paul's first imprisonment, plus Philemon 24, show that Mark was at that
time associated with Paul. We know that after that
Mark was with Peter in Rome, and that Mark wrote
his Gospel at the request of the Romans. That Gospel
is composed of what Mark had heard Peter present
to his hearers again and again so that Mark's writing
earned him the designation Peter's "interpreter." In
the year 64 Peter was crucified in Rome. Now we discover that Mark is again the assistant to Timothy,
surely by direction of Paul; and Paul wants him as
well as Timothy to hurry to Rome.

We see why Paul says that Mark is useful to him
"for ministry." We should properly understand this
diakonia. Mark is not to be a *famulus* of Paul. Mark
had been in Rome with Paul (Col. 4:10; Philemon 24)
and after that with Peter and knew Rome and the
Roman Christians, as many as were still left, so well
that he was certainly a most useful man for Paul to
have about him in Rome under present conditions.
Would that we had the pertinent details! Yet those
that are indicated seem assured.

13) This explains the next remark: **Now
Tychicus I am commissioning for Ephesus.** This is
an epistolary aorist. Some have made the comparison:
Demas *abandoned* me — Crescens and Titus *went away*
— Tychicus *I sent away.* Yet the second verb is true
of Demas as well as of Crescens and Titus. Not for
one moment should we think that Crescens and Titus
had abandoned Paul; the apostle sent them away
on important missions to Galatia and to Dalmatia. If
he had sent Tychicus in the same way, i. e., if ἀπέστειλα
were indeed a historical aorist, Tychicus would be
named directly after Titus and, like Crescens and
Titus, without the insertion of another verb.

Tychicus is mentioned *after* Paul asks that Timothy
bring Mark along. These two, on leaving their field
at Paul's request, are having a substitute sent by Paul,

namely Tychicus. Hence the parenthetical δέ which
inserts what provision Paul is making for Ephesus;
hence also the phrase: "I am commissioning for Ephesus," and not, "I am sending or I sent (ἔπεμψα) *to thee.*"
Tychicus will, of course, carry this letter to Timothy,
but Paul is "commissioning him for Ephesus," to fill
the position there during Timothy's absence. This will
be a long absence, for if Timothy gets to Rome by winter (v. 21), no matter what happens to Paul, Timothy
and Mark will not be able to return to Asia until
spring. Shipping stopped during the winter, and some
transshipping was necessary even if most of the trip
was to be made by land.

**The cloak which I left back in Troas with Carpus
on coming be bringing** (along), **and the books, especially the parchments.** The main point is that Paul
had been in Troas. When? Not three or four years
ago (see the introduction) but on his very recent journey to Rome. In tracing Paul's movements between
his two imprisonments this halt at Troas, like the stop
at Miletus (v. 20), must be properly placed.

On the spelling and the derivation of the word
meaning cloak see the dictionaries and the grammars.
Some have thought that this was a receptacle for the
book rolls and the parchments, Milligan defending
the meaning "book wrap" until he changed his mind
We are safe in translating this word "cloak" (the
papyri have this meaning): a long cape made of the
heaviest material, which one would not want to carry
along during the summertime in those warm latitudes.
Paul needed it for the approaching winter (v. 21). The
supposition that Paul had been forced to flee from
Troas because he was suddenly threatened with arrest,
and that he had, after all, been captured and then
conveyed to Rome, contains so many improbabilities
that we dismiss this hypothesis. The βιβλία, it seems,
were papyrus rolls; more valuable were "the parchments" which were also rolls, but made of skin.

There has been much surmising regarding these documents, and many questions have been asked as to why Paul needed them. It is generally supposed that the parchments were a copy of the LXX. Whatever these book rolls may have contained, our personal guess is that Paul did not want them for personal reading or study but as aids in his trial, to lay before the court as evidence that he was teaching no *religio illicita*, but a religion that was as legitimate legally as that of the Jews because it used the identical sacred writings as its source. These his own book rolls which he had used for many a year were the ones he needed and not some others that were borrowed from other Christians, say from the elders of the church at Rome. Of these "the parchments" would be most valuable if they were, indeed, a copy of the LXX.

Offense has been taken at the fact that Paul should mention such articles, especially the cloak. Some also ask whether inspiration is needed for a verse like this. The answer to the latter is that, if inspiration is able to watch over what we deem as the great utterances of Scripture, why should it not guide also what some of us may deem the most minor ones? The Holy Spirit certainly does not need the advice of men to tell him what to inspire and what not. As for Christians who look askance at the "unimportance of this statement," the best advice is to let the Holy Spirit judge regarding the importance.

Is it so unimportant for us to know how much Paul needed that warming cloak in a cold, damp dungeon during the coming winter? What would we not give if we had more of such little details about Jesus and about any of his apostles! It is not a healthy spirituality that forgets a saint's physical needs. The thought of Paul's faraway cloak has its bit of comfort to bestow on poor fellow sufferers of the apostle who must lie shivering in similar dungeons for the gospel's sake. Jesus, too, had not where to lay his head. On the cross he cried, "I thirst!" Your comfortable circumstances and mine have not been those of all other believers. Paul's missing cloak is material enough for a sermon.

Paul's First Hearing Before the Court Leads Him to Expect the Worst

14) **Alexander, the coppersmith, did me much damage. The Lord will duly give to him in accord with his works; against whom do thou also guard thyself, for he greatly withstood our own statements.**

The sense of this passage is much debated. The idea that at this point of his letter Paul is speaking of a person who opposed him during the trial in connection with his first imprisonment, and that this person was a Gnostic, is not tenable. That this Alexander was the man mentioned in I Tim. 1:20, who was expelled from some church in Asia Minor several years ago, is scarcely probable; for in this second letter he is identified as "the coppermith." If this was the same man, then Timothy knew him; and if identification was necessary, the proper one would be a reference to the man's expulsion as stated in I Tim. 1:20 and not to his trade. This supposition also entails the necessity of transferring this Alexander from Asia Minor to Rome. Neither can this be the Alexander mentioned in Acts 19:33, 34. For that Alexander was a Jew who was at one time thrust forward by the Jews in Ephesus, not against Paul, but to shield the Jews; his occupation is not known. He cannot be considered in this connection although his name was Alexander.

This name was as common as Smith or Jones is now. That is why Paul adds "the coppersmith." In Acts 19:24 it is Demetrius who is called "a silversmith," which is not the same as "a coppersmith" although this word means a worker in brass or metal. This smith in Rome is Alexander, the smith in Ephesus was Demetrius. Paul has nothing but his trade by which to identify him so that when Timothy gets to Rome he may be on the lookout for him. What the religion of this Alexander was nobody knows.

"He showed me much baseness" = did me much mean damage. So much that Paul adds: "The Lord will duly give him (repay him; ἀπό as in the verb in v. 8) according to his works." These are almost the words of Ps. 62:12. The reading that has the optative (A. V.) makes this an imprecation: "May the Lord repay him!" But this reading is too poorly attested textually. It is unfair to Paul to say that, when it came to loving enemies, the apostle himself did not exactly excel. What Alexander was doing was to damage the cause of the gospel in the person of Paul which is something rather different from venting personal spite on Paul.

15) When and where was this damage done? Unless it was done right here in Rome a day or two ago, at the time of Paul's first hearing before the imperial court, this matter regarding Alexander would be out of place at this point in Paul's letter. Thus Paul adds the statement that Timothy is to watch out and to guard himself against the man, which means when he and Mark arrive in Rome. Paul adds a little more to cast light on the way in which Alexander damaged him: "for greatly he withstood our own statements." These are the *logoi* or statements made a day or two ago before the court at the time of the hearing. The emphatic personal adjective ἡμετέροις is much stronger than the mere pronoun ἡμῶν would be. This means: the statements made at the trial on *our* side, on the side of the defense, over against "their own" statements, those on the side of the prosecution.

To say that these *logoi* "were expressions of doctrine common to all Christians" and to think that *logoi* refers to "our preaching" (A. V. margin), is to overlook the force of the possessive adjective. "Our own" is not the majestic plural. Paul did not stand absolutely alone during that first hearing before the imperial court; he had witnesses with him, but only witnesses, no more. Against what Paul and his few witnesses stated, οἱ ἡμέτεροι λόγοι, this Alexander, who was either the chief and most violent witness for the prosecution or the complainant and accuser, brought the strongest contradictions, severely and meanly damaging Paul's case in the eyes of the court. We hear still more.

16) **At my first defense no one was at my side; on the contrary, all abandoned me. May it not be reckoned up to them!**

Paul speaks of his first hearing before the court. His case was not tried by Nero himself who, it seems, was in Greece at that time, but ἐπὶ τῶν ἡγουμένων (Clemens), in one of the two basilicæ named after L. Æmil. Paulus who built the one and restored the other, large halls where hundreds could be present and hear the proceedings. Of the presiding judge who was most likely Helius Cæsareanus, the freedman of Claudius who was prefect of Rome and Italy, Dio Cassius says that, as Nero aped the minstrels, this freedman aped Nero.

Ἀπολογία is the "answer" (A. V.) which the defendant is called on to make to the indictment lodged against him; compare such defenses in Acts 7:1, etc.; 24:10, etc.; 26:1, etc. When Paul says that no one was at his side but that all abandoned him he does nor refer to witnesses but to assistants such as the Roman courts allowed. These appeared in the capacity of *patroni et amici* of the accused, παρά (in the verb), to stand by him at the trial, to lend their prestige before the court.

These had to be men of importance and influence, whose word and whose action in favor of the defendant would have weight with the court to incline the judge either toward acquittal or toward mitigation of the severity of the sentence. Conybeare writes regarding

Paul at this hearing: "No advocate would venture to plead his cause, no *procurator* to aid him in arranging his evidence, no *patronus* (such as he might have found, perhaps, in the powerful Æmelian house) to appear as his supporter and to deprecate, according to ancient usage, the severity of the sentence." It is not necessary to think only of Christians who might be able to act in this capacity for Paul; the apostle had other friends. In Asia, for instance, the high Asiarchs acted as his friends (Acts 19:31). Alas, at this first hearing not a single man of this kind had the courage to appear at Paul's side, all abandoned him. The reading varies between the aorist which simply states the fact of abandoning and the imperfect which describes the act. There seems to be little reason for preferring the latter.

If we understand the function of such patrons in a Roman court we see that men like Luke, Tychicus, or any of Paul's own assistants, and men like those named in v. 21 were not competent to act in this capacity. It is not necessary, therefore, to offer excuses for them as some do. None of these men had sufficient, yea, any standing with the imperial court. We have no means of knowing to whom Paul refers when he writes: "all abandoned me." All we know is that several men, whether they were Christians or non-Christians, could have acted as patrons for Paul but failed to do so. Their reason was, we may be sure, the nature of the indictment against Paul and the great danger of acting as a patron before the court in behalf of a man who was under such an indictment.

Only a few years before this time Rome had been burned (July, 64); to avert the suspicion of incendiarism from himself Nero and his partisans charged the crime against the Christians and caused some to be crucified, others to be dressed in wild beasts' skins and hunted to death by dogs, and still others to be wrapped in robes of pitch and set on fire to illuminate the Vatican circus and Nero's gardens while that monster played the charioteer. Christianity, which was now distinguished from Judaism, became a *religio illicita*, its promulgation a capital crime. To act as a patron for a man who was charged with this crime and one whose only defense was the claim that it was not a crime, was almost to appear as *particeps criminis* and was dangerous, indeed.

So Paul had no one at his side, and this vicious Alexander was able to damage Paul greatly. Whether it was also charged that Paul was one of those who had had a hand in the burning of Rome, and whether several points were charged against him, we are unable to say. Some conclude that "in my first defense" refers to one charge, and that other court sessions that followed heard the other charges; also that, despite the damage done by Alexander, this first charge (implication in the burning of Rome) was dismissed because witnesses proved that Paul was in distant Spain at that time. In our opinion "my first defense" refers to the preliminary hearing on the one capital indictment on which Paul was bound to be condemned to death at the completion of his trial.

"May it not be reckoned up to them" means by the Lord. Here we have the optative in a prayerful wish; it may be the case that because of this optative the future indicative of v. 14 was changed into a corresponding optative in some texts. Paul asks the Lord not to hold against these men their fear of standing by him. Paul makes the best of his disappointment although his life hangs in the balance. His example is worthy of emulation.

17) Although he was abandoned by all who might have acted as his patrons, Paul was not left alone at that first hearing. **But the Lord stood at my side and put power in me so that through me the herald proclamation got to be fully completed, and all the Gentiles got to hear it.**

The Lord was Paul's *patronus* and as such stood "by him" or "at his side." He did more than to influence the judge, he put power into the prisoner according to the promises given in Matt. 10:19, 20; Mark 13:11-13; Luke 12:11, 12; 21:14, 15. In order to understand the next clause we shall let Conybeare reconstruct the memorable scene:

"At one end of the nave was the tribune, in the center of which was placed the magistrate's curule chair of ivory on a platform called the tribunal. Here also sat the council of assessors, who advised the prefect upon the law though they had no voice in the judgment. On the sides of the tribune were seats for distinguished persons as well as for parties engaged in the proceedings. Fronting the presiding magistrate stood the prisoner with his accusers and his advocates. The public was admitted into the remainder of the nave and aisles, which was railed off from the portion devoted to the judicial proceedings, and there were also galleries along the whole length of the side aisles — one for men, the other for women. The aisles were roofed over as was the tribune. The nave was originally left open to the sky. The basilicas were buildings of great size so that a vast multitude of spectators was always present at any trial which excited public interest. Before such an audience it was that Paul was now called to speak in his defense. His earthly friends had deserted him, but his heavenly Friend stood by him. He was strengthened by the power of Christ's Spirit and pleaded the cause, not of himself only, but of the gospel. He spoke of Jesus, of his death and his resurrection, so that all the heathen multitude may hear."

The ἵνα clause denotes result, here even actual and completed result: "so that through or by means of me the herald proclamation (κήρυγμα) got to be fully completed, and all the Gentiles got to hear it." By the Lord's empowering of Paul in that great first hearing before the emperor's court the capstone was placed upon Paul's whole "herald proclamation"; it was brought to full completion. "Through me" = as far as this proclamation was entrusted to me, to make it to all the Gentiles. Epexegetical *καί* helps us to understand in what sense the final completion of the proclamation has now been achieved "through Paul": "all the Gentiles got to hear it." The Gentiles were the multitudes present at the first hearing in the great court. With this, as far as Paul was concerned ("through me" in the emphatic position), his work was done.

To understand what Paul here says we should know that Paul's first imprisonment opened up to him the great Jewish work in Rome. See the author's exposition of Acts 28:17-31. As far as Gentiles are concerned, see the author on Phil. 1:12-14. The hearings at the close of Paul's first imprisonment were not public, were not regarding an indictment — Festus had not been able to transmit anything of that kind to Rome — but hearings on Paul's appeal to Caesar before the Roman court alone —only the court heard Paul. He was acquitted, went to Spain, and since that time had no other Roman province to enter. Now, with this great hearing in Rome itself, Paul considered his *kērugma* accomplished. "All the Gentiles" does not mean every last one of them but all the Gentile nations. Paul had planted the gospel in every one of them, taking in all the Lord had allotted to him, Rome itself now closing the list.

Those who regard this as a purpose clause must wrestle with the subjunctives, which they refer to the future: in order that at some future time the herald proclamation might get to be fully accomplished through Paul and that at some future time all the Gentiles might get to hear it. There is no question that this whole letter is written in the prospect of death

(v. 6), and Paul did die. Yet he says emphatically "through me." If the clause is a purpose clause and thus refers to the future, to what future time do these aorist subjunctives refer? One writer states that the news of Paul's testimony here in Rome would eventually penetrate to all nations of the Gentiles. Yet much more had already penetrated, Paul himself had made it penetrate by personal presence and by work, and these nations had heard.

Another writer thinks that by means of others the news would penetrate, and that "through me" signifies only that this penetration would have ceased if Paul had been recreant in this supreme hour of his first hearing. Still another places the whole verse into the trial that was held during Paul's first imprisonment. Still other opinions are offered; all of them seek to find something in the thought of purpose, something that refers to the future. Ἵνα expresses completed result. In fact, it states for what the Lord empowered Paul; the aorist "did empower me" says that this result or object was then and there achieved by the Lord.

This was accomplished at Paul's first defense, **and I was rescued out of lion's mouth,** an echo of Ps. 22:22: "Rescue me out of lion's mouth!" LXX. We again have many opinions as to the meaning of this. Although Paul says "lion's mouth," *Loewenrachen,* some refer this to Nero as though Paul had written *"the* lion's mouth." Some think of being condemned to "the lions" although no Roman citizen could receive such a sentence. I Pet. 5:8 is introduced, but this passage is of no help. Those who regard the previous clause as a clause of purpose with a reference to the future think of a prolongation of Paul's preaching; but Paul's dungeon was not a pulpit. Some speak of a spiritual rescue, that Paul's soul escaped the devil at this first hearing. The sense of the figure is simply this, that at his first hearing the Lord kept him from being sent to execution at that time.

18) That explains the next statement: **The Lord will rescue me from every wicked work and will save me for his kingdom, the heavenly one; he, to whom** (belongs) **the glory for the eons of the eons. Amen.**

"Did rescue — shall rescue," a significant repetition. The rescue of a day or two ago when Paul expected to be sent to his execution, this wonderful rescue which was due wholly to the Lord, is to Paul an assurance of the next far greater rescue when the Lord will take him to his heavenly kingdom. This is not a thought of the prolongation of life for more gospel work, not a thought even of receiving another opportunity at a coming hearing to utter the great herald proclamation of the gospel in the court basilica before assembled crowds. That next appearance in court, when it is finally ordered, will most likely end with the sentence of the judge, that and nothing more. Paul hopes that Timothy may yet reach him before that day and hour. We hope that he did.

'Από and εἰς are contrasted: from every wicked work (πονηρός, viciously wicked) unto, into, or for his kingdom, the heavenly one (added like an apposition, R. 776). On "kingdom" see v. 1. There is no thought of wicked work which Paul might do but only the thought of wicked work (such as Alexander's, v. 14) which men might inflict on Paul. "Will save me" refers to both the saving act of placing into heaven and the continuing safety that follows. Christ's kingdom here on earth is where he rules with his grace and his gospel; Christ's heavenly kingdom is where he rules with heavenly glory.

Here we have one of the clear passages of Scripture regarding what happens when our souls leave their bodies at death: we shall at once enter the heavenly kingdom, that is, heaven, where the heavenly King is enthroned. Phil. 1:23: "to be with Christ." There is no intermediate place for the soul, no *Totenreich* with two compartments: one, "paradise," for the righteous, the other, beneath it, an antechamber of hell for the wicked. Those who invent this fiction which darkens the true Christian hope contradict all the clear passages of Scripture. The body shall, indeed, sleep in the grave, but the soul shall be where Stephen's soul went at death, where Moses and Elijah are (the latter even with his body), in the very presence of God and Christ. The souls of the damned go to hell at once. At the time of the resurrection the body will be raised from the dust, will be glorified like the soul, will be joined to it, thereafter also to partake of all the bliss of that heavenly kingdom.

Paul's heart is deeply moved as he pens these words. Instead of uttering a sad complaint at the thought of a cruel death, his soul is filled with the glow of golden hope and expresses its joy in the form of a doxology. The relative pronoun is emphatic (compare Rom. 2:29; 3:8; 3:30) : *"he,* to whom (belongs) the glory," etc. Note the article: all the glory, praise, and honor that creatures are able to bestow. And this "for the eons of the eons," the strongest Greek way of saying "for all eternity." The human mind, having no conception of timelessness, is compelled to use expressions of time. Thus the Greek first pluralizes "eon" and then makes this plural superlative by a duplication with the genitive plural. So vast and *unuebersehbar* is just one eon; now take any number of them, and in every one of these place any number of others, making eons of eons — incomprehensible, staggering. But for all of them this glory is due to God.

A solemn, impressive "Amen" is added like a seal of verity from the fullest assurance of faith. It is the transliterated Hebrew word for "truth" which has passed into the other languages.

Thus Paul faced the end, and it is thus that he finally bowed his head before the executioner's sword or his ax and went to his eternal reward.

Salutations

19) Salute Prisca and Aquila and the house of Onesiphorus. Erastus remained in Corinth, but Trophimus I left in Miletus sick. Be diligent to come to me before winter. There salutes thee Eubulus and Pudens and Linus and Claudia and the brethren all.

On "salute" see Rom. 16:3. We last saw Prisca and Aquila in Rome (Rom. 16:3) but are not surprised to find them back in Ephesus when we think of the burning of Rome and Nero's persecution of the Christians in consequence. As was done in Romans, the wife's name is placed first, she being the abler of the two; see Acts 18:18-28. In the long list given in Rom. 16 these two are placed first; so they here deserve to head the list, since they are inexpressibly dear to Paul (Rom. 16:4). On the questions raised about "the house of Onesiphorus" see the remarks concerning 1:16-18.

20) Paul does not account for Erastus and Trophimus because he had received a letter from Timothy which asked about them but most likely because Timothy would think of them and wonder why they were not with Paul, and why, if they were, they were not at least sending salutations. So Paul states where he had left them. It is probably best to believe that "Erastus" is the man named in Acts 19:22, but not the one mentioned in Rom. 16:23 (see the latter passage). Regarding Trophimus, who is mentioned in Acts 20:4 and 21:29 and then does not appear until now, we are unable to add anything further. The

important point is Paul's naming Corinth and Miletus
as places where he has just recently been; with these
we must associate Troas (v. 13). How the naming of
these places helps us to trace Paul's movements just
before his arrest in Rome the introduction attempts to
show.

21) Paul repeats the request voiced in v. 9. Since
this is a repetition it shows us how earnestly Paul
pleads for Timothy's coming. After saying "quickly"
he now says at least "before winter"; why before winter, is stated in connection with our comment on v. 9.

Linus eventually became bishop of the original
congregation of Rome. See Smith's *Bible Dictionary*,
where also the stories about Pudens and Claudia are
properly discussed, vol. 1, p. 469, etc. Eubulus is not
mentioned in tradition. These four are mentioned by
name probably because they were personally known to
Timothy. When we look for names in the list given in
Rom. 16 we should remember two things: 1) Rom. 16
names the important persons and those personally connected with Paul; 2) this old, original Christian congregation was sadly wrecked in 64 when Nero mar-
tyred so many of its members.

Καὶ οἱ ἀδελφοὶ πάντες, "and the brethren all," leaves
us with various questions. Who were these brethren
all? All those with whom Paul was in some kind of
touch through Luke? All the survivors of Nero's
persecution in the old, original congregation? Or these
plus the Jewish Christians in Rome? We accept the
first of these three answers because we take it that
Paul sends greetings from persons who know that
he is writing and who want their greetings sent.
These could not be all the Christians in Rome, not even
all who still belonged to the original congregation. See
the story (introduction) of the Epistle to the Hebrews
and the exposition of Acts 28:17-31.

During his first imprisonment in Rome (two years)
Paul had converted a multitude of Jews. Rome had

seven synagogues; three or four of them were converted to Christianity, remained in their own large synagogues, escaped bloody martyrdom (Heb. 10:32-34, see the exposition) because they were still popularly considered to be Jews, suffered during the persecution only because they tried to help the victims that belonged to the original congregation, and, now that Paul faced death, were entirely unable to do anything to help him. This is a mere sketch. Some regard all these Jews that were converted by Paul's labors during his first imprisonment as members of the original congregation and thus run into serious difficulties regarding the situation in Rome. When Paul writes "all," we do not think that he includes all the converted Jews in these three or four Christianized synagogues.

22) **The Lord** (be) **with thy spirit!** This is Paul's own prayer-wish for Timothy. **The grace,** i. e., his grace (be) **with you!** μεθ' ὑμῶν, plural, without further specification. "You" means Timothy and all fellow Christians who may be with him when this letter is placed into his hands. These are the great apostle's last words.

Soli Deo Gloria

St. Paul's Epistle to Titus

St Paul's Epistle to Titus

CHAPTER I

The Greeting

1) Paul, slave of God and apostle of Jesus Christ in accord with (the) faith of God's elect and (their) realization of (the) truth that (is) in accord with godliness, on the basis of (the) hope of life eternal which (life) the God who does not lie promised before agelong times, but he now made public in their own periods his Word in (the) herald proclamation with which I on my part was entrusted in accord with (the) order of our Savior God: to Titus, genuine child in accord with (the) common faith: grace and peace from God, (the) Father, and Christ Jesus, our Savior!

Titus has a position on the island of Crete which was similar to that which Timothy had in the great Roman province of Asia. Both men are representatives of the apostle; both are to attend to the work that Paul would do if he were in their place; they are his apostolic agents. The field of Titus is smaller than that of Timothy. Timothy is to remain in his field indefinitely; before the winter sets in, Titus is to be relieved by Artemas or Tychicus (3:12). The field of Titus is new, the churches are not so fully developed as are those that are under Timothy's supervision.

Paul gives similar instructions to both men, but those given to Titus are briefer and reflect the simpler conditions obtaining in his field. In the field of Titus, for instance, there are no deacons and no women deacons and no elders who have already served for some years. Yet they confront dangers of the same order although those obtaining in Crete are not so fully de-

(887)

veloped. First Timothy and this letter to Titus were
written, it would seem, on the same day.

Save for the greeting found in the great letter to
the Romans, the greeting of this little letter to Titus is
longer than those used in Paul's other epistles. The
writer expands especially the first member, "Paul."
This is, however, not due to the new relation to Paul
into which the office of Titus placed him. Titus had
before this time acted for Paul on most important com-
missions; remember the two on which he was sent to
Corinth. This letter with its long preamble regarding
Paul himself is to constitute the written commission
and authorization for Titus. He who here describes
himself at such length lends his powers to his genuine
child to act for him in the matters contained in this
letter. Some people might challenge Titus, might at
least question this or that which was done or taught by
Titus. Well, here is Paul's own letter, which settles
such things with finality.

For Titus himself, who was for so long a time
associated with Paul, such a long preamble is not
needed. It was not needed for Timothy in First Timothy although this letter served the same object in the
case of Timothy, for Paul and his whole office were
well known in Ephesus and in the many churches in the
province. Crete was a new field, and although Paul
had just been there and had left Titus there (v. 3),
although the people knew him, their knowledge was
imperfect, and thus Paul tells them at length who he is.
Everything depends on who that man really is for
whom Titus is acting in Crete. Here is Paul's own
written statement regarding who he is. Whoever refuses to heed Titus thereby refuses to heed the apostle
himself.

We see that this preamble applies to the contents
of this entire letter. The instructions it contains are
certainly not new to Titus. He had known these things

for many a year. When Paul parted from him, we feel
sure that the two talked over just what Titus was to
do as Paul's representative. As far as Titus was concerned, this was enough. Yet, when dealing with the
Cretans, it was a great advantage to have the main
things in written form. Paul sends them in this letter
just as he does to Timothy in First Timothy. Study
the letter in this light; its purpose and its contents will
thus be clearer.

In our translation we indicate the fact that the articles are absent in the Greek. The English needs the
articles. These verses offer a good instance of this
difference in these languages. In the Greek any genitive already makes the noun it modifies definite, an
appended relative clause does so likewise; in English
such modified nouns generally also have the definite
article. The Greek at times also uses the article with
proper nouns and again it does not; we have examples
of both: τοῦ (article) σωτῆρος ἡμῶν Θεοῦ and ἀπὸ Θεοῦ
Πατρός (no article).

"Slave of God" could, in the English, be "the slave
of God," compare Rom. 1:1; Phil. 1:1. The point is
not that a "slave" works for his owner but that a
slave's will is entirely the will of his owner. All Christians are such slaves of God; they have no will of their
own but make God's will theirs in everything. With
this designation which he puts at the very beginning
Paul associates himself with all the Cretan Christians,
their fellow slave here instructs Titus, and all this
instruction applies to Paul as well as to Titus and to
them.

"Apostle of Jesus Christ" is added with δέ. This
δέ often merely adds; its difference from καί is only this,
that it adds something that is different. We have no
connective that corresponds to this δέ and must use the
non-differentiating "and"; "but" is too adversative. As
Jesus Christ's apostle Paul belongs to a distinct class

of men, he and the Twelve were especially commissioned by Jesus Christ to found the church and were
especially equipped for this great work.

In I Thess. 2:6 "apostles" is used with reference to
Paul, Silvanus, and Timothy; but this extension of the
term indicates only that these two were helping Paul
to do the apostolic work. In all the epistolary greetings in which Paul calls himself "apostle" he has no
such extension of this title in mind. Since he was commissioned by Jesus Christ, this slave of God has one
and only one function to perform, namely to execute
that commission as Jesus Christ requires. By writing
this letter to Titus, Paul, the commissioned one, is
doing that very thing. As far as his authority is concerned, all of it lies in this commission, and thus all of
it goes back to Christ. Matt. 10:40; Luke 10:16.

This connection of Paul with God and Jesus Christ
suffices so that here Paul's appointment by "the will
of God" is not added. The thing that Paul wants to
emphasize in view of what he here writes for the benefit of the recently formed churches in Crete is his connection with the entire gospel and its eternal blessings
and with all true Christians who are joined with him
in all that this gospel bestows on them. When, in
dealing with the Cretans as Paul's representative,
Titus shows them this their connection with Paul, they
will all be glad to heed Titus and back of Titus, Paul,
and back of both, God and Jesus Christ, for they, too,
want to be God's elect in this eternal gospel with all its
eternal blessings. These recent converts need to have
this connection pointed out to them. Paul knows
what he is doing when he writes this full statement
about himself. He has no thought of self-glorification
or of extending his authority but only the thought of
conveying all blessing possible. As already said, this
applies to the contents of the entire letter.

Here we have a good example of Paul's mastery in
compactness of expression; immense concepts are con-

cisely and perfectly combined so that many pages
would be required to expound all that is here said. The
flexibility of the Greek enables Paul to weld such great
thoughts together. "Slave" and yet "apostle"; Paul is
both "in accord with (the) faith of God's elect and
(their) realization of (the) truth that (is) in accord
with godliness." There is no reason to say that this
κατά phrase expresses either a purpose or a norm. No
less than four κατά appear in close succession; all are
evidently to be understood in the same sense. Paul's
being the slave and apostle he is cannot be "for the
purpose of" bringing God's elect to faith as if faith
were something that is intended only for the elect (Calvinism). Paul's being the slave and apostle is not
"normated by" the faith the elect have and by their
knowledge as if God and Christ looked at that faith
and so designed Paul's Christianity and apostleship.
Is Paul himself not one of the elect?

Paul's slavery and apostleship are "in accord with"
the elects' "faith and realization of truth." These four
harmonize, they do so in all respects as regards all the
elect of God, Paul included, even as true faith and
knowledge exist in them. The accord and harmony are
found between what Paul is and what God's elect have,
namely their saving faith and knowledge. Every word
that Paul will write in this letter he will write as God's
slave and Jesus Christ's apostle, and every word will
thus accord and harmonize with the saving faith and
knowledge of God's elect. In this very first phrase
Paul and all God's elect are joined heart and soul; in
this harmonious circle, whose center is God and Jesus
Christ, the Cretans are included.

God has his elect whom he himself chose in eternity
(I Pet. 1:2) ; with their faith and their realization of
the truth Paul's whole condition and position are
agreed; God and Christ made them so. There is no
need to restrict the elect to those living at that time,
for Paul ever sees the entire *Una Sancta*. The **whole**

doctrine of election lies in the word ἐκλεκτοί, all that is said elsewhere in Scripture about them and their election. They are the true πιστοί and ἅγιοι, Eph. 1:1, 4. Paul combines their "faith and realization of truth," ἐπίγνωσις, full inner apprehension of divine reality, and with the article states that he refers to the truth which is "in accord with godliness." So he welds into one: faith — heart-knowledge — gospel truth — godliness; and instead of leaving them abstract he makes them most concrete by planting them in God's elect. All who belong to this number, who prize this truth, who have faith, knowledge, and godliness, will heed what this slave of God and apostle of Jesus Christ writes to Titus.

2) The ἐπί phrase is parallel to the first κατά phrase: Paul is God's slave and Christ's apostle "on the basis of (the) hope of life eternal which (life) the God who does not lie promised before agelong times," etc. One who in his own person and in his whole office rests on this basis here sends instruction to Titus regarding the Cretans. He stands on the hope of life eternal. All this faith, knowledge, and godliness reach their climax in this hope of finally receiving the life of blessedness that never ends. This life the God who does not lie (adjective ἀψευδής), who never breaks his word and promise, promised, and not just recently, but ages ago, to all the ancient patriarchs as far back as Adam. Although the Cretans have only recently come to know and to believe these promises, they have stood solid during all the past ages. The Greek has no word for "eternal" and so uses αἰώνιος, which in other connections as here in the πρό phrase signifies only "agelong." Rich as the language is, its poor pagan conceptions hampered it in many of its concepts.

3) So old are these promises of the never-lying God. Why the Cretans did not know about them until recently, and how these promises have now been brought to them, are added with a compact statement.

Yet Paul does not continue the relative clause but
begins an independent sentence: "but he now made
public in their own seasons (or periods) his Word" —
how? "in (the) herald proclamation with which I on
my part was entrusted in accord with (the) order of
our Savior God." These καιροί are in contrast with the
long χρόνος; the periods since the Word (with its promises of life eternal and its truth of godliness) was published had been brief, for the publication began at
Pentecost and even then did not fully get out into the
Gentile world until some years later. The dative of
time "in their own seasons" refers to the seasons determined by God for this great publication. Paul does not
merely say "his (God's) Word," namely all that God
has to say to men, but at once connects this with his
own office: "with which (Word) I on my part was
entrusted in accord with (the) order of our Savior
God."

Every term fits exactly. The great proclamation
was given in the form of "a herald's message" which
was given to him to be shouted out in public so that all
men might hear. With this message Paul was entrusted
by God (the accusative after a passive). The very
verb conveys the idea that Paul ought to be faithful to
that great and honorable trust. The verb and the subject are transposed in order to emphasize both; ἐγώ
itself is emphatic: "I on my part." A special order of
God (see I Tim. 1:1) to Paul conveyed this trust. The
genitive sheds a flood of light upon the whole clause:
in accord with (the) order "of our Savior God"; "Savior" as in I Tim. 1:1, the double genitive as in I Tim.
2:3; compare 4:10.

Three times in First Timothy and four times in
Titus, Paul uses "Savior," which shows that the letters
were written at the same time. "Our" Savior is highly
confessional. Paul and Titus have salvation; and when
the Cretans hear the Word they will in the same way
confess: "Our Savior!" But the main point is that

this truth, promise, Word, plus the order to Paul, the apostle who was to be the great herald, emanate from "our Savior God." The one thing that was brought was salvation, eternal life (v. 2) ; faith, knowledge, godliness, hope accepted this salvation. "Our Savior God" (read as a unit) crowns Paul's whole introduction of himself. As an instrument of this Savior he sends these instructions for the Cretans, as such Titus will submit them, and the Cretans will receive them.

We have only skimmed the content of these verses; let the reader dwell on each concept and on the way in which they are combined. The mine is deep and rich. We remark that no forger could possibly have introduced Paul in this letter in this way.

4) The second member of the greeting is brief: "to Titus, genuine child (duplicate of I Tim. 1:2) in accord with (the) common faith" (I Tim. 1:2: "in faith"). "Child" expresses dearness, and "genuine" an acknowledgment that Titus (like Timothy) runs true to his spiritual parentage and will so transmit these instructions. Once more we have κατά: "in accord with (the) common faith," the significant adjective bringing Paul and Titus into fullest concord just as κατά itself does. "Common" reaches farther, for this is the faith which places all of God's elect into fullest concord, harmony, communion (v. 1). In this concord and common faith Titus is to apply these instructions, all of which have only one purpose, namely to aid the concord of the common faith.

The third member of the greeting is like others found in Paul's letters save that to "Christ Jesus" is added "our Savior" just as in v. 3 it modifies God. Both are equally "our Savior"; the salvation they bestow is the same. All three persons unite in our saving. The repetition emphasizes the great purpose of this letter in its service to the Cretans. This slave of God is slave of "our Savior God," this apostle of Jesus Christ is an apostle of "Christ Jesus, our Savior"; all

he writes as their slave and apostle is for the further-
ance of their work as Saviors.

Concerning Elders and Errorists

The Type of Elders to Be Ordained

5) To treat the greeting (v. 1-4) superficially is
to lose much as regards the body of the letter. This
verse reads like the introductory verse found in I Tim.
1:3. Both men have similar tasks. In First Timothy,
Paul begins with the disturbers and speaks about the
elders in 3:1, etc.; in Titus, Paul begins with elders
(v. 5-9) and then takes up the disturbers (v. 10-16).

**For this reason I left thee in Crete that thou fur-
ther put in order the things (still) lacking and place
into office elders city by city as I on my part directed
thee: if one is unaccused, one wife's husband, having
believing children, not in accusation of dissoluteness
or refractory.**

On the work done in Crete and how Paul stopped
at the island when he left Rome for Ephesus after his
first imprisonment, see the introduction to these letters. There is no reason for adopting another reading than the aorist: "I left thee," ἀπό in the verb: "I
left thee back" (behind). Paul writes τούτου χάριν in
Eph. 3:1, 14: "in favor of this," i. e., for this reason,
and ἵνα adds what it is, namely further to put in good
order the things still lacking in these recently formed
congregations. Ἐπιδιορθώσῃ is the first aorist middle
subjunctive; if ς is appended, we have the first aorist
active subjunctive. In such congregations quite a number of things would need attention. Καί adds the most
important one, the placement of elders in each congregation. Paul writes "city by city" (distributive κατά).
Work must have been done in a number of cities.

It may well be possible that, when Paul was in
Crete, he himself helped Titus with this work; but

much was yet to be done by Titus. Here again we meet the viewpoint that, because Paul tells Titus to go on with the completion of this work, Titus had been slack. Another idea is that Paul is answering a letter he had received from Titus, but when Paul answers a letter he says so at least by the way in which he answers. Congregations needed an adequate number of elders and more of them as the membership increased. All congregations were to be properly manned. The verb does not mean "to ordain" (our versions) although they were actually ordained by the laying on of hands; Paul speaks of placing them in office, having them elected by the congregations and then ordaining them; the former is the main thing. This is not a new direction for Titus but the one given him when Paul left him. It is here put in writing as an authorization which Titus may show when it becomes necessary, which also explains ἐγώ, "I on my part."

6) The "if" clause is a part of the directions and thus needs no apodosis. A man that is to be put into this office must be "unaccused," *unbeschuldigt*, not one about whose past or present accusations are being circulated among the people. A man's record must be clean (I Tim. 3:10). Next, "one wife's husband" as discussed in I Tim. 3:2, 12: whose married life has been clean. He will usually have children, and since older men were chosen as elders, Paul wants only men who have believing children, τέκνα πιστά, not men whose sons and whose daughters are still pagans. A handicap such as that would be too great for an elder. These children will be grown up, and even if they are professing Christians, Paul wants only the father of children "not in accusation of dissoluteness," *Liederlichkeit* (see Eph. 5:18). If the sons and the daughters must have their gay times, their father remains ineligible. This is also true if they are known to be "refractory," literally, "not made subject," refuse to bow to parental author-

ity. I Tim. 3:5 shows how this circumstance most certainly disqualifies the father.

7) Note the "if" and the "must" in I Tim. 3:1, 2; we now have the latter: **For it is necessary that the overseer be unaccused as God's steward, not self-pleasing, not quick-tempered, not (sitting long) beside wine, not a striker, not out for shameful gain; on the contrary, devoted to hospitality, devoted to what is beneficial, sober-minded, just, true to moral obligation, self-controlled, clinging to the faithful Word in accord with the doctrine, that he may be able to exhort in the teaching that is healthful and convict those speaking against it.**

Δεῖ indicates any necessity, here the one suggested by "as God's steward," οἰκονόμος. This steward was often a slave (v. 1) who was capable and able and was by his wealthy master placed over one of his estates to manage it and perhaps had many other slaves under him; see the *oikonomos* mentioned in Luke 16:1. God's "steward," "the overseer" in one of God's congregations, must of necessity have the qualifications here listed. Here we have one of the plain passages in which "elder" (πρεσβύτερος) and "overseer" (ἐπίσκοπος) are used side by side as designations for the same office. "Must be as God's steward" is to be construed with all the predicates.

The first five are negative, the next seven positive. The first and the last are comprehensive. "Unaccused," which is repeated from v. 6, means: so that before any forum nothing can be said against the man, first, on the score of his family life, his wife and his children; second, on any of the points now added in v. 7-9. No one is to be able to charge him with being αὐθάδης, literally, "self-pleasing," in disregard of others set on having his own way in everything and in this sense "self-willed" (our versions) or "arrogant." Nor is anyone to be able to charge that he is "quick-tempered," easily flaring up in anger; or that he loves to sit long beside the wine (see I Tim. 3:3), a winebibber; or that he is "a striker," quick with his fists in a dispute; or "out for shameful gain" (see I Tim. 3:3, 8). These the candidate for overseership is *not* to be, his record on these points must be clean.

8) The positive points are even more numerous. First, "devoted to or a lover of hospitality" as explained in I Tim. 3:2, gladly opening house and home to travelling or to persecuted Christians. This indicates that a man who could do this did not need congregational pay for his office. The companion virtue is: "devoted to or a lover of what is beneficial," ἀγαθόν, good and helpful to others. This expands the idea contained in generous hospitality. One great motive in the minister's heart must be this love of doing good to others. Yet both of these "lover" virtues are to be sanely exercised, hence we have the addition "sober-minded" (I Tim. 3:2), not extravagant and lacking balance in his opinions and judgments like some who want to be too hospitable, too good to others in a morbid way and thus spoil what good they would do and do no little harm.

A second three are added. The first two are again a pair and are balanced by the third. Δίκαιος and ὅσιος are often found together in classical Greek (Trench) but not in the meaning "just and *holy*" — on the latter see the notes under I Tim. 2:8: "unpolluted" in the sense of "true to one's moral and religious obligations." The word used is not ἅγιος or the equivalent of what we call "holy." Nor does "just" or "righteous" refer to men, to the observance of the second table of the law, and the other word to God, to the observance of the first table (Trench). The first means conduct that meets the approval of the divine Judge (forensic); the second, conduct that observes the true and established ordinances of the Lord. In this way the two are a pair, the one looking to the Lord's verdict, the other to the Lord's requirements as set down in his law.

Thus the third: "self-controlled," literally, "in control of strength," goes with the two: always having strength enough to check anything that would be unjust or would contravene the ordinances (Trench illustrates by the case of Joseph, see I Tim. 2:8).

9) "Unaccused" in regard to any of the five negatives and also in regard to anything connected with the six positives, the candidate for office must have the final qualification: "holding or clinging to the faithful Word in accord with the doctrine," etc. This is a fuller statement of what "able to teach" means in I Tim. 3:2. Note how the Greek makes both the phrase and the adjective attributive by placing them between τοῦ . . . λόγου and having the phrase modify the adjective, literally: "the in accord with the doctrine faithful or trustworthy Word," i. e., the Word whose doctrine makes it so reliable and worthy of confidence and faith. But for that doctrine it would not be πιστός. Verbs of holding to anything take the genitive. The expression is compact and unites in one concept: the Word — its doctrine — its trustworthiness; the Word — its great contents — its supreme quality. Every elder is to be a man who holds solidly to this Word, who knows it, makes it his whole stay.

An elder must cling to the Word, not only for his own person, but also — and that is the point to be noted here — "in order that he may be able to exhort in the teaching that is healthful and (in order that he may be able) to convict those speaking to the contrary." Note the difference between "the doctrine" (διδαχή) and "the teaching" (διδασκαλία). The latter presents the former, and all admonishing or exhortation to faith and Christian living (παρακαλεῖν) is in most vital connection with "the teaching," the substance of which is "the doctrine"; all other exhortation is without inner basis although so many pulpits today offer nothing better. Nine times in these letters Paul uses "healthful," participle and adjective; here four times in succession (1:13; 2:1, 2, 8). Who wants diseased teaching? Diseased animals are not offered to the public for consumption, they are taken out and buried, but some pulpits today offer such diseased matter. Follow out the further implications yourself.

If there be any who speak to the contrary, the elder must be able to convict such people, namely in connection with the healthy teaching, i. e., convict by showing convincingly that they are wrong. This need not secure their admission that they are wrong; some would not be convinced by the Lord himself; but it does mean a conviction that is plain to true believers, one that in not a few instances will also make a convert of the gainsayer.

Titus is to instruct the churches city by city, to choose only such properly qualified men. When such elders lead the congregations, the latter will prosper.

The Dangerous Errorists

10) When Paul continues with γάρ he does not intend to base the required qualifications of elders on the present situation obtaining in Crete so that, if these errorists were not present, less might be required of elders. No, these requirements are necessary for the church as such and for all time. The situation obtaining in Crete reveals only how especially necessary proper qualifications for elders are at this time. We thus do not restrict the ἀντιλέγοντες mentioned in v. 9 to the errorists now named nor identify their conviction with stopping the mouths of these errorists. These errorists are a special class. Something more is to be done with them than with Christians or with outsiders who may need conviction.

**For there are many refractory idle talkers and
mind-deceivers, especially the circumcised, whom it
is necessary to gag (because they are) such as turn
upside down whole houses by teaching what they
must not for shameful profit's sake.**

"There are many" introduces this miserable lot;
unfortunately, they are numerous in Crete as Paul
found when he was there. "Refractory vain talkers
and mind-deceivers" describes them first as talkers
whose talk does not lead to the goal and next as men
who do nothing but mislead and deceive the mind. In
both of these actions they are "refractory" (compare
v. 6), refuse any control whatever. "Especially the
circumcised" ("they from circumcision"), of Jewish
extraction. Ancient writers tell us that Jews were
numerous in Crete. These were, however, neither genuine Jews nor Judaizers like the ones mentioned in
Acts 15:1, 5, nor those found in Galatia and in Corinth. We shall see that they were of the same type
as those with whom Timothy had at this very time to
deal in his field so that we may say that a connection
existed between them.

11) Titus should do but one thing with these people, namely gag them, stop their mouths and silence
them by main force. Paul does not say how this was to
be accomplished; in I Tim. 1:4 he wants Timothy to
order them to stop their contrary teaching. This
means that in any congregation the elders were per-
emptorily to silence them when they tried to talk at
the services. That is why Paul writes this to Titus.
Some elders and some church members might think
this too severe a procedure, might want these men to
have at least a chance to be heard. Paul here backs
the authority of Titus for gagging them completely.
If it becomes necessary, Titus may show these directions that were written by Paul himself. That, too, is
why Paul fortifies his orders as he does: refractory

talk that leads to no proper goal (μάταιος), that only deceives the mind, simply has to be silenced as every sensible person will agree.

Οἵτινες has qualitative and thus also at times causal force. Here it has the latter: Think of it, these fellows want to speak at the congregational services when they are "such as turn whole houses topsy-turvy by teaching what they (simply) must not," and do this "for shameful profit's sake." Just because they are "such," every attempt of theirs to get into the public services with their talk must be stopped without hesitation. First they "creep into the houses" (II Tim. 3:6), and when they have secured some victims they count upon their support when they speak in the congregational services.

When Paul requires that the elders in the churches were not to be lovers of money (I Tim. 3:3), "not out for shameful gain" (Tit. 1:7), this, of course, had its general bearing, namely that mercenariness disqualifies for an unselfish office; but it also had a very specific bearing for the churches that were under Timothy's (I Tim. 6:5) and Titus' supervision inasmuch as the errorists who were disturbing their congregations operated "for shameful profit's sake." The fact is that, apart from some fanatics and zealots, the majority of deceivers would soon stop if their evil work produced no financial profit. Modern history has some notorious examples where great sums were secured by the leaders and shared in by their lieutenants. The Cretans had a bad reputation for heeding itinerating prophets who worked for profit. This is testified to by Polybius, Livy, and Plutarch (R., *W. P.*).

12) Paul refers to this: **There said one of them, a prophet of their own: Cretans always liars, base beasts, lazy bellies.** Paul adds: **This testimony is true.**

This hexameter, which is scanned by R. 422, is quoted from the poet Epimenides who was a Cretan

born at Cnossos. Plato dates him at 500 B. C. Aris-
totle at 630. Callimachus (somewhere between 310
and 240 B. C.) quoted the first words: "Cretans always
liars," in a hymn to Zeus so that some commentators
refer to him as the source of this quotation, and since
Callimachus proclaimed the immortality of Zeus while
the Cretans claimed to be able to point to the grave of
Zeus, they thought that Paul agreed with this poet over
against the Cretan liars. Paul, however, quotes Epimenides, "one of them" (partitive ἐκ), who thus certainly
ought to know his own people. "One of their own
prophets" means only one of their notable spokesmen.
Their representation as liars dates far back; their
claim to have the grave of Zeus may be in part responsible. The fact that they were still liars, even in Paul's
time actually makes the old Cretan poet's line as sound
as a prophecy. These Cretan deceivers were the latest
exemplification of base lying.

More than that: "base beasts," κακὰ θηρία, "low-
grade wild beasts," who are always prowling around
for prey (in I Tim. 3:6 we have the same trait but
another figure); "slow bellies" (A. V.), literally "bellies lazy," inactive, that want to be filled without ex-
ertion in earning an honest living by honest work. The
present deceivers met the old poet's specifications quite
completely. As for their being "of circumcision," it
should be noted that the Cretan population was mixed,
that there had been Jews in Crete for ages, and that
thus these Jewish deceivers were as much Cretans as
all the rest. Ovid (twice), Cicero, and Apuleius refer
to the Cretan lying; in fact, as Κορινθιανίζομαι meant to
whore like the Corinthians, so Κρητίζω meant to lie like
Cretans.

13) When Paul calls this testimony true he means
that it is still true; but the evidence for this fact are
these "mind-deceivers" against whom Titus and all the
elders are to warn the churches. Paul would not say
that he refers to all the Cretans in Crete and also to

all the church members. Why should he? Besides, it
would not be true. When a country has a bad reputation, that does not mean that all its people are guilty,
but that only a certain percentage is. In a country
that is notorious for liars Christians must be the more
on guard. That is the point Paul would make for Titus
and for the Cretan Christians. This business of lying
and all other wickedness the gospel had come to stamp
out, and since these lying deceivers were busy in the
young churches right now, there was no use to mince
words. This apt quotation from a Cretan himself was
certainly convincing.

Paul continues with a relative: **for which cause
keep convicting them sharply so that they may be
healthy in the faith, not giving heed to Jewish myths
and commandments of men turning away from the
truth.**

Because the poet's word about Cretans is true as is
evidenced by these many deceivers that were troubling
the churches, therefore Titus is to keep convicting
"them," i. e., the people under his charge, any who
may need it, and he is to do that ἀποτόμως, as one cuts a
thing off with one blow of the ax, namely "sharply."
The elders are to be able to do the same thing (v. 9),
note the same verb. Titus *is* doing this, the present
imperative tells him to keep on. This convicting does
not refer to the deceivers; they are to be gagged,
silenced in all the churches. But if these deceivers get
into a house, Titus is to see to it that the church members in that house are sharply taken to task, are decisively warned of their danger.

Ἵνα may express purpose, "in order that," or contemplated result, "so that they may be healthy (present subjunctive: continue to be) in the faith," *fides
quae creditur,* the doctrine which constitutes the Christian faith. Some think of *fides quae creditur,* personal,
subjective faith; but v. 14 shows that "the faith" =
"the truth" as the opposite of "Jewish myths and com-

mandments of men who have turned away from this truth." This does not disregard personal faith, for "to remain healthy" in the objective faith is to have healthy personal faith. Personal faith becomes unhealthy when it feeds on unhealthy teaching (compare the remarks on "the healthy teaching" in v. 9).

14) Paul says that the Cretan deceivers spread "myths," the identical term he used in I Tim. 1:4; 4:7, where we described these myths. In 3:9 Paul adds "genealogies"; in I Tim. 1:4 myths and genealogies are mentioned together. The fact that they were "Jewish" we saw in First Timothy; here Paul calls them so. When he adds "commandments of men who have turned away from the truth" he refers to the same kind of men that he called the "teachers of law," which he fully describes in I Tim. 1:6, etc., so that the whole exposition of I Tim. 1:4-11 should be inserted also here. The deceivers who were found in and around Ephesus and those that were active in Crete were of the same type; there was evidently a connection between them; in both places many of them were Jewish; they dealt with the genealogies of the books of Moses, inserted fictitious names into these genealogies, and spun fabulous stories around these names; at the same time they put fancies into the law of Moses so that it no longer struck the consciences of sinners (I Tim. 1:8-11), as Paul's own conscience was once crushed in contrition (I Tim. 1:12-17). With such teaching they crept into houses and then tried to get into the public services.

From "the truth," the true law and gospel, they ever "keep turning away" whenever it is offered to them; they see no financial profit in the truth but secure a good deal by their silly fables, etc. Like pestiferous wild beasts they prey on simple Christian souls, like wild boars they uproot whole houses and feed their lazy bellies.

15) **All things** (are) **clean to the clean, but to those who have been stained with filth and**

(to the) unbelieving nothing (is) clean; yea, even their mind and their conscience has been stained with filth.

The fact that "all things" includes "every creature of God" mentioned in I Tim. 4:4, 5 (compare Col. 2:16-23) is plain; yet here πάντα includes still more, namely the Word of God itself. "All things" are clean "to the clean," to those who have been made clean in mind, in heart, and in life. They thus use everything that is clean in a clean way, especially also the clean, healthy teaching (v. 9).

But to those who have been and as a result are still befouled, polluted, stained with filth (*besudelt*), and unbelieving not a thing is clean. One article combines the figurative perfect passive participle (from μιαίνω) and the literal adjective "unbelieving," the adjective explains the participle. Even the healthy teaching, the truth, the faith are not clean to them but are treated as unclean, as so much filth in which they root like κακὰ θηρία, wild hogs. The holy, lovely garden of the Word and of the church they invade as if these were full of the vile stuff they feed on. So men today still root around in the Bible, tear it up, find their lies and errors in it, befoul everything.

Ἀλλά is not adversative but climacteric (R. 1185-6), a climax to the preceding δέ: "yea, even their mind and their conscience has been stained with filth" (the repetition emphasizes this drastic verb). Their pollution is not merely on the outside, it has entered the very center of their being. The νοῦς is not merely the intellect but the whole mind as directing the will; as such it is here combined with the conscience, the inner moral judge of what is right and wrong, who ever holds us responsible. When these two have themselves become fouled, nothing touched by them, however clean and holy it may be, is any longer so to them, nor do they treat it so.

Here we have one of the psychological insights into the pathology of mind and of conscience which is verifiable in deceivers of all kinds, especially also in the field of religion. It will repay study to get Paul's full meaning. In fact, his entire psychology, especially in these days of psychological decadence, deserves thorough study; Paul's letters are full of the best material, and there is no better teacher than he save Jesus himself.

16) **God they keep professing to know, but with their works they deny, being abominable** (or detestable) **and disobedient and for every good work tested out as spurious.**

They indeed confess that they know God, know him far better than the true Christians; εἰδέναι is the proper verb and not γινώσκειν, see the difference in II Tim. 1:12. They profess that they are fully informed about God. They would, of course, also confess that they have fully "realized" God *cum affectu et effectu.* Paul challenges them already regarding their professed εἰδέναι, for to judge from their words, which are the loudest and most reliable confession any man makes, they flagrantly deny God. Their works are vain talk and deception of mind. The way in which they operate with these (v. 10, 11), their turning away from the truth, etc. (v. 14), are works indeed! Do not think only of the little things that occur in ordinary daily life.

The participial addition substantiates: "being abominable," despicable in the sight of God and of God's people. Why? The next two terms answer: "disobedient" (see "the sons of the disobedience" in Eph. 2:2; 5:6: Col. 3:6), namely to the Word of God, the truth, the healthy teaching. To confess to be informed regarding God and yet to disobey the very Word of God is to confess and to deny in the same breath, than which nothing can be more abominable. The effect, being abominable, is placed first; the cause, substantiating the effect, is placed second, their being disobedient. With this goes an intermediate effect: "for every good (beneficial) work ἀδόκιμοι, tested out as spurious." Yet this last is like a final judgment. Like coins or metals that are tested as to genuineness these confessors of God are found spurious, utterly to be rejected.

Paul is dealing with the Cretan churches through Titus, his apostolic representative. These directions are Paul's aid to Titus, which he is to show wherever it may become necessary, whenever Titus has to squelch the Cretan deceivers, and when some of the church members think him too severe.

CHAPTER II

Concerning the Natural Groups in the Congregation

The Old Men

1) This verse is the preamble. Δέ is merely transitional. **Now thou, do thou continue to utter the things that are becoming for healthy teaching.**

As in 1:13, the present imperative supports and acknowledges what Titus has been doing and tells him to go on steadily in his course. The fact that Titus is ever teaching the healthy teaching of the pure gospel is taken for granted. On "healthy" see 1:9. All that Paul adds is that, whatever Titus may say to any of the members, is to be fit, proper, and becoming to this healthy teaching of his. There is a contrast with the deceivers mentioned in 1:10-16 in the pronoun "thou" but not in δέ. There is no contrast regarding the great difference in doctrine but only regarding the conduct to which Titus is to admonish the people: they are to grace the doctrine with a becoming life, and Titus is to keep on telling them what things are becoming.

2) Thus, to start with: **that old men be temperate, sober-minded, healthy as regards the faith, the love, the patience.**

These are not official elders but "old men" as such, who ought to be a good example to the rest of the members. The two adjectives are like those found in I Tim. 3:2: "temperate" (II Tim. 4:5: "in all things"), not specifically regarding drink, but temperate in thought, word, and act; in particular, not rushed off their feet by any flighty teaching. The companion term "sober-minded" merely enhances this virtue: always sound and balanced. The old men ought to be the balance wheel of every congregation.

The third term (a participle) makes this still clearer: "healthy as regards the faith," etc., (datives of relation); in 1:13 we have healthy "in the faith." "Being healthy" is twice ascribed to "the teaching"; see especially 1:9, and note 2:1. Twice to the people themselves (here and in 1:13 — see the latter). In both of these passages "the faith" is objective. In fact, unlike I Tim. 6:11, all three datives are articulated because they are objective: "the faith, the love, the patience" set before us in the Lord's Word, to be achieved in a healthy way, by the healthy teaching of that Word in our hearts. These three cover the entire domain in which the old men should prove themselves leaders. On "love" and "patience" see the definitions in I Tim. 6:11.

The Old and the Young Women

3) **The construction with** εἶναι **continues: that old women (be) likewise in demeanor as befits sacred persons, not slanderers, not enslaved by much wine, teachers of excellence in order that they may make sober-minded the young women to be devoted to husbands, devoted to children, sober-minded, chaste, housekeepers, good, subjecting themselves to their own husbands in order that the Word of God may not be blasphemed.**

Paul's arrangement is chiastic: the old men and the young men first and last; the old and the young women between, these two being also closely combined. "Likewise" is general: as Paul points out some things for the old men, so he likewise points out some for the old women.

The first item is comprehensive: "in demeanor as befits sacred persons." This word is not compounded with ἅγιος but with ἱερός, which does not emphasize the idea of "holiness" and "holy women" (A. V. and margin) but rather leads us to think of conduct and bearing such as becomes a ἱερεύς in the ἱερόν, a priest in the sacred place, hence: "reverent in demeanor" (R. V.).

The two negatives concur with this: "not slanderous," garrulously gossiping and exchanging the latest scandals — Christian old women have something more priestly to do; "not having been (and thus still being) enslaved by much wine" — no priest was allowed to function when he drank and thus disgrace his office. The comment that this shows the disreputable Cretan character is unwarranted. Whoever has traveled in Oriental countries knows not only that wine is the common drink but that, since the condition of the water is as it is, wine is almost a necessity. This explains the references to the drinking of wine in I Tim. 3:3, 8; Titus 1:7; and here in the case of old women. Moreover, these churches were new; the old converts had lived a long pagan life. When these things are remembered, we shall understand.

4) The fourth item is again positive so that here, too, we have a chiastic arrangement of the four, the two positives excluding what the two negatives mention. For "teachers of what is noble or excellent" or "teaching in a noble way" is the occupation of reverent old women and not of slanderous or bibulous tongues.

5) Whom they are to teach and what follows in a purpose clause: "in order that they may make soberminded the young women (feminine adjective) to be devoted to husbands," etc. This verb repeats the adjective "sober-minded" which occurred in v. 2 as well as the one that follows here in v. 5 and means "with sober-mindedness to make others sober-minded." We

see how great a stress Paul lays on sober-mindedness; in fact, the young men are also "to be sober-minded." Christianity lends balance of mind to all its members, old and young, men and women, and fortifies them against all flighty deceivers who would unsettle them.

Seven items are noted in the case of the young women; the first two are a pair: "devoted to husbands, devoted to children," husband-lovers, children-lovers; these two are themselves a sermon for young women: truly affectionate wives and mothers, an ideal so sadly missing today. Now we again have "sober-minded," and with "chaste" or "pure" in every way these two form a pair. The same applies also to the next two: οἰκουργούς (or οἰκουρούς), "caring, working for the home" (or "keeping at home," domestic, the reading varies), their home is to be their kingdom. With this goes ἀγαθάς, "good" in the sense of doing what is good and beneficial to others (here husband and children). This is a picture of homebodies and housekeepers as they dispense all good things in this domain. Homes that have such wives and such mothers are good homes, especially when they are filled with the Christian spirit.

We have a seventh item: "subjecting themselves to their own husbands," a matter that is constantly stressed by Paul lest anyone think that the gospel altered the relation between husband and wife. Paul's fullest presentation is found in Eph. 5:22, 23, in the light of which all his other brief references should be read. These things the old women must teach the younger. The texts vary between the subjunctive σωφρονίζωσι and the indicative σωφρονίζουσι. The latter is not a "corruption" or a mistake in copying but the beginning of the use of the present indicative after ἵνα, which is common in the later Greek (R. 984, bottom).

Paul has more to say regarding the young women than regarding any other class of members. Why this

is the case is indicated by the purpose clause which,
however, extends back also to the old women because
they are to be qualified for producing all this sober-
mindedness in the young women. If the women fail
in what Paul here asks, he fears "lest the Word of God
be blasphemed," lest the whole gospel be vilified. So
much depends on the women, in great part on the
young women, of the church. The world will to a great
extent judge the churches by the character which the
gospel produces in the women.

The Younger Men

6) **The younger men likewise continue to
admonish to be sober-minded.** In the case of these
everything is summarized in the one infinitive "to be
sober-minded," which, however, receives special
force because of its repetition, for in 1:8 the adjective is used regarding an elder, in 2:2 regarding
old men, in v. 4 the verb is used with reference to
both old and young women, and the adjective is
again used regarding the latter. Since it is thus
repeated, when it is now asked of younger men the
word is weighted with meaning.

"Younger men" (the masculine adjective) means
all who are younger than the old men, say from
65 or 60 on down. We may note that in the case of
the women Paul does not use a comparative adjective. This is due to the fact that "young women"
are in his estimation those who may still bear children; those who are beyond that age are regarded
as "old." Some wish to add περὶ πάντα: "to be sober-
minded concerning everything." This addition does
not improve the sense, especially since such an addition does not appear with sober-minded in the previous verses. Moreover, if one *is* sober-minded, will
he be so only in some things so that "concerning all
things" must be added?

7)   Since this verse begins with the phrase περὶ πάντα, some think that more emphasis is given to σεαυτόν; but the reflexive pronoun with a verb that is already reflexive, this pronoun being even placed ahead of that verb for the sake of emphasis, needs no further help. If this phrase is made a part of v. 6, Titus is to be an example only for the younger men. That would be strange in view of I Tim. 4:12 where Timothy is to be the example for the believers generally.   This is also true with regard to Titus: **in regard to all things continuing to furnish thine own self as an example of excellent works, in the teaching uncorruptness, gravity, healthy statement, nothing to be found against it, so that he who is opposed may be shamed as having nothing ill to say in regard to us.**

Although it is joined to the foregoing by only a participle, this clause applies to all that has been said regarding the men and the women. We see at once that there is a connection with v. 1, "the healthy teaching," which v. 7 resumes with "in the teaching . . . healthy statement," etc.   Paul uses a participle on purpose because a participle makes all that he says about Titus being an example subordinate to the preceding, which exactly what is to be conveyed.

First the inclusive statement that in regard to everything Titus is in his own person to provide an example of noble and excellent works.   The present participle implies that he has been doing this, and that Paul expects him to continue to do so.   The idea is not that Titus is in danger of forgetting although all church officers should welcome reminders such as this, but that all these people may know from Paul's own written word that he first and foremost obligates Titus and also himself (note ἡμῶν) to what they both require of others.   So it should always be: the people looking to their pastors as examples, and they and the pastors looking to their higher church officers as still better examples, and that περὶ πάντα, "in regard to everything."

With the phrase and the following accusatives supply παρεχόμενος; some think that the active participle is to be supplied, but the middle is perfectly in order: "continuing to furnish on thy part." Now, however, Paul specifies the main thing that Titus is to continue to furnish for the people, namely "in the teaching uncorruptness" as far as substance is concerned; "gravity" as far as the manner of the teaching is concerned; "healthy statement" as far as all individual statement (λόγος) is concerned, every statement is to be so that "nothing can be legally found against it." The whole of this forms a unit. "Uncorruptness" has nothing to do with a moral motive in Titus as some suppose. The word is used to match "health" and refers to the contents of the teaching; in no part is there to be the least taint or degeneration. As in substance sound to the core, so in the presentation the teaching is to be furnished with "gravity," the dignity which accords with such teaching.

8) In fact, every statement made must be "healthy" (see 1:9), this healthiness being mentioned now for the fifth time, the word connecting directly with v. 1 and 2; so healthy that no judge shall be able to find a single indictment against it, ἀκατάγνωστον, *nichts dagegen erkennen,* a legal expression. Ἵνα expresses contemplated result: "so that the one opposed," the opponent who may listen in order to get hold of something as the Pharisees watched every *logos* that came from Jesus' lips, "may be shamed" for doing such a thing, "finding nothing ill to say in regard to us" (this pronoun includes Paul himself). This is to be the main thing among all the excellent works of Titus in which he is to provide an example. It is the main thing for two reasons. All this sound, healthy teaching is to be the spiritual food of the people; and at the same time it is to be the pattern, type, and illus-

tration of how they are to teach, from their elders on downward.

The Slaves

9) **Slaves to be in subjection to their own masters in all respects, to be well-pleasing, not answering back, not taking things for themselves, but showing all good fidelity in order that they may adorn the teaching about our Savior God in all respects.**

The construction continues with another accusative after παρακάλει. R. 944 regards the infinitive as a legal (imperative) infinitive. We feel constrained to draw ἐν πᾶσιν forward in this verse just as we do in v. 10; moreover, this phrase is purely adverbial: *in jeder Hinsicht* (B.-P. 1012), "in all respects," not "in all things." The fact that slaves were to be in subjection to their masters need not be stated, they *were* that; but the fact that Christian slaves were to be subject voluntarily *in all respects,* that needed to be said. By having become Christians the slaves were not exempted from any part of their obligation as slaves. "To be well-pleasing" is coordinate, hence it is also an infinitive, which means that this clause is an explanatory apposition to the preceding one: in subjection in all respects = trying to please well. That is the kind of subjection Paul means, not one that is sullen and reluctant, but one that is eager and glad to please.

The two negative participles name two subordinate points. These are common faults of slaves and of subordinates in general, which Christian slaves will therefore note and shun with special care: "not answering or talking back" as though knowing better and thus able to contradict their masters; secondly, "not diverting anything for themselves," anything not intended for them by their masters; the German *entwenden.*

10) No; instead of anything of that kind Christian slaves are to show forth "all good fidelity." Πίστις

is here not to be taken in the active sense as a confidence that the slaves place in their masters but in the passive sense as a confidence which their masters may have in the slaves, the German *Treue;* and it is to be one that is ἀγαθή, "good" or beneficial for their masters. In brief, Christian slaves are always to show themselves worthy of being fully trusted by their masters in anything that serves their masters' interests.

In v. 5 ἵνα indicates the negative motive behind truly Christian conduct: "that the Word of God may not be blasphemed" as producing no good in its adherents; here the motive is positive: "so that the teaching about our Savior God may be adorned in all respects" by true Christian conduct in its adherents (ἐν πᾶσιν as in v. 9). Paul often uses negatives and positives in this way; but when the negative is used, this already implies the corresponding positive: not blasphemed = praised; thus the positive adorned = not disgraced. Doctrine and teaching are universally judged by their product in the lives of those who believe them. All Christian teaching welcomes this test. Judge a tree by its fruits. It is a bad thing, therefore, when Christians profess to believe the teaching they receive and yet deny it by their lives and their words (1:16).

Note well that the highest interest of Christians is always to be, not that of self, but that of "the Word of God" (v. 5), which is the same as "the teaching of our Savior God" — the genitive is probably objective: "about our Savior God"; "our Savior" is inserted attributively as it was in 1:3; in 1:4 it is added appositionally. When it is regarded as being objective, this genitive would indicate the contents of "the teaching" or of "the Word of God," namely that God as "our Savior" saves us. Thus the whole salvation of God in Christ Jesus would be introduced in a direct way. When it is regarded as a possessive genitive or as a genitive of source, this saving idea of "the teaching" would be indicated less directly. Would that all of us, whatever our age, sex, or station in life, even if the latter be the lowest and humblest in the social scale, might make the gospel of salvation our supreme interest and motive in life!

11) The fact that Paul is thinking of the contents of the teaching appears from v. 11-14 where he presents a beautiful summary, γάρ meaning: "for this is what I mean by teaching of our Savior God." **For there has appeared** (second aorist passive, the aorist stating only the past fact, to express which we use the English perfect) **the grace of God, saving for all men, educating us, that, after denying** (once for all) **the ungodliness and the worldly lusts, we** (definitely) **live sober-mindedly and righteously and godly in this present eon,** (ever) **expecting the blessed hope and epiphany of the glory of our great God and Savior Jesus Christ, he who gave himself for us so as to ransom us from all lawlessness and to cleanse for himself a people select, zealous for excellent works.**

This summary of "the teaching" presents the salvation purchased and won for all men, but as one that changes their whole lives from ungodliness to good works. Paul reserves this summary until the last because it is not pertinent only to "slaves" (v. 9), for he admonishes *all* the different classes of Christians to do good works. He speaks of slaves only as being one of these classes; nor can this gospel summary be restricted to slaves. "For" reaches back through the whole chapter.

We get the correspondence of terms when we translate "there was made an epiphany" (aorist passive ἐπεφάνη) of the grace, etc. — expecting "the epiphany" (v. 13). There are two epiphanies: one in the past, another yet to come. When did the action of this aorist occur? The church has answered this question by using v. 11-14 as its epistle lection for Christmas Day in accord with Luke 2:10: "Behold, I bring you

good tidings of great joy, which shall be to all people,"
also Luke 2:14. The thought is not that this first
epiphany stops with the incarnation and the birth; as
an epiphany it includes the ransoming that followed.
Scarcely a better epistle text could have been selected
for Christmas Day.

"The grace of God" is the *favor Dei* of his infinite,
incomprehensible love for our fallen race. Χάρις always
denotes unmerited favor when it is predicated of
God in regard to men; it is in the highest degree unmerited. The great connotation is the *guilt* of fallen,
sinful men who deserve justice and eternal punishment as the guilty, convicted criminal deserves death
at the hands of a just judge. "Grace" brings the opposite; how it does this is shown in Rom. 3:24, etc.,
where God's grace is shown as being in perfect harmony with his righteousness, for God's grace, as here
in v. 14, includes Christ's ransoming, the propitiation
by means of his sacrificial blood.

Σωτήριος πᾶσιν ἀνθρώποις is predicative to ἡ χάρις: "the
grace . . . saving for all men." Here is the universality of this saving grace, which is in direct contradiction to Calvin's limited grace, who writes in his Commentary, published in Geneva in 1600, p. 542: *Interea
non intelligit singulos homines, sed ordines potius no-
tat, aut diversa vitae genera,* "Yet, he (Paul) does
not understand individual men but rather notes orders
or diverse genera of life," i. e., "classes in life," and
he does this because slaves have just been mentioned
as being one such class. To Calvin "all men" = some
slaves, some young men, some young women, some old
women, some old men. He has a similar exegesis of
other passages, for instance, John 3:16: "God so loved
the world," regarding which he says that "the world"
is mentioned only because there was nothing in the
whole world to call forth God's love.

12) This wondrous grace which is "saving for all
men" is now operative in us (in Paul, Titus, the Cretan

Christians), "educating (or training us as a παῖς or boy is educated, this verb is found also in I Tim. 1:20; II Tim. 2:25) us, that, having denied the ungodliness . . . we live sober-mindedly," etc. Ἵνα introduces the object clause and is equal to an infinitive: our constant education by saving grace effects this, that, after saying "no" to all ungodliness, we live in true godliness. Paul stresses the moral effect of God's saving grace because of the moral admonitions that he is sending to Titus for the Cretans. See this again at the end of v. 14. But this entire effect on Christian life is the fruit of the faith which embraces "the Word of God" (v. 5), "the teaching of the Savior God" (v. 11), "the ransoming" effected by Christ (v. 14), the fruit of the regeneration in baptism (3:5). The present durative participle states that this education is a process, in fact, one that continues throughout our present life.

What this educating process produces is expressed by effective aorists, for these things are actual, definite. The negative effect is expressed by a participle because it is subsidiary to the positive effect. "Having denied (this verb is used also in 1:16: said "no" to) the ungodliness and the worldly lusts," means that by a divine act we broke with them, disowned and ousted them as being abominable. The double object is emphatic; doubling is one form of emphasizing. It is Pauline to place side by side a comprehensive singular, "the ungodliness," and an unfolding plural, "the worldly desires" (ἐπιθυμίαι is commonly used in the evil sense so that we write "lusts").

When it is viewed in detail, "the ungodliness" consists of worldly lusts, at least manifests itself in them. Both are specific and well known, hence the articles are used. "Worldly" means that the desires are connected only with life in this cosmos and seek their satisfaction in nothing higher. The two terms sum up the whole inwardness of man in his sinful state. The break made in this denial is due wholly to God's saving grace,

its saving power saves us from the grip of this ungodliness and these lusts and their fearful ultimate effects.

The positive side is that "we live (effective aorist)
sober-mindedly and righteously and godly in the present eon." Regenerated by grace, we live a new and
totally different life which is here characterized by
three adverbs over against the two preceding nouns.
The arrangement seems to be chiastic: "the ungodliness . . . godly" at the extremes, the other terms between. "Sober-mindedly" runs through the preceding
(1:8; 2:2, 4, 5, 6): the mind has become balanced by
grace and is free of the former senseless follies. This
is apparent to men. "Righteously" means so that
God's judgment approves the life we live, which takes
us into his sight. Finally, the highest feature of all:
"godly," i. e., truly pious in worship and in communion
with God, the opposite of "the ungodliness." The
worldly lusts even men regard as vicious; sober-mindedness is the opposite of these, for lusts carry away
while soberness makes steady. The worldly lusts bear
their mark of condemnation; righteous living is again
the opposite, for it has God's approval.

This is what God's saving grace does for us, it edu-
cates and trains us in the new life. No greater Christmas gift could be given to bless us.

13) All of this work of grace is connected also
with the second epiphany of Jesus. We have come to
live in this way "(ever) expecting the blessed hope
and epiphany of the glory of our great God and Savior
Jesus Christ." Our expectation of Christ's second
epiphany moves us to live as we do. Instead of stating it in so bare a way: "expecting the epiphany of
Jesus Christ" — which is the heart of what he says —
Paul expands both the object ("the epiphany") and
the genitive ("of Jesus Christ"). It helps to clarify
when this is noted. We have an expansion of just
two points: epiphany and Jesus Christ. When Paul

thinks of what we expect, the wonderfulness of it makes him expand in loftiest description.

This is what we expect: "the blessed hope and epiphany of the glory." Here "hope" is objective and = the thing for which we hope. Καί is epexegetic: our blessed hope is "the epiphany of the glory" of Jesus. To show this relation the two nouns "hope" and "epiphany" are placed under one article. As for the genitive τῆς δόξης with ἐπιφάνειαν, this cannot be adjectival as the A. V. has it: "the glorious appearance," for "of the glory" (articulated) is definite. Blessed, indeed, is what we hope for, namely the epiphany, the visible appearance at the last day of the δόξα of Jesus, of the sum of all his divine attributes shining forth on his judgment throne in his human nature.

Moulton, *Einleitung*, 134, etc., and R. 785, etc., state that we should divide the genitives: τοῦ Θεοῦ καὶ σωτῆρος ἡμῶν is one concept, "our God and Savior," and Ἰησοῦ Χριστοῦ, "Jesus Christ," is its apposition. In other words, Jesus Christ is here called our God and Savior. *One* person is referred to and *not two*.

There has been much discussion in regard to this grand genitive. Winer and others state that we have an ambiguity and that we cannot be certain as to whether one person is referred to or two. Winer decides that there are two. Some introduce dogmatical reasons; Meyer subordinationism. As far as we are concerned, it makes no difference whether Jesus is here once more called God or not; deity is ascribed to Jesus in so many Scripture passages that the addition or the subtraction of this passage is immaterial. The grammar and the language decide. Here these are decisive and are supported by the context: it is the epiphany of the deity in Jesus Christ that constitutes our blessed hope. The analogy of Scripture corroborates this view, Luke 9:26: "When he (the Son of man who is man and more than man) shall come in the glory of himself and of the Father," in this glory which is one and belongs equally to both persons. White (*Expositor's Greek New Testament*) thinks that Luke 9:26 decides that two persons are mentioned in our passage. Yet the Scriptures know about only the one epiphany, this of Jesus, which constitutes our hope.

The adjective "great" is not decisive as though it could be applied only to Jesus as God and not to the Father as God. The article τοῦ simply unites Θεοῦ καὶ σωτῆρος ἡμῶν and makes this one designation with "Jesus Christ" as the apposition. In the same way the article τὴν combines ἐλπίδα καὶ ἐπιφάνειαν. A division cannot be made at καί so that we should have 1) "the great God," one person, 2) "and our Savior Jesus Christ," a second person. Winer, Meyer, and others call Θεός and Σωτήρ "attributes" and then assert that in the analogy of Scripture the attribute "God" is never applied to Jesus but only the attribute "Savior." But the *person himself* is here called "our God and Savior." In II Pet. 1:1 he is again called: τοῦ Θεοῦ ἡμῶν καὶ σωτῆρος, the apposition Ἰησοῦ Χριστοῦ following in the same way. Elsewhere he is called "God" and "the Son of God." "Jesus Christ" is only his earthly and his official name and thus only an obvious apposition which states to whom Paul refers. The R. V. is without question right, its margin and the A. V. are unacceptable.

After all this discussion we should not fail to absorb Paul's full meaning: We Christians live the lives we do because our Savior-God's boundless grace has saved us and keeps educating us to live such lives, and because we ourselves "in this present eon" look forward to another eon when our great hope, the appearing or epiphany of the glory of Jesus Christ, shall at last arrive. Then he who in his own person is "our God and Savior" (ἡμῶν modifies both terms) will come in all his glory, in his second epiphany, which shall transcend all that we are able to imagine.

14)   With what we may call a demonstrative relative Paul now expounds "our Savior": "he who gave
himself in our stead in order to ransom us from all
lawlessness," etc.   That is Christ's work as the Savior.
Turn to I Tim. 2:6 so that we may not need to repeat;
add Eph. 5:2 and Gal. 1:4.   This is our Savior's voluntary, expiatory, substitutionary sacrifice, his "ransoming" and ransom.   All are expounded under the
passages cited.   He is the One whose epiphany of glory
we are expecting.   Now we revel in grace, then we
shall share all his glory.

Yet Paul here fortifies his admonition to holy living.   That is why he says that Jesus "ransomed us
from all lawlessness," i. e., paid the price to buy us
free and take us away from all lawless living (ungodliness and worldly lusts, v. 12) "and cleanse us for
himself as a people select, zealous for all excellent
works."   As the second verb has the reflexive pronoun,
so the first verb is itself reflexive: "ransom us for
himself," pay the ransom so that we may belong entirely to him.   Λαός is often used as a designation for
the chosen people Israel.   The added adjective περιούσιος
makes this strongly emphatic: *auserlesen, erlesen, auserwaehlt*, B.-P. 1038; see I Pet. 2:9; John 10:14-16 for
Paul's whole thought in other words.   Shall we not be
such a "select people"?   Shall we ever think of again
running with the world in the old excess (I Pet. 4:4)?

15)   Paul closes this part of his letter: **These
things continue to utter and to admonish and to
impress with conviction, with all imperativeness!**
The present imperatives imply that Titus is busy doing
this very thing and ask him to keep on.   The three
form a climax.   Titus is ever to say these things; more
than this, he is to urge them in admonition; even more
than this, he is to drive them in so as to produce conviction.   Even more than this: he is to use with it
all every form of ἐπιταγή, command, authoritative or

ders which brook no disobedience. Some sinners will listen when he speaks to them; some require admonition; some even sharp conviction (1:9, 13), yea, direct orders.

Let no one disregard thee! Paul will not permit any man to disregard his representative. The verb used, literally, "to think around," is not καταφρονεῖν, "to think down on" or despise, but the German *sich hinwegsetzen ueber*, "to disregard," with his thinking go around and so evade thee, to keep on in any kind of sinful conduct in spite of all thy orders. We still have to watch that kind of men.

CHAPTER III

Concerning the Position of Christians Among Men Generally

A Summary Statement of the Conduct

1) The wording is most compact, *multum in parvo*. **Continue to put them in remembrance to be in subjection to rulerships, to authorities, to be obedient, to be ready for every kind of beneficial work, to blaspheme no man, to be non-fighters, yielding, showing all meekness toward all men.** In short, Christians are ever to be good citizens among all their fellow citizens.

Polybius and others remark about the seditious character of the Cretans so that some commentators think that this is the reason for Paul's injunction. They refer to I Tim. 2:1, 2 where the Christians in Asia are asked to pray for their rulers and say that here they are asked to be in subjection and to obey. But a look at Rom. 13:1, etc., does not substantiate such a view. Besides, Paul uses only four words, which are entirely too few for such a pointed reference to a national characteristic. Moreover, he continues with admonitions regarding general conduct as citizens among other citizens. We have here a brief outline of the Christian obligation of a citizen with regard to the government and with regard to his fellow citizens. Christianity holds us to the things which are compactly stated here. We are content to be in subjection to our governmental authorities and of our own will to be obedient to the laws they make for the communities in which we live. We have the very highest motive for this, namely our Lord's will. This makes the very best citizens, such as obey for Christ's and for conscience's sake.

(926)

The two datives are abstract terms: "rulerships, authorities," and thus say more than terms that name certain kinds of rulers and magistrates would do. Our submission and obedience is to be rendered to government as such irrespective of its particular form or of the persons in whom it is vested. All that the New Testament says on this matter is so important and far-reaching because the government of those days was pagan and in the hands of pagans, who were generally corrupt. We need think only of Pilate, of Felix who detained Paul in the hope of receiving a bribe, of Festus who denied Paul simple justice. A bright spot were the Asiarchs who warned Paul during the riot in Ephesus. What the Jewish Sanhedrin was its treatment of Jesus and of Stephen shows.

Yet ever Christians are to be subject, are to obey. The only limit to this subjecting is their own religion which, while it holds them to submission and obedience in all things secular and thus makes them the very best citizens, for that very reason forbids them to give up this their religion at the behest of any governmental demand even if the severest punishment and death itself be inflicted in consequence. The fact that such inflictions were bound to come Jesus himself plainly told his followers; his words soon proved true.

"To be ready for every beneficial work" means as citizens under their government and among their fellow citizens. The motive is again purely Christian and truly religious. This positive excludes the corresponding negative, all works that are evil, that do harm to others, and also failure to do beneficial works when opportunity for doing them offers itself. The clause is brief but covers everything.

2) "To blaspheme no one" means with curses and vicious epithets, denouncing some magistrate or some fellow citizen. As bad as some of these may be, the Christian does not give way to an ugly temper and to sinful language. "To be non-fighters," picking up no

casus belli, is followed by its opposite: ἐπιεικεῖς, Luther's beautiful *gelinde,* "yielding" or "gentle"; we lack a real equivalent in both the Latin and the English. See Phil. 4:5 *in extenso.* People who are ever fighting are wretched citizens and neighbors; people who are willing to yield in gentleness are admirable, especially when they follow the gentle spirit of Jesus.

Paul amplifies: "showing all meekness toward all men." Trench distinguishes between "yieldingness" and "meekness," the former referring to conduct, the latter to the inward virtue back of it; hence Paul also uses the participle which urges us to show our meekness. The former yields what we might call our rights; it ever remembers that we are sinners among sinners and thus bears what the sins of others inflict upon us. The latter is the temper which does not make us assert ourselves; it is an unassuming, passive spirit, the opposite of harshness and haughtiness. Here it is referred to as governing us in regard to all men; elsewhere meekness is the right attitude also toward God.

Here we have an excellent text on Christian citizenship as far as our relation to government as well as to our fellow citizens is concerned. It rests on the new life which makes us citizens of heaven; our supreme interest in this world is to grace the gospel so as to win men to its banner.

What We Once Were and What We Now Are

3) "For" indicates that we are to note what is now said in regard to the previous injunctions. **For we were at one time also on our part devoid of understanding, disobedient, deceived, slaving for lusts and pleasures of all kinds, leading lives in baseness and envy, detested, hating each other.**

This describes what we on our part also *were,* what the ungodly around us still *are;* note "also" we. Paul includes himself although he had been a Jew. The

argument is strong: Shall we, after having been
delivered from such a state, again fall back into it?
The picture here drawn is only a partial presentation
because the reference of v. 1, 2 is to our lives among
men; this then, Paul says, is how we ourselves once
lived among men.

'Ανόητοι = mindless and thus without understanding = "in the vanity of their mind (νοῦς)," Eph. 4:18.
The mind, which controls thought and will, functions
in the unregenerate in a way that is wholly perverted.
The first evidence is the fact that it leaves them "disobedient," the opposite of the obedience noted in v. 1,
and even more, namely "disobedient" to what the mind
itself according to proper reason, nature, experience,
and the natural conscience, should dictate.

"Deceived," made to wander from the true and
proper course, points to all the deceptions against
which the unregenerate are so helpless. The next feature of this state is: "serving as slaves for motley lusts
and pleasures," letting them dictate their will and
following such dictation, the mind being blind to what
must result. Thus "leading lives (διάγοντες, sc. βίον) in
baseness and envy." Κακία denotes everything that is
morally inferior, and then Paul names "envy" as one
bad specimen. "Detested" is the passive outcome, to
which is added the active "hating each other."

Let the Cretans look back at their former condition; let them also look at what they see in the unregenerate about them at the present time. Then, as γάρ
indicates, they will understand Paul's injunction the
better.

4) **When, however, the benignity and the love
of our Savior God for men appeared, not as a result
of works in connection with righteousness which we
on our part did, but in accord with his own mercy
did he save us by means of the bath of regeneration
and renewing by the Holy Spirit, whom he poured
out upon us richly through Christ Jesus, our Savior,**

so that, by having been declared righteous by that One's (God's) grace, we got to be heirs in accord with eternal life's hope.

This, Paul says, is what we became, what God made of us. The whole gospel is here compressed into one rich sentence. Here there are four terms to designate our Savior God's love. So many are unusual even in the case of Paul: χρηστότης — φιλανθρωπία — ἔλεος — χάρις. "Savior" is twice used. The saving work for all men is compressed into the one verb of the first clause so that the saving deed of God effected in our hearts is unfolded by the rest of the statement and ends with what we thereby got to be, namely heirs of life eternal.

The reason for Paul's using "the benignity" and "the love of men" lies in the preceding verses. Both terms are forms of God's ἀγάπη or "love" for the whole world of men. The former appears in Rom. 4:2; it is more than "the kindness" of our versions, more also than "the goodness." See Trench who subscribes to Jerome: *Benignitas sive suavitas,* in which strength is blended with lenient, bland, tranquil association, apt for all good things, inviting to familiarity, sweet in address, etc.

While the two articles make the two concepts stand out in their distinctness, God's benignity and his *phil-anthropia* or affection for human beings (*Menschen-liebe*) are well placed side by side. The latter word is rare in the New Testament; it is used in Acts 28:2 regarding the humanitarian feeling of pagans and in Acts 27:3 (adverb) regarding the humane act of Julius. Only in our passage is the word used with reference to God. While Paul brings out these two sides of God's love he presently adds his mercy and his grace. A singular verb may be used with two subjects, the nature of which is so much alike.

Ἐπεφάνη, second aorist passive, repeats this verb from 2:11 where it is used regarding "the grace of our Savior God" which appeared as an epiphany "to

all men." The remarks made in 2:11 apply also here;
in both places the aorist refers to the love of God
which appeared in Jesus and in his whole redemptive
work. "When" that made its epiphany, God "saved
us"; yet that does not mean that these acts occurred
together in point of time; the modifier of the second
verb excludes such simultaneousness. Paul received
baptism at a later time, and the Cretans received it
still later. Note the stress that is laid on saving: "our
Savior God — *saved* us — through Jesus Christ, our
Savior." This is the stronger because in 1:3, 4 we
already had: "our *Savior* God — Christ Jesus, our
Savior"; and in 2:10, 11, 13, where God is twice called
Savior and Jesus once. The great act of saving and
placing into eternal safety gives this title to both
persons who, each in his own way, were and are active
in man's salvation. "Our Savior" is confessional and
altogether in place as a possessive to characterize those
in whom God's and Christ's salvation is actually being
realized.

5) The main part of the sentence begins at this
point, and the two contrasting phrases are placed before the main verb for the sake of emphasis, which
enables Paul to add all the further modification which
is so highly important in this connection. Verses 4-7
are a perfectly constructed statement. "Not as a
result (or outcome, ἐκ to indicate source) of works, of
those in connection with (some kind of) righteousness, which (works) we on our part did (the English
idiom is: have done) did God save us." Let no one
harbor such an idea or imagine that he has either
done such works or that such works are possible.

Bengel and others divide this phrase and this relative clause and analyze them into several thoughts,
but the combination forms a unit and states out of
what our having been saved did *not* flow: *not* out of
anything in the way of "works" (no article), works
(τῶν) in connection with (ἐν) anything that can be

called "righteousness," works which *"we* on our part (emphatic ἡμεῖς) *have done"* (the verb and the subject are transposed so that the verb, too, is emphatic). The description of what works are utterly excluded is not complete until we reach the last word of the combination.

In his act of saving us God could not take and did not in any way take into consideration any works that had been done by us, for which we might in any way claim righteousness, i. e., such a quality accorded us by a verdict pronounced on us by God. Verse 3 shows the total absence of such works in our unregenerate past and the presence of nothing but the opposite kind of works. The remark that Paul does not say "works of law" is pointless; for if they were to be connected with "righteousness" the works done by us would have to meet some δίκη or norm, some law, in accord with which some judge could rightly declare us righteous.

Δικαιοσύνη is a forensic term. No norm exists according to which a righteous judge, in particular God, could declare us righteous; if any judge ever did such a thing he would thereby condemn himself as being unrighteous; his verdict would be false. In other words, Paul says more than that we did not meet the righteous requirements of the Mosaic law; we did not meet the requirements of any code of true moral law. We deserved utter condemnation as being unrighteous in all our works, yet in spite of this "our Savior God," being a "Savior" indeed, "saved us," his very name "Savior" and the very act "saved" pointing to us as such who were hopelessly lost with all our works.

His act of saving us was *in toto* an act of mercy: "in accord with *his* mercy," αὐτοῦ is in contrast with ἡμεῖς. As distinguished from "grace," ἔλεος or mercy implies our wretched, miserable state (sketched in v. 3). God's act accorded with the pity which *he* had for us in our sad state. As the Savior God he had such mercy, and this he followed when saving us. If he had followed any other norm (κατά) such as the works which we ourselves had done he would have abandoned us, and we should have perished forever.

He saved us by the means that he himself had prepared (διά). Here Paul does not, however, name "the redemption in Christ Jesus" as he does in Rom. 3:24 but the subjective means of applying this redemption to the individual sinner "dead in his transgressions and his sins" (Eph. 2:1): "he saved us by means of the bath of regeneration and renewing by the Holy Spirit," etc. Paul's other great passage regarding baptism is Eph. 5:26 where we discuss λουτρόν at length: "the bath of the water in connection with spoken word," and reject the R. V. marginal translation "laver." As far as finding immersion in the word "bath," this would be curious, indeed, when all of us constantly take baths without immersion. Our versions use "washing," which conveys the meaning well. The genitives make the expression definite as so many genitives do. Christians know of only *one* "bath of regeneration," etc.

It seems to make little difference whether these genitives are regarded as possessive: "bath belonging to regeneration"; or qualitative: "regenerating bath"; or objective: "bath effecting regeneration." Any one of these genitives retains the main point, namely that this bath and this regeneration plus the renewing are inseparably connected: where the bath is, there the regeneration and the renewing are. And this bath is the means (διά) which God used when he saved us. This interpretation is, of course, troublesome to the Baptist Robertson (and to all others who deny baptismal regeneration) in his *W. P.,* who offers the exegesis: "Man submits to the baptism *after* the new birth to picture it forth to men." He regards this bath as being only a picture that men are to see, a mere symbol for the eye. Paul excludes this idea in a double

way: God *saved* us by means of the bath, etc., — this
is the "bath of regeneration." How can anyone think
Paul would say: "God saved us by means of (διά) a
picture of regeneration"? Compare Jesus' own words
to Nicodemus in John 3:3, 5.

Παλιγγενεσία occurs only once more in the New Testament, in Matt. 19:28, in a connection that is entirely
different from baptism and personal regeneration; but
the New Testament is full of the new birth, the new
life, and all the imagery that goes with regeneration;
we have mentioned John 3:3, 5, add at least I Pet. 1:3,
23. While this word is used frequently by pagan
writers and appears also in the mystery cults, the gulf
between Paul's meaning and the pagan meaning is
absolute; for paganism had no conception of the generation of a spiritual life in a sinner, a ζωή implanted
by the Holy Spirit, to make spiritually alive a life that
passes unharmed through physical death into glory
and blessedness with God and Christ. Πάλιν in the
compound "*re*-generation" (ἄνωθεν, John 3:3) is in contrast with our natural generation: this is a second generation, one that is spiritual, that starts a spiritual
life; note John 3:4, 6. Yet this spiritual life affects
not only our "spirit"; it affects the whole man, body
and soul, makes him a child of God that is "born of
the Spirit" and by this generation and birth becomes
an heir of heaven.

'Ανακαίνωσις = "renewing," and καινός is in contrast
to the old nature and life; it is new as being wholly
different; see "the old man" and "the new man" in
Eph. 2:22-24, where we also have νέος in the infinitive
"be renewed," the other Greek word for "new," namely
in the sense of never having been in us before. Regeneration is accompanied by a newness that is totally
different from the former oldness (v. 3), yea, a newness nothing of which existed before.

Some would erase the difference between the two
words for "new" and restrict us to our one English

word "new," but this is done without justification.
Here the "renewing" that contrasts with the old life
is the proper term since the old life has just been
described (v. 3). The difference between "regeneration and renewing" as here used is that the former
kindles the new life by an instantaneous act, the latter
continues and develops this life by a constant growth
and progress.

In the language of the Church *regeneratio* is used
in both this narrow sense as it is here used by Paul,
yet also in the wider sense as including the renewing
(*C. Tr.* 921, 20). The genitive "of the Holy Spirit"
(no article, proper name) designates the agent who
regenerates and renews. We connect this genitive
with both "regeneration and renewing" and not only
with the latter. It is said that "regeneration" is an
intransitive or passive term and cannot receive such a
genitive and thus also a *genitivus auctoris*. It would
be strange, indeed, if Paul would name the one who
does the renewing and fail to say who does the regenerating.

God saved us by means of baptism. Baptism is a
bath of regeneration and renewing, in both of which
the Holy Spirit is the actor. That is why God could
use baptism as such a means (διά), why baptism is by
no means a mere symbol or picture but a true means
of divine grace. It is not an *opus operatum* as when
a crowbar turns over a stone but as when spiritual
grace operates spiritually by the Holy Spirit's entering the heart with his grace and kindling the new life.
As physical generation and natural life are still an
unsolved mystery to present-day scientists (Graebner,
God and the Cosmos), so the spiritual rebirth is still
more of a mystery. For this reason the regenerating
agent is named here and in John 3, and for this reason
Jesus spoke v. 7, 8 to Nicodemus. For adults, who
must first hear and believe the Word, baptism still
remains the efficacious "bath" which Paul declares it

to be. For Word and baptism, faith and regeneration
ever go together. To reject baptism is to confess the
absence of regeneration. Baptism seals regeneration
for the adult, which is as close as we are able to define
its regenerating effect in the adult.

6)   The relative οὗ is not to be construed with the
neuter "bath" but with the "Holy Spirit," the genitive
case being attracted from the accusative. Since the
Spirit is a person, we translate "whom he poured out
(aorist, not imperfect) upon us richly." To be poured
out richly cannot be predicated of a bath, not even of
one that has much water; it can be predicated only of
the Spirit. This is not a reference to Pentecost when the
great outpouring took place through Jesus Christ but
to baptism and the outpouring of the Spirit that takes
place in this sacrament. This is true, the Spirit's outpouring in the sacrament, and his effective coming and
work in the Word and the Eucharist, rest on the great
act that occurred at Pentecost; the great outflow continues with every individual application of Word and
sacrament. The subjects reached by the Spirit grow
more numerous. "Richly" means in abundant measure
so as to effect the results that God, our Savior, desires,
namely actually "to save us."

This outpouring that occurs in every baptism is
ever "through Jesus Christ, our Savior." Paul might
have used a verb and a wording with ὑπό, "by"; he uses
διά, "through," which matches John 14:16; 15:26 to
correspond to God's pouring out, God uses Jesus as the
personal medium. Thus the three persons are connected with baptism: God, the Father, as our Savior,
Jesus Christ, our Savior, as our Mediator (διά), and
the Holy Spirit as our gift from both, as the person
who effects our regeneration and renewing, he being
the one to whom *per eminentiam* this work has been
assigned as the work of redemption is that of the Son.
We see that this agrees with Matt. 28:19. It agrees
with what the Scriptures reveal in regard to all the

opera ad extra; they are all *communa.* All three persons are engaged in them, each in his own way.

7) Here ἵνα expresses more than purpose; it expresses actual result: "so that, by having been declared righteous by that One's grace, we got to be heirs in accord with eternal life's hope." This is not purpose, which still leaves the question as to whether the purpose came to be attained in us or not; it *was* attained, which means result. Our versions read as though the result may not have been attained, or as though the outpouring of the Spirit wrought only the potentiality or possibility ("might be," etc.) of our getting to be heirs. No; we then and there, in and by baptism, in and by the Spirit bestowed in baptism, actually "became heirs," etc., (the passive form γενηθῶμεν is always used in the sense of the middle; the Koine formed such passive forms of intransitive verbs and had a special liking for them). We regard the aorist as ingressive: "we got to be." Once getting to be such heirs means that we remain what we got to be.

The terms match: this regeneration or new birth makes us God's children, God's sons, and thus heirs, even heirs by birth (John 3:8b). "Heirs" own but do not yet enjoy their inheritance; it is not yet paid out to them. Paul therefore says: "We got to be heirs in accord with eternal life's hope." "Life" matches "regeneration." By baptism we were saved from our spiritual death; the true spiritual life was kindled in us by the Spirit; as children of God we then and there became heirs of God who are waiting in hope for the great inheritance, "life eternal" in glory. Κατά says that what we got to be is "in accord" with this hope. The genitive is objective: hope "for life eternal."

Now we understand the aorist ἔσωσε, "God, our Savior, did save us" in baptism; this aorist is not eschatological, is not dated in the future, but is dated at the time of baptism; then and there "he did save us," but as yet only as heirs with the glorious life of heaven yet to be given them although, as heirs, we already own it. Our Savior God and Jesus Christ, our Savior, are placed on the same level by this word "Savior" and in this act of saving us just as in 1:3, 4 "Savior" says this about both persons, and 2:10, 11 about God, and v. 13 about Christ.

The result clause would be complete without the participial addition, but its addition is most valuable. It specifies the judicial act which established us as heirs: "by having been declared righteous by that One's grace." Ἐκείνου refers to the more remote antecedent "our Savior God," the subject of all the previous verbs, and not to "Jesus Christ, our Savior," the subject of no verb but only the genitive with a preposition. If the grace of Jesus were referred to, αὐτοῦ should be used and not ἐκείνου. Paul makes the same statement here that he made in Rom. 3:24 so that all the comment given there can be repeated. Only the tense differs, for the present participle used in Rom. 3 describes how God continually declares believers righteous by his grace (the dative being the same as in our passage) while the aorist refers to the declaration already made regarding Paul and Titus who are baptized. So we repeat only this much: the participle is forensic: in heaven God, the Judge, pronounced the verdict that declared righteous and by that verdict cancelled all guilt. This he did "by his grace," the pure undeserved favor extended to the guilty; yet this was not done arbitrarily, for the ransoming of the guilty, mentioned in Rom. 3, has here been mentioned in 2:14 and thus needs no repetition. This grace is intended for all men, yet it can act only in the case of believers as far as justifying is concerned; the rest spurn the ransom as well as the grace. See all that is said in connection with Rom. 3:24.

8) Paul closes this paragraph regarding what we were and what we now are by adding the strong assurance: **Faithful the statement,** the one just con-

cluded (compare this formula in I Tim. 1:15; 3:1; 4:9; II Tim. 2:11). Hence Paul adds: **and concerning these things I intend that thou speak with confidence so that they who have believed God may keep devoting care to excellent works to take the lead** (in them).

On βούλομαι, "I intend," see I Tim. 2:8 (also 5:14). Titus has been and is still carrying out Paul's intention as his ready and willing apostolic representative. Titus is to keep on in his confident, assured affirmation "concerning these things," the plural now spreading out what "the *logos* or statement" embraces. As sure and trustworthy as this *logos* is, which sums them up, so assured Titus is to be in presenting all that is contained in this *logos*. He is not to act like those mentioned in I Tim. 1:7, who do not even know the things about which they are making confident affirmation; Titus is to affirm what *is* sure, what he knows to be so. His own confident assertions are not to rest on his own convictions but on this Word and its real and objective contents. The infinitive is middle and not passive.

Ἵνα expresses intended result: "so that they may continue to devote thought and care on excellent works." The genitive is to be construed with this verb, which, as a verb of emotion, governs this case (R. 509.) Some would construe it with the following infinitive. This infinitive is added only to enhance the idea.

This verb does not mean "to maintain" (our versions); the R. V.'s margin is also faulty, for it leaves the impression that doing good works means "managing matters of business," the honest profession of Christians being to do good works. Goodspeed follows Field's lead in this and draws the genitive to the infinitive: "make it their business to do good," which M.-M. 451 approve. The infinitive means "to preside" (I Tim. 5:17), "to take the lead in" (R., *W. P.*). It thus enhances the idea of devoting care to excellent works, such care that will make these Christians stand foremost like elders who preside. They are not to lag or to be dragged along but are to have their place in the front rank. The meaning but not the word is "so as to excell." The subject, which is saved until the end, is emphatic: "they who have trusted God," i. e., since their conversion and on into the present. By their devotion to excell they are to show that they have put their fullest confidence in God. The participle is to be construed with the dative and not with a preposition and means: trusted in God as regards what he says and promises.

We make a new paragraph at this point; others make it at verse 8.

What and Whom to Shun

At the end of the letter Paul says a few words on this point. **These things are excellent and profitable for men,** not only for Christians, but also for others with whom Titus and the Christians come into contact. Since they are noble, excellent in themselves, these things are certainly also profitable for men. Both adjectives are intended to be understood spiritually. Nor need we debate regarding what "these things" signify; they are all the excellent things that this letter contains, which are certainly spiritually profitable to human beings (generic article). Titus has the blessed work of leading all the Cretan Christians in bringing these things to their fellow men. It is still our task today.

9) Now the negative side: **But silly questings and genealogies and strifes and battles about the law continue to turn thy back on, for they are unprofitable and in vain.**

Paul refers to silly, foolish seekings, questings and questionings, by which people want to find or to find out things that amount to nothing (see the compound noun in I Tim. 1:4). "Genealogies" have been explained in I Tim. 1:4, which see. These first two nouns belong together, for the silly questings were to a large extent concerned with filling in the genealogies recorded in the books of Moses and spinning stories around these fictitious names.

The next two also belong together: "strifes" or disputes about such things; and then, again specifying, "battles about the law"; the Greek has a mere adjective: νομικάς. This recalls the senseless, ignorant "law teachers" mentioned in I Tim. 1:6, who did not know what the law was for and turned it into fancies. On all four nouns compare II Tim. 2:23; Tit. 1:14. We have already said that the Cretan and the Ephesian errorists seem to have been of the same type. They were full of a lot of silly stuff that was unworthy of serious attention and created nothing but fussing and fighting with true Christians and deceived those Christians who were not yet well grounded.

These things, Paul says, "continue to turn thy back on," the same present middle imperative which is used in the similar direction to Timothy (II Tim. 2:16, which see). Paul means, "treat them with contempt because it is useless to do anything else." Such things are "unprofitable," no advantage or profit can be derived from them; and they are at the same time "in vain," *erfolglos* (as distinguished from κενός, *gehaltlos*, with no content), no proper goal being reached by discussing them. Paul's judgment is corroborated by all Christian experience.

10) **A heretical person, after one and a second admonition, disdain to be bothered with, knowing that such a one has been perverted and sins, being self-condemned.**

C.-K. 86 says that αἱρετικός means *ketzerisch*, "heretical," also in this passage. He then defines αἵρεσις and says that we should not go to the philosophical schools for getting the sense of the word but to passages like

I Cor. 11:19; Gal. 5:20; II Pet. 2:1. Schlatter remarks that the *hairetikos* is the possessor of a definite will which obtains its contents from the context while αἵρεσις in its later significance characterizes the man who holds to it. Paul passes from reprehensible opinions to a man who holds and seeks to spread them. How the opinions are to be treated v. 9 states; how the man is to be treated we are now told, namely in the same way as his noxious opinions. The precise opinions referred to we know sufficiently from I Tim. 1:4, etc., which see. Yet this statement is concerned with any heretical person, no matter what heretical opinions he holds.

It is confusing to introduce distinctions such as fundamental and non-fundamental, for these need careful definition before they are used in any connection, to say nothing of the present one. An αἱρετικός is one who holds an αἵρεσις or a number of them, a chosen view of his own apart from the teaching of the Scripture. In Acts 24:14 Paul denies the charge that he holds to an αἵρεσις, and he does that because he believes all things which are written in the Law and the Prophets (i. e., the Old Testament) and has no opinion of his own on a single point.

We thus have no difficulty in understanding the adjective. Paul says that a man is *hairetikos* who holds to such things as the myths, the genealogies, and the ignorant teaching of law mentioned in I Tim. 1:4-11, empty, ignorant, phantastic, vain though they were. Thus any teaching that forsakes Scripture and certainly such as contradicts Scripture stamps a man as *hairetikos*. He chooses for himself what the church, by choosing Scripture, must repudiate and disown. Whether this be little or much makes little difference since to the extent to which he chooses his own ideas to that extent the person concerned is *hairetikos*. One additional point, we think, lies in the word, namely that the *hairetikos* comes out and stands for his separatistic, antiscriptural opinions (call them "views") to the damage of true Christians; he may, of course, also be an agitator.

What is to be done? One or two admonitions or remonstrances are to be administered. Νουθεσία is "the word of remonstrance, of reproof, of blame, where these may be required" (Trench). There is to be nothing like strife and battle (v. 9). An earnest, thorough talking-to is what is meant. One application may suffice and succeed. If not, "a second" is to follow, of course, not *pro forma*, but deeply serious. If that too fails, and if it appears that further efforts are useless, then "disdain to be bothered with" such a man. That applies not merely to Titus but to the churches as well. The imperative is iterative and applies to every man of this kind. On the verb see I Tim. 4:7; II Tim. 2:23.

To be sure, men of this sort want to remain in the congregation. Why does Paul then not demand their expulsion? Because their *hairesis* already excludes them, and disdaining to be bothered with them settles the matter. We may note Rom. 16:17, 18. What would become of the church if it continued its fellowship with such people? Every organization discards and shakes off its discordant members. If it fails to do so it suffers the consequences. Matt. 12:25. The church is greater than any other organization or body.

11) The participial clause is causal: since Titus knows. And the thing he knows is obvious, namely that "perverted has such a one been," the verb is placed forward for the sake of emphasis. The passive leaves unsaid who perverted him, the perfect tense states that this is now his condition. R., *W. P.*, makes the meaning of the verb too strong: "turned inside out"; it means "turned out from," namely out of the true doctrine and teaching in which all true Christians must remain. The passive leads us to think of the father of lies who did this turning. Paul puts his finger on the main point: this man has allowed himself to be separated from the divine truth and has frustrated the

efforts to bring his heart back to that truth. *He* is the separatist, his *hairesis* makes him sectarian to whatever extent it has carried him. Paul says that Titus knows that, and since Titus leads the Cretan churches, they, too, will know it and will disdain to continue fellowship with such a person.

"And is sinning" points to this man's guilt. Paul says that it is known. A man who is wrong and remains so despite the "admonition" certainly "sins," ἁμαρτάνει, the common word for sinning. How does such a man "sin"? The participle answers and even states the gravity of the sin: "as being self-condemned," as himself pronouncing an adverse judgment upon himself. Neither Paul nor Titus and the church need to condemn him, the *hairetikos* himself does this. His guilt and this verdict upon himself agree as they, of course, ought to. The very word *hairetikos* implies that this man has the truth before him but rejects it and prefers his own contrary ideas. Then comes the *nouthesia* or remonstrance; this, too, the man rejects. His guilt is evident, also his self-condemnation, for his rejection is the adverse judgment pronounced by himself. He is not a pagan who never heard the truth, who is wrong because of invincible ignorance.

Today thousands openly disagree with Paul. When one has been turned away from the true teaching of God and Christ, this is not considered as sinning and as self-condemnation. Such men are not blamed in the churches, they often receive no remonstrance, they are often highly honored, nor do the leaders of the churches or the churches themselves obey v. 9; they themselves may have been turned and in varying degrees become *hairetikoi*. Although they themselves are guilty they naturally seek to acquit themselves, and thus they also acquit others. Paul's word to Titus still stands, and *its* verdict Christ himself confirms.

The Conclusion of the Letter

12) **Whenever, I shall send Artemas to thee or Tychicus, be diligent to come to me to Nicopolis, for there I have decided to winter.**

The indefinite temporal clause states that at some time soon to be determined Paul intends to send either Artemas or Tychicus to Titus. When he does so, Titus is to proceed with diligence to Nicopolis to join Paul who has decided to spend the winter in that city. It is a fair conclusion that one of these two men is to take the place of Titus in Crete; which one is as yet undetermined. Titus may thus arrange his work and his plans accordingly. We know nothing further about Artemas (perhaps an abbreviation of Artemidorus). Only this seems plain, that he was one of Paul's able and trusted assistants who was in the same class with Titus and Tychicus. This adds another man to the group of Paul's assistants. Tychicus we know quite well.

Zahn, *Introduction,* II, 53, etc., lists nine cities that have the name Nicopolis in commemoration of some victory or other. Paul refers to the one in Epirus, which was by far the most important and famous city of this name and had been founded by Augustus as a memorial to the victory at Actium. Here Paul intends to spend the winter, of course, for work in which Titus is to be his assistant. Paul was not yet at Nicopolis; the letter was not written in this city. We do not know where Paul was when he wrote this letter; he was apparently somewhere in Macedonia (I Tim. 1:3). See the introduction.

13) **Zenas, the jurist, and Apollos send forth with diligence on their journey that nothing may be lacking to them.**

Like a general, Paul moves his lieutenants into strategic positions. Zenas is new to us. It is debated whether νομικός, which is evidently added to distinguish this man from some other Zenas, signifies a Roman jurist or lawyer or a former Jew who was learned in the Old Testament law. This man's name is Greek; hence he seems to be a jurist, a *juris consultus* or *jurisperitus* (the Latin terms). Apollos is the man named in Acts 18:24, etc., last named in I Cor. 16:12. He now appears as one of Paul's assistants.

The verb means "to outfit and to expedite for a journey." This implies to provide necessary funds, clothing, and baggage, and usually also to accompany a part of the way. We cannot assume that these men were now with Titus; for Paul would then have sent them salutations and would have stated whither they were to go. They were with Paul, had received their directions from him, and carried this letter to Titus who was to help in sending them on. We have no means of knowing their ultimate destination, not even whether both were bound for the same place.

14) Besides, let also our people be learning how to take the lead in excellent works for imperative need so that they may not be unfruitful.

This statement is typical of Paul. He looks out for the two travelers and at the same time has the spiritual benefit of the Cretan Christians in mind. Titus does not, of course, have sufficient means to send Zenas and Apollos on; his diligence is to be exercised in getting what may be needed from the churches. Δέ adds the thought that thus "our own" (people) are to be learning how to stand in the front line in good works for imperative needs; translate it "moreover" or "besides." We do not find a contrast in the substantivized possessive adjective "our own" as though it were said in oppotion to people who are *not* our own, pagans, errorists, false Christians.

When it is used with an infinitive μανθάνω = to be learning *how* and not to be learning *that* (R. 1041).

Here the Cretans have an opportunity to practice a little. On the infinitive "to take the lead" see v. 8. "Our own" are to stand forward, in the front line, when it comes to "excellent works for imperative needs." We read the genitive and the phrase together. The infinitive is placed between them in order to make the whole a unit. The last clause expresses contemplated result: "so that they may not be unfruitful." For if our people do not step forward with good works when necessities are to be provided they will scarcely learn how to do other good works and will thus remain unfruitful.

15) **There salute thee all those in my company** (μετά), i. e., all Paul's assistants who are at this moment with him on his tour through Macedonia. These are salutations for Titus personally. **Salute those who love us in faith.** "Us" = Paul and those in his company. Titus is to convey the salutation of these to all who love them with fraternal affection (φιλέω). The implication is that all Cretan believers do, indeed, so love Paul and his associates.

Grace with all of you is briefer than in II Thess. 3:18 but has the same sense.

Soli Deo Gloria!

St. Paul's Epistle to Philemon

INTRODUCTION

There is universal admiration for Paul's letter to Philemon. Even the critics have found no fault with it. Luther sees in it "a masterfully lovely example of love," like the love of Christ for us: "For we are all his Onesimi if we will believe it." Bengel sees in it a fine specimen that shows how Christians ought to treat *res civiles ex principiis alterioribus*. This epistle is the Biblical answer to the question of slavery. Here we have no law of outward compulsion to forbid slavery but a gospel spirit of love which so changes the heart that slavery automatically withers and becomes impossible.

Philemon was a man of wealth and general importance, who was converted by Paul (verse 19) and probably came into contact with the apostle in Ephesus. He may have lived in Ephesus for a time and then moved to Colosse, or he may have been in Ephesus on business, and thus have heard the gospel from the apostle. Apphia is generally regarded as his wife. Archippus may have been his son or at least a relative of his. The church in Colosse was founded by Epaphras (Col. 1:7, 8; 4:12, 13).

Onesimus was a slave that belonged to Philemon. This slave had run away to Rome, where he somehow came into contact with Paul and was not only converted but also became so closely attached to Paul that Paul would have liked to keep him, not as a slave, but as a friend and helper. Then Epaphras, the spiritual leader of the Christians in Colosse, Laodicea, and Hieropolis, came to visit Paul in Rome in order to obtain counsel and help against a peculiar, superstitious type of Judaizers who had begun to trouble the churches in Colosse and Laodicea. Acting on the information brought by Epaphras (Col. 1:8), Paul wrote his letters to the Colossians and to the Laodiceans and to the Ephesians and sent Onesimus back to his master under the protection of Tychicus with a personal letter to Philemon. We see how events converged so that these four letters were written and dispatched by the hand of Tychicus. It was not safe to send Onesimus back alone because the slave catchers might have arrested him, especially when he neared Colosse. After he was placed in the care of Tychicus he was safe. See further details in the introductions to Ephesians and to Colossians.

Paul shows perfect tact in this letter. He calls out all that is noble in Philemon. He touches all the motives that will induce Philemon to receive Onesimus back in a Christian manner. No excuse is offered for the slave's running away. He ran away as a pagan, Paul returns him as a Christian. Philemon lost a heathen slave who had never served his master except in his heathen way; Paul gives him back a Christian slave who comes back to his master of his own accord, impelled by a Christian conscience, to make good his past grave fault and henceforth to serve his master in a truly Christian way. Read Eph. 6:5-8; Col. 3:22-25 and see how these passages were written with Onesimus in mind. Paul's letter meets the case with such perfection that every line becomes precious to those who desire to emulate the apostle's spirit and the perfect way in which it reaches out toward another's heart. The whole letter is of pure gold. No wonder the church placed it into the canon.

THE LETTER

1, 2) Paul, a prisoner of Christ Jesus, and Timothy, the brother.

This statement associates Timothy with Paul in writing these lines to Philemon. One who is suffering a long imprisonment for the sake of the gospel together with another who is a spiritual brother of this prisoner and of Philemon join in asking of the latter what this brief letter contains. If Philemon will respond he will rejoice the heart of this prisoner of Christ Jesus and will show that Philemon, too, is a brother, indeed. The genitive is merely possessive and as such distinguishes this prisoner and his entire state from the host of other prisoners who are held for reasons that have nothing to do with Christ. Philemon, too, belongs to Jesus Christ but enjoys his liberty; when he reads these lines from one of Christ's prisoners, his heart will be moved and deeply touched. Since they likewise come from a brother, a close associate of this prisoner and one who is with all his soul devoted to this prisoner's great work, these lines will move Philemon the more to respond in a brotherly spirit.

The two appositions are simple and restrained and the more effective for this reason. One need only imagine himself in Philemon's place. Here we have no sentimentality but only a manly touch and no more.

To Philemon, our beloved and (our) fellow worker, and to Apphia, our sister, and to Archippus, our fellow soldier, and to the church in thy house.

This letter is intended for Philemon, but his action regarding the slave Onesimus will affect his family and also the group of Christians who are accustomed to gather in his house. We are unable to say whether the

(953)

whole Colossian congregation or only a part of it made
Philemon's home its headquarters. Philemon will consider these others who will also influence and advise
him. "Our beloved" = whom we, the writers, sin-
cerely love. "Our fellow worker" indicates the reason
for this love. According to his station and his ability
Philemon worked in the same cause that was so dear
to Paul and to Timothy. Love bound them together.
This bond justifies the appeal made in this letter and
will move Philemon to respond.

Apphia must have been Philemon's wife. The
Greek uses only the article "*the* sister," which has the
sense of the pronoun "our." Archippus, mentioned in
conjunction with the other two, may have been their
son. Col. 4:17 (see this passage) helps to explain
"our fellow soldier." We take it that he was in charge
of the work during the absence of Epaphras. If he
was the son he would be comparatively young for such
a position, yet for this very reason Paul may have
added Col. 4:17 to spur him on in his labors and to
urge him not to be timid because of his youth. Yet we
cannot be entirely certain; we have only the little information that the two letters afford.

The father is called "our fellow worker," the son
"our fellow soldier," which latter expression says more,
for it makes Archippus a captain like Paul and Timothy, who was fighting the Judaizers in Colosse during
the absence of Epaphras. The κατά phrase is like those
found in Col. 4:15 and Rom. 16:5: "pertaining to thy
house." With the pronoun "thy" the letter begins to address Philemon personally although it never forgets
the fact that all the others addressed are concerned.
This letter will be read in the presence of all of them.

3) The greeting is like that found in other letters; see its exposition in Eph. 1:2.

*   *   *

4) I thank my God every time I make mention of thee in my prayers, hearing of thy love and faith which thou hast toward the Lord Jesus Christ and for all the saints, that the fellowship of thy faith may be energetic in full knowledge of every good thing in your midst regarding Christ.

Πάντοτε means "always" and "every time" just as πᾶς may mean "all" or "every." The adverb is usually construed with the main verb: "I thank my God always when I am making mention," etc.; but the sense is quite the same when it is construed with the participle: "every time I make mention," etc. Paul finds delight in writing this about Philemon. But he hopes that Philemon will afford him an additional reason for thanksgiving to God by the fact that he receives back Onesimus in the way in which Paul desires him to do so. Ἐπί = "on the occasion" of my prayers.

5) The iterative present participle: "hearing of thy love," etc., refers to what Onesimus is telling Paul about Philemon and includes what Epaphras adds. One may mention love first and faith second; their relation remains the same, love is ever the fruit of faith. This ἀγάπη is the love of intelligence and corresponding purpose. There is a difference of opinion among interpreters as to the relative clause and as to v. 6. We cannot agree with those who say that σου is to be construed with τὴν ἀγάπην, and that as "thy love" has "thy" as its modifier, so "faith" has the relative clause as its modifier. The fact that "thy" is placed before the nouns argues that it is to be applied to both nouns: "thy love and faith." The relative clause also refers to both nouns: "which (love and faith) thou hast toward the Lord Jesus and for all the saints." The very change of prepositions makes it clear that "*toward* the Lord Jesus" refers to Philemon's faith, and "*for* all the saints" to his love.

The phrases are not arranged as a chiasm to "love and faith," for they are found in a relative clause,

and thus the phrase pertaining to faith is properly
placed first, the other last. As far as construing πίστις
with πρός is concerned, I Thess. 1:8 answers the claim
that the word does not here mean "faith" but "faithfulness." If the latter were meant, namely faithfulness to Christ and toward all the saints, Paul would
have used the same and not different prepositions.

Furthermore, Paul uses the relative clause because
it enables him to use "thou hast." In Rome, Paul does
not hear of the love and faith which were exercised by
Philemon in the past but of these as Philemon continues to have them. In this letter Paul asks Philemon
to use both in regard to Onesimus. If he added each
phrase to its noun only by means of an article (or
without an article) he would lose this pertinent point.
One might think that "love" would be enough here.
This would be especially pleasing to those who emphasize love to the neglect of faith. Onesimus is to be received as a brother in the faith and thus in Christian
love.

6) The ὅπως clause does not denote purpose. It
is an object clause; it is construed *ad sensum;* it modifies nothing that precedes. The reference to Paul's
thanks in his prayers implies that he also asks something of God for Philemon; v. 6 states *what* he asks
without adding a verb of asking. Ὅπως is used after
verbs of asking (B.-D. 369, 4; also 388; 392, 1). The
matter is rather obvious; it would be strange if Paul
only thanked God for Philemon's love and faith and did
not also ask God to bless Philemon, especially in a letter which calls on Philemon to exercise his love and
faith in a special case that is close to Paul's heart. Remember, too, that the Greek mind catches the implication involved far more readily than do our English
minds although they, too, have no difficulty here.

What Paul, in his thankful prayers, asks for Philemon is "that the fellowship of thy faith may be energetic in connection with full knowledge about every

good thing (objective genitive) in your midst **regard-ing Christ.**" Κοινωνία does not mean "contribution" **or** "liberality," a meaning which has been given to it **in** II Cor. 8:4; 9:13; Rom. 15:26; Heb. 13:16, and also here. This word means "fellowship." "Of thy faith" is the subjective genitive as the predicate shows: "may be active or energetic." Philemon's faith puts him into fellowship with all the saints (v. 5). The faith of some lets this fellowship remain rather passive; it takes whatever good this fellowship directs its way but does little or nothing toward its Christian brethren; it also lets the flesh lame its activity. Paul prays that Philemon's fellowship may be energetic. One might regard the verb as an ingressive aorist: "get to be ac-tive," but this would imply that Philemon has hitherto lacked such activity, which is contradicted in v. 5 where Paul mentions the love for all the saints which he had evidently shown. The aorist is constative: "may be active" without a break.

And this "in full knowledge of every good thing in your midst as regards Christ," i. e., really under-standing all the good which is in possession of the Colossians as pertaining to Christ. One's exercise of fellowship must not be ignorant; so much of it is. We often do not properly know the good in our own midst and fail to make use of it in our brotherly fellowship. The neuter ἀγαθόν is used in the classic fashion like an abstract noun; but "every good" means "everything good for our salvation," "what we possess in Christ" (C.-K. 5: *heilbringend*). This is made certain by the added phrase "in regard to Christ."

Philemon needs only to know fully this good as it already exists among the brethren in Colosse, ἐν ὑμῖν. Why should the reading be ἐν ἡμῖν, "among us" (which, according to v. 2, 3, would refer only to Paul and to Timothy)? Knowing the purpose of this letter, we see what Paul has in mind, namely that Philemon will make his faith's fellowship active in full intelligence

also toward Onesimus, who is now his brother in the
faith and to be loved as a Christian brother. But the
expression is still broad and general. "In your midst"
is so pertinent because a number of the brethren in
Colosse were undoubtedly slaves. This lends pertinency
to *"every* good thing as regards Christ"; a number of
these things referred to the standing of slaves as brethren in the church (Gal. 3:28; I Cor. 12:13; Col. 3:11).

7) **For I had great joy and comfort over thy love
because the viscera of the saints** (their compassionate feelings, see Phil. 1:8) **have been refreshed
through thee, brother.** That is why Paul lets Philemon know what he asks of God for him. Philemon
has in the past shown his love by kindly acts of fellowship also toward slaves; he may have had Christian
slaves in his own household, who would be included in
"the church in thy house" (v. 2), and they, too, would
hear this letter read. Philemon had refreshed and
stimulated (perfect tense so that the effect continued)
the tender compassions of the saints by the Christian
love he exercised in fellowshiping slaves as brethren.
That brought Paul much joy when he heard it from
Onesimus and from Epaphras, it also brought him
παράκλησις, "comfort or encouragement," so that he now
sends Onesimus back to him a slave but now a brother.

The final address, "brother," is highly effective;
it is a full acknowledgment that in all these acts Philemon had shown himself a true brother of Paul and a
call now to show himself such a brother by the way
in which he received Onesimus. Ἔσχον may be regarded an ingressive aorist: "I got to have much joy,"
or a simple statement of fact: "I had."

8) Paul now comes to the burden of his letter.
**Wherefore, although having much frankness in
Christ to direct the fitting thing for thee, I am
rather urging (thee) for the sake of love, being a
person like Paul, an old man, moreover now also**

a prisoner of Christ Jesus. Urging thee am I concerning my own child whom I begot in this imprisonment, Onesimus, the one-time for thee useless one, now, however, for thee and for me a useful one, whom I sent back to thee, him, that is my own heart.

"Wherefore" takes up what Paul has written in v. 4-7 about his thankfulness and his joy because of Philemon's faith and love and applies to the whole statement now made. The participial clause is concessive: "although I have." Paul says that after what has been told him about Philemon he really has no hesitation regarding his actually directing him as to what is the proper thing for him to do, namely in the matter about which Paul is writing. A man like Philemon would not be offended when he is frankly told what he ought to do.

This is a sincere compliment to Philemon. Not every Christian is ready to bow to direction from others; we, too, often feel that we cannot frankly tell them what is the proper thing for them to do in a given case. Philemon is a man of a higher type. Παρρησία is frank and open speech without hesitation or holding back due to a fear of offending the other person's susceptibilities. "In Christ" limits this frankness, for Paul's openness is exercised only in connection with Christ.

Paul does not say that, since he is an apostle with high authority, he might simply command Philemon, but that in this case he will not give such a command. Nowhere in this lovely letter does Paul give an intimation of authority or a hint that Philemon needs authority in order to move him. Paul knows a much more powerful motive, namely the appeal to Christian love, which has been aptly called the greatest thing in the world. He is writing to Philemon as to a "brother" (v. 7), and as a brother Philemon will respond. No higher compliment can be accorded to any Christian.

Although Paul might frankly tell Philemon what is the fitting thing for him to do, knowing that Philemon would respond to such a direction, Paul says, "I am rather urging (thee) for the sake of love." "Beseech" is not the proper translation; Paul is not humbly beseeching or begging; he is urging, and that solely on the score of "the love" of which he has spoken in v. 5 and 7 (the article is the article of previous reference). "Rather" means that Paul prefers to put the whole matter solely on this highest plane of pure love, intelligent and purposeful Christian love. This means that Paul knows Philemon has such a love and will exercise it when he is urged to do so. Paul thus doubles his sincere compliment. "For the sake of love" needs no "my," "thy," or any other qualification.

9) It makes no difference whether we construe v. 9 with v. 8 or with v. 10, for in either case the reference to Paul's own person must be construed with παρακαλῶ, "I am urging." The ordinary reader would pass immediately to v. 9 since nothing indicates that a stop is to be made at the end of v. 8. "I am rather urging thee for the sake of love, being a person (such a one) as Paul, an old man, moreover now also a prisoner of Christ Jesus." Paul speaks of himself objectively: being such a one as Paul, old and now even in addition to that a prisoner of Christ Jesus. On the latter see v. 1. Paul touches upon two points: his age and his imprisonment. Some think he mentions three points, but we fail to see that being "Paul" is a third point.

An old man means that Paul has been in the work for a long time; from such a person one might well take a frank and open order that is given in Christ's name but not so readily from a younger man, a beginner in the work. Paul has been in the work for a long time and is now even suffering because of that work, is to that extent a martyr in the great cause in which Philemon, too, was a joint worker (v. 1). One would, therefore, all the more take an order frankly given in Christ from such an old man. Paul knows that Philemon would certainly do so.

By all means note the nobility of the motives that are here called forth by Paul. He always knows the right springs to be touched in men's hearts, and he touches them in the right way. This fact made it so difficult for men to resist him. Here he calls out all that is noblest and highest in Philemon's heart. The very fact that he appeals only to the highest lifts Philemon up to that level and impels him to act on no lower level. Paul could do that so perfectly because he himself lived altogether on that high level. This is why we fail, for often we try to move people to act on this high level when so much in our lives shows that we ourselves do not move on it. That makes our urging insincere, and no insincerity in this field has ever been successfully hidden; people detect it intuitively.

Paul was about sixty years old at this time. At the time of the stoning of Stephen he is called a *νεανίας,* "a young man" (Acts 7:58), but that word should not be understood in our sense of a youth. That word designated a man who had passed the age of thirty. R., *W. P.,* reports that Hippocrates calls a man "old" (a *πρεσβύς*) when he is between forty-nine and fifty-six, after that he is "aged" (*γέρων*). Our versions translate as though Paul had used this latter word. Some twenty-six or twenty-seven years had elapsed since the incident recorded in Acts 7:58 occurred; our estimates must be according.

We prefer the reading *πρεσβύτης,* "an old man," to the inferior reading *πρεσβευτής,* "an ambassador," which some commentators prefer by appealing to Eph. 6:20: "I am acting as ambassador in a chain." Even the correct reading "an old man" has been taken to mean "an ambassador" because only old and experienced men were as a rule sent as ambassadors. The whole

idea of ambassadorships is, however, incongruous to
the present connection; no commentator has been able
to work it into Paul's thought in a convincing way.

10) "Urging thee am I" repeats the significant
παρακαλῶ and now adds what is on Paul's heart: "concerning my own child whom I begat in this imprisonment, Onesimus," etc.   The possessive adjective "my
own" is stronger than the pronoun "my."   Onesimus is
Paul's own "child."   All the tender love that lies in
this word is enhanced by the relative clause: "whom I
begot (we should use the perfect: have begotten) in
this imprisonment"; the article has the force of "this"
or of "my."   Δεσμά or δεσμοί = "imprisonment" with
or without fetters: δέσμιος (v. 9), "a prisoner."   Paul
is the spiritual father of this "child" (I Cor. 4:15).
In Gal. 4:19 Paul uses the figure of a mother.   In addition to the tender love that is contained in this expression there lies in it the thought of immaturity:
Onesimus is only a child as yet and in this condition
needs much tender care lest his young spiritual life
suffer or die.   Paul places these words before the name
"Onesimus" so that they may immediately touch Philemon's heart.

11)   Paul knows that there will at once flash into
Philemon's mind the thought as to the kind of a fellow
he has known Onesimus to be.   The very fact that Paul
converted him is due to his having run away to Rome.
Paul meets this at once and takes out of this thought
the effect it might produce: "the one-time for thee
useless one, now, however, for thee and for me a useful
one, whom I sent back to thee, him, meaning my own
heart."   All the ill occasioned by Onesimus is overcome
by the immense good brought about by Paul.

Some note a play on the meaning of the name "Onesimus."   Derived from ὀνίνημι, it means "the useful
one"; the play would be on the fact that his one-time
uselessness is now turned into the greatest usefulness.
But ἄχρηστος and εὔχρηστος are derived from a different

verb, χράομαι. This mars the supposed pun or play on terms, the more so since Paul could have used two derivatives from ὀνίνημι. He failed to do so. In a real pun the words must have at least a similar sound; not even that is the case here. For our part we say that a pun at this place in Paul's letter would be a mistake.

"Once useless to thee" = when he ran away. We decline to extend this and to say that he was useless when he served, even before he ran away. It is a Christian rule never to make a case worse than it is. Besides, a useless slave would soon be roused out of his uselessness by his master; and if he proved incorrigible he would be promptly sold. "Now, however, for thee and me a useful one" is an incomplete thought, which is completed by the next clause.

12) He is now useful because Paul is sending him back to Philemon. The aorist is epistolary: "I sent," and refers to the time when this letter is read by Philemon. Useless while he was gone; again useful when he is returned. But how is he useful also for Paul? As the slave sent to Philemon by Paul, as the converted slave who will serve Philemon in the way in which Paul taught him (Col. 3:22-25; Eph. 6:5-8). This is really turning matters around. It is Paul who is proving himself useful to both Philemon and Onesimus. Yet it is true, this is the very thing that Paul regards as being useful to him. If Onesimus now faithfully served Philemon as Paul had taught him, Paul would be served by that service to the delight of his heart.

The A. V. follows an inferior reading: "thou, therefore, receive him," σὺ δὲ αὐτόν with προσλαβοῦ. We retain αὐτόν but do not regard it as an intensive pronoun with the relative ὅν (R., W. P.), nor as meaning "in his own person" (R. V.), but as a pronoun in apposition with the relative :"whom — him, that is, my very own heart," a construction that enables Paul to add τοῦτ' ἐστι. When Paul says that he is sending "him" he tells Philemon that he is sending "his own σπλάγχνα," the

nobler viscera (heart, liver, lungs), the seat of the feelings. We have no corresponding idiom and must be
content to convey the thought. In Onesimus, Paul
sends his own heart, a part of himself, all his own
tender emotions as they are centered in Onesimus.
Can there be a question as to how Philemon will treat
what Paul sends him?

13) Paul has not yet completed the description
of the relation of Onesimus to himself. So dear has
this slave come to be to him that he adds: **whom I
was wishing to retain for mine own self that in thy
stead he might be ministering to me in my** (article;
or: in this) **imprisonment for the gospel, but without
thine own decision I resolved to do nothing in order
that this favor of thine be, not as by way of compulsion, but by way of free volition.**

We see from this that the language Paul used in
v. 10-12 is not extravagant. Onesimus, once converted,
became so devoted and so helpful to Paul that Paul
desired to retain him as a personal attendant to wait
on him during the time that he remained a prisoner
in Rome. How long that would be Paul could not tell.
When Paul was freed, Onesimus would, of course, be
sent to his master. This slave had learned to be a most
competent servant and upon his conversion had put
his entire heart into competently serving Paul so that
Paul doubly loved the man.

The imperfect ἐβουλόμην is used for the sake of cour-
tesy as is so well explained in R. 919 and not to express
an unfulfilled wish (B.-D. 359, 2). It is like our: "I
was wishing." Ὑπὲρ σοῦ plainly means "in thy stead"
(substitution), R. 631; "in thy behalf" is incongruous.
Paul is not intimating that Philemon ought to serve
him but only that Philemon might like to supply Paul
with a servant who might serve the latter during his
imprisonment, the servant substituting for his necessarily absent master. Some think that this would in-

volve setting Onesimus free. Not at all; when Paul needed no further personal service, the slave would return to Philemon.

14) Paul had this wish but gave up the idea. Without Philemon's own decision (γνώμη) Paul resolved to do nothing in this direction lest, if he did, the favor from Philemon (τὸ ἀγαθόν σου, the good thing Philemon thus did for Paul) be by way of compulsion or constraint and not by way of a free volition made without even a suggestion by Paul or by anybody else (ἑκούσιον is used as a noun). The very fact that Paul says this about his wish and his resolve shows that he has no thought that Philemon is to send Onesimus back to Paul to act as his servant. Once having told about his wish, Paul could now not accept such a favor. For what Paul says is said wholly in the interest of Onesimus; Philemon is to know how highly Paul had learned to prize this converted slave.

Note the change in tense and then first the courteous imperfect (v. 13) and then the epistolary aorist "I resolved" (English: "it is now my will"). When Philemon reads this he will note a past preference over against a past decision (R. 886). The imperfect, moreover, leads the reader to expect the aorist that follows; the former leaves the matter open, the latter definitely closes it. The genitive τοῦ εὐαγγελίου is objective: "imprisonment for the gospel."

15) With γάρ Paul explains that the probable providence of God in bringing about the contact of Onesimus with Paul went far beyond the matter of his having a dear and devoted servant for the time of his imprisonment; this peculiar providence only incidentally pertained to Paul, God used him only as an instrument for higher ends. **For perhaps for this reason he was separated (from thee) for a time that thou shouldest duly have him back forever, no longer as (just) a slave, but beyond**

**a slave, a brother beloved, especially to me but how
much more to thee both in the flesh and in the
Lord.**

Paul says "perhaps," for God's providential purposes are veiled; even Paul can speak of them only ten-
tatively. This slave ran away, which fact, of course,
rightly angered Philemon. Now he comes back. Let
Philemon consider what God seems to be doing in this
matter. Yes, the slave was gone for a time, Philemon
was deprived of his labor and was provoked at that.
But does it now not seem as if in God's providence this
running away for a time means that Philemon is to
have his slave back forever? The Greek uses the adjective αἰώνιον whereas we use the adverb; ἀπό in the
verb = "duly have back"; God duly returns him,
wanted to take him from his master only for a ὥρα, a
short time. The ἵνα clause is in apposition to διὰ τοῦτο.

16) The thought of "forever" is incomplete: forever "no longer as (just) a slave" as before and as he
would have been if he had not run away. God, Paul
suggests, wanted to bless Philemon by taking away
his slave in order to return to him as one "beyond a
slave," namely as one who is now to be a "brother
beloved," a Christian slave, who as such would serve
his master in the conscientious and devoted way that
no pagan slave achieves, hence "beloved" for his
Christian character and devotion. What a gain for
Philemon? When he thinks of this purpose of providence he cannot possibly be harsh with his slave who is
now so wonderfully changed.

This is not all. Yes, "a brother beloved." But how
did God change this pagan slave into such a brother?
Why, through Paul. Moreover, Paul has already
learned to love this slave — how much he loves him
he has just said (v. 10, etc.). Philemon is receiving
back this slave as a brother beloved "especially to me"
(Paul). Onesimus is *Paul's* dearly beloved brother.

Will he, then, not be this "by much more to *thee*" (Philemon)? For, now that Paul sends him away, Paul will no longer have him "in the flesh," but from now on Philemon will have him "both in the flesh and in the Lord." The longer he has this slave of his who is again physically present in Philemon's house and at the same time united with Philemon in the Lord, the more will Philemon find him beloved, more beloved than Paul had found him during their brief contact in Rome.

This is the true light in which Paul sees this remarkable case and seeks to find God's purpose in it all. Philemon is to see it in the same divine light. Paul is content to have served as God's tool; content in having this new beloved brother, whom he himself has won, separated in the flesh. Paul is happy that Philemon will have more than this in Onesimus. This slave is Paul's brother as eternally as he is Philemon's. We fail to find the least hint that Philemon ought to set Onesimus free. Yet this has been found in Paul's words.

17) Since this slave is coming back to Philemon as 'a brother, Paul adds: **Accordingly, if thou hast me as one in fellowship, receive him as myself.** The condition is one of reality. In his heart and thought Philemon most certainly regards Paul as a κοινωνός, which means more than "a partner" (our versions) or a companion, for this word is derived from κοινωνία, "fellowship," and hence means "one in true Christian fellowship." Hence, since Onesimus is returning as a brother in the Lord, Paul says that Philemon is to "take him to himself" (προσλαβοῦ, aorist, to take him definitely) as he would take Paul himself if Paul came to him. "As me" = as if it were I that thou art receiving to thyself. We need not extend this into an identification; it is enough that Onesimus is now a brother in full Christian fellowship with Philemon just as is Paul himself although the one is a slave,

the other an apostle. The fellowship is equal; Philemon shoud make no difference.

18) There might be one drawback to this arrangement; Paul removes it completely. **But if he did thee wrong in any respect or owes anything, charge this to me — I, Paul, write it with my own hand, I myself will duly pay! — that I say not** (charge it) **to thee, seeing that even thine own self thou owest to me in addition. Yes, brother, I** (am the one who) **would like to make a profit off thee in the Lord! Refresh my heart in Christ!**

"Or" is not disjunctive but conjunctive. "Wronged thee in some respect" is one way of stating it, "or" is another, more specific way: "or owes" thee anything. The condition of reality assumes this as a fact. Yet the conditional form leaves it to Philemon to decide whether he, too, will consider that Onesimus did him a wrong and thus owes him the making good of that wrong.

The oftener we read this conditional clause, the less can we bring ourselves to accept the general interpretation which lays all the stress on the second verb and thus concludes that Onesimus stole money from his master when he fled, and that he did this in order to enable him to flee or that he first stole and then fled for fear of detection and punishment. We ask ourselves how Paul could then write "if." He should simply acknowledge the fact; Onesimus surely confessed his crime. Paul should ask pardon for Onesimus, nothing less. Restitution by Paul would not be enough. An offer of repayment on the part of Paul, and least of all a conditional offer that is coupled with the hint that Philemon might well cancel the loss to himself in view of what he himself owed to Paul, cannot be ascribed to the apostle. Such ethics are not sound; we cannot bring ourselves to ascribe them to Paul. The matter is not helped when Paul is supposed

to be writing ethics like this in a joking way. Ethical
obligations cannot be treated in a jocular fashion. The
Christian must confess theft as a sin, must do whatever may be possible in the way of making restitution. No cry of "brother, brother," puts any Christian beyond that.

We thus decline to accept the idea of a theft. This
"if" and the two verbs "wronged thee or owes" mean
that the wrong done to Philemon may be considered as
a debt. Philemon may well consider it so, and Paul
takes it that Philemon has a right to do so. Now the
wrong done was the fact that Onesimus fled and deprived his master of his services. That could be
reckoned in dollars and cents, it had cost so and so
much to pay for the work that Onesimus should have
done for Philemon and did not do. Philemon might
think of this as a loss of this amount of work because
it remained undone, or as the cost of having it done
by another. Thus "if" becomes clear; Philemon may
reckon thus, and "if" he does, Paul will not object or
haggle about the amount of the loss. Whatever the
amount, Paul says: "Charge it to me."

There is more in this offer than is generally thought.
Why does Paul not make an offer that Onesimus work
overtime? Paul had precious little money; when could
he hope to pay? Can we assume that Paul says:
"Charge this to me!" when he knows that Philemon
would not think of doing such a thing and could not
possibly take a cent from Paul? First of all, Onesimus is Paul's child (v. 10). A child's debt is its
father's. Paul is sending this child of his to Philemon
and wants him received as a child, yea, "as mine own
self" (v. 17), and absolutely nothing is to interfere
with such a reception. Therefore, if this loss or in-
debtedness comes into Philemon's mind, he is to treat
it as if Onesimus were Paul himself and not the debtor
so that, as he would receive Paul himself no matter
what he considered that Paul owed him, thus he would

also receive Onesimus and not think or say that a debt must first be paid.

19) "Charge this to me!" = hold nothing against this my child that might interfere with your receiving him as my child, yea, as mine own self. To make this certain, to enable you to do it, I here and now give you my promissory note: "I, Paul, write it (epistolary aorist) with my own hand, I myself will duly pay" (in a number of verbs ἀπό has the sense of "duly," here it means to pay an acknowledged debt). This is not written in a playful manner, for Paul is deeply concerned about removing this last hindrance that might delay the wholehearted reception of Onesimus. Luther notes this similarity: as Paul takes over the entire debt of Onesimus, so Christ takes over our entire debt, but in a higher sense. "For we are all his Onesimi if we believe it." Some think that Paul took the pen from his scribe's hand and himself wrote this verse. We prefer to assume that Paul wrote this entire, most personal letter with his own hand.

The usual rendering is: "that I say not unto thee how that thou owest to me even thine own self besides" (R. V.; the A. V. is less exact). But this translation does not seem to fit. Why do we have the pronoun σοι with λέγω, which is seemingly so unnecessary? Why προσοφείλεις, "thou owest in addition or besides"; in addition to what? We prefer Wohlenberg's rendering: "that I say not (charge it) to thee, seeing that (consecutive ὅτι, R. 1001) even thine own self thou owest to me in addition." This balances the pronouns ἐμοί (v. 18) — σοι — then also σεαυτόν — and again μοι. It takes care of the verb: besides whatever Philemon charges as a debt that is due from Onesimus, Philemon owes his very own self to Paul and "in view of that" (ὅτι) may well charge to himself and not to Paul (despite Paul's strenuous offer) this debt of Onesimus. "That I say not (charge it) to thee" is termed *paraleipsis*, after all saying something that one prefers not to say. B.-D. 495.

Philemon owes a double debt to Paul, "his own self," which means that Paul converted him, probably when Paul was in Ephesus, and when Philemon met Paul there. And now he owes Paul something "besides" (πρός), namely the return of his runaway slave who is a better slave than he had lost. With ἵνα μὴ λέγω Paul only suggests that Philemon may consider this debt of his to Paul and thus not dream of charging the least thing to Onesimus. Yet to all that Paul has already done for Philemon, to what he is now doing in addition (returning his slave as a Christian) Paul will most happily add also this other payment: making good for anything Philemon may think Onesimus owes him.

Let us not lose the main point because of the details: the one thing Paul desires is the removal of anything whatever from the mind of Philemon that might hinder him from genuinely receiving Onesimus as a child of Paul's. Paul had converted both of them, and the latter was as dear to him as the former. At any sacrifice or cost to himself Paul wants the two to be in perfect Christian fellowship.

20) "Yes, brother," Paul confesses, "I (am the one who, emphatic ἐγώ) would like to make a profit off thee in the Lord!" The second aorist optative states Paul's wish. Note that ἐγώ σου are juxtaposed, both are strongly emphatic: *I — off thee*. Yet this is no more than a wish for this one instance (aorist). But look at the profit that Paul would like to make; all of it is "in the Lord." His happiness is what he desires, happiness in seeing these two converts and spiritual children of his joined in truest Christian fellowship although the one is a master, the other only a slave. A nobler sentence has seldom been written. Ah, Philemon will delight to let the apostle to whom **he** owes so much, make this profit "off him."

Ὀναίμην is the verb from which Ὀνήσιμος is derived, and thus some regard it as a play on the verb: "Onesimus," the profitable one — "I would make a profit." But Paul wants to make this profit off Philemon, which rather interferes with a play on the verb. Besides, the word "Onesimus" occurs in v. 10, rather far away for a play on words. "Yes, brother" = yes, it is as you may surmise, I want to make profit off you, the most brotherly that one brother could desire off another and that one brother would let another make.

"Refresh my heart in Christ," my viscera (v. 12; M. M. 584)! This drops the figures and states literally what Paul desires from his brother Philemon; this is the profit.

21) Paul is not waiting until Tychicus returns and reports how Philemon received his slave; he is happy now in anticipation. **Having confidence in thy obedience I write to thee, having come to know that thou wilt do even beyond what I say.**

The perfect participle has its present implication. Paul's whole letter rests on his confidence in Philemon's obedience. "Obedience" is not to be restricted to the present case; Philemon has constantly shown it although he is wealthy and prominent. The aorist of the verb is the epistolary aorist. The aorist participle is ingressive: Paul has arrived at this knowledge on the basis of all that Epaphras and Onesimus have told him; he knows that Philemon will do not only what Paul asks of him but something far beyond that. This is not a hint to send the slave back to Paul to be Paul's servant. "Beyond what I say" is to be understood in a spiritual way. Ὑπακοή is not what we call "obedience," i. e., to a command. Paul has given no commands. The word means "hearing and heeding" what is said to a person and thus matches "the things I say."

22) **Moreover, at the same time be making ready for me lodging, for I hope that through your**

prayers I shall be granted to you. Paul means "at
the same time" that Philemon will do more than Paul
asks; also this he asks, that Philemon prepare him
lodging since he hopes God will answer the prayers
made for him and grant his friends in Colosse the
opportunity to see him again. The imperative is the
present tense, hence it does not urge a special hurry.
One might think that in a home such as that which
Philemon possessed Paul would find accommodation
at any time even if he came unannounced. Yes, if Paul
were to arrive alone, this might be true. But he always traveled with companions, and we may be sure
that after he was released his party would be more
numerous than usual.

Paul says that he "hopes," etc. This surely means
that he has information to the effect that his case will
soon be heard by the imperial court. When he writes
the Epistle to the Philippians, the trial is in progress.
The interval between the writing of these epistles was,
therefore, comparatively brief. Paul promises the
Philippians a visit; here he also promises his friends in
Colosse a visit. We see that he is planning for the
future and that he intends to revisit the eastern
churches that are already established. The contention
that these plans do not fit his imprisonment in Rome
but only his imprisonment in Cæsarea, is untenable;
for then these plans hung fire for almost three years.
Then, too, Paul had no prospect of release while he was
imprisoned in Cæsarea. The plural "you" refers to all
the persons addressed in v. 1, 2.

23, 24) **There salutes thee Epaphras, my fellow war captive in Christ Jesus, Mark, Aristarchus,
Demas, Luke, my fellow workers.**

These do not salute all those mentioned in v. 1, 2
but only "thee," because these associates of Paul that
are now present with him are evidently personally
known to Philemon. As far as those mentioned in v.

1, 2 are concerned, they are included in the greetings that were sent in the letter to the congregation as such. Jesus, called Justus, it appears, was not personally known to Philemon (Col. 4:11); hence he is not included. "Fellow war captive," which is applied to Epaphras and in Col. 4:10 to Aristarchus, has caused much useless discussion. The term is figurative. The idea that these men were imprisoned with Paul is not tenable. Paul separates Epaphras from the other four simply because he is the founder and leader of the Phrygian churches. Compare Col. 4:10-14.

25) **The grace of our Lord Jesus Christ with your spirit! Amen.** See Gal. 6:18, and Phil. 4:23. "With you" includes all of those addressed in v. 1, 2. Thus closes the loveliest epistle written by Paul.

Soli Deo Gloria